HANDBOOK ON THE ECONOMICS OF LEISURE

Handbook on the Economics of Leisure

Edited by

Samuel Cameron

Professor of Economics, University of Bradford, UK

Edward Elgar
Cheltenham, UK • Northampton, MA, USA

Published by
Edward Elgar Publishing Limited
The Lypiatts
15 Lansdown Road
Cheltenham
Glos GL50 2JA
UK

Edward Elgar Publishing, Inc.
William Pratt House
9 Dewey Court
Northampton
Massachusetts 01060
USA

A catalogue record for this book
is available from the British Library

Library of Congress Control Number: 2011926836

ISBN 978 1 84844 404 1 (cased)

Typeset by Servis Filmsetting Ltd, Stockport, Cheshire
Printed and bound by MPG Books Group, UK

Contents

Contributors

Victoria Ateca-Amestoy, UPV-EHU, Bilbao, Spain.

Gerben Bakker, London School of Economics, UK.

Alessandro Balestrino, University of Pisa, Italy.

Subhojit Banerjee, VBS Purvanchal University, Jaunpur, India.

Grant Black, University of Indiana South Bend, IN, USA.

Samuel Cameron, University of Bradford, UK.

Alan Collins, University of Portsmouth, UK.

Andrew Cooke, Nottingham Trent University, UK.

Joe Cox, University of Portsmouth, UK.

Gillian Doyle, University of Glasgow, UK.

Peter E. Earl, University of Queensland, Australia.

Vincent G. Fitzsimons, University of Bradford, UK.

Véronique Flambard, Université Catholique de Lille, France.

Mark Fox, University of Indiana South Bend, IN, USA.

Stephanie Hussels, Cranfield University, UK.

Karen Jackson, University of Bradford, UK.

David Lane, University of Indiana South Bend, IN, USA.

Gretchen Larsen, King's College London, UK.

Liam J.A. Lenten, La Trobe University, Melbourne, Australia.

Lauren Mintz, University of Maryland, College Park, MD, USA.

Daragh O'Reilly, University of Sheffield, UK.

David Paton, University of Nottingham, UK.

Ti-Ching Peng, National Dong-Hwa University, Taiwan.

Rajesh K. Pillania, Institute for Strategy, New Delhi, India; Asia Fellow, Harvard, Boston, MA, USA and Faculty, MDI, Gurgaon, India.

Simeon Scott, Bradford College, UK.

Andrew B. Trigg, The Open University, Milton Keynes, UK.

Nicolas Vaillant, Université de Reims, France.

Deborah L. Wheeler, US Naval Academy, Annapolis, MD, USA.

François-Charles Wolff, Université de Nantes, France.

Introduction

The field of leisure represents something of a problem in economics. Since the very beginning of the formalization of economic theory there has been a concept of leisure in economic models. As leisure industries generate substantial revenues there have also been applied economic studies of leisure. More recently the focus of economics has shifted to the measurement of subjective well-being or happiness in particular looking for answers to the crass and ancient question of 'what makes us happy?'.

Despite these three threads, we do not have a consistent body of study of the economics of leisure. Partly this is because leisure is a difficult and complex commodity to fit into a maximization-based framework. It is to be hoped that the subjective well-being vogue will bring advances in the integration of leisure activities into the main body of economics. It is unlikely that this can be achieved without some interdisciplinary cross-fertilization. Accordingly, this volume brings together a number of scholars who are primarily economists, but it also takes account of various useful ideas from marketing, anthropology and psychology.

1 Overview of the economics of leisure
Samuel Cameron

INTRODUCTION

To illustrate the increasing importance of leisure, let me begin by quoting from the publicity burb of Trust (a Dutch company that supplies low-cost computing accessories and peripherals):

> Trust Computer Products provides a complete, innovative and affordable range of technological products. The key principle in developing products is to offer variation, pleasure, relaxation and excitement to the user, a principle Trust aims to fulfill.

Thus a computer mouse or USB hub is designed to bring me variation, pleasure, relaxation and excitement. These are all things that I might reasonably expect to get from leisure. I would also be pleased to get them from work but probably would not be morally offended or mortally wounded if I did not. What has all this got to do with economics? It would be nice to be able to report that there was at least one journal of leisure economics and some kind of association of economics of leisure which has regular meetings. Alas, it is not so.

However, there are related items in existence. For example, there are such journals as: *Leisure Studies*, the *Journal of Cultural Economics*, the *Journal of Sports Economics*, the *Journal of Media Economics*, the *Journal of Leisure Research*, the *International Journal of Sport Marketing and Sponsorship*, the *Journal of Sport Behavior*, *Leisure Sciences*, *Sport Marketing Quarterly* and also many tourism research-related journals. There are associations in the fields suggested by this list of journals. For example, the ACEI (Association of Cultural Economics International) meets biennially to present papers on such things as restaurants, cinema, visual art pricing, theatre cost functions, music downloading and so on. It should be noted, as will be apparent in many of the early chapters in this volume, that economists have frequently used the word 'leisure', and a concept of it, since the formalization of economic theory began in earnest.

Clearly all this activity has something to do with the broad topic of leisure in the sense of covering a range of activities which are pursued outside work. In the words of the Trust corporation they bring 'variation, pleasure, relaxation and excitement'. In leisure-specific research the notion of some kind of 'flow' or freedom from responsibility allied with 'meaning' in the activity undertaken is mentioned (see, for example, Csikszentmihalyi and LeFevre, 1989; Csikszentmihalyi, 1990). Admittedly, the individual who engages in amateur dramatics or team sport will feel some perform-ance responsibility to their colleagues. However, this will be largely in some 'spirit of fun', which differs from a work commitment. Such a notion of leisure may free us from the possible definitional problem of being unable to distinguish between consumption in general and leisure. In par-ticular, this problem arises in Becker's (1965) model of household produc-tion where household consumption becomes production.

SIGNIFICANCE OF LEISURE TO THE ECONOMY

The best-known attempt to link leisure to the economy is in Thorstein Veblen's *Theory of the Leisure Class*, published in 1899, which gave us such terms as 'conspicuous consumption'. Veblen's thinking belongs much more in the field of economic sociology, rather than pure economic theory, and thus he has always been hailed as significant in institutional and heterodox economics. His ideas on leisure are intrinsically linked to class distinctions, as is rather obvious from the title of his book. The leisure class were essentially parasitic in extracting their incomes by 'force and fraud' from the working class. This extracted income, and spare time, had to be displayed in formats which reinforced the superior social status of the leisure class. This can be seen in the novels of writers such as Henry James where ostentatious living and frequent glamorous trips abroad are the prerogative of 'superior' families. The leisure class in Veblen's time (and to a lesser extent now) also engaged in sporting activities distinctly different from those of the working class. This might be characterized in the UK context by the comparative positions of polo (and horse-related leisure more generally) and soccer. While polo has not become a pursuit of the masses, over time, soccer has become less of an exclusively working-class interest (something typified in the post-therapy thinly veiled autobiography of Nick Hornby's 1992 novel *Fever Pitch*). Indeed, polo and horse-related leisure are still sometimes to be found as marks of arrival by those who have come into wealth from humble origins. Horse-related leisure continues to be expensive; it is not something that can be substituted by cheap alternatives or digital copies. Being expensive it has conspicuous consumption attributes. It also signifies being a leisure-class member in a heightened inverted way because the origins of horse use lie in the working usefulness of the horse.

Later writers in a broadly 'economic sociology' vein have commented on the role of leisure in the economic system. The passing of leisure choices to the working classes was sometimes seen as compensatory as per the Beatles quote given later in this chapter. A dull, uninteresting and grinding job could be made more bearable. Interestingly, this notion was very prominent in the focus group marketing research for the advertising campaign for the return of rock group AC/DC in 2009.

As part of the general 'lonely crowd' (explored further in Chapter 22) thesis, Riesman and Glazer (1961) were quick to doubt the wider viability of the compensation argument, claiming:

> [L]eisure itself cannot rescue work, but fails with it, and can only be meaningful for most men if work is meaningful, so that the very qualities we looked for in leisure are more likely to come into being if social and political action fight the two-front battle of work-and-leisure.

This chimes with the ideas of modern leisure-specific writing that leisure activities must have 'meaning' lest they become mere 'free' or 'idle' time that runs the risk of degenerating into boredom (see Chapter 5). We should pause to note the gender politics of the time in this statement, as it refers only to men. The presumption may be that women only work for 'pin' money and do not get much leisure because they are primarily deployed in raising children. There is still a dearth of research on the economics of female leisure which is only partially redressed in this volume. The main contribution in this regard is Chapter 23 by Deborah Wheeler and Lauren Mintz which looks at the empowering effect of internet use in a male-dominated culture.

The issue of empowerment opens up another aspect of the use of leisure as work compensation which highlights the active/passive leisure distinction. Compensation can take the form of escapism, fantasy or even rampant hedonism such as promiscuous weekend clubbing and drinking. However, it could also occur in the traditional use of a 'hobby' interest where an individual is developing skills that do not find an outlet at the workplace. Besides the development of skills, hobby activities facilitate the exercise of power and control that may be unobtainable at work.

The current significance of leisure in the economy is breathtakingly obvious. It can be seen simply by switching on the television, walking down any high street and, in addition, going into a shop selling magazines. From a Marxist perspective, capturing workers' leisure time allows it to be turned into another profit opportunity. That is, their 'free time' is then not just time spent in recuperating for another bout of work. Perhaps workers would like to simply sit on the back step and listen to the birds or just go for a walk in their everyday attire. These leisure choices add nothing to the measured national output and the individual finally escapes the marketplace assuming, that is, that it is not burrowing away in their subconscious while they do these relaxing things. From the perspective of the needs of the capitalist economy, these distractions constitute a time surplus which could be utilized in forms of activity which sell commodities. Going outside may seem onerous and the weather may be offputting. If they do go outside they may have bought some leisure-specific outdoor clothing. This need not have a functional 'outdoors' role in terms of providing a use not provided by other clothing which might be worn for work or shopping. Instead, there may be lifestyle or relaxation symbolism in the clothing. Thus we have a leisurewear industry and we find people, who have no intention of doing any sporting activity, wearing tracksuits or shellsuits for long periods

People could stay inside and put on a relaxation aid (CD, video images, odour generator) in lieu of communion with nature. In lieu of walking about outdoors they could get on a treadmill or switch on their Wii and enjoy the pleasures of its exercise routine. Even if they still fancy totally passive 'doing nothing' uses of time there is still the possibility of the market intervening. For example, by selling a course on meditation or even a course or products for 'de-stressing' and time management.

Media-based industries are especially well situated to expand the consumer's leisure spending. This is reflected in the present volume in chapters on films, magazines and the increasingly important sector of video games. We do not offer any specific chapters on music or gambling. There are many economic writings on these topics. However, little interest is shown in these as leisure phenomena, as other headline topics grab attention. In the case of music, in recent times the issue of digital copying seems to have virtually assassinated all other possible research topics in the field. Although we may note that from the leisure perspective, it appears that participation in music is growing, partly aided by the facilities provided by personal computers. This observation brings up some issues raised by Bourdieu (whose work is discussed in Chapter 3) who saw the boundary between producer and consumer as somewhat blurred. Historically, music and movie consumption have been somewhat passive as leisure activities. The artists were viewed, by most, as being the only people fit to deliver the product and the consumer would, for the most part, not dare to attempt emulation. They were thus consigned to the status of a fan.

Technological advances in general and the internet in particular, have reduced the traditional class barriers in these fields. Video game playing (discussed in Chapter 19) raises the level of production in consumption as the player will, to a greater or lesser extent, achieve something (a score or a move to the next level) rather than simply saying 'I just watched a great movie/concert/sports event'. This productive activity does not necessarily have any great social or personal meaning. It is likely that, were he alive today, David Riesman would argue that video gaming further personifies the 'lonely crowd' problem as the individual, thus engrossed, is forgoing much of his/her social interaction needs.

Gambling involves money and risk, therefore it raises issues about rational choice. The wider field of the study of gambling is also concerned with its addiction and social problem dimensions. In terms of its economic significance, casinos are, in some territories, seen as vital parts of a development strategy. Historically, this is what saved Atlantic City on the east coast of the United States from its decline as a seaside resort. The 'walk down the high street' form of research, in the UK at any rate, suggests that after some rocky periods, the betting shop based mainly on sporting outcomes is making a resurgence. This is despite a general decline in retail centres and competition from online gambling. The general culture of gambling has changed in the UK. No doubt this has been helped by the introduction of a National Lottery in addition to the amount of advertising for gambling that is found on the internet. Television is particularly prone to promote gambling. Given its possible negative connotations as a social activity, such promotion is very much as a leisure activity, the bet is then 'a bit of fun'. Hence, bingo companies are allowed to sponsor daytime 'social issue' programmes. On top of this, the arrival of free-to-air digital television has meant that late night/early morning television is full of gambling broadcasts as well as more-or-less pornography in the form of telephone conversation presentations. This is somewhat ironic at a time when smoking sponsorship and advertising is not allowed at any time of the day.

The economy requires some kind of aggregate balance between work and leisure to function as a self-reproducing system. As John Lennon sang, in the Beatles song, 'Girl': 'A man must break his back to earn his day of leisure'. The prospect of leisure, bringing the 'variation, pleasure, relaxation and excitement' promised by Trust computer products, is a carrot inducing people to do more hours of work or work harder in the hours they do work. The latter incentive requires a connection between effort and earnings either directly or in the longer run through enhanced prospects of promotion. This carrot is circumscribed by the social organization of working time, which is discussed in Chapters 6 and 7. Working weekends, limited holidays, long hours, shift systems and high travel-to-work times limit the opportunity to enjoy the leisure that has been earned. That is, even if individuals have the capacity to enjoy their leisure time to the full, they may find that time schedule-related constraints are a hindrance as well as income constraints. For-profit firms (and also many non-profit organizations such as government departments) are expected to deliver efficient outcomes for shareholders/stakeholders. It is not their function to look after the well-being of the worker unless it directly impacts on production efficiency.

Depending on the mode of production, the firm may then severely circumscribe leisure opportunities because of the way work time and tasks are allocated. The arrival of machine-based production meant that machines needed to be kept working for long periods at high levels of capacity to attain efficient cost levels. This may require that workers do sustained and concentrated shifts with relatively few breaks. This creates tiredness and boredom (a subject discussed in Chapter 5). Regardless of the mode of production, a national desire to compete in world markets may bring 'time-lumpy' systems as in current Chinese industrial estates. All of these factors ensure that there is not a simple one-for-one correspondence between having more money and being able to have more leisure. In other words, it is not always the case that more leisure can be 'bought' as a money–leisure bargain is not always on the table as equivalent to a money–effort bargain. This is contradictory to the basic traditional neoclassical microeconomic income–leisure individual choice model.

SIGNIFICANCE OF LEISURE TO THE ECONOMIC THEORY OF INDIVIDUAL CHOICE

When the economics of individual choice first became formalized, the term 'leisure' was commonly used. Its use was very simple. Leisure is time spent not being paid to work. In this time one has, of course, to sleep and find food to eat and so on, but economists did not concern themselves with this. If pressed, one could argue that the quantity of sleep and eating time was predetermined by biological needs and social restrictions. There is a large amount of technical economic theoretical writing within this format and it is still used in many economic models as discussed by Balestrino in Chapter 2. He also discusses the minor revolution in the concept of leisure adopted by economists stemming from Becker (1965). Becker's framework is the key methodological element in the landmark study of time-use data (Aguiar and Hurst, 2007) which has come to the startling conclusion that hours of work have not fallen substantially, yet leisure has increased substantially. This is due to technological advances most notably in time-saving domestic appliances such as vacuum cleaners. Some (Frey et al., 2007) have taken this further to argue that modern Americans have gained six hours per week of leisure time which most of them spend watching television. Television watching is also often associated with unhealthy eating habits which may further reduce the capacity for leisure and reduce life expectancy. The idea that unwise (irrational) use of leisure time is causing health problems is particularly prominent in Australia. Bloomfield (2005) attempts to explain the unduly high morbidity rates of Australian males in terms of them 'killing time' in bored, lonely, passive unfulfilling leisure activities.

The suggestion that people do not know how to use their leisure time wisely seems contradictory to mainstream neoclassical economics. Yet this very proposition was offered by Alfred Marshall. Looking at the fifth edition of his *Principles of Economics* published in 1907, we find that leisure has three entries in the index, the last of which is separately tagged as 'difficulty of using it well 719–720'. The full quotation is as follows:

> But unfortunately human nature improves slowly, and in nothing more slowly than in the hard task of learning to use leisure well. In every age, in every nation, and in every rank of society, those who have known how to work well have been far more numerous than those who have known how to use leisure well.

Marshall retained these comments up until his final edition even though there are passages elsewhere which contradict them. His other remarks are confined to the simple need for leisure as rest and recuperation for the labour force. Marshall does not address the conflict between his quoted remark and the rational choice utility-maximizing model. The neglected work of Scitovsky (1992), discussed in more detail in Chapter 5, echoes Marhall's remarks. He says that many 'are unskilled and unprepared for making enjoyable and socially acceptable use' of their leisure time.

The more general point, about capacity to develop enjoyment, is now being taken up by economists influenced by Amartya Sen's writing on capabilities. Chapter 4, by Victoria Ateca-Amestoy, takes us further into the matter of subjective well-being (or 'happiness' to use the quick and easy populist label) and leisure. Those who cannot use leisure well or wisely cannot attain happiness no matter how much their resource base may have expanded. One possible reason for such failings, besides lack of capacity, is shifting of aspirational goals in terms of what is to be achieved during one's leisure time. This is now subject to the influence of virtual social networks discussed in Chapter 22. Fundamental targets of well-being can become invested with aspirational aims. Ostensibly, physical well-being, in terms of health and fitness (see Chapter 8), is an unambiguously desirable goal. It should expand the available utility from leisure, in any time period, and should also increase one's life span, thereby increasing total potential utility. In mainstream microeconomic models this would be embodied in a unidimensional concept of 'health capital'.

There are very few studies of the economic rationality of health and fitness decisions. In a climate of concern about 'couch potato' laziness, obesity and immobile media consumption, it might seem that any physical fitness activity embodies rational corrective behaviour. In a rare exploration, Della Vigna and Malmendier (2003), address this question using a panel dataset from three US health clubs with information on contract choices and day-to-day attendance. They studied 7,978 health club members over three years. On average, users on monthly contracts forwent $700 during their membership as they attended too infrequently to outperform, on costs, paying per visit. They say that the empirical results are difficult to reconcile with the standard assumption of time-consistent preferences and rational expectations. A model of time-inconsistent agents with overconfidence about future patience is used to explain their findings. The agents overestimate the future attendance and delay contract cancellation whenever renewal is automatic. This still leaves us without an explanation of why people should be overconfident about their own future patience. We might note that similar displays of behaviour and explanations could be used for the DIY/home improvement cases discussed by Earl and Peng in Chapter 10.

Leaving aside the analytical domain, we cannot avoid a very obvious fact about the economics of leisure. There has been a massive shift in the set of consumption/production opportunities. Three hundred years ago relatively few people had the opportunity to consider how to spend their time, as most of their time had to be spent ensuring survival. They also faced low life expectancy, meaning that they would not have faced a problem about allocating time and resources to leisure in a retirement period. Leisure (although the word was not then current) was the preserve of the rich and titled and it could be spent in a small number of well-defined ways. The revolution which has saved six hours a week according to Aguiar and Hurst is mainly a byproduct of the mechanical and electronic innovations generated in production industries.

The dominant technical influences in the changing use of leisure have been the car/transport, broadcasting and now the personal computer/phone/internet. The uses of these can be combined into movement and communication. Expansion in the capacity for movement for leisure has brought scope for holidays and 'day-trip' excursions, but it has been accompanied by an expansion in the time spent actually getting to and from work. This leads us into the thesis of the 'harried leisure class' touched upon in Part I, which forms something of a counter to the claim of Frey et al. (2007) cited earlier that time gained has been squandered in lazy television watching.

The same kind of 'double-bind' argument applies to the increased range and productivity of communication methods. These could, in theory, free one up from work in terms of both time and space (specifically in the form of working from home, discussed in Chapter 7) and also increase the productivity of leisure. In practice, improved forms of communication mean more risks (identity theft, for example) and greater potential for surveillance of individuals by both their employer and the government. On top of this, there is the possible issue of the tools for increased pleasure becoming the instruments of increased oppression as the communication gains are almost solely derived from computing in some shape or form. So, individuals find their pleasurable leisure time further curtailed by equipment malfunction and shortcomings of various types.

AIM AND SCOPE OF THIS BOOK

The collection of chapters in this volume is diverse in terms of topic, ideology and methodology. Most chapters draw on some kind of empirical evidence, some of which is newly produced. No attempt has been made to suggest that any specific approach is universally most useful in analysing leisure. Nor do we suggest that a magnificent synthesis which fully encapsulates the subject is about to be forthcoming. The work presented is interdisciplinary to some extent as some chapters blend economics and other ideas.

I decided not to arrange the selections by topic. Rather the division is as follows:

- Part I   Economic dimensions of leisure;
- Part II   Work/leisure balance;
- Part III   People and places as leisure;
- Part IV   Spectating and events; and
- Part V   Diversions and perversions.

Thus, Part I largely contains discussions of the standard income–leisure trade-off model, the introduction of Becker's time allocation model and some broader issues. Part II looks more at problems around the welfare the individual derives from leisure, and thus goes to the heart of the matter which concerned Alfred Marshall. We then have three more specifically applied parts. The first of these (Part III) looks at both intimate and virtual relationships as forms of leisure. Part IV looks mainly at entertainment and sport. These share high production costs in terms of time intensity and a high degree of rivalry in the overall time-use marketplace. Some contributions here look at individual motivations, while others look more at the strategic responses of suppliers. Finally, we come to Part V on 'Diversions and perversions'. These concern primarily things that bestow some kind of sense of freedom and, in certain cases, a degree of idling inactivity.

Inevitably there is a degree of overlap and some chapters might have been placed in other parts, but overall we hope this is found to be a useful flow of material. One thing that has been attempted is to bring to light some neglected areas such as popular music festivals (Chapter 13). The cultural economics area has featured many articles on the rather select and elitist area of specialist festivals mainly with respect to the impact of subsidy. Earlier in this chapter, comment was made on some of the areas that do not appear in the present work such as gambling and musical activities. Some of these could not make it to full-blown chapters due to lack of willing contributors. In terms of activities located mainly inside the home, we do not have a chapter on cooking as leisure although we do have a chapter on the home improvements/DIY field (Chapter 10).

Outdoor domestic time use is a particularly neglected area and one which is important in a number of ways. Gardening/farming-type activities can bring a number of health and environmental benefits and they also generate revenues for companies supplying seeds, plants, fertilizers, tools and so on. Nevertheless it is hard to find much relevant research pertaining to the leisure aspect of horticulture from an economic point of view.

A burgeoning area in business research concerns the domestic pet sector. This is briefly touched on in Chapter 6 on work–life balance, although it has not received much specific attention from economists (but see Schwartz et al., 2007). The business research arose from studies of family spending which discovered that pets were being regarded as family members. Pet ownership also seems to be correlated with spending on one's self, and is often claimed to raise the subjective well-being of the pet owner.

Pets take us to another area not specifically highlighted in this volume – the role of children in leisure time. The leisure time of the child and the impact of children's use of time on parents are both of economic significance. Expanded consumption opportunities and intensive marketing potentially expand the passive leisure of children, causing substitution away from study (investment in human capital) and reducing income of parents and thereby their leisure time, although there may be a countervailing effect due to less time spent directly in child-rearing. Declining birth rates in developed economies may reflect a preference for leisure time over investment in children, although it could also show a preference for 'quality' of children over quantity.

CONCLUSION

This chapter has given a very broad account of leisure activities and some of the key concepts in the core and fringes of economic analysis relating to them. Some of the themes taken up in the following chapters have also been highlighted. In addition, we have noted those areas where there is a shortage of research.

REFERENCES

Aguiar, M. and E. Hurst (2007), 'Measuring trends in leisure: the allocation of time over five decades', *Quarterly Journal of Economics*, **122**, 969–1005.

Becker, G. (1965), 'A theory of the allocation of time', *Economic Journal*, **75**, 493–8.

Bloomfield, L.J. (2005), 'Killing time: the effect of boredom during unstructured leisure time on men's health', unpublished PhD thesis, Victoria University, Australia.

Csikszentmihalyi, M. (1990), *Flow: The Psychology of Optimal Experience*, New York: Harper & Row.

Csikszentmihalyi, M. and J. LeFevre (1989), 'Optimal experience in work and leisure', *Journal of Personality and Social Psychology*, **56**, 815–22.

Della Vigna, U. and S. Malmendier (2003), 'Overestimating self-control: evidence from the Health Club Industry', Research Paper No. 1800, Research Paper series, Stanford Graduate School of Business, Stanford, CA.

Frey, B.S., C. Benesch and A. Stutzer (2007), 'Does watching TV make us happy?', *Journal of Economic Psychology*, **28** (3), 293–313.

Marshall, A. (1907), *Principles of Economics*, 5th edn, London: Macmillan.

Riesman, D. with Nathan Glazer (1961), '*The Lonely Crowd*: a reconsideration in 1960', in S.M. Lipset and L. Lowenthal (eds), *Culture and Social Character: The Work of David Riesman Reviewed*, New York: Free Press of Glencoe, pp. 349–69.

Schwarz, Peter M., Jennifer L. Troyer and Jennifer Beck Walker (2007), 'Animal house: economics of pets and the household', *The B.E. Journal of Economic Analysis and Policy*, **7** Article 35, available at: http://www.bepress.com/bejeap/vol7/iss1/art35.

Scitovsky, Tibor (1992), *The Joyless Economy*, rev. edn, New York: Oxford University Press.

PART I

ECONOMIC DIMENSIONS OF LEISURE

2 On economics, leisure and much more[1]
Alessandro Balestrino

INTRODUCTION

Sometimes even economists, dismal as they may be, go to the cinema in their free time. A straightforward application of the law of large numbers tells us that, given enough cinemas and enough economists, at least one of them must have watched *Vicky, Cristina, Barcelona* (2008) directed by Woody Allen. In fact, the author of this chapter did – which proves the proposition. He liked the film, and was intrigued by the way in which the director had portrayed the different attitudes to leisure of Europeans and Americans: the former are quite a relaxed lot, who enjoy their creativity and take their time to do what has to be done, while the latter always look busy, hurrying from one task to the other without pause. This is in fact an old theme in the arts, and Allen has at least a significant predecessor that he himself mentioned in interviews: Henry James, one of the most important authors in English literature. James was American, but lived most of his life in London, and a large part of his novels and stories are centred around the contrast between America and Europe. Sometimes this contrast is about the attitudes to leisure: for example, in *Washington Square*, written in the late nineteenth century, he describes the United States as a country where a man who does not earn his income is not well considered in society – this is of course as opposed to the European ideal of the gentleman who lives off his land.

The debate about the different way in which leisure is perceived on the opposite sides of the Atlantic is not limited to literature or the cinema. It can be found in journalism, and has recently made its way into economics as well. The question why Americans' working hours are so much longer than Europeans' is a challenging one for economists, and a few years ago was the subject of a dispute between Prescott (2004) and Alesina et al. (2005). The former argued that the whole difference is due to the different taxation level (higher in Europe), while the latter claimed instead that the main reason is the strong unionization of the European labour market, in which working hours have been reduced in order to curb unemployment. To explain the differing attitudes, Blanchard (2004) underlines the cultural differences between Europeans and Americans, an argument that is very much in line with the Henry James view, as we may call it, according to which Americans tend to be much more active than Europeans. However, Alesina et al. dismiss this line of reasoning and remark that the divergence in terms of working hours is a relatively recent one, as Europeans worked more or less the same as Americans as late as the 1960s.

Actually, cultural influences certainly are not deterministic forces, so that fluctuations are always possible (in the late nineteenth century, still according to the Henry James view, upper-class Americans worked much harder than upper-class Europeans); hence, this sort of criticism is hardly decisive. In fact, it is easy to see behind it the standard dismissal of cultural factors as vague and unmeasurable. However, the role of culture, intended as a set of beliefs about the environment in which the agents live, has recently been made the subject of increasing attention by certain economists (see, for example, Fernandez, 2007 for a review), and we shall follow their lead whenever it may prove fruitful. Indeed, the explanation advanced by Alesina et al. (2005) begs the questions why the European market is so much more unionized than the American one, and why unions have chosen a 'work less, work all' objective rather than other conceivable objectives. Could there be some 'cultural' factor at work behind the scenes? Could it be that European unions insist on shorter working hours out of a time-honoured respect for the man of leisure? In his book on the rise of economic inequality in the US, Frank (2007) argues that income is a positional good for Americans while leisure is not – a positional good being one that is enjoyed not only in itself but also inasmuch as it allows the individual to rank higher on some socioeconomically significant scale. Although Frank does not make the inference, it is possible to suggest that, on the contrary, Europeans tend to see 'leisure' as a positional good, and this attitude could be behind the unions' requests. This would be consistent with Veblen's old argument that, in the American society of his time, status was signalled by conspicuous consumption and the presence of idle household members rather than by the direct enjoyment of leisure time, as had been the case in more ancient times (Veblen, 1899), and may still be the case in societies as deeply rooted in the past as most European ones are.

This sort of discussion, which involves historical and sociological elements, is relatively new in mainstream economics.[2] Veblen's contributions have routinely resurfaced and have sometimes been taken as the basis of orthodox approaches, but neoclassical economists have by and large taken a narrow view of leisure as 'non-working time'. The focus of the analysis is typically on labour, and whatever is concluded to determine the labour supply would also determine leisure time as a residual. For example, in public finance one would study the effect of taxes on labour – although of course the effects on leisure are speculative; if a tax is raised on labour income, the shadow price of leisure is reduced; that is, leisure is effectively subsidized. In recent years, interdisciplinary efforts have become fashionable among economists, especially after the psychologist Daniel Kahneman was awarded the Nobel Prize in economics in 2002. But until then, the most significant departure from the standard approach to leisure was Becker's household production theory (Becker, 1965), especially in the Gronau (1977) version which distinguished between pure leisure and time employed in non-market production activities. Becker's approach brings the time allocation problem to the forefront of the agent's decision process, as utility is taken to depend on domestically produced commodities, with purchased goods and time as inputs. Moreover, household economics recognizes explicitly that the household is a multiperson entity, and models the interactive process whereby actual consumption decisions are taken. Becker's own solution to the problem, that of assuming an altruistic head of the family who decides for all taking everybody's desires into account, is not particularly satisfactory, but more elaborate proposals, on which we shall touch briefly in what follows, have been made in later contributions.

In this chapter, I shall review briefly the evolution of the economists' notion of leisure over the years, touching on the various authors and issues that we have mentioned in the Introduction. The usual space limits, and, more importantly, limits of the author's knowledge, prevent us from treating the question in a truly exhaustive manner. Indeed, I have deliberately sacrificed the scope of the review in order to keep the presentation more fluid and homogeneous.

THE ALLOCATION OF TIME

Let us begin with a brief sketch of how neoclassical economics usually deals with time allocation issues. In the basic models, it is normally assumed that agents have a fixed endowment of time, and that there are two possible time uses: market labour and leisure. Formally, this requires that the utility function is defined over consumption and time:

$$u = u(c, l),$$

where c may be a vector or a composite commodity, and l is labour. There are two constraints, the standard budgetary one, and a time constraint:

$$pc = wl;$$
$$h + l = T,$$

where p is the (vector of) price(s), h is leisure, and T is the time endowment. Labour enters the utility function as a bad, rather than a good (that is the partial derivative with respect to l is negative); the agents are supposed to dislike labour, and correspondingly, to appreciate leisure – the latter is indeed usually conceived as a normal good. More refined models may employ a variant of Lancaster's (1966) characteristic approach, and assume that labour time has both positive and negative traits, but the bulk of the literature sticks to this very straightforward view. The solution of the maximization problem is very simple; at the optimum, the marginal rate of substitution equals the price ratio.

Note that even an extremely simple model like this is often able to yield valuable insights, when applied to real-world problems. Nevertheless, whatever its merits, the basic dichotomy between labour and leisure tends to lump together very different uses of non-working time. Indeed, when an agent is not at work, he/she can do a variety of things, such as watching TV (which is close to what we think of as leisure) but also cooking, tending the garden, or helping the children with their homework. There is in fact a vast variety of tasks that one can perform while not working but that we intuitively perceive as being not exactly leisurely in nature.

This intuition is at the root of Becker's approach which transformed the view that economists have of time allocation issues (Becker, 1965).[3] He suggested that the goods that we purchase on the market should not enter the utility function directly; rather, we should consider that these goods are normally combined with time to yield products which are ultimately what we care for (the objects of our preference ordering). Hence, utility functions are defined over domestically produced commodities in which marketed items and time uses appear as inputs. I buy spaghetti, garlic, extra-virgin olive oil and then, combining them with a portion of my time endowment (as well as some fixed inputs), I cook a home-made pasta; the latter is what actually gives me utility.

Formally, this requires that we specify household production functions of the type:

$$z^i = z^i(x^i, t^i),$$

where z^i is a domestically produced commodity, x^i is a (vector of) marketed good(s) that are used as inputs in the production of z^i and t^i is the portion of time allocated to that specific production process. The purchase of what we may call 'inputs' is subject to the usual budget constraint:

$$\Sigma_i p^i x^i = wl;$$

and the time uses are also subject to a constraint:

$$\Sigma_i t^i + l = T.$$

The utility function represents preferences over the z-goods (the commodities):

$$u = u(z^1, z^2, \ldots, z^n).$$

At the optimum, the marginal rates of substitution between the commodities equal the 'shadow price' ratios; a shadow price is defined as the average cost of production (in which the opportunity cost of time is of course also included).

It is worth noting that the very notion of leisure becomes ill-defined in this context. What we can say is that different commodities will of course require a different ratio of time to purchased input; the ones whose production processes are more time intensive will presumably be those that we intuitively think of as leisure. For example, if a person is in the mood for playing golf, we can say that by using a relatively large amount of time and relatively few purchased inputs this person produces entertainment for him/herself – and this corresponds to the usual meaning of leisure (unless we believe that he/she has just ruined a good walk). However, if the person of our example is a businessman who is playing golf over the weekend with potential clients or providers, then the distinction between leisure and labour becomes blurred. Our man is probably having a good time, but also building a relationship that may be quite useful in business terms. This suggests that we should be careful not to oversimplify when we interpret the ways in which economic agents employ their time.[4] Nevertheless, it has become common to gather all the most time-intensive domestic production processes under the heading of leisure, retaining a more complex structure for the other time uses (this approach has been popularized by Gronau, 1977). In certain cases, this has no negative consequences.

From our perspective, the household production approach matters because it has shown forcefully that the activities carried out during the time not allotted to market work are just as worthy of economic analysis. Running a household is an activity that requires careful decision making and is just as complex as running a small business (and indeed in the not-so-distant past, families were in fact a small business for the most part; think, for example, of farms). Henceforth, home activities can be studied with the same toolbox and the same attitude employed for market activities; the interconnections between the two spheres of economic action are so relevant that ignoring them does a disservice to the interpretative capabilities of economics. And, importantly, the time allocation process lies at the core of the whole analysis.

In particular, the household economics perspective emphasizes that what goes on inside the family matters for the economy at large. For example, many of the activities in which the economic agents engage at home produce outputs that are substitutable for market goods. The implicit competition must be understood for a proper economic analysis, and for forming sensible policy prescriptions (Sørensen, 1994). Also, the family is heavily involved in the creation of an agent's marketable skills. To pick up just one example out of many, what are the economic implications, for a girl, of having received an education centred on the ability to perform household chores? Does this affect her career choice because it biases the formation of her human capital towards a specific direction (Dale, 2009)? And, perhaps even more importantly, the reproductive decisions – how many children to have, how much to invest in them – must be seen not only as accounting for the signals coming from the economic environment, but also as affecting the environment itself. In other words, within the household production perspective, fertility choices are the outcome of a rational process in which well-informed parents decide the quantity and quality (of life) of their offspring by balancing the costs and benefits of each option, as determined by the general economic situation in which they live – the demands of their jobs, the nature of public help, and so forth. In turn, these choices affect the economic situation for the current as well as the future generations, for example because the quantity and the quality of the children have an impact on public expenditure in childcare and schooling now, but also on the sustainability of social security and more generally on the tax revenue of the government in the years ahead, when the children, now adults, enter the job market and pay the contributions for the pay-as-you-go pension system as well as taxes in general (Cigno et al., 2003).

Even choosing among the home production activities those that we can regard as instances of leisure, the connection with market forces remains as strong as ever: listening to music is certainly something that people do (mainly) in their free time, but it requires the purchase of CDs and of hi-fi equipment, or a trip to the venue of the concert (with the ensuing travel and accommodation costs). Moreover, and maybe more relevantly, many non-market activities carried out in one's free time deserve careful economic analysis in their own right. An interesting example is the economics of love.[5] Zelder (2009) investigates the production of love in an existing couple, and more specifically proposes to see love as a perhaps unintended byproduct of joint actions by the partners in a couple. An evening at home (time), good music and a glass of wine (marketed goods) can produce entertainment as the intended outcome of the production process, and also a feeling of love as a possibly unintended consequence.

Zelder argues that in a family, several circumstances (such as monopoly power and free-riding) may arise that induce a less-than-optimal production of love. It is methodologically interesting to see how well-known inefficiency-generating situations play their role in the reasoning here. It is a brilliant example, I believe, of how household production models allow economists to make non-trivial statements about subjects that at first sight might appear very far from the ones with which they are usually concerned.

PUBLIC FINANCE STUDIES

One of the branches of economics that has paid relatively much attention to leisure almost since its inception is public finance. The problem of optimal taxation was famously anticipated by Ramsey (1927), and then became central to economic theory thanks to Corlett and Hague (1953) and others. Due to the need to finance public expenditures aimed at remedying the market failures of second-best economies, a certain amount of revenue has to be raised, and therefore a tax system has to be designed. The original question posed was that of designing it so as to minimize the efficiency loss inherent to its use. Later, the problem was amended to include equity considerations, and the aim became that of designing a tax structure that realized the best possible compromise between the two often contradictory objectives of minimizing inefficiencies and realizing the amount of redistribution implied by the social preferences.

Of course, the reference model in public finance was, at the beginning, of the standard labour/leisure variety, as the early studies pre-date the household economics revolution. We shall therefore start from presenting the main issues within that framework, and revert to the household production view towards the end. Within the basic dichotomic approach, leisure has played a crucial role in the development of the theory of optimal taxation. Partly this role has been substantial, and partly purely formal, the result of choices made basically for convenience and not necessarily for the purpose of making the model more realistic. To see this, we need to provide a few details on how optimal tax analysis is usually conducted.

It turns out that optimal tax analysis is especially simple if one assumes constant returns to scale in the production sector. For one thing this ensures that any tax levied on the production side will be translated 100 per cent forward, which makes it unnecessary to distinguish between production and consumption taxes. More importantly, it freezes any impact that changes in the production (that is, pre-tax) prices (denoted by p) may have on the consumer demand. In fact, the latter is in principle homogeneous of degree zero in the vector (q, m), where q is the consumption (that is, post-tax) prices and m is the lump-sum profit distributed by the firms to the consumers. However, with constant returns to scale, $m = 0$ always. Therefore, changes in pre-tax price do not affect either m or the consumer demand functions. This means that we can normalize the vector of production prices and choose a numeraire; at the same time, we can normalize the vector of consumption prices *independently* and choose an untaxed good. Since the two normalization processes do not interfere with each other, a good can be simultaneously the numeraire and the untaxed good: that is, both its production price and its consumption price equal unity. In turn, the normalization is useful to highlight the fact that, in a general equilibrium perspective, only relative prices matter; the optimal tax design gives prescriptions in terms of relative, as opposed to absolute, prices. That is, if at the optimum it turns out that good 1 must be taxed or good 2 must be subsidized, this must not be taken literally: what the result really means is that good 1 must be taxed less heavily than the numeraire/untaxed good, and good 2 more leniently.

Although nothing requires that leisure is chosen as the numeraire/untaxed good, in the early optimal tax literature it became common to do so, possibly because those early models had a fixed time allocation, and no income tax. Results were often phrased with reference to leisure specifically rather than to the numeraire/untaxed good in general, which has been the source of a dangerous misunderstanding. Indeed, and this is crucial in models with time allocation choices, some practitioners did not realize that the missing tax on labour income, that is to say the missing tax on the shadow price of leisure, was just an artefact of the model, the outcome of the normalization procedure; they actually interpreted it as a reflection of the fact that leisure was 'untaxable'. Nothing could be more wrong: it would in fact mean that one cannot have an income tax, which is of course untrue. On the contrary, in a standard labour–leisure choice model the presence of the income tax implies an effect on the shadow price of leisure – any positive tax on labour is in fact a negative tax, that is, a subsidy,[6] on leisure. To avoid this misunderstanding, it has later become common, in income tax models, to use a consumption good as the numeraire/untaxed good.

In this wider perspective, the substantial part played by leisure in the interpretation of optimal tax results becomes clear. Indeed, these results point consistently in the direction of suggesting that *commodities that are complementary with leisure should be taxed particularly heavily*. The chain of arguments leading to the above prescription can be summarized as follows. The presence of the income tax distorts the time allocation away from labour towards leisure as it reduces the shadow price of the latter, determining a substitution effect that is taken to be dominant over any income effect that may act in the opposite direction.[7] The optimal design of a second-best tax system calls then for counter-distortions that induce the agents to work more and enjoy less leisure. Adding a further distortion in the opposite direction as the original one contributes to reducing overall inefficiency (incidentally, this shows that the unfortunately too common practice of counting distortions in order to assess how much an economy is far away from the first best is incorrect). Since leisure cannot be taxed independently from labour, we can act indirectly by taxing goods that are complementary to the former. Therefore, all the activities that agents carry out in their free time – say, going to the cinema, playing golf or fishing – should be taxed more or subsidized less than the numeraire.

These findings are at the centre of a wide debate on the role of commodity versus income taxation. Some authors have emphasized the importance of the former type of tax in the perspective that we have just outlined, remarking that commodity takes are extremely helpful for attaining a reasonable compromise between equity and efficiency objectives – income tax may be designed in a progressive fashion, ensuring the desired amount of redistribution, while commodity taxes take care of the ensuing efficiency problems. Others have been influenced by a well-known result originally developed by Atkinson and Stiglitz (1976) in a seminal contribution. These authors argued that if the most complete income tax system that could be devised in second best – a system in which tax rates vary continuously with income – is implemented, and leisure is weakly separable in the utility function, then commodity taxes are useless. Weak separability implies that the marginal rates of substitution between any pair of commodities are independent of the level of leisure enjoyed; the basis for indirect taxation (that is, the differences in degrees of complementarity with leisure) then disappears. Those who believe that weak separability is a good assumption tend then to support the abolition of commodity taxes – although they forget that the Atkinson–Stiglitz result also requires a very powerful income tax, one that is very far from what we can find in the real world.

As mentioned, optimal tax analysis has also been performed within household production theory (Sandmo, 1990 is at the origin of this branch of the literature; see also Anderberg and Balestrino, 2000 for a detailed analysis and further references). Public finance studies have normally followed the Gronau (1997) specification, in which all time-intensive uses of time are gathered under a common denominator and labelled 'leisure'. This format is especially convenient for studying the direct versus indirect tax controversy in a wider setting. Once household production is factored in, standard optimal tax results must be revised – the very language in which they are usually presented may become misleading, if not downright meaningless. For example, the Atkinson–Stiglitz result that we discussed at the end of the previous section cannot even be stated correctly in a full-blown household production model, because, as we saw, there is no such thing as leisure, so one cannot say whether it is separable or not. In the Gronau version, the notion of weak separability of labour regains its meaning, but loses its effect on the design of the tax system: for, even if leisure is weakly separable, the other uses of time for less time-intensive production processes are not, so that the logic of the Atkinson–Stiglitz reasoning fails.

Once we take household production into account, a role for commodity taxation remains no matter how effective the income tax schedule we are able to devise. This role remains similar to the one it has in the optimal tax design when a standard labour/leisure model is adopted, but the specific prescriptions (tax that good lightly, tax that other good heavily) depend now on the role of the marketed goods in household production. There are some goods that are clearly inputs in domestic production processes, and others that act as substitutes for the output of such processes. Food is again a good example: raw foodstuff has a definite role as input, whereas restaurant meals, or even pre-cooked items, tend to replace home-made meals. Thus, the general aim remains that of counteracting the distortions away from market work induced by the income tax, but the exact way in which this is achieved, in this setting, is by taxing inputs in home production more heavily than market substitutes.

LEISURE AND WELL-BEING

A question that economists seem strangely reluctant to tackle is whether having more free time makes people happier. Neither household production nor public finance practitioners are prepared to answer this sort of question: economists are trained to look at behaviour, and at how it could be influenced by policy choices. Certainly, economists presume that behaviour is dictated by the maximization of an objective function that represents utility. But the utility function is unknowable, and the study of its determinants is believed by many to lie outside the scope of economics.[8] Welfare economics should take care of these aspects, and in a sense does so at a theoretical level, recovering an interpretation of utility as well-being as opposed to a mere preference ordering. However, its efforts are less convincing at the applied level, inasmuch as it identifies utility with real income, completely sidestepping the issue of consumer satisfaction (or better, assuming it away on the basis of the implicit postulate that more income necessarily makes the economic agent more satisfied).

Discussions on the value of leisure for human well-being were more common before marginalist economics became dominant from the 1930s onwards. For example, Marshall in his *Principles* comments, although in a characteristically unsystematic fashion, on the importance of using leisure time appropriately – see, for example, the quote and the brief comments in Chapter 1. Going even farther back in time, it may be instructive to remind the reader that Thomas Carlyle's famous (or infamous) attribution of the epithet 'dismal science', to political economy originated amidst a controversy on the uses of time. Carlyle (1849) argued that the emancipation of slaves in the West Indies had determined a shortage of labour because the natives were not interested in working beyond the minimum that ensured them a basic sustenance and were instead prone to spend the time on wasteful activities; and he saw the liberal political economists, in their role as opponents of slavery, as responsible for favouring a displacement of appropriate uses of time (such as working) by idle and empty ones – hence the accusation of practising a dismal science.

After several decades, however, happiness studies have recently become once more popular among economists, and although they have not yet reached mainstream status, they have become a recognized field of research (see, for example, Easterlin, 2001). The starting-point is often the observation that, beyond a certain level, increases in income do not automatically imply more happiness, usually intended as subjective well-being – but see Kahneman et al. (1997) for an exploration of the concept of objective happiness. The focus on leisure as such is not particularly prominent (however, see Chapter 6 in this volume). Still, even the simple labour/leisure models seem very well-suited for these sorts of study, as they recognize explicitly the dual nature of working time, and highlight the trade-off between consumption and leisure. Household production models are even more appropriate, as they allow an explicit representation of the paradoxical situation in which an economic agent is bound to find him/herself (at least in Western societies): the agent needs to devote time to the effort of earning the money needed to boost his/her consumption, but since consumption also requires time, the more the agent earns, the less he/she can enjoy what he/she buys.

Implicitly, a representation of the time allocation problem similar to the one supplied by the household production approach, an idea, that is, of consumption technology, is behind two pathbreaking works of the 1970s that shed a rather critical light on the increasing reliance on consumer spending as the engine of economic growth: Linder's (1970) analysis of the scarcity of time and Scitovsky's (1976) critique of the consumer society. At the time, the impact of these two works was minimal, but today they are being rediscovered. Indeed, they are two remarkable examples of early studies in what we know these days as the economics of happiness, and, furthermore, they happen to be extremely topical, as if they had been guided by some benevolent anachronistic hand. Their subject is perhaps more relevant today, after the 2008 Wall Street crisis, than it was back in the 1970s. The emphasis on consumer spending had never been brought to consequences as extreme as those that have led to the financial disasters of 2008, in particular the explosion of private debt.

Linder's argument is multifaceted, and we cannot discuss it here with the level of detail that it would deserve. One side that is especially relevant in our context starts from the observation that increases in productivity make working time more valuable, and determine therefore a change in time allocation – a reduction of the time available for domestic consumption activities. This may be construed as implying that increases in productivity induce economic growth at the expense of creating a greater scarcity of time. There are also some consequences of how people tend to employ their non-working time. Certain activities, which are necessarily time intensive, such as those related to the creation of interpersonal relationships or the cultivation of the mind, will have to be sacrificed; as for others, the input ratio can be made less time intensive by an appropriate selection of the marketed goods, perhaps a more expensive version that allows a shortened domestic production process (such as pre-cooked meals rather than raw foodstuff to prepare lunch).

Scitovsky's analysis is also very rich. First, it is remarkable for its interdisciplinary approach; at a time when the boundaries in social science were mostly closed, Scitovsky tried to develop, from the vantage point of economics, a 'psychology of human satisfaction'. As has now become standard practice in happiness studies (see above), his starting-point was the fact that in what he saw as an extremely affluent society, more affluent than ever, people did not seem to be happier than before. Scitovsky argues that this happened because the tendency had been towards an increase in the consumption of what he calls 'comfort goods' (TV shows, luxury cars, sports watches, and so on), that is, goods that allow immediate pleasure but soon become a source of addiction and consequently of boredom. He sees the individual as constantly oscillating between strain and boredom,[9] trying to avoid excesses in both directions – an argument that he develops using discoveries from clinical psychology and neuropsychiatry (today, we would call him a neuroeconomist!). The idea, therefore, is that if a good does not trigger a minimum of arousal, if it does not induce in the individual some degree of activation, then it will not yield a lasting sense of satisfaction. On the other hand, there are consumption activities that are capable of delivering a type of satisfaction that may actually *increase* over time, such as practising a sport, listening to good music, learning a new language, building social relationships – more generally, all those goods that are related to our culture and to our sense of community. But, as we noted above when discussing Linder's analysis, these forms of consumption are costly, especially because they require time, more particularly when one is in the early phases: before enjoying the pleasure of reading the Latin poets in their own language, one has to actually learn Latin, and that may take years of often challenging and difficult exercises. The temptation to indulge in comfort goods may therefore be overwhelming, given the tendency to avoid strain.

Scitovsky's view of comfort goods as a source of addiction suggests yet another connection with Becker's work apart from that with household production models. One of the subfields Becker helped to create is indeed the economics of addiction, with the explicit aim of showing how rational choice theory could accommodate addictive behaviour (Becker and Murphy, 1988). The argument is that a rational consumer can predict that a certain substance will 'hook' him/her, but will accept this because of an expectation of net benefit. Scitovsky's view is somewhat different but not impossible to reconcile – however, it has a far wider reach and might include the most extreme situations (drug addicts or chain smokers) as a subcase. Scitovsky sees most ordinary, everyday goods as potentially addictive, and this seems to capture the essence of addiction in a very deep sense – just think of how clothes or shoes can become objects of compulsive behaviour *à la* Becky Bloomwood (the heroine of the *The Secret Dreamworld of a Shopaholic* series by Sophie Kinsella). There is again an astonishing topicality in Scitovksy's work: more that 30 years ago, working from the perspective of economics, he had basically anticipated today's discoveries of neuroscience, pointing out that addiction is not only about mind-altering substances, but also about a general attitude towards the achievement of pleasure through consumption in general. This in turn relates to the hypothesis that addiction seems to arise from the fact that we, as a species, are attracted towards things that give us pleasure, because we perceive them as important to our survival (see, for example, Paulus, 2007). This is clearly an advantageous attitude from an evolutionary standpoint, but has the drawback that sometimes the hard-wired programming is started from substances that have long-term, not easily foreseeable, negative consequences, and sooner or later become indispensable to its activation. The point that neuroscientists make today, just as Scitovsky did in his book, is, however, that not only what we commonly call drugs may be responsible for this: everything that is inherently enjoyable can turn into an addiction – food, TV, video games, sex, gambling, shopping, the internet.[10]

Taking Linder's and Scitovsky's analyses together, we obtain an uncannily accurate rendition of how most people live today in our societies

– more accurate than if we still were in the 1970s. One could also take a further step, and attempt a normative statement. If one held the view that culture- and community-related activities (reading a book or listening to music, spending quality time with one's relatives or friends) are essential to one's well-being, it is clear that what passes today for a 'normal' way of living will be judged as normatively unacceptable. The ancient Greeks' ideal of a life dominated by contemplation, poetry and political debate is very hard to achieve these days.

ECONOMICS AND SOCIAL STATUS

A branch of the literature that often crosses the path of happiness studies is the economics of social status. A possible explanation of why more income does not necessarily make us happier is that if others also experience the same or a similar income rise, we do not acquire a higher status relative to them. As long as we care for status, this may offset the impact of the increase in income. Certainly, mainstream economics has usually downplayed the importance of status-seeking as a motivation of behaviour. Among anthropologists, sociologists and social psychologists, the idea is instead largely accepted; there might be no general consensus on exactly how important status is, but social scientists in general would agree that it matters to some extent.

However, it is also possible to find within economics important contributions on the subject. The first systematic study of social comparison in economics, and one in which leisure plays a vital part, is famously due to Veblen (1899). Veblen's argument has anthropological roots. He noted that in primitive societies the ruling-class members kept for themselves jobs such as hunting and fighting which held high symbolic importance, but at the same time allowed them to enjoy much more leisure than everyday jobs like farming. Hence, he argued, the very fact of having free time became a signal for a high social rank. He saw the same factors at work in the American society of the late nineteenth century in which he lived, and deduced that the search for status had been, and still was, the primary driving force behind all human actions. The specific ways in which status was signalled had, however, changed over the years. In his time, he saw that businessmen, unlike tribal chiefs, were kept very busy by the demands of their profession, and had thus replaced consumption for leisure as a way to signal their status. Of course, this form of consumption had to be highly visible to perform this task – it had to be 'conspicuous'. Rich industrialists had to live in large mansions, give magnificent receptions and so on. Also, they employed a host of servants and carefully kept their wives and daughters free from work duties, using the fact that they could afford to keep so many members of their household fundamentally idle as a further proof of their status.

Although Veblen was highly critical of marginal utility and neoclassical economics,[11] nothing would prevent us from casting the above arguments using the standard array of economic tools and devices, and indeed several contemporary economists have worked along these lines. The notion of the utility-maximizing, self-centred agent who allocates his/her scarce resources efficiently is by no means incompatible with that of the status-seeking agent, as utility functions incorporating the desire to do better than some reference standard are easy to define. For example, Ireland (1994) and Falk and Knell (2004) have studied social status and social comparisons; Bernheim (1994) and Bagwell and Bernheim (1996) have used signalling games to characterize the emergence of fashions and fads in social equilibria; Boskin and Sheshinski (1978), Corneo and Jeanne (1997) and Ireland (2001) have performed optimal tax analysis under the assumption that agents are interested in status.

But important examples can also be found going farther back in time. Before the permanent income hypothesis (Friedman, 1957) became dominant in the 1950s, an influential theory of consumption was the 'relative income hypothesis', which maintained that consumption decisions are taken on the basis of two main frames of reference, to wit the living standards of important others and one's previous living standard (Duesenberry, 1949). As Frank (2005) argues, the relative income hypothesis does better than the permanent income one in terms of interpreting empirical puzzles and outlining possible tendencies, such as explaining the fact that consumption decisions are often less responsive to income fluctuations than one might expect, but it was easily supplanted by Friedman's alternative approach. Why Duesenberry's view was set aside so abruptly remains somewhat unclear. Here, we advance the following explanation. The 1950s were the years in which Friedman's positive approach to economics, according to which the quality of an economic model should not be judged from the accuracy of its assumptions on behaviour, but from the reliability of its predictions, gained a large following among economists (Friedman, 1953). It is interesting to note how strongly such an approach was influenced by the prevalent theoretical position in psychology at the time, 'behaviourism'. At the heart of behaviourism, as developed in the works of Watson (1924) and later of Skinner (1938) among others, lies the idea that those aspects of the psychological functions that cannot be observed, what goes on in one's consciousness or one's mind, cannot be subjected to a proper scientific treatment. It was proposed instead to make *observable behaviour* the only object of scientific studies. According to this view, behaviour is the result of responses to environmental stimuli, which can act as positive reinforcements (when the stimulus is applied) or negative ones (when the stimulus is withheld). Each iteration reinforces the probability that antecedent behaviour will be repeated. Clearly, the stimulus–response framework is echoed in Friedman's characterization of positive economics. The relative income hypothesis, on the other hand, was too reliant on unobservable comparisons that are supposed to take place in one's mind to survive the shift in the direction advocated by Friedman.[12]

Another important concept that is relatively popular among economists, and is related to status-seeking behaviour, is that of positional good, originally presented by Hirsh (1976) and later refined in the works of Frank (1985, 1999, 2007).[13] The point here is that certain goods yield a satisfaction that depends not on the absolute level of consumption, but on the relative position of the one who consumes them in some economically meaningful hierarchy. Education is the best-known example: it is true that the more educated you are, the higher is the salary you may expect to earn, but if more and more people manage to arrive at the same level of education that you have, then your chances to do so diminish. It is not the fact that you have a PhD *per se* that makes you valuable on the labour market; it is the fact that you have it while others do not. It is said that these positional externalities are a common feature of contemporary economies, and are socially wasteful, as they induce a sort of arms race (sometimes referred to as 'expenditure cascade') in which agents run in an effort to remain at least in the same position as they were before the race began. This leads to an impoverishment of the middle class, as an increasing part of their income is spent on items whose only utility is that of allowing them to keep up with the Joneses (Frank, 2007).

Duesenberry's and Frank's arguments are perfectly in line with Veblen's. Apparently, there is a difference because leisure is not at the centre of the analysis – social competition is taken to be based on income. Indeed, the consensus seems to be that net income and consumption are positional goods in American society – not leisure (Frank, 2007). But after all, this is also what Veblen argued, since he remarked that leisure had been substituted by conspicuous consumption as a status-signalling device in the America of his time. And what about Europe? We noted in the Introduction that in the arts Europeans are usually portrayed, at least since the industrial revolution, as more prone to enjoy leisure than Americans. Blanchard (2004) remarks that, at the beginning of the twenty-first century, productivity levels are more or less the same in the European Union and in the United States, but Europeans have transformed part of the productivity increase into more leisure rather than more income, while Americans have done just the opposite. If we believe that status-seeking is a universal trait possessed by Americans and Europeans alike, then it may be the case that, among the latter, at least part of this increased consumption of leisure serves the purpose of satisfying the agents' desire to achieve and to signal a high social rank.

The question is that, while the search for status might be common to all humanity, the exact way in which such a status is acquired and made public varies across space and time. Native Americans signalled their rank using combinations of feathers on their head, while modern and contemporary Europeans seem to conceive of leisure as a positional good: having more free time than others is a sign of high status. One of the characters in Jane Austen's *Sense and Sensibility* – the young man who will in the end marry the sensible sister – would like to earn a living as a lawyer but does not dare to do this because of the social stigma that his mother feels would then be attached to the family: having a close relative who actually *works* would be unbearable. If Austen has portrayed her characters this way, it must have been because this was how people in her class felt about these issues. The set of shared beliefs and understandings that we call 'culture' was at the time such that status was strictly associated with idleness: a gentleman was expected to pursue gentlemanly interests, and perhaps to be a good dancer, certainly not to *earn* his income. Considering how cultural traits survive over time, albeit often in modified form, it is little wonder that today people in Europe compare how they spent their holidays, and how long they could stay on holiday, in order to assess their relative status. This is consistent also with the argument put forward by Alesina et al. (2005), according to which the phenomenon, observed by Blanchard (2004), that Europeans, unlike Americans, have turned productivity increases into an opportunity for more leisure rather than more income, must be due to the presence in Europe of a strongly unionized labour force that has pursued a 'work less, work all' objective. Indeed, one of the deep motivations for this objective might have been the desire to let the workers acquire more social status by having more free time – not necessarily the only motivation, but perhaps one that has contributed to making the workers more prone to support it. After all, the unions could have asked to employ the resources freed by the productivity increases for developing marketing strategies and winning new markets for European products, and then pursue a 'work the same, work all' objective. However, would the workers have reacted to this proposal with the same enthusiasm? Would the possibility of earning more income have been as enticing as that of having more free time?

It is important to stress at this point that to claim that the diverging perceptions of leisure and income across the Atlantic might be due to cultural differences is by no means equivalent to saying that there is no economic argument we can employ to explain them. On the contrary, it is a way to suggest that economists should study the emergence of cultures, their impact on the agents, the changes they undergo, and so on using their own methodology.[14] A few contributions in this vein have emerged recently: for example, Fernandez and Fogli (2006) have studied the impact of culture on fertility outcomes. It would be an interesting and ultimately rewarding task to investigate how culture can affect the perception of a good as being positional or not, or how different cultures identify different devices to signal status, and so on. The application of a rigorous economic approach could definitely bring fresh insights to our understanding of culture, if only economists could overcome their diffidence on these issues. In particular, if one also introduced public finance considerations, it could be checked whether a model of this sort can make sense of the fact that in recent years Europeans have tended to exploit productivity increases in order to enjoy more free time, and at the same time explain the nature of the European tax systems. Thereby, we would turn full circle to the heart of the debate between Prescott (2004) and Alesina et al. (2005) from which we started our discussion.

CONCLUDING REMARKS

An inference that one may be tempted to draw from the analysis so far, is that a book on the economics of leisure would never have been written if household production models had not been introduced in economic theory. Without the insights offered by those models, the simplistic opposition between leisure on one side and work on the other would have forced us economists to focus exclusively on the latter. However, while it is true that household economics did open the door for economics to deal with a vast variety of issues, not only the ones that will be covered in the present book but also many others,[15] it is also true that it retained the 'orthodox' methodological stance. In fact, Becker's approach was deemed innovative because it proposed to study 'social', as opposed to narrowly defined 'economic', issues using the standard economists' toolbox – the *Homo oeconomicus* framework. This represented, in the mind of those who have embraced household economics, a distinctive trait relative to the softer, less analytical, approaches favoured by other social sciences such as sociology or psychology.

However, 45 years have passed since the household economics revolution started, and in the meantime something has changed in the perception of what constitutes the essence of the economic methodology. There have always been heterodox approaches that did not share the mainstream economists' insistence on assuming full rationality of the decision makers, and even within the orthodoxy it has sometimes been possible to introduce bounded rationality. But in the last decade, and especially after psychologist Daniel Kahneman had been awarded the Nobel Prize in economics for his work on the economics of risk and uncertainty, the idea that *Homo oeconomicus* may be subjected to some adjustments without losing its identity has been gaining momentum among economists.

Household behaviour seems to be an eminently suitable ground on which to test the effectiveness of these adjustments. This is because within a household there are many instances of non-repeated choices for which the standard argument in defence of full rationality does not seem to work. This argument maintains that in many economic environments agents repeat their choices so often that they soon become able to follow a rational and efficient course of action. Indeed, for many market situations this is an entirely sensible assumption. However, within the realm of household economics, there are several non-market or clearly non-repeatable decisions that call for different assumptions. It is true that authors such as Browning and Chiappori (1998), Chiappori (1988), and Bourguignon et al. (2006) have argued that a marriage is a prototypical example of game-theoretic repeated interaction, and hence by the Folk theorem ought to sustain efficient outcomes. However, the Folk theorem as such does not tell us that these efficient outcomes are the only equilibria, nor that they will be more likely to be chosen than inefficient ones. Moreover, as noted, for example, by Lundberg and Pollak (2003), several decisions normally taken within a marriage are not frequent and very costly to reverse once taken: for example, decisions about location, reproduction, retirement, education of the children and labour force participation.[16]

While the explicit consideration of this fact does not call for a complete overhauling of the *Homo oeconomicus* approach, it does suggest that models relying on a form of bounded rationality may be well suited to investigate the issues at hand. Certainly, this is already commonly done in the area of household economics, since many authors have looked at the family as a non-cooperative situation, and assumed a Cournot-type behaviour (for example, Konrad and Lommerud, 1995 and Anderberg and Balestrino, 2007). The Cournot model is commonly accepted among orthodox economists, so that we tend to forget that it already incorporates a limited rationality assumption, because it implies that the agents make the wrong predictions about the behaviour of their opponents. An elegant model that does not presuppose efficiency at the outset has been proposed by Lundberg and Pollak (2003), who view marriage as a non-stationary, multistage game, in which some decisions taken today affect the distribution of bargaining power starting from one period ahead; in the absence of a commitment mechanism, these games admit inefficient outcomes. Moving a bit further away from strict orthodoxy, it would be interesting to try out the effectiveness of other models of bounded rationality: the social psychology literature offers a wealth of evidence supporting the claim that, especially for difficult and irreversible decisions, individuals systematically make mistakes, often of a cognitive nature, such as misreading the available information, or relying on heuristic rules of thumb (see, for example, Tversky and Kahneman, 1982a, 1982b). Coupling this sort of assumption with the powerful analytical machinery of economics seems like a promising move, as it would present both the advantage of being in line with what evidence we have and that of having a deep interpretative capability.[17]

Leisure-related (or more generally time allocation) choices, in particular, seem to be the perfect playing-field for trying out this sort of cross-fertilization exercise, in which economics borrows insights from other social sciences such as psychology or sociology. Just go back to the list of examples we gave above concerning not easily reversible choices within a household (to repeat: location, reproduction, retirement, education of the children, labour force participation). All of them involve possibly complex time allocation decisions: children, for instance, are especially time-intensive goods to produce, as they require care, education, and so on. But also when a family decides to relocate to another town because, say, one of the partners has got a new job, the time schedules of both partners will of course have to be adjusted, and the same will be true if one of them decides to join or leave the labour force or goes into retirement.

These remarks point to the following conclusion. It would be legitimate to see this book as motivated by a broader view of economics than is usually assumed in mainstream circles. But it would also be possible to find a motivation from inside the orthodox view: household economics has made it clear that economists can fruitfully study the sort of choices and decisions that agents take concerning their non-working time, and the new openness of economic methodology to insights coming from other disciplines has permitted this sort of study to be particularly innovative. It can be hoped that some lessons can be learned this way, and that they become in turn useful for original analyses of more standard subjects.

NOTES

1. The author would like to thank Sam Cameron for providing the initial stimulus to write the present chapter, and for his insightful remarks on previous drafts.
2. It would be more correct to say 'in what is now perceived as mainstream'. Marshall, whom we all regard as a fully orthodox economist, took cultural factors very seriously in his theory of consumption (see, for example, Marshall, 1920, Book III, Chapter 2).

3. See Gronau (1997) for a more recent retrospective view on these models.
4. For example, how can we distinguish labour from leisure when we work from home? A discussion of this point can be found in Chapter 7 of the present volume.
5. While there have been studies on this subject for quite some time, not many have really focused on love as an emotion, as Zelder (2009) does. However, recently, there have been a few attempts at building an economics of the emotions. This has been favoured by the fact that psychology today sees emotions as cognitive acts, rather than irrational upheavals. See Balestrino and Ciardi (2009) for a discussion and some references; relatedly, see also Cameron (2009) on the economics of hate.
6. Taxes may be perceived as the 'opposite' policy instrument from subsidies, and indeed they may have opposite redistributive effects. But in so far as efficiency is concerned, their impact is the same – second-best subsidies are just as distortionary as second-best taxes.
7. Leisure is believed to be a normal good. Whenever a subject sees his/her income reduced, as is the case in the presence of an income tax , the subject should therefore also reduce his/her consumption of leisure due to the income effect. Normally, this effect is taken to be small, and indeed the labour supply curve is usually depicted as increasing in the net wage rate. If, at relatively high income levels, the income effect becomes dominant, we have a 'backward-bending' labour supply curve.
8. In the next section, we shall comment upon the connections between this attitude and a (by now rather outdated) branch of psychology known as 'behaviourism', which was particularly fashionable at the time when economics was ripening as a social science, between the 1930s and 1950s, and has influenced the development of several landmark models, such as Paul Samuelson's revealed preferences or Milton Friedman's positive economics.
9. See Chapter 5 in this volume for a discussion of the economics of boredom.
10. Interestingly, most of these activities have a strong impact on the way time is allocated – see Chapters 21 through 24 in the present volume.
11. This stance has been maintained and defended by those who have continued in the wake of Veblen's work ('institutionalism').
12. Incidentally, note that if the above explanation is correct, it points out a systematic bias that has affected economics until recently. Indeed, economics has remained faithful to the spirit of behaviourism long after the latter has receded from mainstream psychology, possibly because economics had severed relations with the other social sciences for several decades after the 1930s (see Bruni and Sugden, 2007) and has thus missed the changes that occurred there from the 1960s onwards, when behaviourism was supplanted by a cognitivist approach in mainstream psychology.
13. See Kashdan and Klein (2006) for a critique of Frank's position.
14. Other social sciences, such as sociology, have been studying the relation between ethno-religious traits and attitudes towards leisure for a long time: just think of Weber's work (Weber, 1922).
15. Such as crime, marriage and divorce, and so on.
16. Taking a step backward and considering the formation and dissolution of a household, rather than its day-to-day management, note that also the choices to marry or to divorce are not frequently repeated and are costly to reverse.
17. For an attempt in this direction, with specific reference to household formation, see Balestrino and Ciardi (2008).

REFERENCES

Alesina, A., E. Glaeser and B. Sacerdote (2005), 'Work and leisure in the U.S. and Europe: why so different?', *NBER Macroeconomic Annual 2005*, Cambridge, MA: NBER, pp. 1–64.
Anderberg, D. and A. Balestrino (2000), 'Household production and the design of the tax structure', *International Tax and Public Finance*, **7**, 565–86.

Anderberg, D. and A. Balestrino (2007), 'Non-cooperative households and the size and composition of public expenditure', *Economics of Governance*, **8**, 61–81.

Atkinson, A. and J. Stiglitz (1976), 'The design of tax structure: direct versus indirect taxation', *Journal of Public Economics*, **6**, 55–75.

Bagwell, L. and B. Bernheim (1996), 'Veblen effects in a theory of conspicuous consumption', *American Economic Review*, **86**, 349–73.

Balestrino, A. and C. Ciardi (2008), 'Social norms, cognitive dissonance and the timing of marriage', *Journal of Socio-Economics*, **37**, 2399–410.

Balestrino, A. and C. Ciardi (2009), 'Love, bonding, value: discussing the economics of love', *Teoria*, **29** (2), 151–63.

Becker, G. (1965), 'A theory of the allocation of time', *Economic Journal*, **75**, 493–508.

Becker, G. and K. Murphy (1988), 'A theory of rational addiction', *Journal of Political Economy*, **96**, 675–700.

Bernheim, B. (1994), 'A theory of conformity', *Journal of Political Economy*, **102**, 841–77.

Blanchard, O. (2004), 'The economic future of Europe', *Journal of Economic Perspectives*, **18**, 3–26.

Boskin, M. and E. Sheshinski (1978), 'Optimal redistributive taxation when individual welfare depends upon relative income', *Quarterly Journal of Economics*, **92**, 589–601.

Bourguignon, F., M. Browning and P.-A. Chiappori (2006), 'Efficient intra-household allocations and distribution factors: implications and identification', CAM Working Papers 2006-02, University of Copenhagen.

Browning, M. and P.-A. Chiappori (1998), 'Efficient intra-household allocations: a general characterization and empirical tests', *Econometrica*, **66**, 1241–78.

Bruni, L. and R. Sugden (2007), 'The road not taken: how psychology was removed from economics, and how it might be brought back', *Economic Journal*, **117**, 146–73.

Cameron, S. (2009), *The Economics of Hate*, Cheltenham, UK and Northampton, MA, USA: Edward Elgar.

Carlyle, T. (1849), 'The nigger question', reprinted in *Miscellaneous Essays*, London: Chapman & Hall, 1988, **7**, pp. 79–110.

Chiappori, P.-A. (1988), 'Rational household labor supply', *Econometrica*, **56**, 63–90.

Cigno, A., A. Luporini and A. Pettini (2003), 'Transfers to families with children as a principal–agent problem', *Journal of Public Economics*, **87**, 1165–77.

Corlett, W. and D. Hague (1953), 'Complementarity and the excess burden of taxation', *Review of Economic Studies*, **21**, 21–30.

Corneo, G. and O. Jeanne (1997), 'Conspicuous consumption, snobbism and conformism', *Journal of Public Economics*, **66**, 55–71.

Dale, K. (2009), 'Household skills and low wages', *Journal of Population Economics*, **22**, 1025–38.

Duesenberry, J. (1949), *Income, Saving and the Theory of Consumer Behavior*, Cambridge, MA: Harvard University Press.

Easterlin, R. (2001), 'Income and happiness: towards a unified theory', *Economic Journal*, **111**, 465–84.

Falk, A. and M. Knell (2004), 'Choosing the Joneses: endogenous goals and reference standard', *Scandinavian Journal of Economics*, **106**, 417–35.

Fernandez, R. (2007), 'Women, work, and culture', *Journal of the European Economic Association*, **5**, 305–32.

Fernandez, R. and A. Fogli (2006), 'Fertility: the role of culture and family experience', *Journal of the European Economic Association*, **4**, 552–61.

Frank, R. (1985), *Choosing the Right Pond: Human Behavior and the Quest for Status*, Oxford: Oxford University Press.

Frank, R. (1999), *Luxury Fever: Money and Happiness in an Era of Excess*, Princeton, NJ: Princeton University Press.

Frank, R. (2005), 'The mysterious disappearance of James Duesenberry', *New York Times*, June 9, available at http://www.robert-h-frank.com/PDFs/ES.6.9.05.pdf.

Frank, R. (2007), *Falling Behind: How Income Inequality Harms the Middle Class*, Berkeley, CA: University of California Press.

Friedman, M. (1953), *Essays in Positive Economics*, Chicago, IL: University of Chicago Press.

Friedman, M. (1957), *A Theory of the Consumption Function*, Princeton, NJ: Princeton University Press.

Gronau, R. (1977), 'Leisure, home production and work – the theory of the allocation of time revisited', *Journal of Political Economy*, **85**, 1099–124.

Gronau, R. (1997), 'The theory of home production – the past ten years', *Journal of Labor Economics*, **15**, 197–205.

Hirsh, F. (1976), *The Social Limits to Growth*, London: Routledge & Kegan Paul.

Ireland, N. (1994), 'On limiting the market for status signal', *Journal of Public Economics*, **53**, 91–110.

Ireland, N. (2001), 'Optimal tax in the presence of status effect', *Journal of Public Economics*, **81**, 193–212.

Kahneman, D., P. Wakker and R. Sarin (1997), 'Back to Bentham? Explorations of experienced utility', *Quarterly Journal of Economics*, **112**, 375–405.

Kashdan, A. and D. Klein (2006), 'Assume the positional: comment on Robert Frank', *Econ Journal Watch*, **3**, 412–34.

Konrad, K. and K.-E. Lommerud (1995), 'Family policy with non-cooperative families', *Scandinavian Journal of Economics*, **97**, 581–601.

Lancaster, K. (1966), 'A new approach to consumer theory', *Journal of Political Economy*, **74**, 132–57.

Linder, S. (1970), *The Harried Leisure Class*, New York: Columbia University Press.

Lundberg, S. and R. Pollak (2003), 'Efficiency in marriage', *Review of Economics of the Household*, **1**, 153–67.

Marshall, A. (1920), *Principles of Economics*, 8th edn, London: Macmillan.

Paulus, M. (2007), 'Neural basis of reward and craving – a homeostatic point of view', *Dialogues in Clinical Neurosciences*, **9**, 379–87.

Prescott, E. (2004), 'Why do Americans work so much more than Europeans?', *Federal Reserve Bank of Minneapolis Quarterly Review*, **28**, 2–13.

Ramsey, F. (1927), 'A contribution to the theory of taxation', *Economic Journal*, **37**, 47–61.

Sandmo, A. (1990), 'Tax distortions and household production', *Oxford Economic Papers*, **42**, 78–90.

Scitovsky, T. (1976), *The Joyless Economy*, New York: Oxford University Press.

Skinner, B. (1938), *The Behavior of Organisms: An Experimental Analysis*, New York: Appleton-Century-Crofts.

Sørensen, P.B. (1994), 'Public finance solutions to the European unemployment problem', *Economic Policy*, **25**, 223–64.

Tversky, A. and D. Kahneman (1982a), 'Availability: a heuristics for judging frequency and probability', in D. Kahneman, P. Slovic and A. Tversky (eds), *Judgment under Uncertainty: Heuristics and Biases*, New York: Cambridge University Press, pp. 163–78.

Tversky, A. and D. Kahneman (1982b), 'Judgment under uncertainty: heuristics and biases', in D. Kahneman, P. Slovic and A. Tversky (eds), *Judgment under Uncertainty: Heuristics and Biases*, New York: Cambridge University Press, pp. 3–20.

Veblen, T. (1899), *The Theory of the Leisure Class*, New York: Macmillan.

Watson, J. (1924), *Behaviorism*, New York: Norton.

Weber, M. (1922), *Die Protestantische Ethik und der Geist des Kapitalismus*, Tübingen: I.C.B. Mohr (English translation, *The Protestant Ethic and the Spirit of Capitalism*, London: Penguin Classics, 2002).

Zelder, M. (2009), 'The essential economics of love', *Teoria*, **29** (2), 133–50.

3 Towards a Bourdieusian economics of leisure
Andrew B. Trigg

INTRODUCTION

An economic analysis of leisure has to position itself in relation to the neoclassical core of the economics paradigm, either as an extension or as a modification of its principles, or in contrast as an alternative perspective. In neoclassical economics, individuals draw on their exogenous preferences to maximize utility, making a key choice between income and leisure. Unemployment, for example, is interpreted as a voluntary choice of leisure over income from work, as is the non-participation of female workers in the labour market, or a preference for part-time work. The price mechanism is critical to such decisions, with wages per hour of employment representing the price of leisure. At its core, the neoclassical system consists of individual atoms choosing between outcomes that are feasible within a market price mechanism.

Alternatives to the dominant neoclassical paradigm abound, both within economics itself and across the social sciences. They inevitably lack the coherence of the neoclassical system, with its choice-theoretic starting-point. But an important opposing theme is the lack of choice available to people in a market-based system. In economics, symbolic of this alternative perspective has been the revival of the father of macroeconomics, John Maynard Keynes, in the wake of the global economic recession that started in 2008. People in their millions have been forced by systemic failure into involuntary unemployment, as was identified by Keynes in the 1930s. In the wider social sciences, structural approaches have focused on the constraints placed on people by society as a whole. The rallying point for championing the cause of those that lack choice, condemned by their social position in society to destitution and despair, is provided by the discipline of sociology. As observed by Duesenberry (1960, p. 233), 'Economics is all about how people make choices. Sociology is about why they don't have any choices to make'.

The purpose of this chapter is to suggest alternative foundations for economics drawing on the discipline of sociology as a starting-point. The study of leisure and culture provides a possible vehicle for developing this alternative, since it has provided the main focus of one of the most important sociologists of the twentieth century, Pierre Bourdieu. The analysis of lifestyles in his main work, *Distinction* (1984), has been ranked as one of the key contributions to social sciences during the twentieth century (Swartz and Zolberg, 2004, p. 1). Key to Bourdieu's approach, and its relevance to the economics of leisure, is his attempt to bridge the divide between economics and sociology. Bourdieu reaches out to economics by allowing individuals to make choices about their lifestyles, showing how cultural innovation can break down economic and cultural constraints. But constraints are not a supplementary addition to the theory; they are fundamental to how society functions. An individual's position in society has an immensely powerful impact on his/her adopted lifestyle. How individuals speak, eat, drink and dress are all driven by societal forces which are not necessarily explained by individual choices.

Bourdieu's contemporary approach is rooted in the analysis of leisure provided by Thorstein Veblen, one of the first thinkers to consider himself both a sociologist and an economist. His great work, *The Theory of the Leisure Class* (1899), viewed the pursuit of leisure as the most important driver of social and economic change. Veblen's work is also important since some of his ideas, in particular the concept of conspicuous consumption, have become part of the vernacular of neoclassical economics. But what is not so widely known is the importance that leisure has in underpinning conspicuous consumption. For Veblen, leisure does not just have a price based on forgone wages: it is symbolic of not having to work, of having the status that is associated with a particular position in society.

The next section will show the importance of leisure to Veblen's theory, in preparation for the third section in which Bourdieu's approach is introduced. In addition to providing an alternative to neoclassical theory, Bourdieu's approach also has implications for how statistical analysis should be carried on in the light of sociological theory. The fourth section provides an example of how correspondence analysis can be used to identify lifestyle patterns, using survey data in the UK, of the type developed by Bourdieu. The final section concludes.

VEBLEN'S THEORY OF THE LEISURE CLASS

Veblen's theory of the leisure class is based on a social and economic analysis of cultural evolution. In the various stages of evolution, economies have become able to produce a surplus, which allows part of the population the privilege of not working. From slave societies through to modern industrial capitalism, a non-working leisure class has evolved, able to enjoy the fruits of surplus produced by the working part of the population.

This economic divide has inevitably led to a cultural divide. Those that do not work develop an antipathy to those that do. 'The performance of labour has been accepted as a conventional evidence of inferior force; therefore it comes itself, by a mental short-cut, to be regarded as intrinsically base' (Veblen, 1899, p. 24). Those that carry out the menial tasks of productive labour may actually take pride in their work, but for members of the leisure class, work is repugnant because of its association with low status. Veblen provides the example of Polynesian chiefs who were prepared to starve to death rather than stoop so low as to even feed themselves. Honour and esteem can only be established by being a member of the leisure class (ibid., p. 27).

The counterpart to this antipathy to work is a pursuit of conspicuous leisure in order to establish and reinforce higher positions in the social hierarchy. Members of the old aristocracy spent most of their social calendar hunting, fishing and horse racing: anything but a day's work. The young Winston Churchill's time in the 4th Hussars, for example, was 'devoted largely to horse-riding, drill, playing polo, eating in the mess, and gambling and drinking in the evenings' (Ponting, 1994, p. 18). Whereas the working classes may hunt animals for subsistence, the leisure class develops a form of hunting that is sport, for game rather than material sustenance. 'It is this latter development of the chase – purged of all imputation of handicraft – that alone is meritorious and fairly belongs in the scheme of life of the developed leisure class' (Veblen, 1899 [1994], p. 26). The leisure class therefore seeks a non-productive consumption of time because of its intrinsic disgust for labour and its wish to promote its position in the social hierarchy through conspicuous leisure.

Conspicuous consumption, which involves the allocation of money rather than time, is seen by Veblen as an additional means by which positions of property and status can be displayed. As society becomes more mobile, with less social contact between individuals, consumption can be preferred over leisure as a vehicle for display. But these two undercurrents are intimately linked – hunting and the purchase of fine horses, for example – and both have a role to play in modern capitalism, as it has evolved from previous stages of society.

Those at the bottom of the social hierarchy are also forced to engage in conspicuous consumption and leisure. A trickle-down approach to culture is suggested in which the lower social strata emulate the consumption and leisure of their superiors. Veblen identifies a cultural powerlessness, in which the oppressed are compelled to participate in the culture of the dominant class, even when they are living in destitution. 'Very much of squalor and discomfort will be endured before the last trinket or the last pretence of pecuniary decency is put away' (ibid., p. 53).

This is all a far cry from the neoclassical theory of leisure. First, as a theory of social class, Veblen's approach brings into question the individualist basis of neoclassical theory. A social class analysis is required to explore how leisure pursuits have developed as part of the evolution of culture. Second, preferences are not exogenous, but rather depend on an individual's position in the social hierarchy, and interdependent with the preferences of other members of the same social strata and other social strata. Third, individuals are not free to choose their preferences for leisure. The poor are constrained by their capacity for leisure, and are culturally dominated by the leisure class. Even the rich are enslaved by the obligations of the social hierarchy, having to distinguish their tastes from the vulgarities of menial work. Finally, individuals are not restricted to the maximization of utility as rational agents: Velben's framework is radically more general, with individuals in large part unconsciously following habits that have evolved as part of a historical process.

Only when grounded in Veblen's original writings can concepts of conspicuous leisure and consumption be fully appreciated as a theoretical alternative to neoclassical theory. Rather than being interpreted as a quirky exception to neoclassical economic theory, Veblen's approach can be drawn on as an original perspective in which sociological structures take centre stage in the economic framework of analysis. This economic dimension is further developed in the next section by turning to the writings of Pierre Bourdieu.

BOURDIEU'S SYSTEM OF LIFESTYLES

The building blocks of Bourdieu's contribution to economic analysis are his attempt to provide an alternative to Gary Becker's theory of human capital (Becker, 1962). Whereas Becker emphasized the potential that each individual has to invest in his/her own capacities to earn income, Bourdieu examined the constraints placed on individuals. In order to directly engage with economic theory, Bourdieu introduced his own concepts of capital, of which there are two main species: economic and cultural.

Economic capital captures the economic power of an individual, including both accumulated wealth and the capacity to earn income. Cultural capital is an individual's accumulated stock of knowledge about the products of artistic and intellectual traditions. Of critical importance is the unequal distribution of these two types of capital. Some individuals are born into wealthy and well-educated families, in which both types of capital are passed on from parents to children. The advantage enjoyed by some children can range from inherited property, and a private education, through to a familiarity with art, music and books.

Familiarity with classical music is highlighted by Bourdieu as an example of how cultural capital is unequally distributed. He observes:

> [W]hen a child is introduced at an early age to a 'noble' instrument – especially the piano – the effect is at least to produce a more familiar relationship to music, which differs from the always somewhat distant contemplative and often verbose relation to those who have come to music through concerts or even only through records. (Bourdieu, 1984, p. 75)

Early familiarity with music produces a casual ease, which makes the higher cultural capital of certain individuals seem natural.

Bourdieu places primary importance on economic capital, as the fulcrum of inequality: 'economic capital is at the root of all the other types of capital' (Bourdieu 1986, p. 252). He follows Karl Marx in viewing the defining feature of capitalism as its accumulation of money capital. Cultural capital complements and extends the power of money capital, however, by performing a remarkable role in making the social hierarchy seem natural and based on merit. Not only do those at the bottom of the social hierarchy lack economic resources, they also lack cultural capital.

Bourdieu's concept of cultural capital can be seen as a development of Veblen (Trigg, 2001). Like Veblen, Bourdieu views attitudes to work, and the necessity to work, as key to the evolution of cultural tastes. Manual labour, for example, creates the economic basis for particular popular tastes towards food: the most filling and economical foods that would tend to be favoured by manual workers in order to replenish calories and are affordable at the wages earned by a manual worker. In a further echo of Marx, such popular tastes for food are based on 'the necessity of reproducing labour power at the lowest cost which is forced on the pro-letariat as its very definition' (Bourdieu, 1984, p. 177). Recognizing, with Veblen, that working-class culture is dominant, Bourdieu sees the 'art of eating and drinking' as 'one of the few areas in which the working classes explicitly challenge the legitimate art of living' (ibid., p. 179).

The aesthetic tastes of the bourgeoisie, however, are based on an aversion to popular tastes. Those higher up the social hierarchy must establish their distance from popular tastes. 'By contrast, the taste of the professionals or senior executives defines the popular taste, by negation, as the taste for the heavy, the fat and the coarse, by tending towards the light, the refined and the delicate' (ibid., p. 185). Such differences in taste are so powerful that they can transcend economic constraints. Individuals that move up the social hierarchy, breaking free of the constraints of manual labour and low income, can still cling on to popular tastes that they have been brought up with. As shown in Trigg (2004), this can provide the cultural basis for understanding the Engel curve between income and consumption.

Differences in taste, based on differentiation between social classes, generate important biological differences. Whereas those that engage in manual work may develop heavy bodies based on their tastes for fatty foods and alcohol, according to Bourdieu those higher up the social hierarchy develop a 'cult of health', 'often associated with an aesthetic exaltation of sobriety and controlled diet' (Bourdieu, 1984, p. 213). With food and diet as an example, we see the basis for different lifestyles, which are based on social positions with respect to work.

Sport is highlighted by Bourdieu as an arena for differentiated lifestyles. Those at the top of the social hierarchy seek to distance themselves from popular sports. He refers to the 'most prestigious activities, far from vulgar crowds', 'expressed in yachting, open-sea swimming, cross-country skiing or under-water fishing' (ibid., p. 219). In addition to a preference for battles against nature rather than other human beings, at its extreme the bourgeois aesthetic is to avoid the collective element of team sports. Tennis, golf, skiing, horse riding and show jumping are all examples of individual-based sports which tend to depend on early parental encouragement, private clubs, individually chosen partners, and relatively less physical exertion than team sports. When the privileged do take part in team sports, differentiation can evolve within the team, as exemplified in rugby by the use of working-class forwards to provide physical strength. And once participation in a sport by the working classes becomes widespread, those at the top of the social hierarchy will tend to withdraw from that sport, as exemplified by the evolution of football from its early aristocratic roots.

Examples abound, of course, of working-class show jumping champions and physically brutal rugby forwards educated at Harrow. It should be emphasized, however, that Bourdieu's system only emphasizes the dominant society-wide *tendencies* that shape the formation of cultural differences. Where the Bourdieu system is perhaps more sophisticated than that of Veblen, is in its capacity to model exemptions and counter currents to these dominant tendencies in a framework in which class inequalities are reproduced. Of particular importance is the way in which Bourdieu classifies lifestyles horizontally. The traditional class hierarchy is vertical, starting with the working classes at the bottom, moving up to the elite social classes at the top. By examining the structure of both cultural and economic capital, Bourdieu is able to introduce a horizontal dimension. This is illustrated in Figure 3.1, in which the cultural capital is represented

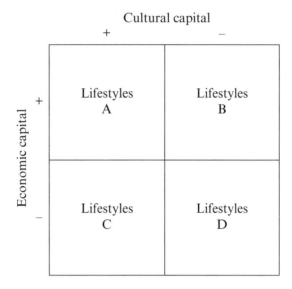

Cultural capital

Source: Rosengren (1995).

Figure 3.1   Bourdieu's classification of lifestyles

by the horizontal axis and economic capital by the vertical axis. The elite lifestyles (group A) are associated with high economic and cultural capital. This may involve, for example, top lawyers who visit the opera. The lowest status lifestyles (group D) are associated with low cultural and economic capital: the traditional working-class lifestyle associated with low-budget popular culture. However, the off-diagonals of Bourdieu's framework allow for more sophisticated combinations. Those in group B have high economic capital, but low cultural capital, which could be lifestyles that characterize the self-employed, who are upwardly mobile but have low inherited levels of cultural capital. Group C lifestyles could be those of say teachers, high in cultural capital, so very much on the cutting edge of avant-garde culture, but lacking in economic resources.

Key to this framework is Bourdieu's concept of the habitus. This is a system of probabilities in which individuals are at the same time constrained by and able to shape the system. Consider first the constraint that individuals are not free to choose the combination of economic and cultural capital that they inherit. The combination of capital that they inherit is structurally determined, depending on the economic and cultural capital of their parents. Children with different inherited volumes and combinations of capital have markedly different probabilities of social mobility. A child from a low-skilled working-class family has a very low probability of going to university; a child from a professional background has a high probability of going to university. Inequalities in the distribution of economic and cultural capital between these occupational classes are reproduced for society as a whole.

The habitus is like a particularly unfair game of musical chairs. Ten children of professional parents are vying for nine chairs (a 1 in 9 probability of success), while 10 children of unskilled parents are vying for only one chair. Instead of physically constraining social mobility, as in previous slave or peasant societies, class inequalities are reproduced through this system of unequal probabilities. Low probabilities, it must be emphasized, do not amount to the same thing as zero probabilities. The former UK Labour leader, Neil Kinnock, pronounced that he was the first Kinnock ever to go to university. With his social background, Kinnock had a low probability of such social mobility, but managed to be the exception to the rule. Similarly, there is a low probability that some individuals with professionally educated parents do not go to university, and suffer downward social mobility. This illustrates the second dimension of the habitus, which is that structural inequalities do not determine all outcomes. 'The habitus is not only a structuring structure, which organizes practices and the perception of practices, but also a structured structure' (Bourdieu, 1984, p. 170). Though the structure dominates practices, there is also room for practices to shape the structure.

The habitus thus allows for some degree of agency on the part of individuals. Those at the top of the social hierarchy are continually attempting to influence the probabilities. They innovate in their cultural tastes, developing 'strategies for outflanking, overtaking and display' (ibid., p. 282). And for those at the bottom of the social hierarchy there is a continual struggle between forces of emulation, on which Bourdieu places less emphasis than Veblen, and popular tastes based on necessity. Popular tastes can at times become in vogue, with the upper strata viewing them as having none of the pretensions to art (or power) which inspire the ambitions of the 'petit bourgeois' (ibid., p. 62). As argued in Trigg (2001), a 'trickle round' of tastes can be posited, in which there is a trickle down of tastes from the top, but also a trickle up of tastes from the bottom as those at the top try to outflank the middle class.

CORRESPONDENCE ANALYSIS

An important dimension to Bourdieu's approach is its grounding in empirical observation. Most notably, he carried out a questionnaire survey of cultural practices and competencies in France during the early 1960s

(Bourdieu, 1984). With these data, Bourdieu championed correspondence analysis, which has been used mainly by French social scientists (see Benzecri, 1992). Correspondence analysis is a descriptive technique that explores structural patterns in data, visualized using geometric diagrams.

Data are presented here from the Cultural Capital and Social Exclusion Survey, a 2004 sample of representative adults living in the UK. Just over 1,500 respondents were asked questions designed to explore their cultural capital – for example, visits to museums, number of books in the home, and activities such as sport or newspapers purchased (see Bennett et al., 2009 for more information about the survey). Variables used are reported in Appendix 3A. To consider these variables together, as a way of building a cultural map of the UK, we employ multiple correspondence analysis (see Greenacre and Blasius, 1994). Using this technique, the objective is to explain total inertia (chi-squared/N) with a small number of joint plots. The axes of each plot are referred to in correspondence analysis as 'dimensions'. This can be thought of as an extension of principal component analysis to categorical data. The dimensions produced by correspondence analysis are equivalent to the underlying factors produced by principal component analysis.

The first three dimensions of our analysis of the UK survey data produced inertia counts of 27.4, 16.8 and 14.5 per cent, giving a total of 58.7 per cent inertia accounted for. Figure 3.2 reports a joint plot for the first of these two dimensions – the two best dimensions that one could choose to bring out the structure in the data. Note that there is no preconceived assumption about what these dimensions represent; this comes out of how the data are interpreted. This has some advantages over the hypothesis-testing approach used in econometrics, for example, in which a dependent variable has to be chosen alongside exogenous regressors. Correspondence analysis is open about the possible structures that might be revealed by the data.

Each point on Figure 3.2 represents one category of a variable. For example, one of the variables in the survey has categories that denote how many books individuals have in their home. Points on the diagram represent the categories of this variable. The variable representing which newspapers individuals read has categories Telgr/Times (the *Daily Telegraph* or *The Times* broadsheets) in the top left of Figure 3.2, and Sun/Star (tabloids *The Sun* or *Daily Star*) in the bottom right.

The relative positions of points in Figure 3.2 offer insights into associations between variables that may exist in the data. In the top left quadrant, for example, there is a close association between points representing the reading of broadsheet newspapers (Telgr/Times), possessing more than 250 books (>250bks), and watching the television channel BBC2. Also

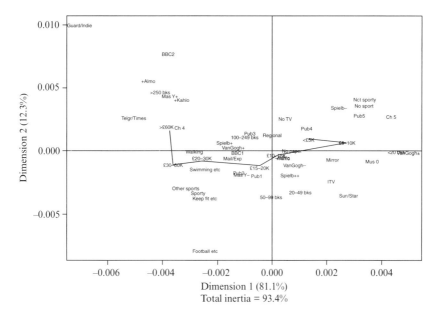

Figure 3.2 Joint plot of culture survey data

forming part of this cluster are points indicating knowledge of the avant-garde Spanish film director Pedro Almodovar (+Almo) and the Mexican artist Frida Kahlo (+Kahlo). The close distance between these data points suggests a clustering of high cultural capital. Reading an established broadsheet newspaper like *The Times* could be interpreted as a legitimate taste; but knowledge of the film director Almodovar suggests a more inno-vative profile (see Hill, 2004 for examination of the relationship between film and cultural capital). Bennett et al. (2005, p. 20) also associate admir-ing the works of Frida Kahlo with the 'greatest taste risk takers, suggesting an avant-garde rather than a legitimate taste formation'. The possession of books and watching BBC2, a somewhat highbrow public service channel in the UK, may be associated with both innovative and legitimate tastes.

This cluster of high cultural capital is also associated with high income, with the data point representing the highest level of income (>£60K) located in close proximity. Following Bourdieu (1984), we can interpret the income variable as an indicator of economic capital. Hence, the cluster in the top left quadrant of Figure 3.2 can be interpreted as representing high cultural and economic capital at the top of the social hierarchy.

Points representing different levels of economic capital are joined up using the line displayed in Figure 3.2. The horizontal trajectory of this line suggests an interpretation of the horizontal axis (dimension 1) as capturing economic capital. Moving right to left on Figure 3.2, low levels of economic capital such as £5–10K build up to the highest level of economic capital (>£60K) at the far left. Low levels of economic capital are associated with low levels of cultural capital: reading tabloid newspapers (Mirror), not visiting museums (Mus0) and watching the largest commercial/popular channel in the UK (ITV). This snapshot provides some evidence that particular lifestyles that might be regarded as less legitimate are associated with low income – as might be explained by Bourdieu's class habitus.

Figure 3.2 does not, however, precisely reproduce the schematic framework shown in Figure 3.1. Instead of economic and cultural capital having their own dimensions, as Bourdieu found using French data, for the UK one dimension seems to represent both cultural and economic capital.

CONCLUSIONS

With its roots in Veblen, Bourdieu's analysis offers a way of uncovering the unequal structures that are hidden by market capitalism. These structures are primarily based on economic inequality, but are reinforced by unequal distributions of cultural capital. Segments at the top of the social hierarchy evolve lifestyles that seem natural but are characteristic of a leisure class, formulated in direct opposition to working-class necessities and associated popular culture. In this probabilistic framework, some choice and innovation is of course allowed, giving a perception of a fluid and meritocratic society. But the lifestyles of those at the top of the social hierarchy restrict social mobility, reproducing class inequalities, in a much more subtle and ingenious way than previous caste or feudal ties. The case made in this chapter is that an economics of leisure, across fields such as sport, reading and cinema, should be set in this type of society-wide context.

ACKNOWLEDGEMENTS

This chapter draws on data produced by the research team for the ESRC project Cultural Capital and Social Exclusion: A Critical Investigation (Award no. R000239801). I am grateful to Tony Bennett (Principal Applicant) and the project team for permission to use this data. Special thanks are also extended to Andrew Bertie for his assistance with the data analysis, and helpful comments from Tony Bennett, Roberto Simonetti and Mike Savage.

REFERENCES

Becker, G.S. (1962), 'Investment in human capital: a theoretical analysis', *Journal of Political Economy*, **70** (5), 9–49.

Bennett, T., M. Savage, E. Silva, A. Warde, M. Gayo-Cal and D. Wright (2005), 'Cultural capital and the cultural field in contemporary Britain', Working Paper No. 3, CRESC Working Paper Series, University of Manchester, Manchester.

Bennett, T., M. Savage, E. Silva, A. Warde, M. Gayo-Cal and D. Wright (2009), *Culture, Class, Distinction*, Abingdon: Routledge.

Benzecri, J.-P. (1992), *Correspondence Analysis Handbook*, New York: Dekker.

Bourdieu, P. (1984), *Distinction: A Social Critique of the Judgement of Taste*, London: Routledge.

Bourdieu, P. (1986), 'The forms of capital', in J.G. Richardson (ed.), *Handbook of Theory and Research for the Sociology of Education*, New York: Greenwood Press, pp. 241–58.

Duesenberry, J. (1960), 'Comment on "An Economic Analysis of Fertility"', in NBER (eds), *Demographic and Economic Change in Developed Countries*, New York: Columbia University Press, pp. 225–56.

Greenacre, M.J. and J. Blasius (1994), *Correspondence Analysis in the Social Sciences: Recent Developments and Applications*, London: Academic Press.

Hill, J. (2004), 'UK film policy, cultural capital and social exclusion', *Cultural Trends*, **13** (2), 29–39.

Ponting, C. (1994), *Churchill*, London: Sinclair-Stevenson.

Rosengren, K.E. (1995), 'Substantive theories and formal models – Bourdieu confronted', *European Journal of Communication*, **10** (1), 7–39.

Swartz, D.L. and V.L. Zolberg (2004), *After Bourdieu*, Dordrecht: Kluwer.

Trigg, A.B. (2001), 'Veblen, Bourdieu and conspicuous consumption', *Journal of Economic Issues*, **35** (1), 99–115.

Trigg, A.B. (2004), 'Deriving the Engel curve: Pierre Bourdieu and the social critique of Maslow's hierarchy of needs', *Review of Social Economy*, **62** (3), 393–406.

Veblen, T. (1899 [1994]), *The Theory of the Leisure Class*, New York: Dover.

APPENDIX 3A   DEFINITION OF VARIABLES USED IN SURVEY ANALYSIS

Ever play sports/any physical exercise? (2 modalities)
- Sporty [yes]
- Not sporty [no]

Favourite sport/exercise (6 modalities)
- Football etc [soccer, rugby, hockey, cricket]
- Swimming etc [swimming, water polo, cycling, gymnastics, martial arts, skiing, tennis]
- Walking [includes walking the dog, rambling]
- Keep fit etc [keep fit, aerobics, gym, body building, weights training, jogging/running]
- Other sports [golf, basketball, any other sport not listed above, unclassifiable]
- No sport

How often go to museums (3 modalities)
- Mus Y+ [more than once a year]
- Mus Y– [once a year or less]
- Mus 0 [never]

How often go to pubs? (5 modalities)
- pub1 [at least once a week]
- pub2 [less often but at least once a month]
- pub3 [less often, at least several times a year]
- pub4 [once a year or less]
- pub5 [never]

Newspaper read most often (7 modalities)
- No paper [does not read a daily newspaper]
- Mirror [*Daily Mirror* or *Daily Record*]
- Sun/Star [*The Sun* or *Daily Star*]
- Guard/Indie [*The Guardian* or *Independent*]
- Telgr/Times [*Daily Telegraph*, *The Times* or *Financial Times*]
- Mail/Exp [*Daily Mail* or *Daily Express*]
- Regional paper [*Metro*, regional, foreign & other newspapers]

Number of books group (5 modalities)
- <20 bks
- 20–49 bks

- 50–99 bks
- 100–249 bks
- >250 bks

Heard of Frida Kahlo (2 modalities)
- +Kahlo [heard of]
- –Kahlo [not heard of]

Seen/liked Van Gogh (3 modalities)
- VanGogh+ [have seen works by him and liked]
- VanGogh– [have seen works by him and did not like]
- VanGogh+– [not seen works by him or not heard of]

TV channel watch most often (6 modalities)
- BBC1
- BBC2
- ITV [ITV/NI:UTV]
- Ch 4 [Channel 4/S4C]
- Ch 5 [Channel 5]
- No TV [never watches TV, never watches any of above]

Heard of Pedro Almodovar? (2 modalities)
- +Almo [heard of]
- –Almo [not heard of]

Watch Stephen Spielberg film? (3 modalities)
- Spielb++ [would make a point of watching]
- Spielb+ [might watch]
- Spielb– [would probably not watch or haven't heard of him]

Income of respondent before tax, after deductions (K = 1,000)
- < £5K
- £5–10K
- £10–15K
- £15–20K
- £20–30K
- £30–60K
- >£60K

4   Leisure and subjective well-being
Victoria Ateca-Amestoy[1]

INTRODUCTION

In September 2009, the Commission on the Measurement of Economic Performance and Social Progress, a project launched by French President Nicolas Sarkozy and chaired by the Nobel laureate Joseph Stiglitz, released its results with wide media coverage (Stiglitz et al., 2009). The final report identified the limitations of GDP as an indicator of economic performance and social progress. It also sent out messages on the need to go beyond productive factors to measure economic performance and people's actual well-being. Among those messages, it highlighted the need to measure non-market activities such as leisure or unpaid domestic work. The commission recognized the contribution of leisure to subjective well-being, and pointed out that 'changes in the amount of leisure over time and differences between countries represent one of the more important aspects of the situation of well-being in these respects' (p. 37). It singled out the importance of developing indicators of 'both leisure quantity (number of hours) and quality (number of episodes, where they took place, presence of other people), as well as measures of participation in cultural events and of "poor leisure"' (p. 49).

The possibility of using indicators that go beyond materialistic objective measurements is not new in economics. However, economists have been reluctant to incorporate subjective outcomes into economic analysis (at least with respect to other social sciences). In an article published in 2002 in the *Journal of Economic Literature*, Bruno Frey and Alois Stutzer present a survey under the title 'What can economists learn from happiness research?', offering analytical foundations and providing a raft of fields of application (Frey and Stutzer, 2002). The most prominent antecedent in the economic use of subjective indicators is the so-called 'Easterlin Paradox', which refers to the finding made in the 1970s by the American economist Richard Easterlin whereby even if material standards in Western countries increase, the happiness levels of individuals remain quite constant (Easterlin, 1974). Although there is still no consensus on the limitations of adopting subjective measures to perform empirical economics, certain precautions have been acknowledged. The analysis of subjective well-being becomes an economic topic when the use of economic models can advance the knowledge of that subject (Hamermesh, 2004).

This chapter proposes an analytical framework for studying the role of leisure in achieving a good quality of life. We discuss the contributions of economics and other social sciences in order to explain the determinants of subjective well-being that are related to individuals' leisure experiences. Interdisciplinary work, or work from related areas, is also considered with a view to its one day being included in economic models.

Throughout, we provide arguments and evidence to sustain two main points. First, we contend that researchers are able to adopt a comprehensive approach and capture unobservable dimensions of leisure, a condition that goes far beyond free time, if they analyse individual leisure through the use of a subjective well-being framework. Second, we introduce the dimensions of theoretical leisure analysis (for example, the strategic complementarity of time and social resources, or the non-positional nature of leisure as an economic good) and relate them to empirical evidence.

Leisure is 'not just' free time, that is, time that is not dedicated to either market work or household chores. It is not even discretionary time (Goodin et al., 2005), time of 'temporal autonomy' and 'discretionary control', which is not limited by compulsory activities derived from subsistence needs or contracts (residual time), time in which freedom of choice prevails when choosing what to do, when and with whom. In order to enjoy leisure, of a reasonable quality, other circumstances apart from free time are needed. Within the conceptual framework we propose, leisure is a human need to be fulfilled by household production and consumption of what we may call 'leisure experiences'. Those experiences are commodities that fall directly within the individual's determination and assessment of his/her quality of life. This means that leisure is one of the arguments of the individual's utility function, one of the instances from which he/she will achieve well-being. By doing this, we shall adopt a Beckerian approach (Becker, 1965, 1990).

Leisure is accompanied by other commodities that correspond to basic needs such as sleep, accommodation, appearance, nourishment, childcare, health, travel and miscellaneous needs (Gronau and Hamermesh, 2006). Commodities are produced inside the household in such a way that it maximizes the gain to the members. The material constraints are time and money. Concerning the list of commodities, when focusing on those produced with different combinations of time and goods, researchers have found evidence that leisure is the most time-intensive one: leisure time will be an essential input for the production and consumption of enjoyable leisure. As we shall discuss in due course, there are strong complementarities among the productive factors of enjoyable experiences.

There is a second distinct feature of leisure as a commodity: the 'first person criterion'. Needs are fulfilled by the production and consumption of commodities. For all the other commodities, the production process can be carried out by a third party, with its output being subsequently consumed by the individual. Leisure, however, has to be produced and consumed by the individual him/herself. While childcare or food can be bought on the market (a third party produces those commodities), so we can directly enjoy the caring and eating processes by devoting time solely to their consumption, there is no way of separating the production and consumption processes for leisure experiences. It is always the individual who has to embark upon the production and consumption of enjoyable leisure.

THE CONCEPTUAL SETTING

Each person defines what leisure does or does not mean to them in a different way. We believe that those answers would be based on individual tastes, and on the different resources available for fulfilling their needs. Not everyone enjoys the same amount of free time, not everyone is good at sports or music, not everyone likes attending crowded places, and so on and so forth. Furthermore, two different people who have enjoyed the same 'leisure condition' may rate it differently depending on social norms, their past experiences, personal aspirations and social influences. One of them may find that the experience has been 'terrific', whereas the other may qualify it as 'just average'. In the first subsection, we review concepts and economic models of leisure. In the second, the subjective well-being and domain approaches are introduced.

Alternative Approaches to Leisure

Since using a purely personal definition of leisure would make any analysis impossible, we shall present the four constructs of leisure proposed by Kelly (1982). The first approach is the most basic one, which defines leisure as quantifiable leisure time, either residual or discretional, based on the freedom to choose. The second defines leisure as the activity that is chosen at a given time and place, so there are certain attributes of the activity that define it as leisure. The third defines leisure as a subjective condition on the grounds of a freely chosen experience based on intrinsic motivation. The fourth, the integrative approach proposed by Kelly, is the one that we prefer for this chapter, since leisure is recognized as an action that takes place at a given time, is an activity that we can identify and, more importantly, brings pleasant experiences to the person involved in that action.

The first approach has been adopted in research that uses reported survey data on free time (such as recording the amount of free time in the German Socio-Economic Panel). The second has mostly relied on data from time-use surveys, in which a register of activities is kept by means of time diaries (Aguiar and Hurst, 2007). The third approach seems hard to observe or approximate for empirical analysis. The last concept – subjective and not directly observable as some of its elements might be – can be studied by means of leisure satisfaction research (Ateca-Amestoy et al., 2008). When presenting the relevant domain satisfaction measures, we shall further illustrate these conceptual approaches to leisure.

We refer to the fourth approach either as leisure or as leisure experience. In fact, in our opinion it is particularly suitable for fitting the extended analytical framework of Becker (1965) and Gronau (1977). It is also suitable for supporting the following definition of leisure satisfaction by Beard and Ragheb (1980). For these authors, leisure satisfaction is the

> positive perceptions or feelings that an individual forms, elicits, or gains as a result of engaging in leisure activities and choices. It is the degree to which one is presently content or pleased with her general leisure experiences and situations. This positive feeling of pleasure results from the satisfaction of felt or unfelt needs of the individual (p. 21).

The amount of time devoted to arbitrarily set lists of activities considered to be leisure (Aguiar and Hurst, 2007) has been widely studied, sometimes in an attempt to explain the significant differences between countries in the time allocated to activities outside the market. A noticeable contradiction in contemporary societies lies in the fact that they have simultaneously become richer in material terms and poorer in terms of time. The allocation of time that is not chosen freely produces time stress; modern societies impose labour contracts and ties that constrain individual decisions. Even if time is the only scarce resource that is equally distributed among every human being, people can suffer time as well as money poverty (Hamermesh and Lee, 2007).

Even if some authors consider that time is the ultimate source of utility (Zeckhauser, 1973), time by itself is of no use to individuals, since the mere passing of time does not fulfil any human need (except possibly for sleeping). That amount of time must have some particular properties. It should be a period in which freedom of choice operates. Yet that discretionary nature is not the only attribute of leisure (if we want to think about leisure in hedonic terms as a multidimensional economic good with a bundle of characteristics). Such discretionary time has to be scheduled in particular ways, so other productive inputs may concur. Hence the reason we highlight a basic feature of leisure: the presence of enjoyable others. This aspect has only recently been introduced in the economic analysis of leisure (Osberg, 2008).

Time devoted to leisure must have certain properties, such as timing, and the social dimension of leisure requires the company of people. Own-time availability, together with enjoyable others' time availability are inputs with strategic complementarity in the production of the leisure commodity (Jenkins and Osberg, 2005). Individuals may enjoy synchronous leisure and 'togetherness' (Hamermesh, 2002). Household composition, marital status and number of children could also be relevant, in the sense that individuals may prefer to enjoy leisure with their closest relatives. *What is done* both as a primary and secondary activity, *when* and *who with* can be captured by time-use registers – a very valuable source of information. In fact, some of the questions that arise in what follows could be complementarily and ideally studied by checking certain testable hypotheses with both happiness and time-use data.

Jenkins and Osberg (2005) consider that the marginal utility of each individual's leisure depends on the choices made by other people. Therefore, there is strategic complementarity between the time allocated for the enjoyment of leisure and the allocation decisions made by others. Many of the things people do in their leisure time involve other people, and are distinctly more pleasurable if done with others; indeed, many things are impossible without the concurrence of others. We may synthesize this presence by the inclusion of 'companionable others' in the discussion. This presence is sometimes measured by means of social capital variables. Warde and Tampubolon (2002) point to the relevance of social capital in leisure consumption by studying how personal involvement in family and friendship ties determines differences in leisure choices.

Apps (2003), Aguiar and Hurst (2007) and Burda et al. (2007) identify leisure with activities. Apps explains how individual time decisions are conditioned by the allocation decisions of others, so family has to be taken into account from an analytical point of view, offering support for Beckerian approaches. Burda et al. find a negative relation between GDP per capita and the gender difference in total work time (including work for pay in the market and work at home). There is a 'leisure gap' between men and women. This gender difference cannot be explained in terms of differences in opportunity cost and marital bargaining power, but is probably due to social norms. Gender effects are also found by Bonke et al. (2009), who explore the relations between time and money as inputs for commodity production and financial and leisure satisfaction. They find gender differences in the technology used for the production of commodities. The differences in the productivity of materialistic or social inputs for leisure production by gender may also be shaped by social norms.

By means of tacit agreements or enforceable laws, individuals are able to coordinate their actions in a particular time, and typically enjoy leisure time with a fairly normalized schedule: weekends, summer holidays. This possibility of synchronization in leisure guarantees the presence of our pleasurable others and the building of bonding social capital (Merz and Osberg, 2006). Social norms determine not only objective outcomes, such as the synchronization of schedules, but also differences in factor combinations (preferences and skills due to early socialization), or in aspiration levels that may be different for either sex. Clark (1997) explains how social norms shape aspirations. A higher unemployment rate for women with respect to men has a positive effect on the female valuation of job status. We can explain the high contribution of leisure to quality of life in terms of aspirations. Leisure is not the opposite of work (indeed, leisure time does not complement work time); however, there are high interrelations between both spheres (Gershuny, 2000).

The main challenge facing economic research in this field is to determine how an unobservable, such as leisure, can contribute to individual welfare. In this case, the researcher faces a double black box for individual judgement, far from the solid consumer theory based on preferences revealed by observable choice. The first difficulty arises because not everyone defines leisure in the same way and because not everyone produces leisure experiences by using the same technology or the same inputs. Own time will be crucial for everyone; however, for some people the presence of others will be far more necessary than for other people. There could be individuals who are much more materialistic than others, and that personality trait could influence both the way they satisfy their leisure need and the way they value certain leisure conditions. Some people could be much more efficient in the production of pleasurable experiences because of their higher education. We know that leisure helps to enhance people's quality of life, but the valuation of those experiences is determined by societal norms and arrangements and by personal aspirations, past experiences and comparison effects; so a second difficulty is due to heterogeneity in the valuation process.

Both the definition of leisure satisfaction made by Beard and Ragheb (1980) and the complex production of enjoyable leisure experiences make it especially suitable now to present how happiness research in economics has sought to discover why personal involvement in leisure has positive effects. Since we have no means of observing the final leisure output, subjective assessment could be a reliable approach to that particular subjective condition.

The Subjective Well-being Approach in Economics

Traditional research on quality of life has relied heavily on objective and materialistic indicators of living conditions. GDP has been the 'champion' indicator when studying the evolution of living standards and comparing economies. Within the realm of objective indicators, nearly all non-market activities and many aspects of human development, such as leisure, have been neglected, especially non-material aspects of well-being, such as social relations, autonomy and self-determination (Frey and Stutzer, 2002). Happiness research has become something of a fashionable and popular topic (Layard, 2006), and more importantly, it has provided solid arguments for incorporating its insights into social science analysis. After a period of reticence by orthodox economists overly focused on revealed preference, there is now a growing interest in incorporating the subjective well-being approach. Happiness is now considered a satisfactory empirical proxy for individual utility.

Among other reasons for the flourishing literature on subjective well-being, we can highlight the following: (i) the approach offers richer insight into individual utility and quality of life, (ii) there is plenty of survey information available about living conditions, opinions and perceptions of people and societies, (iii) this approach can help to evaluate the net effects of alternative economic policies in terms of individual utilities, being therefore useful for informing economic policy decisions, (iv) it can help to determine the effect of different institutional conditions (such as quality of governance, social capital or societal decision-making processes) over individual well-being, and finally (v) it appears to be an alternative way of assessing the value of non-market goods and evils, such as environmental quality or chronic diseases (Frey and Stutzer, 2002; Van Praag and Ferrer-i-Carbonell, 2008).

Happiness, life satisfaction and subjective well-being are often used synonymously in economics, although not in other social sciences. Relying on Diener and Seligman's definition, well-being 'includes all of the evaluations, both cognitive and affective, that people make of their lives and components of their lives', while life satisfaction can be defined as a 'global judgment of well-being based on information the person believes is relevant' (Diener and Seligman, 2004, p. 4). These authors contend that life satisfaction is one of the expressions or elicitations of well-being, together with positive and negative affects and satisfaction with salient domains of life. In this way, life satisfaction is a dimension of well-being; life satisfaction is the cognitive dimension of well-being and happiness is the affective one (Kim and Kim, 2009). The indiscriminate use of happiness, life satisfaction and subjective well-being in surveys and in empirical economic contributions is due to their high positive correlations (Ferrer-i-Carbonell, 2002; Frey and Stutzer, 2002; Van Praag and Ferrer-i-Carbonell, 2008). Experienced utility and well-being can be measured with some degree of accuracy by means of the exploration of happiness and subjective well-being data.

If the overall judgement of well-being is life satisfaction, the judgement of particular aspects of life is domain satisfaction. The link between the evaluation of the whole and of the parts is explored by the so-called 'bottom-up' approach to the analysis of subjective well-being (Van Praag et al., 2003; Rojas, 2006; Easterlin and Sawangfa, 2007; Van Praag and Ferrer-i-Carbonell, 2008). Overall life satisfaction is determined by domain satisfaction. Individuals are able to distinguish various aspects of their life, and evaluate each one of them. Each domain satisfaction is determined by the evaluation of one's own personal situation in different dimensions of life, such as: financial situation, housing conditions, health, leisure, job or education, among others. The domain approach uses the 'bottom-up' or 'two-layer' model. It states that life can be approached as a general construct of many specific domains, and that life satisfaction can be understood as a result of satisfaction in these domains of life. Those domain satisfactions have a 'mediator' role to determine overall happiness.

In what follows, we shall consider that leisure satisfaction has leisure experiences as the main input, and that higher leisure satisfaction will contribute, in turn, to higher overall satisfaction or happiness (Ateca-Amestoy et al., 2008).

LEISURE SATISFACTION

We begin by reporting how leisure satisfaction is measured in different surveys. We then comment on empirical findings of research in an attempt to account for the individual's underlying decision-making process. Several authors have studied the mediating role of leisure satisfaction in order to determine the contribution of individual objective characteristics to happiness by means of a two-layer model (Van Praag and Ferrer-i-Carbonell, 2008). In our opinion, this approach is more consistent with economic decision making, when compared with the modelling of the direct effect of leisure on life satisfaction.

If a unique economic definition of leisure is somewhat difficult to propose, it is still more difficult to differentiate the resource (time or free time) from the outcome (leisure experience) when looking at social surveys. The difficulty increases when considering different languages, since in some of them, the differences are more subtle than in others.

Large social surveys measure leisure satisfaction in different ways. In the British Household Panel Survey (BHPS), leisure satisfaction is split up into two subdimensions, namely, satisfaction with the amount of leisure and satisfaction with the use of leisure time (Van Praag and Ferrer-i-Carbonell, 2008). The first one is measured by the statement 'how satisfied you are with the amount of leisure time'; the second one corresponds to 'how satisfied you are with the way you spend your leisure time'. We argue that the statement on how satisfied the individual is 'with your social life' captures further dimensions of leisure social involvement (in so far as social involvement is not productive, we may consider that it is leisure). The German Socio-Economic Panel (GSOEP) measures how satisfied the individual is with his/her 'free time' (*Freizeit*, in German); the 2008 questionnaire also includes a question on the number of hours dedicated to hobbies and free-time activities on an average weekday, as well as a report about the frequency of participation in different leisure activities. The Household, Income and Labour Dynamics in Australia Survey (HILDA) asks about satisfaction with the 'amount of free time'. The European Community Household Panel (ECHP), a large-scale survey conducted over the 1994–2001 period, considered only satisfaction 'with leisure time'. The *Latinobarómetro*, a comprehensive survey for 17 countries in Latin America and the Caribbean, includes only satisfaction with the amount of leisure, how satisfied the respondent is with his/her 'free time' (with the amount of available *tiempo libre*, making a literary translation from Spanish, the original language). The AsiaBarometer – for a changing group of countries – asks about satisfaction with 'leisure'. Other major surveys, such as Gallup, the World Value Survey or the European Social Survey also include measures of domain satisfactions. Typically, respondents are asked to score on some Likert scale the manner that, in their opinion, best describes how dissatisfied or satisfied they are with certain aspects of their life (for the implications of the ordinality of the satisfaction variable on the estimation procedures, see Ferrer-i-Carbonell and Frijters, 2004 and Van Praag and Ferrer-i-Carbonell, 2008).

We can identify several subdomains that are leisure related: the amount of free time itself (leisure as the amount of time, thus, an economic resource), the way that time is used (leisure as experience, so a commodity that is produced and consumed), and social relations (the relational dimension of leisure). Any one of these is consistent with the Beckerian approach previously discussed. First, we focus on the overview of findings for satisfaction with leisure (*Freizeit* for the GSOEP used in Erikson et al., 2007 and in Van Praag and Ferrer-i-Carbonell, 2008; *ocio* for the Spanish regional survey used in Ateca-Amestoy et al., 2008).

Since leisure is a time-intensive commodity, time is perhaps one of the most influential factors on individual satisfaction with the leisure experience. This is indeed the case, as the number of working hours has a negative and significant impact on leisure satisfaction (Ateca-Amestoy et al., 2008; Van Praag and Ferrer-i-Carbonell, 2008). Temporal autonomy has an effect on satisfaction with the amount of leisure time. Both the quantity of time devoted to leisure activities and the discretionary nature of that time contribute to a better quality of life (Erikson et al., 2007).

Income should have a positive effect on leisure satisfaction. More income can be used in the production of the leisure commodity. In two of the studies above, it has no statistically significant effect; the household income variable has a poor empirical performance. It could be that wealth or some measure of permanent income determines consumption decisions, since in some models income has an effect, albeit not changes in income. Some studies find that leisure-orientated goods have a positive influence, therefore capturing the materialistic component of leisure production (such as leisure equipment or holiday homes).

Labour status determines leisure satisfaction. Being self-employed has a negative impact, and this is leisure-domain specific. This does not necessarily happen with other domains, such as job satisfaction, for which there is evidence that self-determination has a positive impact. For the comparison between the self-employed and the employed, we find that this outcome is intuitive: we would expect employees to be less uncertain about when they can use their leisure-time resource. The labour status of those less satisfied with their leisure time is related to a greater uncertainty about the distribution of leisure time throughout the day. This would introduce a technological argument: time is not so productive when available at irregular intervals or in unpleasant schedules. Unemployed people systematically report lower levels of satisfaction in each domain of life; the same happens with leisure satisfaction. Here we have another argument for the use of comprehensive approaches to leisure that depart from the mere computation of residual time. It is difficult to assume that unemployed people produce and consume more leisure commodity because they have more time to dedicate (Ahn et al., 2005).

One of the shortcomings of these datasets is the difficulty in gathering precise information on wages in order to impute the opportunity cost of leisure time. For household income – the materialistic dimension of leisure – the level effect is weakly positive. There is evidence that the value of time determines the effect of time allocation decisions and subjective outcomes. For instance, Frey et al. (2007) find that the distress due to heavy TV watching is higher for people with a high opportunity cost. Hamermesh and Lee (2007) explore time stress, concluding that people with high wages are stressed not only because they work more, but also because they possess such a command over goods that they are busy spending their income.

Family composition also influences the opportunity cost of leisure time. One might think that a couple would synchronize their schedules in order to enjoy shared leisure (Hallberg, 2003; Hamermesh, 2009). This is not the case in all the empirical studies. For instance, in the above-mentioned analysis by Van Praag and Ferrer-i-Carbonell, people living alone in Germany have a greater probability of enjoying higher leisure satisfaction. This is a surprising finding but the effect of companionable others may be culturally dependent.

Family composition also induces differences by gender in the valuation of leisure experiences. Where statistically significant differences are found, males have a higher probability of more leisure satisfaction, all other things being equal. A plausible explanation for this could stem, in our opinion, from the fact that the measurement of leisure time through the indirect computation of number of hours or by activity often overestimates the availability of this resource for women. They typically spend more time than men involved in some activities lying on the borderline between leisure and household work, such as childcare. They are also more likely to be performing a secondary household activity simultaneous to the primary leisure activity (for instance, reading the newspaper while cooking, or walking in the park pushing the buggy). The number of children and dependants reduces leisure satisfaction. Childbearing has a negative effect on parental time stress (Nazio and MacIness, 2007; Ateca-Amestoy et al., 2008).

The state of one's health is closely related to the capacity for producing quality leisure. We can conceptualize health in terms of personal capital, determined by a genetic endowment that accumulates by means of investment in healthy lifestyles, and that deteriorates due to age and unhealthy habits. Therefore, people with better health are more likely to have a better quality of life. However, the causation is not clear: being in good shape (mental and physical) certainly contributes to being able to produce better leisure and enjoy it more. At the same time, involvement in high-quality leisure contributes to better health. The effect of age on leisure satisfaction has an inverse U-shape (the minimum reached at some point in the 30s). This finding is interpreted frequently in terms of changes in aspiration levels throughout life. This regularity holds for every domain of life satisfaction.

The reverse of the discretionary nature and the fact that freedom of choice is a vital attribute of leisure arise from hedonic adaptation features and from its perverse effects: routine, boredom and lack of excitement.

People learn to adjust to the good and bad circumstances of their lives. We incorporate achievements and adjust aspirations upwards. The effects of adaptation may be of a different sign depending on the type of leisure experiences. The frequency of sporting activities leads to some capital accumulation and positive addiction features, and the same may be true for some types of cultural participation (Becker, 1990), but we cannot ignore the fact that the novelty or scarceness of an experience may increase its enjoyment (Lyubomirsky et al., 2005; Michalos and Kahlke, 2008, 2010). Good attributes of pleasurable experiences should include certain ingredients, such as good matching between activities, the right amount of effort, optimal timing and an element of habit, motivation and social support. Again, individual heterogeneity may determine what the right combination of ingredients is for each individual, for instance because of idiosyncratic risk aversion.

Individual happiness depends on an individual's own relative situation or status, and the comparison with others could expose individuals to negative externalities in terms of 'peer-effects' (Luttmer, 2005) in utility and/ or consumption. Positionality in terms of consumption matters far more for some commodities than for others (Frank, 2007). Frijters and Leigh, (2008) relate conspicuous leisure and conspicuous consumption to social turnover. Their hypothesis that individuals living in societies with a high turnover prefer to allocate resources to conspicuous consumption rather than leisure is supported by data for the United States. Status is exhibited in more materialistic terms, moving away from Thorstein Veblen's traditional description (1899).

A converse positive influence of social interactions may arise from social relationships and other 'relational goods' (Gui and Sugden, 2005; Bruni and Stanca, 2008; Stanca, 2009) or social capital. The ability to incorporate social components has a positive effect on the quality of the leisure experience. This effect could be mediated by the individual's preference for social involvement with respect to introspective leisure activities. This social involvement may have a direct effect on the possibility of community identity building and, consequently, on the accumulation of social capital. Social capital and meaning creation through leisure involvement may enhance quality of life. Many of the non-economic studies that investigate those effects distinguish between individual quality of life and societal quality of life (Scottish Executive Social Research, 2005). Social capital has been found to be highly correlated with health (physical and mental). However, causal relationship is always an issue, being hard to disentangle, since it may operate in both directions: enjoying high levels of well-being would determine high social capital endowments or, alternatively, high social capital may contribute to high well-being at the individual level.

Empirical approximations to social capital – such as trust, social contacts and membership of associations (among them, recreational ones) – have been widely used as explanatory factors in individual well-being (Putman, 2000; Helliwell, 2003; Powdthavee, 2008). One of the conclusions reached is that social capital influences well-being through different and independent channels. Potentially, the ability to enjoy good quality leisure experiences is one of them.

So far we rely on 'How satisfied you are with your leisure/your free-time/the leisure that you enjoy' type of questions. We would now like to review the main findings of the domain estimation by Van Praag and Ferrer-i-Carbonell (2008) on data from the BHPS (1996–98 waves). They consider a model for satisfaction with the amount of leisure time, a second one for satisfaction with the use of leisure time, and a third one for satisfaction with social life. It is quite difficult to assess what individuals are evaluating when answering the question on satisfaction with the amount of leisure time. Nazio and MacIness (2007) say that it measures time stress. In economic terms, as individual preferences are non-satiated and leisure has a positive marginal utility, since leisure time has a positive marginal product in the leisure production function, more leisure time would strictly be preferred to less. A plausible explanation may be that highly satisfied individuals have been able to implement an unconstrained allocation of resources, whereas highly unsatisfied individuals have been driven to corner solutions, due to binding time constraints. Regarding the second question, satisfaction with use of leisure time, we believe that it asks individuals to evaluate their leisure experience. We have decided to include the last question, satisfaction with social life, in this discussion due to the critical relevance of the social dimensions of leisure.

The findings for satisfaction with amount of leisure time go in the expected direction for the number of working hours (strong negative effect), but statistically insignificant effects are found for the amount of leisure hours in the case of workers. No conclusive evidence is found for income. Regarding the presence of other members in the closer circle, evidence for the UK suggests that singles have a lower probability of being satisfied with the amount of leisure time with respect to childless couples (supporting the Hallberg, 2003 explanation). When estimating valuation functions for men and women in the same couple separately to test for different gender effects, the negative effect of children on satisfaction with the amount of leisure time is much stronger for women. This could be due to the higher opportunity cost of time for mothers.

To measure satisfaction with the use of leisure time we need a valuation question that embodies qualitative dimensions of leisure. Van Praag and Ferrer-i-Carbonell report the non-effects of household income and the amount of leisure time. The effect of the number of children is negative. The separate analysis by gender reports the more prominent negative effect of children on women and the fact that the number of leisure hours has a more positive effect for men.

The pattern for satisfaction with social life is nearly the same as the one for explaining satisfaction with leisure use, with people living together being strictly better off. There is a gender effect that favours men over women. The differentiated gender models draw a more subtle picture: available household income has a strong positive effect on female valuation, while not being statistically significant for men. Van Praag and Ferrer-i-Carbonell conjecture that women are able to substitute income for time by reducing housework, when buying it on the market. The number of children in the household reduces female satisfaction with this domain, but not the male's. This social dimension is the aspect of leisure evaluation in which more gender asymmetries arise.

When considering life/work balance issues, one may wonder whether subjective well-being research can contribute to a better understanding of the matter. Job satisfaction is positively correlated with satisfaction with the amount of leisure time, an indicator of the social nature of the time perception (stress) of work and leisure (Nazio and MacIness, 2007). A positive correlation between those domains is also found for Denmark in the study by Bonke et al. (2009). Job satisfaction and leisure satisfaction are complements, even though job and leisure compete with one another in terms of time allocation. We may add that it is a problem not only of allocating a number of hours, but also of the timing of the assignment and its stability. The rivalry between working time and leisure time is not just a problem of quantity. Unfriendly work schedules (awkward timetables or random shifts) may severely compromise leisure satisfaction, and it could be that extra income cannot compensate for the damaging effect on life satisfaction.

The contribution of leisure satisfaction to life satisfaction has been measured in a number of studies that have adopted the aforementioned two-layer model (domain satisfactions are mediators of life satisfaction). Ateca-Amestoy et al. (2008) perform an analysis for a representative sample in the Spanish region of Andalusia and find a zero-order correlation of +0.393 between leisure satisfaction and general satisfaction, with partial correlation of +0.1718 when controlling for the influence of other domain satisfactions, namely, environment, finance, housing, health and job. Pratt's indices of relative importance are computed for that two-layer model: the index for leisure satisfaction (5.6 per cent) ranks fourth, after financial satisfaction (63.9 per cent), housing (19.8 per cent) and health (7.2 per cent), but ahead of environment (3.1 per cent) and job (0.07 per cent). Van Praag and Ferrer-i-Carbonell (2008) study the four samples of the population represented in the GSOEP (East and West, and distinguishing between workers and non-workers) and find level effects for the different domain satisfactions as explanatory factors of overall happiness. The leisure satisfaction coefficient is of smaller magnitude than the level effects for financial, health and job and of greater size than the effects for housing and environmental satisfaction (with level effects somewhat higher in the Eastern sample).

LEISURE AND LIFE SATISFACTION

Instead of considering the mediating role of leisure satisfaction, one could focus directly on the effect of leisure on some measure of overall subjective well-being, such as happiness or life satisfaction. There is ample evidence of the beneficial effects of leisure (Haavio-Mannila, 1971; Eriksson et al., 2007). How does leisure contribute to a 'good life'? Donovan et al. (2002) report some evidence: for most people leisure is a less important source of satisfaction than job, marriage or family, but for a minority leisure is more important; happiness is correlated with satisfaction with leisure activities at around +0.40, declining to +0.20 when controlling for employment, social class and other factors.

We now look at studies dealing with the link between leisure and subjective well-being. We focus on studies that have a more economic approach (in the sense of Hamermesh, 2002, 2009), but do not discard contributions involving other disciplines. Economic research in this field has been scarce. Economic researchers have sought to concentrate on objective personal circumstances to study the determinants of life satisfaction. This makes leisure a somewhat unattractive candidate to enter as an explanatory variable in a life satisfaction regression, due to the difficulties of definition and measurement. We shall comment on certain items of research based on participation in one particular leisure activity, TV watching (Corneo, 2005; Frey et al., 2007; Bruni and Stanca, 2008; Frey and Benesch, 2008). We then extend to (sometimes non-economic) research on cultural participation and other leisure activities. TV watching is by no means an anecdotic activity; it is the most time-consuming form of leisure in OECD countries. There is a surprising positive correlation between working hours and hours dedicated to TV watching across countries (more working time reduces available time to be allocated to competing commodities). Corneo rationalizes this outcome in a model that considers two types of leisure: a social type (leading to the production of relational goods and subject to strategic complementarities) and a solitary type. There is also evidence that TV watching is not the most rewarding type of leisure. Many people report that they watch more TV than they consider good for them and, when compared with alternative leisure activities, it ranks lower in terms of the reported level of enjoyment (Frey et al., 2007). According to those two subjective measures (consuming 'too much' and 'level of enjoyment') people choose to produce experiences that lead to lower utility than certain other alternatives. Why then are people choosing an apparently non-optimal outcome? TV watching can turn into an addictive habit and produce low-quality leisure experiences, but as a commodity it has some good properties: it is an easily accessible leisure alternative with low material and social input requirements (Bruni and Stanca, 2008). It is time intensive, but relatively inexpensive in monetary terms. It is not very demanding since it does not require a good physical or mental condition. Some enjoyment may be gained even from tiny slots of time. Last but not least, it does not require companionable others; when no one is around, we switch on the TV.

Frey et al. explain this in terms of self-control problems and of the lag that goes from instantaneous benefit to future underpredicted costs. The negative effect of that 'wrong' decision is aggravated by the misprediction of the future utility of socializing and the perverse change in aspiration levels. TV watchers replace their comparison standards; the peers are replaced by life portrayed on TV (more violent, with more chaotic relations, more affluent people and more luxurious than real life). Therefore, the negative impact of peer effects for material comparisons is aggravated for heavy TV watchers. Heavy watching is correlated with lower financial satisfaction, having more materialistic attitudes (importance of being affluent), feeling less safe, trusting people less (therefore having less social capital), and thinking they are involved in fewer social activities than their peers. The negative relation between TV watching and life satisfaction can be partially explained by the differences in preferences and in beliefs among people who watch more TV. Furthermore, the negative effect is more pronounced for people with a high opportunity cost of time. TV plays an important role in crowding out relational activities through two mechanisms (Bruni and Stanca, 2008). There is an indirect one: the negative effect of the substitution of freely chosen socialization patterns by socialization patterns imposed by TV (in the spirit of Frey et al., 2007). The direct one is that there is less time available for relational goods. Relational goods are focused on the dimensions of identity and genuineness of interpersonal relations, that is, on the non-instrumental nature of social interaction. Making a distinction between life satisfaction and individual happiness, Bruni and Stanca find that the intrinsic motivation in leisure engagement contributes most to life satisfaction (the cognitive dimension), whereas the genuineness component of relational goods is particularly relevant for happiness (the affective dimension).

Again, strategic complementarity in the presence of others is an alternative explanation to the misprediction of the utility of personal interaction that leads to heavy non-optimal TV watching, or to the addiction processes. Relational types of leisure – substitutes for non-rewarding TV – are constrained by immediate costs in terms of time and effort, by coordination with other people, and by intensive engagement for long periods. All those aspects appear again as crucial determinants of the quality of leisure. They clearly influence the transformation of time into leisure by means of some production function that has yet to be sufficiently analysed. This analysis of the most popular leisure activity leads to a quite negative view of the contribution of leisure to well-being. However, let us complete the discussion with (i) other types of media-related leisure, (ii) other types of artistic and cultural participation leisure, and (iii) cultural and physical activity leisure.

Frey and Benesch (2008) extend the analysis of media use: TV, radio and newspapers are examined. Radio and newspapers are positively related to higher life satisfaction. Why then do people systematically choose the wrong alternative? The question is difficult to answer due to comparability problems: the three activities have different characteristics. The greatest fraction of TV consumption is done for entertainment, and the degree of concentration needed differs: highest for newspapers and lowest for listening to the radio, which is often a secondary activity. Nevertheless, for TV the cognitive and physical costs are low and the instantaneous reward is high (relaxation and fun). This may make the activity very attractive in relative terms. The results are not very conclusive, but we can learn that each of those activities induces leisure of different quality, satisfies different needs, and is evaluated in different ways due to our expectations of the enjoyment that we are about to experience. Were leisure satisfaction to be analysed, the distinct impact of each type of activity could probably be quantified.

A pioneering study of the relationship between the arts and quality of life involves a paper on social indicators written by Michalos (2005). The author, editor of *Social Indicators Research* (a journal widely cited in the reference section), qualifies the study of the impact of the arts on the overall quality of life as the area *most understudied* and *underrated* in the field of social indicators research. In his first study, he conducts a survey with questions on participation and frequency of participation in 66 artistic activities, together with satisfaction derived from participation, attitudinal questions on beliefs and feelings about the arts, socio-demographic questions, and health and quality of life issues. Different activities correlate differently with different health and quality of life dimensions. Playing a musical instrument is positively associated with general health. Gourmet cooking has the highest positive correlation with life satisfaction and with happiness, as well as with subjective well-being. The results from multi-variate analysis lead Michalos to conclude that, relative to satisfaction obtained from other domains of life, the arts have little impact on quality of life for his sample. That study is supplemented by two subsequent ones (Michalos and Kahlke, 2008 and 2010). It is interesting to note how individuals perceive the most rewarding artistic activities to be ones that are not necessarily the most frequent ones. This may have to do with the demand for variety, with the need to avoid hedonic adaptation or, again, with the intrinsic differences in the quality of different artistic activities. In those studies they also conclude that the contribution of involvement in artistic activities is not great in relative terms, again for a regional sample in Canada.

Cultural activities, as conceptualized in Kim and Kim (2009), have a positive impact on subjective well-being. The authors contribute to the study of the impact of cultural participation on quality of life, and analyse data for Korea. Cultural capital (as per Bourdieu, 1984) is operationalized through cultural participation (Seaman, 2006). More precisely, by means of (i) the previous year's number of cultural experiences, (ii) the number of different types of experiences, and (iii) the monthly average expenditure on cultural activities. They study the impact of those three dimensions on the affective dimension of well-being (happiness) and the cognitive one (life satisfaction). Differences in well-being are found among those with cultural capital and those with no cultural capital at all. As expected, people with more frequent and diverse experiences and with higher expenditure record more life satisfaction. Frequency seems to correlate more with life satisfaction, whereas diversity (an omnivorous type of cultural consumer) seems to have a stronger correlation with happiness. The three variables are statistically significant for both measures of well-being, though of smaller magnitude than sex, income, education, health or social relations. We might be dealing with a misspecification problem, since empirical studies on the demand for cultural goods show how cultural participation is determined by all those variables (ibid.). Active involvement in the arts in a representative Italian sample is measured by Grossi et al. (2011a, 2011b), together with a measure of quality of life (the Psychological General Well-Being Index). Data are analysed by means of artificial neural network analysis, so no causation can be interpreted.

A pitfall of identifying arts with formal cultural participation is the neglect of non-use values of cultural goods. This point is an interesting one in the discussion by Michalos and Kahlke (2008). Cultural value is a difficult concept to handle from an economic point of view, but there is wide consensus that cultural goods embody both use and non-use values (in this aspect, they are very similar to environmental goods). For instance, take the example of material cultural heritage. One can distinguish between use and non-use values. Users experience the good in a visit and enjoy that leisure experience, but even non-users may attach positive value and derive utility from the good (due to any one of these sources of value: existence, option and bequest value). Along these same lines, we may expect that living in a place with easy access to cultural heritage will lead to higher levels of quality of life (of course, accounting for an adaptation process that influences valuation). First, because there is the open possibility of using that item of cultural heritage any time in the future as a productive result to produce pleasurable leisure experiences. This may be explored in the future by operationalizing Amartya Sen's capability approach. Second, because of the value of existence and of symbolic value that may contribute to the sense of belonging and may make social capital accumulation grow faster.

A comprehensive analysis of cultural and sports activities is performed by Rodríguez et al. (2008), testing for alternative conceptual frameworks of the link between leisure and life satisfaction. The first theory that they test is the activity theory, which states that the greater the frequency and the intimacy in the activity, the greater the life satisfaction. For the competing explanation, the need theory, need satisfaction has a positive effect on an individual's subjective well-being. Although the results are not conclusive, we shall comment on certain points. First, frequency of participation does not provide information about the quality of the experience. Second, different activities satisfy different psychological needs and to different extents, so we recall again the advantages and drawbacks linked to each one of the four definitions of leisure discussed in this chapter. As a result of this study, it seems that some so-called leisure activities contribute more to achieving higher life satisfaction because they contribute more to the satisfaction of such needs as autonomy (which appears to be especially relevant and associated with higher self-esteem and positive affects) and social interactions. It could be that the satisfaction of needs has a mediating role on the influence of leisure activities for determining high life satisfaction.

Economic contributions to explain how leisure influences subjective well-being are scarce. One of the possible reasons may be the difficulty in using the right concept of leisure. If an activity approach can be used to exert good control over the individual decision-making process, it is simply by focusing on one activity. When comparing two or more activities, such as in the contribution made by Frey and Benesch (2008), the unobservable leisure dimensions that determine the quality of the experience make the analysis harder.

CULTURE AND INSTITUTIONS MAKE A DIFFERENCE

Up to this point, we have mainly discussed the common features that link leisure and quality of life. We have found common factors and other empirical findings that differ for the sample being used. A multicultural context should be taken into account to discuss the diverse effect of leisure on quality of life. Leisure experiences are socially and culturally constructed (Iwasaki, 2007). We argue that, with leisure being a social and cultural concept, there may be special institutional and cultural traits that have not yet been considered. Leisure is a realm of self-realization that produces relational goods and meaning, all of which are products that are culture dependent. Cross-country analysis of leisure has mainly focused on time distribution patterns (Aguiar and Hurst, 2007). We have commented on the scarcity of studies that relate leisure and well-being; this fact becomes more prominent in cross-cultural studies.

With the exception of some works that use data from the ECHP survey, there is little comparative economic work in this field. Hamermesh and Lee (2007) conduct a time stress analysis for national representative samples in Australia, Germany, the US and Korea. A non-economic approach can be found in Manrai and Manrai (1995), who investigate a sample of international students (both local and from other countries and cultures) in the US. For them, leisure attitudes depend on three aspects of time that determine time use: time-activity (polychronic versus monochronic), time priority (work versus leisure) and time-setting (individualistic versus collectivistic). For Iwasaki (2007), culture plays a key role in facilitating the 'meaning-making' and the 'life-quality-enhancement' of leisure. This statement is based on the review of examples for Asian, Middle Eastern, and indigenous contexts. Culture is operationalized in terms of religiosity in Jagodzinski (2010), who finds higher influences of social and cultural context in Asian countries with respect to Europeans. Time distribution, leisure and leisure satisfaction also depend on other contextual factors, such as the type of welfare state, which contribute to people's well-being in many different ways (Esping-Andersen, 2002). Rice et al. (2006) propose the measure of 'temporal autonomy' to characterize the contribution welfare (taxes, transfers and childcare subsidies) and gender regimes make to people's autonomy (they run a comparative for the United States, Australia, Germany, France and Sweden). Some empirical findings that we have reviewed may indicate which aspects of the link between leisure and quality of life may depend on cultural and institutional differences.

We have discussed the jointness and togetherness hypotheses for leisure (a couple would seek to synchronize schedules in order to enjoy leisure together, Hallberg, 2003). Empirical research has determined that, for some countries, being single determines higher cultural participation (Seaman, 2006) or leads to higher leisure satisfaction (in the German study by Van Praag and Ferrer-i-Carbonell, 2008). However, in other countries, the presence of companionable others increases the leisure satisfaction reported by the individual, potentially by means of the higher quality as defined in Mediterranean countries (Ateca-Amestoy et al., 2008; Demoussis and Giannakopoulos, 2008) or in the UK (Van Praag and Ferrer-i-Carbonell, 2008). It seems that leisure can be more orientated to autonomy need fulfilment in certain societies, while more orientated to community-belonging aspects in others. Gender differences could also be due to cultural transmission patterns. This informs our interpretation of the findings for Denmark, whereby men prefer goods-intensive types of leisure compared to women, who prefer types that are more intensive in social relations (Bonke et al., 2009).

The degree of positionality could also be culturally dependent. For instance, we have commented on the finding that leisure is not as positional as other economic goods (Frank, 2007). However, this has to be considered together with the contribution made by Frijters and Leigh (2008). In the model they test, the conspicuous nature of leisure and income is modulated by cultural arrangements. In societies where mobility and turnover are relatively high, people tend to concentrate their efforts to gain status on conspicuous consumption, rather than on conspicuous leisure. Again, social norms determine the allocation of resources and the enjoyment of leisure.

After concluding the discussion on the relevance of the cultural and institutional framework, it seems obvious to mention that those factors should be present in future research. By conducting empirical research and by looking at the findings of other social disciplines, we shall learn more about what links productive resources for leisure (time included) with satisfaction. Time-use surveys will undoubtedly continue to be valuable sources of information. The underlooked aspects of the diaries will throw up results that will enrich the concepts of primary and secondary activities, the places for leisure and the contribution of the place to the quality of the experience, the jointness of participation in leisure activities for members of the family, and the scheduling of the leisure analysis of the places in which the action takes place. This time-use research should be complemented with further evidence of how different leisure conditions contribute distinctly to create leisure satisfaction.

New insights can be gained if researchers overcome the one-dimensional time quantity approach and substitute it by the multidimensional leisure quality approach. Ultimately, good and pleasant leisure contributes to a satisfactory life.

NOTE

1. The author thanks Arantza Ugidos for helpful comments and suggestions. She also acknowledges the financial support from the Basque government (research grants HM 2009-1-18 and IT-241-07), the Spanish Instituto de la Mujer (I+D+I 2007-031), and the Spanish CICIT (SEJ 2006/10827).

REFERENCES

Aguiar, M. and E. Hurst (2007), 'Measuring trends in leisure: the allocation of time over five decades', *Quarterly Journal of Economics*, **111**, 969–1005.

Ahn, N., J.F. Jimeno and A. Ugidos (2005), 'Mondays in the sun: unemployment, time use and consumption patterns in Spain', in D.S. Hamermesh and G.A. Pfann (eds), *The Economics of Time Use*, Amsterdam: Elsevier, pp. 237–59.

Apps, P. (2003), 'Gender, time use and models of the household', Institute for the Study of Labor (IZA) Discussion Paper 789, IZA, Bonn.

Ateca-Amestoy, V., R. Serrano-del-Rosal and E. Vera-Toscano (2008), 'The leisure experience', *Journal of Socio-Economics*, **37**, 64–78.

Beard, J.G. and M.G. Ragheb (1980), 'Measuring leisure satisfaction', *Journal of Leisure Research*, **12**, 20–33.

Becker, G. (1965), 'A theory of the allocation of time', *Economic Journal*, **75**, 493–517.

Becker, G.S. (1990), *The Economic Approach to Human Behavior*, Chicago, IL: University of Chicago Press.

Bonke, J., M. Deding and M. Lausten (2009), 'Time and money: a simultaneous analysis of men's and women's domain satisfactions', *Journal of Happiness Studies*, **10**, 113–31.

Bourdieu, P. (1984), *Distinction: A Social Critique of the Judgment of Taste*, London: Routledge & Kegan Paul.

Bruni, L. and L. Stanca (2008), 'Watching alone: relational goods, television and happiness', *Journal of Economic Behavior and Organization*, **65**, 506–28.

Burda, M.C., D.S. Hamermesh and P. Weil (2007), 'Total work, gender and social norms', Institute for the Study of Labor IZA Discussion Paper 2705, IZA, Bonn.

Clark, A.E. (1997), 'Job satisfaction and gender: why are women so happy at work?', *Labour Economics*, **4**, 341–72.

Corneo, G. (2005), 'Work and television', *European Journal of Political Economy*, **21**, 99–113.

Demoussis, M. and N. Giannakopoulos (2008), 'Analysis of domain satisfactions: evidence from a panel of Greek women', *Journal of Socio-Economics*, **37**, 1347–62.

Diener, E. and M. Seligman (2004), 'Beyond money: toward an economy of well-being', *Psychological Science in the Public Interest*, **5**, 1–31.

Donovan, N., D. Halpern and R. Sargeant (2002), *Life Satisfaction: The State of Knowledge and Implications for Government*, London: Strategy Unit.

Easterlin, R. (1974), 'Does economic growth improve the human lot?', in P.A. David and W.B. Melvin (eds), *Nations and Households in Economic Growth*, Palo Alto, CA: Stanford University Press, pp. 89–125.

Easterlin, R. and O. Sawangfa (2007), 'Happiness and domain satisfaction: theory and evidence', Institute for the Study of Labor (IZA) Discussion Paper No. 2584, IZA, Bonn.

Eriksson, L., J.M. Rice and R.E. Goodin (2007), 'Temporal aspects of life satisfaction', *Social Indicators Research*, **80**, 511–33.

Esping-Andersen, G. (2002), *Why We Need a New Welfare State*, Oxford: Oxford University Press.

Ferrer-i-Carbonell, A. (2002), 'Subjective questions to measure welfare and well-being: a survey', Tinbergen Institute Discussion Paper 2002-020/3, Amsterdam.

Ferrer-i-Carbonell, A. and P. Frijters (2004), 'How important is methodology for the estimates of the determinants of happiness?', *Economic Journal*, **114**, 641–59.

Frank, R.H. (2007), 'Does context matter more for some goods than others', in M. Bianchi (ed.), *The Evolution of Consumption: Theories and Practices*, Advances in Austrian Economics, Vol. 10, Bingley, UK: England Group Publishing, pp. 231–48.

Frey, B.S. and C. Benesch (2008), 'TV, time and happiness', *Homo Oeconomicus*, **25**, 413–24.

Frey, B.S. and A. Stutzer (2002), 'What can economists learn from happiness research?', *Journal of Economic Literature*, **40**, 402–35.

Frey, B.S., C. Benesch and A. Stutzer (2007), 'Does watching TV make us happy?', *Journal of Economic Psychology*, **28**, 283–313.

Frijters, P. and A. Leigh (2008), 'Materialism on the march: from conspicuous leisure to conspicuous consumption', *Journal of Socio-Economics*, **37**, 1937–45.

Gershuny, J. (2000), *Changing Times: Work and Leisure in Postindustrial Society*, Oxford: Oxford University Press.

Goodin, R.E., J.M. Rice, M. Bittman and P. Sanders (2005), 'The time pressure illusion: discretionary time versus free time', *Social Indicators Research*, **73**, 43–70.

Gronau, R. (1977), 'Leisure, home production and work: the theory of the allocation of time revisited', *Journal of Political Economy*, **85**, 1099–124.

Gronau, R. and D.S. Hamermesh (2006), 'Time versus goods: the value of measuring household production technologies', *Review of Income and Wealth*, **52**, 1–16.

Grossi, E., P.L. Sacco, G. Tavani-Blessi and R. Cerruti (2011a), 'The impact of culture on the individual subjective well-being of the Italian population: an exploratory study', *Applied Research Quality Life*, forthcoming, DOI 10.1007/511482-010-9135-1.

Grossi, E., P.L. Sacco, G. Tavani-Blessi and R. Cerruti (2011b), 'The interaction between culture, health and psychological well-being: data-mining from the Italian Culture and Well-Being Project', *Journal of Happiness Studies*, forthcoming, DOI 10.1007/510902-011-9254-x.

Gui, B. and R. Sugden (2005), 'Why interpersonal relations matter for economics', in B. Gui and R. Sugden (eds), *Economics and Social Interaction Accounting for Interpersonal Relations*, Cambridge: Cambridge University Press, pp. 1–22.

Haavio-Mannila, E. (1971), 'Satisfaction with family, work, leisure and life among men and women', *Human Relations*, **24**, 585–601.

Hallberg, D. (2003), 'Synchronous leisure, jointness and household labor supply', *Labour Economics*, **10**, 185–203.

Hamermesh, D.S. (2002), 'Timing, togetherness and time windfalls', *Journal of Population Economics*, **15**, 601–32.

Hamermesh, D.S. (2004), 'Subjective outcomes in economics', *Southern Economic Journal*, **71**, 2–11.

Hamermesh, D.S. (2009), 'It's time to "do economics" with time-use data', *Social Indicators Research*, **93**, 65–8.

Hamermesh, D.S. and J. Lee (2007), 'Stressed out on four continents: time crunch or yuppie kvetch?', *Review of Economics and Statistics*, **89**, 374–83.

Helliwell, J.F. (2003), 'How's life? Combining individual and national variables to explain subjective well-being', *Economic Modelling*, **20**, 331–60.

Iwasaki, Y. (2007), 'Leisure and quality of life in an international and multicultural context: what are the major pathways linking leisure to quality of life', *Social Indicators Research*, **82**, 233–64.

Jagodzinski, W. (2010), 'Economic, social, and cultural determinants of life satisfaction: are there differences between Asia and Europe?', *Social Indicators Research*, **97**, 85–104.

Jenkins, S.P. and L. Osberg (2005), 'Nobody to play with? The implications of leisure coordination', in D.S. Hamermesh and G.A. Pfann (eds), *The Economics of Time Use*, Amsterdam: Elsevier, pp. 113–45.

Kelly, J.R. (1982), *Leisure*, Englewood Cliffs, NJ: Prentice-Hall.

Kim, S. and H. Kim (2009), 'Does cultural capital matter? Cultural divide and quality of life', *Social Indicators Research*, **93**, 295–313.

Layard, R. (2006), *Happiness: Lessons from a New Science*, London: Penguin.

Luttmer, E. (2005), 'Neighbors as negatives: relative earnings and well-being', *Quarterly Journal of Economics*, **120**, 963–1002.

Lyubomirsky, S., K.M. Sheldon and D. Schkade (2005), 'Pursuing happiness: the architecture of substainable change', *Review of General Psychology*, **9**, 111–31.

Manrai, L.A. and A.K. Manrai (1995), 'Effects of cultural-context, gender, and accumulation on perceptions of work versus social/leisure time usage', *Journal of Business Research*, **32**, 115–28.

Merz, J. and L. Osberg (2006), 'Keeping in touch – a benefit of public holidays', Institute for the Study of Labor (IZA) Discussion Paper 2089, IZA, Bonn.

Michalos, A. (2005), 'Arts and the quality of life: an exploratory study', *Social Indicators Research*, **71**, 11–59.

Michalos, A. and P.M. Kahlke (2008), 'Impact of arts related activities on the perceived quality of life', *Social Indicators Research*, **89**, 193–258.

Michalos, A. and P.M. Kahlke (2010), 'Arts and the perceived quality of life in British Columbia', *Social Indicators Research*, **96**, 1–39.

Nazio, T. and J. MacInnes (2007), 'Time stress, well-being and the double burden', in G. Esping-Andersen (ed.), *Family Formation and Family Dilemmas in Contemporary Europe*, Bilbao: Fundación BBVA, pp. 155–83.

Osberg, L. (2008), 'Leisure' in S.N. Durlauf and L.E. Blume (eds), *The New Palgrave Dictionary of Economics*, Basingstoke: Palgrave-Macmillan.

Powdthavee, N. (2008), 'Putting a price tag on friends, relatives and neighbours: using surveys of life satisfaction to value social relationships', *Journal of Socio-Economics*, **37**, 1459–80.

Putnam, R.D. (2000), *Bowling Alone: The Collapse and Revival of American Community*, New York: Simon & Schuster.

Rice, J.M., R.E. Goodin and A. Parpo (2006), 'The temporal welfare state: a cross-national comparison', Levy Economics Institute WP 449, Levy Economics Institute of Bard College, New York.

Rodríguez, A., P. Látková and Y.Y. Sun (2008), 'The relationship between leisure and life satisfaction: application of activity and need theory', *Social Indicators Research*, **86**, 163–75.

Rojas, M. (2006), 'Life satisfaction and satisfaction in domains of life: is it a simple or a simplified relationship?', *Journal of Happiness Studies*, **7**, 467–97.

Scottish Executive Social Research (2005), *Well-being and Quality of Life: Measuring the Benefits of Culture and Sport: Literature Review and Thinkpiece*, Edinburgh: Scottish Executive Education Department.

Seaman, B.A. (2006), 'Empirical studies of demand for performing arts', in V. Ginsbourgh and C.D. Throsby (eds), *Handbook of the Economics of the Arts and Culture*, North-Holland: Elsevier, pp. 415–72.

Stanca, L. (2009), 'With or without you? Measuring the quality of relation life throughout the world', *Journal of Socio-Economics*, **38**, 834–42.

Stiglitz, J.E., A. Sen and J.P. Fitoussi (2009), 'Report by the Commission on the Measurement of Economic Performance and Social Progress', European Commission.

Van Praag, B.M.S. and A. Ferrer-i-Carbonell (2008), *Happiness Quantified: A Satisfaction Calculus Approach*, 2nd edn, Oxford: Oxford University Press.

Van Praag, B.M.S., P. Frijters and A. Ferrer-i-Carbonell (2003), 'The anatomy of well-being', *Journal of Economic Behavior and Organization*, **51**, 29–49.

Veblen, T. (1899 [1965]), *The Theory of the Leisure Class*, Augustus M. Kelley, New York.

Warde, A. and G. Tampubolon (2002), 'Social capital, networks and leisure consumption', *Sociological Review*, **50**, 155–80.

Zeckhauser, R. (1973), 'Time as the ultimate source of utility', *Quarterly Journal of Economics*, **87**, 668–75.

PART II

WORK/LEISURE BALANCE

5. The economics of sleep and boredom
Samuel Cameron

INTRODUCTION

It might be deemed reasonable to include a chapter touching on boredom in a book on leisure, as 'leisure boredom' is one of the indices used in empirical studies of boredom. In their study of high school dropout rates in Cape Town, South Africa, Wegner et al. (2008) define 'leisure boredom' as 'the perception that leisure experiences do not satisfy the need for optimal arousal' (p. 421). The use of the term 'optimal' ought to pique the interest of economists. Boredom scholars also use scales for sexual boredom which might be deemed to be relevant to leisure boredom in some contexts. Sleep is an area in which there have been some mainstream economics papers, and its leisure relevance is hard to ignore as most people spend a figure approaching a third of their life doing it. In the corner solution, where we could rid ourselves totally of the need to sleep, then we would have in the region of over 2,700 hours a year 'extra' to earn money and enjoy ourselves in leisure activity.

Sleep and boredom are not areas of leisure which we find addressed in government policy initiatives very often[1] yet they are important for a number of obvious reasons. It is claimed that boredom can have deleterious health consequences particularly for the young by causing self-damaging consumption choices and also leading to depression. Too much or too little sleep influences both the quality and productivity of work and leisure activity through accidents, health changes and loss of motivation. Sleep problems can also induce resort to both sedating and activating drugs depending on the context. The need for sedating drugs is obvious. Stimulating drugs may be resorted to in order to keep people awake and having fun or indeed working beyond their inherent capacity. The most common form of this is caffeine-based drinks but we also have the non-hedonic use of cocaine, as in its nickname of 'Bolivian Marching Powder'.

The relevance of sleep to leisure is also evident in volume terms. The pure biological needs of the human body determine that people (even low sleep hyperactives of the Ian Paisley/Margaret Thatcher variety) require a very large amount of sleep relative to other activities. If one has a full-time job then it is quite difficult for enough of the time left to be dedicated to any other single activity that would take up as much time as sleep without

Table 5.1   Distribution of sleep hours in USA, 1998–2009: weekday

	1998	2001	2002	2005	2009
Hours (per day) (%)					
<6	12	13	15	16	20
6–7	23	18	24	24	23
7–8	28	31	29	31	27
8+	35	38	30	26	28
Mean (hours)	na	7	6.9	6.8	6.7
Median (hours)	na	7	7	7	7
N = 1,000					

Source: National Sleep Foundation (2009).

Table 5.2   Distribution of sleep hours in USA, 1998–2009: weekend

	1998	2001	2002	2005	2009
Hours (day) (%)					
<6	8	7	10	10	14
6–7	14	10	12	15	16
7–8	23	21	22	24	24
8+	53	61	52	49	44
Mean (hours)	na	7.8	7.5	7.4	7.1
Median (hours)	na	8	8	7.5	7
N = 1,000					

Source: National Sleep Foundation (2009).

long-term health effects. There has been concern about an emerging 'sleep deficit' whereby modern citizens sleep many fewer hours than their counterparts of a century ago with the current average reported at around 7 to 7½ hours. The main source of headline news stories on sleep trends is the survey 'Sleep in America' published annually since 2001 by the National Sleep Foundation. Some pertinent data from this, showing declines in sleep, are shown in Tables 5.1 and 5.2.

'Sleep in America' is a 20-minute phone poll of about 1,000 people mainly focused on 7–10 key issues which are not the same every year in which the survey is undertaken. Questions fluctuate due to topicality, for example, the effect of 9/11 was investigated in the 2002 survey. This is the most systematic data we have although it would obviously need to be more rigorous to be entirely satisfactory. The main concern about bias is that the sampling frame has tended to overrepresent older people.

The 2009 report shows that average weekday sleep is only 6 hours 40 minutes, and that weekend catch-up prospects are not good as the figure rises by only 27 minutes to 7 hours 7 minutes. Only 49 per cent say they had a good night's sleep every night. The studies show growth in both prescribed and non-prescribed sleep medication. In addition to these data, the 2009 report indicates that 19 per cent of those who are clinically obese say they are too sleepy to engage in leisure activities compared with 13 per cent of those considered to be of normal weight (weight judgements are based on body mass index).

If true, this apparent shortage of quality sleep and impairment of leisure activity would seem to suggest serious efficiency and quality of life issues that may justify government intervention. The argument has, however, been disputed, most notably by sleep researcher Jim Horne (see Harrison and Horne, 1995; Horne, 2004; Anderson and Horne, 2008) who claims that the assertion that we sleep less nowadays is largely a result of misinterpretations of historic data. He also disputes proposals that healthy adults, without complaint of daytime sleepiness, can have a sleep debt or underlying chronic sleepiness. Horne says that these are derived from unreliable experimental procedures being generalized inappropriately. The public's understanding of the terms 'tiredness' and 'fatigue', which could indicate sleep debt, have much wider connotations, and can be mood states unlikely to be rectified by extra sleep. Horne claims that sleeping beyond one's norm can be through boredom or pleasure rather than physiological need. He strongly argues against any policies to increase the amount of sleep that people get. He would hardly need to worry, as it seems unlikely that a market-driven economy is going to allow consumption and production time to slip away for health maintenance reasons (even if misguided).

As we have just seen, the validity of time-series claims about sleep data (whether it be actual sleep taken or perceived sleep deficit) has been questioned. Although we do not have time-series data on the volume of boredom, there is a general sense that complaints of boredom are a growing feature of modern life, particularly in the case of young people. This feature is illustrated tangentially in the next section.

BOREDOM IN POPULAR CULTURE

There have been sporadic discussions of the position of boredom in culture such as literature and philosophy (see Healy, 1984; Spacks, 1995; Bargdill, 2000; Moran, 2003; Milgram, 2004; Silver, 2006). The philosopher Svendsen (2005) in a whole book on the philosophy of boredom begins by telling us that a friend of his lost his life due to boredom. This would seem a mistaken ascription of depression to another label. Svendsen goes on to give a rather selective treatment of boredom in popular culture in his book. He focuses mostly on the 'Generation X'/'slacker' mentality found in Brett Easton Ellis's novels and their film adaptations. He also discusses music, notably direct quotations from Iggy Pop's 'I'm Bored' which, in essence, seems to be paradigmatic of an archetypal form of boredom. That is, energetic youthful frustration of unfulfilled potential giving rise to angry boredom. In current popular song this is exemplified in 'Never Miss A Beat' by the Kaiser Chiefs which features a narrator rejecting in a sarcastic manner things offered to them (presumably by a parent) and professes that it is 'cool to know nothing'. Consideration of other popular songs will provide a useful entry into the categorization of types of boredom.

States or feelings of boredom have been expressed in popular culture before the advent of pop music and rock and roll. The general belief is that boredom as a term in some form (such as 'ennui') only came into use in the eighteenth century. This is discussed by Silver (2006), who looks at its use in literature and problems of translation of the concept into different languages. More explicit use of the term is found since the shift to mass popular songs post-Beatles. The biggest successes of the period did not pen any overt boredom ditties. The Rolling Stones 'Satisfaction' did offer a rather drole commentary on the frustrations of modern life but did not indicate a state of boredom *per se*. However, The Lovin' Spoonful (1966), Procol Harum (1969) and the Buzzcocks (1977) offered songs simply called 'Boredom' while the Pet Shop Boys (1990) contributed 'Being Boring' to the digest. The last named is, however, a song about *not* being bored and thus involves use of the term in an ironic context. To jump forward briefly to the psychological studies of boredom, this is subversion of concept validity. That is, psychological scales are premised on the assumption that the respondents mean what they say.

These different songs might give us a quick introduction to the facets of boredom as a social construct. The Buzzcocks song falls ino the same category as Iggy Pop's 'I'm Bored' as it appears to be about youthful pent-up frustration as per the BBC television comedy 'The Young Ones'. The chorus is actually the word 'Boredom' shouted over and over again in a mocking 'punk' style. The Lovin' Spoonful song is about having nothing to do because of being stuck in an uneventful place with no acquaintances. The type of boredom evinced here could thus be cured with an internet connection and a mobile phone, or so it might seem. It is more redolent of typical adult boredom. The Procol Harum song is pretty much just a list of differences of opinion both minor and polar opposites ('some say they're looking yet some say they're seeing') with a chorus expressing lack of interest in the matter. It thus shades into the ennui school we discuss next, although it lacks either fey witticism or the sneering arrogance one might look for in this as defining characteristics.

ENNUI AND JADEDNESS

So far we mainly encounter boredom as states of having 'nothing to do' or states of frustration at not being able to do what one wants to do or even worse not knowing what this might be. The ennui variety of boredom is opposite to this, as it is a state in which the bored subject implies that his/her boredom is indicative of some kind of superior personality which the everyday world, populated by inferior mortals, is unable to live up to. There are older literary allusions (see Silver, 2006) to a person classified as a bore, which do not go on to consider the ambient or endogenous state of bored thoughts or emotion. In Oscar Wilde's *A Woman of No Importance* and Lord Byron's *Don Juan* there are dismissive comments about the pain of having to listen to bores. Here the bore is an inferior person and the person being bored by them is a superior person, or so they think.

So, the full birth of the ennui variety may be found in the work of Noel Coward, particularly his song 'I Get a Kick Out of You' which lists a lack of interest in alcohol, cocaine and flying in a plane. These are, however, counterpoints to an expressed romantic enthusiasm and thus cannot be seen as a precursor to the 'slacker/Gen X' mindset where nothing at all is of interest and thus nothing matters and ultimately morality might collapse. This mindset leads to singing in a disconnected sneering voice, a style which began in punk but was later denuded of its energy in Kurt Cobain's delivery in Nirvana. The true harbinger of this is to be found in the public persona of Andy Warhol. Warhol's career consisted of orchestrating supposedly shocking and exciting events throughout which he looked and sounded thoroughly disinterested. This might be seen as ironic mockery of a culture where everything has to be made to seem more exciting than it really is, in order to ensure sustained consumption and economic growth. This generates a drive which promotes sensation-seeking to the level of an addiction. The need for sensation-seeking as an alleviation to boredom can be seen in various film and novels particularly, the work of J.G. Ballard but also even in quite old films such as Alfred Hitchcock's *Rope* (1948).

We might also suggest that the current trend of youth complaints about boredom is not of the ennui/jadedness variety but likewise demonstrates status acquisition. For example, older people and their cultural interests might be deemed boring as a way of further indicating their social inferiority. This is demonstrated by the distorted parsing of the word as 'bo-ring', with the first part being distended to indicate additional contempt.

THE RELATIONSHIP BETWEEN SLEEP AND BOREDOM

All of us will at some time have heard the claim that 'I was so bored I nearly fell asleep', perhaps in connection with the monotonous sound of a lecturer's voice delivering tedious material as demonstrated in British comedian Ken Dodd's portrayal of the world's most boring lecturer in the film version of Lewis Carroll's *Alice in Wonderland*.

Relatively few academic studies look at the relationship between sleep and boredom. Kass et al. (2003) looked at the correlation of daytime sleepiness, insomnia, boredom proneness and attention deficit in a sample of 148 college students' scores on the Epworth Daytime Sleepiness Scale and Athens Insomnia Scale, the perception of time passing slowly, and feelings of constraint. Perhaps what is most interesting methodologically in this study is that people are asked about 'feelings of constraint'. Constraints have generally been taken as given and objective in economic theory so one would tend not to ask people about feelings of constraint. However, there is an implicit drift to examining this in current empirical work on subjective well-being (SWB)/happiness (see Chapter 4) which draws on Amartya Sen's capabilities approach.

On a more populist level, *The Sun* newspaper (UK), on 29 March 2008 got its reporter Nick Francis to stay awake for as long as possible in response to reported claims, from University of California researchers, that people's need for sleep was not a necessity but an atavistic hangover from earlier times. He attempted to keep himself awake by online discussions with readers and his blog was reported. After a few nights he reports 'I can't settle on one activity for very long before getting bored'. There is thus reciprocity between sleep and boredom as sleep reduces capacity to derive pleasure from arousal, and boredom may reduce sleep due to lack of sufficient arousal in the waking state. The two activities are clearly opposite in the sense that one has to be awake in order to be bored although it would be possible to have a dream in which one was bored.

THE THEORETICAL ECONOMICS OF SLEEP AND BOREDOM

The key notion to which sleep and boredom relates in theoretical economics is that of equilibrium and disequilibrium. This is hinted at in the definition used in boredom studies as per the quote we gave at the beginning which uses the crucial word 'optimal' in discussing the amount of arousal. In standard microeconomics, individuals are assumed to be long-run utility maximizers who face given constraints of time and money. The time limit means that one may be forced to fall short of equilibrium sleep and the money limit may mean that one simply cannot find enough goods to produce excitement and sensation and therefore becomes forced to endure boredom. Theoretical economics was applied to sleep by Bergstrom (1976) and Hoffman (1977). I am not aware of any similar specifically applied directly to boredom, although Scitovsky's now neglected work, *The Joyless Economy* (1992), deals with boredom at various points as does Stonebraker in 'The Joy of Economics' (2005) which is largely an exposition of Scitvovsky. To Scitovsky, solving the problems identified by Alfred Marshall (see Chapter 1 in this volume), requires the cultivation of culture as the source of skilled consumption. To get skilled consumption, we need culture. And to get culture, we need education. Recent trends in educational curricula have not pushed consumption skills; they have pushed production skills instead.

Boredom could be viewed as a state of disequilibrium which would never occur if an individual had sufficient resources which might be expanded to include skilled cultural consumption capital. This is only strictly true in a social context if we define resources to include other people, as boredom may arise due to not being able to find sufficient numbers and variety of others to interact with. This point is illustrated in the context of sexual swinging in Chapter 24 by Alan Collins.

These constraint ideas can be illustrated in a standard microeconomic choice diagram such as Figure 5.1. Here we use two aggregate commodities. One is 'diversions' which provide sensation-seeking and interest and the other is simply 'all other goods'. We ignore any household production structure between these two types of good. Sleeping is ignored here. The indifference curves (IC) show the marginal rate of substitution between diversion and other goods. We assume that both goods are 'normal' goods in terms of the standard economic definition. The budget line shows the relative prices of the two activities. The person will maximize utility at the point where the budget line is tangential to the indifference curve (E_1). If there is a fall in the relative price of diversions then they will move to a new equilibrium (E_2) where they are better off and have more diversions but also more other goods due to the income effect of the price fall.

There seems to be no intrinsic reason why the individuals should describe themselves as 'bored' in either case. Boredom could be introduced in a number of different ways. One common type of boredom such as experienced by reviewers of arts/entertainment, or attendees at academic conferences, is time 'wasted' which could have been spent doing something else when one is obligated not to get up and leave. This would effectively be a change in the constraint where there is a shortfall in the volume of

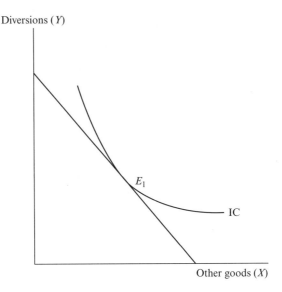

Figure 5.1   Consumer equilibrium without boredom

diversions due to random exogenous events, for example, a theatre critic might get to review a play he/she likes one week and not the next week. Similarly, a student who is forced to attend a lecture which appears to have no particular usefulness or relevance to the field of study he/she has elected to follow. This state is shown in Figure 5.2. where the amount of diversion is limited by the enforcing line ZZ in addition to income and prices.

Following Elster (1982, 1993, 1998), we could look at this as an emotional ascription of meaning to the state. This may not be problematic for the psychologists who study boredom, but for economists it may cause difficulties which we explore below. If this emotional statement is to be modelled in economic terms, then we could relate the expressed 'boredom proneness' (BP as we may as well use the terms already established by psychologists) to the magnitude of the shortfall induced by ZZ. This may seem rather trivial but as we are talking about perceptual gaps there is the issue of social mediation. That is, boredom can arise due to being unable to meet real or imagined levels of activity achieved by others in one's reference group (be they classmates, workmates, neighbours or superstars).

The treatment so far covers mainly frustration boredom although social mediation via tribalism may take us into the ennui and jadedness variants. These are all emotional ascriptions which an economist might dismiss as 'not real'. A more fundamental problem is where the boredom comes to represent a substantial decline in the individual's capacity to experience

Diversions (*Y*)

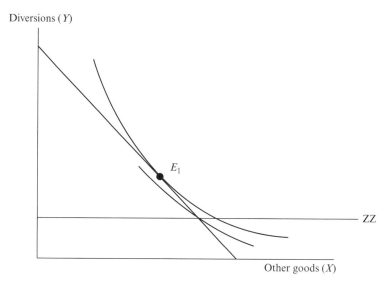

ZZ

Other goods (*X*)

Figure 5.2   Consumer equilibrium with boredom

pleasure, excitement and emotion in any activity. This wider notion of boredom, as not just a constraint problem, is symptomatic of a degeneration of the utility function. That is, there is an attenuation of the capacity to enjoy as opposed to the satiation problem. The satiation problem is due to a superabundance of goods. That is, the individual has so much pleasure-giving activity that he/she is simply unable to produce any further marginal increases in enjoyment for him/herself. Marginal utility has declined to zero. We accept, for example in the case of food, that this may be a short-run event which abates as the body adjusts and the person returns to a state of desire. The same would apply to sexual activity and the consumption of entertainment goods. The problem of satiation might arise in a slightly different form due to information overload in an information society which was explicitly identified quite long ago by Klapp (1986). That is, our brains and emotions become fatigued by the sheer amount of stimulus and information, to a degree that may overwhelm even the high levels of skilled cultural consumption in a Scitovskian utopia. There is something of a paradox here. Far from achieving bliss, in situations of abundance, we find ourselves slumping into states of apathy and boredom.

In contrast, the economic theory of sleep consists mainly of turning what was once a (largely undiscussed) constraint into a choice variable. Sleep then becomes a commodity subject to income and substitution effects. Its 'price' then is effectively the offered wage rate, although into this could be factored the relative price of leisure activities. Econometric studies based on time-use data by Biddle and Hamermesh (1990) garnered some media attention, but there has not been a lot of similar research following in their wake. Recently, better data have been investigated by Szalontai (2005), using South Africa's first time-use survey finding negative effects of wages and education on sleep consistent with previous international findings. This suggests that sleep is a commodity which can be competed into lower use by other commodities. The study claims that differing sleep patterns across countries can be explained by economic factors, seemingly implying that they are not a reflection of cultural or biological differences.

This is an intrinsically equilibrium view of the universe as sleeplessness in the daytime and feelings of excess tiredness could indicate that optimal choices, implied by discussions of this empirical work, have not been made. The data in routine time-use studies do not cover these subjective elements although they are covered in one-off studies and in 'Sleep in America' as discussed above.

Let us now look for a while at the sleep industry to consider some issues that the Biddle–Hamermesh type of work does not look at. To the uninitiated it might seem strange to talk of the 'sleep industry'. If we think of beds, pillows and so on as sleep technology then they are part of this industry. Adding sleeping tablets and other sleep-assisting products to it we seem to have a potentially vital economic sector. In the USA, the term 'sleep market industry' is used. An annual consultancy report (costing over two thousand dollars for an online download) called 'The U.S. Sleep Market' is published by Market Data Enterprises. This discusses the effect of the recession and provides forecasts for about five years ahead. It identifies growth due to general increases in sleep problems and specific areas such as sleep apnea (being wakened by inability to breathe). Pillows and mattresses are identified as a steady replacement market. The profitable areas are identified as drugs, sleep labs and sleep apnea devices. Before moving on to the issues of economic analysis of the effect of the sector, it is instructive to present a full list of the 'sleep devices' identified:

- sleep lamps/light therapy: used for seasonal affective disorder, dawn simulation, light boxes;
- sound machines/white noise machines;
- eye shades and sleep masks;
- earplugs;
- sleep pods;
- sleep/insomnia books; and
- miscellaneous retail products and services: hotels and spas are making rooms 'sleep friendly' to add value to a normal room.

In addition to this, we may note that regular goods are sometimes enhanced with sleep-assistance characteristics which are claimed to add around 50 per cent to the retail price. This has recently been the case with 'sleep milk' in the UK, which is locating itself in a niche formerly dominated by the iconic brand 'Ovaltine'. The sleep market is therefore somewhat like the diet market. Products can be promoted on the basis of solving lifestyle problems for increasingly anxious individuals. Sleep, diet and fitness efforts might be expected to conspire to make an individual more beautiful or attractive. The claims do not in general need to have scientific validity. Dietary products are subject to more stringency in terms of misleading advertising than sleep products.

Let us consider how the industry output operates in an economic model. For the individual, sleep may be pure leisure but the sleep market industry would find this a poor source of profit growth. If the individual has 'sleep problems' it is more appropriate to see sleep not as pure leisure but as an input into the stock of health capital (HK) which is an indirect source of utility through prolonging life and the capacity to enjoy it. Let us designate sleep health capital as ZZHK. The equation for production of this can be written as:

$$ZZHK = f(SHW, SSW, SET, SIP, SPL, X, ZTu), \qquad (5.1)$$

where:

SHW is sleep hardware = beds and mattresses. These items are the basic fixed capital of sleep. Sleeping on the floor (which may be superior for certain complaints) and other household items is possible but most individuals require a dedicated bed and mattress. Typically, an individual will only have one bed and mattress to sleep on and may share this with others.

SSW is sleep software such as pillows, blankets, duvets and sleep-specific bed attire. Unlike sleep hardware these are variable capital items. There is flexibility in how many of these are owned and used.

SET is sleep-enhancing technology – what the sleep market industry report identifies as 'sleep devices'. In some cases technology will be embedded in beds or pillows if they have special features such as odour or manoeuvrability.

SIP is sleep-inducing pharmaceuticals which may be synthesized in a laboratory or an organic product like untreated Valerian.

SPL is the labour of 'sleep professionals' in assisting the individual to sleep. This will include not only specifically designated sleep professionals but also others such as hypnotherapists and lifestyle consultants advising on Feng Shui and so on.

ZT is time spent in bed.

X is all other goods and activities and u is a random disturbance term independent of the other inputs to ZZHK.

More generally ZZHK would feature in the allocation of time problem in the household production model in which the ultimate objective is utility maximization. To highlight the salient policy issues here, let us assume that the objective is to generate a given level of ZZHK* efficiently. Assume that the individual has a given income/wealth and that the relative prices of the above factor inputs are fixed. We would expect that ZZHK* can be produced in a relatively more or less capital-intensive way. Typically an individual cannot increase the literal amount of bed or mattress in the short run, although he/she can expand its quality in the long run. There would then be a potential trade-off between hardware quality and other inputs, most conspicuously SET and SIP. In a state of perfect information, the ratio of these to SHW expenditure would be optimal and determined by their relative prices. We should note that there may be additional interdependency between factor inputs in that SIP will to some extent be prescribed by sleep professionals (or general doctors), operating as agents, rather than independently purchased in the market.

There are a number of possible reasons for market failure centred on risk and information problems. First, individuals may be poorly informed of the efficacy and health risks of using SIPs. This can arise due to asymmetric information and also systematic representation by manufacturers and sleep professionals. The September 2006 issue of *Consumer Reports* (www.ConsumerReports.org/health) argues that the use of sleeping pharmaceuticals in the United States is generally correlated to the growth in direct-to-consumer advertising of sleep medications. There were 43 million prescriptions in 2005, a 32 per cent increase from 2001. Prescription insomnia medications brought pharmaceutical companies more than $2.7 billion. Unesta, introduced by Sepracor in April 2005, was supported by $227 million on advertising that year. Prescriptions increased from 98,471 in April 2005 to 477,877 by year end.

It has to be added that, from an economic point of view, these data do not by themselves indicate that pharmaceutical companies are evil drug-pushers brainwashing the sleep deprived into addiction to pills. Unesta may simply be a superior product which deserves to oust its rivals from the market. The volume of advertising may be incidental to its success or could be simply giving the consumers information they need to know.

Notwithstanding, the facts just cited show that there seems to be substantial and growing prevalence towards pharmaceutical inputs in sleep production. One obvious reason for this is relative price. Pills are cheap and may have a degree of disguised pricing to the end user who may be receiving them at zero or discounted marginal cost, consequent to having made prior health investment expenditures. Improving one's bed is a fixed capital decision which is comparatively expensive and for which the benefits may be not so easily demonstrated.

There are additional sources of market failure other than pharmaceutical. Potentially the supply of beds could be distorted in that manufacturers may be inclined or induced to promote suboptimal beds in terms of their sleep productivity. To give one example, the height and shape of beds have at various times been influenced by the provision of under-bed storage. Given the difficulties of monitoring the degree to which beds are entirely fit for purpose there is no regulation in the output of beds. Beds may also be chosen for aesthetic reasons which conflict with sleep productivity. In addition to this, the custom of individuals, in intimate relationships, of sleeping together means that the bed, and the general sleeping environment, may be joint choices which are disadvantageous to the sleeping optimum of one individual.

There may be misperception of ZZHK required. It is difficult to specify how much quantity and quality of sleep an individual is receiving and the extent to which it falls short of what he/she needs. These difficulties create the market in sleep labs. Historically, sleep labs were found only in sleep research centres in universities where individuals volunteered as 'guinea pigs' in return for payment. The sleep lab is an expansion of the role of paid market monitoring of one's lifestyle, as instanced in the health and fitness sector discussed by Scott in Chapter 8.

Finally, let us give a bit more consideration to the random disturbance term. This would represent other factors such as stress from work, children, study and so on. There would be a biological component. Individuals tend to have different body clocks which could function on the basis of the need for a set amount of sleep at the same time each day, or they could exhibit 'drift' or discontinuities.

Pharmaceuticals address neurotransmitters in the brain and would potentially disrupt the individual's adjustment processes. The possibility of endogenous adjustment is undermined by competition from market solutions. Although these may have risks, they appear to offer more certainty. That is, if one input does not seem to be working it can be replaced by another of the same type or a different type of input. But sitting and waiting for things to rectify themselves offends the desire for control and regulation of the body/lifestyle. Thus the sleep market industry constitutes a movement towards the medicalization of sleep in the same way that fitness, health and beauty have been medicalized by intervention.

Some of the issues discussed above have been dealt with in the sporadic sociological literature on sleep (for example, Aubert and White 1959; Barbalet, 1999; Williams and Boden, 2004). Economists, however, have shown no interest in this particular source of market failure.

SENSATION-SEEKING, BOREDOM AVERSION

Thus far, pure economic theory has a limited amount to say about sleep and boredom. This limit is due to the assumption of given tastes which preclude an analysis of stimulus–response problems and dysfunctionality. In other words, the machine of individual happiness in the economic model is never assumed to be irreparably broken. Current economic literature on the issue of happiness or 'subjective well-being' (SWB) as it is termed more circumspectly in the professional academic discourse (see the application of this to leisure by Victoria Ateca-Amestoy in Chapter 4) still essentially ties in to mainstream economics.

The only economist to consistently countenance openly this kind of problem, as mentioned earlier, was the now largely forgotten Tibor Scitovsky who went so far as to entitle his book *The Joyless Economy* (1992). One of the areas that Scitovsky focuses on is variety-seeking. This term tends to be used in marketing literature (see, for example, Van Trijp, 1995) where it has been linked to boredom in such issues as choice of brand of butter. That is, it is argued that people will seek out alternative brands of butter just because they are bored and not because there is necessarily any intrinsic reason to seek different characteristics in butter as a commodity. There has also been research on which type of boredom state is most conducive to young people being induced, by advertising, to buy different types of goods.

Scitovsky's fundamental point would be that humans have an intrinsic need for variety. The existence of variety is not necessarily ruled out by assumptions of fixed tastes and a fixed bundle of goods so long as the bundle of goods on offer is sufficiently large and the tastes include a variation term of taste for variety. However, one of the potential market failures of a capitalist system is that it throws up 'boring variety', that is, lots of choice between more or less identical products as per the Bruce Springsteen song '57 Channels and nothing on'.

This complaint has also been made about the recent vogue for creative economies/cities/industries. For example, an internet posting by Karrie Jacobs (2005), argues that the cities which are vaunted as high points of creativity are in fact anything but. She says: 'One cool business district looks pretty much like the next, just the way one suburban mall looks pretty much like the next. And once you start thinking about creativity in terms of class, hipness as a monoculture seems like the inevitable outcome.' In terms of our current discussion, she would seem to be saying that 'latte towns' are boring because they lack variety.

So, the mere existence of a range of choices is *not* enough to guarantee the consumer a subjective feeling of variety. Even if the choices are varied, there is a kind of 'meta-variety' problem which contradicts the 'independence of irrelevant alternatives' assumptions of basic consumer theory. That is, if the set of wide-ranging alternatives has not changed for some time the individual may experience dissatisfaction even if he/she has no intention of choosing from the expanded set of choices. If we take the archetypal 'iPod therefore I am' problem – someone who has 10,000 songs on his/her device and is only likely to listen to say a tenth of those regularly may still develop variety loss if the set of 'never listened to' songs is fixed. Thus a loss of satisfaction can then be ascribed as 'boredom' by the economic agent who may *not* be suffering from the constraint problem considered in the early part of this chapter.

On a social level, this variety option problem may be driven by fashion cycles. These can involve the rejection of items which are older not because they have been superseded in their intrinsic technical content but simply because they are older. Designating these items as 'boring' is one method of speeding their exit from the menu of fashionable items. There can be rediscovery and rebranding of such discarded items as newly fashionable as such or ironically with a veneer of kitsch (Thompson, 1979).

This raises the issue of the role of stimulus in consumption choices. Possibly there is also the problem of stimulus addiction which economists have, so far, failed to touch upon in models of addiction. In the psychology-based boredom research these matters are touched upon in the area of 'sensation-seeking'. Indeed (see Vodanovitch, 2003b) boredom research is more properly seen as a subgenre of sensation-seeking research. There is a Boredom Susceptibility (BS) subscale of the Sensation Seeking Scale. Empirical work on boredom is primarily carried out by psychologists using scales constructed from answers given to a questionnaire. Boredom scales are correlated with scales for other attributes (from other questionnaire scales) and/or experimentally generated performance outcomes; for example, performance on a laboratory task. The primary boredom measurement tool is the Boredom Proneness Scale developed by Farmer and Sundberg (1986). Vodanovich and Kass (1990) investigated the factor structure of this scale which is thought to have at least five factors. The unpacking of the overall idea of boredom has involved job boredom, leisure boredom, sexual boredom, state boredom and trait boredom. Kass and Vodanovich (1990) conclude that boredom proneness and sensation-seeking were found to be similar in regard to the need for a

Table 5.3   Summary of empirical boredom studies

Item correlated with boredom	Positive	Negative
Positive and negative affect	+	
Productivity performance		–
Attention deficit		–
School dropout rates		–
Procrastination	+	
Impulsiveness	+	
Career planning		–
Gambling	+	
Absenteeism	+	
Job satisfaction		–
Job tenure		–
Mental health problems		–
Physical health problems		–
Daytime sleepiness		–
Age		–
Gender Males vs Females*	+	

Note: * In the study with race, black females were found to be more boredom prone than white males.

varied, novel and exciting environment. This is a general statement of the 'iPod therefore I am' problem discussed above.

THE QUANTITY OF BOREDOM: BRIEF NOTE ON EMPIRICAL WORK

Psychologists who study boredom extensively tend to till the convenient sample of college students, so there are issues about the generalizability of the results. Where people other than students are sampled, it is often a somewhat arbitrary comparison sample to the students. Boredom itself is assessed from a concatenation of a set of questionnaire responses into indices. It is obviously not possible to quantify boredom in an accurate cardinal way. It is therefore not feasible to attempt international or historical comparisons of the amount of boredom. Table 5.3 shows a list of the factors which have been correlated with boredom in psychological studies. This table simply shows a list of variables rather than identifying dependent and independent variables. Although a few studies use multiple regression, many are based on correlations and do not seek to specifically attribute any direction of causality between variables. The itemization in this table is based on studies cited elsewhere in this chapter plus Hamilton et al. (1984), Blaszcsynski et al. (1990), Vodanovich et al. (1991), Seib and Vodanovich (1998), Vodanovich and Rupp (1999), Watt and Vodanovich (1999), Sommers and Vodanovich (2000), Wallace et al. (2003) and Wegner et al. (2008).

Some of the more intriguing results are to be found in Watt and Vodanovich (1992), yet another study of undergraduates ($n = 381$). The results indicated that blacks ($N = 202$) were significantly more boredom prone than whites ($N = 176$). In addition, black females were found to possess the highest level of boredom proneness, followed by black males, white males, and white females. Walt and Vodanovich suggest that further research is needed to look at how race may mediate the relationship between boredom proneness and its correlates (for example, substance abuse, depression, low academic achievement). They make no attempt to explain the gender and race differentials *per se*.

The male–female ordering is confirmed in other studies which do not take account of race. Vodanovich and Kass (1990) found that males had a higher need for varied external stimulation than females. Gender differences were found on the Boredom Susceptibility subscale of the Sensation Seeking Scale–Form V with males scoring significantly higher than females. Vodanovich and Watt (1999) using students ($N = 338$) from the Republic of Ireland and the United States found that gender was a significant predictor of boredom proneness in the US sample (with males being associated with higher boredom scores) but was not a significant factor among the Irish. It is difficult to establish any ethnic dimension to this as it would require such things as measuring the ethnic origins of the US sample, some of whom may be of Irish origin.

DISCUSSION

Sleep and boredom are not seen as mainstream topics in economics or in leisure studies. Yet they are obviously very important. Complaints of boredom, too much sleep or not enough sleep are indicative of problems in allocating resources to leisure such as an inability to match the work/life balance (see Chapter 6 below). The traditional economic analysis of sleep which originates from Bergstrom (1976) overlooks these issues as sleep is yet another choice variable. Pervasive societal boredom might be seen as the ultimate problem of economic success in that individuals do not reach a point of bliss (as depicted in traditional microeconomics textbooks) when their marginal utility declines to zero from saturation of consumption, but instead experience a total loss of the capacity to enjoy.

On the other hand, one can construct the argument that boredom can be a beneficial disequilibrium state. This is put forward in Martin (2003) in a speculative book of essays and also by Vodanovich, the major author of empirical psychological studies in boredom. Vodanovich (2003a) argues that there is a conceptual bias in the available research on the construct of boredom. That is, the 'constructive' nature of boredom has been either ignored or underreported by researchers. His review of positive benefits of boredom comes from non-empirical writings given that the psychological literature has overlooked these. He proposes that future research should focus on examining the potential benefits of boredom, particularly as it relates to identifying how and why boredom leads to positive versus negative outcomes. One possible outcome is creativity from the frustration type of boredom which leads one to seek something new. However, it may be a fallacy to attribute boredom as being a 'cause' of innovation as it may just be an epiphenomenal transitory stage of creative endeavours. That is, we may be cautious of jumping to the conclusion that it may be a good thing to encourage boredom in order to get the beneficial products of it.

This caution takes us back to the labour market issues in the light of Riesman and Glazer's (1961) remark, quoted in Chapter 1, that leisure cannot compensate for lack of fulfilment in work but rather requires satisfying work to be pleasurable. Boredom at work is periodically greeted as a new important issue mainly in areas of personnel psychology – for example, recently by Game (2007) and Mann (2007). Game argues that there have been no previous studies of 'boredom coping' at work and argues that workers should receive training in boredom coping skills along with job redesign initiatives. A little further back, Fisher (1993) and Fisher and Hadrill (1994), looked at similar issues.

Going much further back (Whittaker, 1998), we find that, in 1922, sweet manufacturer Rowntrees took on a psychologist to look at these very problems. In 1934, the UK's Manpower Research Council (MRC) published *Incentives in Repetitive Work* (Wyatt, 1934) which claimed, in words which would now be deemed unacceptable: 'Too high a degree of intelligence may be detrimental to success and satisfaction in repetitive work, while a low degree of intelligence affords greater ability to endure monotony' (p. 92). The economist Sargent Florence included boredom as a human cost of work along with fatigue and injury in his book *The Economics of Fatigue and Unrest* first published in 1924.

Some of the work of Vodanovitch, summarized in Table 5.3, looks at these labour market issues. Kass et al. (2001b) provide evidence possibly contradictory to the above MRC claim that the trait of boredom proneness is predictive of performance on monotonous tasks within the first 10-minute block of trials but no difference in performance occurred on subsequent blocks, suggesting that as state boredom increases, differences between individuals diminish. Kass et al. (2001a) find that those high in job boredom possessed significantly greater absenteeism and longer organizational tenure.

These kinds of findings take us back to the human costs of work boredom and indeed the costs of sleep deprivation. To evade or shift such costs the individual would need to be able to adjust the framing of his/her consumption behaviour and to be offered redesigned workplace environments. The reframing of consumption is what Scitvosky hoped cultural education would be able to achieve. As for the workplace measures which Game (2007) advocates, these face economic barriers.

First, employers are sensitive about their jobs being described as boring. In 2009, 16-year-old Kimberly Swann was sacked for calling her administrative job, in Clacton (UK), boring on her Facebook page. Such sensitivities surely stand in the way of providing 'boredom coping' training as, by providing such training, the employer admits that the job is boring. Such training is a substitute for job redesign as job redesign could potentially remove the boringness of a job. The economic problem with job redesign is that real or imagined falls in output may occur. This depends on the nature of the work and the payment contract. In a time limited (such as packing orders for a deadline) payment-by-results set-up, one would rather the workers were bored as an incentive to finish as soon as possible and get out.

I do not pursue this issue further here as this is a book about leisure, not work. We may conclude by going back to Riesman and Glazier again to note that perhaps the promotion of better work environments would synergically elevate the worker's capacity to enjoy leisure time in a way that would please Marshall and Scitvosky.

NOTE

1. Periodically some concern is expressed about the risks of sleepiness in drivers of vehicles. A few years ago there were campaigns (in the UK) to get them to pull over and take breaks but this seems to have died down again.

REFERENCES

Anderson, C. and J.A. Horne (2008), 'Do we really want more sleep? A population-based study evaluating the strength of desire for more sleep', *Sleep Medicine*, **9**, 184–7.

Aubert, V. and H. White (1959), 'Sleep: a sociological interpretation I', *Acta Sociologica*, **4**(2), 46–54.

Barbalet, J.M. (1999), 'Boredom and social meaning', *British Journal of Sociology*, **50**(4), 631–46.
Bargdill, R. (2000), 'The study of life boredom', *Journal of Phenomenological Psychology*, **31**(2), 188–219.
Bergstrom, T.C. (1976), 'Toward a deeper economics of sleeping', *Journal of Political Economy*, **84**(2), 411–12.
Biddle, J. and D. Hamermesh (1990), 'Sleep and the allocation of time', *Journal of Political Economy*, **98**(5), 922–43.
Blaszcsynski, A., N. McConaghy and A. Frankova (1990), 'Boredom proneness in pathological gambling', *Psychological Reports*, **67**, 35–42.
Elster, J. (1982), 'Sour grapes – utilitarianism and the genesis of wants', Ch. 11. in A. Sen and B. Williams (eds), *Utilitarianism and Beyond*, Cambridge: Cambridge University Press.
Elster, J. (1993), 'Some unresolved problems in the theory of rational behaviour', *Acta Sociologica*, **36**(3), 179–90.
Elster, J. (1998), 'Emotions and economic theory', *Journal of Economic Literature*, **36**(1), March, 47–74.
Fasmer, R. and N.D. Sundberg (1986), 'Boredom proneness: the development and correlates of a new scale', *Journal of Personality Assessment*, **50**, 4–17.
Fisher, C.D. (1993), 'Boredom at work: a neglected concept', *Human Relations*, **46**, 395–417.
Fisher, C.D. and C. Hadrill (1994), 'Interrruptions, task type and the experience of boredom', Discussion Paper No. 55, Bond University School of Business, Robina, QLD, Australia.
Game, A.M. (2007), 'Workplace boredom coping, safety and HR implications', *Personnel Psychology*, **36**(5), 701–21.
Hamilton, J.A., R.J. Haier and M.S. Buchsbaum (1984), 'Intrinsic enjoyment and boredom coping scales: validation with personality, evoked potential and attentional measures', *Personality and Individual Differences*, **5**, 183–93.
Harrison, Y. and J.A. Horne (1995), 'Should we be taking more sleep?', *Sleep*, **10**, 901–7.
Healy, Sean (1984), *Boredom, Self, and Culture*, Rutherford, NJ: Fairleigh Dickinson University Press.
Hoffman, Emily P. (1977), 'The deeper economics of sleeping: important clues toward the discovery of activity X', *Journal of Political Economy*, **85**(3), 647.
Horne, J.A. (2004), 'Is there a sleep debt?', *Sleep*, **27**, 1047–9.
Jacobs, K. (2005), 'Why I Don't Love Richard Florida', MetropolisMag.com, posted February 22, 2005.
Kass, S.J. and S.J. Vodanovich (1990), 'Boredom proneness: its relationship to Type A behavior and sensation seeking', *Psychology: A Journal of Human Behavior*, **27**, 7–16.
Kass, S.J., S.J. Vodanovich and A. Callander (2001a), 'State-trait boredom: the relationship to absenteeism, tenure and job satisfaction', *Journal of Business and Psychology*, **16**, 317–27.
Kass, S.J., S.J. Vodanovich, C.J. Stanny and T.M. Taylor (2001b), 'Watching the clock: boredom and vigilance performance', *Perceptual and Motor Skills*, **92**, 969–76.
Kass, S.J., J.C. Wallace and S.J. Vodanovich (2003), 'Boredom proneness and sleep disorders as predictors of adult attention deficit scores', *Journal of Attention Disorders*, **7**(2), 83–91.
Klapp, O.E. (1986), *Overload and Boredom. Essays on the Quality of Life in the Information Society*, New York: Greenwood.
Mann, S. (2007), 'The boredom boom', *The Psychologist*, **20**(2), 90–93.
Martin, P. (2003), *Counting Sheep*, London: Flamingo.
Milgram, E. (2004), 'On being bored out of your mind', Meeting of Aristotelian Society, London, January.
Moran, J. (2003), 'Benjamin on boredom', *Critical Quarterly*, **45**(1–2), 168–81.
National Sleep Foundation (2009), '2009 Sleep in America Poll Summary of Findings', prepared by WBA Market Research, Washington, DC.
Riesman, D. with Nathan Glazer (1961), '*The Lonely Crowd*: A reconsideration in 1960', in S.M. Lipset and L. Lowenthal (eds), *Culture and Social Character: The Work of David Riesman Reviewed*, New York: Free Press of Glencoe, pp. 349–69.

Sargent Florence, P. (1924), *Economics of Fatigue and Unrest*, London: George Allen & Unwin and New York: Henry Holt.

Scitovsky, T. (1992), *The Joyless Economy*, rev. edn, New York: Oxford University Press.

Seib, H.M., and S.J. Vodanovich (1998), 'Cognitive correlates of boredom proneness: the role of private selfconsciousness and absorption', *Journal of Psychology*, 132, 642–52.

Silver, D.A. (2006), 'On the introduction of boredom', paper presented at the annual meeting of the Midwest Political Science Association, Palmer House Hilton, Chicago, II, 9–12 November.

Sommers, J. and S.J. Vodanovich (2000), 'Boredom-proneness: its relationship to psychological- and physical-health symptoms', *Journal of Clinical Psychology*, 56, 149–55.

Spacks, Patricia Ann Meyer (1995), *Boredom: The Literary History of a State of Mind*, Chicago, IL: University of Chicago Press.

Stonebraker, R.J. (2005), *The Joy of Economics: Making Sense Out of Life*, Winthrop University, Rock Hill, SC (date given is last modification of web page).

Svendsen, L. (2005), *A Philosophy of Boredom*, trans. J. Irons, London: Reaktion Books.

Szalontai, G. (2005), 'The demand for sleep: A South African study', *Economic Modeling*, 23(5), 854–74.

Thompson, M. (1979), *Rubbish Theory: The Creation and Destruction of Value*, Oxford: Oxford University Press.

Van Trijp, J.C.M. (1995), 'Variety-seeking in product choice behavior: theory with applications in the food domain', Mansholt Studies No. 1, Wageningen Agricultural University.

Vodanovich, S.J. (2003a), 'On the potential benefits of boredom: a neglected area in personality research', *Psychology and Education*, 40, 28–33.

Vodanovich, S.J. (2003b), 'Psychometric measures of boredom: a review of the literature', *Journal of Psychology*, 137, 569–95.

Vodanovich, S.J. and S.J. Kass (1990), 'Age and gender differences in boredom proneness', *Journal of Social Behavior and Personality* (Special Issue), 5, 297–307.

Vodanovich, S.J. and D. Rupp (1999), 'Are procrastinators prone to boredom?', *Social Behavior and Personality: An International Journal*, 27, 11–16.

Vodanovich, S.J. and J.D. Watt (1999), 'The relationship between time structure and boredom proneness: an investigation between two cultures', *Journal of Social Psychology*, 139, 143–52.

Vodanovich, S.J., K. Verner and T. Gilbride (1991), 'The relationship between boredom proneness and positive and negative affect', *Psychological Reports*, 69, 1139–46.

Wallace, J.C., S.J. Vodanovich and R. Restino (2003), 'Predicting cognitive failures from boredom proneness and daytime sleepiness scores: an investigation within military and undergraduate samples', *Personality and Individual Differences*, 34, 635–44.

Watt, J.D. and S.J. Vodanovich (1992), 'An examination of race and gender differences in boredom proneness', *Journal of Social Behavior and Personality*, 7, 169–75.

Watt, J.D. and S.J. Vodanovich (1999), 'Boredom proneness and psychosocial development', *Journal of Psychology*, 133, 303–14.

Wegner, L., A.J. Flisher, P. Chikobvud, C. Lombard and G. King (2008), 'Leisure boredom and high school dropout rates in Cape Town', *South Africa Journal of Adolescence*, 31, 421–31.

Whittaker, N. (1998), *Sweet Talk: The Secret History of Confectionery*, London: Phoenix Books.

Williams, Simon J. and Sharon Boden (2004), 'Consumed with sleep? Dormant bodies in consumer culture', *Sociological Research Online*, 9(2), available at: http://www.socreson line.org.uk/9/2/williams.html.

Wyatt, S. (1934), *Incentives in Repetitive Work: A Practical Experiment in a Factory*, Industrial Health Research Board Report No. 69, London: HM Stationery Office.

6 Half full or half empty: the economics of work–life balance
Samuel Cameron and Mark Fox

INTRODUCTION

> All life we work but work is a bore, if life's for livin' what's livin' for?
> ('Oklahoma U.S.A.', composed by Ray Davies and released by the Kinks
> in 1971)

Here we develop, in a more applied context, some themes covered in earlier chapters. We do this by examining an issue that has become prominent in modern life – that is, the issue of balancing one's work with one's life. We use the term 'life' as in 'having a life' and 'quality of life'. The idea of achieving work–life balance implies that the enjoyment of leisure is a respite from work and other pressures. As evidenced in the well-known work of Linder (1970), work–life pressures have had an increasing effect on women as market economies have moved towards the norm of a working mother, who may also be pursuing a career in an ambitious manner. Today, divorced and single-parent households are also commonplace. Furthermore, in many Western societies we see ageing populations, with employees increasingly juggling work obligations with providing care for elderly relatives.

Increased business competition adds to the challenges of work–life balance. Technology provides the means for customers and suppliers to contact employees anytime and anywhere, with the expectation of a quick response. Technology also blurs the lines between work and 'life' by enabling employees (while ostensibly working) to communicate with family members and friends, and to take care of personal matters such as shopping or arranging to meet friends (Simmers et al., 2008). Some of the issues arising from social networking are dealt with further in Chapter 22.

Key metrics of work–life balance differ markedly around the world; see Table 6.1 for data from OECD countries. For example, in Greece the average hours worked per year are 2,120, compared to only 1,389 hours in the Netherlands. Workers in Finland, Brazil and France often receive as many as 30 statutory holiday days a year and around 10 days of public holidays per year. In contrast, Canadian employees are entitled to only 10

Table 6.1 Key metrics of work–life balance

	Average annual hours worked	Statutory minimum holidays (days)	Public holidays (days)	Maternity leave (weeks)	FTE paid maternity leave	FTE paid paternity leave	FTE paid parental leave	Life expectancy at birth (years)
Australia	1,721	20	8	6	0	..	0	81.4
Austria	1,631	25	13	16	16.0	0.4	16.7	79.9
Belgium	1,568	20	10	15	11.3	1.2	2.6	79.5
Canada	1,727	10	9	15	8.3	..	19.3	80.6
Czech Rep.	1,992	20	12	28	13.7	..	50.3	76.4
Denmark	1,610	25	9	18	18.0	2	32	78.2
Finland	1,728	30	10	17.5	16.9	5.7	35.8	79.5
France	1,542	30	10	16	16.0	2	31.1	81.0
Germany	1,432	20	10	14	14.0	..	34.8	79.8
Greece	2,120	25	12	17	17.0	0.4	..	79.1
Hungary	1,988	23 (age 31/32)	10	24	16.8	1	72.8	73.3
Iceland	1,807	N/A	N/A	13	10.4	10.4	..	81.7
Ireland	1,601	20	9	48	18.2	0	..	79.7
Italy	1,802	20	11	21	16.0	..	7.8	81.1
Japan	N/A	20	16	14	8.4	..	31.2	82.7
Korea	N/A	19	15	15	15.0	..	42.3	79.2

101

Table 6.1 (continued)

	Average annual hours worked	Statutory minimum holidays (days)	Public holidays (days)	Maternity leave (weeks)	FTE paid maternity leave	FTE paid paternity leave	FTE paid parental leave	Life expectancy at birth (years)
Luxembourg	1,555	25	10	16	16.0	0.4	12.1	79.4
Mexico	1,893	N/A	N/A	12	12.0	..	..	76.0
Netherlands	1,389	20	8	16	16.0	0.4	..	79.8
New Zealand	1,753	20	11	12	6.0	..	..	80.1
Norway	1,422	25	10	9	9.0	6	38.4	80.5
Poland	1,969	26	10	18	18.0	4	16.1	75.5
Portugal	1,745	22	13	17	17.0	2	..	78.6
Slovak Rep.	1,769	20	15	28	15.4	..	30.7	74.6
Spain	1,627	22	14	16	16.0	2	..	80.7
Sweden	1,625	25	11	12	9.6	9.3	52.8	80.8
Switzerland	1,643	20	9	16	12.8	..	..	81.7
Turkey	N/A	N/A	N/A	12	7.9	..	..	71.7
United Kingdom	1,653	28	8	39	9.3	0.3	..	79.3
United States	1,792	No requirement. Typical is 15 days	10	12	0.0	..	..	79.1

days of statutory holidays and can also have 9 days of public holidays per year. Parental leave provisions invariably favour women who are typically entitled to significantly more days of both paid and unpaid leave than men. Such state-assisted programmes reinforce cultural expectations about the primary role of child-rearing by making it financially unattractive for men to take paternity leave.

ECONOMIC ANALYSIS OF WORK–LIFE BALANCE

Neoclassical economics invariably views work as an undesirable activity that is endured to obtain income. This view is still held by some economists today. For example, in a model of labour supply, McAfee (2006) states: 'We set L to be leisure rather than labour supply because it is leisure that is the good thing, whereas most of us view working as something we are willing to do provided we're paid for it'. As this quote illustrates, economists typically define work as an exchange of labour for monetary compensation, or to entrepreneurial endeavours that improve one's net worth. Further, it is implicit that work is engaged in for productive ends – and for monetary compensation that can be used to purchase goods. In contrast to the neoclassical view of work, Gary Becker's economic theory of the family (see Chapters 2–6) views household activities as inputs to household production, with paid work providing further inputs. When adopting this view, there is no need for work to be seen as providing disutility.

The concept of work–life balance presupposes that work and life are distinct domains and that it is desirable to have a balance between these domains. As the following quote illustrates, work–life balance is often seen as a juggling act of sorts: 'Work–life balance is about effectively managing the juggling act between paid work and other activities that are important to us – including spending time with family, taking part in sport and recreation, volunteering or undertaking further study' (New Zealand Work Life Balance Project, 2003).

The very notion of work–life balance assumes that achieving balance is desirable not only for ourselves, but for those with whom we interact. When work–life imbalance occurs, this may have costs to us personally (in the form of, say, lack of sleep and general malaise); to our families (as we have less time for family chores or to devote to our spouse or children); and to our employers, co-workers and customers (for example, as we make more mistakes and act in ways that frustrate customers).

The standard microeconomic approach to work–life balance can be expressed in simple indifference curve diagrams which assume utility

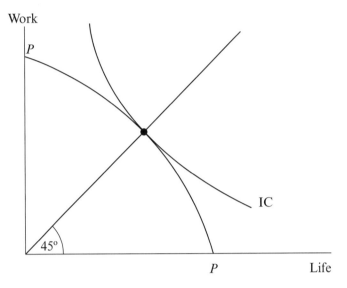

Figure 6.1   Work–life balance

maximization subject to known and fixed constraints. We presume a utility function of the form:

$$U = f(W, L),$$

where W is work and L is life. There may be areas of positive and diminishing marginal utility for both arguments. Further, we assume that some kind of standardization can be made, such that life and work can be converted into comparable (if imaginary) units. This is necessary as time alone does not properly index these activities (for one thing, there is the issue of quality). Figure 6.1 shows three things:

1. An indifference curve (IC) for the work–life choice which in the region drawn assumes diminishing marginal utility (at different rates).
2. A constraint in the form of a production possibility frontier (P) which will be determined by stocks of human capital and (at any point in time) past choices such as job, marriage and housing.
3. A 45-degree line to show equality between work and life.

In Figure 6.1, our hypothetical individual is in balance in the sense of choosing equality of work and life. Their utility is maximized on the 45-degree line. Figures 6.2 and 6.3 show, respectively, an individual with a

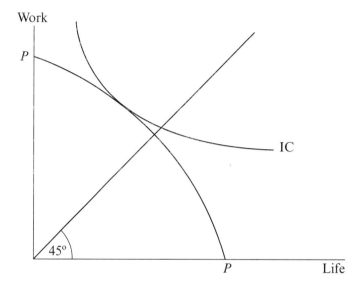

Figure 6.2   Work-biased choice

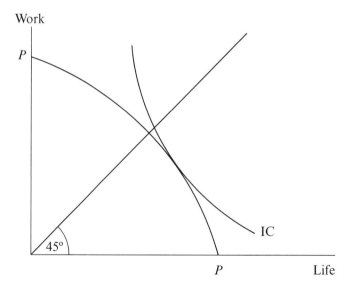

Figure 6.3   Life-biased choice

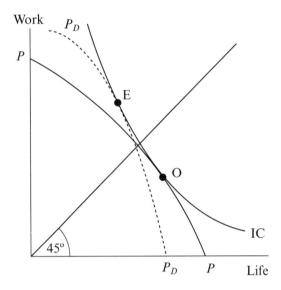

Figure 6.4   Distorted view of production possibility frontier

work-biased choice and one with a life-biased choice. In these two figures, it is assumed that the individuals are identical, except for their tastes for work versus life. Neither individual can be said to be suffering from an imbalance, even if some people might depict 6.2 as a 'workaholic' and 6.3 as work-shy.

In the examples shown thus far individuals do not suffer from imbalance in their own terms, even if they show literal imbalance. Figures 6.4 and 6.5 show situations where imbalance occurs due to mistakes. IC_D and P_D in these situations represent 'false' or 'distorted' relationships that the individual believes to be true. The position shown as E is the mistakenly chosen one, whereas O is the optimum based on the true data. The specific mistake in Figure 6.4 is a distorted view of the production possibility frontier. For example, individuals may be deluded about what they may be able to achieve in terms of output at work; or, conversely, they are deluded about their ability to achieve in 'life'. For example, they may imagine that when they get home from work that they are the world's greatest guitarist. Figure 6.4 shows only a delusion about work capacity and the individual is not (in this specific diagram) worse off due to it. However, the individual is showing more work centredness than he/she would if he/she used non-distorted information.

Figure 6.5 shows the alternative of mistakes about preferences. The specific case shown is where the individual imagines that he/she has a greater

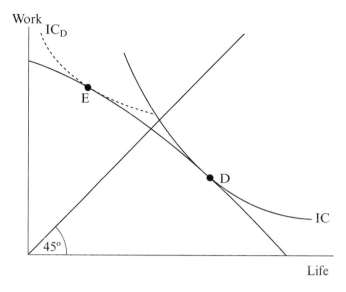

Figure 6.5 Delusion about work capacity

enjoyment of work (relatively). In the case shown, this results in a literal overbalance of work to life. However, this does not have to be so. If the individual's initial preferences were sufficiently life oriented, it would be possible to have an individual with a perceptual distortion in this direction who ends up on the right hand side of the 45-degree line.

In the basic theoretical models of neoclassical microeconomics, it is not possible to have a work–life imbalance, except in the sense that imbalance may arise through rigidities or through a shortage of resources. The crudest example of this is the 'working poor' who are so impoverished that they have to work relentlessly to sustain a required standard of living. Poverty is an impediment to having as much time available as one would ideally like to pursue other activities (for example, spending time with family, leisure activities and other forms of relaxation). Poverty also gives rise to work–life issues for children. Worldwide, there are over 186 million child labourers (ILO, 2002). When households are unable to meet their basic economic needs, children are more likely to work. The incidence of child labour decreases as income levels rise and as opportunities for investing in the future of children (in particular, through education) emerge (Edmonds, 2002).

As we shall discuss later, rigidities may arise due to inflexible working hours and other job characteristics and through anomalies generated by governments' packages of taxes and subsidies. However, before our discussion progresses, we need to revisit Nobel Laureate Gary Becker's influential work on families (see, for example, Becker, 1965, 1991).

Becker's Economic Theory of the Family

Becker proposes that households/families are formed because people expect net gains from three things:

1. having and raising children who are local public goods (who may become impure public bads if they develop antisocial behaviour);
2. economies of scale and scope in consumption – for example, couples may share fuel bills and recreational sexual activities, in which case the transaction costs of looking for someone with whom to copulate are reduced; and
3. external effects, including social approval.

In Becker's model, the timing and spacing of children is viewed as a rational choice process so that, for example, rising wages will lead to a lower demand for children if the substitution effect outweighs the income effects of children as normal goods. In such a model, family members provide time inputs into production processes which are deemed to be leisure and thereby enhance the ability to 'have a life'. This is because the family context often expands the scope for the production of leisure activities as families enable people to share in activities, which may raise the gains from those activities.[1] On the other hand, families can also constrain the pursuit of leisure. The extreme case of this is when the consumption demands of children restrict resource availability for parents to pursue a 'life'.

Our ability to balance work and non-work domains can be compromised by the characteristics of partners or children (or, for that matter, pets). Pressures arising from the partner one has chosen can be seen as a mistake of partner choice (or as a risk), in the sense that the partner has changed in ways that were not easily predicted. There is also the possibility that partners are selected for certain characteristics (such as appearance or social standing), which are bundled with other constraining characteristics. In the case of children and pets, risk occurs as it is difficult to anticipate how much of a constraint they will be. The limit case of this is when a child is born with serious disabilities and guilt and social pressures lead reluctant parents to keep and care for them. Depending on how the individual frames the situation, this may be a corner solution, where there is no 'life' and only work, due to the demands of caring.

FRAMING OF WORK AND LEISURE

Decisions about work–life balance can be framed in a number of ways. One way of framing such choices is to look at our current needs in the light of historic work–life balance decisions. As decisions about work–life balance take place over time, individuals may see their 'ideal' work–life balance differently depending on factors such as their life stage.[2] For example, retirement may be viewed as an opportunity to lead a more balanced life to compensate for excessive hours worked during a traditional working life. However, in making work–life balance decisions there are problems of risk and imperfect time substitution. Postponing leisure activity until one is older may curb the possible enjoyment of leisure due to declining faculties, illness and contracting social networks. Alternatively, premature death may curtail the ability to attain sought-after balance (although some religious individuals may rationalize excessive work hours during 'life' on the basis that they will be rewarded for this in an afterlife). Cultural context also influences our sense of entitlement about work–life balance. Some cultures place more value on leisure and on family time. Others cultures value work or put pressure on individuals to work harder and longer than might otherwise be seen as desirable.

The view of leisure or time for worship as a right often has religious origins. Several religions incorporate the notion of Sabbath days or various holy days (times when believers may rest and engage in religious rituals). For religious adherents there may be costs associated with not observing holy days. These costs may arise from psychological distress (so that working on the Sabbath may yield less utility compared to working at other times). In some societies religious holy days have become official 'holidays' that are widely observed and provide days of rest and worship for believers – and a respite from work for most.[3] Other countries recognize differences in religious beliefs among their populace and mandate that employers make reasonable accommodations that are based on individual religious practices or observances.[4] In contrast to state-sanctioned holidays that favour one religion and do not recognize the religious practices or observances of others, such legislation may more equitably improve work–life balance across society.

We now turn our attention to theories that attempt to explain work–life balance.

WIDER ECONOMIC THEORIES TO EXPLAIN IMBALANCE

In the Becker family/time allocation models, imbalance only occurs through mistakes such as bad choice (of job or partner) or from unforeseeable events (such as children having highly divergent preferences to their parents). Individuals would not (knowingly) inflict imbalance on themselves as this would seem to be irrational (that is, choosing to purposefully pursue suboptimal time allocation). In general, if one does this and regrets it, this would seem to be a form of neurosis. Needless to say, economic models do not countenance neurotic behaviour. Hence, we need to look for wider explanations for seemingly self-harming lifestyle choices. The previous section on the framing of decisions ushered in a more behavioural economics kind of approach (see, generally, Schwartz, 2008). Behavioural economists are not wedded to traditional economists' views of humankind. Instead, they propose that standard economics models are unrealistic in assuming that we have unbounded rationality, unbounded willpower and unbounded selfishness (Mullainathan and Thaler, 2000). Owing to our limited cognitive abilities and to incomplete information we often make decisions based on various heuristics/rules of thumb. Hence, we use 'behavioural scripts' when making decisions. Such scripts indicate the 'appropriate' behaviour that should be pursued – they act as a knowledge structure and a guide to behaviour (Lord and Kernan, 1987).

Now we turn our attention to some ways in which people rationalize apparent work–life imbalance and to the scripts they may use when doing so.

Pseudo-moral Obligations

Weber (1905) proposed that religious beliefs contributed to the spirit of capitalism. Accordingly, the Protestant (or Puritan) Work Ethic was thought to contribute to capitalism by encouraging hard work, dedication to work as a calling, self-denial and thriftiness. In Christianity, the idea of work as a form of punishment has a long history – as shown by God's banishing Adam and Eve from the idyllic Garden of Eden, 'to till the ground from whence he was taken' (King James Bible). In explaining the rise of capitalism in Europe in the sixteenth and seventeenth centuries, Tawney notes that the Puritans were 'an earnest, zealous, godly generation, scorning delights, punctual in labour, constant in prayer, thrifty and thriving, filled with a decent pride in themselves and their calling, assured that strenuous toil is acceptable to Heaven' (2008, p. 211). These notions of devotion to arduous work and of pleasure as a sinful distraction from getting closer to God provide early examples of pseudo-moral obligations.

In modern life, an extreme example of work–life imbalance is the Japanese notion of 'karoshi' – death by overwork. Japan legally recognized karoshi as a cause of death in the 1980s. Some researchers attribute karoshi as the cause of up to 10,000 deaths per year (Nishiyama and Johnson, 1997). Karoshi arises from the deep feelings of commitment that workers feel toward their employers and to Japanese cultural imperatives about the role of work itself:

> To the Japanese work . . . is the process of carrying out obligations owed to society and to oneself as a social being . . . Work, to the Japanese, can be viewed as a religious experience: 'When you toil, your heart is at peace', says Zen Buddhism. If you work hard, the gods will favour you. Work hard, not necessarily smartly. Working hard is an end in itself. It is simply what one does in life if one is a good person. Work is a moral, not instrumental, act. It is associated with good, not utility, and workers who slack off are not just unproductive but downright bad. (Herbig and Palumbo, 1994, p. 14)

Karoshi is thought to have its origins in 'ganbatte' – a social imperative that says that one should have a selfless, long-suffering commitment to completing a task. These values carry over into the workplace, with the result that being seen to be working hard is often more important than being efficient at work; or, 'presence is equal to productivity' (ibid., p. 11). A similar focus on excessive devotion to work at the expense of employee's personal lives is evident in some workplaces in the West. For example, Jill Andresky Fraser (2001) uses the term 'white-collar sweatshops' to refer to businesses where excessive workload and technology blur the lines between work and family in ways that are harmful to individuals and to the functioning of families.

The key point from these examples is that an excessive work focus may arise from internalizing workplace or social values (pseudo-moral obligations), rather than something that is enforced by market constraints.

Moral Crusading

Economic progress has made the notion of work as a calling redundant for most. The increasingly specialized nature of individual jobs and the use of technology have resulted in the situation whereby the 'majority of mankind has been alienated from its product' (see, for example, Scitovsky, 1992, p. 207). Hence, opportunities for creating meaning through one's work are not as common as they once were. Nevertheless, some people hold various socially minded objectives that cannot be pursued through their work by, say, showing a concern for the environment, helping others or preventing animal cruelty. In these cases, leisure activities may be chosen to provide an outlet for moral crusading. Such leisure activities may be self-organized (for example, organic gardening) or they may involve volunteering (for example, taking care of animals at a pet shelter).

In the United Kingdom around 59 per cent of the population participate in volunteer activities for various organizations every year, contributing on average 11 hours' helping during the last four weeks they volunteered (National Centre for Social Research and the Institute for Volunteering Research, 2007). While standard labour substitution models propose that people volunteer less when the cost of time (wages) is higher, Freeman (1997) found that the opportunity cost of labour accounts for relatively little of the propensity to volunteer.

Opportunistic Investments in Career

Opportunistic investments can directly or indirectly help people gain greater rewards from their current career, or prepare them for a future career. Individuals with few family commitments will typically have more time available to make such investments. Direct investments involve activities that are undertaken for fun in a person's own time, while also developing skills for future employment. For example, someone (who does not do this kind of work for a living, but finds doing so enjoyable) writing and distributing non-work-related software in his/her own time. Another example of direct investments is Toastmasters District 32 (2011) – who trumpet themselves as the 'most efficient, enjoyable and affordable way of gaining communication and leadership skills'. Direct investments help build skill levels; establish a reputation in the area where one wants to work or to advance further in; or provide contacts that may lead to future employment in an area that is currently a hobby. Opportunistic investments inevitably have uncertain payoffs; however, as such activities often comprise a leisure component and develop personal as well as professional competencies, it is easy to rationalize these activities as being worthwhile. Also, as one is unsure as to when the skills themselves will become useful it is easy to see a future, if indefinite, payoff.

Some opportunistic investments are largely intended to build social capital (as per Putnam, 2000), as they bring people into contact with others who may be useful in advancing their career. Such indirect investment activities may also be influenced by the leisure pursuits of a given social class (for example, golf or sailing). These activities may hone leisure-related skills that can be an adjunct to career success in some fields, for example, developing a low golf handicap (the Executive Women's Golf Association promotes golf by stating that 'Golf has long been a sport for doing business – don't let your résumé be without it'). However, opportunistic investments can be time-consuming and costly. In the case of golf, equipment costs, membership fees, green fees and the cost of lessons can be substantial.

Unfortunately, opportunistic investments may entail engaging in activities that some people find inherently unenjoyable or objectionable, for example, after-work drinks with colleagues. Also, as the following quote illustrates, career investment opportunities may be limited to only some organization members, such as the 'old boys' network':

> These informal networks are often exclusive to men and revolve around social events, sporting events and/or drinking establishments. Career success is often built through these informal networks and women's access to these networks is restricted . . . Furthermore, important decisions are often made at many of these informal gatherings, leaving female managers out of the decision making process. (Jeavons and Sevastos, 2002, p. 3)

In addition to the scripts that we have just examined, there are characteristics of work itself that can contribute to work–life imbalance. We shall discuss four of these work characteristics now: overtime, shift work, burnout inducing work, and commuting time.

Overtime

Compared to hiring additional employees, having existing employees work overtime may prove less costly for employers as it typically does not increase training costs and may only increase some fringe benefit costs. Mandatory overtime is commonplace in some occupations (for example, nursing), but it may contribute to burnout and poorer-quality patient care. Similarly, in the US auto industry increased overtime is associated with more employee injuries (Smith, 1996).

The impact of overtime on work–life balance depends on whether the extra hours worked are voluntary or mandatory. Mandatory overtime gives less control over work–life balance. Golden and Wiens-Tuers (2007) found that fatigue that carried over into the home was significantly associated with mandatory overtime, but not with voluntary overtime. Employees with mandatory overtime also suffered greater work–family time interference when compared to those whose overtime was voluntary. Golden and Wiens-Tuers propose that the lack of choice in additional work hours for mandatory overtime workers may account for these findings.

In light of concerns about the consequences of excessively long working hours for employee health and safety, some governments have issued working hours directives.[5] For example, the European Working Time Directive states that the average working time within each seven-day period should not exceed 48 hours.

Shift Work

Shift work was historically concentrated in manufacturing industries (to increase plant utilization) and in areas such as healthcare and emergency services (where around the clock services are essential). However, with globalization and the emergence of 24/7 economies, shift work is increasingly common in retail and service settings (Bambra et al., 2008). In the UK there are over 3.5 million shift workers (Health and Safety Executive, 2009). In the US around 15 per cent of full-time employees work shifts (Bureau of Labor Statistics, 2005). Of these US employees, over half report that they undertake shift work as it is the 'nature of the job'. Other reasons for taking shift work include: 'personal preference' (11.5 per cent), 'better arrangements for family or child care' (8.2 per cent), 'could not get any other job' (8.1 per cent) and 'better pay' (6.8 per cent). Many of these motives indicate that shift work improves work–life balance for some employees. However, shift work is associated with well-documented deleterious health effects. Most of the health consequences of shift work result from disruptions to circadian rhythms (Bambra et al., 2008). These damaging consequences include problems with sleeping and with daytime functioning (including increased fatigue) and gastrointestinal problems. Bambra et al. also observe that shift work leads to 'considerable social desynchronization' as it involves working at times when it is difficult to maintain balanced family and social lives. Several studies support this view. For example, White and Keith (1990) found that shift work reduces marital quality and increases the likelihood of divorce. Shift work can also lead to higher accident rates in the workplace – perhaps owing to increased fatigue and attention problems (Smith et al., 1998; National Institute for Occupational Safety and Health, 2004).

In economic terms, shift workers (as with those facing the post-retirement leisure issue) face imperfect time substitution as sleeping outside of normal circadian rhythms and social hours is an imperfect substitute for conventional sleep.

Burnout

Burnout is typically viewed as comprising three elements: emotional exhaustion, depersonalization/detachment and a sense of reduced personal accomplishment (Maslach and Jackson, 1986). In a review of the job burnout literature, Halbesleben and Buckley (2004) observe that one of the antecedents to burnout is job and role characteristics. Much of the early research on job burnout focused on the nature of interactions with clients, leading Cordes and Dougherty to observe that interactions that are 'more direct, frequent, or of longer duration, for example, or client problems that are chronic (versus acute) are associated with higher levels of burnout' (1993, p. 628). Role conflict and ambiguity also contribute to burnout. Role conflict occurs when we have conflicting expectations from others about what our appropriate behaviour should be within a given role (Kahn et al., 1964). Role ambiguity occurs when there is insufficient clarity regarding how to perform job tasks or about how performance is evaluated.

Various forms of role overload have been associated with burnout. Overload can be qualitative (feeling one lacks the skills to perform a given task well) or quantitative (feeling that the volume of work cannot be completed in the available time).

Commuting Time

Aside from the characteristics of work itself, time spent commuting to and from work also affects work–life balance. People use commuting time in different ways – including unwinding by drinking or socializing on a long train trip home or by working more. De Grazia (1994) observes that in many European countries people make their way home leisurely; whereas, say, in the US, people tend to be in a frenetic rush to get home. One of the explanations de Grazia gives for this (apart from distances travelled) is that in some European countries afternoon naps or leisurely lunches may provide a respite from work in the middle of the day. If imbalance is a source of utility loss then rational individuals should seek abatement strategies. If the costs of imbalance are also borne by others, then employers and governments have incentives to assist individuals who suffer from imbalance. It is, therefore, convenient for us to look first at strategies pursued by individuals and, then, at external efforts to provide balance.

ATTEMPTS BY INDIVIDUALS TO REMEDY IMBALANCE

Attempts to restore work–life balance may involve overcompensation and tend to be risky.

Workplace Shirking

Workplace shirking helps restore individual perceptions of inequity in the workplace. Adams's (1965) equity theory proposes that employees compare their inputs and outcomes with others and, based upon these comparisons, evaluate whether they are being (un)fairly compensated. Inputs include time, effort, educational attainment and experience. Outcomes include monetary compensation, office size and location, benefits and praise from one's boss. If employees believe that they are being treated inequitably, one way to restore balance is by reducing inputs, for example, a salaried worker may put forth less effort, take longer lunch breaks, come into work later or spend work hours on enjoyable non-work activities, for example, surfing the internet or social loafing.

Workaholism

Many people regard workaholics as engaging in irrational behaviour. This is because workaholics spend less time than others enjoying leisure activities owing to long hours spent working and to the physical and psychological effects of overwork. Workaholics may turn to work in a misguided effort to find satisfaction or to distract themselves from family issues that leave them feeling frustrated or unfulfilled (Morrison and Deacon, 2003).

The question that naturally arises when looking at workaholics is: why do they pursue behaviour that many of us regard as irrational? One possible explanation is found in Becker and Murphy's (1988) theory of rational addiction. Becker and Murphy propose that their model can be used to help explain addiction to a wide variety of behaviours and not just to, say, alcohol, drug use and smoking. Rational addiction models propose that individuals accumulate a stock of addiction over time that, in turn, influences future behaviour. The accumulated stock of addiction (work hours, in the case of workaholics) leads to an increase in the marginal utility of additional (future) working hours and to a reduction in the marginal utility of leisure time. Using such a model, the impact of being a workaholic is to ensure a form of 'addiction', whereby the future value of work is increased and the future value of leisure is reduced.

Hyper-leisure Activities

Hyper-leisure activities may be used to counteract problematic work environments (for example, work environments that are stressful or boring, or where bullying occurs). Some hyper-leisure activities occur away from the workplace and result in less time being spent at work. One example is the employee who – rather than attending to his/her workplace responsibilities – seeks refuge in a favourite hobby. Other hyper-leisure activities occur in the workplace itself (for example, spending large amounts of time surfing the internet).

Boredom at work may promote or facilitate hyper-leisure activities. As Scitovsky observes, 'Perfect comfort and lack of stimulation are restful at first, but they soon become boring, then disturbing', encouraging us to seek stimulation (1992, p. 31). Dyer-Smith and Wesson (1997) found that boredom at work was associated with absenteeism which, in turn, would increase leisure time. Another study, by Game (2007), refers to disengagement strategies (that is, strategies associated with avoiding sources of boredom) and found that the most common of these strategies was social loafing (that is, informal interactions with co-workers). However, employees who experience more workplace autonomy (the ability to decide when to work and how work gets done) are more likely to engage in shirking behaviours (see, for example, Garrett and Danziger's 2008 research on cyberslacking).

Relaxing

As with hyper-leisure activities, relaxation activities may be pursued to counteract work stress. Common forms of relaxation include: watching television, internet surfing and social networking, playing video games, and drug and alcohol use. Needless to say, these activities need not be mutually exclusive. Some of these activities may produce unintended consequences in the form of dysfunctional overstimulation. Such is the case for the person who is hyperactive after playing video games and has trouble sleeping.

It is worth noting that television and the internet have altered time use more than any other development since the automobile. While watching television is generally relaxing (Csikszentmihalyi and Kubey, 1981), this may depend on what is being watched. In this regard, an experimental study found that 15 minutes of news watching led to increases in the state of anxiety and total mood disturbance (Szabo and Hopkinson, 2007).

Powernaps

While sleep was the focus of Chapter 5, here we focus on 'powernaps'. Powernaps can result in increased post-nap functioning. For example, naps of 10 to 20 minutes improve post-nap functioning. However, napping for 30 minutes or more can lead to sleep inertia when one wakes; hence, if we nap too long we risk decreasing our immediate post-nap functioning and mood (Hayashi et al., 2004). Workplace naps are circumscribed by cultural norms. In some countries there is no tradition of sleeping in the day and, therefore, napping during work hours would be seen as signs of possible senility, illness or general deviance (even if naps are taken during lunch breaks). Illicit naps are taken by employees when they are expected to be awake and working. Illicit naps can potentially be costly as they could lead to dismissal or to a loss of professional reputation. They could also lead to damage or death to customers.

BUSINESS AND STATE ATTEMPTS TO GIVE BALANCE

Having looked at some approaches that individuals can take to restore imbalance, we now examine corporate and state attempts to facilitate balance.

Holiday and Other Entitlements

Work–life balance depends on legally prescribed rights (for example, maternity/paternity leave, working hours or statutory holiday entitlements). As the UK's Department of Trade and Industry observes: 'The ability to spend time away from the workplace is an important component of work–life balance and can help reduce stress' (2006, p. 10). We demonstrated at the start of this chapter that holiday entitlements differ considerably from country to country.

Parental Leave and Childcare

Parental leave provides time to invest in a child's well-being. Several studies illustrate this point. Tanaka (2005) found that paid parental leave is associated with lower post-neonatal mortality rates. Bernal (2008) found that when mothers work full-time, while using childcare facilities, this is associated with a reduction in children's cognitive ability. Parental leave helps protect jobs while parents take care of their children. However, the time spent away from work may impact on career progression when parents return to work. For this reason, parental leave that can be taken by either mothers or fathers allows parents to split the burdens of childcare – and to share in any detrimental career consequences that arise from spending time away from work.

Eldercare

The human lifespan is lengthening. This trend, combined with the post-Second World War baby boom, means that the care of elderly relatives is an increasing concern. In the UK, the proportion of people aged 65 and over is projected to increase from 16 per cent in 2006 to 22 per cent by 2031 (Office for National Statistics, 2006). In the US the proportion of those aged 65+ is projected to increase from 13 per cent in 2010 to 19 per cent in 2030 (US Census, 2008). Around 40 per cent of those who care for elderly relatives still have childcare responsibilities (Labour Project for Working Families, 2002). These individuals (the so-called 'sandwich generation') face unique work–life balance pressures.

In some countries, eligibility for medical assistance is asset and income based (for example, Medicare and Medicaid benefits in the United States). Policies such as these encourage the elderly to create trusts and give assets to others in order to meet healthcare eligibility criteria (Wiener and Stevenson, 1997).

Flexible Work Arrangements

Flexible work arrangements can enhance work–life balance. Such arrangements include flexitime, telecommuting and compressed workweeks. Flexitime allows employees to have some choice about when their work is scheduled. This provides more flexibility in meeting both work and family obligations. Telecommuting allows employees to work from home or from another remote site. A compressed workweek typically allows employees to condense their workweek into, say, four days. Of the various flexible work arrangements, flexitime and telecommuting are the most beneficial to managing work–life balance. In contrast, a compressed workweek tends to lead to diminished work performance owing to longer work hours during the days being worked.

FEASIBILITY OF ACHIEVING WORK–LIFE BALANCE

As mentioned at the start of this chapter, individual attempts to achieve work–life balance are largely influenced by various family considerations. Also, the nature of some work will inherently help or constrain employees from engaging in balancing behaviours.

Within organizations, the development of work–life programmes is typically undertaken by the human resources (HR) function. However, HR professionals will invariably only view work–life balance initiatives as strategically desirable inasmuch as they facilitate achieving organizational goals. Work–life balance may lead to beneficial consequences for employees and others, but not necessarily for the organization. Benefits that do accrue to organizations may come in the form of helping recruit, train or motivate staff (Nord et al., 2002). In some cases, a perfectly rational HR strategy is to choose not to invest in work/life programmes and suffer the consequences (low job satisfaction, high turnover, dysfunctional behaviours and so on). This occurs in environments where the labour market is loose, the nature of the work is straightforward, labour is effectively a replaceable commodity and training time is minimal. Hence, employees with higher skill levels and those in positions where talent is scarce are more likely to find that employers are amenable to providing work–life balance initiatives. This helps explain why flexible work arrangements are better suited to some types of work – such arrangements tend to be initiated by individual employers (or at the request of employees), rather than being government mandated. Flexible work arrangements may be particularly important for women as they have historically played a greater role in homemaking and caregiving (Burgess et al., 2007).

We shall now look at a few examples of attempts by organizations or governments to provide balance and how these may be thwarted or lead to disparate outcomes. First, consider that (whatever their entitlements) employees may choose not to take all of their paid holiday and leave entitlements. For example, one Australian study found that 58 per cent of employees do not take their full entitlements (Denniss, 2004). This may be because banking current leave for future use can be seen as a means of increasing utility from a future holiday – by increasing the length of that holiday and/or enabling it to fit in with the schedules of other family members. However, the downside of paying employees for unused leave is that this undermines the purpose for which leave is granted (namely, rejuvenation) and encourages behaviours detrimental to the employer (for example, coming to work with the flu and infecting co-workers). Other employees may not take leave as their workplace cannot function without them.

Second, eldercare benefits typically result in disparate outcomes for women. Traditionally, housework and care activities tend to fall more upon women than on men; hence, the care of elderly relatives will more often negatively affect women's careers. As Moen and Yu (2000, p. 315) observe:

> [W]orking fewer hours (typically the strategy of women managing work and family roles) in a society which equates long hours with productivity and commitment, can have long-term deleterious consequences for security, seniority, rewards, and advancement, as well as reproducing gendered roles at home and at work. It also may not be conducive to life quality in a society that gives primacy to paid work.

Further, it appears that eldercare is less demanding for married caregivers. Moen and Yu found that compared to married workers with a stay-at-home spouse or dual-career couples, non-married workers experienced the highest levels of overload and the lowest levels of coping/mastery.

Third, childcare costs hit solo parents and the working poor the hardest (Kalb, 2009). These costs are typically higher for parents with younger children as older children are more likely to be cared for in school or in daycare centres that are often less expensive than the one-on-one care that infants require. Research indicates that the cost of childcare is strongly negatively associated with the labour supply of married women and that wages have a strong positive effect on women's labour force participation (Ribar, 1992). It is likely that fiscal policies that effectively increase incomes for married women (or that reduce the costs of childcare) will increase both the use of childcare and labour force participation by women (ibid.; Kalb, 2009). Paid leave policies may not entirely compensate for lost earnings as not all leave is paid at 100 per cent of earnings. However, the higher the proportion of earnings covered by paid leave, the less the gender equality in taking leave (Ray et al., 2008). Higher earnings coverage makes it increasingly attractive for the higher-earning individual in a couple to take parental leave. As we saw in Table 6.1, most countries' parental leave policies make it unattractive for men to take paternity leave but typically provide incentives for women to take maternity leave.

On a national level there are systemic impediments to achieving work–life balance. These impediments often arise from the pursuit of economic goals rather than – or at the expense of – broader social welfare. Linder proposes that, whereas economic growth had historically been trumpeted as something that would lead to 'a tranquil and harmonious life, a life in Arcadia' (1970, p. 1), it has instead contributed to what he, paradoxically, calls the 'harried leisure class'. This idea is captured in the Linder theorem: that is, 'a rise in real wages ('productivity') will lead to a reallocation of time to the disadvantage of cultural and other time-consuming pursuits' (Baumol, 1973, p. 629). This is because higher real wages make the cost of time more expensive and the pursuit of cultural goods (which tend to be more time intensive) relatively less appealing.

Ezra Mishan in *The Costs of Economic Growth* goes so far as to argue that economic growth 'is more likely on balance to reduce rather than increase social welfare' (1971, p. 219). Part of the logic behind such criticisms is that, while governments invariably track economic measures, such as gross national product, happiness is rarely measured. This is the case even when, as in the US, the 'pursuit of happiness' is guaranteed by the Constitution.[6] Oswald observes that politicians and policy makers often assume that 'by raising its output and productivity a society truly betters itself' (1997, p. 1816). This leads to the question of the link between income and happiness.

Generally, increased wealth is associated with increased happiness; however, at higher income levels additional income does not raise happiness as much as it does at lower income levels (Frey and Stutzer, 2002). Yet, increases in overall per capita income do not raise average happiness. Thus Easterlin (1974) proposes that happiness is relative (that is, it is based on comparisons that we make with others). This observation is often called the 'Easterlin Paradox'. A recent example of the Easterlin Paradox is found in research by Di Tella and MacCulloch (2008), whose dataset comprised 350,000 people in 12 OECD countries and covered the period from 1975 to 1997. Happiness was indeed found to be positively correlated to income and to the welfare state, but was negatively correlated with the average number of hours worked and to economic variables such as inflation and unemployment. However, only small changes in happiness occurred over time due to increases in incomes. Aside from the concept of happiness being based on comparisons with others, aspirations tend to rise with higher incomes, creating a hedonic treadmill (Binswanger, 2006). Rising aspirations act to reduce the satisfaction gained from current income levels. The notion of a hedonic treadmill is consistent with the observations of Scitovsky, who proposes that we become addicted to a certain standard of living that is satisfying at first, but then this gives way to the 'motivation of wishing to avoid the pain and frustration of giving up a habit to which one has become accustomed' (1992, p. 137).

SOME THOUGHTS ON RETIREMENT

So far we have largely discussed the issue of balance during the years when people are indeed working. This leaves the issues of what promotes the retirement decision and of achieving balance during the retirement years.

Labour force participation follows an inverted U-shape, peaking in mid-life (Rettenmaier and Saving, 2006). The decline in participation among older workers is partly a result of social security and private pension plans. This decline also occurs because of an inverted U-shape of earnings over the life cycle, making it attractive for employees to substitute work for leisure in midlife and postpone more leisure until later in life when leisure has a lower opportunity cost (Kaufman and Hotchiss, 2005).

Personal wealth is also associated with retirement decisions. A life-cycle model indicates that individuals will accumulate wealth when younger (and have higher earnings power) and then draw upon their accumulated wealth during retirement (Coronado and Perozek, 2003). Retirement decisions are based on beliefs about future wealth, health, financial needs of dependants and the health of significant others. A study of early retirement decisions by older employees in the Netherlands found that males and females were both influenced by their partners' views in making their own retirement choices (however, men were more influenced by their female partners); the number of shared leisure activities affects support for a partner's retirement; and that the health consequences of retirement are important – 'social pressure by the partner to retire early may reflect an attempt on the part of one of the partners to protect the other's health' (Henkens and van Solinge, 2002, p. 68).

Several government-related considerations also play a key role in decisions about the timing of retirement, namely the provision (and size) of retirement benefits and the provision (or subsidization) of healthcare benefits by the state. In some countries, the issue of retirement is something of a moot point owing to the lack of state-provided pensions or to low life expectancy.

With retirement, one issue that arises is that those who have spent much of their adult life working suddenly have significantly more leisure time, but now lack whatever stimulation their work may have provided. Hence, boredom is a common problem in retirement. As Scitovsky observes, 'If they are unskilled consumers, they soon find their sources of stimulation inadequate; the result is the heartrending spectacle of elderly people trying desperately to keep themselves busy and amused but not knowing how to do so' (1992, p. 235). Scitovsky astutely observes that some leisure activities (for example, television watching) can be satisfying when our demands for stimulus enjoyment are relatively low, such as at the end of a tiring work day. However, when we have more time (and capacity) to enjoy leisure, we often have a greater need for novelty from the stimulation that leisure provides. Some retired persons may look for stimulation through exciting distractions that may become addictions (for example, gambling). Roman and Johnson (1996) observe that increased alcohol consumption may occur for some retirees – who are simultaneously seeking to fill their leisure time and to cope with the changes in life that retirement brings.

Finally, subsidies of various forms may influence the leisure pursuits of older citizens. For example, subsidized access to public transport, to museums, and to cinemas may encourage the elderly to engage in these activities. In many cases, these subsidies take effect prior to the age of retirement, thereby providing older citizens with the opportunity to sample these activities.

NOTES

1. As with children, pet ownership provides households with various gains. Pets confer health benefits on their owners in the forms of reduced blood pressure, reduced cholesterol, and improved triglyceride levels (National Center for Infectious Diseases, 2009). Spending time with pets also reduces feelings of loneliness, is fun and relaxing, and facilitates opportunities for social interaction. And, owning pets that require regular exercise is complementary to a healthy lifestyle. Also see Hirschman (1994) and Schwarz et al. (2007).
2. Positive work-to-family spillover is a function of ageing and of the time spent in a given job (tenure). Grzywacz et al. (2002) propose that, with experience, employees become

better at managing the fit between work and family responsibilities. Employees who are unsuccessful in managing work–family balance may opt out of their current workplace by finding positions elsewhere that are a better fit (or they may be fired). Work–life balance issues can also derive from the value systems of demographic cohorts. For example, the different value systems of Generation Xers, Yers and Boomers drive different needs and, consequently, drive employer/human resources programmes to accommodate those needs.

3. For example, in New Zealand, Christmas, Good Friday and Easter Monday are statutory holidays mandated by the Holidays Act 2003. Likewise, countries with a significant Buddhist population (for example, Thailand and Sri Lanka) have statutory holidays that comprise Buddhist observances.
4. In the United States, Title VII of the Civil Rights Act 1964 prohibits (in organizations with 15 or more employees) discrimination on various grounds, including religious beliefs.
5. Laws that mandate overtime payments at a significantly high multiple of hourly pay have also been adopted by governments in an effort to reduce unemployment. High overtime rates make it increasingly attractive for organizations to employ additional part-timers, rather than simply paying existing employees to work longer.
6. One interesting attempt to measure the opposite of happiness is found in the Misery Index (the unemployment rate added to the inflation rate). The basic idea is that as the Misery Index increases, people feel worse off.

REFERENCES

Adams, J.S. (1965), 'Inequity in social exchange', *Advances in Experimental Social Psychology*, **62**, 335–43.
Bambra, C.L., M.M. Whitehead, A.J. Sowden, J. Akers and M.P. Petticrew (2008), 'Shifting schedules: the health effects of reorganizing shift work', *American Journal of Preventative Medicine*, **34** (5), 427–34.
Baumol, W.J. (1973), 'Income and substitution effects in the Linder theorem', *Quarterly Journal of Economics*, **87** (4), 629–33.
Becker, G.S. (1965), 'A theory of the allocation of time', *Economic Journal*, **75** (299), 493–517.
Becker, Gary S. (1991), *A Treatise on the Family*, enlarged edn, Cambridge, MA: Harvard University Press.
Becker, G.S. and K.M. Murphy (1988), 'A theory of rational addiction', *Journal of Political Economy*, **96** (4), 675–700.
Bernal, R. (2008), 'The effect of maternal employment and child care on children's cognitive development', *International Economic Review*, **49** (4), 1173–209.
Binswanger, M. (2006), 'Why does income growth fail to make us happier? Searching for the treadmills behind the paradox of happiness', *Journal of Socio-Economics*, **35** (2), 366–81.
Bureau of Labor Statistics (2005), 'Workers on flexible and shift schedules in May 2004', available at: http://www.bls.gov/news.release/pdf/flex.pdf (accessed 29 November 2009).
Burgess, J., L. Henderson and G. Strachan (2007), 'Work and family balance through equal employment opportunity programmes and agreement making in Australia', *Employee Relations*, **29** (4), 415–30.
Cordes, C.L. and T.W. Dougherty (1993), 'A review and an integration of research on job burnout', *Academy of Management Review*, **18** (4), 621–56.
Coronado, J. Lynn and M. Perozek (2003), 'Wealth effects and the consumption of leisure: retirement decisions during the stock market boom of the 1990s', available at: http://www.federalreserve.gov/pubs/feds/2003/200320/200320pap.pdf (accessed 29 November 2009).
Csikszentmihalyi, M. and R. Kubey (1981), 'Television and the rest of life: a systematic comparison of subjective experience', *Public Opinion Quarterly*, **45** (3), 317–28.
de Grazia, Sebastian (1994), *Of Time, Work and Leisure*, New York: Vintage Books.

Denniss, R. (2004), 'Paid annual leave in Australia: an analysis of actual and desired entitlements', *Labour and Industry*, **15** (1), 1–16.

Department of Trade and Industry (2006), 'Success at work: increasing the holiday entitlement – an initial consultation', available at: http://www.berr.gov.uk/files/file30011. pdf (accessed 29 November 2009).

Di Tella, R. and R. MacCulloch (2008), 'Gross national happiness as an answer to the Easterlin Paradox?', *Journal of Development Economics*, **85**, 22–42.

Dyer-Smith, M.B.A. and D.A. Wesson (1997), 'Resource allocation efficiency as an indicator of boredom, work performance and absence', *Ergonomics*, **40** (5), 515–21.

Easterlin, Richard (1974), 'Does economic growth improve the human lot? Some empirical evidence', in Paul A. Davis and Melvin W. Reder (eds), *Nation and Households in Economic Growth: Essays in Honor of Moses Abramowitz*, New York: Academic Press, pp. 89–125.

Edmonds, Eric V. (2002), 'Globalization and the economics of child labour', available at: http://www.dartmouth.edu/~eedmonds/nzzessay.pdf (accessed 29 November 2009).

Fraser, Jill Andresky (2001), *White-Collar Sweatshop: The Deterioration of Work and its Rewards in Corporate America*, New York: W.W. Norton.

Freeman, R.B. (1997), 'Working for nothing: the supply of volunteer labour', *Journal of Labour Economics*, **15** (1) (Part 2), S140–S166.

Frey, B.S. and A. Stutzer (2002), 'What can economists learn from happiness research?', *Journal of Economic Literature*, **40** (2), 402–35.

Game, A.M. (2007), 'Workplace boredom coping: health, safety, and HR implications', *Personnel Review*, **36** (5), 701–21.

Garrett, R. Kelly and James N. Danziger (2008), 'On cyberslacking: workplace status and personal internet use at work', *CyberPsychology and Behaviour*, **11** (3), 287–92.

Golden, Lonnie and Barbara Wiens-Tuers (2007), 'Overtime work and family consequences', available at: http://ssrn.com/abstract=988203 (accessed 29 November 2009).

Grzywacz, J.G., D.M. Almeida and D.A. McDonald (2002), 'Work family spillover and daily reports of work and family stress in the adult labour force', *Family Relations*, **51** (1), 28–36.

Halbesleben, J.R.B. and R.M. Buckley (2004), 'Burnout in organizational life', *Journal of Management*, **30** (6), 859–79.

Hayashi, M., Y. Chikazawa and T. Hori (2004), 'Short nap versus short rest: recuperative effects during VDT work', *Ergonomics*, **47** (14), 1549–60.

Health and Safety Executive (2009), 'Shift work and fatigue', available at: http://www.hse. gov.uk/humanfactors/shiftwork (accessed 29 November 2009).

Henkens, K. and H. van Solinge (2002), 'Spousal influence on the decision to retire', *International Journal of Sociology*, **32** (2), 55–73.

Herbig, P.A. and F.A. Palumbo (1994), 'Karoshi: salaryman sudden death syndrome', *Journal of Managerial Psychology*, **9** (7), 11–16.

Hirschman, E.C. (1994), 'Consumers and their animal companions', *Journal of Consumer Research*, **20** (4), 616–32.

International Labour Organization (ILO) (2002), 'Every child counts: new global estimates on child labour', December, available at: http://www.ilo.org/ipecinfo/product/viewProduct.do?productId=742 (accessed 29 November 2009).

Jeavons, Simone and Peter Sevastos (2002), 'A matched cohort study of career progression: glass ceiling effect or sticky floors?', available at: http://www.psychsavvy.com.au/PDFS/ SJMasters_paper.pdf (accessed 29 November 2009).

Kahn, Robert L., Donald M. Wolfe, Robert Quinn, J. Suduck Snoek and Robert A. Rosenthal (1964), *Organizational Stress: Studies in Role Conflict and Ambiguity*, New York: John Wiley & Sons.

Kalb, G. (2009), 'Children, labour supply and child care: challenges for empirical analysis', *Australian Economic Review*, **42** (3), 276–99.

Kaufman, Bruce and Julie Hotchiss (2005), *The Economics of Labour Markets*, 7th edn, Mason, OH: Thomson South-Western.

Labour Project for Working Families (2002), available at: http://ist-socrates.berkeley.
edu/~iir/workfam/home.html (accessed 29 November 2009).
Linder, Staffan B. (1970), *The Harried Leisure Class*, New York: Columbia University
Press.
Lord, R.G. and M.C. Kernan (1987), 'Scripts as determinants of purposeful behaviour in
organizations', *Academy of Management Review*, **12** (2), 265–77.
Maslach, Christina and Susan E. Jackson (1986), *Maslach Burnout Inventory Manual*, 2nd
edn, Palo Alto, CA: Consulting Psychologists Press.
McAfee, R. Preston (2006), *Introduction to Economic Analysis*, available at: http://www.
mcafee.cc/Introecon/IEA.pdf (accessed 29 November 2009).
Mishan, Ezra (1971), *The Costs of Economic Growth*, New York: Praeger.
Moen, P. and Y. Yu (2000), 'Effective work/life strategies: working couples, work conditions,
gender, and life quality', *Social Problems*, **47** (3), 291–326.
Morrison, David E. and David A. Deacon (2003), 'Organizational consequences of family
problems', in Jeffrey P. Kahn and Alan M. Langlieb (eds), *Mental Health and Productivity
in the Workplace: A Handbook for Organizations and Clinicians*, San Francisco, CA:
Jossey-Bass, pp. 254–75.
Mullainathan, Sendhil and Richard H. Thaler (2000), 'Behavioural economics', in
International Encyclopedia of the Social and Behavioural Sciences (Massachusetts Institute
of Technology), available at: http://www.iies.su.se/nobel/papers/Encyclopedia%202.0.pdf
(accessed 29 November 2009).
National Center for Infectious Diseases (2009), 'Health benefits of pets', available at: http://
www.cdc.gov/HEALTHYPETS/health_benefits.htm (accessed 29 November 2009).
National Centre for Social Research and the Institute for Volunteering Research (2007),
'Helping out: a national survey of volunteering and charitable giving', available at: http://
www.cabinetoffice.gov.uk/media/cabinetoffice/third_sector/assets/helping_out_national_
survey_2007.pdf (accessed 29 November 2009).
National Institute for Occupational Safety and Health (2004), 'Overtime and extended work
shifts: recent findings on illnesses, injuries and health behaviours', NIOSH Publication No.
2004-143, available at: http://www.cdc.gov/niosh/docs/2004-143 (accessed 29 November
2009).
New Zealand Work Life Balance Project (2003), available at: http://www.dol.govt.nz/work
life/index.asp (accessed 29 November 2009).
Nishiyama, K. and J.V. Johnson (1997), 'Karoshi – death from overwork: occupational
health consequences of the Japanese production management', *International Journal of
Health Services*, **27** (4), 625–41.
Nord, W.R., S. Fox, A. Phoenix and K. Viano (2002), 'Real-world reactions to work–life
balance programs: lessons for effective implementation', *Organizational Dynamics*, **30** (3),
223–38.
Office for National Statistics (2006), 'National projections: UK population to rise to 65m
by 2016', available at: http://www.statistics.gov.uk/cci/nugget.asp?id=1352 (accessed 29
November 2009).
Oswald, A.J. (1997), 'Happiness and economic performance', *Economic Journal*, **107** (455),
1815–31.
Putnam, Robert D. (2000), *Bowling Alone: The Collapse and Revival of American Community*,
New York: Simon & Schuster.
Ray, Rebecca, Janet C. Gornick, and John Schmitt (2008) 'Parental leave policies in 21
countries: assessing generosity and gender equality', Center for Economic and Policy
Research, London, September, available at: http://www.cepr.net/documents/publications/
parental_2008_09.pdf (accessed 29 November 2009).
Rettenmaier, A.J. and T.R. Saving (2006), 'Planning for your golden years', Private
Enterprise Research Center, January, available at: http://www.tamu.edu/perc/perc/
Publication/jan06.pdf (accessed 29 November 2009).
Ribar, D.C. (1992), 'Child care and the labour supply of married women', *Journal of Human
Resources*, **27** (1), 134–65.

Roman, P.M. and A.J. Johnson (1996), 'Alcohol's role in work-force entry and retirement', *Alcohol Health and Research World*, **20** (3), 162–9.

Schwartz, Hugh H. (2008), *A Guide to Behavioural Economics*, Falls Church, VA: Higher Education Publications.

Schwarz, P.M., J.L. Troyer and J.B. Walker (2007), 'Animal house: economics of pets and the household', *The B.E. Journal of Economic Analysis and Policy*, **7** (1), available at: http://www.bepress.com/bejeap/vol7/iss1/art35 (accessed 29 November 2009).

Scitovsky, Tibor (1992), *The Joyless Economy: The Psychology of Human Satisfaction*, New York: Oxford University Press.

Simmers, C.A., M. Anandarajan and R. D'Ovidio (2008), 'Investigation of the underlying structure of personal web usage in the workplace', *Academy of Management Proceedings*, 1–6.

Smith, L., S. Folkard and I. Macdonald (1998), 'Work shift duration: a review comparing eight hour and 12 hour shift systems', *Occupational and Environmental Medicine*, **55**, 217–2.

Smith, M.L. (1996), 'Mandatory overtime and quality of life in the 1990s', *Journal of Corporation Law*, **21** (3), 599–622.

Szabo, A. and K.L. Hopkinson (2007), 'Negative psychological effects of watching the news on the television: relaxation or another intervention may be needed to buffer them!', *International Journal of Behavioural Medicine*, **14** (2), 57–62.

Tanaka, S. (2005), 'Parental leave and child health across OECD countries', *Economic Journal*, **115** (501), F7–F28.

Tawney, Richard H. (2008), *Religion and the Rise of Capitalism: A Historical Study*, New York: Mentor Book Language.

Toastmasters District 32 (2011), 'What Toastmasters can do for you', available at: http://www.district32toastmasters.org/joomia/abouttm.html (accessed 18 May 2011).

US Census (2008) 'Percent distribution of the projected population by selected age groups and sex for the United States: 2010 to 2050', available at: http://www.census.gov/population/www/projections/summarytables.html (accessed 29 November 2009).

Weber, Max (1905 [1958]), *The Protestant Ethic and the Spirit of Capitalism*, trans. Talcott Parsons with a foreword by R.H. Tawney, New York: Charles Scribner's Sons.

White, L. and B. Keith (1990), 'The effect of shift work on the quality and stability of marital relations', *Journal of Marriage and the Family*, **52** (2), 453–62.

Wiener, J.M. and D.G. Stevenson (1997), 'Long-term care for the elderly and state health policy', available at: http://www.urban.org/UploadedPDF/anf_17.pdf (accessed 29 November 2009).

7 Working from home: leisure gain or leisure loss?

Samuel Cameron and Mark Fox

INTRODUCTION

Chapter 1 of this volume highlighted the fact that, due to the inflexible nature of work arrangements, workers cannot always readily exchange leisure for money. This reality was further developed in Chapter 6, which showed the difficulties of achieving work–life balance. These discussions assumed a straightforward division between the workplace and the home. In a theoretical Becker model, 'work' occurs in the home and leisure may take place at work, but work and home remain separate domains that are distinguished by whether or not one is paid by someone else. However, where one is employed by others, then taking leisure at work will often be detrimental to the aims of the employer. This would occur regardless of whether the leisure involves, say, taking too many breaks, watching porn or playing games on an office computer. Chapter 5 indicated that when work is particularly boring, such activities may be productivity enhancing, if they enable higher effort levels and lead to lower labour turnover. While this is possible, most firms would still seek to curtail such behaviour. In fact, recent cases suggest that firms are highly sensitive about this.

Since the industrial revolution, employers have typically compensated workers for their time, their knowledge/attention/skills, and their presence. As Gajendran and Harrison (2007) observe, 'Employees mainly transact their time, rather than their products with employing firms. That time is tightly bound to task and place' (p. 1524). The most logical way to escape from employer control over one's work–leisure choices might seem to be by becoming one's own boss. If self-employment leads to a growth in activity, the individual will become the boss of other people, which may require frequent attendance at the workplace where these employees are located. This would restrict the scope for the owner–manager to work from home. Generally, working from home (WFH) seems to have expanded in potential due to technical change and owing to the private and social costs of attending workplaces, which homeworking would help circumvent. These costs centre round travel and its spillover costs, such as environmental pollution, stress and accidents. Information and communication technologies (ICTs) have also made traditional '9 to 5' employees reachable outside traditional work hours by customers, co-workers and bosses. As Tan-Solano and Kleiner observe, 'With the emergence of sophisticated digital technologies, the concept of people converging to a common space for productive output seems redundant' (2001, p. 123). As we shall see, the use of the word 'redundant' is a rather extreme comment on the actual situation.

VARIETIES AND NATURE OF WORKING FROM HOME

What is working from home? What first springs to mind is the person who runs a business from home or who performs some part of a job which has a workplace somewhere else, without going there during normal working times. It might appear simple to define working from home and it might seem that the simple three-word phrase is sufficient to encapsulate its features. However, the literature in management and personnel psychology contrives to muddy the waters. Those disciplines tend to talk about 'telework' and 'telecommuting', terms that were first introduced by sociologist Jack Nilles in 1973 (see Nilles, 2004). Teleworking was originally conceived as home-based or mobile work and involved moving the work to the person; whereas telecommuting involves the use of ICTs (JALA International, 2010). Today, terms relating to working from non-employer locations have different meanings that often vary depending upon where the terms themselves are being used (Baruch and Yuen, 2000). Accordingly, we suggest that the clearest way to deal with WFH is to look at two key features of work, namely (i) the contractual basis of the work itself, and (ii) the nature of constraints on transfers of labour time to the home from the workplace. The following is a list of broad types based on the contractual basis for work:

1. *A fixed effort, conventional job that is performed at home, during work hours, on a regular basis* This is not possible for certain jobs. A car assembly plant worker cannot, to any feasible extent, take work home, as this would disrupt production flow and reduce overall productivity. However, knowledge and information-based work can, in terms of certain discrete tasks, be performed at home. This is especially the case if the worker has comparable (or better) computing facilities at home than those of his/her employer. An estimated 30 to 40 per cent of jobs in the US are thought to be suitable for telecommuting (Cambridge Systematics, 2007).

2. *Designated award of a period of time away from the workplace to com-plete a specific piece of work*   This is similar to a leave of absence, except that there is an expectation of producing something specific within the leave period. This can be, to some extent, a substitute for maternity leave (although one would have to question whether joint production in child-minding and paid work, in a domestic residence, counts as 'leisure'). In many universities, sabbaticals are an example of a lump-sum allowance. Here, time is given on the basis of complet-ing a project that may require more dedicated focus and freedom from other activities.

3. *Running a business from home*   This has obvious applicability for office and information-based work. The case of self-employed farmers shows a more intimate work–home intersection. For home-based businesses, the loss of the business may also involve loss of the home. This will occur when contracts with loan agencies tie the work and home together. The case of farmers is excluded in the general litera-ture on WFH and has not attracted attention in the subjective well-being literature. As empirical evidence for the stress on farmers of work–home intersection, we note that (at least in the UK), they have actuarially high suicide rates.

4. *Doing employed work only from home*, for example, mundane internet paid work, stuffing envelopes or toys. The contractual basis for this work is pay by results (PBR), and the situation approximates the simple intermediate microeconomics income–leisure choice model as workers can fully flexibly decide their levels of effort and time input and consequent leisure access. The snag is that the work undertaken will be for relatively low returns as there is typically a ready supply of low-cost labour, who seek flexibility or who have limited employment opportunities elsewhere. Thus, this type of contract does not expand leisure opportunities.

5. *Day extenders, who bring home work, over and above their regular work hours at a remote workplace*   This is essentially unpaid overtime (Song, 2009). Using BLS data from the US, Eldridge and Pabilonia (2007) find that WFH results in an underestimation of hours worked (for national productivity calculations) of between 0.8 and 1.1 per cent.

6. *Engaging in illegal activity at home*, such as growing and selling drugs or various services (prostitution, sex chat lines, homebrew, porn sites), which fall outside government regulations. Illegal activity is not neces-sarily different from legitimate enterprise as it could still be pursued at a remote workplace. Examples include digital piracy 'factories' and brothels. Some of these activities would be legal in some cities. Illegal

homeworkers receive an extra income effect boost as, of necessity, they will not be paying taxes on their revenues. In terms of their well-being, this will be adjusted downwards to some extent by the risks of detection and compensation.

As far as time management goes, illegal homeworkers will be constrained to a greater or lesser extent depending on the nature of their work and the level of income they can generate. One obvious example is 'high-class' prostitutes, whose services are in great demand and who may be able to pick and choose the volume and timing of 'work' (that is in the day/night/weekend and so on) to fully maximize their welfare. In the case of drug-dealers, the kinds of work–life balance issues that we discussed in the previous chapter can arise. If individuals run a prosperous illicit business, they may have a traditional entrepreneurial attitude which leads them to work harder and to have less leisure than they would in a conventional paid job. It is reasonable to suppose that a high-powered gang boss may exhibit the same leisure bind as the stressed-out CEO of a legitimate corporation.

SOME ATTRACTIONS OF WORKING FROM HOME

Working from home allows possibilities for joint production (such as the ability to combine work tasks with caring for children or dependent relatives). This appears to be more of a motive for women than for men (Popuri and Bhat, 2003). For example, in 28 structured interviews (14 with teleworkers from a Canadian financial services institution and 14 with their co-residents) childcare concerns were the major reason for homeworking for women, but not for men (Sullivan and Lewis, 2001). These women tried to work when their children were at school, or later at night when their children had gone to sleep. Likewise, in a survey of 63 male and 65 female information technology (IT) professionals, respondents were asked for their views on whether telecommuting did (or would) allow them to undertake various activities (Beasley et al., 2001). Women were significantly more likely than men to say that telecommuting would allow them more time with their children; provide flexibility in work hours; allow for more time with their spouse; and provide opportunities to combine home upkeep with job requirements. In contrast, men were more likely than women to say that telecommuting would allow them to work at home because they do not have time to do so at the office, or to use company equipment for personal interests. These findings reinforce the idea that traditional role expectations regarding childcare and household chores are more important considerations for women than for men.

Working from home can reduce employees' travel time and costs. Increased productivity may result through reducing the time that a traditional commute involves (Siha and Monroe, 2006). Commuting provides a mixture of imperfect substitutes for leisure and imperfect substitutes for work. People may, for example, work and play on their laptops during a train journey. Nevertheless the quality and scope of such experiences is less than they would be in a less constrained environment. Commuting (particularly by car) can be stressful and time-consuming, particularly in congested cities or in extreme weather. Commuting by train or bus can also pose various stresses (such as people who talk or play music loudly, unpleasant smells, or being uncomfortably close to strangers). Productivity gains can arise from the ability to work without the distractions that traditional workplaces offer (colleagues who wish to gossip, impromptu meetings and so on). For example, many teachers who are generally workplace-centric nevertheless elect to do their marking at home if this is permitted.

Working from home could contribute to more effective time allocation. Some jobs may require breaks due to boredom or needing to wait for tasks to be completed before progressing further. The range of things to do during breaks may be greater at home than in a traditional workplace (for example, washing dishes while a computer is printing a document). Breaks may also take the form of leisure activities such as watching television or playing with children. Working from home can also have restorative aspects as it may allow one to escape from work problems (for example, rampant hatred of colleagues) which are temporary and could be ameliorated by doing some work at home. All of these observations are entirely consistent with Gary Becker's allocation of time/household production model.

CONSTRAINTS WHEN WORKING FROM HOME

A meta-analytic literature review by Gajendran and Harrison (2007) reviewed 46 teleworking studies that had taken place in natural settings, with a total of 12,883 employees. Telecommuting was generally found to have a small, but positive impact on perceived autonomy and in lowering work–family conflict. Telecommuting also improved ratings on job satisfaction, performance, turnover intent and role stress. However, when telecommuting was more intensive (defined as more than 2.5 days per week), this accentuated the positive effects on work–family conflict, but *harmed* relations with co-workers. It was thus detrimental to leisure when it was significantly increased in amount.

One obvious constraint on working from home concerns the ease of communication with co-workers and third parties. The location of residence may be crucial to this as broadband speeds differ drastically between and within countries. Cambridge Systematics (2007, pp. 2–4) note that technology is a key barrier to telecommuting and:

> The lack of technology or, more specifically, the lack of speedy technology hampers telecommuting. If, for example, a worker requires particular software that is only licensed at the office, he or she cannot telecommute. If workers cannot access files at the office, have slow connection speeds, have unreliable connectivity, cannot access e-mail, or have difficulty staying abreast of client and home office needs, it is likely that telecommuting will not provide a viable replacement for office work.

In a study of 43 telecommuters who mainly worked for IBM Australia, Ilozor et al. (2001) found that job satisfaction was correlated with the clarity of communication by management; with the clear communication of deadlines; with regular communication; with the use of telecommuting social groups; and with reviewing work regularly.

While working from home may improve work–life flexibility, such arrangements pose challenges as the overlap between work and domestic lives is 'greatest when work is carried out in the places where people conduct their daily lives – bedrooms, kitchens, dining rooms and so on' (Felstead et al., 2001, p. 216).

The conventional workplace provides distractions in the forms of other people and opportunities for non-work use of work equipment. However, being in the home often provides more distractions (that come in different forms) from a remote workplace. Chief among these may be partners and children. On the equipment level, the homeworker can now have all-day access to television as well as online audio visual media. We should note that the possibility of eating, consuming alcohol, or drug use, as a distraction is typically much greater in the home.

Johnson et al. (2007) conducted a study of 18 Canadian women rehabilitation consultants who worked from home. From these interviews, the authors proposed three ways in which work can intrude on the home – through the reallocation or alteration of household space to accommodate working activities; through the visual evidence of work throughout the house; and through auditory intrusions. In the light of such intrusions, working from home requires considerable personal discipline, or as Felstead and Jewson (2000) refer to this, 'managing the self'.

Broadly speaking, we expect work to have an atmosphere of work and home to have an atmosphere of home. Also, the lack of transparency of being seen to be 'at work' by colleagues and supervisors can, for some work, make it easier to feel that there is limited accountability (or few social costs) for not working. Home may be too comfortable for some individuals to feel sufficiently motivated to get work done. Thus, one finds songwriters such as Nick Cave and Diane Warren going to an 'office' to write songs, instead of working from home, which they are entirely free to do. Warren is arguably the world's most successful living songwriter and her 'office' has old and mediocre equipment that falls well short of technical levels of most domestic PCs for music-making. Thus her *not* working from home cannot be explained by equipment needs. Revealingly, Warren attributes her success more to 'turning up' than to inspiration or hard work.

Working at home may induce a 'time elasticity illusion' in other household members, who may believe that time spent at home can be used for household production without detracting from time spent in paid work. Thus, a homeworker may be under pressure from his/her partner to undertake household chores or increase childcare responsibilities. This is borne out in a study conducted in Ireland (Russell et al., 2007) in which women experienced higher levels of work–life conflict than men. Interestingly, these researchers observed that the number of flexible work arrangements, present in the workplace, significantly reduced work–life conflict for men, but not for women.

There is evidently a conflict between work contracts and the constraints of specific locations where work is undertaken. When an individual is located at the employer's premises, the employer has an incentive to ensure that constraints will not lead to performance that falls short of what has been contracted for (for example, to ensure that computers do not break down or that the individual is not prevented from working by colleagues). Working from home shifts constraint management to the individual. One consequence of this is that workers who did not previously have individual deadlines may find themselves in deadline situations. Thus, the contribution to company output becomes more visible and identifiably traced to one individual than would be the case if they worked at a remote workplace. Here we have issues that would not arise in the standard labour market model of mainstream microeconomics as uncertainty of outcomes arises due to location constraints. Dealing with these issues properly requires some notion of effort determination in the work bargain which we look at in the next section.

THE EFFECT ON LEISURE: INDIVIDUAL CHOICE MODEL

From the last section, we see the paradox that working at home may actually involve a loss of 'at work' leisure through various pressures.

For example, Hyman et al. (2003) in a study of software developers in Scotland observed that when these employees had to take work home, this adversely affected health and led to stress and exhaustion. In the standard microeconomic income–leisure trade-off model, income effects of reduced costs of various types would mean that the employee can both do more work and have more leisure. This would be defined in terms of units of effort and leisure rather than just time spent. There would potentially be a win–win for employers and employees as a cause of efficiency loss (namely, rigidities in the work contract) would be reduced.

The problem that we need to consider is the risk of variability of effort: will the individual be able to maintain the same or greater effort at home? To be consistent, the same approach should be taken to determine effort, irrespective of whether the effort is being made at the workplace or in the home. The pioneering works of Leibenstein (1976) and Akerlof (1982) on effort determination were concerned with the traditional workplace. Akerlof's major idea is that labour contracts are a 'partial gift exchange'. For employees, the 'gift' given to employers is work/effort beyond the minimum specified in a contract. For employers, the gift given to employees is any wages, or other benefits, above the level offered if they left their current position. Conceptually, this is not a surplus or economic rent as it would not then typify a gift relationship.

The mere act of working from home is not automatically a gift, as this depends on the subjective evaluation of the situation by the worker. It may be a gift when workers deem WFH to have value in and of itself. In this case, employees may be inclined to work harder as they feel greater loyalty and trust towards their employer. In some cases, WFH will be a gift from the worker to the firm, where they are taking work home in addition to that for which they are contractually obligated. These gifts may be of the nature of the potlatch system where one gives donations in the expectation of a future, but uncertain, return, in that an expectation may hold of mutual insurance (for example, such workers will be given preferential treatment in the future if they find themselves having personal problems).

This is effectively a situation where implicit contracts supplement formal contracts. In contrast to Akerlof, Leibenstein did not specifically consider trust and loyalty. Instead, he proposed the APQT (activity, pace, quality, time) taxonomy to describe the worker's effort decision. In a traditional mass manufacturing workplace, economies of scale from the division of labour would mean that some workers largely perform one core activity, leading to possible alienation, frustration, boredom and so on. Employee choices then mainly come down to pace and time, as quality would be heavily constrained by the restrictive working environment. Quality and pace may be circumscribed by colleagues. For example, one response to a boring job would be to complete it faster in order to finish it sooner (or just to create a distraction), but if the effort is group determined then the individual will be forced to agree to the group effort levels.

Working from home potentially shifts the APQT boundaries, as is evident in the use of the term 'flexitime', which suggests that the T component can be moved, with implications for APQ. Where individuals work at home, they may escape a variety of formal and informal supervisory monitoring. Formal monitoring may be technologically restored, as we discuss shortly. Informal monitoring (such as opinions of colleagues) will still exist to some extent, so long as the worker still makes frequent visits to the formal work-place environment. With the arrival of information technologies, this may also take the form of electronic communications from colleagues.

The core idea in these more diverse economic analyses of labour markets is that notions of fairness/equity will be important in determining behaviour. If individuals experience dissatisfaction on fairness grounds then they may withdraw effort as they no longer see the labour contract as a partial gift exchange. This could arise because of leisure constraints. A boring, tiring job which has extensive and problematic time demands could lead to feelings of unfairness because the worker has such poor-quality and low-quantity leisure time. Workers would then be reluctant to take work home as a partial gift exchange for the employer. Employees may feel that time at home should be used to get completely away from the workplace and engage in the compensatory leisure ethos questioned in Chapter 1, with reference to the work of Riesman and Glazer (1961).

THE EFFECT ON LEISURE OF WORKING FROM HOME: EMPLOYER CONTROL

It would appear irrational for an employer to allow WFH if all it does is increase worker well-being at the expense of employers. Conversely, welfare economics would judge there to be a Pareto improvement if the workers were better off and the firm was not worse off. However, this may be difficult to achieve due to symbolic control disputes. The employer can lose even without malfeasant activity by employees if the workers are able to deliver less effort than they are contracted for. Conversely, the employer could still experience a net gain even when there is malfeasant activity by employees. Benefits to employers may arise from reducing costs (for example, the costs of traditional office space), increased productivity, increased loyalty, flexibility and so on. There may also be a contractual gain if the compensation package depends on time spent in the workplace. The removal of certain workers from the workplace may reduce a time-wasting culture (so that, for example, it will be less possible to hold essentially pointless meetings and engage in other group displacement activities the fewer people there are). It may help solve conflict situations as less output is lost than through giving 'pure' leave to someone to remove them from a hostile situation.

Research by Felstead et al. (2003) shows that firms tend to adopt multiple approaches to monitoring, involving: (i) introducing new surveillance devices; (ii) activating the surveillance capabilities of existing devices; (iii) setting short- or medium-term targets for output, and monitoring these; (iv) home visits by managers; and (v) emphasizing trust. Based on 202 interviews with managers and employees in 13 organizations, Felstead et al. found that monitoring efforts are typically ad hoc, rather than strategic, that is, they were not 'part of a planned, co-ordinated and deliberate action in pursuit of a wider objective' (p. 246). Hence, the key problem for employers is to ensure that their WFH scheme is efficiently designed. In an ideal world this would require no monitoring to ensure delivery of output. So, we first discuss the design of the scheme in a world with no monitoring and then look at monitoring issues.

Optimal Structure of the WFH Scheme

To highlight the issues involved in determining the operation of a WFH scheme, consider a highly stylized abstract model. In addition to assuming that there is no need for monitoring, we make the following assumptions:

1. For any given firm, we assume that there is only one simple scheme in operation.
2. Monday can be made a WFH day for any of the workers at equal costs and benefits for both sides, including the absence of economies of scale issues and comparable productivity levels at work versus home.
3. WFH does not incur any additional non-output-related costs or benefits imposed by the employer – for example, one does not get a different contract or payment due to sometimes working at home, nor does the firm experience any effects from the behaviour of its competitors.
4. Workers have identical work–home preferences.
5. Workers reveal their preferences truthfully – no one lies about how much they like or dislike WFH.
6. Employers will not force workers to have Mondays at home if they do not want this.

The decision to be made involves determining the optimal percentage of workers to be given a Monday to WFH, and a means of deciding which workers should get the day and frequency (that is, do they get it once a week, once a month and so on). Under the assumptions made, this would be quite a simple problem as all homeworkers should all get the same result – assuming the absence of returns to scale issues. How many workers are given Monday WFH depends on the nature of the workplace and the technological requirements.

However, consider a second scenario wherein workers have different preferences for WFH, then some difficulties arise for the allocation decision. The simplest case is to assume a split of those who like WFH (L) and those who dislike it (D) with homogeneous preferences within these groups. That is, at equal net reward, Ls will always prefer WFH and Ds will always reject it. As a fraction we must have $L + D = 1$ but the proportions of L and D could vary by workplace. If there is a technological necessity that some workers must be present on Monday then there will be a threshold L^*, above which WFH allowances cannot go. As in the original case, we could still propose arbitrary sharing as the optimal solution, but this time only *within* the L group as the D group is not interested in WFH.

If we stick with assumption (6) the firm will have little incentive to facilitate WFH if D is sufficiently high. However, D workers have some incentive to trade offered entitlements to L workers. This incentive would be greater if we relaxed assumption (5) as 'real' Ds could pretend to be in the L group in order to sell their entitlements for more. A situation where workers collaborate over their work entitlements would take us out of the classical theory of the firm into the direction of worker-cooperative or labour-managed firm situations. Small numbers of versions of these may be found in the so-called 'creative industries'. The disruptive potential and transaction costs of opportunistic bargaining over WFH entitlements constitute barriers to the adoption of such schemes.

Monitoring of WFH is necessary if workers cannot be trusted to deliver the effort that is expected. Lupton and Haynes (2000) note that the major barriers to teleworking are managers with a traditional view of work manifested in a lack of trust. Kowalski and Swanson (2005) propose that trust is 'Probably the most critical factor for success in teleworking' (p. 243). Employees' trust in their managers is also important. Staples (2001) found that when employees work remotely, 'interpersonal trust of the employee in their manager was found to be strongly associated with higher self-perceptions of performance, higher job satisfaction and lower job stress' (p. 3). Further, a study mentioned earlier (Felstead et al., 2003), which looked at 202 managers and employees, noted that both groups 'found their relative invisibility within established systems of surveillance to be disturbing, making it difficult for them to demonstrate their honesty, reliability and productivity' (p. 245).

The fundamental prerequisite for monitoring is information about worker activity. If monitoring is to have any effect there must also be penalties for shortfalls. Penalties could be explicit in terms of reduced pay or (ultimately) by termination. They could also be more tacit, for example in terms of decreased possibilities of promotion. The worst type of monitoring, from the employer's point of view, is one of low impact on performance, but high costs of operation. In some cases, shifting the costs of information gathering to employees through voluntary audits could be counterproductive as more output may be lost in complying with the monitoring than is gained in effort supply.

One example of a system of self-monitoring is the 'Transparency Review' in the UK higher education sector which audits time allocation of staff explicitly, as it requires workers to state what they did on Saturday and Sunday (days in which they are not expected to be at the workplace). It does not ask what leisure activities they were doing when they were not engaged in formal work. It does, tacitly, condone working from home and leisure shifting as an individual could in principle submit an acceptable return with 20 hours of work at the weekend compensated by a reduction in the weekdays.

With the prevalence of IT, employers can engage in more high-impact/low-cost monitoring, by establishing that the homeworker is in fact logged on to a workplace database for X hours a day.

Given the presence of monitoring costs, we must look at the employer's monitoring cost function (MN). We would expect this to rise with the number of workers on WFH allowances ($NWFH$). We might posit a function of the form:

$$MN = b_0 + b_1 NWFH^x,$$

where $b_1 > 0$ and its first derivative is expected to be decreasing if there are economies of scale in monitoring. This is a simple static cost function derived from technology where perfect knowledge and no risk is involved. It would determine the degree of adoption of WFH along with the D/L ratio and other factors discussed above.

If we introduce risk and psychic costs, these further reduce the adoption of WFH. Risk could be represented by allowing for the employer to operate on expected MN where the variance is taken into account. Psychic costs of the threat to control may be a complex function of the amount of WFH and its dispersal over categories of workers.

In a long-run, dynamic situation, we may have decreasing psychic costs due to a demonstration effect whereby employers discover that they do not risk a loss of control. If employers are risk neutral they will be indifferent to changes in the variance of expected returns with a fixed mean.

If employees are risk averse, then higher variances will be a deterrent to adoption of WFH.

EVIDENCE ON INCIDENCE

WFH appears to be an inverted U-shaped phenomenon. That is, those who are poor and in low-quality jobs may have access to it, as do those in higher-status professional ranks; however, most of us have limited access to WFH. For the disadvantaged, Felstead et al. (2002b) observe that working from home is a job requirement, 'they have no choice, once gainfully employed in deciding whether to work at home or on the premises of the employer' (p. 205). Based on UK data from the Workplace Employee Relations Survey and the Labour Force Survey, Felstead et al. conclude that those who have the option to work at home (even if just for one day per week) tend to be 'male, highly educated, better paid on average and in higher grade occupations' (2002b, p. 221). The same research also concluded that working at home was more likely to be permissible in the public sector, in larger firms, and where employees were responsible for the quality of their own outputs. Research in the UK by Moore (2006) also supports the contentions of Felstead et al. (2002b) and distinguishes the motivations of traditional versus professional homeworkers. Moore finds that traditional homeworkers were significantly more motivated by family considerations than were professional homeworkers. The latter were more motivated by flexibility and financial reasons than were the former.

Comparative WFH data is difficult to find, and complicated by definitional issues. Most of the data is on telecommuting which involves ICTs. The Status Report on European Telework New Methods of Work (1999) looked at the percentage of the workforce who telework, and found the highest rates in Finland, Sweden and the Netherlands (all of which had telework percentages of over 14 per cent). The UK rate was only 7.6 per cent, and the average for European countries was 6 per cent (see White, 2000). More recently the (now defunct) Statistical Indicators Benchmarking and Information Society (SBIS) reported rates of teleworking for European countries and for the US, as of 2002–03. SBIS found the highest rates of teleworking in the Netherlands (26 per cent), Finland (22 per cent), Denmark (22 per cent) and Sweden (19 per cent). The UK, Germany and Sweden all had teleworking rates of 17 per cent, and Spain had a low teleworking rate of only 4.9 per cent (reported in Australian Telework Advisory Committee, 2005).

More recent data on teleworking are shown in Table 7.1. A very basic exploration of the relationship between teleworking and some proxies

Table 7.1   Incidence of telework in the EU27 and Norway, 2005 (%)

	% involved in telework at least 'a quarter of the time' or more	% involved in telework 'almost all of the time'
Czech Republic	15.2	9.0
Denmark	14.4	2.6
Belgium	13.0	2.2
Latvia	12.2	1.8
Netherlands	12.0	1.9
Estonia	11.8	1.4
Finland	10.6	1.6
Poland	10.3	2.3
Norway	9.7	1.3
Sweden	9.4	0.4
Austria	8.6	3.2
United Kingdom	8.1	2.5
Slovakia	7.2	3.4
Greece	7.2	1.4
Spain	6.9	1.5
Lithuania	6.8	0.7
Slovenia	6.7	1.9
Germany	6.7	1.2
France	5.7	1.6
Cyprus	5.7	0.0
Luxembourg	4.8	0.0
Ireland	4.2	0.5
Hungary	2.8	0.5
Romania	2.5	0.7
Italy	2.3	0.5
Portugal	1.8	0.4
Bulgaria	1.6	0.0
Malta	0.0	0.0
EU27	7.0	1.7

Note: Results are based on responses to the question: 'Does your main paid job involve: telework from home with a PC?'

Source: http://www.eurofound.europa.eu/docs/eiro/tn0910050s/tn0910050s.pdf (pp. 4–5).

is given in Table 7.2. This table shows zero-order bivariate correlations between the two measures of telework and nine other variables representing economic prosperity, environment, level of development and technological access. The only statistically significant relationship of interest to us is the coefficient of 0.529 between depth of internet use and the 'quarter

Table 7.2   Partial correlation coefficients of teleworking measures from Table 7.1 with some additional variables

Variables	Partial correlation coefficients										
Quarter or more	1										
Almost all	0.65**	1									
Human Development Index	0.18	-0.15	1								
Per capita GDP (2003 $ PPP)	0.08	-0.05	0.79**	1							
Annual population growth (% 1970–2003)	-0.23	0.2	0.44*	0.46*	1						
Tertiary education – spending as % of total education spending	0.4	0.22	0.45*	0.52**	0.2	1					
Cellphone – subscriptions per 1,000 people (2003)	0.14	0.15	0.72**	0.73**	0.34	0.55**~	1				
Internet users per 1,000 people (2003)	0.53	0.13	0.55**	0.43*	0.01	0.22^	0.37	1			
Annual growth rate GDP % 1990–2003	0.14	-0.04	0.34	0.39*	0.32	0.1	0.27	0.09~	1		
Carbon dioxide – emissions per capita (2002)	0.17	0.14	0.46*	0.78**	0.36	0.56*	0.65**	0.36~	0.45*~	1	
Female/male earned income ratio	0.14	0.14	0.04	-0.05	-0.15	0.35~	0.03	-0.04~	-0.09	0.08	1

Notes:
** Correlation is significant at the 0.01 level (2-tailed); * Correlation is significant at the 0.05 level (2-tailed).
All other data are taken from Human Development Report; there are 28 observations except where ~ indicates 24 and ^ = 21.

Table 7.3 Regression equation to predict rates of teleworking: EU27 and Norway 2005

Independendent variables	Dependent variable	
	Share of quarter or more of time spent teleworking	Share of almost all time spent teleworking
Per capita GDP	0^	−0.00007 (1.07)
	(1.04)	
Cellphone use	0.005	0.005 (1.69)
	(0.8)	
Internet use	0.021	0.002 (0.58)
	(2.76)	
GDP growth rate	0.18	−0.142 (0.45)
	(0.29)	
Constant	−0.23	−0.95 (0.49)
	(0.6)	
R-squared	0.34	0.165
N	23	23

Note: Figures in brackets are absolute '*t*' ratios; ^ = this figure is not actually zero but is zero here due to rounding.

plus' teleworking percentage. As far as magnitude goes, this is a statistical association of just over 25 per cent between the two variables.

These results may be somewhat coloured by the outlier status of Luxembourg which has much higher GDP per capita and carbon dioxide emissions than other nations. Accordingly, we omitted Luxembourg and recomputed this matrix (not shown, but available upon request) and also ran some simple regressions for the technological and economic growth variables with it included and excluded. However, the omission of Luxembourg does not bring any notable differences. The most inclusive regression equation estimated was:

$$QOM \text{ or } ALMA = f \text{ (Per Capita GDP, Annual Growth GDP, Cellphone Subscriptions, Internet Use, } u)$$

where u is the normal and independently distributed classical disturbance term. QOM is a quarter or more teleworking and ALMA is almost all.

The results are shown in Table 7.3 and stick to the basic linear formulation. The positive and statistically significant relationship between the quarter + teleworking measure and internet use is confirmed. Further experimentation with this equation does not make much difference to our results.

As teleworking is in percentages and internet use is per 1,000 people, the coefficient of 0.021 indicates that an increase of about 50 people per 1,000 using the internet is required to generate a 1 percentage point increase in people reporting at least 25 per cent of their work time spent teleworking. The equation for 'almost all' work time teleworking shows only one (as it falls near the 5 per cent level on a one-tailed test) statistically significant relationship. This relationship is for cellular phones rather than internet use. The equivalent number to that just given is 500 more cellular subscriptions to predict a 1 percentage point rise in reported 'almost all' time spent teleworking. A study by Lal and Dwivedi (2009) provides some insights into why homeworkers use mobile phones. These authors conducted in-depth interviews with 25 respondents from a telecommunications organization, and concluded that social interaction with co-workers is more of an issue for those employees who largely work from home. They observed:

> In the absence of face-to-face interaction, respondents highlighted that changes had to be made in their patterns of communication. This involved a significant number of homeworkers using their work provided mobile phones in order to engage in social interaction with colleagues. In total, 18 out of the 25 respondents used their mobile phone for this purpose, specifically for exchanging information about other colleagues, developments and changes within the company, as well as for information regarding how to complete work tasks. Interaction as such was not maintained with all colleagues; rather, it was used as a medium for developing and maintaining social relationships with colleagues who comprised their small network of close associates, which they had built up during their working life with the company. (pp. 268–9)

Research also shows that, generally, rates of WFH appear to be increasing. Using Labour Force Survey data for the UK, Felstead et al. (2002a) observe that the percentage of employees working *mainly* from home increased from 1.5 per cent in 1981 to 2.5 per cent in 1998. In the UK, teleworkers (those who use phones and computers to work mainly from home), more than doubled between 1997 and 2005, rising from 4 per cent of all employees in 1997 to 8 per cent in 2005 (European Working Conditions Observatory, 2007). The World at Work (2007) organization shows an increasing trend for telework in the US from 2002 to 2006. Employee teleworkers rose from 7.7 per cent of all employees in 2002 to 12.4 per cent in 2006. Contract teleworkers increased from 13 to 16.2 per cent over the same period. Teleworkers were defined as those who performed all or some of their work at a remote location.

The American Time Use Survey gives some indication of WFH for the US. From 2003 to 2008, the proportion of Americans doing some or all of their work from home (even if their usual workplace was outside the home) increased from 19 to 21 per cent (Bureau of Labor Statistics, 2004, 2009). Full-time employees who worked fully or partially from home increased their average hours of homeworking from 2.60 hours in 1993 to 3.01 hours in 2008. For part-time employees, the average hours worked from home increased from 2.29 hours to 2.36 hours.

Many businesses are started from home and are often referred to as home-based or micro enterprises. Working from home appears to be more commonplace for the self-employed. The December 2008 Labour Force Survey data from the UK indicate that 74 per cent of those who worked mainly at or from home were self-employed (Department of Enterprise, Trade and Investment, 2009). In the UK it is estimated that around 60 per cent of businesses are started from home (Enterprise Nation, 2007) and home-based businesses comprise around 28 per cent of all employment (around one-third of the workforce). Those operating home-based businesses also count as homeworkers. In Canada, it is estimated that as many as half of all those who self-identify as self-employed work from home (Lowe, 2002). In Australia those working from home comprise 67 per cent of small business operators (Australian Telework Advisory Committee, 2006). In a study of 76 female and 184 male Australian home-based business owners, women were more likely than men to have been motivated to go into business for a flexible lifestyle (63 per cent of female respondents and 39 per cent of male respondents) (Walker and Webster, 2004). Also, women were more likely than men to cite the need to balance work and family (55 per cent of women versus 20 per cent of men). Research based on data from Statistics Canada (Pérusse, 1998) shows that when there were no children, rates of homeworking among the self-employed were similar (50 per cent for women and 33 per cent for men). Self-employed women homeworkers were more likely than their male counterparts to have children aged under six (77 versus 50 per cent) or between 6 and 15 (60 versus 50 per cent).

Research on day extenders is somewhat sparse. In a New Zealand study, Callister and Dixon (2001) found that, during weekdays, 15.5 per cent of non-agricultural workers worked at both a remote workplace and at home (also 8.3 per cent worked entirely from home and 74.2 per cent worked entirely from a remote workplace). Day extenders appear more likely to work at home during the evening, rather than in the morning. Around 30 per cent of hours worked between 8pm and midnight on weekdays were done in workers' homes. Some employees completed more than average amounts of paid work at home (including corporate managers, physical science professionals and teachers). In the US, Eldridge and Pabilonia (2007) used BLS data and found that between 8 and 9 per cent of non-farm business employees brought some work home.

GOVERNMENT POLICIES

The International Labour Organization (ILO) views homeworkers as predominantly disadvantaged relative to regular wage earners: 'Homeworkers, the majority of whom are women, constitute a particularly vulnerable category of workers on account of their often informal status and lack of legal protection, their isolation and their weak bargaining position' (ILO, 2010). However, coordinated international efforts to address working conditions for homeworkers have been largely unsuccessful. For example, the ILO's Home Work Convention of 1996 was intended to promote equality of treatment between homeworkers and regular wage earners in various areas including: the right to establish or join organizations such as unions; protection from employment discrimination; occupational health and safety protection; compensation; social security protection; access to training; minimum age requirements; and maternity protection (ILO, 1996). Only seven countries ratified this convention (Albania, Argentina, Bosnia and Herzegovina, Bulgaria, Finland, Ireland and the Netherlands).

The major focus of the EU has been on teleworking, rather than WFH in general. The foremost initiative in this regard is the 2002 Framework Agreement on Telework. This agreement was motivated by the EU's desire to promote growth and jobs, and to modernize labour markets in light of the use of ICTs within an increasingly knowledge-based economy (Commission of the European Communities, 2008). The Framework Agreement was developed with the cooperation of the European Trade Union Confederation and includes provisions to provide the same legal protections to teleworkers as those at employers' premises. The implementation of this framework has largely been considered a success (Welz and Wolf, 2009).

Governments may influence the choices of individuals regarding WFH and its impacts either directly, with explicit policies, or indirectly, through other policies. For example, if a policy to greatly reduce traffic congestion were introduced, it would cause substitution away from the WFH choice due to decreased travel to work costs. Likewise, the tax treatment for using part of the house as an office would impact on WFH choice. Working from home is also thought to reduce the overall risks of infection from disease among the workforce when a possible pandemic is being faced (Christensen, 1987). At a national level, telecommuting may increase employment opportunities for people who may otherwise be excluded from the workforce (Baruch and Yuen, 2000), including those with primary care responsibilities, those with disabilities, people in remote locations and those in areas with high unemployment.

Strategies and incentives to promote telecommuting include: marketing campaigns; free consulting services or funding for organizations that wish to design and implement telecommuting; education and outreach; cash incentives for using alternative modes of travel; prizes for using a particular alternative mode of transport; and tax moratoriums on telecommunication fees and tax credits (Cambridge Systematics, 2007). However, there is no evidence that incentive programmes influence participation rates (by organizations or by employees) in telecommuting (ibid.).

Working from home can reduce the externalities that commuting to work imposes on others (Christensen, 1987). These externalities include transport-related costs (such as fuel usage and pollution). In the United States, the 1990 Amendment 1 to the Clean Air Act encouraged telecommuting programmes as one means of coping with requirements that organizations in the 11 states with the worst air quality reduce daily commuters by 25 per cent during peak travel periods. Subsequently, several large companies (Prudential Insurance, AT&T and Georgia Power) initiated WFH programmes that were motivated by this legislation (Pearce, 2009). Firms were required to create a compliance plan within two years and demonstrate compliance within four years. As Allenby and Richards (1999) observe, approaches such as telecommuting constitute part of the triple-bottom-line philosophy for organizations; that is, the simultaneous pursuit of economic, social and environmental objectives. However, telecommuting will only benefit the environment if telecommuters use less energy (and do so in ways that are less harmful) compared to traditional employer-site-based workers. Needless to say, determining the net energy use of telecommuters is complex and needs to take into account their commuting and transport use patterns, their use of energy for work-related purposes (including, for example, the consumption of paper products), and whether telecommuting impacts on urban sprawl. Research on these issues is sparse (Nilles, 2004; Rhee, 2009), but does tend to indicate that telecommuting tends to involve fewer environmental impacts than traditional work (Allenby and Richards, 1999).

Government policies can also constrain the development of telecommuting. For example, local ordinances may prohibit work (or certain sorts of work) from occurring in the home. Occupational safety and health laws may increase the risk for employers who permit employees to work at home, as the home may then be considered a workplace, but monitoring of the home workplace may be more problematic (Australian Telework Advisory Committee, 2006; Cambridge Systematics, 2007). Also, in some cases, double taxation of telecommuters may occur. Taxes may apply at the location of both the employer's home office and the employee's home/workplace.

DISCUSSION

This chapter has continued the theme of Chapter 6 of workplace constraints on the availability and productivity of leisure. In this case we are looking mainly at a specific method of evading rigidities in the nature of the work–employment bargain. Technology has facilitated the expansion of WFH for many jobs, but it operates within wider social constraints. Institutional rigidities arise from the legacy of previous modes of production. Large organizations inherited a philosophy of organizing work that is premised on the notion that all workers should be in a building, all of the time (unless specifically called to another place to conduct business). This is not a given in all previous modes of production, as in the case of, say, lace manufacture. The current emphasis on the importance of the creative economy in its extension of the post-industrialism thesis suggests that traditional working places will break down as the role of machine production declines. This has been suggested by past futurologists. For example, at the World Future Society's Conference in 1982 it was predicted that before long, one-third of workers in industrialized countries would be teleworking (Skelly, 1983). In *The Third Wave*, futurist Alvin Toffler (1980) had proposed the idea of an electronic cottage. He foresaw that:

> The leap to a new production system in both manufacturing and the white-collar sector and the possible breakthrough to the electronic cottage, promise to change all the existing terms of debate, making obsolete most of the issues over which men and women of today argue, struggle and sometimes die. (p. 223)

We might then frame a futurist-come-creative economy hypothesis that WFH should have increased by more than it has. So, we then need to look at the constraints that have limited growth. These fall into three categories: external restrictions by governments and by employers, and internal restrictions felt by workers.

At the cultural level, workers impose inhibitions on themselves preventing the use of WFH to improve their welfare:

- They may simply feel guilt due to not being 'at work'.
- They may have more profound difficulties in being able to enjoy themselves.
- Going beyond such notions as peer pressure and the Protestant Work Ethic, Marcuse uses the notion of the 'psychic thermidor' (see Marcuse, 1955 and Geoghegan, 1981) which is an inbuilt tendency for individuals to defeat their own basic emotional desires via succumbing to repression.

- They may miss the social interactions offered by a traditional workplace.
- They may fear a loss of advantage in their post due to reduced access to information, gossip and so on, and/or reduced opportunities to personally influence those in a position to promote them.

Employer Restraints

Employers may be influenced by the same cultural factors as workers. In the sections above we also identified the further symbolic issue of control.

Government Restraints

Finally, we come back to the role of government. In developed liberal economies, the last 50 years or so have seen governments increasingly intervene in employment contracts by providing specific rights and entitlements. These have covered such things as fairness of treatment in the workplace, occupational health and safety, and freedom from discrimination in wages (whether by, say, gender, race, ethnicity or age, severance, or insurance). The effect of these policy interventions is to raise the cost of labour. Among this raft of measures, the chief step towards breaking the traditional continuity of time at work in a job has been parental leave entitlements. This is beneficial to firms who want to retain parents who have significant levels of specific (idiosyncratic) human capital. However, as we observed in Chapter 6, such policies also tend to favour women over men and reinforce caregiving stereotypes.

Government policies are driven by the need to seek election or re-election. In this respect, their chief labour market target is the unemployment rate. This focus is partly driven by fear of other unwanted social consequences that may flow from this. In the UK this focus has moved on to the fear of growing unrest from NEETs (not in employment, education or training), especially in large urban areas. Given the above, the relevant questions about WFH concern its attractiveness as a right/entitlement or its possible usefulness as a way of reducing the unemployment rate or NEET total. It seems difficult to establish substantial access to WFH as a basic right as this represents a radical shift to freedom of the worker under employment contracts, as opposed to merely being given protection from unfairness.

Working from home and associated types of employment flexibility would seem to be growing *but* they are still a very minor part of the economy. Although they offer the potential to overcome rigidities in the scope for leisure in a market economy, there seems little evidence that this has actually been the case. Instead of the promise of the electronic cottage, it may well be the case that (particularly for women), with increased workplace flexibility, 'Leisure time acquires an industrial tone when the demand for time efficiency in home activities tramples on emotions and symbols which provide meaning in life. The house comes to feel like work: an assembly line of household duties, including child care' (Gephart, 2002, p. 337).

REFERENCES

Akerlof, G.S. (1982), 'Labor contracts as partial gift exchange', *Quarterly Journal of Economics*, **97** (4), 543–69.
Allenby, B. and D.J. Richards (1999), 'Applying the triple bottom line: telework and the environment', *Environmental Quality Management*, **8** (4), 3–10.
Australian Telework Advisory Committee (2005), 'Telework – International Developments', available at: http://www.archive.dcita.gov.au/__data/assets/file/0018/25254/ATAC_Paper_3_-_International_final.rtf (accessed 23 March 2010).
Australian Telework Advisory Committee (2006), 'Telework for Australian Employees and Businesses: Maximizing the Economic and Social Benefits of Flexible Working Practices', available at: http://www.workplace.gov.au/NR/rdonlyres/39378CEC-A47E-4981-9DA0-004502E8F433/0/ATACReportTelework.pdf (accessed 23 March 2010).
Baruch, Y. and Y.K.J. Yuen (2000), 'Inclination to opt for teleworking: a comparative analysis of United Kingdom versus Hong Kong employees', *International Journal of Manpower*, **21** (7), 521–39.
Beasley, R.E., E. Lomo-David and V.R. Seubert (2001), 'Telework and gender: implications for the management of information technology professionals', *Industrial Management and Data Systems*, **101** (9), 477–82.
Bureau of Labor Statistics (2004), 'Time Use Survey – First Results Announced by BLS', available at: http://www.bls.gov/news.release/History/atus_09142004.txt (accessed 30 December 2009).
Bureau of Labor Statistics (2009), 'American Time Use Survey – 2008 Results', available at: http://www.bls.gov/news.release/atus.nr0.htm (accessed 30 December 2009).
Callister, P. and S. Dixon (2001), 'New Zealanders' working time and home work patterns: evidence from the Time Use Survey', Occasional Paper 2001/5, available at: http://www.dol.govt.nz/PDFs/OP2001-5s.pdf (accessed 15 January 2010).
Cambridge Systematics (2007), 'Congestion Mitigation Commission Technical Analysis: Telecommuting Incentives', available at: https://www.nysdot.gov/programs/repository/Tech%20Memo%20on%20Telecommuting.pdf (accessed 15 January 2010).
Christensen, K.E. (1987), 'Impacts of computer-mediated home-based work on women and their families', *Information Technology and People*, **3** (3), 211–30.
Clean Air Act (1990), 'To amend the Clean Air Act to provide for attainment and maintenance of health (Enrolled as Agreed to or Passed by Both House and Senate)', available at: http://thomas.loc.gov/cgi-bin/query/D?c101:5:./temp/~c1015ml6z5 (accessed 2 January 2010).
Commission of the European Communities (2008), 'Report on the Implementation of the European Social Partners', available at: http://ec.europa.eu/social/BlobServlet?docId=463&langId=en (accessed 2 January 2010).
Department of Enterprise, Trade and Investment (2009), 'Special feature – homeworking', *LFS Quarterly Supplement*: January, available at: http://www.detini.gov.uk/section_10-special_feature_home_workers.pdf (accessed 30 December 2009).
Eldridge, L.P and S.W. Pabilonia (2007), 'Are those who bring home work really working longer hours: implications for BLS productivity measures', BLS Working Papers 406, available at: http://www.bls.gov/osmr/pdf/ec070050.pdf (accessed 27 December 2009).

Enterprise Nation (2007), 'Facts and figures about home businesses', available at: http://www.enterprisenation.com/detail/Facts_and_figures_about_home_businesses/1285/43.aspx (accessed 15 January 2009).

European Working Conditions Observatory (2007), 'Place of work and working conditions – UK', available at: http://www.eurofound.europa.eu/ewco/studies/tn0701029s/uk0701029q.htm (accessed 30 December 2009).

Felstead, A. and N. Jewson (2000), *In Work, At Home: Towards an Understanding of Homeworking*, London: Routledge.

Felstead, A., N. Jewson, A. Phizacklea and S. Walters (2001), 'Working at home: statistical evidence for seven key hypotheses', *Work, Employment and Society*, **15** (2), 215–31.

Felstead, A., N. Jewson, A. Phizacklea and S. Walters (2002a), 'Opportunity to work at home in the context of work–life balance', *Human Resource Management Journal*, **12** (1), 54–76.

Felstead, A., N. Jewson, A. Phizacklea and S. Walters (2002b), 'The option to work at home: another privilege for the favoured few', *New Technology, Work and Employment*, **17** (3), 204–23.

Felstead A., N. Jewson and S. Walters (2003), 'Managerial control of employees working from home', *British Journal of Industrial Relations*, **41** (2), 241–64.

Gajendran, R.S. and D.A. Harrison (2007). 'The good, the bad, and the unknown about telecommuting: meta-analysis of psychological mediators and individual consequences', *Journal of Applied Psychology*, **92**, 1524–41.

Geoghegan, V. (1981), *Reason and Eros: The Social Theory of Herbert Marcuse*, London: Pluto Press.

Gephart, R.P. (2002), 'Introduction to the brave new workplace: organizational behavior in the electronic age', *Journal of Organizational Behavior*, **23** (4), 327–44.

Hyman, J., C. Baldry, D. Scholarios and D. Bunzel (2003), 'Work–life imbalance in call centers and software development', *British Journal of Industrial Relations*, **41** (2), 215–39.

Ilozor, D.B., B.D. Ilozor and J. Carr (2001), 'Management communication strategies determine job satisfaction in telecommuting', *Journal of Management Development*, **20** (6), 495–507.

International Labour Organization (ILO) (1996), 'C177 Home Work Convention, 1996', available at: http://www.ilo.org/ilolex/cgi-lex/convde.pl?C177 (accessed 27 February 2010).

International Labour Organization (ILO) (2010), 'Other specific categories of workers', available at: http://www.ilo.org/global/What_we_do/InternationalLabourStandards/Subjects/Otherworkers/lang--en/index.htm (accessed 27 February 2010).

JALA International (2010), 'Definitions', available at: http://jala.com/faq.php (accessed 17 January 2010).

Johnson, L.C., J. Andrey and S.M. Shaw (2007), 'Mr. Dithers comes to dinner: telework and the merging of women's work and home domains in Canada', *Gender, Place and Culture*, **14** (2), 141–61.

Kowalski, K.B. and J.A. Swanson (2005), 'Critical success factors in developing teleworking programs', *Benchmarking: An International Journal*, **12** (3), 236–49.

Lal, B. and Y.K. Dwivedi (2009), 'Homeworkers' usage of mobile phones; social isolation in the home-workplace', *Journal of Enterprise Information Management*, **22** (3), 257–74.

Leibenstein, Harvey (1976), *Beyond Economic Man: A New Foundation for Microeconomics*, Cambridge, MA: Harvard University Press.

Lowe, G.S. (2002), 'Employment relationships as the centrepiece of a new labour policy paradigm', *Canadian Public Policy/Analyse de Politiques*, **28** (1), 93–104.

Lupton, P. and B. Haynes (2000), 'Teleworking – the perception–reality gap', *Facilities*, **18** (7), 323–8.

Marcuse, Herbert (1955), *Eros and Civilisation*, Boston, MA: Beacon Press.

Moore, J. (2006), 'Homeworking and work–life balance: does it add to quality of life?', *Revue Européene de Psychologie Appliquée*, **56** (1), 5–13.

Nilles, J.M. (2004), 'Telecommuting and urban sprawl: mitigator or inciter?', *Transportation*, **18** (4), 411–32.

Pearce, J.A., III (2009), 'Successful corporate telecommuting with technology considerations for late adopters', *Organizational Dynamics*, **38** (1), 16–25.

Pérusse, D. (1998), 'Home-based entrepreneurs', *Perspectives on Labour and Income* (Statistics Canada, Catalogue No. 75-001-XPE) **10** (3), 31–4, available at: http://www.statcan.gc.ca/studies-etudes/75-001/archive/1998/5018538-eng.pdf (accessed 27 February 2010).

Popuri, Yasasvi D. and Chandra R. Bhat (2003), 'On modeling the choice and frequency of home-based telecommuting', TRB 2003 Annual Meeting, available at: http://www.ltrc.lsu.edu/TRB_82/TRB2003-001314.pdf (accessed 17 January 2010).

Rhee, H.K. (2009), 'Telecommuting and urban sprawl', *Transportation Research Part D*, **14**, 453–60.

Riesman, D. with N. Glazer (1961), '*The Lonely Crowd*: a reconsideration in 1960', in S.M. Lipset and L. Lowenthal (eds), *Culture and Social Character: The Work of David Reisman Reviewed*, New York: Free Press of Glencoe.

Russell, H., P.J. O'Connell and F. McGinnity (2007), 'The impact of flexible working arrangements on work–life conflict and work pressure in Ireland', ESRI Working Paper No. 189, available at: http://www.esri.ie/UserFiles/publications/20070427094523/WP189.pdf (accessed 17 January 2010).

Siha, S.M. and R.W. Monroe (2006), 'Telecommuting's past and future: a literature review and research agenda', *Business Process Management Journal*, **12** (4), 455–82.

Skelly, F. (1983), 'Address to the world's Futures Society 1982 Assembly', as cited in P. Eder, 'Telecommuters: the stay-at-home workforce of the future', *The Futurist*, **17** (3), 30–35.

Song, Y. (2009), 'Unpaid work at home', *Industrial Relations*, 48 (October), 578–88.

Staples, D.S. (2001), 'A study of remote workers and their differences from non-remote workers', *Journal of End User Computing*, **13** (2), 3–14.

Status Report on European Telework New Methods of Work (1999), August, available at: www.eto.org.uk.

Sullivan, C. and S. Lewis (2001), 'Home-based telework, gender and the synchronization of work and family: perspectives of teleworkers' and their co-residents', *Gender, Work and Organization*, **8** (2), 123–45.

Tan-Solano, M. and B.H. Kleiner (2001), 'Effects of telecommuting on organisational behaviour', *Management Research News*, **24** (3/4), 123–6.

Toffler, Alvin (1980), *The Third Wave*, New York: Morrow.

Walker, E. and B. Webster (2004), 'Gender issues in home-based businesses', *Women in Management Review*, **19** (8), 404–12.

Welz, Christian and Felix Wolf (2009), 'Telework in the European Union', available at: http://www.eurofound.europa.eu/eiro/studies/tn0910050s/tn0910050s.htm (accessed 17 January 2010).

White, Rebecca (2000), 'Background document N: a literature review of aspects of teleworking research', Environmental Change Institute, University of Oxford, available at: http://www.eci.ox.ac.uk/research/energy/downloads/40house/background_doc_n.pdf (accessed 17 January 2010).

World at Work (2007), 'Telework trendlines for 2006', available at: http://www.publications.parliament.uk/pa/cm200506/cmhansrd/vo060323/text/60323w09.htm (accessed 17 January 2010).

8 Contradictions of capitalism in health and fitness leisure

Simeon Scott

INTRODUCTION

This chapter investigates the origin, and subsequent development, of keeping healthy and fit as a leisure activity. Definitions of 'healthy' tend to stress freedom from disease, whereas being 'fit' is defined as ability to perform tasks. However, there is often considerable overlap in definitions of these terms. During the last three decades, government agencies, such as the Department of Health, have issued increasing amounts of information on public health and fitness issues, with particular reference to a number of leisure-related activities such as eating, exercise, alcohol consumption and smoking. For example, the UK Department of Health-sponsored Foresight Report (2007, 17) stresses problems associated with obesity:

> In recent years Britain has become a nation where overweight is the norm. The rate of increase in obesity, in children and adults, is striking. By 2050, Foresight modelling indicates that 60% of adult men, 50% of adult women and about 25% of all children under 16 could be obese. Obesity increases the risk of a range of chronic diseases, particularly type-2 diabetes, stroke and coronary heart disease and also cancer and arthritis. The NHS [National Health Service] costs attributable to overweight and obesity are projected to double to £10 billion per year by 2050.

Similarly, the marketing literature of health and fitness centres refers to good reasons for exercising during leisure periods and adopting a healthy diet. Trainers in the industry typically list the benefits of regular exercise as increases in life expectancy, greater physical energy and stamina, along with improved mental and emotional well-being. Personal trainers argue that a combination of exercise and a good diet will result in more regular sleep patterns, a slimmer body shape and a greater sense of self-worth.

Partly as a result of such information, there have been significant changes in the proportion of leisure time devoted to health and fitness-related activities, particularly in private, profit-driven, fitness centres. The central argument of this chapter is that this marketization of health and fitness activities is both cause and effect of a number of social contradictions. For instance, the benefits of health and fitness are not spread equally within the population: those on medium to high incomes generally devote a higher proportion of their time to health and fitness-related activities as compared with those on lower incomes; see Department of Health (2008) for the UK and Smith Maguire (2008) for the US. As these two texts indicate, accompanying this trend in the health and fitness leisure market has been a rise in levels of obesity, along with growing physical and mental health problems. Since the early 1980s, health and fitness, obesity, diet and related issues have generally been subsumed into a personal responsibility, market-orientated, approach to leisure. For instance, the Foresight Report (2007, 2 in Key Messages) argues: 'Although personal responsibility plays a crucial part in weight gain, human biology is being overwhelmed by the effects of today's "obesogenic" environment, with its abundance of energy dense food, motorised transport and sedentary lifestyles'.

In order to understand the origins of contemporary trends in health and fitness, including its gradual integration into the leisure/lifestyle industry, we begin with a discussion of work and leisure in largely egalitarian, hunter-gatherer tribes. Focusing on the health and fitness issues of our later ancestors, the next section examines the relevance of the social differentiation that marked the transition to early agriculture. The implications of this differentiation for work, leisure and health underpin subsequent sections, which discuss the transition from early agriculture to slavery, through feudalism and on to contemporary capitalism. Against the backdrop of the widening gap in income and wealth in many Western countries, health, fitness and diet are considered in the context of their commodification in the contemporary leisure industry, with sections devoted to social exclusion and conspicuous consumption. The chapter ends with a summary of the results of some primary research on health, fitness, diet and leisure, along with some concluding remarks.

THE GENESIS OF THE WORK/LEISURE DIALECTIC

The subject of leisure is often approached in a one-sided way. For example, Veal (1992) describes leisure as recreation accompanied by a state of mind which is optimistic and peaceful; leisure as an end in itself. He presents contemporary leisure as a process that is both self-reproducing and creative, akin to Aristotle's notion of *telos*. Veal's description of leisure as relaxation, which includes diversion, creativity and the like, is limited to the extent that it is not located in the contemporary struggle to assert human subjectivity against an ongoing struggle centred around work, commodification and clock time.

In order to explore the origins of this struggle, we turn to the writings of anthropologists and archaeologists, the majority of whom believe that our earliest ancestors were tribal nomads who were generally well fed and healthy. They obtained their subsistence by hunting and gathering, they had a relatively egalitarian ethic and more leisure time available to them than people in any subsequent mode of production. However, a minority of researchers take issue with this view of hunter-gatherers. There are still residues of a nineteenth-century colonialist 'state of nature' perspective, which presented hunter-gatherers as ignorant 'savages' engaged in a survival of the fittest free-for-all. More recently, drawing on the axioms of neoclassical economics, a more sober minority view has emerged. For instance, Beinhocker (2007, 7) writes: 'we can imagine' such people 'sat in the dust of the savannah and traded tools'. He claims this is 'the beginning of the human "economy"', advocating 'the great benefits of trade'. Citing research on a surviving South American hunter-gatherer tribe, the Yanomamö, Beinhocker compares their estimated income with that of the 'average' New Yorker, concluding that the latter is 400 times better off and has a much wider range of 'economic choices'. Unfortunately, Beinhocker's analysis tells us little about either the work/leisure balance or the health and fitness of these hunter-gatherers. We shall return to Beinhocker's theme that the harder one works, or 'trades', the more goods one obtains, with his corollary that leisure activities are unproductive.

A contrasting view is provided by Gowdy (1992, 130–48). Dispelling myths that hunter-gatherers engaged in 'trade', he comments on both the relative egalitarianism, including gender equality, and sustainability of the hunter-gather lifestyle. Gowdy argues that original hunter-gatherers typically 'had a rich and varied diet, lived relatively long lives and had plenty of leisure time'. He cites research indicating that adults in the African !Kung tribe 'spent only 2–3 hours per day in activities directly related to subsistence . . . about 40% of the !Kung population, children, young adults (aged 15–25) and elderly (over 60) were not expected to work and did not contribute to the food supply'. Emphasizing the absence of market-orientated social relations, he writes of 'an open and free supermarket', asking rhetorically: if 'everyone has free and open access to the supermarket, why would anyone take more than they need?'.

In a classic text on the subject, Sahlins (1974, 14) reports how members of Palaeolithic hunter-gatherer tribes tended to be slim and, relative to Neolithic agriculturalists, healthy. Anticipating the advice of contemporary personal trainers, he notes that hunter-gatherers travelled frequently, though often at a leisurely pace, restricted their food consumption and had a healthy diet. They 'work less than we do', Sahlins argues, their 'food quest is intermittent, leisure abundant, and there is a greater amount of sleep in the day time' as compared with 'any other condition of society'. These men and women spent their extensive periods of leisure engaged in such activities as embroidery, visiting relatives, entertaining guests, dancing, pipe smoking, playing games of chance or just 'doing nothing'. In terms of the gender mediation of the balance between work, leisure and productivity, female gathering typically provided more of the food than male hunting. However, Lewis-Williams and Pearce (2009, 32) make an important point with regard to the relationship between work and leisure for members of these tribes. On artistic activities, such as 'image making', as compared with 'practical matters of making a daily living', they write: 'such a distinction is probably ours rather than one made by the people themselves'. It seems that work and leisure were part of a continuum, with hunting as a largely male group experience and gathering a largely female collective activity, with older members of groups passing on their knowledge and skills to the young.

We must be careful not to idealize this egalitarian, leisurely and relatively healthy mode of being. In order to maintain food sources and an ecological balance, nomadic hunter-gatherers kept only what they could carry and were therefore restricted in the number and range of their practical, artistic and cultural artefacts. To maintain an optimum age and size, tribal subgroups would, according to Sahlins, in the extreme, practise infanticide and senilicide. In contrast to the egalitarian tribal ethic, it is likely that relations between tribes were sometimes hostile and occasionally violent. In short, for all its advantages in terms of leisure and health, hunter-gathering was a culturally and technologically stagnant mode of production.

WORK, LEISURE AND HEALTH IN SOCIETIES BASED ON AGRICULTURE

Some tribes moved from hunter-gathering to agriculture and trade during the Neolithic period. Work and leisure became separated, with work tasks becoming increasingly arduous. Leisure thus ceased to be part of an egalitarian social totality and became a refuge from extensive and oppressive periods of work. Writing of a 'Neolithic Revolution', related to the appearance of 'complex burials and, above all, art', Lewis-Williams and Pearce (2009, 17–20) argue that the development of domesticated plants and animals and a more spatially restricted lifestyle coincided with climate change and rising populations. Relative to hunter-gathering, agriculture and herding was more intense and arduous, of longer duration, less satisfying, repetitive, involved less walking, and was therefore less healthy.

The authors note the new threats of 'catastrophic disease' to crops and animals, soil erosion and degradation. Health and fitness were undermined by diseases spreading in more densely populated areas and by the heavy work required for irrigation.

Summarizing anthropological research on life expectancy and other health indicators, along with the likelihood of mass starvation, Gowdy (1992, 142) agrees 'that the transition to agriculture represented a step backwards for humans in terms of health, the availability of leisure time, and social freedom'. Later, during the Bronze Age and into the ancient city states beginning around 3,000BC, for the subordinate classes, including the slaves that resulted from wars, work was largely physical, repetitive, intensive, of long duration and imposed by fiat. In general, the lower one's place in the social hierarchy the less the time available for leisure, the poorer one's health and the shorter one's life expectancy. Whereas, the higher a person's place in the hierarchy the more likely he or she was to engage in a conspicuous display of leisure-related consumption, most noticeable in the orgies and other entertainments of ancient Rome. Thus, the egalitarian ethic of the hunter-gatherers was eclipsed by modes of production in which social differentiation and exploitation were fundamental. The stage was set for the antagonistic work/leisure relationships that were typical of the feudal period and early capitalism.

WORK, LEISURE AND HEALTH IN CAPITALIST SOCIETY

As the enclosure movement accelerated in Britain during the late feudal period, peasants and agricultural labourers were driven off the land into the new urban centres of capitalism. Capitalism radically transformed the landscape and social structure of Britain. There are detailed historical descriptions of the work, leisure and health of workers during the genesis of capitalism. These descriptions include Mandeville's (1724 [1989]) eighteenth-century text, Engels's (1842–44 [1993]) mid-nineteenth century research on Manchester and Marx's (1867 [1976]) later nineteenth-century work taken from factory inspectors' reports. Such texts indicate that, for these workers, life was typically short and unhealthy. They performed repetitive, often arduous and dangerous jobs for long hours, with little time, and few resources available for leisure. Unhealthy and unsanitary conditions were the norm for these workers, both in the workplace and in the overcrowded slum housing built near to the factories.

Members of the new working class were being forced into a working regime centred on 'clock time'. This involved an arbitrary splitting up of the day into hours, minutes and seconds, which underpinned the value creation process at the core of wage labour. As the eighteenth-century Scottish economists, such as Adam Ferguson (1767 [1966]), indicated, labourers were constantly obliged to increase their output per homogeneous unit of time. This would often involve repeating a narrower range of tasks more quickly, with fewer and shorter leisure breaks. Work time thus became the period during which operatives experienced the alienating effects of the labour process, with significant implications for their physical fitness and mental health. Away from the workplace, the limited haven of leisure was located in 'subjective time'. Here the passage of time varied according to the subjective experience of the worker temporarily engaged in leisure. While time at work appeared to move slowly, leisure time moved more quickly, especially as the hour to recommence work approached. We are reminded here of the aphorism: 'time flies when you are having fun'.

Thus, unlike hunter-gatherer society, in the capitalist mode of production work time came to be related to necessity and leisure time to freedom. However, during the post-1945 period, the ratio between formal work time and leisure time improved for most workers in the advanced capitalist nations, with corresponding improvements in diet, health and fitness. But, claims that Western economies would soon become leisure-centred societies, with short working weeks, proved to be unfounded. Wright Mills (1951, 226–7) argued that workers tended to live a schizophrenic existence where leisure time during evenings, weekends and holidays provided a sanctuary away from the alien environment of the workplace. This is implicit in the Americanism 'quality time', which is used to describe some leisure activities.

Between 1945 and 1975, most Western capitalist countries experienced a period of unprecedented economic growth. Yet, as better-paid members of the working class moved to the leafy suburbs or countryside, the extra travelling time added to the totality of the work process. While it could be argued that increasing amounts of time in traffic jams present leisure and status display opportunities, such time is potentially stressful, physically uncomfortable and detrimental to commuters' physical and mental health. However, these developments must be understood in the context of the internal contradictions of capitalism. As explained in Scott (2007, 35), the contradictions arise from the zero-sum struggle between wages and profits. While these contradictions are relatively dormant during periods of economic growth, in Britain and elsewhere, they surfaced during the early 1980s. For example, the collapse in manufacturing employment was accelerated by what has been called 'globalization', a wage-cutting process in which companies moved production to export zones in low-income developing countries. Many millions of Western manufacturing workers, the majority of them male, found themselves on training courses or claiming Enterprise Allowance benefits (a scheme which promoted self-employment) or in enforced 'leisure', that is, unemployed and unable to obtain work in the growing service sector.

Thus began the formation of what Tony Blair (2006) called the 'socially excluded'; also known as the modern 'underclass' or 'lumpen proletariat'. According to the British tabloid press, following the 1980 recession, there developed a 'benefits culture', which involved a turning upside down of the capitalist work/leisure philosophy. It was argued that a growing number of the 'socially excluded' could obtain enough from state benefits, sometimes supplemented by other income-generating activities, to enable them to live a life in which, despite their work/leisure imbalance, necessities and some luxuries were affordable. Eschewing euphemisms, one pro-market journalist referred to the work/leisure imbalance of this 'benefit-addicted underclass, bereft of aspiration, trapped in dependency and unable or unwilling to escape'. The Karen Matthews case, where a mother was found to have kidnapped her daughter for financial gain in 2008, argued the journalist, 'pulled back the curtain to allow us a glimpse of this netherworld of taxpayer-funded fecklessness'. The journalist referred to people who 'spend an entire lifetime wedded to a belief that the rest of society will continue to subsidise their idleness'. There is a 'culture of dependency that saps ambition and undermines any notion of personal responsibility', argued the journalist, the state is 'propping up a large number of people who have never worked' (Telegraph, 2008). As we shall see, the theme of 'personal responsibility' is central to the contemporary commodification of health and fitness.

Other social changes accompanied the late twentieth-century polarization of Britain. For example, new jobs in the expanding service sector typically featured a culture of working long hours, with low-income women often taking on several part-time jobs. Overall, there has arisen a two-thirds/one-third society, with a widening gap between the rising real incomes of the overworked majority and the stagnant, or even falling, real incomes of the minimum wage or 'benefits culture' minority. As we shall see, such radical changes to the pre-1980 work/leisure balance were to have a negative effect on the diet and health of low-income groups. However, the 2007 world banking collapse, the recession, the growing proportion of the population over 65 requiring retirement benefits and rising government debt are likely to exacerbate contemporary work/leisure contradictions.

Capitalism has become, according to one early critic using philosophical parlance, an all-consuming super-subject; an 'alien power', reducing human subjects to the status of predicates; as explained by Marx (1867 [1976], 716). As a result, a range of non-work activities typically used for preparation and rejuvenation for the next round of work are subsumed within the work cycle and subject to the tyranny of clock time. Linder (1997, 65–7) unwittingly confirms the thesis that, in seeking to overcome its contradictions, capitalism routinely seeks to commodify leisure time or 'consumption time'. It is axiomatic, he argues, that all areas of human existence are actual or potential arenas for buying, selling and consuming commodities. Thus, Linder argues: 'work takes time just as experiencing the pleasures of a good cup of coffee takes time'. 'Time spent in leisure activities', he writes, 'must then also produce a higher yield to keep pace with the increased yield on time at work. For example, socializing may be orientated towards meeting business contacts'. Linder is therefore critical of those who assume that non-working time is non-economic time. In effect, he wants to complete the commodification of 'free time' or '*idleness time*, which is the amount of time spent being passive and experiencing a slow pace of life' (original italics). In seeking to commodify leisure, Linder implicitly corroborates a key contradiction of capitalist social relations: capital's need to create ever-more opportunities to realize profits; a need which underpins the growth of the health and fitness sector of the leisure industry.

DIET AND CLASS DIFFERENTIATION

As the marketing literature of the health and fitness industry, and government reports, indicate, diet profoundly affects health and fitness. The report 'Health Inequalities; Progress and Next Steps' (Department of Health, 2008, 54) cites data indicating increasing 'obesity prevalence' for both men and women of lower income. Ellaway and Macintyre (2000, 52–9) point out that the poorest sections of the working class consume a less healthy diet and have an increased risk of health problems. Members of this class, they argue, live 'in deprived areas where the consumption of fruit and vegetables is low' and 'the price of certain "healthy foods" is higher'. Patel (2007, 269 and 273) argues similarly for the United States. Fast-food restaurants, according to Patel, are concentrated in neighbourhoods of poor people, and people of colour. For the poorest sections of the working class, lack of education and impoverished cultural norms tend to limit food choices, rather than any intrinsic inability to make informed choices.

According to the World Health Organization (2010a, webpage, on 'Obesity and Overweight'), 'Body Mass Index (BMI) is a simple index of weight-for-height. It is defined as the weight in kilograms divided by the square of the height in metres (kg/m^2). For example, an adult who weighs

70kg and whose height is 1.75m will have a BMI of 22.9.' While BMI is a crude measure of obesity, it is worth noting that, as Table 8.1 indicates, Americans have the highest BMI in the world, followed by Mexico and the UK. According to the Weight Control Information Network (2010), 'More than 85% of people with type-2 diabetes are overweight'. With regard to explaining this state of affairs in America, Drewnowski (2008) eschews the notion of lack of personal responsibility, arguing that the evidence suggests that obesity is the consequence of a 'failing economic environment'. Drewnowski insists that obesity and diabetes follow a social gradient; he refers to the illusion of freedom of choice where unhealthy foods are good tasting, readily available, and cheap. Whatever the amount of leisure time available to those participating in the benefits culture, having the time to shop around is unlikely to significantly increase their food choices.

HEALTH, FITNESS AND CLASS DIFFERENTIATION

Since 1980, the number of publicly funded healthy leisure options has declined in the UK. Jackie Ashley (*The Guardian*, 2 January 2006) argues there are now far fewer publicly owned swimming pools and other sporting facilities than 30 years ago, a situation compounded by the selling off of schools' sports fields. Ecoversity (2010) explains how hikers have noted deteriorating access to rights of way and poor maintenance of paths by local authorities. Child safety issues, due to traffic increases and fears of abduction, have resulted in young people spending more time inside the home using computer games, mobile phones, iPods and the like. The limited number of wooded or grassed spaces in inner towns/cities provide potential sites for drug dealing, tipping of waste and other antisocial activities. In contrast, higher-income parents are more likely to provide healthy activities, such as visits to the countryside, for their children.

Wilkinson and Pickett (2009, Chapters 5, 6 and 7) present data on health and fitness correlated with the level of income *inequality* which, they argue, shows that a much higher percentage of the population suffer from mental illness in more unequal countries. On heart disease among UK civil servants, the authors report on research which indicated that men 'in the lowest grades (messengers, doorkeepers, and so on) had a death rate three times higher than that of men in the highest grade (administration)' (p. 75). Linking low job status to other conditions, the authors report that lower grades were indeed more likely to be obese, to smoke, to have higher blood pressure and to be less physically active. Commenting on the social inequality of the US, the authors quote statistics indicating that black men in Harlem were less likely to reach the age of 65 than men in Bangladesh.

Table 8.1   Obesity by country

Rank	Country	Amount (%)
# 1	United States	30.6
# 2	Mexico	24.2
# 3	United Kingdom	23.0
# 4	Slovakia	22.4
# 5	Greece	21.9
# 6	Australia	21.7
# 7	New Zealand	20.9
# 8	Hungary	18.8
# 9	Luxembourg	18.4
# 10	Czech Republic	14.8
# 11	Canada	14.3
# 12	Spain	13.1
# 13	Ireland	13.0
# 14	Germany	12.9
= 15	Portugal	12.8
= 15	Finland	12.8
# 17	Iceland	12.4
# 18	Turkey	12.0
# 19	Belgium	11.7
# 20	Netherlands	10.0
# 21	Sweden	9.7
# 22	Denmark	9.5
# 23	France	9.4
# 24	Austria	9.1
# 25	Italy	8.5
# 26	Norway	8.3
# 27	Switzerland	7.7
= 28	Japan	3.2
= 28	Korea, South	3.2
	Weighted average	14.1

Note: Obesity measured as percentage of total population who have a BMI (body mass index) greater than 30 kg/m^2 (data for Australia, Austria and Portugal are from 2002. All other data are from 2003). Obesity rates are defined as the percentage of the population with a BMI over 30. The BMI is a single number that evaluates an individual's weight status in relation to height (weight/height^2, with weight in kilograms and height in metres). For Australia, the United Kingdom and the United States, figures are based on health examinations, rather than self-reported information. Obesity estimates derived from health examinations are generally higher and more reliable than those coming from self-reports, because they preclude any misreporting of people's height and weight. However, health examinations are only conducted regularly in a few countries (OECD).

Source: OECD Health Data 2005.

THE HEALTH AND FITNESS INDUSTRY AND CONSPICUOUS CONSUMPTION

Growth of the health and fitness industry has been most noticeable in the advanced capitalist economies. In Sweden, Lagrosen and Lagrosen (2007, 45–8) summarize the results of observations and interviews with customers and staff at a number of upmarket fitness centres. Health and fitness was marketed as part of a package which included 'self-esteem' and 'beauty'; the latter being defined as 'the various aesthetic objectives of the customer in terms of appearance – such as a slimmer body, enhanced muscle mass, smoother skin or a generally "healthy look"'. Customer 'beauty' was enhanced through such techniques as massage, spa treatments, yoga, meditation and the like. One aspect of 'service quality', report the authors, is building size which needs to be 'spacious enough to avoid overcrowding', but not too large to be 'impersonal'. Emphasis has increasingly been put on the relationship between exercise and eating green and organic products, along with a range of therapies and complementary medicines. Similarly, identity markers, such as race or gender images, are used by health industry marketers to expand the propensity to consume of its clients.

In Britain, many of the larger private fitness centres have swimming pools, climbing walls, sports pitches and more. While many local authority centres have been closed or sold off, those remaining are, in some cases, comparable with middle-market private centres. In other cases, publicly owned centres have a limited range of facilities, with such evidence of neglect as broken lockers, antisocial behaviour and a somewhat chaotic atmosphere. Centres with lower membership and lower admission charges are likely to be the leisure choice of lower-income people who wish to keep fit and avoid obesity in a socially inclusive environment. While other exercise options are available for those on lower incomes, such as running, cycling or walking, such people tend to work longer hours and have fewer holidays than their better-off counterparts, meaning less time for leisure and health and fitness-related activities. The cost of upmarket branded sports clothing and footwear, key indicators of social status, is likely to exclude some lower-income family members. While the falling cost of sporting equipment for the home does increase low-income access, data suggest that regular home-based exercise is not common among low-income families.

Over a century ago, Veblen (1899 [1994]) described the phenomenon of conspicuous consumption among America's social elite. He explained how, in societies differentiated by social classes, natural functions, such as sleeping, and consuming food and drink, are undertaken in ways expressive of socioeconomic, moral, cultural and artistic norms. Veblen famously explained how, as industrial production developed in the United States, the new 'upper' or 'leisure' class used conspicuous consumption to demonstrate its social distance from the new industrial working, or 'lower', class. The dialectical term 'reification' has been used to explain how particular commodities come to signify social differentiation. Such commodities *appear* to have the power to generate class differentiation, whereas in *essence* it is the social relationships which manifest themselves through the buying and consuming of these goods. In the next section, *inter alia*, we shall consider how contemporary conspicuous consumers of the products and services of the health and fitness industry seek to differentiate themselves from the poorer sections of the working class, particularly the 'socially excluded' underclass.

THE COMMODIFICATION OF HEALTH AND FITNESS

At the core of the transformation of health and fitness into conspicuous consumption is the need to commodify the products and services offered by the industry. With the Charles Atlas adverts, 'the world's most perfectly developed man', as a model, the American health and fitness industry began to turn its various products and services into saleable commodities on a mass scale in the early 1970s. The mass marketing of health and fitness-related products and services began by promoting jogging, body building and aerobics. Featuring a philosophy of self-improvement and personal responsibility, there followed the modern gym, health club, fitness magazine, fitness video, fitness instructor and personal trainer. Marketing resources, and increasingly sophisticated techniques, were used to create environments which were conducive to mutual affirmation, a place for display and the formation of a competitive hierarchy of fitness. This process ran counter to the trend towards home-centred leisure activities; with growing numbers of middle- and higher-income consumers patronizing what was to become a multi-billion dollar industry in the US, soon turning into a lucrative source of profits on a global scale.

Linking the industry to the contradictions of capitalism, Smith Maguire (2008) points out that the US has 'the world's largest fitness industry and, at the same time, the highest rates of population obesity and inactivity' (p. 22). She comments that in the US, as elsewhere, manual jobs are disappearing, with rising numbers of desk bound jobs, often involving interaction with VDU screens. Similarly, the expansion of credit has allowed more members of the working class and lower middle class to acquire the latest labour-saving devices for their homes. These developments pose questions regarding the contemporary meaning of health and fitness and its relation to the work/leisure dialectic. For example, as physical capacity becomes less significant in post-industrial working environments, the ends to which such capacity is directed and the means by which it is developed become problematic. Contemporary work/leisure contradictions emerge when we compare our lifestyle with that of hunter-gatherers. The latter would be unlikely to run a marathon, or do 100 press-ups – which today would typically combine keeping fit with raising money for charity. In contrast, the ability to perform relevant physical tasks would be built into the lifestyle of hunter-gatherers. Similarly, their egalitarian ethic would obviate the need for charity, which is a microcosm of the social contradictions of contemporary capitalism. In contemporary Britain, some workers do develop the fitness to do a 12-hour shift on a building site, or fight on the front line in Afghanistan. Yet others, who may work in call centres, might struggle to carry bags of shopping up flights of stairs when the lift to their flat is out of order. Challenging the idea that health and fitness is mainly indicative of strength, endurance and resistance to disease, the marketing of the industry has turned its focus to social encounters in the competitive environment of the workplace, dinner party and elsewhere. For many, health and fitness are indicative of status, cleanliness, mental and emotional well-being, sleekness, attractiveness and sexiness. In this context, we may note that, in Britain, a sexually attractive person is often described as being 'fit'.

Most countries have an egalitarian amateur ethos which underpins traditional team sports and other health and fitness activities. However, rather like the threat to local food and clothing cultures posed by global brands, the profit-driven health and fitness industry promotes *individual* attainment, stressing post-modernist notions of personal image and identity. For those seeking to rise in the early twenty-first-century social hierarchy, status depends less on work output and more on image, or presence – the packaging and branding of the human form. Hence, for the ambitious, it is a question not just of keeping fit, slim and having a good body shape, but also of joining the *right* health club or aping the *right* celebrity image – a process in which the body becomes less utilitarian, more symbolic. Ostergaard and Jantzen, in Beckham and Elliot (2000, 18–20), might well have been referring to this industry when they describe marketers treating the consumer as 'a member of a tribe where the product symbolism creates a universe for the tribe . . . they are searching for the "right" *symbols* so that they can be *recognised* by other members of the same tribe . . . instantaneously differentiating him or her from other groups' (original italics).

Increasing numbers of middle-class and skilled working-class people, argues Smith Maguire, have adopted a narcissistic cult of body worship. Converts to this cult constantly monitor their weight, calorific intake and related fine-tuning indices. They repeatedly update their dietary, medical and anatomic knowledge from personal trainers, other cult members and a growing health and fitness media. In this context, Smith Maguire refers to the advent of the health 'professional', who is part entrepreneur and part fitness evangelizer. Typically, 'professionals' and their clients discuss such issues as choice of clothing, footwear, equipment use and number of exercise sessions per week. 'Professionals' are frequently made aware of the contradictions between corporate profitability and the interests of their clients. If a personal trainer wears a particular branded good, asks Smith Maguire, is he/she endorsing the product?

The cheapness and availability of home gym equipment means that keeping fit is, in theory, possible for all. The home equipment market has, however, stalled since 2004 and there are doubts over the extent of after-sales use of such equipment, since motivation is difficult in social isolation. On current trends in the industry, one report explains:

> Many of the affluent consumers have switched their allegiances away from competitive sports requiring equipment [in favour of] joining a gym, swimming, jogging, or cycling. Furthermore, they have less time for organised sports such as squash or cricket. Joining a health club can also absorb most of consumers' budgets for sport and fitness. (Sports Equipment Market Report, 2007; summary)

PRIVATE 'SOLUTIONS' TO SOCIAL PROBLEMS

The health and fitness industry, Smith Maguire argues, is predicated on the idea that obesity and poor health are a direct result of a lack of personal responsibility – a weakness which, as we have noted, the media often associates with the underclass. The industry has a vested interest in opposing the idea that these are *public* health issues requiring environmental change and collective behavioural prescriptions. Thus the growth of the industry, she argues, coincides with a rising disillusionment with state-run leisure facilities and a rejection of the idea that social issues are best addressed by collective intervention. Barber (2007, 143) captures the mood:

> [T]hrough the magic of marketing, such profoundly public terms as *liberation* and *empowerment*, once reserved for a civic discourse associated with democracy and citizenship, are made over into tools of consumerism and merchandising – the new banners of a 'consumer revolution' whose aim is to destroy the public selves (citizens) our political revolution once constituted (original italics).

Health and fitness issues have thus become a part of what marketers refer to as 'lifestyle choices'. So, for instance, depletion of the ozone layer is treated as an opportunity to ritually apply a branded lotion to prevent skin cancer rather than an environmental issue requiring social intervention. Socioeconomic and environment issues are only part of the health and fitness industry's agenda in so far as they are a potential source of profits.

SOME PRIMARY RESEARCH ON HEALTH, FITNESS AND DIET

A Focus Group

In November 2009, a group of around 30 postgraduate students, some of whom were employed as full-time managers, acted as an improvised focus group, providing data relevant to some of the themes explored in this chapter. Members of the focus group referred to the trend for health and fitness clubs to replace gyms in order to attract higher-spending clients. They reported that the premium brands, such as Fitness First and Virgin Active, use price to reinforce social exclusion. These brands, argued the students, had centres in West Yorkshire and were notable for their after-training social activities centred round the coffee bar. Members of the focus group noted class, gender and racial differentiation in the centres and gyms, comparing, for instance, a local college fitness centre which is free and a university centre which is in the medium price range. Group members confirmed the claim that gyms located in run-down inner-city areas tend to have a predominantly male, pumped-up ethos. The group indicated that there are also women-only gyms, where Muslim women, for instance, feel able to exercise away from male eyes. Focus group members reported that their experiences confirmed the conspicuous consumption thesis with regard to health and fitness. The industry was big business, said some of the students, and subject to the imposition of clock time. Some fitness centres, they argued, were more like a working environment, rather than a leisure-orientated space with a more subjective time atmosphere.

A Gym and Fitness Centre Compared

As part of an investigation into ways in which health and fitness activities are socially mediated, in December 2009 the author visited an establishment describing itself as a gym, located in a run-down industrial area of Bradford, a city of around half a million people located in the north of England. Inside, the atmosphere was Spartan, with poor lighting and mirrors making the interior look larger than it was. The equipment seemed to be mainly weight-lifting orientated and members seemed to be exclusively young Asian males. At the reception desk, two friendly Asian young men informed me that the gym welcomed female members, but lacked appropriate 'facilities' and as a result no women came. A trainer at a more upmarket fitness centre claimed that this gym's membership charges were relatively low, adding the claim that most members of this gym wanted to cultivate a 'pumped-up' look. Comparing the gym with the middle-range fitness centre which the author has visited twice a week for a couple of years, it was a case of chalk and cheese. The fitness centre is state of the art, with excellent facilities, fully trained staff and a wide range of activities, including swimming, climbing, Pilates, massage and the like.

Edited Interviews with Two Personal Trainers

In December 2009, a male trainer at a middle-market fitness centre associated with a university was keen to transform the lives of his clients. Clearly caring deeply about the health and fitness of clients, he acknowledged that the prices charged at his centre inevitably excluded some 'lower-class' people. Such people, he argued, had 'other priorities' for their spending; however, the centre did offer lower prices for 'community groups' and those 'referred by their doctors'. The centre is aware of its 'image', the trainer indicated, priding itself on a relaxed race and gender mix. It is, he explained, 'not too posh' but neither is it for those who just want to look 'pumped up'. He made the point that steroids, and other drugs, would not be tolerated on the premises. The trainer was aware that health and fitness could be addictive, but argued that this was good for the client up to a certain point. Such addiction could be counterproductive if, he added, it leads to anorexia or other obsessive forms of behaviour.

This trainer argued that the government had failed in its commitment to health and fitness. Spending on the NHS, he argued, would be much reduced if illnesses were *prevented*, rather than cured. He claimed that government policy on smoking was hypocritical, allocating resources to discourage smoking while obtaining substantial income from duties on tobacco products. The trainer was aware of the somewhat artificial, clock-time-orientated, regime in the centre. Wanting to see more resources devoted to free health and fitness in schools, the trainer argued for more such resources in community centres, churches, mosques and the like. He stressed the importance of a good diet and wanted to see more relevant information and resources made available in the workplace. Finally, he was strongly in favour of creating dedicated cycle paths, walkways and improved park facilities

A second trainer told me that she was aware of the restrictive environment in the fitness centre, preferring to exercise in a local park, especially on hot summer days. On prices at the centre, she indicated that there are commercial pressures; however, as 'a trainer I try to make up for this by giving my clients as much information and education within sessions or programmes so that they get the most out of their money'. 'The very low bracket of income is definitely excluded' from fitness centres, particularly personal trainer services, she argued; 'therefore it is vital that people learn to pursue health and fitness in their own four walls and outdoors. Centres should offer more programmes/sessions to citizens, as quite often one of the restrictions is general access and affordability.' Our staff and public members, she reported, 'are generally middle class'. Following refurbishment of the centre, she explained:

> [T]he number of students has drastically increased and there is a bigger amount of young guys trying to get big. Considering that we do not sell bodybuilding specific supplements or specialise in 'hardcore' equipment or even have mirrors it is clear that we try to keep numbers of the 'muscle freaks' at bay. Still, if customers aim to develop such a physique me as a trainer will help them achieve it as long as they pursue it in a natural way (no drugs) . . . Nowadays there is probably more advertising going out promoting general fitness, showing people smiling, running around, looking sporty, whereas, in the '80s it was very much about ladies in leotards or men in short shorts, both showing off their muscles. The long, sleek, lean look is dominant over the bulky look: Arnold Schwarzenegger would nowadays not be used to advertise for a gym, it would be the fit, happy looking, average person from next door. This is what most big fitness chains (Virgin, Fitness First, Canons, Esporta, etc.) are aiming at; and it is all business related. How many Arnolds can they find out there in comparison to how many 'average' people. There is still a market for the 'pumped' look, but I think it is very much receding.

On the contradictions between leisure and relaxation, on the one hand, and the clock-time, counting-orientated, environment typical of the health and fitness industry, on the other, she said:

> I think any trends or cults can end up in obsession. It is all about how a person perceives such ideas and if they are able to do things in a balanced way. For me fitness is part of leisure (as well in the sense of relaxation) as it gives you peace of mind, stress relief, good body image, social well-being etc. Very often it depends on the people themselves, how they deal with such trends, if they take them to an extreme; it depends on their surroundings, such as: type of gym, peer groups, quality of trainers and media influence. Counting and measuring can be very intimidating and off-putting for new, inexperienced customers. For them it should be about learning how to exercise properly, how they should *feel* during exercise/activity and what they have to take care of.

However, she added,

> [F]or more experienced members it is vital that they check their progress regularly as the benefits of exercise will otherwise stall. Personally I do not encourage measuring of calories, rather aiming for progress in strength, stamina, flexibility or change of body *shape*. Losing weight is all nice and well and at times essential for people, but they should never forget the other positive effects healthy living can have.
>
> In order to keep fitness sessions up, they *need* to be enjoyable in one way or another. At the same time people have to realize that sometimes this enjoyment might not be while they are exercising (the pain/discomfort might be prominent) but that the relief and boost comes after the session and usually lasts for the whole of the day or even longer (not only physically but also mentally). As mentioned above I always try to show clients the various benefits of fitness or weight management programmes. The main aim for people is obviously 'to lose weight' or 'to tone up'. I aim to distract from these terms and from the apparent importance of kilos/pounds. For me it is about someone feeling better, being happier (with themselves), gaining confidence, having a longer and healthier life. I do not just measure their weight or body fat; a big aspect is the increase in cardiovascular fitness, strength and even more important (especially for very deconditioned customers) the ability to get around in daily life: to be able to get out of a chair, to walk to the next shop, to lift a bag off the floor etc. Of course I enjoy it if someone comes to me just for the purpose of being put through their paces, but once again I thrive off it because I know they thrive off it too. I always try to raise awareness about possible risks that come with exercising or other effects a change of lifestyle may have. There will be bad feelings, there will be pain, there may even be injuries (they are more likely to happen in the house though), there will be time difficulties, etc. Yet, in my opinion the overall effects are extremely positive.

On fitness mediated by gender and race, the trainer said:

> [T]rends are still slightly gender specific. As before, women tend to prefer cardiovascular training, aerobics classes, weight loss regimes, diets. Nevertheless, I was pleased to see that when we introduced our new equipment, that there were now more female customers using the resistance equipment, too. They still have the fear or misconception of becoming 'too big' but luckily I am proof that heavy weights don't necessarily get you bulky. Men still are dominant with the weight training, and I think this will probably always be the case.

For men, she argued,

> [I]t is either about 'losing that belly' or 'putting on mass'. Working in a facility that has a big base of Asian customers it is clear to say that women rarely train with weights (unless it is for their abdominals or thighs) and that men 'hit the weights hard'; probably too hard as I encounter a lot of bad technique and too heavy loads just for the ego! Oriental customers are generally somewhere in between. I think they mostly aim for good overall fitness; they use the rest of the facilities (swimming, badminton etc.) quite often. Unfortunately their

knowledge of how to pursue fitness correctly (technique and progress basics) seems to be under par: very often they seem to 'play around' with the equipment rather than commit to a proper routine.

On government policy on health and fitness, she said:

> I think overall the government is already trying harder to promote healthier living. There are various campaigns by the NHS, council related programmes etc. I think Social Services should get more involved, as this might improve the lives of their clients. I would honestly like to put a ban on any (media advertised) crash diet out there. They actually cause problems such as obesity, mental disorders (eating disorders, depression etc.). As well, there should be a law that every employer needs to provide appropriate fitness facilities (this could include grounds to walk in), healthy food availability and acceptance of regular eating. If the working world could be improved and if employers encouraged healthy living it would definitely make people at least more aware . . . Doctors/ GPs should be better educated when it comes to health and fitness. This sounds ridiculous but unfortunately most doctors do not even exercise themselves, they smoke and their breakfast consists of black coffee!

Finally, on diet, the trainer reported:

> [H]ealthy eating is still a huge issue. There is great misunderstanding as to what is healthy or very often even even ignorance about it. We are surrounded by take-aways, and they are certainly well used; on the other hand, people come to me telling me they never eat breakfast, they eat twice a day or 'I don't have carbs, because they make you fat'. It makes me angry, because it is plainly about them getting proper information, education and support.

Diet and Social Class

Manchester is the largest city in the north of England. A report on the city, by the Centre for Social Justice (Duncan Smith, 2007), highlighted the widening gap between the underclass and other social classes. Describing the 'two Manchesters', the report argued that many of Manchester's people are 'being left behind', despite the economic success of the city over the last 15 years. With this report in mind, a team of staff and students from Bradford College conducted research on healthy eating in Manchester and Bradford in April 2008. In Manchester, the main healthy eating café/shop in the city centre is located near the university. In the café, the staff/customer profile appeared to be disproportionately white, and arguably more affluent, as compared with the population elsewhere in the city centre.

The city of Bradford is notable for its Asian community, particularly people of Pakistani origin. Poorer members of this community tend to live within a 1 to 2 mile radius around the city centre, occupying properties vacated by the mainly white, but increasingly better-off Asian, flight to the suburbs. Significant numbers of East European immigrants have taken up residence in the inner city ring, although, with the onset of recession, some are returning home. One observation session in Bradford took place in a healthy eating café, located next to the university, staffed mainly by volunteer students. Some of the volunteers were from overseas, while others might well have been what marketers call 'social strugglers'; that is, from working-class backgrounds but committed to political, environmental, vegetarian and healthy eating causes. Of the customers at the café, who were mainly staff and students from the university and college, a few black and Asian faces were noted, but the majority were middle class, as indicated by their accents, and white. One building worker came to the café regularly; however when interviewed, he turned out to be a trainee electrician with a degree in photography. During another interview, a member of staff acknowledged that the café's organic and Fair Trade products were likely to be beyond the budgets of typical Bradford working-class people.

There are other healthy eating cafés in Thornton, a village on the outskirts of Bradford, in the nearby town of Halifax and in Leeds, the largest city in the area. Similar remarks could be made about both the social class and race/ethnicity of their staff and customers. More mainstream cafés, restaurants and coffee bars in and around Bradford city centre are notable for their lack of healthy options. There are many Asian, that is Pakistani and Indian, cafés; however, apart from vegetarian and occasional low-fat options, there is little that is specifically *healthy* on their menus. The eating houses typically frequented by poorer white working-class people, for example, public houses and cafés located in the markets, had few healthy options on their menus. Real ale public houses occasionally have organic beers available; such pubs have, however, largely become niche markets located in the leafier suburbs. In an interview, a black male lecturer expressed concern about the plight of those on lower incomes who, he argued, generally bought poor-quality food at the lowest prices. Some overseas students interviewed in Bradford indicated that healthy eating products had already become a symbol of affluence in their country of origin. Students from Gulf states reported that there were large numbers of immigrants working as drivers, labourers, cleaners and cooks in their country. These immigrants, they explained, typically shop at discount supermarkets where, as in Britain, few, if any, healthy products were available.

CONCLUSION

While the primary research sample is small, the evidence does offer support for the thesis that a number of activities associated with health and fitness have been commodified and subject to clock time. On the contrast between the slim healthy body shape and the more pumped-up look, the latter being associated with working-class males, respondents spoke of a hierarchy of health and fitness providers, with the branding of fitness centres, sports clothing, footwear and equipment correlating with a culture of conspicuous consumption. The thesis of exclusion of those on low incomes from contemporary fitness centre culture is tentatively supported in the pilot research. There was evidence of gender exclusion in one gym, with data indicating that race and gender mediate health and fitness choices. Unfortunately, due to time factors, an investigation of ways in which contemporary trends in health and fitness are related to declining political and social participation was not possible. However, the reader is referred to a study, by Thomas et al. (2009), on Sheffield, a large city in the south of Yorkshire, which investigates the health and fitness implications of social exclusion. On diet, the research presented here did provide evidence of social differentiation with regard to healthy eating choices in Manchester and West Yorkshire. Evidence from the two personal trainer interviews suggested ways of resolving some of the contradictions in government policies on health and fitness. For instance, the trainers pointed to a lack of opportunities for people to cycle, walk or run, as an alternative to the use of private cars or public transport for both work and leisure.

Raising similar issues, the Foresight Report (2007, 3 in Key Messages) calls for fundamental change on health and fitness in Britain:

> [A] bold whole system approach is critical – from production and promotion of healthy diets to redesigning the built environment to promote walking, together with wider cultural changes to shift societal values around food and activity . . . Many climate change goals would also help prevent obesity, such as measures to reduce traffic congestion, increase cycling or design sustainable communities. Tackling them together would enhance the effectiveness of action. There are also synergies with other policy goals such as increasing social inclusion and narrowing health inequalities since obesity's impact is greatest on the poorest.

We may also note the World Health Organization (2010b, 26) Report, which refers to the 'toxic combination of bad policies, economics, and politics', which is 'in large measure responsible for the fact that a majority of people in the world do not enjoy the good health that is biologically possible. . . . Social injustice is killing people on a grand scale'. Such arguments point the way to the need for radical changes in our socioeconomic relationships. Specifically, we need to overcome the fetter, the de facto veto, of profitability that underpins work and leisure in capitalist society. For many people today, leisure is for the most part an opportunity to recharge their depleted batteries at the end of a bout of, often alienating, work. Such work is the price to be paid for the relative freedom of leisure time. In order to sublate this impasse, we need to integrate work and leisure in a democratically planned mode of being in which our needs and abilities are brought together for the benefit of all of humanity rather than the profits of the few. Healthy eating and a fit body and mind could be a routine part of everyone's life, rather than a potentially addictive symbol of social achievement, subject to the discipline of clock time.

DEDICATION

Dedicated to the Memory of David Stark, a tireless campaigner for social justice.

REFERENCES

Barber, B. (2007), *Consumed: How Markets Corrupt Children, Infantilize Adults and Swallow Citizens Whole*, New York: W.W. Norton.
Beckham, S.C. and R.H. Elliot (2000), *Interpretive Consumer Research Paradigms, Methodologies and Applications*, Copenhagen: Copenhagen Business School Press.
Beinhocker, E.D. (2007), *The Origin of Wealth: Evolution, Complexity, and the Radical Remaking of Economics*, London: Random House.
Blair, A. (2006), available at: http://www.number-10.gov.uk/output/Page10037.asp (accessed 26 June 2008).
Department of Health (2008), 'Health Inequalities; Progress and Next Steps', available at: www.doh.gov.uk (accessed 11 June 2009).
Drewnowski, A. (2008), 'The dual burden of being overweight and undernourished', *Seattle Post Intelligencer*, available at: seattlepi.com (accessed 8 June 2009).
Duncan Smith, I. (2007), 'Manchester people "left behind"', available at: news.bbc.co.uk (accessed 12 February 2008).
Ecoversity (2010), available at: http://www.brad.ac.uk/admin/ecoversity/travel/index.php (accessed 12 January 2010).
Ellaway, A. and S. Macintyre (2000), 'Shopping for food in socially contrasting localities', *British Food Journal*, **102** (1), 52–9.
Engels, F. (1842–44 [1993]), *The Condition of the Working Class in England*, Oxford: Oxford University Press.
Ferguson, A. (1767 [1966]), *An Essay on the History of Civil Society*, Edinburgh: Edinburgh Paperbacks.
Foresight Report (2007), 'Tackling Obesities: Future Choices – Summary of Key Messages', available at: http://www.foresight.gov.uk/OurWork/ActiveProjects/Obesity/KeyInfo/Index.asp (accessed 12 January 2010).
Gowdy, J.M. (1992), 'The bioethics of hunting and gathering societies', *Review of Social Economy*, **50** (2), 130–48.
Lagrosen, S. and Y. Lagrosen (2007), 'Exploring service quality in the health and fitness industry', *Managing Service Quality*, **17** (1), 41–53.
Lewis-Williams, D. and D. Pearce (2009), *Inside the Neolithic Mind*, London: Thames & Hudson.
Linder, S.B. (1997), 'The increasing scarcity of time', in N.R. Goodwin, F. Ackerman and D. Kiron (eds), *The Consumer Society*, Washington, DC: Island Press, pp. 64–6.

Mandeville, B. (1724 [1989]), *The Fable of the Bees*, London: Penguin Classics.

Marx, K. (1867 [1976]), *Capital*, Vol. 1, London: Penguin.

Patel, R. (2007), *Stuffed and Starved: From Farm to Fork, the Hidden Battle for the World Food System*, London: Portobello Books.

Sahlins, M. (1974), *Stone Age Economics*, London: Tavistock.

Scott, S. (2007), 'Corporate social responsibility and the fetter of profitability', *Social Responsibility Journal*, **3** (4), 31–9.

Smith Maguire, J. (2008), *Fit for Consumption: Sociology and the Business of Fitness*, London: Routledge.

Sports Equipment Market Report (2007), available at: www.researchandmarkets.com/reports/544232 (accessed 12 January 2010).

Telegraph.co.uk (2008), 'Karen Matthews and the underclass thrive on Labour's welfare state', 6 December (accessed 8 June 2009).

Thomas, B., J. Pritchard, D. Ballas, D. Vickers and D. Dorling (2009), 'A tale of two cities: The Sheffield Project', available at: http://www.shef.ac.uk/sasi (accessed 12 January 2010).

Veal, J. (1992), 'Definitions of leisure and recreation', *Australian Journal of Leisure and Recreation*, **2** (4), 44–8.

Veblen, T. (1899 [1994]), *The Theory of the Leisure Class: An Economic Study in the Evolution of Institutions*, New York: Dover.

Weight Control Information Network (2010), 'Do you know the risks of being overweight?', available at: http://win.niddk.nih.gov/publications/health_risks.htm#type2 (accessed 11 January 2010).

Wilkinson, R. and K. Pickett (2009), *The Spirit Level: Why More Equal Societies Almost Always Do Better*, London: Allen Lane.

World Health Organization (2010a), available at: http://apps.who.int/bmi/index.jsp?introPage=intro_3.html (accessed 11 January 2010).

World Health Organization (2010b), 'Closing the gap in a generation', available at: http://whqlibdoc.who.int/publications/2008/9789241563703_eng_contents.pdf (accessed 11 January 2010).

Wright Mills, C. (1951), *White Collar: The American Middle Class*, New York: Oxford University Press.

PART III

PEOPLE AND PLACES AS LEISURE

9 Dating as leisure
Véronique Flambard, Nicolas Vaillant and François-Charles Wolff

INTRODUCTION

Becker's analysis of marriage (1973, 1974) is built on the hypothesis that the social process by which men and women meet is a market phenomenon, implying both material and psychological gains for (potential) partners. This market, frequently referred to as the 'marriage market', can be analysed by defining social relationships as a special case of consumer behaviour. Levy and Zaltman (1975) have termed exchanges on this market 'intimate marketing'. One of the most cited papers on this issue is that of Hirschman (1987), who analysed the behaviour of advertisers using 'lonely hearts' columns. Hirschman's analysis of dating advert users explores the role of consumption in human courtship and the idea of 'marital exchange' through the developments of the theory of resource exchange (Foa and Foa, 1974, p. 150). Hirschman deals with the demand for partners in terms of Lancaster's economic theory of consumer behaviour (1966). Each potential partner is treated as a bundle of characteristics, including age, level of education, physical appearance and intelligence, among others. Consumption of these characteristics during the dating process will, to some extent, be a form of leisure.

Becker's seminal analysis of marriage (see Grossbard-Shechtman, 1995, 2003) has been followed by a number of works looking at the economics of the partner selection process more generally. There is empirical work on personal advertisements by Cameron and Collins (1997, 1999, 2000a, 2000b) and on marriage bureaux by Cameron and Vaillant (2006) and Le Guirriec and Vaillant (2005). Using data from a speed-dating experiment, where random matching of subjects was generated, Fisman et al. (2006) show that women put greater weight on the intelligence and race of partners, while men respond more to physical attractiveness. Moreover, men do not value women's intelligence or ambition when it exceeds their own and women exhibit a preference for men who grew up in affluent neighbourhoods. Finally, male selectivity is invariant to group size, contrary to female selectivity. In another contribution, Fisman et al. (2008) extend their findings by examining racial preferences in dating. Gender, but also subjects' backgrounds, age and physical appearance seem to affect racial preferences.

Partner selection occurs naturally and informally, but it may also be organized through commercial intermediaries facilitating mating and dating (Quah, 1990; Vaillant, 2004a). According to Ahuvia and Adelman (1992), people who use commercial intermediaries do so in exchange for three services: (i) searching, that is, defining who are potential mates; (ii) matching, that is, obtaining information about the potential right partners; and (iii) interaction, that is, interacting in order to form or reject a relationship. Matchmaking agencies, personal advertisements and online dating services allow individuals to reduce the extensive costs of mate search, by easily locating potential partners (Vaillant, 2004b). Therefore, weighting costs and benefits, individuals with a relatively high income level experience substantial opportunity costs by searching for the right mate (Gronau, 1977, p. 118). They are more likely to use commercial intermediaries to reduce them, except if their high opportunity cost is more than compensated by a rich social life. Indeed, networks increase their pool of potential partners, especially when they seek partners with similar professional characteristics (Batabyal, 2001).

Furthermore, people who are characterized by features of low market value, or people who are picky about their prospective partners are more likely to buy matchmaking services of one sort or another. Speed-dating drastically reduces searching and matching costs, by eliminating a large amount of leisure interaction per date. Moreover, it greatly increases the number of dates per unit of effort. It might then be aimed at increasing the efficiency of dating leisure by attempting to increase matching.

Recent institutional, technical and social changes have altered the pool of individuals looking for dates, at all ages and at different moments in their lives (Stevenson and Wolfers, 2007). In particular, the rise in household appliances over the last century has made leisure and consumption complementarities more important drivers of couple matching than the production capabilities emphasized by Becker (1981). Gould and Paserman (2003) argue that rising wage inequalities have increased the return of a partner search and decreased the value of remaining unmarried. Caucutt et al. (2002) claim that rising returns to labour market experience raise the incentive for highly educated women to develop stronger prospects in both the labour and marriage markets.

With the increasing value of the search for a partner, online dating becomes more and more attractive. David Evans, an online dating consultant, estimates at 30 million the number of persons that will log on in 2009 to one of the 1,500 estimated online dating services in the United States. European internet users are far more engaged in online dating than those in North America. According to ComScore World Metrix, 18 per cent of European internet users (38.2 million) visit online personal sites each month (in 2006). France, Germany and England represent the largest market shares. According to JupiterResearch, online dating services are the third-largest attractor in internet users for paid content, after music and games, earning 10 per cent of the online audience in 2007. Online search offers a larger set of potential partners and anonymity than offline search. Those facing difficulties meeting potential mates are more likely to use the internet. Online search also allows for the selection of partners with similar leisure preferences (for example, with the use of conditions 'must love travel').

Clearly, people using online services may be distinguished according to at least two categories: candidates for marriage who are involved in mating rather than dating on the one hand, that is, people who are trying to 'invest' in marriage; and individuals who have short-run intentions on the other, that is, people trying to 'consume' human relationships. Thus, the continued existence of online dating services simply reaffirms that it meets the needs of individuals of both categories.

From an economic viewpoint, time devoted to dating can be analysed either as a cost for individuals who are seeking to marry, or reciprocally as a consumption good for dating consumers, in so far as this activity in itself provides satisfaction. In the first case, the cost can be both explicit, subscriptions to an online site or restaurant expenses for example, and implicit (since time spent on dating cannot be devoted to paid work (it is leisure time). In the second case, dating is a consumption good, a form of leisure. Of course, other activities can serve as a substitute or a complement to dating activities (such as social networks, hotline, sex toys, porn movies and so on), but their impact on dating is not discussed here.

In this chapter, we specifically consider individuals who express a demand for dates. The remainder of our text is organized as follows. In the next section, we present a theoretical model of dating behaviour explaining why improved economic conditions may have ambiguous effects on dating. We turn to an empirical analysis in the following section. Using a vector error-correction model and original French time-series data, we investigate the relationship between online dating, the economic sentiment (a proxy for economic wealth and people's confidence in the future) and decrease in dating opportunities (measured by the lagged fertility rate). The final section concludes.

THE ECONOMICS OF DATING

To explain optimal investment in dating activities by individuals, we turn to the expected utility theory and consider a simple microeconomic model of time allocation *à la* Gronau (1977). Dating is viewed as an additional possible time use, which extends the usual trade-off between leisure and working activities. The model could be modified to consider not only the implicit cost of dating (time), but also the associated expenses. Here, instead the latter are pooled with private consumption without allowing any distinction of marginal utility for different expenses. For example, one euro spent on a movie or visit to the theatre may (or may not) bring the same marginal utility as one euro spent in a bar, but here the marginal utility is treated as identical.

The Model

We assume that there are only two states of the world in our model: either the representative agent is successful in meeting singles (state s), or he/she is unsuccessful (state u). Let q be the probability of the 'bad' outcome, so that $1 - q$ is the probability associated with s. Whatever the outcome, the individual level of utility U is expected to depend on his/her level of private consumption C, on leisure l and on the number of potential partners met (D^u or D^s). We denote, respectively, $U^s(C, l, D^s)$ and $U^u(C, l, D^u)$ the individual utility functions in both states.[1] The individual's expected level of utility EU may be expressed as:

$$EU = (1 - q) \cdot U^s(C, l, D^s) + q \cdot U^u(C, l, D^u) \tag{9.1}$$

We assume that the number of meetings in successful and unsuccessful situations (respectively, D^s and D^u) is affected by time spent in dating activity. We rely on the following parametric specifications:

$$D^s = n^0 + N(d), \tag{9.2}$$

$$D^u = n^0, \tag{9.3}$$

where n^0 is an exogenous variable reflecting the number of random meetings, independently of the effort of the agent.

With more time spent in dating (denoted by d), the individual is expected to meet more potential partners. We rely on the sequel of decreasing returns for these dating activities, that is, the dating technology is concave ($N' > 0$ and $N'' < 0$).

Let us now turn to the individual resource constraints. First, the total amount of time T is devoted to hours of work h, leisure l and dating activities d, so that $T = h + l + d$. Second, there is the standard budget constraint such that the individual devotes his/her income to private consumption C (prices being normalized to one). There are two sources of earnings: labour income $w \cdot h$, with w the hourly wage rate, and an exogenous non-labour income Y (including bequests or public transfers, for instance).[2] From the corresponding constraint $C = w \cdot h + y$ and using the time constraint, we get the following full-budget constraint:

$$C + w \cdot l + w \cdot d = w \cdot T + y. \tag{9.4}$$

The maximum attainable level of income is given by $w \cdot T + y \equiv Y$. From (9.4), it is clear that the opportunity cost of one hour spent in dating activities and the opportunity cost of leisure are similar, given by the wage rate.

The problem for the consumer is hence to maximize his/her expected utility level by choosing the amount of time to spend in dating and leisure. Formally, the optimization problem is:

$$\max_{l,d} EU = (1 - q) \cdot U^s[Y - w \cdot l - w \cdot d, l, n^0 + N(d)]$$

$$+ q \cdot U^u(Y - w \cdot l - w \cdot d, l, n^0). \tag{9.5}$$

In what follows, we denote by U_i^s and U_i^u, respectively, the first derivative of the individual utility function, evaluated, respectively, at D^s and D^u with respect to the ith argument, with $i = 1,2,3$. The utility functions are supposed to be strictly quasi-concave, that is, $U_i^s > 0$, $U_i^u > 0$ and $U_{ii}^s < 0$, $U_{ii}^u < 0$ (with $i = 1, 2, 3$). We further assume some complementarity between private consumption and the time inputs ($U_{1i}^s > 0$, $U_{1i}^u > 0$, $i = 2, 3$), but some substitutability between the time inputs l and d ($U_{23}^s < 0$, $U_{23}^u < 0$).

The corresponding first-order conditions $\partial EU/\partial l = 0$ and $\partial EU/\partial d = 0$ are:

$$(1 - q) \cdot (-w \cdot U_1^s + U_2^s) + q \cdot (-w \cdot U_1^u + U_2^u) = 0, \tag{9.6}$$

$$(1 - q) \cdot (-w \cdot U_1^s + N'U_3^s) + q \cdot (-w \cdot U_1^u) = 0. \tag{9.7}$$

The interpretation of these conditions is as follows. From (9.6), the marginal expected cost of one hour of leisure in terms of forgone income $(1 - \theta) \cdot \omega \cdot Y_1^\sigma + \theta \cdot \omega \cdot Y_1^\nu$ is equal to its marginal expected benefit $(1 - q) \cdot U_2^s + q \cdot U_2^u$ since utility is increasing with leisure. From (9.7), the marginal expected cost of one hour spent in dating activities $(1 - \theta) \cdot \omega \cdot Y_1^\sigma + \theta \cdot \omega \cdot Y_1^\nu$ is equal to its marginal expected benefit $(1 - q) \cdot N'U_3^s$. Combining (9.6) and (9.7) leads to:

$$(1 - q) \cdot (U_2^s) + q \cdot U_2^u = (1 - q) \cdot N' U_3^s. \tag{9.8}$$

Equation (9.8) means that the marginal expected benefit from one hour of leisure $(1 - q) \cdot (U_2^s) + q \cdot U_2^u$ should be equal to the marginal expected benefit from one hour spent in dating activities $(1 - q) \cdot N' U_3^s$ at the equilibrium. When this equality does not hold, a better outcome can be reached by reallocating time between leisure and dating.

Economic Conditions and Dating

We are interested in the comparative static properties of the model in order to know the impact of a change in the exogenous income y and the wage rate w on both the optimal amounts of leisure and dating. From the second-order derivatives, it can be shown that the derivatives $\partial d/\partial Y$ and $\partial d/\partial w$ can be either positive or negative. As in standard models of time allocation, the impact of a change in the individual level of income on dating activities will be given by the sum of a substitution effect and an income effect.

Consider an agent with few economic resources and consider an increase in his/her wage rate. The substitution effect will first dominate and the individual will increase his/her number of hours worked. This mechanically reduces time devoted to dating, especially if dating and other leisure are complementary goods. Now, with a substantial rise in income, the income effect is expected to be larger than the substitution effect. The additional utility gained from an extra hour of dating becomes greater than the utility derived from the additional income earned, and more effort will be devoted to dating activities. Note that this marginal benefit also depends on the effectiveness of the dating activity, measured through the shape of the dating technology $N(\cdot)$.

The relationship of online dating with the business cycle is not documented either. During a recession, people tend to rethink their priorities. It is true in business, but also in the personal life sphere. The need to get through it together, to feel part of a community, to create social and affective links, can be stronger in difficult periods. Moreover, for those looking for a mate, the perspective of income and risk pooling may also be an incentive during economic slowdown. In an article published in *The New York Times*, Ellin (2009) reports that dating interest is up, both with online and offline matchmakers, during the fourth quarter of 2008 (during a period of recession). Dr Pepper Schwartz, a professor of sociology at the University of Washington and the relationship expert at perfectmatch.com, reports in this article a 51 per cent increase in new members in the fourth quarter of 2008 compared to 2007. During the previous economic downturn in 2001, a similar increased interest in dating was observed. With the average cost of offline dating being higher than the monthly cost of online dating, both the substitution and the income effects tend to encourage online dating compared to dating during hardship. Unemployed and underemployed people, with more time on their hands, can devote more time to surfing the web.

At the same time, it is also possible that during an economic recession, people feel less confident and that, as a result, socialization and in particular dating are less successful. Dating (online or otherwise) may hence be correlated in a complex way with the income level as we just discussed, but also with the level of uncertainty, the attitude of people and their confidence. It follows that the sign of the correlation between the business cycle and online dating remains ambiguous even if anecdotal evidence suggests a negative correlation between online dating and the wealth of the economy.

THE EMPIRICAL MODEL

Our empirical analysis is based on a time-series analysis. We use a French monthly dataset covering the period from January 2004 to August 2008 (56 observations). Specifically, we focus on the relationships between demand for dating (*MEETIC*), economic sentiment (*ESI*) and a proxy for the decrease in dating opportunities (measured by the lagged fertility rate denoted *invOP*) in France.

Data

In order to test the relationship between online dating and income, one could use micro data with information on time (and more generally financial resources) allocation between work, consumption and dating as well as information about wealth and labour income. Such data have never been collected as far as we know. Alternatively, we may rely on macro data, which will be relevant to assess the relationship between confidence and the business cycle. By adding other variables, we could extend the analysis to other covariates. For example, it would be interesting to study the link between dating interest, confidence and sexual health (STIs, HIV, AIDS, pregnancies). Using data from the San Francisco Stop Aids Project, Geoffard and Méchoulan (2004) show that improvements in treatments against HIV (in 1996) provoked an increase in the risk level, by diminishing the cost associated with risk for those individuals who have opted for testing. Although they studied the relationship between sexual health and one aspect of confidence (confidence in physicians' competence which may also reflect a general form of optimism), they did not study the relationship with dating interest.

Existing sex surveys provide some descriptive statistics, but do not offer any analysis and explanations. For instance, the Durex Sexual Wellbeing Global Survey presents findings from 26 countries every year, investigating people's attitudes to sex. Since 2005, Durex Company also publishes yearly reports called 'Face of global sex',[3] with a different question each year. In 2008, directly relevant to a study that would investigate confidence, dating interest and sexual health, the focus was on confidence. A sexual confidence scale assesses confidence aspects of sexual health (avoiding STIs/HIV/AIDS and pregnancy) as well as other dimensions of confidence, that is, sexual fulfilment and where to find guidance on various sexual issues.

The Endogenous Covariates

The variable *MEETIC* was built using http://www.google.fr/trends, which counts the number of times the word 'MEETIC' has been searched on google over a one-month period. 'MEETIC' is the dating site by far the most viewed in Europe and France.[4] Interestingly, the use of online web search queries, submitted daily by millions of users around the world, is employed by public health specialists to monitor health-seeking behaviour. Indeed, the relative frequency of certain queries (for example, 'cough') is highly correlated with the percentage of physician visits for that condition (that is to say, for 'cough' in the example).

Economic conditions are captured by the economic sentiment indicator of consumers from the 'Joint Harmonised EU Programme of Business and Consumer Surveys'.[5] About 40,000 consumers are currently surveyed across the EU. Answers obtained from these questions are aggregated in the form of 'balances' which are constructed as the difference between the percentages of respondents giving positive and negative replies. The European Commission calculates confidence indicators as arithmetic means of answers (seasonally adjusted balances) to a selection of questions related to the confidence indicator they are supposed to monitor. Sentiment indices are widely believed to have predictive power for the performance of the macroeconomy. Some empirical support for this belief is provided by research findings, which indicate that the sentiment index contains information about future changes in the economy beyond what is contained in past values of other available indicators (Carroll et al., 1994; Ludvigson, 2004).

Finally, dating also depends on the opportunities for success (correlated

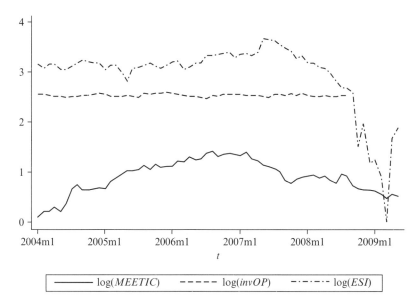

Figure 9.1   Demand for dating, economic sentiment and the inverse of the available opportunities of dates

with the number of people looking for a date). As a proxy for the decreased opportunities of dating (*invOP*) in France, we use the $t - 9$ month rate of fecundity. We can reasonably think that a woman who is pregnant is less likely to look for a date. Therefore, when the share of pregnant women increases, the share of single women looking for a date is decreasing. This proxy variable does not take into account the proportion of males that are available, but since two persons are needed for a date, it is related to the availability of possible matches. It should be kept in mind that this remains only an approximation. Stevenson and Wolfers (2007) report that according to data from Forrester Research, over one-third of those using online dating are currently married. Hence, we cannot rule out that some of them may be married to women who are expecting a baby.

All of the variables were expressed as logarithms and seasonally adjusted. Note that we add +38 to each observation of the economic indicator, in so far as it presents negative values (min(*ESI*) = –37). Figure 9.1 depicts the evolution of the various variables.

When studying time series, we need to know first whether the variables are integrated or not. If they are integrated of the same order, a stable long-run relationship may exist which can be taken into account using

Table 9.1 Descriptive statistics (whole sample)

	Mean	SD	PP (level)		PP (1ˢᵗ diff.)	
			Z (rho)	Z (t)	Z (rho)	Z (t)
Log(*MEETIC*)	0.907	0.332	−4.833	−2.218	−57.122	−7.283***
Log(*ESI*)	2.960	0.690	−5.000	−1.426	−80.682	−10.374***
Log(*OPP*)	2.547	0.026	−27.298	−4.093***	−68.665	−9.445***

Note: *** Significant at the 1% level. PP = Phillips–Peron.

error-correction models. We therefore apply unit root tests to establish the order of integration in each of the four variables. Specifically, we turn to the unit root test developed by Phillips and Perron (1988). Basically, the Phillips–Perron test is a modification of the standard test proposed by Dickey and Fuller (1979). The Phillips–Perron test estimates the Dickey–Fuller test and modifies the *t*-ratio of the unit root coefficient so that serial correlation does not affect the test statistic. Table 9.1 presents the results for the unit root test for a model with an intercept.

The variables log(*MEETIC*) and log(*ESI*) appear to be non-stationary in levels, and stationary when differenced. In other words, we can conclude that these series are integrated of order one ($I(1)$). The Phillips–Perron test on the variable log(*invOP*) rejects the existence of a unit root. We thus conduct a Dickey–Fuller generalized least-squares (GLS) test, which is a modified Dickey–Fuller *t*-test for a unit root in which the series has been transformed by a GLS regression. The DF-GLS statistic for the series does not exceed the critical values in absolute terms at the 1 per cent level of significance (−2.36 > −2.62). When we take the first difference of each variable, it does, which means that log(*invOP*) is integrated of order one (or $I(1)$).

A Vector Error Correction Model (VECM) Approach

The results described above indicate that there may be one or several stable long-run relationships between the variables and that we should test for cointegration before specifying the multivariate model. The concept of cointegration was formalized by Engle and Granger (1987). We say that variables are cointegrated when we can form a linear combination of them that is stationary; this linear combination can be considered as a long-run relationship between the variables. If one or several cointegrating relationships are identified in a multivariate system, the long-run relationship can be included as error-correction terms in the vector autoregressive set-up.

Table 9.2   Length of the vector auto-regressive model

lag	LL	LR	df	P	FPE	AIC	HQIC	SBIC
0	150.571				0.000	−4.703	−4.222	−3.4409
1	263.565	225.990	9.000	0.000	3.0e–08*	−8.8626*	−8.25099*	−7.2565*
2	270.518	13.905	9.000	0.126	0.000	−8.781	−8.038	−6.83044
3	274.586	8.137	9.000	0.520	0.000	−8.583	−7.710	−6.28902
4	283.074	16.975*	9.000	0.049	0.000	−8.563	−7.558	−5.92435
5	286.843	7.538	9.000	0.581	0.000	−8.354	−7.218	−5.37095
6	292.385	11.086	9.000	0.270	0.000	−8.215	−6.949	−4.8885

Note: * Significant at the 10% level.

Engle and Granger and Johansen (Johansen, 1988; Johansen and Juselius, 1990) tests can be used to determine the number of relations of cointegration. The latter is often preferred due to its one-step approach and its ability to handle more than one cointegrating relationship. Another drawback with the original Engle and Granger test is the importance of the choice of dependent variables. In the Johansen test, it is assumed that all variables are endogenous and the test is therefore not sensitive to structure choice.

Before performing the Johansen procedure, it is necessary to specify the lag length of the vector auto-regressive (VAR) model. The results of diagnostic tests proposed by Sims (1980) are shown in Table 9.2.

The final prediction error (FPE), the Schwarz Bayesian information criterion (SBIC), the Hannan and Quinn information criterion (HQIC) and the Akaike information criterion (AIC) indicate vector autoregressions of order 1, whereas the likelihood-ratio test statistics (LR) conclude to a four-lag order. Both lag 1 and lag 4 will be considered in the Johansen procedure, but we only report the results for four lags. The Johansen procedure produces trace and maximum Eigen-value tests, presented in Table 9.3, from which the number of cointegrating vectors can be identified. We proceed sequentially by first testing for H_0: $r \leq 0$, with r the number of cointegrating vectors. If H_0 is rejected, we then test for $r \leq 1$ and so on until the null hypothesis cannot be rejected.

The Johansen procedure clearly rejects the null hypothesis of zero cointegrating vector against the alternative, at both 1 and 5 per cent levels, when considering only one lag in the underlying VAR model (results are not presented). Table 9.3 indicates that the null hypothesis of no cointegration relation cannot be rejected at 1 per cent, but is rejected at 5 per cent in favour of at most one statistically significant cointegrating vector. Considering the results of the Johansen procedure that rejects

Table 9.3   Johansen procedure (with constant in cointegration)

No. of cointegrating vectors	Eigenvalue	Trace test
$r = 2$ (alternative: $r = 3$)	0.04326	2.299
$r = 1$ (alternative: $r = 2$)	0.16222	11.504*
$r = 0$ (alternative: $r = 1$)	0.30487	30.414*

Note: * Significant at the 10% level.

the null hypothesis of no cointegration relation at 5 per cent (with one or four lags), we shall consider a model with four lags and one relation of cointegration.

The dating equation is identified by normalizing the estimated coefficient on $\log(MEETIC)$ to 1. The estimated relation of cointegration is (with standard errors in parentheses under the coefficients):

$$\log(MEETIC) = 124.72 - \underset{(0.073)}{2.97} \cdot \log(ESI) - \underset{(0.000)}{44.60} \cdot \log(invOP), \tag{9.9}$$

where the vector of coefficients represents the cointegrating vector defining the linear combination of variables that are $I(0)$. These can be described as long-run equilibrium.

First, the dating demand is negatively related to both the economic sentiment and the fertility rate, which indicates that it is positively related to the number of potential partners. The estimated coefficient associated with $\log(ESI)$ indicates that a 1 per cent increase in ESI will decrease the demand for dating by 3 per cent in the long run. When people are more confident in the economy and have more income, they tend to spend less time on MEETIC. On the contrary, during economic downturns, they appear to increase their demand for online dating.

Our results are consistent with anecdotal evidence suggesting that some people have more time to invest in online dating (those that are not employed full-time) and that the marginal utility of dating increases during economic recession ('people want to go through it together'). Besides, the dating demand increases with the number of potential partners: the latter raises the marginal utility of dating, which can explain why it becomes more attractive to invest in dating.[6]

The next stage consists in studying the nature of the short-run relationship using a VECM. In this representation, short-run fluctuations are represented with the lagged first differences. Any changes in the dependent variables are a function of the level of disequilibrium in the cointegration relationships (measured with the error-correction term, ect):

$$\Delta MEETIC_t = a_{MEETIC} + \sum_{i=1}^{4} b_{i,MEETIC} \Delta MEETIC_{t-i} + \sum_{i=1}^{4} c_{i,MEETIC} \Delta ESI_{t-i}$$
$$+ \sum_{i=1}^{4} d_{i,MEETIC} \Delta invOP_{t-i} + e_{MEETIC} ect_{t-1} + \varepsilon_{1t} \qquad (9.10)$$

$$\Delta invOP_t = a_{MEETIC} + \sum_{i=1}^{4} b_{i,invOP} \Delta MEETIC_{t-i} + \sum_{i=1}^{4} c_{i,invOP} \Delta ESI_{t-i}$$
$$+ \sum_{i=1}^{4} d_{i,invOP} \Delta invOP_{t-i} + e_{invOP} ect_{t-1} + \varepsilon_{2t} \qquad (9.11)$$

$$\Delta ESI_t = a_{ESI} + \sum_{i=1}^{4} b_{i,ESI} \Delta MEETIC_{t-i} + \sum_{i=1}^{4} c_{i,ESI} \Delta ESI_{t-i}$$
$$+ \sum_{i=1}^{4} d_{i,ESI} \Delta invOP_{t-i} + e_{ESI} ect_{t-1} + \varepsilon_{3t}, \qquad (9.12)$$

where ect_{t-1} is the lagged error correction term and the vector e represents the weight or adjustment speed. In other words, it measures how fast the stationary variable ect_{t-1} feeds back into the system. The ε_t are serially independent errors with mean zero and finite covariance matrix.

Table 9.4 presents estimates of the short-run equations (9.10), (9.11) and (9.12). We can observe that the demand for meeting and the fertility rate appear to be the variables that adjust to any disequilibrium from the long-run relation (through the error correction term) in the previous period. Standard Granger-type causality tests can be performed in a VECM. Following Granger (1969), *ESI* causes *invOP* if the prediction of *invOP* is improved when including past values of *ESI*. In the short run, the *t*-test applied to the lag of each explanatory variable in each of the three equations indicates the statistical significance of the short-run causal effects (and the strict Granger exogeneity or endogeneity of the dependent variables).

Here, the variable *ESI* is deemed to cause *invOP* if one or more of the lagged coefficients of *ESI* is statistically different from zero. Our data suggest that this is indeed the case. In other words, when economic agents are optimistic about the economy, the fertility rate tends to increase and the opportunities for dating fall. The other variables appear to be strictly exogenous to each other. Again, this result is robust to other specifications, for instance that including a model with one lag and one cointegration relation.

Table 9.4   VECM estimation results

	D[Log(*MEETIC*)]		D[Log(*invOP*)]		D[Log(*ESI*)]	
	Coef.	*p*-value	Coef.	*p*-value	Coef.	*p*-value
CE	−0.027	0.074	−0.013	0.000***	0.010	0.600
D[Log(*MEETIC*)]						
t − 1	0.010	0.946	−0.009	0.807	0.144	0.441
t − 2	−0.090	0.577	−0.188	0.631	−0.077	0.690
t − 3	0.031	0.847	−0.056	0.158	0.221	0.258
t − 4	0.081	0.625	−0.030	0.458	0.271	0.179
D[Log(*ESI*)]						
t − 1	−0.558	0.404	−0.020	0.901	−0.580	0.474
t − 2	0.594	0.378	0.257	0.121	−0.612	0.452
t − 3	0.358	0.591	0.374	0.022**	−1.010	0.210
t − 4	0.924	0.144	0.174	0.262	−0.097	0.899
D[Log(*invOP*)]						
t − 1	−0.027	0.849	0.018	0.596	−0.027	0.873
t − 2	−0.035	0.790	0.093	0.004***	−0.055	0.729
t − 3	0.009	0.948	0.088	0.013**	0.057	0.744
t − 4	−0.008	0.956	0.034	0.355	0.096	0.599
Intercept	−0.002	0.900	−0.004	0.197	−0.011	0.514
R-squared	0.300		0.4436		0.1474	
Chi-squared	15.854	0.322	29.501	0.009	6.397	0.955

Note: *** Significant at the 1% level; ** significant at the 5% level.

DISCUSSION AND CONCLUDING COMMENTS

With some exceptions, little attention has been paid to the question of time devoted to partner choice. However, recent institutional, technical and social changes have altered the pool of individuals looking for dates, for all ages and at different moments in their lives. It should renew the interest in research on partner choices and the time devoted to it.

Search models, risk-pooling models and expected utility models of arbitrage between working time and leisure focus on different dimensions of choice of the individual. In particular, the first two can explain the different mechanisms that tend to extend the search period and that modify the costs and benefits of marriage (or cohabitation). Rising returns to labour market experience raise the incentive for highly educated women to seek to develop stronger prospects in both the labour and the marriage markets. If individuals view marriage as an insurance against income risks, those who are more risk tolerant will accept a delay in marriage. But clearly, not all people using online services are looking for a life partner. The motivations are therefore very different from the ones just traditionally analysed. To take into account both forms of dating, we use a model where the time has to be allocated between leisure and work. We have chosen to explore this last dimension, which has yet to be explored, by focusing on one growing form of partner search: online dating.

In this work, we sought to understand the relationship, if any, between dating and the business cycle, and more exactly between online dating and the business cycle. Online search offers a larger set of potential partners and anonymity than offline search. Moreover, it is likely to become more attractive in an economic recession as the former appears as a cheaper substitute for the latter.

We relied on a simple microeconomic model of time allocation. Dating was viewed as an additional possible time use, which extended the usual trade-off between leisure and working activities. As in standard models of time allocation, the impact of a change in the individual level of income on dating activities was given by the sum of a substitution effect and an income effect. Hence, in general, we cannot predict the direction of the effect of a change in the economic sentiment on the demand for dating. In simple microeconomic models where workers are supposed to choose their hours, the relationship between time devoted to dating and income should be U-shaped. What should happen then in aggregate under real-world conditions? From our own viewpoint, additional issues should lead to a much more complex, undetermined relationship. In fact, the marginal utility of dating for an individual also depends on the effectiveness of the dating activities, on their risk aversion, on their own risk of income variation and on their desire to pool risk with a mate among other factors.

The economic theory is therefore not able to predict the effect of a recession on the industry of online dating, as we could for a traditional normal good or inferior good. It is therefore interesting to explore this question empirically and to study whether, as reported in newspapers, economic recessions tend to stimulate the online dating industry in aggregate.

For that purpose, we have used monthly observations covering the period from January 2004 to August 2008 on the demand for online dating in France through the MEETIC website, on the economic sentiment (*ESI*) and on a proxy for the rate of missed opportunities of dating (*invOP*) in France through the lagged fertility rate. The results are as follows. The three series are integrated of order one. One relation of cointegration is identified, which can be described as a long-run equilibrium between the three variables. The dating demand is negatively related to both the economic sentiment and the fertility rate. So, during economic downturns, people appear to increase their demand for online dating, which is consistent with anecdotal evidence suggesting that some people have more time to invest in online dating and that the marginal utility of dating increases during economic recession. In conclusion, our empirical tests indicate that for the last recession the demand for online dating increased with the deterioration of the economic sentiment in the long-run trend. But nothing can be said about short-run fluctuations around the equilibrium, regarding the relationship between the economic sentiment and the demand for dating. Our study offers a first investigation of this interesting and puzzling question of the effect of income on the demand for dating. More work is needed on this topic to better understand how income may have an impact on the demand for dating, both theoretically and empirically. It would be worthwhile to collect both macro data in order to predict long-term trends for the dating industry, but also micro data on both users and non-users of these online dating services. This would allow us to shed light on the selection process in online dating and to better understand individual strategies to find a partner through these services. All these issues are of interest for future work.

NOTES

1. These utility functions are supposed to be continuous and twice differentiable.
2. Note that we do not account for the potential income of the spouse in the case of a successful meeting.
3. See: http://www.durex.com/en-sg/sexualwellbeingsurvey/pages/default.aspx.
4. See: http://www.businessweek.com/bwdaily/dnflash/feb2005/nf2005028_4806_db089. htm or for a more recent source: http://www.onlinepersonalswatch.com/files/meetic_res-q309_vfengfinale.pdf.
5. See: http://ec.europa.eu/economy_finance/db_indicators/surveys/documents/userguide_en.pdf.
6. When estimating a model with one lag and one cointegration relation, we reach very similar conclusions.

REFERENCES

Ahuvia, A. and M. Adelman (1992), 'Formal intermediaries in the marriage market: a typology and review', *Journal of Marriage and the Family*, **54**, 452–63.

Batabyal, A.A. (2001), 'On the likelihood of finding the right partner in an arranged marriage', *Journal of Socio-Economics*, **33**, 273–80.

Becker, G.S. (1973), 'A theory of marriage: part one', *Journal of Political Economy*, **81** (4), 813–46.

Becker, G.S. (1974), 'A theory of marriage: part two', *Journal of Political Economy*, **82** (2), S11–S26.

Becker, G.S. (1981), *A Treatise on the Family*, Cambridge, MA: Harvard University Press.

Cameron, S. and A. Collins (1997), 'Estimates of a hedonic ageing equation for partner search', *Kyklos*, **40** (3), 409–18.

Cameron, S. and A. Collins (1999), 'Looks unimportant? A demand function for male attractiveness by female personal advertisers', *Applied Economics Letters*, **6**, 381–4.

Cameron, S. and A. Collins (2000a), 'Random utility maximizer seeks similar: an economic analysis of commitment level in personal relationships', *Journal of Economic Psychology*, **21**, 73–90.

Cameron, S. and A. Collins (2000b), *Playing the Love Market: Dating, Romance and the Real World*, London: Free Association Books.

Cameron, S. and N. Vaillant (2006), 'A goods characteristics model of the hedonic ageing equation: evidence from a French marriage bureau', *Brussels Economic Review*, **48** (4), 341–54.

Carroll, C.D., J.C. Fuhrer and D.W. Wilcox (1994), 'Does consumer sentiment forecast household spending? If so, why?', *American Economic Review*, **84**, 1397–408.

Caucutt, E., N. Guner and J. Knowles (2002), 'Why do women wait? Matching, wage, inequalities, and the incentives for fertility delay', *Review of Economic Dynamics*, **5** (4), 815–55.

Dickey, D.A. and W.A. Fuller (1979), 'Distribution of the estimators for autoregressive time series with a unit root', *Journal of the American Statistical Association*, **74**, 427–31.

Ellin, A. (2009), 'The recession. Isn't it romantic?', *The New York Times*, 11 February, available at: http://www.nytimes.com/2009/02/12/fashion/12dating.html, last accessed 24 May 2011.

Engle, R.F. and C.W. Granger (1987), 'Cointegration and error correction: representation, estimation and testing', *Econometrica*, **55**, 251–76.

Fisman, R., S. Iyengar, E. Kamenica and I. Simonson (2006), 'Gender differences in mate selection: evidence from a speed dating experiment', *Quarterly Journal of Economics*, **121**, 673–97.

Fisman, R., S. Iyengar, E. Kamenica and I. Simonson (2008), 'Racial preferences in dating', *Review of Economic Studies*, **75**, 117–32.

Foa, U.G. and E.B. Foa (1974), *Societal Structures of the Mind*, Springfield, IL: Charles C. Thomas.

Geoffard, P.Y. and S. Méchoulan (2004), 'Comportements sexuels risqués et incitations: l'impact des nouveaux traitements sur la prévention du VIH', *Revue économique*, **55** (5), 883–900.

Gould, E. and D. Paserman (2003), 'Waiting for Mr Right: rising inequality and declining marriage rates', *Journal of Urban Economics*, **53** (2), 257–81.

Granger, C. (1969), 'Investigating causal relations by econometric models and cross-spectral methods', *Econometrica*, **37**, 424–38.

Gronau, R. (1977), 'Leisure, home production and work – the theory of the allocation of time revisited', *Journal of Political Economy*, **85** (6), 1099–124.

Grossbard-Shechtman, S. (1995), 'Marriage market models', in M. Tomassi and K. Ierulli (eds), *The New Economics of Human Behavior*, Cambridge: Cambridge University Press, pp. 99–112.

Grossbard-Shechtman, S. (2003), 'A consumer theory with competitive markets for work in marriage', *Journal of Socio-Economics*, **31**, 609–45.

Hirschman, E. (1987), 'People as products: analysis of a complex marketing exchange', *Journal of Marketing*, **51**, 98–108.

Johansen, S. (1988), 'Statistical analysis of cointegrating vectors', *Journal of Economic Dynamics and Control*, **12**, 231–54.

Johansen, S. and K. Juselius (1990), 'Maximum likelihood estimation and inference on cointegration – with applications to the demand for money', *Oxford Bulletin for Economics and Statistics*, **52**, 169–210.

Lancaster, K. (1966), 'A new approach to consumer theory', *Journal of Political Economy*, **74** (2), 132–57.

Le Guirriec, G. and N. Vaillant (2005), 'From libertinism to marital commitment: an economic analysis of the marital research's differentiated objectives', *Journal of BioEconomics*, **7** (1), 84–95.

Levy, S. and G. Zaltman (1975), *Marketing Society and Conflict*, Englewood Cliffs, NJ: Prentice-Hall.

Ludvigson, S. (2004), 'Consumer confidence and consumer spending', *Journal of Economic Perspectives*, **18**, 29–50.

Phillips, P.C. and P. Perron (1988), 'Testing for a unit root in time series regressions', *Biometrika*, **75**, 335–46.

Quah, E. (1990), 'Optimal search, matchmaking and the factors affecting age at first marriage', *Indian Economic Journal*, **37** (4), 74–80.

Sims, C. (1980), 'Macroeconomics and Reality', *Econometrica*, **48**, 1–48.

Stevenson, B. and J. Wolfers (2007), 'Marriage and divorce: changes and their driving forces', *Journal of Economic Perspectives*, **21** (2), 27–52.

Vaillant, N.G. (2004a), 'Estimating the time elapsed between ending a relationship and joining a matchmaking agency: evidence from a French marriage bureau', *Journal of Economic Psychology*, **25** (6), 789–802.

Vaillant, N.G. (2004b), 'Discrimination in matchmaking: evidence from a French marriage bureau', *Applied Economics*, **36** (7), 723–9.

10 Home improvements
Peter E. Earl and Ti-Ching Peng

INTRODUCTION

Home improvement activities tend to be seen by government statisticians as a form of production, not as part of leisure. However, a recurrent theme in ethnographic work on do-it-yourself (DIY) activities (for example, Shove et al., 2007; Watson and Shove, 2008) is the satisfaction people get from self-expression arising from all the hard work that goes into upgrading their homes. The amount of time people spend on home improvement activities is difficult to determine because surveys of time use tend to include this area within, for example, 'repairs and gardening' (Lader et al., 2006) or 'core non-market work' (Aguiar and Hurst, 2007). It is tempting to infer that declining hours spent by men in market-based work have, to some degree, been offset by increased time spent on home improvements, thus contributing to the sense of 'harried leisure' in modern society identified by Linder (1970). Impressions of women spending more time in home improvement activities would be difficult to confirm from US data, since the pattern is for sharply deceasing time in non-market work as women have increasingly taken paid work (Aguiar and Hurst, 2007, p. 976). What is clear, however, is that expenditure on repairs and home improvements represents a major growth area that, by 2002, was approaching $200 billion annually in the US (Baker and Kaul, 2002), with the UK DIY industry worth over £20 billion annually by 2004 (Williams, 2008, p. 312). Associated with this has been the increasing dominance of the retailing of home improvement products by 'big box' warehousing chains such as Home Depot in North America, B&Q in the UK and Bunnings Warehouses in Australia (see Hernandez, 2003, for a case study of the changing face of DIY retailing in Canada). Although home improvement choices have been studied even in countries with low per capita incomes, such as Vietnam (see Phe, 2002), big box DIY retailing may not suit such economies. For example, Home Depot's 1998 attempt to expand into Chile was a dismal failure and the firm exited after three years (Bianchi and Arnold, 2004).

The economic significance of home improvement activities goes well beyond their opportunity costs in time for other leisure activities and their contribution to aggregate demand. Work that results in bigger homes and/or higher-quality accommodation also has significance in areas such as:

- *The measurement of rates of inflation* Rises in median house prices may to some degree reflect rising housing quality or house sizes brought about by home improvements (Leventis, 2007).
- *Greenhouse gas emissions* The long-lived nature of residential properties and the small annual increment from the construction of new homes means that improvements in average energy efficiency largely depend on improvements to existing homes (Lane et al., 2008).
- *The costs of ensuring the welfare of an ageing population* Regular investment is required to keep housing in good functional order and thereby increase the prospects for elderly people to avoid the need to move into care homes. Policies aimed at facilitating home improvements by the elderly may thus have major payoffs via reduced social welfare expenditure (Tinker, 1998; Saville-Smith et al., 2008).
- *Homelessness* Gentrification of inner city areas may contribute to a growth in the number of homeless people by driving up property values in these areas, displacing those who relied on access to cheap, low-quality rental accommodation (see the study of this issue in Washington, DC, by Williams, 1996).

This focus of this chapter, however, is on the challenges that home improvement activities present to consumers, what drives their behaviour and how they make their choices about what improvements to make and how to get them done. It is probably helpful to begin by considering the range of meanings embraced by the term 'home improvements'.

WHAT DO WE MEAN BY 'HOME IMPROVEMENTS'?

This chapter takes a very broad view of the term 'home improvements'. Table 10.1 is a taxonomy showing the range of activities it encompasses. Many of these activities are commonly referred to by the term 'renovation', but the latter can sometimes have a much narrower formal definition. For example, the Australian Bureau of Statistics (2002) defines renovations as including alterations and additions (taken to mean those changes to the structure or footprint of a property for which local authority planning consent is required) but excludes repairs and maintenance even though these excluded categories involve similar capabilities and types of inputs.

Table 10.1   Taxonomy of home improvement activities

Type of activity	Examples
Rehabilitation of derelict residence	Turning a ruined farmhouse in another country into a holiday home
Conversion of non-residential building to residence	Barn or warehouse conversion
Conversion of existing single residence to multiple residence, or vice versa	Apartment conversion Granny flat
Creating new living space within existing structure or changing functions of existing spaces	Loft conversion Conversion of integral garage into a study, an additional bedroom or family room Media room/home theatre
Changing internal floor plan	'Knocking through' to make one room from two Adding an en-suite bathroom
Major structural additions	Extension to offer extra bedroom Patio or conservatory Carport or garage
Changes to built-in equipment and facilities	Kitchen or bathroom makeovers Remove open fire and install central heating system
Cosmetic changes	Interior redecoration Stucco rendering to exterior or other change of siding material
Repairs and maintenance	Fixing cracked walls or floors Rewiring Replacement of clay sewerage pipes by PVC pipes Replacement of rotting floors or joinery in dampness-prone areas Restumping a timber house

MOTIVATIONS FOR UNDERTAKING HOME IMPROVEMENT ACTIVITIES

When attempting to understand what drives home improvements, an obvious economic starting-point is to contrast investment-related motives with 'nest-building' consumption-related activities, as in the work of Munro and Leather (2000), who emphasize the importance of the latter. However, these activities can be seen in a more fine-grained way as means to a larger variety of ends, some of which can be served simultaneously by a single project:

1. *Enhance the market value of the property or its potential rental yield*   A better set of characteristics may enable a property to command a higher price. However, making improvements purely to achieve an investment return requires that the person undertaking them has a different set of opportunity costs from buyers as regards alternatives to working on home improvements or incurring transaction costs of outsourcing work, and willingness to incur dislocation costs associated with the work. Improvements in market value may also arise indirectly via network externalities associated with conforming to the standards being set by neighbouring homes or prompting neighbours to improve their homes (Park, 2008). Such considerations have underpinned public policies aimed at raising the average quality of housing by promoting home improvement activities, for example via the provision of improvement grants. However, such policies are frequently confounded by the willingness of homeowners to continue to put up with properties that are in a poor state of repair unless they can use the policy measures to satisfy other motivations (Munro and Leather, 2000). Such behaviour may not merely reflect factors such as dislocation costs that policy makers had not brought into their calculations. They may also, according to Stewart (2003), reflect an environment in which house prices seem to rise even for homes in poor condition, leading homeowners to underestimate the additional value that improvements might generate.

2. *Increase the property's marketability*   This is a variant on the previous point, focused on scope for increasing the probability of finding a buyer within a particular period if it is put on the market at a particular price (see Earl, 1995, pp. 274–6). Two distinct kinds of improvement may be necessary to achieve this, though both are related to the problems of bounded rationality faced by prospective buyers. To simplify the choice process, buyers may use non-trade-off checklist-based decision rules to draw up a shortlist of properties to inspect (Earl, 1986, Ch. 7) in contrast to the picture offered by Lancaster's (1966) model of choice among rival characteristics bundles. A single failing could thus cause a property to be 'ruled out'. Improvements aimed at diffusing buyers' potential objections and encouraging them to take a serious look at the property may necessitate quite major investments, such as adding an en-suite bathroom to the master bedroom to ensure that a large 30-year-old house matches the list of features offered by much newer 'executive homes'. Much less costly are improvements that will help the property make a good 'first impression' if viewed on-site by the prospective buyer (Fortes and McCarthy, 2009).

Table 10.2   Lifestyle-related home improvements

Lifestyle goal	Example of means to achieving goal
Enhance comfort, security and health	Install new heating system or air conditioning
	Replace carpets with timber-style floor coverings to reduce allergy problems
	Install/replace security doors and screens
Reduce environmental burden	Double-glazing
	Cavity wall insulation
	New shower heads and dual-flush toilets
	New light fittings
Improve ergonomic functionality	Replace step-up-and-in shower with walk-in shower
	Change kitchen layout and design of storage systems
Enhance aesthetic and tactile appeal	Modernize exterior by rendering brickwork or adding new siding material
	Change in colour scheme for décor
	Replace curtains with blinds
	Change from laminated to granite bench-tops
Maintain fit with changing family requirements	Add extension to accommodate growing family
	Remodel part of house into a 'granny flat'

3. *Enable the homeowner to meet new or existing lifestyle aspirations more cheaply than by selling up and buying an alternative property*   Table 10.2 gives some examples of how home improvements can help home-owners meet such goals. Moving may be a less cost-effective strategy either because of significant transaction costs or because available alternative properties that meet their requirements offer more than what they require in some respects and carry corresponding price pre-miums. Though some acts of home improvement are a consequence of changing domestic circumstances, such as having more children, that disturb an existing match between the household and the property, it would be a mistake to assume that the homebuyer achieves equilib-rium at the time of purchasing a property. It is common for proper-ties to be bought with an intention to embark on improvements after moving in because buyers could find nothing that was exactly what they wanted (Seek, 1983; Littlewood and Munro, 1997).

4. *Enable the homeowner to enjoy enhanced social standing*   That is, the improvements are a form of conspicuous consumption or a means of living up to expectations that society has evolved for how people in particular social roles should live.

5. *Meet psychological goals via the process of achieving the improve-ment*   Scitovsky (1981), for example, includes renovation activities as

a means towards satisfying a desire for excitement that arises where comfortable affluent lifestyles do not generate enough novel stimuli. In a related vein, Shove et al. (2007) report that, for example, kitchen upgrades can serve as an antidote to the alienation caused by the grinding routine of everyday life as they enable even council-house occupants to put their own stamp on their domestic environment. Likewise, Chaplin (1999) shows how the effort involving in upgrading a cheap holiday home in France is seen by some as a way to escape from the pressures and routine of life in Britain. In addition to being an antidote to boredom, home improvements also provide opportunities for people to test hypotheses about their capabilities or the possibility of turning their current residence into their dream home (Kelly, 1955; Earl, 1986; Watson and Shove, 2008).

It might be expected that heritage preservation is a motivating factor when owner-occupiers spend on improving listed buildings. However, Hills and Worthing (2006) found that owners of such buildings invested in maintaining them to avoid discomfort and costs of allowing further deterioration and to get the satisfaction that went with keeping them in 'good order', rather than for cultural reasons.

TO IMPROVE OR NOT?

The existence of wants or needs for home improvements does not guarantee that they will be undertaken, except in cases of emergency repairs such as dealing with burst pipes. This is largely an area of discretionary expenditure in which the assumptions of given tastes and rationality are not particularly apt. Although changing household needs often drive home improvements, Baker and Kaul (2002) also show the importance of recent experience, implying that consumers develop tastes for making improvements, while Bendimerad (2005) finds that age and generation (baby boomer, X, Y) both help explain differences in the propensity to make home improvements. Since older people and those who have been living in a property for a long time are less likely to be focused on making capital gains by moving on, they are generally less likely to do repair work, being less concerned with making capital gains (Littlewood and Munro, 1996). Neglect of properties may be associated with self-neglect (McDermott et al., 2009), as where elderly people with pathological hoarding tendencies live in increasingly cluttered squalid conditions that make rooms very difficult to clear before work can begin.

Cognitive processes may also prevent consumers from seeing the need to make improvements that expert observers may see as rational. For example, Gram-Hanssen et al.'s (2007) study of responses to energy labels reveals that consumers often fail to make rational home improvement choices in response to them because they are prone to question expert knowledge rather than simply 'take it in'. In some cases, people with plenty of spare time, such as those in retirement, opt to allow their homes to suffer serious decay even though they would not find it financially challenging to address the problems and restore their quality of life. Rather than addressing the problems, they may simply deny their existence, or underestimate their scale, as with the case of many elderly New Zealanders in the study by Saville-Smith et al. (2008). They block information to avoid cognitive dissonance (see Akerlof and Dickens, 1982; Earl and Wicklund, 1999) if friends and family attempt to demonstrate the absurdity of the situation.

From the standpoint of psychological economics this is easy to understand. Although it might appear to a mainstream economist that a householder is irrationally delaying dealing 'merely' with, say, dysfunctional plumbing, loose tiles, rotting timber or flaking paintwork, the situation is actually one of high 'involvement' that has implications for the core of the householder's self (see Earl, 1986; Laaksonen, 1994):

- Consumers may suffer anxieties about their competence in DIY activities. Prior experiences are crucial here: as Watson and Shove (2008, p. 86) conclude, 'each project and each task of which each project is made is of consequence for the development of competence, skill or disillusionment, and so for the formulation, or otherwise, of new projects'.
- Anxiety may also be due to a lack of familiarity with relevant products and suppliers and perception that one lacks good decision rules for avoiding ending up dealing with 'cowboy' builders (see Holt and Edwards, 2005) (with knowledge getting more out of date the longer the work is postponed).
- Consumers may be concerned about how disruptive the work will be to established routines and about the trustworthiness of contractors.
- It may even be the case that some householders have phobias about interacting with tradespeople over the telephone to arrange for them to visit to give quotations, or feel concerned about how they will deal with tradespeople whose quotations they reject or whose work does not meet their expectations. Signs that there may be gender-based anxiety in this respect, due to male tradespeople treating men and women very differently as clients, might be inferred from the emergence of directories of female tradespeople.

In other words, self-confidence is a prerequisite for embarking on home improvements. Consistent with this, Peng (2009) found that although the likelihood of renovation was affected by fundamental factors such as the age of the property and household demographics, predictions were considerably improved by adding a psychological variable based on subjects' own ratings of themselves as renovators.

From the standpoint of conventional economics, deferral of home improvements has to be explained rather differently. One possibility is that it makes strategic sense: the initial empirical work by economists on renovation did not focus on its place in leisure choices but on choices made by owners of rental properties regarding whether or not to let them decay, thus saving renovation costs but reducing potential rental earnings (for example, see Arnott et al., 1983; Spivack, 1991).

Somewhere between the anxiety-based and rational neglect perspectives on failures to make home improvements comes an interpretation, via the work of Akerlof (1991) and O'Donoghue and Rabin (1999), of procrastination associated with time-inconsistent preferences. Such preferences may arise due to people discounting the future hyperbolically rather than exponentially and thereby giving undue weight to immediate costs (or benefits) versus longer-term benefits (or costs). People who behave as if they are discounting in this way will tend to postpone an action until tomorrow without realizing that when tomorrow comes they will delay the action yet again.

The likelihood of procrastination is increased by the fact that decay that necessitates repairs or replacement of the fabric, fixtures or fittings of a home is something that householders typically cannot address continuously. Some may try to keep their properties looking new by continually cleaning and polishing, but fixed costs and indivisibilities force even the more obsessively houseproud to tolerate the slide into entropy for significant periods. Redecorating a room, for example, involves fixed costs of acquiring materials and getting ready to deploy them without making a mess. Although some areas may be more prone to suffer from damage via the sun or from scuffing in everyday use, it is often necessary to repaint entire walls or the entire room in order to ensure that colours end up being consistent. The issue of consistency may also arise with fittings that come in sets whose parts wear out at different rates: for example, when one element in a set of matching bathroom fittings ceases to work properly or breaks, it may be impossible to buy a replacement on its own, not merely due to strategic behaviour by suppliers but because the service life of the products is long and the design in question is no longer in production.

Barriers to continuous upkeep of a home may mean, however, that the timing of restoration work is decided in ways that differ from what one would expect from conventional economics. If consistency in appearance is an issue for the householder but decay takes place at different rates in different areas, then restoration costs will be increased by the need to work both on the parts whose decay is a source of dissatisfaction and on other parts that, considered in isolation, would not need attention at the moment. The costs of maintaining consistency increase the costs of dealing with the immediate source of dissatisfaction and therefore will tend to delay remedial action. In the interim, members of the household may go through long periods of, for example, putting up with taps that initially can still be turned off fully with a big effort but eventually start to drip with increased rapidity no matter what one does. The eventual choice to put up with the situation no longer is likely to involve breaching a threshold of tolerance of some kind – a psychological discontinuity – rather than something in keeping with standard marginalist economic thinking. In other words, this seems an area that can be framed in terms of Simon's (1955) 'satisficing' view of choice.

SHOPPING FOR IDEAS AND INPUTS

Even for those who do not engage in DIY at the stage of executing their renovation projects, considerable leisure time can be consumed working out which renovation projects should be embarked upon, designing the end result and shopping for inputs of goods and services. While mainstream economists would tend to presume that people have pre-existing preferences in characteristics space, the reality is probably that most people may only have strong renovation preferences in some limited sense (for example, a visceral sense of the ghastly when they see it). Otherwise, their preferences are largely shaped socially or with the aid of what Earl and Potts (2004) call the 'market for preferences' in conjunction with the kind of 'market institutions' to which Hodgson (1988) has drawn attention. Watching renovation programmes on television, reading home renovation magazines and visits from design consultants are all means for the would-be renovators to size up what is possible and desirable from home. Similar roles can be played by trips to external market institutions such as bathroom centres, tiling and floor-covering stores and hardware supermarkets (often conveniently grouped as small 'Marshallian business districts') along with periodic 'home-show' exhibitions or visits to display homes in new housing developments.

There is certainly no shortage of inspiration via television: in a typical week, Halliday (2005) counted 16.5 hours of shows on terrestrial stations in the UK focusing on home improvements, particularly as a means of adding value to one's property. Such programming may seem a contemporary craze but it actually began with the BBC screening programmes hosted by DIY expert Barry Bucknell (1912–2003) in the 1950s, many of which were aired live with all the hazards that this entailed. This was followed by a 39-episode series, 'Bucknell's House' in 1962 in which he renovated an entire run-down property in Ealing, London. This series kick-started the modern DIY industry in the UK (Milmo, 2003): millions watched it and many viewers sought to emulate Bucknell's achievements. Bucknell's preferred style, with its straight edges and lack of ornamentation, could be described as 'modernist', a preference that continues to be evident in current home makeover programmes despite consumers from differing social backgrounds having a much wider range of visions of how their dream home should look. By including ordinary consumers, these programmes are supposedly suggesting a democratizing of taste (something that DIY has also been argued to facilitate: see Atkinson, 2006). However, sociologists see them as preaching that modernism is the style that the masses should pursue (see the Bourdieu-inspired analysis by Philips, 2005, and Silva and Wright, 2009), while Halliday (2005, p. 73) sees them as denigrating feminine taste through their focus on functional, less-is-more design, not decoration and ornamentation.

The outsourcing of preferences can produce sharp divisions about what kinds of home improvements display good taste. In his book *Rubbish Theory*, Thompson (1979) draws on his own experiences in the renovation sector in London in the 1970s, and contrasts the behaviour of two groups with sharply differing world-views. One consists of upward-aspiring working-class renovators (whom he calls the 'Ron-and-Cliffs') who focus on trying to make their houses look newer than they are. The other group consists of members of *The Guardian*-reading chattering classes (whom he calls the 'Knockers-Through') who set out to gentrify properties by making them look more 'original' as they attempt also to make them suit better their functional requirements.

In seeking to undo what they see as the damage done by previous owners who had 'modernized' in a crass and tasteless manner, the Knockers-Through were keen to lay their hands on the panelled wooden doors and old fireplaces being discarded by the Ron-and-Cliffs as the latter install aluminium joinery and central heating. Much of this 'damage' was probably done a decade or so earlier by fans of Barry Bucknell. Gyrating preferences – which Thompson tries to model using graphical techniques from catastrophe theory – are similarly evident with bathroom surfaces: white tiles, basins and toilets were in the 1970s portrayed as fit only for institutional environments and were hence replaced by coloured tiles and ceramic bathroom suites, whereas nowadays clinical white is seen as classy.

The challenges that home improvement-related shopping presents are particularly evident when seen in terms of the search good, experience good and credence good distinction associated with the work of Nelson (1970) and Darby and Karni (1973). Because home improvements are specific to a particular residence and involve creating a system of related elements, it is often hard to be sure what the end result will look like before a financial commitment is made. To some extent, computers enable improvement choices to fall more readily into the 'search good' category: for example, the digital photography revolution has made it possible to see how a room will look in particular colour schemes simply by taking a photograph of it and then editing the colours on one's computer, while interior and exterior design consultants can provide 3-D simulations of new kitchens, patios and suchlike. Retailers can help to reduce risks by supplying test-pots of paint, providing classes for those who know their skills are limited, and offering no-quibble refunds for mistakenly purchased items that are returned in as-new condition (for example, fittings that turned out to look wrong or would not fit). Otherwise, though, this is the territory of experience goods, where the end result can only be judged after the work has been done, or credence goods, where customers may have residual doubts, even after the work has been completed, about what was actually done or whether work done because a tradesperson advised that it was necessary really was needed.

Concerns about quality will vary depending on whether the goal is to keep living in the property in the long term or whether the plan is to sell the property soon after home improvements have been done. If the latter is the plan, there is an incentive (moral compunction aside) to skimp on work that might make sense in the long run and to use quick-fix strategies and cheaper, less durable materials. This is an obvious place to apply the 'lemons' analysis proposed by Akerlof (1970): the buyer will find it difficult to judge whether, say, paint has been chosen for its long-lasting qualities in the absence of any evidence on this score. Likewise, even if a building inspection report is purchased, the buyer may still be left uncertain about what work has been done behind new surface finishes, since the inspector can only find out by removing these surfaces. Buyers will tend to presume the worst in cases where a property shows signs of having recently been spruced up and their guesses are likely to be right: such guesses mean that an investment in doing the job really well is unlikely to pay off via a correspondingly higher price (see further Iwata and Yamaga, 2007).

In the face of uncertainty and inexperience, the retailer's advice can be sought. If there is scope for finding out eventually whether the advice was worth having (that is, if the product is not inherently a credence good), then the retailer will have an incentive to ensure that staff provide appropriate advice in order not to jeopardize future sales of other renovation products to the customer. From the standpoint of Klein and Leffler's (1981) analysis of the economics of brands, we should not be surprised to find that hardware stores are increasingly likely to be members of large chains or franchise networks: not only does this give purchasing and advertising economies, it also increases the incentive of the chain to make sure its staff do not give misleading advice or other forms of poor service, for poor performance in one store may have repercussions across the wider network. (Network arrangements also permit leaner stock levels for each store in so far as a branch that is out of stock of a required item can 'helpfully' check with a near neighbour to see whether it is available there and, if it is, advise the customer how to get there.)

Where work is outsourced, institutional components of the markets in question may be predicted to guide choices: businesses that have been around for a long time and are members of relevant trade associations will tend to be favoured over those in the Yellow Pages that are not, while suppliers will seek to allay fears about the quality of the end product by proffering evidence of work done satisfactorily for previous customers. In a large city, many potential suppliers may be signalling their trustworthiness via institutional cues, so a considerable investment of leisure time is necessary if a thorough search for the best-looking deal is to be conducted. This seems likely to be the kind of situation in which search is truncated via the use of simple search rules such as 'get three quotations and choose the cheapest'.

DIY VERSUS OUTSOURCING

Just as preferences for home improvements may be outsourced or personally developed, the actual work involved in turning visions into reality can be outsourced or achieved via DIY. For those who would rather use their leisure time in other activities and economize on transaction costs, there are firms that offer complete package deals that include the design stage and project management of all the tradespeople necessary to bring the project to fruition. It is also possible to employ mixed strategies, choosing to get contractors in for some tasks and doing others personally, while some employ informal outsourcing among their social networks (Adriaenssens and Hendrickx, 2009). In discussing how such choices are made, we proceed *as if* the nature of the home improvement has already been chosen, as per the structure of the chapter so far. However, it should be noted that in some cases, it is actually the desire to engage in DIY and possession of particular DIY tools and skills that shapes the choice of which home improvements to make, rather than the project choice preceding the choice of strategy for executing it (Watson and Shove, 2008, p. 82).

Davidson and Leather (2000) provide a useful study of DIY activities in the UK that draws on data from the Family Expenditure Survey and the English Housing Conditions Survey. They report (p. 748) that, in the UK in 1991, the proportion of work undertaken by DIY was only 15 per cent for major structural improvements but as much as 60 per cent for more cosmetic changes. Although those who engage in DIY can get much more work done for a given financial outlay at the cost of forgoing leisure time from other activities, it is the poor and those with more time available who seem to do less DIY (p. 751). Recent work by Williams (2008) reveals a more complex picture. In his sample, more-affluent households were both more likely to outsource tasks of a routine and mundane kind and tended to undertake a much larger number of DIY tasks. He also identifies two kinds of consumers engaging in DIY: those who embraced it enthusiastically and those who did so only reluctantly.

Although some home improvement work is restricted to licensed tradespeople for health and safety reasons, potential to engage in DIY has increased greatly in the last half a century due to technological progress and changing distribution strategies in the hardware sector. For example, Home Depot sets out to be an unintimidating source of DIY knowledge that removes the separation between 'trade' and public customers (Melchionne, 1999). As already noted, another major factor in opening up DIY as a leisure activity was the advent, half a century ago, of television programmes that sought to share professional skills with viewers. Modern home improvement programmes serve less well as means of learning DIY, for they focus more on design than execution and feature ordinary people. Indeed, as Halliday (2005, p. 66) observes, the message of *DIY SOS* is *don't* DIY, via 'images of failed masculinity, rescued by a heroic team of tradespeople'.

To understand how these choices about the division of labour are made, it is instructive to apply theories of vertical integration from the industrial organization literature. Contrasting perspectives emerge via the ideas of Williamson (1985) and Richardson (1972), with the former redolent of the sentiments of the 'Reluctant DIYers' and the latter more in line with the perspectives of the 'Willing DIYers' identified by Williams (2008).

Williamson's perspective is commonly known as the 'transaction cost' approach to vertical integration because it focuses on the costs of achieving reliable results by transacting with other parties. He contends that market transactions are likely to run into difficulties – and hence be avoided in favour of a strategy of internalization (that is, DIY) – if four conditions are present, namely, bounded rationality, opportunism, small numbers of potential trading partners, and asset specificity. Bounded rationality makes it difficult to specify contracts that cover all possible contingencies without any ambiguity. This would not be a problem if parties to a transaction could be presumed to act in good faith and be willing to cooperate in the event of a difficulty once the contract has been signed. However, if one party has a personal interest in misrepresenting the situation and acts in a guileful manner – that is, with opportunism – then it may prove impossible for the other party to get that for which they thought they had bargained. An opportunistic contractor may be able to stage a 'hold-up', threatening not to implement his/her side of the bargain unless the other party agrees to offer a better deal. But opportunism is unlikely if the other party can readily fire an opportunistic contractor and make a deal with someone else. Even if there is a 'small numbers' problem, an aggrieved party may still be able to get out of the difficulty without loss so long as there is nothing to prevent that party from making other uses of what their money has so far bought in relation to the project. The trouble is, many contracts involve inputs that cannot readily be used in other projects. If all four conditions hold, either or both potential trading partners may judge that it is too dangerous to enter into a contract. Fear that a contract may prove unworkable and an expensive mistake will prompt them to engage in DIY.

Home improvements that involve experience goods or credence goods have considerable potential to run into these kinds of difficulties. Bounded rationality is an inherent problem where tradespeople know more than their clients do about the job at hand, and where projects involve the need to coordinate multiple activities in a particular sequence and/or work that goes beneath the surface of what is visible at the time quotations are being prepared. It is common for renovators to face disruptions due to the non-arrival of materials or tradespeople, or to be told by tradespeople that extra work has been found to be necessary. Delays will impose significant costs on the renovating household if they involve major disruption to everyday life, as with parts of the property being uninhabitable or the kitchen or bathroom being unusable. Suggestions about the need for extra work may have to be dealt with in a state of duress: while it may be work that is genuinely needed but which was not foreseen due to the problem area not being revealed until an old structure was removed, the customer may have trouble judging whether this is so. To try to resolve the credence good problem by seeking a second opinion may not only involve further expense but also be a source of further delays and sour relations with the existing contractor who has suggested that the extra work is necessary.

Risks of opportunism vary depending on context and can arise on either side of a home improvement contract. The client can fail to pay in a timely manner for work that has been done, and may have an incentive to do so if there is no likelihood of needing to hire the same contractor again. However, contractors can require instalment payments as the work proceeds as a means of reducing risks and improving the cash flow of their businesses. In a small community, word-of-mouth reports of bad experiences with particular contractors can have major repercussions for a contractor and serve as a deterrent to opportunism. In a large city, by contrast, the risks of the bulk of the population hearing of a contractor's poor performance are much smaller so there will be more temptation for contractors to behave in an opportunistic manner and greater nervousness among renovators about outsourcing the work.

The enormous choice of tradespeople in the Yellow Pages for a large urban area might seem to imply that renovators can fire unsatisfactory contractors much more readily there than in smaller, isolated communities and hence that, in fact, they have no need to be more concerned about the risk of opportunistic behaviour in the former case. This is not necessarily so: quite apart from the credence good issue (if it is present), a large number of potential suppliers is not the same thing as a large number of potential suppliers who can be hired at short notice if a contractor is fired. Chronic shortages of tradespeople such as plumbers and tilers can co-exist with large numbers of practising suppliers of such services. Where such shortages prevail, tradespeople may become more prone to depart from promised schedules or standards of work due to succumbing to temptations to concentrate their attention on more lucrative contracts with other customers. Premium prices could be asked by some firms in order to ensure that they will not be swamped with work and are able to deliver what they promise. However, there is no guarantee that customers who are concerned with hold-up risks will judge that price differentials provide reliable signals in this respect if their search processes have led them to infer (for example, via difficulties in getting tradespeople even to come and supply a quotation) that there is a major shortage of capacity in this line of business.

Asset specificity is normally discussed in relation to tooling, but in the context of home improvements it is less likely to be a problem in this respect: tools can be used on other jobs and specialized tools of high value are often available on a rental basis. Instead, asset specificity arises here with materials such as paint, piping, building boards and timber, or fixtures and fittings that have already been used in the project in question. For example, once tiles have been cut and fitted, it is difficult to remove and use them in another property if there is a dispute between a renovator and a tiler due to the former changing his/her mind about what to fit or complaining that the latter has not fitted them as per the renovator's instructions.

From Williamson's standpoint, it is easy to see why those making home improvements may prefer to engage in DIY: to get the work done as they wish, and without undue delay, the solution is to take control and limit reliance on contractors. A lack of trust in contractors may thus not only help explain why some people shy away from functionally necessary improvements but also why those who do decide to undertake home improvements opt for DIY even if they are short of leisure time and could afford to pay for contractors (see the discussion of 'rogue builders' in Holt and Edwards, 2005).

Williamson's perspective is called into question by the work of Richardson (1972), who focuses on differences in capabilities as the basis for the division of labour and organization of industry. While outsourcing puts the client at risk of being let down or exploited by contractors, it is a way of reducing the risks of personal injury associated with home improvements and the risks of the work being done poorly, more slowly and with greater waste due to the shortcomings of the renovator's set of skills. The physical risks are not trivial: according to Monash University's Victorian Injury Surveillance Unit, in the state of Victoria in Australia there are 15 renovation-related deaths each year and more than 500 hospital admissions, and a third of eye injuries are related to DIY activities (Hoffman, 2006).

Even if one member of a household is perfectly prepared to shoulder such risks, pressure from a concerned spouse may dictate that the work is handed over to professionals. Although DIY may indeed be an exciting pastime, work that looks overly challenging may be outsourced despite concern about the kinds of risks evident from Williamson's standpoint: even if the contractor acts with opportunism, the end result may be more cost-effective than that achieved via DIY.

So far, the only attempt to model the relative explanatory power of these two views of the DIY/outsourcing choice is that of Peng (2009), where 'the time spent on preparation' is used as a proxy for the scope of a renovation project and hence for its potential to run into complications that contractors could seek to exploit in an opportunistic manner. This factor – which could also be seen as a proxy for the presence of a small numbers problem if preparation time is a function of the difficulty of getting tradespeople to come and give quotations – had a significant *negative* influence on the likelihood of DIY renovation, the opposite of what Williamson's theory implies. This result is, however, consistent with the capabilities perspective from Richardson's analysis as it suggests that renovators are less likely to use DIY when the scope of the project – which will determine the tasks/capabilities involved – is too large for them to handle. Renovation experience was also found to be significant in choices between DIY and outsourcing: what counted were the types, rather than the number, of renovation experiences. That is, those with more experience in hiring others tend to follow the same path in their latest renovation and similarly for those who renovated by DIY: those who began with DIY would thus be likely to get more capable at DIY and be even more likely to continue with this strategy, whereas those who outsourced work would have opportunities to get better at choosing and managing contractors. However, although the scope of renovation projects was associated with choices at odds with Williamson's analysis, the finding that renovators who reported lower 'trust in contractors' had a bigger probability of DIY in their latest renovation projects reinforces his broader message about the significance of potential for opportunism in shaping choices between internalization and outsourcing.

OVERCAPITALIZATION AND COST OVER-RUNS

From the standpoint of rational choice theory it would not normally be expected that people would pour more resources into upgrading their homes than they could hope to recoup via a better resale price for their property. The only exception would be where they recognize that their preferences are unusual and judge that such improvements are the most cost-effective way of getting what they want even despite costing more than the value they add to their property. This may be due to the houses that have what they want offering it jointly only with more of some other features than they want or can afford.

The rational agent perspective seems to be potentially misleading in this context. Non-specialists are unlikely to be inherently more competent in project planning and management than the professionals who run into enormous problems of cost control with major public and corporate projects (classic examples include the Sydney Opera House, the Eurotunnel and the 1976 Montreal Olympic Games). Second, those whose unique new home projects provide the focus of the popular reality TV series 'Grand Designs' almost invariably incur significant cost over-runs, while family researchers such as Goodsell (2008) and journalists (for example, Matterson, 2002; Tilbury, 2004; Swan, 2007) who write about renovators likewise emphasize problems with cost control that add to family stresses associated with delays in completion. Third, it appears that often, instead of projects being embarked upon after a 'grand design' plan has been worked out, the grand design emerges along the way via a process of muddling through as consumers get a taste for making improvements and a growing vision of what is possible (Watson and Shove, 2008, pp. 83–4).

Problems in controlling costs are also to be expected if we examine home improvement choices from the standpoint of behavioural and psychological economics. Consider the following:

1. *Soft budgets*   Home improvers nowadays face much less well-defined budget constraints than rational economic man is presumed to face – not just access to credit cards but also the flexibility provided by home-equity/overdraft mortgages. Peng (2009) found that the probability of overcapitalization was increased if a renovation project was financed by an increased mortgage. In affluent societies, cost escalation is also permitted by the discretionary nature of many other kinds of consumption, since the latter can be postponed if there are pressing alternative calls on funds.

2. *Complexity and bounded rationality*   Other things being equal, more complex projects will be more prone to entail expensive surprises. Peng found that both (a) the probability of overcapitalization was a positive function of the time spent preparing for the project, which may be seen as a proxy for its complexity, and (b) those who obtained more quotations from tradespeople were less susceptible to cost escalation.

3. *The completion imperative*   Once under way, home improvements are often difficult to reverse, but if not completed they may leave the householder with a property that is aesthetically and/or functionally worse than before the work started. If problems are encountered that are expensive to deal with, one strategy is to keep the total bill close to the original budget by scaling back the extent or lavishness of remaining work. This may seem to make poor economic sense, however, for low-budget revisions may have serious implications for the marketability of the property. In any case, the renovator may be locked into contracts with tradespeople, another factor that Peng found to be a significant predictor of overcapitalization. With full hindsight, it might have been wiser not to begin the renovation and to let the next owners of the property run into the unforeseen problems. Put like this, a cost over-run can seem worth sanctioning *ex post* even if the total cost of the project would, *ex ante*, have implied overcapitalization. This case for the extra spending does not involve an irrational treatment of sunk costs and an urge to complete the project 'at all costs' due to 'sunk cost bias' (Thaler, 1980). However, non-rational attitudes to sunk costs – that is, a desire to complete the project *because* of costs already incurred, so as not to admit that money has been wasted – may shape perceptions of the payoffs to letting costs escalate, as may cognitive dissonance between, say, the renovator's self-image

and a vision of a renovated kitchen or bathroom being fitted out less lavishly than planned in order to liberate funds to cover unexpected but unavoidable expenditure.

4. *The sequential problem-discovery trap*   Deficient foresight regarding a succession of problems that surface during a home improvement project can result in the renovator being caught in something akin to the sequential wear-out trap identified by Frankel (1955) in his analysis of how firms get locked into outmoded capital equipment. If all the problems with a project surfaced at an early stage, it might well be best to avoid overcapitalization by incurring the costs of a 'cut and shut' return to something akin to the original situation, abandoning any further work and leaving it to the next owner to discover what has been covered up. However, when there is a succession of unexpected problems, the arguments from the previous paragraph will at each stage tend to favour continuation.

5. *Embarrassment and domestic disruption*   If friends and neighbours have been told about the project, the renovator faces being judged as a poor decision maker if it is abandoned or finished in a reduced version. By contrast, if it is finished as planned, it can be shown off without the inflated actual cost being clearly visible. If consumers who are prone to hyperbolic discounting can stop procrastinating and actually get home improvement projects started, they are likely to behave as if addicted to them (see Ainslie, 1992; O'Donoghue and Rabin, 1999) by giving undue weight to short-term disruption costs. This will make them particularly susceptible to suggestions by tradespeople about strategies that can solve unforeseen problems rapidly but at considerable financial cost compared with what they might achieve if they put the project on hold and shopped around for further opinions, even at the risk of the current contractor quitting.

6. *Framing effects*   Following Thaler (1980), we should expect consumers to focus on proportional increases in costs relative to an initial point of reference rather than on the absolute amount of the increase. Thus an additional $1,000 on a planned $10,000 patio re-roofing project will seems less of a problem than, say, an additional $500 on a planned $3,000 bathroom upgrade (though disruption costs of a non-usable bathroom will probably mean that the extra $500 is spent, too, if this is deemed necessary to get it functioning properly again). Likewise, a further $1,000 on a project that has already escalated by $1,000 will not seem so bad as the first escalation if it is now viewed as a percentage of the already-enlarged budget. Renovators may also adopt inconsistent attitudes towards spending on a project depending on whether the total cost appears potentially still to lie within a

target frame or has already breached it. Once they are out of their initial frame, they may have no particular new goal at hand as a means to rein in further expenditure. For example, if the renovator has a personal goal to be out of debt by a particular point this may result in him/her choosing not to go ahead with some projects because these would compromise meeting that goal. However, if a project the renovator has decided to implement has turned out to be unexpectedly expensive and has made it clear that the goal is no longer feasible, then he/she may be less resistant to further unplanned spending to get it finished than they would have been if, by not authorizing it, his/her target would still be feasible.

Home improvers who anticipate having to consider unplanned increases in spending and who know they are likely to suffer from weakness of will would be wise to follow Ulysses' strategy of binding himself to avoid succumbing to the temptations of the Sirens (Elster, 1979). Outsourcing the entire project to a project management firm for a fixed price is one way of avoiding being talked into spending more, once the project is under way, by individual tradespeople who had previously merely given 'estimates'. Such a strategy may come at some cost due to the firm building a risk premium into its calculations, but it reduces the risk of falling prey to the credence good problem via overservicing or opportunistic suggestions about a now-or-never chance to include something extra in the project. Those engaging in DIY also need strategies that limit how long the work takes. They can increase their motivation to get projects completed in a timely manner if it is possible to break them up into subprojects – for example, focus on giving one room a makeover, and then another, rather than seeing the project in terms of the entire house – and then reward themselves each time they complete a subproject (for other leisure-related applications of motivation-inducing choices of goals, see Earl, 1998, pp. 124–8).

The secret to containing outlays may be to practise precisely the kind of 'mental accounting' that is often portrayed as being irrational – that is, do not treat one's financial resources as fungible but establish a dedicated 'renovation' account (ideally, an actual account with a financial institution, not just a mental one) with a definite budget limit from which all the bills will be paid. Even the latter may take some willpower to administer: if the account is based on an ongoing monthly deposit, for ongoing renovation projects, it will be less of a restraint than one that is project specific, since a cost and time over-run on a project can be allowed at the cost of future projects being delayed. Being hostage to one's spouse, relatives or friends by making pledges about what will be done, by when and for how much, is another strategy implied by behavioural economics: the renovator then has the prospects of being nagged at and social embarrassment as incentives to keep the project under control.

CONCLUSION

Home improvement activities are a common way of using leisure time and discretionary income, but while they are often promoted as means to a more relaxing living environment there is little in the literature to suggest that home improvement activities are particularly relaxing forms of leisure. Such activities are seen as challenging, as sources of excitement and as sources of anxiety and nasty surprises, even if they do provide diversions from the boring routines of paid work. Those most likely to find home improvements a relaxing form of leisure are confident, capable consumers whose jobs offer far bigger challenges than they face when engaging in DIY problem solving or dealing with contractors. Economists who seek to understand home improvement choices from an equilibrium-focused standpoint based upon rational agent assumptions should do so with caution. The choice problem certainly can be seen as focusing on rival bundles of characteristics (as with 'to move or improve') with DIY/outsourcing choices based on comparative advantage. However, this is an area commonly characterized by expensive surprises, where progress with a project often opens the consumer's eyes to potential for making further improvements rather than ending in a state of rest. Those who undertake home improvements may face shifting emotional states along the way and end up not merely with a better place to live but also with an enhanced set of capabilities, new decision rules and better sense of self. Along the way, escalating costs in time and money may have unexpectedly crowded out many other leisure activities. This sounds like an area ripe for further research from the standpoint of behavioural economics.

REFERENCES

Adriaenssens, S. and J. Hendrickx (2009), 'Modes of production in home maintenance: accounting for the choice between formality, off the books and self-provisioning', *International Journal of Consumer Studies*, **33**, 596–603.

Aguiar, M. and E. Hurst (2007), 'Measuring trends in leisure: the allocation of time over five decades', *Quarterly Journal of Economics*, **121**, 969–1006.

Ainslie, G. (1992), *Picoeconomics: The Strategic Interaction of Successive Motivational States within the Person*, Cambridge: Cambridge University Press.

Akerlof, G.A. (1970), '"The market for lemons": quality uncertainty and the market mechanism', *Quarterly Journal of Economics*, **84**, 488–500.

Akerlof, G.A. (1991), 'Procrastination and obedience', *American Economic Review*, **81** (2), May, 1–19.

Akerlof, G.A. and W.T. Dickens (1982), 'The economic consequences of cognitive dissonance', *American Economic Review*, **72**, 302–19.

Arnott, R., R. Davidson and D. Pines (1983), 'Housing quality, maintenance and rehabilitation', *Review of Economic Studies*, **50** (3), 467–94.

Atkinson, P. (2006), 'Do it yourself: democracy and design', *Journal of Design History*, **19** (1), 1–10.

Australian Bureau of Statistics (2002), 'Housing and lifestyle: home renovation', *Australian Social Trends* (cat. no. 4102.0), available at: http://www.abs.gov.au/ausstats/abs@.nsf/2 f762f95845417aeca25706c00834efa/062c1f689e72a59cca2570ec000b922d!OpenDocument (accessed 20 January 2007).

Baker, K. and B. Kaul (2002), 'Using multiperiod variables in the analysis of home improvement decisions by homeowners', *Real Estate Economics*, **30** (4), 551–66.

Bendimerad, A. (2005), 'Understanding generational differences in home remodeling behavior', Working Paper W05–10, Joint Center for Housing Studies, Harvard University, Cambridge, MA.

Bianchi, C. and S.J. Arnold (2004), 'An institutional perspective on retail internationalization success: Home Depot in Chile', *International Review of Retail, Distribution, and Consumer Research*, **14** (2), 149–69.

Chaplin, D. (1999), 'Consuming work/productive leisure: the consumption patterns of second home environments', *Leisure Studies*, **18**, 41–55.

Darby, M.R. and E. Karni (1973), 'Free competition and the optimal amount of fraud', *Journal of Law and Economics*, **16** (1), 67–88.

Davidson, M. and P. Leather (2000), 'Choice or necessity? A review of the role of DIY in tackling housing repair and maintenance', *Construction Management and Economics*, **18**, 747–56.

Earl, P.E. (1986), *Lifestyle Economics: Consumer Behavior in a Turbulent World*, Brighton: Wheatsheaf and New York: St Martin's.

Earl, P.E. (1995), 'Liquidity preference, marketability and pricing', in S.C. Dow and J. Hillard (eds), *Keynes, Knowledge and Uncertainty*, Aldershot, UK and Brookfield, VT, USA: Edward Elgar, pp. 269–92.

Earl, P.E. (1998), 'Consumer goals as journeys into the unknown', in M. Bianchi (ed.), *The Active Consumer: Novelty and Surprise in Consumer Choice*, London and New York: Routledge, pp. 122–39.

Earl, P.E. and J. Potts (2004), 'The market for preferences', *Cambridge Journal of Economics*, **28**, 619–33.

Earl, P.E. and R.A. Wicklund (1999), 'Cognitive dissonance', in P.E. Earl and S. Kemp (eds), *The Elgar Handbook to Consumer Research and Economic Psychology*, Cheltenham, UK and Northampton, MA, USA: Edward Elgar, pp. 81–8.

Elster, J. (1979), *Ulysses and the Sirens: Studies in Rationality and Irrationality*, Cambridge: Cambridge University Press and Paris: Éditions de la Maison des Sciences de l'Homme (rev. edn, 1984).

Fortes, R.M. and I.A. McCarthy (2009), 'Renovate for profit: an exploratory residential case study in New Zealand', paper presented at the Fifteenth Pacific Rim Real Estate Society Conference, Sydney, 18–21 January.

Frankel, M. (1955), 'Obsolescence and technological change in a maturing economy', *American Economic Review*, **45**, 296–319.

Goodsell, T.L. (2008), 'Diluting the cesspool: families, home improvement and social change', *Journal of Family Issues*, **28** (4), 539–65.

Gram-Hanssen, K., F. Bartiaux, O.M. Jensen and N. Cantaert (2007), 'Do homeowners use energy labels? A comparison between Denmark and Belgium', *Energy Policy*, **35**, 2879–88.

Halliday, R. (2005), 'Home truths', in D. Bell and J. Holloway (eds), *Ordinary Lifestyles: Popular Media, Consumption and Tastes*, Maidenhead: Open University Press/McGraw-Hill UK, pp. 65–81.

Hernandez, T. (2003), 'The impact of big box internationalization on a national market: a case study of Home Depot Inc. in Canada', *International Review of Retail Distribution and Consumer Research*, **13** (1), 77–98.

Hills, S. and D. Worthing (2006), 'Private home, public cultural assets: the maintenance behaviour of listed building owner-occupiers', *Journal of Housing and the Built Environment*, **21**, 203–13.

Hodgson, G.M. (1988), *Economics and Institutions*, Cambridge: Polity Press.

Hoffman, L. (2006), 'Home DIY kills, maims and injures', *The Australian*, 4 March, 31.

Holt, G. and D.J. Edwards (2005), 'Domestic builder selection in the UK housing repair and maintenance sector: a critique', *Journal of Construction Research*, **6** (1), 123–37.

Iwata, S. and H. Yamaga (2007), 'Resale externalities and the used housing market', *Real Estate Economics*, **35** (3), 331–47.

Kelly, G.A. (1955), *The Psychology of Personal Constructs*, New York: W.W. Norton.

Klein, B. and K. Leffler (1981), 'The role of market forces in assuring contractual performance', *Journal of Political Economy*, **89**, 615–41.

Laaksonen, P. (1994), *Consumer Involvement: Concepts and Research*, London: Routledge.

Lader, D., S. Short and J. Gershuny (2006), *The Time Use Survey 2005*, London: Office of National Statistics.

Lancaster, K.J. (1966), 'A new approach to consumer theory', *Journal of Political Economy*, **74**, 132–57.

Lane, L., A. Power and N. Serie (2008), '"Teach in" on energy and existing homes – restoring neighbourhoods and slowing climate change', LSE STICERD Research Paper, CASE Report 56, available at: http://sticerd.lse.ac.uk/dps/case/cr/CASEreport56.pdf (accessed 1 October 2009).

Leventis, A. (2007), 'Home improvements and appreciation rates reflected in the OFHEO House Price Index', OFHEO Working Paper 07-2, Washington, DC, Office of Federal Housing Enterprise Oversight.

Linder, S.B. (1970), *The Harried Leisure Class*, New York: Columbia University Press.

Littlewood, A. and M. Munro (1996), 'Explaining disrepair: examining owner occupiers' repair and maintenance behaviour', *Housing Studies*, **11** (4), 503–25.

Littlewood, A. and M. Munro (1997), 'Moving and improving: strategies for attaining housing equilibrium', *Urban Studies*, **34** (11), 1771–87.

Matterson, H. (2002), 'Home renovation survival tactics – rates on the rise', *The Australian*, 9 June, 33.

McDermott, S., K. Linahan and B. Squires (2009), 'Older people living in squalor: ethical and practical dilemmas', *Australian Social Work*, **62** (2), 245–57.

Melchionne, K. (1999), 'Of bookworms and busybees: cultural theory in the age of do-it-yourself', *Journal of Aesthetics and Art Criticism*, **57** (2), 247–55.

Milmo, C. (2003), 'Barry Bucknell, home makeover guru of the fifties, dies at 91', *The Independent*, 22 February.

Munro, M. and P. Leather (2000), 'Nest-building or investing in the future? Owner-occupiers' home improvement behaviour', *Policy and Politics*, **28** (4), 511–52.

Nelson, P. (1970), 'Information and consumer behavior', *Journal of Political Economy*, **78**, 311–29.

O'Donoghue, T. and M. Rabin (1999), 'Doing it now or later', *American Economic Review*, **89** (1), 103–24.

Park, K. (2008), 'Good home improvers make good neighbors', Joint Centre for Housing Studies, Harvard University, W08–2, April, available at: www.jchs.harvard.edu/publications/remodeling/w08-2_park.pdf (accessed 1 October 2009).

Peng, T.-C. (2009), 'A pluralistic analysis of housing renovation choices in Brisbane', unpublished PhD thesis, School of Economics, University of Queensland.

Phe, H.H. (2002), 'Investment in residential property: taxonomy of home improvers in Central Hanoi', *Habitat International*, **26**, 471–86.

Philips, D. (2005), 'Transforming scenes: the television interior makeover', *International Journal of Cultural Studies*, **8** (2), 213–29.

Richardson, G.B. (1972), 'The organisation of industry', *Economic Journal*, **82**, 883–96.
Saville-Smith, K., B. James and R. Fraser (2008), 'Older people's house performance and their repair and maintenance practices: analysis from a 2008 National Survey of Older People and existing datasets', November, Report available at the New Zealand 'Ageing in Place' website: http://www.goodhomes.co.nz/ (accessed 30 September 2009).
Scitovsky, T. (1981), 'The desire for excitement in modern society', *Kyklos*, **34**, 3–13.
Seek, N.H. (1983), 'Adjusting housing consumption: improve or move', *Urban Studies*, **20**, 455–69.
Shove, E., M. Watson and J. Ingram (2007), *The Design of Everyday Life*, Oxford: Berg.
Silva, E.B. and D. Wright (2009), 'Displaying desire and distinction in housing', *Cultural Sociology*, **3**, 31–50.
Simon, H.A. (1955), 'A behavioural model of rational choice', *Quarterly Journal of Economics*, **69**, 99–118.
Spivack, R. (1991), 'The determinants of housing maintenance and upkeep: a case study of Providence, Rhode Island', *Applied Economics*, **23**, 639–46.
Stewart, J. (2003), 'Encouraging homeowners to maintain their homes: initiatives in the Bellenden Renewal Area, Peckham', *Journal of Environmental Health Research*, **2** (1), 10–21.
Swan, K. (2007), 'Home renovations keep pressure on prices', *ABC: Inside Business*, available at: http://www.abc.net.au/insidebusiness/content/2007/s1940963.htm (accessed 10 July 2007).
Thaler, R. (1980), 'Toward a positive theory of consumer choice', *Journal of Economic Behavior and Organization*, **1**, 39–60.
Thompson, M. (1979), *Rubbish Theory*, New York: Oxford University Press.
Tilbury, A. (2004), 'Take time to plan before you go ahead', *The Courier Mail*, 24 July, 82.
Tinker, A. (1998), 'Helping older people to stay at home: the role of supported accommodation', in S. Sutherland (chair), *With Respect to Old Age: Long Term Care – Rights and Responsibilities; A Report by The Royal Commission on Long Term Care*, London: HMSO, Cm 4192-I, Appendix 2 (pp. 265–98) of Research Volume 2.
Watson, M. and E. Shove (2008), 'Product, competence, project and practice: DIY and the dynamics of craft consumption', *Journal of Consumer Culture*, **8**, 69–89.
Williams, B. (1996), '"There goes the neighborhood": gentrification, displacement and homelessness in Washington, DC', in A.L. Dehavenon (ed.), *There's No Place Like Home: Anthropological Perspectives on Housing and Homelessness in the United States*, Westport, CT: Bergin & Garvey, pp. 145–75.
Williams, C.C. (2008), 'Re-thinking the motives of do-it-yourself (DIY) consumers', *International Review of Retail Distribution and Consumer Research*, **18** (3), 311–23.
Williamson, O.E. (1985), *The Economic Institutions of Capitalism*, New York: Free Press.

11 Reconsidering the Silk Road: tourism in the context of regionalism and trade patterns
Karen Jackson

INTRODUCTION

> Today, the business volume of tourism equals or even surpasses that of oil exports, food products or automobiles. Tourism has become one of the major players in international commerce, and represents at the same time one of the main income sources for many developing countries.
> (United Nations World Tourism Organization)

The importance of tourism in terms of income to both developing and developed countries is without question. Therefore it is unsurprising that the body of literature considering the determinants of demand for tourism is vast. Income, price, exchange rate and transport costs are considered to be of particular significance. However, there are challenges in the construction of a number of variables. Problems arise in defining and measuring different types of tourism and marketing effort. This chapter outlines key findings from previous research with a specific focus on the role of trade and regionalism in demand for tourism.

Since the creation of the Silk Road – a network of trans-continental trade routes – trade and tourism have been inexplicably linked. However, there is a limited empirical literature that considers the relationship between tourism and trade. Recent studies have called into question the results from the earlier literature, which either ignore the effect of trade or inappropriately attempt to measure the impact by estimating single equations. Since the Second World War there has also been a huge expansion of regionalism, which may impact on tourism through trade as well as a range of other dimensions. However, the empirical literature almost completely neglects this factor as a potential driver of tourism. This chapter examines channels linking regionalism, trade and tourism, concluding with proposed avenues for future research.

PATTERNS OF TOURISM

Patterns of tourism arrivals and receipts vary dramatically across countries. Despite the intuitive link between tourist arrivals and receipts, a casual look at the data suggests that the link is weaker than it seems at first thought. For example, while tourist expenditure in Germany was the largest in the world in 2007 (Table 11.1) they only attracted the fifth-highest number of arrivals in Europe (UNWTO, 2009). By contrast, the UK had the fourth-highest number of arrivals in Europe (ibid.) but fell behind Germany in terms of receipts (Table 11.1). The fact that receipts weakly follow arrivals will prove interesting when we look at tourism demand modelling.

It is also notable from Table 11.1, detailing the top ten tourism recipients in 2007, that developed countries dominate this list. It is indisputable that tourism income is critically important for developing countries as it may prove a stimulus for economic development. A preliminary look at the data in Figure 11.1 suggests that the broad stagnation in tourist arrivals in the early 2000s is likely to be in part due to the Iraq War. During this decade, Asia and the Pacific have overtaken the Americas in terms of arrivals. However, there is a dip in tourist arrivals for Asia and the Pacific in 2003 due to SARS (severe acute respiratory syndrome). This deepened the already poor performance due to the Iraq War. It is interesting to note from Table 11.1 that the Asian and Pacific dip appears to be reflected in Japanese expenditure, but not significantly so in the case of Chinese expenditure. In fact China's performance in terms of tourist arrivals in 2008 dramatically outstrips other Asian and Pacific countries, with

Table 11.1   International tourism expenditure (billion dollars)

	1995	2000	2003	2004	2005	2006	2007
Germany	60.2	53.0	64.7	71.0	74.4	73.9	83.1
USA	44.9	64.7	57.4	65.8	69.0	72.1	76.2
UK	24.9	38.4	47.9	56.5	59.6	63.1	71.4
France	16.3	17.8	23.4	28.6	30.5	31.2	36.7
China	3.7	13.1	15.2	19.1	21.8	24.3	29.8
Italy	14.8	15.7	20.6	20.5	22.4	23.1	27.3
Japan	36.8	31.9	28.8	38.2	27.3	26.9	26.5
Canada	10.3	12.4	13.4	15.9	18.2	20.5	24.8
Russian Fed.	11.6	8.8	12.9	15.7	17.4	18.2	22.3
Korea, Rep. of	6.3	7.1	10.1	12.4	15.4	18.9	22.0

Source: UN World Tourism Organization (2009).

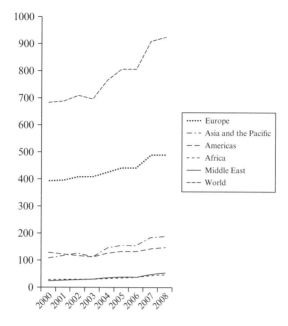

Source: UN World Tourism Organisation (2009).

Figure 11.1   International tourist arrivals (millions)

Malaysia as its closest competitor only receiving less than half the number of tourist arrivals (ibid.).[1] It is possible to connect this strong Chinese performance to the opening up of their economy. The Olympic Games, held in Beijing in 2008, also provide an interesting case study. The World Tourism Barometer (ibid.) notes that host nations of the games often experience a downturn in arrivals due to the expectation of congestion, high prices and tighter restrictions on travel. In addition, the strong performance of Japan in terms of arrivals in 2006–07 (but not translated into receipts) is explained by UNWTO in terms of the recovery of the value of the Japanese currency. Other factors that affected Asian tourism arrivals include political and civil unrest in Thailand.

It is worth considering whether there is any evidence of a correlation between trade, regionalism and tourism. An obvious example to consider is Central/Eastern Europe. Several countries within the Central/Eastern European grouping have recently become EU members, while others have signed another form of regional integration agreement. The detailed data on arrivals in 2007 (UNWTO) shows Ukraine leading the Central/Eastern European region. Nevertheless, it falls behind the Russian Federation,

Poland, Hungary and the Czech Republic in terms of receipts. Yet overall, Central/Eastern Europe has seen the largest increase in arrivals in the European region between 2000 and 2008 (ibid.).

This increase in tourism may be explained by the range of regional integration agreements coming into force. This example provides evidence that the impact of regional integration agreements is worthy of further investigation.

DEMAND FOR TOURISM

In order to investigate the significance of these patterns of tourism there are a number of specifications for modelling demand. Underlying these various models is the utility-maximization problem:

$$\text{Max}_{t,c} U(t, c) \ \ s.t. \ \ P_t t + P_c c \leq I,$$

where $U(t, c)$ is the utility function, t stands for quantity of tourism, c the composite of other goods, P_t the price of a unit of tourism, P_c the price of a unit of composite goods and I stands for income.

One of the simplest models of demand is the log-linear demand function. This equation explains quantity of tourism demanded as a function of the price of tourism, of a country and its competitors, as well as income. The attractive feature of this specification is that the estimated coefficients on prices and income represent estimates of income and price elasticity. However, this popular demand function has a number of weaknesses that mean the general restrictions of classical demand theory are not satisfied. In this chapter it is not necessary to examine this issue in more detail other than to conclude that this has led to questions regarding the theoretical basis of this model.

There has been a general move towards complete demand systems which are able to take into account the mutual interdependence of a large number of commodities. Such systems are consistent with utility maximization. There are four popular systems worthy of mention: the linear expenditure system (LES), the Rotterdam model, the translog model and the almost ideal demand system (AIDS). For a discussion of other models, see Pollak and Wales (1992).

The LES is the simplest and first of the theoretically consistent demand systems as specified and estimated by Stone (1954). However, the linearity of formulation of demand from which the system is derived means that every good must be a substitute for every other good. Hence no two goods in the system are complements and it does not allow for inferior goods.

These assumptions mean that this model can only be applied where the restrictions are viewed as reasonable. In addition, it is not possible to test the classic theoretical restrictions. The Rotterdam model, proposed by Theil (1965) and Barten (1966) can be estimated with and without restrictions that can be tested. This model has been criticized due to the choice of restrictive functional forms to approximate the underlying theory.

Therefore attention has focused on function forms that are considered more flexible as a good approximation to the unknown actual function. One attempt at this is the translog model (Christensen et al., 1975). Yet this form is criticized for not actually being particularly flexible (Deaton and Muellbauer, 1980a). A widely accepted more successful attempt was the AIDS system, which is derived from the standard theoretical framework and uses a general utility function, meaning that it can approximate almost any form (Deaton and Muellbauer, 1980b). However, in comparison to the log-linear form, it requires more calculation to estimate elasticities from the AIDS system. Lastly it is worth noting the gravity model, which could be used to predict flows of tourism between two countries based on variables such as economic size, population and distance between the countries. Recent research has established the theoretical basis of the gravity model and its explanatory power (Deardorff, 1998).

Before turning to the empirical literature, we consider issues in the definition of variables used in modelling tourism demand. Tourism could be viewed as a commodity; for example, the arrival of a tourist at a destination. Alternatively, tourism may be considered as a composite of all the goods that are purchased while one is a tourist; for example travel, food and accommodation. It is also very pertinent to establish the type of tourism being modelled, whether it is recreational, business orientated, a mixture of the two or perhaps a more specific categorization such as cultural tourism. It is expected that each of these types of tourism will be explained by a unique set of variables. For further discussion of the issue of how utility is derived, see Becker (1965) and Lancaster (1971).

Tourism is deeply imbued with risk. There are safeguards in place in case a travel company goes bankrupt, as well as legal recourse if a holiday does not meet the expectations indicated in the travel brochure. In addition, travellers may receive compensation if a delay occurs due to flights being overbooked. However, there is clearly a higher risk associated with the purchase of a holiday/flight/hotel stay than with durable goods such as a new washing machine.

Price elasticity for tourism can also be compared to that of a durable good in that short-run demand is likely to be more elastic than long-run demand. For example, consumers may delay their holiday to a particular destination if the price were to increase significantly. In other words, the short-run elasticity will depend on whether consumers travelling to a destination have the ability to wait until it is off-season. It may be that some consumers have a level of income such that they can choose to go on holiday to a place on a particular date regardless of moderate price changes. This discussion implies that dynamic models may need to be employed.

While tourism may be considered a 'treat', the impact of changes in income on demand is somewhat more complex. A straightforward expectation would be that increases in income would tend to result in an aggregate increase in tourism. Yet it may be that individuals experience no increase in the number of days of leave when their income rises and in addition, some tourists may be very familiar and thus comfortable with a particular destination. This is an illustration of inflexibilities in the work–leisure bargain discussed in earlier chapters. An income increase will not encourage these individuals to purchase a more expensive, or longer, holiday. Alternatively, some destinations may have a 'status symbol' attached to them so that they convey Veblenian conspicuous consumption. For example the government of Mauritius has placed a ban on charter flights landing on the island and therefore tourists who can afford the high prices are attracted to this upmarket, rarely visited destination. Eco-tourism may, in some cases, illustrate an inverse status acquisition as individuals demonstrate their superiority by purchasing more environmentally friendly holidays than those taken by package tourists.

DETERMINANTS OF DEMAND FOR TOURISM

There is an extensive body of literature examining tourism demand as well as a significant number of reviews of this literature (Johnson and Ashworth, 1990; Crouch, 1994; Witt and Witt, 1995; Lim, 1997, 1999). Crouch (1994), and Lim (1997, 1999) all consider a substantial number of studies and focus on identifying the key determinants of the demand for tourism. Crouch examines 85 studies published between 1961 and 1992, whereas Lim (1997) considers 100 studies from 1961 until 1994. However, Lim (1999) goes beyond simply reviewing the literature and carries out a meta-analytic review, which involves a regression analysis of the statistical results found in 70 out of the 100 studies identified in Lim (1997). The review by Johnson and Ashworth (1990) is on a much smaller scale and considers only seven studies from 1980 and 1985, examining tourism flows to and from the UK. There is also a body of literature that focuses on forecasting tourism demand. Witt and

Witt (1995) carried out a review of 40 such studies published between 1966 and 1992. However, this chapter will focus on the determinants of demand for tourism rather than the validity of forecasting attempts although it follows that good demand models should make good forecasting models.

The vast majority of studies are quantitative, using classical regression methods. A range of data types have been used, but limited sample sizes have raised concerns over the reliability of results using annual data. Lim (1997) highlights that, of the 100 publications reviewed, 56 used annual data. In terms of model specification, Lim found that the majority of studies reviewed estimate single-equation models. Log-linear single equations are preferred in 56 of the 100 studies. Lim found only 10 studies that estimated any form of demand system, although there is also a more recent study by Divisekera (2003) that utilizes AIDS when modelling international tourism.

Turning to the variables used in these modelling exercises, first the range of dependent variables will be outlined. Given that some studies considered by Lim (1997) used more than one dependent variable, the total number of estimated equations examined was 119. Of the 119, it was found that 51 studies used tourist arrivals and/or departure as a dependent variable, whereas 49 used tourist expenditures and/or receipts. Yet Johnson and Ashworth (1990) find tourist arrivals and/or departure to be more commonly used, although their review is considerably narrower than Lim's (1997). Nevertheless Johnson and Ashworth suggest that policy makers are likely to be more interested in expenditure rather than number of visits. This view is reinforced by the earlier finding in this chapter of a potentially weak link between arrivals and receipts. Yet Divisekera (2003) also notes the difficulties in obtaining data on aggregate quantities of goods and services consumed by tourists by destination; therefore the author derives a proxy through using tourist numbers and nights. In addition there are other less used dependent variables such as travel exports and/or imports and length of stay. Some studies also differentiate between modes of travel, purpose of travel and type of travel arrangements (Johnson and Ashworth, 1990).

The explanatory variables used include both economic and sociological variables (Crouch, 1994; Lim, 1997). Crouch and Lim both agree that income is the most popular of these variables, judged by the frequency of inclusion in the 100 studies reviewed.

Ideally this variable would measure the income remaining after spending on necessities, but there are obvious measurement issues. Hence, other measures are utilized such as nominal or real per capita personal disposable or national income as well as GNP or GDP (Lim, 1997). Lim suggests real per capita consumption to be less commonly used, while Johnson and Ashworth (1990) mention that Little (1980) uses real per capita consumption without explanation. It is also possible to consider the dynamic effect through the inclusion of both income and lagged income (Lim, 1997). In carrying out a meta-analysis of 70 studies Lim (1999) finds support for the positive relationship between tourism demand and income. Witt and Witt (1995) provide an interesting discussion regarding the magnitudes of income elasticity estimates. They find variability in the estimates, but most exceed unity, suggesting that tourism is a luxury good. The estimates that are below unity concern tourism between neighbouring countries such as Canada/USA and Germany/Austria. There are exceptions when the neighbouring country has a high cost of living, such as in the case of Switzerland.

According to Lim (1997), the second most frequently used variable is relative prices. In terms of data availability, a relative consumer price index (CPI) is the easiest to collect to measure the costs of goods and services that tourists are likely to pay for. The CPI ratio is often multiplied by the exchange rate, which then excludes use of the exchange rate as a separate variable in the estimating equation. Martin and Witt (1987) find this CPI ratio (whether or not the exchange rate is taken into account) as a reasonable proxy for the relative price of tourism. Yet Lim (1997) suggests that the spending pattern of a tourist could well be different from that of an average household. Therefore, rather than use the CPI ratio (and in the absence of a tourist price index) some researchers have used price indices for products that tourists are likely to consume. Crouch (1994) also cites evidence regarding unreliable estimates when the variable proxying relative price does not consider price competition from other countries. Additional considerations are the opportunity cost of travel time as well as representing the higher risk associated with travelling to some destinations (ibid.). The meta-analysis carried out by Lim (1999) finds support for a negative relationship between tourism demand and relative prices. Witt and Witt (1995) find the median estimated value in the studies they consider to suggest inelastic demand, whether travel cost or destination cost is used. However, Crouch (1994) suggests that price elasticities may be underestimated if other destinations are not considered, and that responsiveness will increase over time as increased competition forces down prices. There is evidence in the more recent study of Pritchard (2003) of a higher sensitivity to price when there are substantial price changes in ferry transport from the Canadian mainland. However there is no clear picture emerging from the recent literature (Aslan et al., 2009). Generally it seems that increases in responsiveness to price changes are expected, but this is not yet clearly illustrated by the empirical findings. It is likely that consumers will be less likely to pay a high mark-up for services such as a better flight time as competition increases.

Also the subject of some debate is the responsiveness of tourists to changes in exchange rates, compared to inflation. There is a significant body of literature (Gray, 1966; Artus, 1970; Little, 1980; Lin and Sung, 1983; Truett and Truett, 1987; Tremblay, 1989) suggesting that tourists tend to be better informed about changes in the exchange rate compared to the rate of inflation. However, this has been shown by Edwards (1987) to only matter in the short run, whereas changes in exchange rates and inflation have a similar impact in the long run. Therefore a significant number of studies include exchange rate as a separate variable. However, it is questionable to include both an exchange rate and relative price variables due to multicollinearity (Lim, 1997). Therefore it is reasonable to include a relative price variable multiplied by the exchange rate, or a relative price variable or an exchange rate variable. The choice made may depend on a variety of reasons; for example if the study only considers business travel it may be that volatility in exchange rates is less significant in explaining tourism demand (Crouch, 1994). It is noteworthy that where the exchange rate is included as a separate variable in the studies considered by Witt and Witt (1995), it is found to have a median value of 1.8, suggesting a substantial reaction of demand to exchange rate changes, while such a strong reaction was not found when considering price elasticity estimates.

Lim (1997) finds that 55 per cent of the studies reviewed include a transport cost variable. This would seem surprisingly few since – as Krause et al. (1973) state – the cost of transport is the first consideration in a decision on tourist destination. However, several studies reviewed by Crouch (1994) find multicollinearity between rising real income and falling real transport costs; where other studies fail to find significant results for the variable representing transport costs. Lim (1999) also notes that the meta-analysis does not entirely support a negative relationship between transport costs and tourism demand. Thus the studies that fail to include transport costs use this evidence to explain their decision. For those studies that include a transport cost variable, Lim (1997) reports that this is normally measured by the price of air travel. There are a range of issues surrounding this measure such as the mode, type and class of travel; one issue of particular interest is incorporating travel costs to competing destinations as attempted in the study by Little (1980).

In addition to these key variables there are other factors such as length of stay, tastes of individuals and dummy variables as well as qualitative factors such as gender, age, culture and history. Incorporating dummy variables is considered to be important in tourism demand modelling

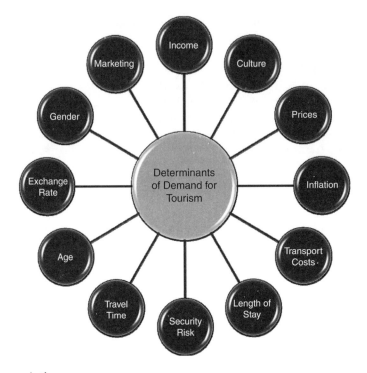

Source: Author.

Figure 11.2   Key determinants of demand for tourism

since the industry is seasonal. In addition, marketing expenditure is clearly relevant, but only considered in seven out of 100 studies reviewed by Lim (1997) due to data issues in constructing the variable. Crouch (1994) also discusses the inclusion of a time trend to account for the changing trends and fashions for various tourist destinations.

The discussion so far is not intended as a complete review of the literature as many others have already attempted this. However, the aim is to shed light on the key determinants of the demand for tourism, namely income, relative prices, exchange rates and transport costs, as well as to indicate the range of other factors considered. The factors highlighted in the literature, alongside those discussed in the earlier section analysing tourism trends, have been summarized in Figure 11.2. It has been found that the complexities and debate around the variables used to proxy the various determinants are in no small part due to data limitations. It is important to note that the literature considered so far has little or no mention of the role of trade, and to an even lesser extent regional trade agreements. The small number of recent studies considering this dimension will be examined in the next section.

THE ROLE OF TRADE IN THE DEMAND FOR TOURISM

The literature discussed so far pays very little attention to international trade as a determinant of tourism demand. The link between trade and tourism could be bi-directional in that international travel may encourage trade, particularly considering business travel that may include other people joining the business traveller for the purpose of holiday travel. The development of trade links may also lead to an increased awareness of a particular country and therefore travel to it. In addition, holiday travel may lead individuals to identify possible business opportunities.

Kulendran and Wilson (2000) published the first study investigating the link between international trade and tourism for pairs of countries. Their study is pivotal since it calls into question the vast body of earlier literature. The authors aim to establish whether the traditional body of literature, examined in the previous section, either incorrectly omitted a trade variable in their estimating equation, or despite the inclusion of a trade variable, failed to take appropriate account of the trade–tourism link in selecting their methodology.

Causality testing was carried out to explore whether trade leads to tourism, tourism leads to trade or the relationship is bi-directional. Yet before causality testing can actually take place, the order of integration of the various time series needs to be established. If the order of integration of two time series is found to be the same, this means that the two series move together over time, in other words the two series are cointegrated. If the series are cointegrated then causality, as established by Granger (1988), must be present in at least one direction. Therefore it is essential to check that the series move together before causality can be tested.

Kulendran and Wilson (2000) considered data for Australia and four of its travel and trading partners: the USA, the UK, New Zealand and Japan. They found that total travel and real exports, as well as total travel and real total trade, between Australia and the USA, New Zealand and Japan were cointegrated. These results also held when holiday or business travel was used instead of total travel. However, only for the UK did they find evidence of cointegration between real imports and total/business/ holiday travel. Now considering Granger causality, it was found for the USA that two-way causality exists between total travel and real total trade, but only one-way causality from real exports to holiday travel. For the UK there is one-way causality from real total trade to total/business travel. Then for the USA and Japan there is evidence of one-way causality from total travel to real exports, and for Japan this result holds when total trade replaces real exports. In addition, results for the USA suggest causality from business travel to real total trade, whereas for the UK causality appears to exist from business travel to real imports. Finally, for Japan there is evidence of one-way causality from holiday travel to real exports and real total trade. The authors suggest that this range of results is to be expected since these partners were chosen due to their various trading relationships; for example the Closer Economic Relationship between Australia and New Zealand as well as the Asia Pacific Economic Cooperation Forum of which Australia, Japan, New Zealand and the USA are all members.

Shan and Wilson (2001) examine data for China and four countries that are major origins of tourists: the USA, Japan, Australia and the UK. All series are found to be integrated of order one. Evidence of two-way Granger causality was found between total trade and total tourists for China and the USA, Australia and Japan.

Al-Qudair (2004) considers data on Islamic countries. There is evidence of cointegration between total tourists and exports, imports and total trade for Benin, Egypt, Jordan, Syria and Tunisia. The results from the Granger causality tests are once again more mixed. There is evidence of one-way causality from total tourists to imports for Egypt, Syria and Malaysia. In addition, there is evidence of one-way causality between total tourists to total trade for Egypt and Syria. For Jordan there is one-way causality between imports and total tourism as well as total trade and total tourists. Lastly, the author finds evidence for Malaysia of one-way causality from exports to total tourists.

Kulendran and Wilson (2000), Shan and Wilson (2001) and Al-Qudair (2004) all find evidence of a long-term relationship between international trade and travel flows. Hence these studies highlight a potential endogeneity issue. Shan and Wilson discuss the failure of previous studies to address this simultaneity bias due to a reliance on estimating single equations. They suggest that the validity of previous results is questionable due to either simultaneity bias or the omission of a trade variable altogether. It is important to note that Kulendran and Wilson, and Al-Qudair present a mixed set of results of the Granger causality test. Yet the role of trade is worthy of further research given these recent studies and the fairly obvious intuitive link between trade and tourism. Thus far, studies have utilized causality testing but there is a need to take the next research step, in that once this testing has taken place trade variables should be incorporated while applying an appropriate methodology.

THE IMPACT OF REGIONAL INTEGRATION AGREEMENTS

Surveying the empirical literature, it is evident that little attention has been paid to the impact of regional integration on the demand for tourism. Kulendran and Wilson consider a range of Australia's trading partners, with whom Australia has various regional integration agreements. The authors attempt to explain the results of the causality testing with reference to these agreements. The empirical literature does not use causality testing to actually investigate the regionalism–tourism link. Furthermore, studies modelling the demand for tourism do not consider regionalism as a possible determinant.

Regional integration agreements involve a variety of policy changes. These changes, and their potential link to tourism, are illustrated in Figure 11.3. The trade–tourism link is highlighted to indicate that this may exist independently of any regional integration agreement. In addition, regionalism results in the lowering of barriers to trade in goods and therefore the trade–tourism link needs to be reconsidered where the driver is a regional integration agreement.

There are also a range of other possible features of a regional integration agreement that may be linked to tourism indicated in Figure 11.3. In addition, it is proposed that there may be a channel from tourism to the deepening of an agreement. In other words it is feasible that an agreement that solely focused on the removal of barriers to trade in goods impacts on tourism; subsequently these changes in tourism

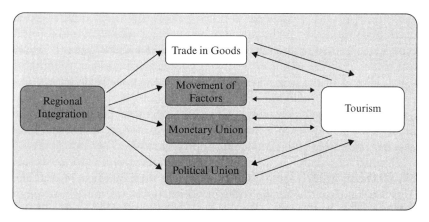

Source: Author.

Figure 11.3 Regionalism–trade–tourism flows

encourage the members to deepen their agreement, beyond barriers to trade in goods.

It is proposed that, depending on the particular case study, the relevant channels indicated in Figure 11.3 are subject to causality testing. Based on the results of these tests, there needs to be appropriate methodology applied to model the demand for tourism.

CONCLUSIONS

This chapter has outlined the current empirical literature examining the determinants of tourism, where the lack of analysis around the impact of trade is a particular cause for concern. By ignoring the importance of trade, this calls into question most of the previous literature. The small number of studies that have considered the link between trade and tourism test causality. While this empirical testing is important, there is a failure to take the next step in modelling tourism, taking into account the impact of trade.

Yet investigating the trade–tourism link is only part of the story. Trade and tourism may be linked in the absence of regionalism; nevertheless regionalism also provides an additional set of channels that may be linked to patterns of tourism. One of these channels is the impact of regionalism on barriers to trade in goods, which in turn may be linked to tourism. However, there are a number of features of deeper integration, apart from barriers to trade in goods, that may also link to tourism.

The current empirical literature is severely lacking in its investigation of trade–tourism and regionalism–tourism links. Therefore further research needs to consider testing the causality between not only trade and tourism but also aspects of regionalism and tourism, where trade–tourism is only one route. This research is critically important given the fact that almost every country in the world is a member of at least one regional integration agreement. In addition, empirical methodologies to model tourism demand need to be reconsidered. Currently there is an absence of gravity modelling and this avenue would be worth exploring, given the good explanatory power of this modelling approach.

This further research is very important given the potential for economic development of developing countries through the expansion of tourism. This is a somewhat neglected route of potential welfare gain for developing countries considering embarking on North–South regional integration. This is particularly pertinent since the welfare gains for the South are often found to be limited.

NOTE

1. The data for Australia are missing and therefore may impact on findings.

REFERENCES

Al-Qudair, K.H.A. (2004), 'The causal relationship between tourism and international trade in some Islamic countries', *Economic Studies*, **5** (19).
Artus, J.R. (1970), 'The effect of revaluation on the foreign trade balance of Germany', *International Monetary Fund Staff Papers*, **17**, 602–17.
Aslan, A., F. Kula and M. Kaplan (2009), 'International tourism demand for Turkey: a dynamic panel data approach', *Research Journal of International Studies*, **9**, January.
Barten, A.P. (1966), 'Theorie en empirie van een volledig stelsel van vraagvergelijkingen' (Theory and empirics of a complete system of demand equations), doctoral dissertation, Netherlands School of Economics, Rotterdam.
Becker, G. (1965). 'A theory of the allocation of time', *Economic Journal*, **75** (299), 493–517.
Christensen, L.R., D.W. Jorgenson and L.J. Lau (1975). 'Transcendental logarithmic utility functions', *American Economic Review*, **65**, 367–83.
Crouch, L. (1994), 'The study of international tourism demand: a survey of practice', *Journal of Travel Research*, **32** (4), 12–23.
Deardorff, A.V. (1998), 'Determinants of bilateral trade: does gravity work in a neoclassical world?', in J.A. Frankel (ed.), *The Regionalization of the World Economy*, Chicago, IL: University of Chicago Press, pp. 7–32.
Deaton, A. and J. Muellbauer (1980a), *Economics and Consumer Behaviour*, Cambridge: Cambridge University Press.
Deaton, A.S. and J.N. Muellbauer (1980b), 'An almost ideal demand system', *American Economic Review*, **70**, 312–26.
Divisekera, S. (2003), 'A model of demand for international tourism', *Annals of Tourism Research*, **30**, 31–49.
Edwards, A. (1987). 'Choosing holiday destinations: the impact of exchange rates and inflation', Special Report No. 1109, Economist Intelligence Unit Ltd, London.
Granger, C.W.J. (1988), 'Some recent developments in a concept of causality', *Journal of Econometrics*, **39**, 199–211.
Gray, P. (1966), 'The demand for international travel by the United States and Canada', *International Review*, **7**, 72–82.
Johnson, P. and J. Ashworth (1990), 'Modelling tourism demand: a summary review', *Leisure Studies*, **9**, 145–60.
Krause, W.G., D. Jud and H. Joseph (1973), *International Tourism and Latin American Development*, Austin, TX: Bureau of Business Research, Graduate School of Business, University of Texas at Austin.
Kulendran, N. and K. Wilson (2000), 'Is there a relationship between international trade and international travel?', *Applied Economics*, **32**, 1001–9.
Lancaster, K. (1971), *Consumer Demand: A New Approach*, New York: Columbia University Press.
Lim, C. (1997), 'Review of international tourism demand models', *Annals of Tourism Research*, **24** (4), 835–49.
Lim, C. (1999), 'A meta-analytic review of international tourism demand', *Journal of Travel Research*, **37**, 273–84.
Lin, T.B. and Y.W. Sung (1983), 'Hong Kong', in E.A. Pye and T.B. Lin (eds), *Tourism in Asia: The Economic Impact*, Singapore: Singapore University Press, pp. 50–62.
Little, J.S. (1980), 'International travel in the U.S. balance of payments', *New England Economic Review*, May–June, 42–55.

Martin, C. and S. Witt (1987), 'Economic models for forecasting international tourism demand', *Journal of Travel Research*, **25** (winter), 23–30.

Pollak, R.A. and T.J. Wales (1992), *Demand System Specification and Estimation*, Oxford: Oxford University Press.

Pritchard, M.P. (2003), 'Tourist price sensitivity and the elasticity of demand: the case of BC Ferries', *e-Review of Tourism Research*, **1** (4), 94–104.

Shan, J. and K. Wilson (2001), 'Causality between trade and tourism: empirical evidence from China', *Applied Economics Letters*, **8**, 279–83.

Stone, Richard (1954), 'Linear expenditure systems and demand analysis: an application to the pattern of British demand', *Economic Journal*, **64**, 511–27.

Theil, H. (1965), 'The information approach to demand analysis', *Econometrica*, **33**, 67–87.

Tremblay, P. (1989), 'Pooling international tourism in Western Europe', *Annals of Tourism Research*, **16**, 477–91.

Truett, D.B. and L.J. Truett (1987), 'The response of tourism to international economic conditions: Greece, Mexico and Spain', *Journal of Developing Areas*, **21**, 177–89.

UN World Tourism Organization (UNWTO) (2009), *World Tourism Barometer*, Madrid: UNWTO.

Witt, S. and C. Witt (1995), 'Forecasting tourism demand: a review of empirical research', *International Journal of Forecasting*, **11**, 447–75.

PART IV

SPECTATING AND EVENTS

12 Leisure tribe-onomics
Daragh O'Reilly

INTRODUCTION

Since the 1990s, there has been a considerable growth in the body of theory which deals with collective consumption or consumer groups. A wide repertoire of terms now exists with which to talk about consumer 'groupness', including user group, brand culture, tribe, neo-tribe, brand tribe, user community, brand community, cult, scene, microculture, subculture and so on. Examples of these groups include many which are linked to leisure activities, for example, musical subcultures such as Goths, punks and metalheads; skydivers; bikers; gay and lesbian subcultures; skateboarders; fantasy and science fiction fans; and yuppies. For those seeking conceptual clarity in this field, the proliferation of academic constructs does not help matters. However, all of these groups have certain issues in common, for example, their boundaries with the outside, membership criteria and assessment, group composition, intra-group hierarchies, group values, group identity, the tension and/or fit between group and individual identities, spirituality/religiosity and heritage. From a leisure economics point of view, the question must be: what are the economic implications of this 'groupness'?

There has been little attention paid within the leisure studies journal literature to notions of collective consumption, and practically none given to notions such as 'brand communities' and 'consumer tribes' which have proven to be very popular within marketing and consumer studies. The social grouping and behaviour of consumers during their leisure activities have a clear economic impact, particularly when these are linked with celebrity and fandom. The aims of this chapter are to bring some of the ideas about consumer tribes and brand communities into the area of leisure and to shed some light on the economic implications.

CONSUMER TRIBES

The idea of consumer tribes is associated perhaps most readily with the work of Bernard Cova (Cova and Cova, 2001, 2002; Cova et al., 2007). He argues that what binds a consumer group together is not so much the brand, but the emotional tie or shared passion of group members about the consumption activity and not necessarily any set of shared or common attributes. The idea of consumer tribes is often assumed to come from the French postmodern sociologist Michel Maffesoli. Certainly, his seminal book *The Time of the Tribes: The Decline of Individualism in Mass Society* (1988 [1996]) is commonly cited in the consumer studies literature. The idea of Maffesoli's which has most captured the imagination of marketing and consumer scholars, is that postmodern or neo-tribes are fluid and rather ephemeral. This is odd, because, from a marketing and economics point of view, it is, on the face of it, going to be hard for anyone to make much money from an ephemeral consumer tribe. This notion of ephemerality has become a kind of *idée reçue*,[1] as Flaubert might have called it (1994). However, the lack of a deeper reading of Maffesoli has resulted in a lot of *idées perdues*,[2] and it is important to recover these ideas if we are to have a fuller understanding of what he appeared to be saying in 1988/1996. Cova et al. (2007) say that the idea of consumer tribes is 'partly inspired' by Maffesoli. It is important, therefore, to go back to Maffesoli to understand his notion of 'neo-tribes' before considering more recent thinking about consumer tribes.

Maffesoli on Neo-tribes

Maffesoli describes neo-tribes in different ways, such as 'networks of solidarity' (p. 72), a 'communion of saints' (p. 73)', 'electronic mail, sexual networks, various solidarities including sporting and musical gatherings' (p. 73), 'youth groups, affinity associations, small-scale industrial enterprises' (p. 75), and 'small community group[s]' (p. 94). It is interesting in the context of this study that tribes are not necessarily made up of consumers only. The willingness to include 'small-scale industrial enterprises' indicates that Maffesoli believed producers could form neo-tribes too.

Maffesoli's book expounds at some considerable length five key themes which he identifies in neo-tribalism as he sees it: the affectual nebula; undirected being-together; the religious model; elective sociality; and the law of secrecy. As far as the affectual nebula is concerned, he sees experiencing the other as the basis of community and it is (p. 36) 'the feeling or passion which, contrary to conventional wisdom, constitutes the essential ingredient of all social aggregations'. He believes that the undirected being-together was 'a basic given of tribes' and that '[b]efore any other determination or qualification, there is this vital spontaneity that guarantees a culture its own *puissance* and solidity'. This notion of *puissance* is important. It is usually translated as 'power'. According to a translator's note (p. 1), the term '*puissance*' in French conveys the idea of the inherent energy and vital force of the people, as opposed to the institutions of power ('*pouvoir*'). The 'religious model' is a key point in his argument. He says: 'The use of the religious metaphor can then be compared to a laser beam allowing the *most complete reading* of the very heart of a given structure' (p. 82; emphasis added). In this regard, he explicitly states (p. 21) that he is 'adopting the perspective of Durkheim and his followers, who always placed the greatest weight on the sacredness of social relationships'. He argued that religiosity should be seen in the most elemental light, that of reliance (p. 77), and that there is a link between the emotional and religiosity (p. 78). He also invoked the notion of the Social Divine (p. 38) – the aggregate force which is the basis of any society or association, and of (p. 41) – demotheism – the people as god. He also makes the point that '[t]here has always been a heavy religious dimension to revolutionary phenomena'. By elective sociality he meant to refer to something which he saw as always having existed, the choice to be with other people. Finally, by the law of secrecy, he meant a 'protective mechanism with respect to the outside world' (p. 90), a secrecy which allows for resistance (p. 92). This '[secret] behaviour . . . was the basis of social perdurability . . . allows us to measure the vitality of a social group'. The secret society was always found on the margins.

These important ideas of Maffesoli, which are absolutely central to his thinking at the time, have not been explicitly worked into tribal marketing and consumer studies discourse. This raises a question about the idea which appears to have gained implicit currency that Maffesoli is some kind of genealogical father to the idea of consumer tribes. It is not clear that it was ever his intention that his tribal thinking would be adapted to talk about consumption. It is important to remember also that Maffesoli does not bring forward any empirical research to support his notion of a neo-tribe. Instead, his book offers a kind of sociological reverie, presumably reflecting on what he himself had observed happening in France and elsewhere in the mid-to-late 1980s, that is, more than 20 years ago. There is a general tendency to assume that the time of the tribes is the late twentieth and early twenty-first centuries, whereas Maffesoli himself clearly states that this tribal time has *always* been there.

Consumer Tribes, the Book

Cova et al.'s edited book, *Consumer Tribes* (2007), contains a range of chapters dealing with different groupings to which the tribal trope is applied. These groups are very varied indeed, including surfers, fans of the British royal family, Swedish yuppies, car cruisers, Warhammer gamers, pipe smokers and fans of Tom Petty and Harry Potter. In their opening chapter, entitled 'Tribes Inc.: The New World of Tribalism', the editors characterize consumer tribes using four metaphors: activators, double agents, plunderers and entrepreneurs. By activators, they mean 'players who activate and enliven a social process of commercial meanings and identity production-consumption' (p. 8). As double agents, consumers are 'sometimes complicit with, but not tricked by' (p. 12) marketing and walk 'a tightrope of resistance and passion' (p. 13); they can be both allies and opponents of the brand at the centre of the tribe. They can be 'plunderers', in the sense that they may commit piracy, or hijack and subvert brands for their own purposes. The editors see plundering as 'less and less of a conscious, revolutionary countercultural action, and more of an aestheticization of the daily experience' (p. 15).

Unlike Maffesoli, they see tribes as playing an important economic role. As entrepreneurs, tribes are 'poised to become collective actors in the marketplace in the same way that companies already are' (p. 16). Marketing is a competency that is available to all communities. And yet, tribes have different ways of working from organizations, and the '(economic) value of coordinating or being part of a tribe is based on perceptions, feelings and emotions' (p. 21). The editors talk of a tribe as 'no longer trying to resist economic actors or the market' but instead becoming 'a legitimate economic actor in its marketplace without losing any of its communitarian nature or forms' (p. 20).

Maffesoli has little to say about economics – or indeed politics (see Muggleton and Weinzierl, 2003: 11). But it is possible to see readily that his combination of puissance, religiosity, emotion, and the sense of secrecy, could lead to the formation of enduring social groups around a focal point. This could clearly have economic implications to the extent that market or exchange relations exist among tribal members or between the tribal members and their 'totem', or between the tribe and outsiders. I suggest that these aspects of Maffesoli's thinking could be quite easily and profitably connected with the notion of the counterculture (Roszak, 1969; Swingrover, 2003; Gair, 2007), which has clear commercial implications (see Frank, 1998; Heath and Potter, 2006). Like Maffesoli, however, the proponents of consumer tribes do not see a political dimension to the tribe. In fact, they see resistance to corporations and the market as being a thing of the past (Cova et al., 2007: 20). The intention in both these discourses is to downplay the idea of resistance. This lack of a political dimension is something which the proponents of consumer tribalism share with Maffesoli. After all, if '[m]odern primitivism is primal partnership, tribal trading and collective capitalism' (ibid.: 20), why should there be any need for politics or for a concept of resistance? The only ideology that is explicitly and readily acknowledged within the 'brand community' literature is religiosity. The idea that the term 'brand community' is ideologically freighted is not widely acknowledged. For all the talk of tribalism and community, the thrust of the inquiry is about ways for marketing people to subtly exploit sociality around products and brands.

BRAND COMMUNITIES

'Brand communities' may be seen as a US-originated construct, in contrast to 'consumer tribes' whose provenance is more European. The idea was first worked up by Muñiz and O'Guinn (2001) and has been one of the most popular marketing concepts of the new millennium. This strand of research takes a more managerial and commercial approach to groups of consumers. The original paper in the branding literature is Muñiz and O'Guinn's work on brand community (2001). This constructs a brand community as 'a form of human association situated within a consumption context' (p. 426), separate from geographical proximity, in which '[m]embers share a social bond around a branded, mass-produced commodity, and believe it is reasonable to do so' (p. 418). These 'brand communities' have three key characteristics: a consciousness of kin, rituals and a sense of moral responsibility. Members have 'a shared knowing of belonging' (p. 413) and 'construct themselves as different or special in some way from others and similar to each other'. They exhibit signs of 'oppositional brand loyalty' (p. 420) in other words they seek to differentiate themselves by comparing other groups unfavourably to themselves on certain key values. As far as community rituals are concerned, members of the community adhere to conventions that set up 'visible public definitions between themselves and other groups' (Douglas and Isherwood, 1979: 65, cited in Muñiz and O'Guinn, 2001) for example, waving or flashing lights to drivers of the same make of car. They celebrate brand heritage and tell stories about their experiences of consuming the brand. Members show a desire to ensure community survival by integrating and retaining members. They also assist each other by providing advice, assistance and information. Key themes in the brand community literature include religiosity (Muñiz and Schau, 2005; Schau and Muñiz, 2007), the role of the brand in relation to the wider community, the instrumental imperative to build stronger brands and successful brand communities (McWilliam, 2000; McAlexander et al. 2002), the dangers of brand communities which become too powerful (Ahonen and Moore, 2005), online brand communities (Kim, 2006) and community typologies (Devasagayam and Buff, 2008). While offering some interesting insights into the social and cultural dimensions of brand communities, this strand of literature is more tied into mainstream managerial marketing, and more concerned with working out systematic implications for marketing and brand managers.

In a recent paper, Schau et al. (2009) identify '12 practices common to an array of brand communities' (p. 40) and suggest that through these practices 'consumers realize value beyond that which the firm creates or anticipates' (p. 30). The practices can be grouped under four headings, 'social networking, impression management, community engagement, and brand use' (pp. 32–3). They 'function like apprenticeships, endow participants with cultural capital, produce a repertoire for insider sharing, generate consumption opportunities, evince brand community vitality, and create value' (p. 30). At the level of marketing practice, the creation of a brand community has become a strategic priority for many brands. Companies have entered the marketplace offering brand community 'solutions'.

Muñiz and O'Guinn (2001) assert that the brand is the social 'tie that binds', yet are careful to say that the 'felt sense of duty' of the brand community members to each other goes only so far. And yet, this is a key issue: because one consumes a bottle of Coke, does this make one a member of the Coca-Cola brand community? What does it mean to be a member of a 'community' along with a multi-billion dollar corporation? How much would a Coke drinker do for another Coke drinker because they happen to consume the same sugared water? How far do the communal bonds stretch?

TRIBES, COMMUNITIES AND SOCIAL IDENTITY

Apart from the lack of a political dimension, neither brand community theory nor consumer tribal theory draws explicitly upon social identity theory (SIT). This theory has some useful things to say about social groups and their identity. SIT was developed by Henri Tajfel and John Turner in the 1970s and 1980s, and it argues that people's psychological processes are qualitatively transformed in group situations and that we can see ourselves as having the attributes of the social group. This is a significant counter to mainstream economic theory which still assumes that consumption is an autonomous individual process even if it is at the level of the family as an uber-individual as per Gary Becker's theory of the allocation of time. Tajfel (1972: 292) defined social identity as 'the individual's knowledge that he belongs to certain social groups together with some emotional and value significance to him of this group membership' (cited in Hogg, 2001: 186). Jenkins (2008: 112–13) summarizes social identity theory along the following lines. Social identity is the 'internalisation of . . . collective identifications' (p. 112). The fact that people belong to groups gives them social identities and enables them to assess themselves. Social group members will tend to favour in-group members and discriminate against out-group members.

This set-up is capable of being analysed within the economic theory of clubs inspired by the work of James Buchanan (1965). However, that still operates at the level of individually determined consumption as the club is merely an instrumental vehicle for the further attainment of individual utility maximization. Nevertheless, group members invest in the maintenance of positive distinctiveness for their in-group. Groups are concerned to differentiate themselves from other groups. 'Self-categorisation as a group member . . . generates a sense of similarity with other group members, and attractiveness or self-esteem' (Jenkins, 2008: 113). Group membership therefore matters to the individual, both in terms of how he or she may seek to warrant and maintain his/her membership and at the same time keep others out. Within marketing and consumer studies, SIT has been used in research papers on country of origin effects in consumer behaviour (Verlegh, 1999), and within management, Hogg (2001) has used it to discuss leadership. It is fair to say, however, that SIT is not widely used within marketing, consumer studies or popular music studies. At a basic level, it offers a way of thinking about the importance of social identity, identification with social groups, group membership, self-esteem, and positive distinctiveness or differentiation. To this extent, it offers potential explanatory power in relation to groups such as 'brand communities' and 'consumer tribes', but these discourses tend to ignore it.

CELEBRITY AND FANDOM

In contemporary 'leisure tribes' (adopting this term for the sake of argument), the totem is often a celebrity. Traditionally, a celebrity was someone with a particular talent, skill, power, or knowledge, for example, a politician, movie star, footballer, model, musician, criminal, artist, or rock band. Nowadays, however, anyone, including the person next door, can be a celebrity. From an economic point of view, the key issue is simply the durability and exploitability of the celebrity 'property', how much celebrity can sell (Pringle, 2004). This has been explored in a book by one of the world's 'leading economic bloggers', Tyler Cowen (2002). Celebrity examples include Beyoncé Knowles, Kanye West, Andy Warhol, Wayne Rooney, Jade Goody, the Olsen twins, L'il Romeo, the Pope, David Lynch, U2, David Beckham (Milligan, 2004) and Brangelina. Celebrities can be read as brands. They project brand identity and personality, and their fans form brand images of them. They enjoy brand equity, they have brand value and they generate revenue streams. By creating celebrity 'properties' – identity monopolies – investors can exploit the crossover, endorsement and merchandising opportunities available within the creative, cultural and sporting industries. Celebrities can also function as endorsers of brands in the marketplace. Celebrities, like products, have life cycles, and it matters economically that they be managed for longevity. The survival of a major celebrity brand matters economically to a lot of people – their agents, magazine proprietors, television and radio, fashion, to name a few. Madonna is an example of a celebrity who has extended her brand life cycle through regular and conscious changes of musical identity, making use of resources and styles already available in culture to make something new, often in a strategically scandalous way. Kate Moss's fall from grace owing to alleged cocaine use is also instructive. After a tabloid scandal, Moss was dropped by the brands which she endorsed, but not long after was earning many times more from a wider range of sponsors, presumably because her darker brand image was a source of economic benefit for them.

The demand-side connection for celebrities is of course the fan (Lewis, 1992; Harris and Alexander, 1998). From being a somewhat derogatory term to describe an individual who is fanatical – that is, almost deranged – about something or someone, the word 'fan' has achieved considerable academic respectability. In popular parlance, one can be a fan of anyone from Barack Hussein Obama to Madonna. Fandom involves emotion, from the serenity of simple contemplation of the object of devotion to the dark desire to stalk and possess it. Providers of goods, ideas, services and experiences for fans seek to mobilize emotional response, engagement, imagination, eroticism, and . . . cash. Being a fan can be seen as having potentially significant economic implications. A fan's enthusiastic adherence to his/her ice hockey club, football team, rock band, television programme, movie actor, favourite singer, theatre director, politician or visual artist can lead to a considerable amount of money changing hands. Depending on the nature of the 'product' in question, fans may pay hard-earned money to attend live appearances, shows, exhibitions, games, conventions, or plays, to acquire audio and audio-visual recordings, and of course a wide range of merchandise, including books, T-shirts, memorabilia and so on. Each fan negotiates his or her own psychological distance from the object of his/her attention and the cost of that relationship. The 'average' fan will not spend limitless amounts of money, but will have to allocate money from a limited set of resources. Some fans develop into collectors or 'completists', fans who must buy everything their favourite artist or football club has produced. Some fans invest part of the domestic budget in season tickets; others are more sporadic in their attendance at events. The attraction to the celebrity provides one axis of fandom, and generally speaking one might reasonably expect that the closer the feeling of attachment, the more meaningful the connection, the more likely the fan is to spend money.

The other axis of fandom is the connection to other fans, the so-called 'tribe' or 'brand community'. For the initiate, more-experienced fans serve as a resource of knowledge about the object of fandom and are useful in terms of gaining more insight and meaning as it were below the surface. Being a fan provides access to a fan culture (Hills, 2002), which provides resources for the construction of a social identity. Fans are both producers and consumers in this culture and circulate texts in social interaction which construct and maintain the fan culture for as long as they wish to remain a part of it, for as long as it remains socially, culturally, politically and economically meaningful to them.

Celebrities need fans, and their business managers need ways of figuring out how to make money from them. Theories about consumer tribes and brand communities offer resources which may help. There are other notions, however, such as the idea of the 'market maven' (Gladwell, 2000; Goldsmith et al. 2003; Clark and Goldsmith, 2005; Geissler and Edison, 2005; Goodey and East, 2008). A market maven is a member of a consumer group who is very well informed on marketing issues and able to signpost other consumers to good deals or information. Identifying these people within the brand community is an important strategy for brand managers. Other strategies include product placement, sponsorship and of course celebrity endorsement, and these are ways in which commercial brands insert themselves into culture and disseminate their identity very widely. The idea of individuals as leaders of demand cycles has been put forward by various economists. As long ago as 1964, Marris proposed the idea of adventurous consumers who are later followed by others. More recently this kind of idea has been fleshed out in much more technical detail in works following Becker's famous 1991 paper on restaurant pricing.

CONCLUSION

The combination of celebrity mediatization and ardent fan groups makes for powerful cultural connections between the supply and demand sides of economic exchanges, and helps to create significant economic opportunities within leisure markets. Although concepts such as consumer tribes and brand communities lack a clear political dimension, and do not consider the individual as citizen or worker, they do offer ways of understanding how social, collective, aspects of consumption relate to market economics. The important issues for the producer in any specific sector or subsector of the leisure economy are, first, to understand precisely how, and the degree to which, these social groupings affect economic exchanges, and, second, how best to 'manage' them.

NOTES

1. Received idea.
2. Lost ideas.

REFERENCES

Ahonen, T. and A. Moore (2005), *Communities Dominate Brands: Business and Marketing Challenges for the 21st Century*, London: Futuretext.
Becker, G.S. (1991), 'A note on restaurant pricing and other examples of social influences on price', *Journal of Political Economy*, **99**, 1109–16.
Buchanan, J. (1965), 'An economic theory of clubs', *Economica*, **32** (1), 1–14.
Clark, R. and R. Goldsmith (2005), 'Market mavens: psychological influences', *Psychology and Marketing*, **22** (4), 289–312.
Cova, B. and V. Cova (2001), 'Tribal aspects of postmodern consumption research: the case of French in-line roller skates', *Journal of Consumer Behaviour*, **1** (1), 67–76.
Cova, B. and V. Cova (2002), 'Tribal marketing: the tribalisation of society and its impact on the conduct of marketing', *European Journal of Marketing*, **36** (5/6), 595–620.
Cova, B., R. Kozinets and A. Shankar (eds) (2007), *Consumer Tribes*, London: Butterworth-Heinemann.
Cowen, T. (2002), *What Price Fame?*, new edn, Cambridge, MA: Harvard University Press.
Devasagayam, P. and C. Buff (2008), 'A multidimensional conceptualization of brand community: an empirical investigation', *Sport Marketing Quarterly*, **17** (1), 20–29.
Douglas, M. and B. Isherwood (1979), *The World of Goods*, New York: Basic Books.
Flaubert, G. (1994), *The Dictionary of Received Ideas*, London: Penguin.
Frank, T. (1998), *The Conquest of Cool: Business Culture, Counterculture, and the Rise of Hip Consumerism*, Chicago, IL: University of Chicago Press.
Gair, C. (2007), *The American Counterculture*, Edinburgh: Edinburgh University Press.
Geissler, G. and S. Edison (2005), 'Market mavens' attitudes towards general technology: implications for marketing communications', *Journal of Marketing Communications*, **11** (2), 73–94.
Gladwell, M. (2000), *The Tipping Point*, Boston, MA: Little Brown.
Goldsmith, R., L. Flynn and E. Goldsmith (2003), 'Innovative consumers and market mavens', *Journal of Marketing Theory and Practice*, **11** (4), 54–64.
Goodey, C. and R. East (2008), 'Testing the market maven concept', *Journal of Marketing Management*, **24** (3/4), 265–82.
Harris, C. and A. Alexander (1998), *Theorizing Fandom: Fans, Subculture and Identity*, Cresskill, NJ: Hampton Press.
Heath, J. and A. Potter (2006), *The Rebel Sell: How the Counter Culture Became Consumer Culture*, Mankato, MN: Capstone Press.
Hills, M. (2002), *Fan Cultures*, London: Routledge.
Hogg, M. (2001), 'A social identity theory of leadership', *Personality and Social Psychology Review*, **5** (3), 184–200.

Jenkins, R. (2008), *Social Identity*, London: Routledge.
Kim, J. (2006), 'Advances toward developing conceptual foundations of internet brand community', *Advances in Consumer Research*, **33** (1), 300–301.
Lewis, L. (ed.) (1992), *The Adoring Audience: Fan Culture and Popular Media*, London: Routledge.
Maffesoli, M. (1988 [1996]), *The Time of the Tribes: The Decline of Individualism in Mass Society*, Newbury Park, CA: Sage.
Marris, R. (1964), *The Economic Theory of Managerial Capitalism*, London: Macmillan.
McAlexander, J., J. Schouten and H. Koening (2002), 'Building brand community', *Journal of Marketing*, **66** (1), 38–54.
McWilliam, G. (2000), 'Building stronger brand through online communities', *Sloan Management Review*, **41** (3), 43–54.
Milligan, A. (2004), *Brand It Like Beckham*, London: Cyan Books.
Muggleton, D. and R. Weinzierl (eds) (2003), *The Post-Subcultures Reader*, Oxford: Berg.
Muñiz, A. and T. O'Guinn (2001), 'Brand community', *Journal of Consumer Research*, **27**, 412–32.
Muñiz, A. and H. Schau (2005), 'Religiosity in the abandoned Apple Newton brand community', *Journal of Consumer Research*, **31** (4), 737–47.
Pringle, H. (2004), *Celebrity Sell*, London: Wiley.
Roszak, T. (1969), *Making of a Counter Culture*, Garden City, NY: Doubleday.
Schau, H. and A. Muñiz (2007), 'Temperance and religiosity in a non-marginal, non-stigmatized brand community', in Cova et al. (eds), pp. 144–62.
Schau, H., A. Muñiz and E. Arnould (2009), 'How brand community practices create value', *Journal of Consumer Research*, **73**, 30–51.
Swingrover, E. (2003), *The Counterculture Reader*, London: Longman.
Tajfel, H. (1972), 'Social categorization', English manuscript of 'La catégorisation sociale', in S. Moscovici (ed.), *Introduction à la Psychologie Sociale*, Vol. 1, Paris: Larousse, pp. 272–302.
Verlegh, P. (1999), 'Ingroups, outgroups and stereotyping: consumer behaviour and social identity theory', *Advances in Consumer Research*, **26**, 162–4.

13 The significance of commercial music festivals

Gretchen Larsen and Stephanie Hussels

INTRODUCTION

During the summer months of 2007, an estimated 485 music festivals, covering every genre of music, were held in the United Kingdom. This figure, which does not include any of the multitude of free festivals that also occur, represents a staggering 38 per cent growth in the number of festivals in just seven years (Mintel, 2008). This phenomenal growth shows little sign of slowing down, as many of the major festivals continue to sell out, some within a matter of hours of tickets being made available. This is attracting much attention from the media and other social commentators who are asking, what is so special about music festivals that attracts such an insatiable interest from all involved – audiences, artists and organizers? Clearly, these festivals are economically valuable (see, for example, O'Sullivan and Jackson, 2002; Gibson and Connell, 2003), but there is some recognition that festivals are also important socially and culturally. Thus, it is only by taking a multidisciplinary approach that we can understand the significance of commercial music festivals in contemporary society.

Before exploring this issue, we must first define the very thing we are aiming to understand. In a very general sense, festivals are special occasions for celebration involving a range of artistic performances, which usually occur over a number of days. The roots of festivals can be traced back to the time of the first Olympic games in Greece, several hundred years BC (Sadie, 2001). Beyond this, there are a multitude of different interpretations of exactly what festivals are. *The New Grove Dictionary of Music and Musicians* gives some indication of this diversity in its entry for 'festivals'.

A generic term, derived from the Latin 'festivitas', for a social gathering convened for the purpose of celebration or thanksgiving. Such occasions were originally part of a ritual nature and were associated with mythological, religious and ethnic traditions. From the earliest times festivals have been distinguished by their use of music, often in association with some kind of drama. In modern times the music festival, frequently embracing other kinds of art, has flourished as an independent cultural enterprise, but it is still often possible to discover some vestige of ancient ritual in its celebration of town or nation, political or religious philosophy, living or historical person. The competitive music festival has also retained combative features reminiscent of festival events of former times. (Ibid.)

This description points to the multitude of complex and related social, cultural, economic, spiritual and political functions of festivals, which contribute to their significance. For example, we can understand festivals as a form of cultural activity in which culture is created, maintained, transformed and transmitted to others. Although on this basis, festivals would appear to be similar to other forms of cultural and artistic activity, they do differ in that artistic production and consumption are concentrated in time and space (Waterman, 1998). The festival is at once a social, cultural, economic, spiritual and political phenomenon, which spreads across a wide range of cultural sectors.

A music festival is an important variant (Shuker, 1998). Perhaps because of their diverse nature, the academic study of music festivals is thinly spread across a range of disciplines (for example, human geography, sociology and business). However, three characteristics of music festivals emerge from the literature which help us define their form and function. The first characteristic is the spatial and temporal form of music festivals, which facilitates the transformation of places from everyday settings into temporary, unique and spectacular environments created for and by specific groups of people (Waterman, 1998; Connell and Gibson, 2003). An important facet of festivals is that they are to do with space, and although they are not necessarily bounded by place 'all festivals have at least one thing in common in that they are ephemeral' (Waterman, 1998, p. 58). The second characteristic of festivals is that they create and maintain cultural meaning and social structure. Festivals can reinforce popular music personas, and create icons and myths in the process (Shuker, 1998). In this vein, King (2004) contends that they can also honour musicians who have made great contributions, preserve a musical (blues) culture and even facilitate racial integration. The final characteristic is the formation of community. Although generally considered to be temporary, some communities of audiences, performers and/or organizers last beyond the spatial and temporal boundaries of the festival itself (Connell and Gibson, 2003). There are potentially many reasons why these communities are drawn together, for example to pay homage to artists (Shuker, 1998) or to 'practice divergent social logics' (Kozinets, 2002, p. 20). These characteristics are apparent in both commercial and non-commercial festivals.

Most contemporary music festivals are explicitly commercial, with various 'stakeholders', such as tour promoters, local government and artists, seeking to benefit financially from them. Perhaps the easiest way to define what makes a festival commercial is to consider what it is not: a free festival. A free festival was initially one where the organizers were not seeking, and did not make, a profit, which was usually organized in protest against capitalism and corporatization. In addition, they also became utopian visions and models of alternative societies. Thus the economy of a free festival is characterized by mutual aid and exchange, rather than by the circulation of money (Partridge, 2006). A commercial festival, on the other hand, utilizes an economy based on money and does seek to make a profit. This profit could be for used for a range of purposes, from increasing stakeholder wealth, to charity, and even simply to grow and develop the festival itself. However, as discussed later, some festivals such as Glastonbury, which are considered commercial by these criteria, can and do offer utopian visions to those who attend and look upon them (Larsen and O'Reilly, 2008).

The aim of the chapter is to develop an understanding of the significance of commercial music festivals from both an economic, and a wider, consumption perspective. To this end, their success is analysed from an economic perspective. Although this analysis clearly demonstrates the economic significance of music festivals, it does not provide any insight into their cultural, social and/or political significance, and therefore is unable to address such questions as: why are music festivals so popular, why do they sell out so quickly, and why are people willing to pay such high prices (and take personal risks) to attend? A consumption perspective facilitates an understanding of such questions, as it draws on social, cultural and political explanations of various participants' involvement in, and experience of music festivals. Thus, following the economic analysis, this chapter will develop a discussion organized around the following benefits of commercial music festivals: social impact; culture and symbolic meaning; community and scenes; and carnival and utopia.

ECONOMIC ANALYSIS OF THE COMMERCIAL FESTIVAL MARKET

Nowadays most cities or regions host music festivals of one sort or another. Thus, while music festivals are not a novelty as such, it is the considerable increase in their number over the years that is astonishing. Festivals encompass a vast number and large variety of events ranging from high-profile national events to amateur music events for which attendees are charged very little. In the UK, music festivals have developed into a massive summer industry with the majority of events taking place between May and September each year. The online social media platform for festival-goers, 'Virtual Festivals', estimated 450 music festivals alone in 2010, which represents an increase of 34 per cent from 2000. Rock/pop festivals are most popular in terms of attendances followed by classical, jazz and opera festivals (Mintel, 2008).

Many of the large commercial music festivals are well known and have been held for many years. These include, for example, Glastonbury, which ran in 1970 for the first time and since then has grown into the UK's largest and one of the world's best-known music and arts festivals, or the Reading Music Festival, which started in 1961 and since then has seen an expansion with the introduction of the partnering Leeds Music Festival.

Music festivals have, however, grown not only in number, but also in terms of scale as measured by attendance and repertoire, see Table 13.1. From 2000 onwards, all of the festivals showed a substantial increase in terms of tickets sold. In line with the increase in number of festivals and level of attendance, an increase in ticket prices across the festivals can be observed as well. So, for example, between 2000 and 2010 ticket prices for Glastonbury, V Festival and the Reading Festival increased by 213 per cent, 234 and 225 per cent, respectively, which means, on average, more than 20 per cent per year. Despite the increase in prices the sell-out rates for the large commercial festivals have been very high with, for example, the 2010 'T in the Park' festival officially selling out within 90 minutes (NME News, 2010).

Box office income continues to be the largest single income for festivals, indicating the importance of attendance development to the festival sector. A survey of 3,000 UK festival fans in 2009 estimated average ticket spend at £140 per head, plus a further £130 on drinks, £60 for food and £100 for travel (Canizal Villarino et al., 2009). The Association of Independent Festivals (2010) surveyed nearly 5,000 festival attendees at 13 of its member festivals about spending habits regarding festivals in the UK. According to the figures, 350,000 people attending independent festivals will spend an average of £346 on festivals in 2010, including ticket prices and contributing to the local economy. When measuring the economic impact of any cultural activity, in most instances, the greatest part of the impact is made by festival attendees spending money on hospitality, accommodation, retail and travel in the economy of a specific geographic location. As an example, in 2004, Brighton Festival generated £22 within the city's economy for every £1 spent on tickets and thereby accounted for over £20 million within the local economy alone. Although Brighton represents the larger end of the festival spectrum, it gives an idea of the secondary impact or 'knock-on' effects that festivals have on local economies and, ultimately, on the UK economy as a whole. According to Reading Council, the Reading Festival brings more than £7 million to Reading and its inhabitants each year as a

Table 13.1 *Major UK commercial music festivals*

Name of festival	Short description and location	Date	Repertoire (artists/acts/ number of stages)	Price per ticket (weekend camping)	Number of tickets sold
Glastonbury	UK's largest and world's best-known music and arts festival. Hosts huge spectrum of attractions from major acts to the obscure. Location: Worthy Farm, Pilton, Somerset	Last weekend of June	2010:	2010: £185	2010: 177,000
			2009: 45 stages	2009: £155	2009: 177,500
			2008: 18 stages/600+ acts	2008: £155	2008: 177,000
			2007:	2007: £145	2007: 177,500
			2006: No festival	2006: No festival	2006: No festival
			2005:	2005: £125	2005: 153,000
			2004: 25 stages/2000 acts	2004: £112	2004: 150,000
			2003:	2003: £105	2003: 150,000
			2002:	2002: £97	2002: 140,000
			2001: No festival	2001: No festival	2001: No festival
			2000:	2000: £87	2000: 100,000
			1999: 300 acts	1999: £83	1999: 100,500
			1998:	1998: £80	1998: 100,500
			1997:	1997: £75	1997: 90,000
			1996: No festival	1996: No festival	1996: No festival
			1995:	1995: £65	1995: 80,000
			1994:	1994: £59	1994: 80,000
			1993:	1993: £58	1993: 80,000
			1992:	1992: £49	1992: 70,000
			1990	1990: £38	1990: 70,000
			1989:	1989: £28	1989: 65,000

Festival	Details	Date	Year	Stages/acts	Price	Attendance
Reading/Leeds Festival	UK's longest-running festival, premier rock and Indie event. Location: Reading and Leeds. Reading Festival started in 1961 (previously called National Jazz and Blues Festival) and Leeds in 1999.	August bank holiday	1987:		£21	60,000
			1986:		£17	60,000
			1985:		£16	40,000
			1984:		£13	35,000
			1983:		£12	30,000
			1982:		£8	25,000
			1981:		£8	18,000
			1979:		£5	12,000
			1978:		£0	500
			1971:		£0	12,000
			1970:		£1	1,500
			2009:		£180	
			2008:	4 stages/100 acts	£155	Reading: 80,000; Leeds: 70,000
			2007:			
			2006:	7 stages/200 acts	£135	Reading: 80,000; Leeds: 70,000
			2005:			
			2004:	6 stages/150+ acts	£105	Reading: 55,000; Leeds: 50,000
			2003:			
			2002:			
			2001:	No festival	No festival	No festival
			2000:		£80	
			1999:		£78	

Table 13.1 (continued)

Name of festival	Short description and location	Date	Repertoire (artists/acts/ number of stages)	Price per ticket (weekend camping)	Number of tickets sold
			1998:	1998: £75	1998:
			1997:	1997: £70	1997:
			1996:	1996:	1996:
			1995:	1995: £60	1995:
			1994:	1994: £55	1994:
			1993:	1993: £49	1993:
			1992:	1992:	1992:
			1991:	1991: £54	1991:
			1990:	1990:	1990:
			1989:	1989: £32.50	1989:
			1988	1988:	1988
			1987:	1987: £25	1987:
			1986:	1986:	1986:
			1985:	1985:	1985:
			1984:	1984:	1984:
			1983:	1983:	1983:
			1982:	1982:	1982:
			1981:	1981:	1981:

			Lineup	Price	Attendance
V Festival	Mainstream pop, rock and dance with strong corporate emphasis. Locations: Highlands Park, Chelmsford, Essex and Weston Park, Telford Staffordshire	Pen-ultimate weekend of August	1980:	1980: £12.50	1980:
			1979:	1979: £10.95	1979:
			1978:	1978: £8.95	1978:
			1977:	1977:	1977:
			1976:	1976:	1976:
			1975:	1975:	1975:
			1974:	1974: £5.50	1974:
			1973:	1973: £4.40	1973:
			2009: 94 acts	2009: £152.50	2009:
			2008: 3 stages/50 acts per site	2008: £145	2008: Highlands: 75,000; Weston: 90,000
			2007:	2007:	2007:
			2006: 4 stages/80+ acts per site	2006: £100	2006: 67,000 per site
			2005:	2005:	2005:
			2004: 7 stages/50+ acts per site	2004: £98.50	2004: 60,000 per site
			2003:	2003:	2003:
			2002:	2002:	2002:
			2001:	2001:	2001:
			2000:	2000: £65	2000:
			1999:	1999:	1999:
			1998:	1998:	1998:
			1997:	1997:	1997:
			1996: 2 stages/one tent	1996:	1996:

257

Table 13.1 (continued)

Name of festival	Short description and location	Date	Repertoire (artists/acts/number of stages)	Price per ticket (weekend camping)	Number of tickets sold
T in the Park	Scotland's rival to Glastonbury and Reading, rock and pop's biggest names along with DJs, hip hop, and dance performances. Location: Ballado, Kinross-shire	Second weekend of July	2010:	2010: £165	2010:
			2009: 180 acts	2009:	2009: 85,000
			2008: 6 stages/110 acts	2008: £130	2008: 80,000
			2007: 11 stages/180 acts	2007:	2007: 80,000
			2006: 9 stages/170 acts	2006: £115	2006: 75,000
			2005: 10 stages/170 acts	2005:	2005: 69,000
			2004: 7 stages/100+ acts	2004: £88	2004: 60,000 per day
			2003:	2003:	2003: 55,000
			2002:	2002:	2002:
			2001:	2001:	2001:
			2000:	2000:	2000:
			1999:	1999:	1999:
			1998:	1998:	1998:
			1997:	1997:	1997:
			1996:	1996:	1996:
			1995:	1995:	1995:
			1994:	1994:	1994: 17,000

Global Gathering	Original dance music festival, includes some of the genre's biggest names. Features adrenaline, village, fairground, hot air balloons and open air cinema. Location: Long Marston, Stratford-upon-Avon	Last weekend of July	2010: 253 acts	2010: £120	2010: 50,000
			2009: 150 acts	2009: £115	2009: 50,000
			2008: 127 acts/music stage/8 areas	2008: £115	2008: 55,000
			2007: 154 acts	2007: £105	2007: 55,000
			2006: 9 stages/147 acts	2006: £105	2006: 45,000
			2005:	2005: £90	2005: 40,000
			2004: 9 stages/105 acts	2004: £47	2004: 35,000
			2003:	2003:	2003: 35,000
			2002:	2002:	2002: 35,000
			2001:	2001:	2001: 25,000

259

result of 80,000 music fans invading Reading at the end of August (Reading Museum Service, 2010). The Association of Independent Festivals (2010), estimates that the music festival business is booming and is contributing more than £1 billion each year to the UK economy. Festivals can hence be seen to make a great contribution both locally and nationally.

Moreover, the commercial festivals indirectly create additional employment. Many big UK festivals outsource food and drink provision. Central Catering Services Ltd, for example, generates £16 million annual income from bar and foodservice management at a dozen or so music festivals in England and Scotland and hires 2,500 temporary employees every summer (Canizal Villarino et al., 2009). Commercial festivals are also seen as a good place to make connections to customers, with brands increasingly teaming up with festivals.

Despite the recent economic downturn, the popularity of festivals continues to grow with most of the major UK festivals in 2009 having sold out immediately. The UK Performing Rights Society (PRS for Music) (2009) explains that most festivals are expected to be fairly recession proof, benefiting from four factors: (i) the UK's weak pound has made staying at home more attractive; (ii) the weak pound will attract more foreign revellers; (iii) festivals tend to attract a younger audience including students – many of whom have yet to be affected by the recession; and (iv) 10 per cent of festival-goers expect to spend more than in previous years.

Despite the commonly recognized economic benefit of commercial music festivals, Gibson and Connell (2005) note that surprisingly little academic work has quantified the economic dimensions of commercial music festivals. Previous economic research on festivals tended to look particularly at publicly funded, non-commercial festivals and has focused mostly on economic impact analysis. There is a notable lack of rigorous sector-wide research within the UK commercial festival sector. The sector is, to a large extent, an entity about which there is only regionally specific, art-form-specific or anecdotal data. As the sector is constantly changing, developing and growing, it is very difficult to 'benchmark' the data and analyse it within the broader, sector-wide ecology. The data presented hence aim to give a general indication on the overall economic importance of commercial music festivals and highlight a growth in number, magnitude and variety of commercial music festivals.

A CONSUMPTION PERSPECTIVE ON FESTIVALS

A consumption perspective facilitates a wider understanding of the significance of commercial music festivals. Festivals, like live music generally, are a form of experiential co-production and consumption which comprises cultural, symbolic, social and emotional dimensions (Botti, 2000) in addition to the political and economic. Thus by drawing on a consumption perspective, we can develop an enriched view of the consumer–fan audience (O'Reilly et al., 2010) and therefore we begin to understand the complex benefits that underpin the 'demand' for commercial music festivals.

In order to take a consumption perspective on commercial music festivals, we must not restrict ourselves to literature published under the consumer behaviour umbrella, but consider literature in the various disciplines that provide a rich and multidisciplinary understanding of arts audiences, for example, business and marketing, human geography, sociology, cultural and media studies, musicology and so on. Across these disciplines four key areas emerge that provide some insight into the wider significance of music festivals: social impact, culture and symbolic meaning, community and scenes, and carnival and utopia. Although these four areas are discussed separately, they are intimately related to one another. All refer to some aspect of social/cultural creative human experience, and therefore could all be considered under the umbrella of the social impact of music festivals. The following section, 'Social Impact' discusses the ways in which commercial music festivals are personally and socially beneficial. The remaining sections focus on particular, important aspects of the social impact of commercial music festivals, which highlights their cultural significance.

Social Impact

Arts activities, including commercial music festivals, have beneficial social impacts at both the individual and collective levels. This has long been acknowledged in the case of festivals, as early festivals were often as much about establishing and strengthening social bonds as they were about celebration and thanksgiving (for example, Sadie, 2001). However, it has only been relatively recently, during the 1990s, that in reaction to the dominance of economic impact reports, researchers, arts organizations and policy makers became interested in defining and measuring social impact (Drummond et al., 2008). One of the first reports on the social impact of the arts, undertaken by Comedia (Matarasso, 1997), outlines that arts activities have individual personal benefits such as personal growth, confidence, the development of skills and education, which can lead to improved social contacts and even employability. The resulting social networks and the mutual understanding that underpins them provide the platform for building local capacity for organization and self-determination, which in turn produces social change. Thus the arts can have a powerful, significant and potentially transformative impact on individuals and communities.

Social change was in fact, the *raison d'être* of the counter-cultural music festivals of the 1960s, which have provided the model for contemporary commercial festivals. These music festivals emerged at a time of social and political upheaval and a related challenge to orthodoxy (for example, Partridge, 2006). Music festivals acted as fuel to the counter-cultural desire for social change by providing spaces where 'one could get away with more risqué behaviour . . . than in other spheres in life – drug consumption, public nudity, protest and performance – an expressiveness not permitted in domestic and public spaces' (Gibson and Connell, 2005, p. 212). Echoes of these early sentiments can still be heard in contemporary commercial music festivals. Many festivals align themselves with a social or political issue with a specific aim to raise public awareness of that issue, for example, Glastonbury's early anti-nuclear link with CND and Live 8's role in the 'Make Poverty History' campaign.

There are, however, a wide variety of social impacts of the arts, of which social change is only one. Jermyn (2001) identified social impacts of community-level participation in the arts claimed in existing research reports. These are outlined below:

- develops self-confidence and self-esteem;
- increases creativity and thinking skills;
- improves skills in planning and organizing activities;
- improves communication of ideas and information;
- raises or enhances educational attainment;
- increases appreciation of the arts;
- creates social capital;
- strengthens communities;
- develops community identity;
- enhances social cohesion;
- decreases social isolation, improves understanding of different cultures;
- promotes interest in the local government;
- activates social changes;
- raises public awareness of an issue;
- enhances mental and physical health and well-being;
- contributes to urban regeneration;
- reduces offending behaviour;
- alleviates the impact of poverty; and
- increases the employability of individuals.

The impacts listed refer to community-level arts, rather than commercial music festivals specifically. However, as a form of art, commercial music festivals will deliver many of the same social impacts. 'Festivals also increasingly take on a wider range of roles as their significance increases, extending from mechanisms to sustain cultural groups, to mechanisms for assuring the acceptance of a particular cultural discourse, to a means of generating local pride, identity and income' (Crespi-Vallbona and Richards 2007, p. 103). Only some impacts have been explicitly discussed in the literature, and these are discussed below.

One of the objectives of many music festivals, particularly smaller festivals, is to enhance the cultural awareness and experience of the local population (Gibson and Connell, 2005), thus contributing to an increased appreciation of the arts. This impact can also be genre specific, as in the case of blues festivals in the Mississippi Delta which through celebration, have revived and preserved the blues (King, 2004). However, as King notes, these benefits are not always without cost, as communities in the Mississippi Delta have been 'repackaged' into an attractive offering for tourists visiting from outside the local community.

It is widely acknowledged that commercial music festivals create and strengthen communities (for example, Shuker, 1998; Waterman, 1998; Gibson and Connell, 2005), and that in doing so they improve understanding of different cultures (for example, Simoni, 2004) and enhance social cohesion (for example, Rao, 2001). These ideas are discussed in depth in the section, 'Community and Scenes'.

A final social impact to highlight here is that of urban regeneration and the alleviation of poverty. Much of the academic research conducted on music festivals has been done within the fields of tourism and geography, and it relates closely to these impacts. Gibson and Connell's (2005) chapter 'Festivals: community and capital' provides a thorough analysis of the role music festivals play in tourism, and the economic strategies that seek to achieve local and regional development through festival tourism.

Culture and Symbolic Meaning

Contemporary music festivals, along with other types of creative output, are significant as a form of cultural activity. Cultural activity 'can be regarded as an expression of, or a contribution to, the culture of a community – its beliefs and understandings about the world. Cultural products have no clear meaning outside their cultural context' (Drummond et al. 2008, p. 19). This quote identifies that an important relationship exists between art, symbolic meaning and culture.

Creative 'products' can have material or economic value, but the value attached to them by those for whom the art is significant, is also symbolic in nature. This particular kind of value is known as 'symbolic meaning', which is meaning that is representative of various elements of culture. It is important to note that these meanings are not fixed, rather they are multiple, fluid, dynamic and socially constructed. Thus cultural activities or 'texts' (Hesmondhalgh, 2002) are carriers of culture, and are important vehicles by which humans construct and interpret their reality (for example, Bowman, 1998). Symbolic meaning is therefore fundamentally important in linking art and culture.

Music festivals as a form of cultural activity, contribute to the production and consumption of culture:

> [A festival] 'can be regarded as a form of cultural consumption in which culture is created, maintained, transformed and transmitted to others. In this sense, festivals differ little from other forms of consumption in similar genres . . . But they are, of course, quite different, in that they usually involve production *and* consumption, *concentrated in time and place*. (Waterman, 1998, p. 65, italics in original)

Temporal and spatial concentration creates an intensity that encourages attendees to immerse themselves in the festival culture (Dowd et al., 2004). In turn, immersed participation creates, shapes and even contests the symbolic meaning of the festival. In fact, Gibson and Connell (2005) suggest that the meaning gained through participation in a festival might actually be the most significant factor for participants.

The symbolic meaning created and received through music festivals can challenge and change both individuals' and communities' understanding of the world we live in. The contesting of culture highlights the political and ideological nature of music festivals. Yazicioglu and Fuat Firat's (2007) study of commercial rock festivals showed how choices to attend and consumption practices at the festival are ideologically informed and driven due to the contested nature of the meaning of rock music itself. One valuable contribution of music festivals, then is, in raising cultural political questions about the relationship between aesthetics, style, taste and power, inequality, oppression, for those who attend, observe and study them. For example, Waterman (1998) explains how elites establish social distance through their support for certain kinds of music festivals.

This notwithstanding, music festivals also play a significant role in the preservation of culture. King's (2004) thorough analysis of blues festivals in the Mississippi Delta illustrates that one of the functions of these festivals is to preserve the culture of blues music and that which it represents. Cultures naturally develop and change; however, as they do, certain cultural activities, such as music, dance, language, folk art and even history, can be lost. Performance and celebration is one way of keeping cultural activities and traditions alive, as it encourages local community members and tourists to develop an appreciation for them.

Finally, festival participants are also able to use the symbolic meanings associated with a festival to create, maintain and communicate both individual and community identities, locating them culturally. Community identity is a fairly widely acknowledged dimension of music festivals (for example, Waterman, 1998; Quinn, 2003; Gibson and Connell, 2005) and is discussed in the following section. Individual identity practices are less well understood in the context of festivals, although Larsen et al. (2009, 2010) detail the symbolic consumption of recorded music. Given the rich symbolic meanings associated with music festivals, individual identity practices are likely to be as ubiquitous.

Community and Scenes

Festival audiences, performers and organizers can be conceptualized as temporary communities. They come together for a few days, and produce and consume the festival, and once the festival is over, all that is usually left are memories. Sometimes these communities do last beyond the spatial/temporal boundaries of the festival itself, such as the networks of performers that develop during a single festival or on the festival circuit (Connell and Gibson, 2003). Shuker (1998) suggests that festival audience communities have 'joined together in homage to the performers and/or the genre' (p. 122) although there might be a range of other reasons why festival audiences are drawn together. For example, although referring to an anti-market as opposed to a commercial festival, research exploring consumer emancipation at the Burning Man Festival in the USA concluded that participants 'successfully construct a temporary hyper community from which to practice divergent social logics' (Kozinets, 2002, p. 20) through which temporary emancipation may be achieved. Thus the formation of community, even if only temporary, facilitates significant experiences that go far beyond appreciation of the music on offer.

One of the most widely acknowledged community-related benefits of music festivals is the creation, maintenance and expression of group/community identity (for example, Shuker, 1998; Waterman, 1998; Connell and Gibson, 2003). Through sharing the production and consumption of the aesthetic and symbolic aspects of a festival, groups and communities can celebrate the shared mythologies, values and meanings that are integral to their identity. Thus the music festival is a '"cultural framework" reflecting the world view of a distinct socio-economic section of modern society'

(Waterman, 1998, p. 59). Festivals enable communities to reify their group identity (Rao, 2001) and this is one of the key reasons why music festivals play an important role in tourism strategies.

By focusing on the identity of groups or communities, we are essentially focusing on processes of distinction. Intimately related to identity, and of equal interest, is the role that festivals play in facilitating social integration and community cohesion. 'The need to create a cohesive community around such identities implies a lessening of social and cultural difference within the local community' (Crespi-Vallbona and Richards, 2007, p. 113). King (2004) shows that even in a highly segregated and fragmented society such as the Mississippi Delta, blues festivals have the power to unite people and create a sense of community, as people from all ethnic groups can develop important connections with one another.

The concept of 'scene' is important in understanding commercial music festival communities, as it refers specifically to communities that occur in relation to music. A scene is a 'cultural space' or a social milieu within which groups of producers, musicians and fans 'collectively share their common musical tastes and collectively distinguish themselves from others' (Bennett and Peterson, 2004, p. 1). Scenes differ from subcultures, because subcultures imply the existence of a commonly shared culture from which it is different and that all behaviours of those belonging to a subculture will adhere to its standards. Scenes present a more fluid and interchangeable sense of belongingness. Bennett and Peterson liken their notion of scenes to Bourdieu's (1979 [1984]) 'field' and Becker's (1982) 'art worlds'. Music festivals are a type of scene. Dowd et al. (2004) show that music festival scenes have three specific characteristics – intensity, boundary work and impact, and that the combination of these characteristics leads to the pilgrimage-like nature of festivals which has the potential to transform participants. Such a study provides valuable insight into the real and potential significance of music festivals.

Carnival and Utopia

Community offers spaces in which people can imagine ideal worlds and societies. As noted in the previous section, the hypercommunity that is created at the Burning Man Festival facilitates emancipation and divergent social logics (Kozinets, 2002). The intense experiences that facilitate such communities were arguably at their height in the rock and pop festivals of the 1960s:

> It was about music and freedom. Music was the medium; freedom was the message. For me the Festival was about free choice . . . values that had been

obscured by the rush of the industrial and technological revolutions. 1969 was the cusp of all the freedom movements of the last part of this millennium. And Woodstock lives on as the call for self-realization on every level for everyone. (Tiber, 1994, p. 267)

Festivals involve the questioning of the status quo, and the imagining and temporary enactment of a better future. The same purpose and process is characteristic of 'ideal societies' literature. There are five distinct types of ideal societies presented in literature: the Land of Cokaygne, Arcadia, the Perfect Moral Commonwealth, Millennium and Utopia (Davis, 1984). At its core, ideal society literature is concerned with how we organize and manage the production and consumption of natural and social resources. The different societies are distinguished by how they approach this issue. Although music festivals can demonstrate characteristics of all of the different kinds of ideal societies (Larsen and O'Reilly, 2008), most of the music festival literature has focused on Cokaygne, through the notion of carnival.

Bakhtin's (1965 [1984]) 'carnival' refers to a specific space and time in a society in which all normal barriers are broken down, hierarchical structures are challenged and the rules that underpin those structures are suspended. The normal order is turned upside down through satire, role reversals, mimicry, derision and excessiveness. In this way, festivals are oppositional. At Glastonbury alone, many examples of the inversion of the normal order and of the grotesque are provided (Larsen and O'Reilly, 2008). The 'kissing coppers' routine performed by actors is a good example:

> A couple dressed in absolutely authentic police uniforms who then start holding hands and kissing. It seemed to fit perfectly at Glastonbury when the police were trying to say they had a new soft image and were there to support the thing. I think the first time they weren't just kissing, they were giving away dope. (Aubrey and Shearlaw, 2004, pp. 212–13)

But, as noted by Gibson and Connell (2005, p. 250): 'in every case, the fact that such inversions and challenges to the established order are usually brief, present in marginal spaces and increasingly festive rather than overtly political, emphasises that they rarely substantially threaten that order'. However, the carnivalesque elements demonstrate how music festivals can provide a critique of the societies we live in.

The role of music festivals in imagining an ideal society is apparent in the utopian elements of the experience and image of music festivals. First conceived by Thomas More (1516), 'utopia' is a place where the beauty of society reigns while the evils of society are removed, therefore being a perfect social, legal and political system that is (maybe) unrealistic and impossible. Utopian societies are extremely detailed because they are generally man-made. Unlike the perfect moral commonwealth, utopia sees man as intrinsically corrupt and therefore he cannot be perfected in any way. Society must instead be designed to curb the worst of his excesses. Therefore utopia is essentially about space. The classic utopias are distinctly closed societies in which spatial controls establish societies that were unchanging and unchangeable. Utopian works idealize space as a means of regulating and controlling attitudes towards consumption. This necessitates the detail of utopian society: every possible measure must be taken to nullify man's sinful nature. Larsen and O'Reilly (2008) demonstrate how *Glastonbury Festival Tales* (Aubrey and Shearlaw, 2004), an account of music festivals, in this case, is characteristic of utopian literature. Therefore *Glastonbury Festival Tales* can be read as an example of contemporary utopian literature which is rhetorically constructed so as to build and maintain the cultural meaning of this iconic festival. The telling of such a story is only successful because it resonates with the experiences of those who have attended Glastonbury throughout its long history. This is telling of a significance of commercial music festivals, which, in addition to the economic, experiential and aesthetic, is critical and ideological.

CONCLUSIONS

Commercial music festivals are complex practices with many layers of meanings. A consumption perspective has provided insight into how the cultural, social and/or political significance of such festivals underpins their economic success. Acknowledging and understanding their wider significance guards against the risks associated with only taking an economic perspective, which is that it could lead to an economic bias and the limited treatment of festivals as commodities. Although commercial music festivals clearly are commodities, they retain and deliver important and meaningful social and aesthetic value beyond their economic value and therefore have not been, and should never be subjected to total commodification.

There are many economic, social, cultural, spiritual and political aspects of commercial music festivals that have not been investigated, but which could potentially yield fascinating insights. A comprehensive economic analysis would illuminate the full economic impact of festivals on those who have a direct investment in their success (for example, artistes, service providers, management) and on the communities that host them. It would also more clearly illustrate the market dynamics which are clearly in play within the festivals themselves, perhaps even providing insights into alternative forms of exchange. At a social–cultural level, further research could illuminate the full significance and contemporary manifestations of a practice which has been central to human celebration, community and the expression of hope for many centuries. We conclude with a quote from Michael Eavis which captures some of the essence of Glastonbury, the festival he has brought to life for 40 years:

> Glastonbury was becoming more than just a name. It was an idea of how life could be for an idyllic midsummer weekend in the Somerset pasturelands, with music, theatre, dance and poetry as well as 'way out' stalls and eccentricity beyond what you could expect probably anywhere else in the world. Green politics and youth fashion all have a huge part to play in what we call our youth culture of today. There will always be something new and unique that can be found in these fields – beautiful things, challenging art and incredible music. Long may the expression of free-thinking people reign over this land! (Aubrey and Shearlaw, 2004, p. 8)

REFERENCES

Association of Independent Festivals (2010), 'Festivals Remain Number One Entertainment Choice for Britons this Summer', available at: http://www.aiforg.com/ (accessed 17 July 2010).

Aubrey, C. and J. Shearlaw (2004), *Glastonbury Festival Tales*, London: Ebury Press.

Bakhtin, M. (1965 [1984]), *Rabelais and his World*, trans. Héléne Iswolsky, London: John Wiley & Sons.

Becker, H. (1982), *Art Worlds*, Berkeley, CA: University of California Press.

Bennett, A. and R. Peterson (2004), *Music Scenes: Local, Translocal and Virtual*, Nashville, TN: Vanderbilt University Press.

Botti, S. (2000), 'What role for marketing in the arts? An analysis of arts consumption and artistic value', *International Journal of Arts Management*, **2** (3), 14–27.

Bourdieu, P. (1979 [1984]), *Distinction: A Social Critique of the Judgement of Taste*, London: Routledge.

Bowman, W.D. (1998), *Philosophical Perspectives on Music*, Oxford: Oxford University Press.

Canizal Villarino, M., B. Whitehall and B. Mecke (2009), 'Music festivals: music and food for the masses', *Food Service Europe & Middle East*, Verlagsgruppe Deutscher Fachverlag, 21 August.

Connell, J. and C. Gibson (2003), *Sound Tracks: Popular Music, Identity and Place*, London: Routledge.

Crespi-Vallbona, M. and G. Richards (2007), 'The meaning of cultural festivals: stakeholder perspectives in Catalunya', *International Journal of Cultural Policy*, **13** (1), 103–22.

Davis, J.C. (1984), 'The history of utopia: the chronology of nowhere', in P. Alexander and R. Gill (eds), *Utopias*, London: Duckworth, pp. 1–17.

Dowd, T., K. Liddle and J. Nelson (2004), 'Music festivals as scenes: examples from serious music, Womyn's music and skate punk', in Bennett and Peterson (eds), pp. 149–67.

Drummond, J., G. Kearsley and R. Lawson (2008), 'Culture Matters: A Report for the Ministry of Research, Science and Technology', University of Otago, Dunedin, New Zealand.

Gibson, C. and J. Connell (2003), '"Bongo Fury"': tourism, music and cultural economy at Byron Bay, Australia', *Tijdschrift voor Economische en Sociale Geografie*, **94** (2), 164–87.

Gibson, C. and J. Connell (2005), 'Music and tourism: on the road again', *Aspects of Tourism*, **19**, London: Channel View Publications.

Hesmondhalgh, D. (2002), *The Cultural Industries*, London: Sage.

Jermyn, H. (2001), *The Arts and Social Exclusion: A Review Prepared for the Arts Council of England*, London: Arts Council England.

King, S. (2004), 'Blues tourism in the Mississippi Delta: the functions of Blues festivals', *Popular Music and Society*, **27** (4), 455–75.

Kozinets, R.V. (2002), 'Can consumers escape the market? Emancipatory illuminations from Burning Man', *Journal of Consumer Research*, **29** (1), 20–38.

Larsen, G. and D. O'Reilly (2008), 'Festival Tales: Utopian Tales', Academy of Marketing Annual Conference, Aberdeen, Scotland.

Larsen, G., R. Lawson and S. Todd (2009), 'The consumption of music as self representation in social interaction', *Australasian Marketing Journal*, **17** (3), 16–26.

Larsen, G., R. Lawson and S. Todd (2010), 'The symbolic consumption of music', *Journal of Marketing Management*, **26** (7/8), 671–85.

Matarasso, F. (1997), *Use or Ornament? The Social Impact of Participation in the Arts*, London: Comedia.

Mintel (2008), *Music Festivals and Concerts – UK – August 2008*, Mintel International Group Limited.

More, Thomas Sir (1516), *Utopia*, London: Penguin Classics.

NME News (2010), 'T in the Park festival 2010 sells out within 90 minutes', 27 February, available at: www.nme.com/news/various-artists/50002 (accessed 19 July 2010).

O'Reilly, D., F. Kerrigan and G. Larsen (2010), 'Re-orienting arts marketing: the new textbook generation', Academy of Marketing Annual Conference, Coventry, UK.

O'Sullivan, D. and M. Jackson (2002), 'Festival tourism: a contributor to sustainable local economic development?', *Journal of Sustainable Tourism*, **10** (4), 325–42.

Partridge, C. (2006), 'The spiritual and the revolutionary: alternative spirituality, British free festivals, and the emergence of Rave culture', *Culture and Religion*, **7** (1), 41–60.

PRS for Music (2009), 'British festivals to generate £450m in 2009', 11 June, available at: www.prsformusic.com (accessed 17 July 2010).

Quinn, B. (2003), 'Symbols, practices and myth-making: cultural perspective on the Wexford Festival opera', *Tourism Geographies*, **5** (3), 329–49.

Rao, V. (2001), 'Celebrations as social investments: festival expenditures, unit price variation and social status in rural India', *Journal of Development Studies*, **38** (1), 71–97.

Reading Museum Service (2010), 'Reading Festival', available at: www.readingmuseum.org. uk/collections/festival.htm (accessed 17 July 2010).

Sadie, S. (ed.) (2001), *The New Grove Dictionary of Music and Musicians*, London: Macmillan.

Shuker, R. (1998), *Key Concepts in Popular Music*, London: Routledge.

Simoni, V. (2004), 'Journeys of expression III: tourism and festivals as transnational practice', *International Journal of Tourism Research*, **6**, 375–6.

Tiber, E. (1994), *Knock on Woodstock*, New York: Festival Books.

Waterman, S. (1998), 'Carnivals for élites? The cultural politics of arts festivals', *Progress in Human Geography*, **22** (1), 54–74.

Yazicioglu, E. Tach and A. Fuat Firat (2007), 'Glocal rock festivals as mirrors into the future of culture(s)', in Russell Belk (ed.), *Consumer Culture Theory: Research in Consumer Behaviour*, **11**, London: Elsevier, pp. 101–17.

14 The rise and decline of drive-in cinemas in the United States

Mark Fox and Grant Black

INTRODUCTION

The drive-in cinema concept was developed during the Great Depression by Richard Hollingshead, Jr. He was motivated by a desire to create a business with good cash flow and a limited reliance on credit. Initially Hollingshead opened a gas station/restaurant where customers could also watch outdoor movies from their vehicles. This concept was intended to take advantage of three of the four things that he believed people would give up last during tough economic times (that is, food, automobiles and movies). After dropping the gas station, Hollingshead worked on modifying the drive-in cinema concept and eventually devised and (in 1933) patented a system of terraced parking ramps that positioned cars so as to not block one another's views. He patented three features of his invention: a fan-shaped parking lot, terraced rows and ramps that tilted cars upward for viewing/parking (Downs, 1953).

The first drive-in cinema opened in New Jersey on 3 June 1933, accommodated up to 400 automobiles, and showed the second-run British comedy, *Wife Beware*. Sound was provided by three loudspeakers. Admission was 25 cents per car and 25 cents per person, with a maximum overall admission fee of a dollar (Segrave, 2006), and a concession stand sold beer and light meals (Shaw-Smith, 2009) (25 cents is the equivalent of $4.16 in 2009 dollars). In comparing his concept to regular four-wall theatres, Hollingshead spoke enthusiastically of the convenience of drive-ins:

> The mother says she's not dressed; the husband doesn't want to put on his shoes; the question is what to do with the kids; then how to find a baby-sitter; parking the car is difficult or maybe they have to pay for parking; even the seats in the theater may not be comfortable to contemplate. (Quoted in Shaw-Smith, 2009, p. 35).

Hollingshead claimed that his drive-in invention solved these problems:

> The drive-in theater idea virtually trans-forms an ordinary motor car into a private theater box . . . In the drive-in theater one may smoke without offending others. People may chat or even partake of refreshments brought in their

cars without disturbing those who prefer silence . . . Here the whole family is welcome, regardless of how noisy the children are apt to be . . . The aged and infirm will find the drive-in a boon. (Quoted in ibid. p. 35)

Subsequently, the industry peaked in the late 1950s with over 4,000 drive-ins in the United States alone. A 1951 article trumpeted drive-ins as 'the most dynamic force in the entire motion picture industry' (Luther, 1951, p. 411). Yet, despite the historic prominence of drive-ins, Bruce Austin observed in 1983: 'Little, however, has been written in a comprehensive fashion about this form of exhibition' (p. 59). This is still pretty much the case today. The multivolume *History of American Cinema* does not mention drive-ins until the volume focusing on the 1960s (and, even then, fewer than two pages are devoted to drive-ins). Douglas Gomery's (1992) book *Shared Pleasures: A History of Movie Presentation in the United States* devotes only about three pages to drive-ins. The academic literature on drive-ins is sparse and has explored the characteristics of drive-in audiences (Luther, 1950a, 1951; Austin, 1983, 1984, 1985), changing exhibition patterns (Horton, 1976; Giles, 1983), the role of drive-in cinemas in the post-war viewing experience (Cohen, 1994), land use (Downs, 1953), technical developments in projection and sound (Underhill, 1950), architectural features (Bell, 2003), the display of comic soft-core films during the 1970s (Waller, 1983), and the development of drive-ins in Australia (Goldsmith, 1999). The only book of note on drive-ins is Kerry Segrave's *Drive-in Theaters: A History from their Inception in 1933* (other books devoted to drive-ins are best described as coffee-table fare – that is, heavy on images, but light on insight and research).

The paucity of research on drive-ins is puzzling when we consider that, at their peak (in the late 1950s), they comprised one-third of cinemas in the US (Kozak, 2007).[1] Drive-ins are also worthy of examination as this form of exhibition is somewhat rare today. By 2008 there were 393 drive-ins in the US, comprising only 6.6 per cent of all cinemas. This begs the question: given their historic prominence, what led to the decline of drive-ins?

This chapter progresses as follows: in the next section we contrast the drive-in experience to that of traditional, indoor cinemas. The third section outlines the early development of drive-ins, and the fourth looks at their rapid growth in the post-Second World War period. The fifth section shows how drive-in owners encouraged addictive consumption by drive-in patrons. In the sixth section we turn our attention to how drive-ins encourage considerate conduct by patrons. The seventh section shows why drive-ins declined in popularity over time. Then, in the eighth section, we look at a modern alternative, inspired by drive-ins, namely guerilla drive-ins and MobMovs (Mobile Movies). The final section concludes the chapter.

THE DRIVE-IN EXPERIENCE

Table 14.1 shows the advantages and disadvantages of drive-ins relative to traditional cinemas and illustrates that these experiences are by no means perfect substitutes. Drive-ins have an advantage over traditional theatres in that they provide a more social atmosphere for patrons. A survey of attendees at a Rochester, New York, drive-in, found that almost one-sixth of attendees felt the most important reason for going to a drive-in was to 'have fun' (Austin, 1983). Drive-ins also offer greater personal privacy and space than traditional theatres, with cars becoming the equivalent of theatre boxes. In the comfort of their own vehicle, drive-in attendees can largely do whatever they choose. Austin's survey of drive-in attendees found that almost 16 per cent ranked privacy as the most important reason for attending.

By reducing constraints on attendance, drive-in theatres are often more family friendly than traditional theatres. Giles summarizes this point thus: 'Rather than pay a baby sitter while they attend a walk-in theater, parents take the children with them to the movies. At the drive-in, the snack bar supplies a wide range of food and drink, children are free to talk and play without disturbing other patrons' (1983, p.70). On the other hand, traditional theatres have increasingly worked to reduce potentially disruptive behaviour by patrons, including increasing audience monitoring, raising penalties for noise, and prohibiting children less than six years of age for evening showings (Gomery, 1992).

Table 14.1   Advantages and disadvantages of drive-ins versus traditional cinemas

	Advantages	Disadvantages

Drive-ins	Social atmosphere
	Privacy of vehicle
	Being outside
	Lower admission cost
	Multiple features
	Family friendly
	Can bring personal
	  belongings
		Limited movie selection
		  compared to multiplexes
		Lower sound quality
		Reliance on weather

Traditional cinema	Wide movie selection
	Convenient locations
	Better sound quality
	Comfortable viewing
	  environment/stadium
	  seating
		Limited privacy
		More restrictions on
		  behaviour
		Less social atmosphere
		Higher cost
		Less family friendly

Drive-ins have struggled to acquire first-run films as easily as traditional theatres (Austin, 1983; Giles, 1983).[2] As a consequence, drive-ins' exhibition costs have also been lower as they have often shown classic movies, or have shown movies after they have already spent several weeks being exhibited in traditional cinemas. Also, while seeing a movie when it is first released is a major reason for attending a theatre, other motives are more important. De Silva (1998) found that the major reason for attending movie theatres was the ability to escape one's daily life (cited as the most important reason for movie attendance by 43.8 per cent of patrons); whereas seeing a movie when it was first released was the major motive for only 10.3 per cent of moviegoers. However, it is unclear whether De Silva's research is focusing on just indoor theatres or on both indoor theatres and drive-ins.

Compared to indoor theatres, drive-ins have typically provided more value for patrons (Loeffler, 2007). A single admission price typically covers a double feature and admission prices for adults are typically lower than for non-matinee sessions at indoor theatres. Compared to indoor cinemas, drive-ins provide patrons with a longer viewing experience per dollar of admission. The average admission price for drive-ins is around $6.66 for adults, with children often being admitted for less (or for free). This compares to an average of $7.18 for all US ticket prices (National Association of Theater Owners, 2009a); however, evening prices for adults often are $8 or more. For most drive-ins this admission price covers a double or a triple feature. In contrast, it is very rare for indoor cinemas to offer double or triple features.[3]

Drive-ins also have various disadvantages compared to traditional theatres. The emergence of drive-ins as a form of exhibition is a way to bring movies to the masses, who were often located in non-urban areas (Segrave, 2006). As urbanization and land values increased, the economic rationale for drive-ins diminished due to their need for large tracts of open land (Giles, 1983; Gomery, 1992). The development of modern multiplex theatres in urban communities provided greater accessibility and increased movie-viewing options compared to existing drive-ins. Moreover, technological advances in movie sound made traditional theatres increasingly attractive relative to drive-ins. Traditional theatres could more readily adopt new sound technologies than drive-ins, which had to rely, first, on loudspeakers, then through personal speakers, and, today, FM radio transmission. All these technologies provided poorer sound quality than technologies used in indoor theatres (Segrave, 2006). Today, the high cost of adopting new digital sound technologies may be prohibitive to many independent drive-in operators, which will only serve to widen the gap between drive-ins and walk-ins.

Drive-ins also face uncertain weather conditions (ibid.). Seasonal changes limit when they can operate, particularly in colder climates. For 2009, we were able to find information on the length of season for 310 of the 383 existing drive-ins. Relatively few drive-ins (12 per cent) were open all year. Most (77 per cent) were open for between five and seven months of the year, during the warmest months.[4] Moreover, inclement weather poses greater economic risks for drive-ins than for traditional theatres (the operations of the latter are rarely affected by weather). While inclement weather can reduce the quality of the drive-in experience or prevent movie showing altogether, it can also dissuade moviegoers from choosing to attend a drive-in (even when weather would permit operation). Despite the inherent weather risks of outdoor movie watching, the lure of the outdoors will likely continue to draw patrons. Austin (1983) found that almost 8 per cent of drive-in patrons considered being outdoors as the most important reason for attendance, while another 2 per cent were drawn to the different movie experience of a drive-in. Aside from generically referring to themselves as 'ozoners' (whereas indoor theatres are known as 'four-walls' or 'hardtops'), drive-ins often have names that play upon their outdoor appeal. It is common to see words such as 'moon', 'moonlight', 'sunset', 'sky', and 'star' in the names of drive-in theatres.

Having explored some of the pros and cons of drive-ins relative to traditional cinemas, we now turn our attention to factors that shaped the growth, and then the decline, of drive-ins.

EARLY DEVELOPMENT OF DRIVE-INS

By 1938, some five years after the first drive-in opened, there were only 50 to 60 drive-ins (Variety, 1938). The Great Depression and then the Second World War hindered the initial growth of drive-ins. Table 14.2 presents the first data on drive-in numbers and locations as detailed by *The Film Daily Year Book*. In early 1942, just after the US entered the war, there were fewer than 100 drive-ins. During the war the number of drive-ins remained relatively stable (by early 1946 there were only 102 drive-ins). There are several reasons for the initial slow growth of drive-ins. Most notably, the start of the war brought their development to a standstill. This was due to: (i) tyre and fuel rationing; (ii) government efforts to discourage 'pleasure driving' (that is, driving that was regarded as unnecessary, such as driving to the cinema. See Maxwell and Balcom, 1946a); and (iii) building restrictions (Bell, 2003). From 1941 to 1944 fuel consumption for passenger cars declined from 1.17 million barrels per day to 0.73 million barrels, a decline of some 37 per cent (Maxwell and Balcom, 1946b).

Table 14.2   Growth of US drive-ins, 1942 to 1952

	1942	1943	1944	1945	1946	1947	1949	1950	1951	1952
Alabama	2	3	3	3	3	3	14	41	73	101
Arizona	2	1	1	1	2	1	5	11	15	20
Arkansas	2	2	2	2	2	3	6	28	50	59
California	4	3	3	3	6	7	57	124	190	238
Colorado								18	38	45
Connecticut	2	2	2	2	2	1	8	12	21	32
Delaware							8	3	5	7
DC								1	1	1
Florida	6	6	6	6	7	7	22	69	109	153
Georgia	5	7	5	5	6	3	20	56	101	133
Idaho							15	20	31	35
Illinois	4	4	4	4	4	4	32	82	126	172
Indiana	4	4	4	4	4	5	40	75	119	150
Iowa							9	35	43	53
Kansas						1	14	36	62	66
Kentucky	1	1	1	1	1	2	21	55	76	88
Louisiana	2	3	3	3	3	5	10	22	48	68
Maine						1	4	15	30	37
Maryland	1	1	1	1	1	1	5	12	14	20
Massachusetts	10	9	9	9	9	11	27	48	71	83
Michigan	3	3	3	2	2	5	38	57	94	108
Minnesota							5	24	32	44
Mississippi	1	1	1	1	1	1	6	17	37	47
Missouri	2	2	2	2	2	4	16	47	81	100
Montana							3	12	24	29
Nebraska							6	18	25	31
Nevada						1	2	3	4	6
New Hampshire	2	2	2	2	2	2	5	16	24	30
New Jersey	1	1	1	1	1	1	9	22	32	42
New Mexico							4	11	23	34
New York	5	5	5	5	6	13	43	98	132	103
North Carolina	3	3	3	3	3	3	88	162	197	267
North Dakota								8	10	13
Ohio	11	11	11	11	11	26	113	181	222	259
Oklahoma							1	23	43	76	94
Oregon							1	6	18	44	56
Pennsylvania	6	5	5	5	5	7	62	152	229	278
Rhode Island		1	1	1	1	2	3	4	7	8
South Carolina	1	1	1	1	1	1	45	85	108	143
South Dakota							4	14	16	18
Tennessee	2	2	2	2	2	4	15	39	71	102
Texas	8	9	9	9	9	22	87	173	280	362

Table 14.2 (continued)

	1942	1943	1944	1945	1946	1947	1949	1950	1951	1952
Utah							14	21	35	43
Vermont							1	12	17	19
Virginia	4	5	5	5	4	3	27	61	75	101
Washington		1	1	1	1	1	17	25	35	45
West Virginia						1	19	69	93	124
Wisconsin	1	1	1	1	1	1	5	35	55	62
Wyoming								15	22	22
Total	95	99	97	96	102	155	983	2,205	3,323	4,151

RAPID GROWTH IN THE POST-WAR YEARS

Following the Second World War, gas and tyre rationing were over and modern automobiles were more available and affordable (Bell, 2003). The post-war years of 1946 to 1952 saw gasoline consumption by motorists increase by 63 per cent (Austin, 1983). Also, after the war suburbanization became widespread, with drive-ins offering one entertainment option for suburbanites.

At an individual level, the demand for moviegoing has been shown to be affected by gender, age, income and location (Collins and Hand, 2005). Movie demand is higher for males, the young, the affluent, and for urban dwellers. Many of these demographics were rapidly changing after the war, contributing to an environment conducive to the growth of drive-in theatres. The *Motion Picture Herald* predicted an increase in post-war drive-in construction, due to, among other factors, the 'resumption of normal restrictions upon the amorous impulses of youth' (quoted in Valentine, 1994, p. 160). The Baby Boom thus provides one explanation for the rapid growth in drive-ins after the war, when 'An ex-GI and his wife hungry for a cheap evening of family entertainment could pack the kids in the station wagon and head out to the new drive-in theater' (Thompson, 1983, p. 47).

The post-war development of drive-ins was also facilitated by a legal ruling that Hollingshead's 'invention' was not patentable after all.[5] On 8 April 1949, the First Court of Appeals ruled that Hollingshead's patent lacked inventiveness and merely constituted a somewhat obvious way of arranging vehicles using landscape features such as ramps (Segrave, 2006). Although many drive-ins had not observed the patent, this legal ruling opened the way for new developers to open drive-ins without the fear of lawsuits from Hollingshead.

As we shall now demonstrate, the growth of drive-ins was also facilitated by exhibition practices that encouraged addictive consumption.

ADDICTIVE CONSUMPTION

In the early years of drive-ins the movies being exhibited were somewhat secondary to the overall audience experience. In advertising their cinemas some drive-ins did not even mention the specific movies that they were showing (Thompson, 1983). Early drive-ins were often family entertainment venues, with playgrounds (complete with attendants), circus acts and big bands, dance floors, or miniature golf. Children were often admitted free as they consumed more concession items than adults. By the 1950s, drive-ins often resembled community recreation centres (Downs, 1953). One example of this phenomenon is a description of the Starlite Drive-in, circa 1956, which was operated by Stanford Kohlberg and located southwest of Chicago:

> Admission for adults is $1.25: youngsters under twelve, as many as can be packed in a car, are free, and each gets a door prize. The $1.25 pays for the movie, for dancing under the stars to music from name bands. It includes free milk for babies and free diapers if young mothers forget them. Kohlberg has a Kiddieland for youngsters too small to be interested in cinema drama. He has a miniature golf course and driving range for anyone in the family not interested in the picture. Three concession buildings purvey soft or hot drinks, pizza pies, hot dogs, hamburgers at popular prices. For one dollar Kohlberg sells his patrons a chicken dinner. One of his more brilliant ideas is the 'Starlite Happiness Book,' good for five or ten or fifteen dollars' worth of entertainment and food, sold on credit to any holder of a department-store or oil-company credit card. Kohlberg bills his charge accounts at the end of thirty days. (Taylor, 1956, p. 249)

The strategy of drive-in operators to foster a broader leisure experience for all family members coincides with the theory of rational addiction, which argues that individuals will engage in addictive behaviour as indicated by increased future consumption based on past consumption to maximize utility (Becker and Murphy, 1988). To increase revenues, drive-ins attempted to cultivate addictive consumption (whether for watching movies, eating at concession stands or engaging in other entertainment activities). Downs (1953) posits that one reason for higher concession sales by drive-ins (compared to four-wall theatres) was their picnic-like atmosphere, the convenience of eating in cars and 'ever-famished children' (p. 151).

While, in general, there is mixed evidence to support rationally addictive behaviour as applied to movie demand (Cameron, 1999; Collins et al., 2009a; Yamamura, 2009), some research suggests that movie watching is indeed influenced by past consumption. Yamamura found that movie theatre attendance in Japan depends on past attendance and that this link strengthens with age. Similarly, Collins et al. (2009b) found that purchases of movies on video increase for individuals who more frequently attend movie theatres, or who rent videos. Thus, drive-ins could increase revenues by encouraging attendance by all family members, each of whom could generate utility from different activities at the venue. For example, parents may like to watch a movie, teens may enjoy the social interaction, and children may like the concessions and other entertainment. By meeting these diverse needs, drive-ins were able to provide a higher level of utility for the collective family unit. Further, as drive-ins proliferated and competition increased, owners increasingly realized that they were also competing with household chores for patrons' time and attention. Given this, some drive-ins provided time-saving household devices so as to make drive-ins more appealing for patrons:

> Some drive-ins had bottle warmers so Mom wouldn't have to stay home with the baby. Others provided household services. Mom could drop off her grocery list and laundry when she arrived and pick up the shopping and clean clothes after the show. Dad could get an oil change or have a flat tire fixed. The family might place a dinner order with an attendant and have it delivered to their car, or take a trip to the concession stand for fried chicken, burgers, or even pizza pie. (Shaw-Smith, 2009, p. 36)

This strategic behaviour is consistent with Becker's (1965) theory of household production and joint utility maximization and the role of the value of time in influencing entertainment choices. Also, as the number of drive-ins rapidly increased in the 1950s and they were increasingly competing with one another, those drive-ins that offered such additional services had a point of differentiation. Movie theatres (including drive-ins) recognized the trade-offs between moviegoing and home-based activities (see, generally, Cameron 1986). By allowing consumers (particularly mothers and fathers) the opportunity to have some household services conducted in conjunction with attending drive-ins, the appeal of these cinemas was enhanced.

Another key appeal of drive-ins is the opportunities afforded for social interactions. However, one problem with leisure activities that involve groups is maximizing the benefits of social interaction while simultaneously minimizing the impact that the disruptive conduct of some has on the enjoyment of others.

ENCOURAGING POSITIVE AUDIENCE CONDUCT

One way that cinema owners encourage desirable audience behaviours is through various rules of conduct. To encourage acceptable public etiquette, traditional theatres generally follow standard policies for patron behaviour. Those rules are often announced, or listed onscreen, prior to the start of a movie (for example, instructing viewers to not talk during the show and to turn off cell phones). Some theatres (typically art-house cinemas and smaller, owner-operated venues) have staff make announcements prior to the start of the movie, thereby reinforcing awareness of theatre rules and safety information. Common rules include: no talking during the movie; no use of personal communication devices; no solicitation; no outside food or drinks; no recording devices; no smoking; no personal bags, such as backpacks; and (at least during some showings) no babies or small children. Likewise, to reduce audience conduct problems that are generally unique to drive-ins and to improve the experience of all patrons, drive-ins often have rules that patrons are expected to follow. Drive-ins.com provides guidance for patrons, including: asking drive-ins in advance of visits whether or not they allow pets; avoiding bringing laser pointers or outside food or drink; not shining headlights on the screen; driving slowly and using parking lights; and following rules regarding horn blowing ('Some drive-in operators encourage the ritual of horn honking to communicate enthusiastic agreement while some drive-in operators consider it rude and inconsiderate').

From their outset, drive-ins were envisaged as a less restrictive environment than traditional theatres. The desire of drive-in operators to provide increased freedom for patrons has persisted over the decades. Yet, like traditional theatres, drive-ins operate with rules governing patrons' behaviour to try to provide the best overall customer experience. In this regard, economic theory argues that society is made better off through each individual pursuing the maximization of his/her own personal well-being (utility), which is, in part, generated by engagement in leisure. Of relevance to this discussion are thoughts on the philosophy of leisure. Aristotle defines felicity as the highest good attainable through human action, which can be exemplified by leisure's idealistic combination of the search for knowledge, the search for virtue and the civil character (Hemingway, 1988). At the core of such reasoning is the belief that the pleasure derived from leisure is based on moral pursuits. However, contrary to Aristotle's ideal, some individuals may generate utility from uncivil or immoral behaviour. Such behaviour often imposes costs (disutility) on others. As a result, collective utility may diminish. In the context of drive-ins, imagine a patron who derives utility from being intoxicated, excessively noisy, and verbally abusive or violent towards others. Conversely, imagine another patron who would be made worse off from not only observing the disruptive patron's condition and rowdiness but who also bears the brunt of any confrontation with this individual. To reduce the risk of facing such disutility, some individuals would choose to participate in activities other than drive-ins (that is, activities that would generate higher individual utility). The ability of these individuals to switch to other activities will depend on the availability of substitute activities. In the case of drive-ins numerous substitutes exist, including watching movies at home. If a sufficiently large decline in drive-in attendance were to result from the abhorrent behaviour of some patrons, then drive-in owners would have an incentive to implement policies to curb uncivil behaviour in order to increase the likelihood of return visits by patrons. Therefore, drive-in theatres regulate patron behaviour through established guidelines to maximize the satisfaction of customers' experiences.

Drive-ins appear more likely than traditional theatres to highlight their rules online. This may be due to patrons being less familiar with drive-ins than with traditional theatres and to the environment in which drive-ins are exhibited. Only two of the ten major North American chains[6] provide any information about rules on their websites, whereas, in a sample of 20 drive-ins, we found that 65 per cent listed rules on their websites. Rules for drive-ins generally address three areas: business operations and profitability, safety, and the theatre experience. Common rules include: paid entry is required, re-entry is not allowed, no outside food or beverages, one allotted space per vehicle and recording devices are prohibited. These rules are designed to maintain or improve the profitability of drive-ins. Other rules aim to improve the safety of patrons and to reduce liability risks for drive-in operators. Such rules include: low speed limits within the premises, no open flames or fireworks, no alcohol or drug use, the need to supervise children, and the requirement that shoes be worn outside vehicles. The remaining rules generally focus on creating and maintaining a pleasant movie experience, including: adherence to typical public etiquette related to behaviour such as language, noise and sexual activity; restrictions on the use of vehicle lighting; designated parking areas for larger vehicles; restrictions on blocking the view of others; no littering; no use of laser pointers; no smoking in common areas; and restrictions on the type of pets that are allowed.

While many general guidelines are common across drive-ins, specific rules are by no means identical. For example, some drive-ins allow no outside food, while others offer paid permits to bring in food or have no restrictions whatsoever on outside food (or cooking) on the premises.

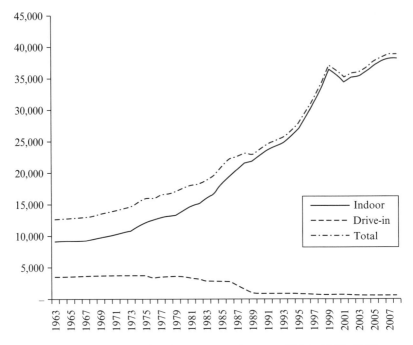

Figure 14.1   Drive-ins and indoor cinema theatres; USA, 1963–2007

Some do not allow pets; others permit only 'friendly' pets. Drive-ins may also vary in their handling of weather and the showing of films. Some offer weather-related refunds, while others do not.

Having just explained the appeal of early drive-ins and how positive audience conduct is encouraged, we now turn our attention to some of the factors that contributed to the demise of drive-ins.

THE DECLINE OF DRIVE-INS

Following their peak in the late 1950s, drive-ins declined rapidly in number. The data in Figure 14.1 (1963–2007) show that from 1963 to 2008 the number of drive-in screens declined from around 3,500 in 1963 to 636 in 2008 (Kozak, 2007; National Association of Theater Owners, 2009b). In this section, we look at some of the key reasons for this decline, namely: the development of television, indoor multiplexes, the changing nature of the industry's cost and revenue structure, and location decisions of the present-day drive-ins.

Impact of Television and Other Forms of Entertainment

Prior to television, the movie industry overcame competition from radio, a less close substitute. Along with subsequent technologies such as DVDs, cable and satellite television, TV proved to be the strongest (but by no means only) competitor to cinema in the twentieth century. Evidence indicates that the growth of television hurt movie attendance. Stuart (1976, 1982) finds that the concentration of television sets had a significant negative effect on theatre receipts in the short run and on the number of operating theatres in the long run. Similarly, Cameron (1986, 1990) finds that the number of colour TVs has a negative effect on the number of movie tickets sold. The impact of television as a viable competitor to attending movies arose not only from television being a close substitute for the cinematic experience, but also from the movie industry's response to television. As Spraos (1962) and Cameron (1986) conclude, television's direct impact as a competitor comes largely from the convenience of home entertainment and from the lower perceived costs of television viewing versus moviegoing. In addition, the movie industry's strategic responses to television were poorly timed and ineffective. At first the movie industry largely ignored TV and did not view TV as viable competitor. The movie industry produced numerous low-quality films that offered little heterogeneity compared to TV, and also struggled to implement profit-enhancing strategies and technologies (Jowett, 1976; Murray, 1977).

Television constitutes a strong substitute to cinema due to its ability to meet basic sociological needs that generate higher levels of utility for individuals. As anthropologist Hortense Powdermaker has observed, 'Modern man is lonely, desperately in need of personal relationships. He goes to the movies, and for two hours he has the illusion of close, intimate, personal contact with exciting and beautiful people' (quoted in Luther, 1950b, p. 167). If this is true, then television provides these same benefits without the necessity of travelling to a cinema. Jowett (1976) suggests that 'the American public was obviously more content to stay at home and watch old movies for free, than pay to see newer ones' (p. 355). By 1957 approximately one-quarter of TV viewing time was devoted to old movies (Jowett, 1976). Downs (1953, p. 160) suggests that television may have had a lesser impact on drive-ins than traditional theatres, since 'attending drive-ins is quite unlike sitting at home' and the desire to get out of the house 'will continue to feed customers into outdoor theaters in spite of television'.

While television was demonstrated as early as 1927, technological challenges, the Great Depression, regulatory restrictions and the Second World War interrupted its development and adoption (Murray, 1977).

Major developments in television subsequently emerged after the war. Within four years after the close of the war, 98 television stations in 58 US cities sprung up reaching 40 per cent of the population (ibid.). As with many technologies, the cost of adoption is typically high early on, and then prices fall due to diminishing production costs. Other deterrents to the early adoption of TV included telecasting initially being restricted to between 5pm and 10pm, which limited the use of television. As these barriers weakened, the adoption of television increased. The screen size, quality of image and sound, number of channels, and breadth of programming have increased for television, thereby increasing TV's substitutability with moviegoing (Cameron, 2003). Only 9 per cent of households had adopted television by 1950, but its adoption accelerated rapidly and reached 90 per cent in 1962 and 98 per cent in 2001 (US Census Bureau, 2003).[7] Also, the ownership of multiple television sets by the same household offered more viewing choices for different household members, thereby strengthening television's competitive position relative to cinemas. Of US households having television, only 4 per cent had multiple sets in 1955 whereas 76 per cent had multiple sets by 2000 (TV History, 2009).

The rapid expansion of technology in the modern computer era has accelerated the emergence of new forms of competition to movie theatres. According to the goods characteristic theory of consumer behaviour, changes in consumption technology (such as home entertainment devices) contribute to competitive pressures for moviegoing (Cameron, 1988). Home entertainment choices quickly gravitated towards new technologies such as video cassettes, DVDs, cable and satellite TV transmission, pay-per-view and the internet. For example, the advent of cable television expanded the choices available to television viewers, enhancing the at-home entertainment experience. In 1965 only 2.3 per cent of US households had cable TV whereas by 2001 cable penetration reached 68 per cent (US Census Bureau, 2003). Cameron (1988) provides evidence that well after television had made its substantial impact on movie attendance, the adoption of home video recorders contributed to the decline in movie ticket sales in the UK. Similarly, in the US, following the development of pre-recorded movies, the development of multiplexes was followed by a decline in cinema attendance in the mid-1980s (Bull et al., 2003).

Aside from television and other forms of in-home entertainment, the appeal of drive-ins waned as indoor multiplex cinemas (often located in shopping malls) became more commonplace.

The Development of Multiplexes

The growth of multiplex cinemas was largely motivated by economies of scale. Multiplexes spread theatre costs across more customers, while also attracting more patrons by showing a wide range of offerings (Pautz, 2002). Single-screen cinemas limit when people can see a movie; however, with multiplexes some movies will typically be shown on multiple screens, thereby providing more possible viewing times and satisfying the needs of those who want to see movies when they are first released. Thereafter, as movies attract smaller audiences, they can be placed in smaller screens, before their run ends (Litman, 1998). As movies tend to be most popular in their early weeks (Krider and Weinberg, 1998), this arrangement increases the overall utilization of theatre seating. For indoor cinemas, part of the attraction of multiplexing is that parents and children can see different movies and then meet after. Stanley Durwood, the then-CEO of AMC Theatres, a pioneer of multiplexes, has stated: 'variety is the key to the multiple-theater operation. Also, adults may attend a picture with adult appeal, while their children are in the adjacent theater attending a film specifically designed for children' (Durwood, 2001, p. 281). Alternatively, with multiplexes located in (or near) malls, parents could leave children to watch a movie and go shopping. Multiplexes, therefore, can reduce the time costs associated with moviegoing. Drive-ins make such arrangements less feasible, although certainly children (or adults) could sit in lawn chairs in one area, while others sat in a vehicle in another.

Multiplexes opened in increasing numbers during the 1960s and by the mid-1960s most new cinemas were multiplexes, typically located in shopping centres. In particular, 1963 saw a major shift in movie theatre construction, with the opening of a cinema in a shopping mall wherein 'two small theaters [are] served by a single projection booth, thus saving significantly on labor and projection costs' (Monaco, 2003, p. 48). Scale economies were gained employing young, unskilled employees who were typically non-unionized and paid relatively low wages. With the development of multiplexes, the 1960s were characterized by 'functionality and commercial efficiency' (ibid., p. 51). From these origins, one of today's largest cinema chains, AMC (American Multi-Cinema), developed.

The growth of indoor multiplexes occurred at a time when, owing to rising land prices, opening or maintaining stand-alone cinemas near to the suburbs was becoming less attractive. Subsequently, by the early 1980s drive-in owners were increasingly being squeezed by competitive pressures. With the widespread development of multiplexes, patrons were increasingly expecting new feature films every week. However, distributors were demanding a greater share of box office revenues and were using their

Table 14.3   Estimated percentages of theaters that are multiplexes

	1977	1982	1987	1992
Not drive-ins	32	49	69	78
Drive-ins	11	15	20	27

Table 14.4   Average revenues and number of screens ($000)

	Number of screens operated				
	1	2	3 or 4	5 to 8	9+
1977 4-wall	162	376	606	1,104	N/A
1982 4-wall	229	406	762	1,361	N/A
1987 4-wall	228	345	675	1,286	3,111
1992 4-wall	275	374	711	1,553	3,036
1992 Drive-in	176	362	838	N/A	N/A

power to negotiate longer exhibition runs (Thompson, 1983). As most drive-ins were small and independently owned, they lacked the negotiating leverage of the major multiplex operators with the result that, over time, drive-ins were less able to book first-run films.

Multiplexing is easier for indoor cinemas than for drive-ins. When drive-ins first started, multiplexing owners were often motivated by reducing traffic congestion resulting from vehicles entering or leaving at around the same time; hence, the same movie would show on multiple screens, with staggered starting and ending times. Further, for drive-ins the natural elements constrain where screens can be placed. The optimal screen position is typically one that ensures an earlier show time relative to the setting sun. For drive-ins, the addition of more screens increases the likelihood that some screens will be facing the setting sun, or be viewable by passing motorists or nearby residents. Hence, compared to indoor theatres, drive-ins were slow to multiplex. By 1970 only 10 per cent of ozoners were multiplexes, compared to 30 per cent of indoor theatres (Segrave, 2006). US Census data give us some idea of the prevalence of multiplexing since that time (see Table 14.3). From 1977 to 1992 multiplexing became more commonplace for both indoor and for drive-in cinemas. (In 1977, 32 per cent of indoor cinemas had multiple screens, rising to 78 per cent in 1992. In 1977 only 11 per cent of drive-ins were multiplexes, rising to 27 per cent in 1992).[8] Data from the National Association of Theater Owners (2009b) provide insights into the incidence of multiplexing in more recent years and show that multiplexing has increased among indoor theatres much more rapidly than for drive-ins. Subsequently, from 1995 to 2008 the number of screens per location for indoor theatres rose from 3.8 to 7.1. During this time, the average number of screens per drive-in increased from 1.4 to 1.7.

Table 14.4 gives us some idea of the revenue benefits derived from additional screens: 1992 was the only year for which revenue and screen data were available for both drive-ins and four-wall theatres. In that year, single screen four-wall theatres averaged $275,000 in revenues per theatre, compared to $176,000 for drive-ins. Adding a second screen increased overall revenues for both types of cinema, but resulted in average revenues of $374,000 for four-wall theatres and $362,000 for drive-ins.

Now we consider issues associated with the location of drive-ins and the competitive pressures they face.

Changing Cost and Revenue Structure

By the 1950s, drive-ins were relatively inexpensive to construct. A 200-car drive-in could be built for around $50,000 and a 500-car drive-in for $75,000 (Downs, 1953). More expensive drive-ins (which incorporated many extra amenities) would cost up to $250 per vehicle, whereas the construction cost of seats in traditional theatres was also about this figure (ibid.). However, the key point is that the average car contained 2.5 paying customers, whereas the typical theatre seat would sit only one paying patron, and drive-in consumers purchase up to four times as much food (ibid.). By the mid-1950s drive-ins often charged admission on a per-car basis, making attendance more affordable for families (Horton, 1976). However, by the end of the 1950s increasing land prices made operating drive-ins less attractive:

> Suburban drive-in theaters constituted an especially good business investment so long as they were located on the fringes of developing areas where land could still be purchased relatively inexpensively. In most places, however, land values had already risen so high by the suburban real estate boom that building drive-ins in ideal locales was rendered financially impossible. (Monaco, 2003, p. 46)

Aside from higher concession sales (compared to indoor cinemas) drive-ins also benefited from the lower costs of the movies they exhibited – at least in the early days when drive-ins typically showed second-run movies that would have considerably lower rental fees (Downs, 1953). Early drive-ins appear to have been very profitable and typically earned net profits of 15 to 20 per cent on capital invested, compared to around 10 per cent for traditional theatres (Luther, 1951). In contrast to their heyday in the early to mid-1950s, the drive-ins of today have been referred to as a 'low-profit labor of love' (Leber, 2008). To some extent this is because their underlying economics have changed dramatically. This is particularly true of the real estate costs. In the late 1940s and early 1950s a disproportionate number of drive-ins were located in smaller towns and semi-rural locations (Monaco, 2003). However, as suburbia expanded, taxes increased and these locations became attractive for other uses, including strip malls and big box stores (Cohen, 1994). Indeed, Austin proposes that rising land prices were 'perhaps the key feature in the decline of ozoners' (1983, p. 70).[9] Today, the United Drive-In Theater Owners Association (UDITOA) puts the cost of a new drive-in (excluding land) at $300,000 to $500,000 for a new single screen facility and $400,000 to $800,000 for a twin screen. The UDITOA suggest that 10 to 14 acres of land are needed for a 500-car drive-in. Given the costs associated with landscaping and equipment, the UDITOA observe that it is often less expensive to re-open an existing, closed drive-in than to create a new drive-in from scratch. On their website UDITOA shows a single screen, 400-car former drive-in location on 11 acres of land for sale for $340,000.

The changing economics of concession revenues have also made an impact on drive-in profitability over time. Historically, concession revenues were particularly important to drive-ins as families with young children were the primary target market. At their peak, many of the entertainment-related attractions of drive-ins were designed to attract children who 'consumed refreshments more avidly than adults' (Downs, 1953, p. 150). For example, from 1952 to 1964 *The Film Daily Year Book* asserted that annual concession receipts for drive-ins were typically four to five times higher than for indoor theatres. The US Census of Business for 1954 observes that popcorn, candy and other concession items were a more significant source of revenue for drive-ins compared to indoor theatres (US Department of Commerce, 1957). In 1948, concessions comprised 13.1 per cent of pre-tax receipts for drive-ins and 6.6 per cent for other theatre types. However, by 1954 concession sales made up 22 per cent of total pre-tax receipts for drive-ins, compared to 10.7 per cent for other theatres. More recently, the 1997 Economic Census reports that concession sales comprise 23.5 per cent of all drive-in receipts and 28.5 per cent of indoor theatre receipts (US Census Bureau, 1999). These figures demonstrate that traditional theatres have increased their reliance on concession revenues, and are now even more reliant on these revenues than are drive-ins. Nevertheless, concession sales remain an important source of revenue for drive-ins with the UDITOA giving the following advice to would-be owners: 'Because you may not always make a lot of money at the box office, you should concentrate on your snack bar/concession business. This is where the money is to be made! In fact, some drive-in owners will tell you that they are actually restaurant owners who play movies!' (UDITOA, 2009).

Location Decisions of the Drive-ins of Today

The changing economics of drive-ins have influenced decisions about the locations of present-day drive-ins. The UDITOA provides the following advice to would-be drive-in operators:

> You will need to check on your potential competition from indoor theaters. If you are nearby an operating drive-in, locate yours in another area. Keep in mind that film companies often favor multiple screen theaters when it comes to permitting them to play first run film product. Their philosophy seems to be that they can make more money on a picture if they release it to a multiple screen indoor theater that can play it on more than one screen several times a day. Therefore, you would likely fare better if you locate your drive-in where it is not close to big multiple screen theaters, if possible. You will want to build your drive-in with at least 2 screens because you will be able to attract more customers by having multiple pictures when you are required to play the same movie for 4 weeks. You also want to make sure that you have an adequate population base to draw from and that the demographics would support attendance at an outdoor theater. (Most drive-ins cater to families and their patronage is generally a mix of teenagers, young families, and the elderly.)

In order to verify the credibility of these claims, in May 2009 we collected data on all 383 open drive-ins in the US.[10] The basic dataset was obtained from Drive-ins.com, who promote themselves as 'The definitive resource for drive-in information'. For each drive-in we looked at how many other drive-ins were within a 30-mile radius.[11] Some 212 of the 383 drive-ins (55 per cent) had no competing drive-ins within 30 miles. For drive-ins located on the US mainland (that is, excluding two drive-ins located in, respectively, Hawaii and Puerto Rico), the nearest other drive-in was, on average, 45.7 miles away. Hence, it does indeed appear that drive-ins typically do not compete with other drive-ins. We did, however, find that drive-ins are often competing with traditional cinemas for patronage. On average there were 13 four-wall theatres within a 30-mile radius of any given drive-in. Also, there was always at least one four-wall theatre within 30 miles of any given drive-in.

Using 2007 Census data, we also looked at the size of the city or town where each drive-in is located. Most drive-ins are located in smaller towns and around half are located in towns with fewer than 10,000 residents. Only 20 per cent are located in towns or cities with over 30,000 residents. This is likely because the cost of land is lower for drive-ins in these smaller towns, and other entertainment options outside the home may be limited in such locales.

We also looked at the number of screens and vehicle capacity of drive-ins (see Table 14.5). Contrary to the advice of the UDITOA, 64 per cent

Table 14.5   Capacity (number of vehicles) of drive-ins, May 2009

Screens	No. of drive-ins	Average total capacity	Average capacity/ screen	Lowest	Highest
1	246	380	380	100	1,200
2	82	574	287	200	1,600
3	24	795	265	450	2,000
4	17	958	240	500	1,700
5	6	1,067	213	500	1,885
6	6	1,695	283	601	3,000
9	1				
14	1				

of drive-ins only had a single screen. As the UDITOA indicate, having a one-screen cinema does indeed limit capacity, with the average capacity of one-screen theatres being 380 vehicles, whereas the average total capacity of two-screen drive-ins is 575 vehicles.

Now we turn our focus to one of the alternatives to traditional drive-ins, namely guerilla drive-ins.

GUERILLA DRIVE-INS AND MOBMOVS

The number of drive-ins has stabilized somewhat in recent years as many new drive-ins opened as older ones closed. This may, in part, be driven by nostalgia:

> [A] funny thing happened on the way to the dinosaur graveyard. Those little kids who fell asleep in the back of the station wagon recalled their fond memories of family outings to the drive-in. If you are lucky enough to live near one of the remaining drive-ins, you know that on a warm summer night under the stars, every row is packed. Little kids play tag beneath the big, white screen before the movie starts, then snuggle up in blankets in the back of pickups and SUVs while Mom and Dad get comfortable in their lawn chairs. As the first ghostlike images begin to flicker over the screen, the air fills once again with the scent of popcorn and bug spray. (Shaw-Smith, 2009, p. 37)

Much of the nostalgic appeal of drive-ins is also found in their modern-day variations. Today, technology enables people with their own projectors and sound (or sound transmitting) equipment to create drive-in like experiences that are known as 'guerilla drive-ins' or 'MobMovs' (Mobile Movies). The first guerilla drive-ins were actually walk-ins that used large grass areas (such as parks), a makeshift screen, a portable projector and a speaker system. Walk-ins involved the use of public, outdoor spaces for movie exhibition, but without the need for a motor vehicle. The pioneer of walk-ins is the Santa Cruz Guerilla Drive-In, located in California. The organizers of this concept propose that it makes use of outdoor space, is a service to the community, and is anti-commercialist:

> The Santa Cruz Guerilla Drive-in is an outdoor movie theater under the stars that springs up unexpectedly in the fields and industrial wastelands. Beyond showing great free movies year-round and bringing a broad community together, part of our mission is reclaiming public space and transforming our urban environment into a joyful playground. (2009).

Similarly, the organizers of the Dolores Park Movie Night in San Francisco, a walk-in outdoor theatre, state:

> We live near Dolores Park, and want to make the most of our beautiful little neighborhood. Dolores Park Movie Night has no affiliations, no causes, no politics and minimal organization. We pay for permits, movie licences, and equipment ourselves and only ask for small donations to cover recurring costs. Dolores Park Movie Night is our small contribution to the local community. (2009)

Participation at MobMovs is organized over the internet. Participants become part of a mailing list and are notified of showings of interest. In order to get a general idea of the appeal and constraints of MobMovs, in June 2009 we reviewed 148 user reviews of the Dolores Park Movie Night that appeared on Yelp.com. These reviews give us a general idea of what moviegoers liked or disliked about this experience (Table 14.6).

Guerilla drive-ins and MobMovs have been made possible by technological developments. Technology has impacted on leisure in complex ways. It affects not only how leisure is engaged in, but what constitutes leisure. According to Gandossy (2007), the 'leisure time of past generations – characterized by greater social involvement and longer chunks of uninterrupted time – does not exist for most of the population' (p. 1). Putnam (2000) argues that leisure has become increasingly privatized due, in part, to technology. Technological advancements have, arguably, strained the broader sense of community. Morse (2008) contends that modern electronic devices have profoundly influenced social interaction in public space: 'It has become increasingly difficult to feel part of the larger community, when everyone seems to be in his or her own private virtual reality . . . Traditional notions of privacy and civility have been suspended, modified, or altogether abandoned' (p. 1). Further, Sclove (1998) suggests that home electronic entertainment devices have a negative social impact as they 'draw people indoors and alone, and thus away from social and civic engagement' (p. 1). Putnam (1996) has gone so far as to propose

Table 14.6   What patrons liked or disliked about the Dolores Park Movie Night

Patrons liked	%	Patrons disliked	%
Can bring or purchase food & beverages	59	Presentation quality of movie	34
Social atmosphere	49	Need to bring blanket and warm clothes	32
The movie itself			
Atmosphere in general	25	Atmosphere	28
Cost	18	Need to arrive early to get a good spot	27
Can bring pets or be around pets			
Presentation quality of movie	18	Crowded	19
	7	Bathroom issues	15
	7	Noise	7
		The movie itself	7

that watching television is the greatest contributor to the decline in civic participation in the US. As evidence of home entertainment's allure, a Pew Research survey found that approximately three out of four adults would prefer to watch a movie at home rather than at a theatre (Gandossy, 2007).

The individualization of leisure, coupled with economic and legal systems that are based on strong property rights, has made an impact on the use of space for public interaction. In a typical modern city public space is often limited and its use constrained. The Project for Public Spaces (2000) defines four attributes common to successful public spaces: accessibility; providing activities; comfort; and opportunities for social interaction. In many cities the lack of quality public space can be attributed to inaccessible space, lack of opportunity for use of space, poor conditions of available space, and weaker social interaction.

Guerilla drive-ins counter some of the negative effects of evolving technology on leisure and social interaction, while also making quality use of public spaces. One organizer of guerilla drive-ins explains a commonly held motive for creating them:

> I think we've reached a point in our social development where a lot of us feel our entertainment and our lives are very governed by commerce, everything we do involves us throwing money out, everything we do is an act of consumption. We're inspired by providing a place where people can interact in a more meaningful way. (Interview with 'Steve', quoted in Ferguson, 2009, p. 1)

A key issue that will influence the longevity and growth of guerilla drive-ins is their legal status. Commercial movies in the US are protected under the Federal Copyright Act. The purchase, rental or lending of a movie does not confer the right to exhibit it publicly outside the home unless it occurs at a location properly licensed for public exhibition. To legally show movies, guerilla drive-ins would need to acquire exhibition licences and get permission from owners of the land where exhibitions would occur. While the cost may not be sizeable, it is foreseeable that guerilla drive-in organizers may willingly bear the risk of noncompliance to reduce time and money costs, as well as for philosophical reasons.[12]

While guerilla drive-ins emerged in the early 2000s they remain relatively unknown today, but their numbers are on the rise. For instance, MobMov.org was founded in 2005 and by December 2009 had 280 chapters worldwide. If guerilla drive-ins become an extensive phenomenon and choose legal noncompliance, their fate will likely follow that of other illegal activities enabled by technology, such as downloading music on the internet through illegal file sharing software such as Napster. Similar to the music industry, movie distributors would likely take action to counter copyright infringement at a large scale.[13]

CONCLUSIONS

A convergence of factors contributed to the rapid decline of drive-ins. Some of these factors were associated with the post-war movement of families to suburbia. This migration, in turn, increased property taxes and real estate prices and made alternative uses of drive-in land more attractive. Suburban sprawl also saw the development of malls, which often had multiplex cinemas. Multiplexes were attractive to moviegoers as they showed more movies than drive-ins and also allowed family members to see different movies (or, for some to watch a movie, while others shopped).

Part of the initial appeal of drive-ins was that they offered other sorts of entertainment and some offered household time-saving devices; however, as entertainment and time-saving devices became more common in the home and in smaller communities, this eroded one of the sources of competitive advantage for drive-ins. Further, having more entertainment options (particularly in the home) made it easier for family members to engage in leisure activities individually, rather than together. As a result, engaging in joint leisure activities outside the home became less appealing for families. Also, as the release window between movies being available at the cinema and then on TV or video declined over time (National Association of Theater Owners, 2009c). This has made watching movies at home more attractive in terms of both cost and convenience.

Changing exhibition practices also played a role in the demise of drive-ins. As large, national cinema chains emerged, drive-ins increasingly struggled to obtain first-run movies. However, with fewer families going to drive-ins, many repositioned themselves to a teen market and became known as 'passion pits', which only further eroded their family appeal and made drive-ins less welcome in their own communities (Austin, 1985).

By 2009, fewer than 400 drive-ins remain in the United States. These are typically located in smaller towns, tend not to compete with one another and face competition from indoor cinemas that will typically have more screens and more movie choices. Recent years have also seen the emergence of guerilla drive-ins and MobMovs, which make use of public spaces, create a sense of community, enjoy the outdoors, and have an anti-commercial sentiment.

NOTES

1. Another puzzling feature of drive-ins is that they are largely a US phenomenon. Segrave states: 'almost no other country adopted the drive-in, even though most things American are widely imitated in other lands' (2006, p. 104). For example, as of May 2009 we found that there were 383 drive-ins in the USA, 76 in Canada, 14 in Australia, 7 in Germany, 5 in South Africa and very small numbers in some other countries. Segrave (2006) attributes the popularity of the drive-in in the US to three factors: the availability of land, an automobile culture, and an affluent population. The social appeal of drive-ins may provide another reason for their popularity in the US, compared to, say, Europe. Horton proposes that drive-ins perform a social function that is not as necessary in Europe (Horton, 1976).

2. The United Drive-In Theater Owners Association advises drive-in owners that, 'Sometimes the studios require that you run seven nights per week, not weekends only – to get first-run films. And even then, they are under no obligation to offer you a particular film. If you have a lot of indoor competition, they may get the picture before you. It may be better financially not to get a film "on the break" but to wait two or more weeks in order to get the percentage down. All of these factors will depend on your particular situation. In general, patrons demand new product. Unless you are in a unique situation, showing old or classic movies will not make a lot of money. Most patrons will not come to see a movie that is available on video. Additionally, there are limited resources for acquiring classic movies on a regular basis' (UDITOA, 2009).

3. Having said this, the physical organization of many multiplexes is such that there is a single point of entry and patrons could choose to see multiple movies, one after the other (even though this is generally prohibited by cinemas).

4. Revenue streams are somewhat limited for drive-ins during their off-season; although some drive-in lots are used for flea markets, swap meets, other forms of entertainment, or have all-year restaurants. The feasibility of such additional revenue sources would depend on weather conditions, with more severe weather increasing the costs of snow ploughing, while also making it less appealing for patrons to visit a drive-in location during the off-season. United Drive-In Theater Owners Association provides the following advice to would-be drive-in owners: 'This will help you to be able to support yourself on your drive-in alone and not have to take an outside job.' (Most drive-in owners have another job in addition to the drive-in.) (UDITOA, 2009).

5. After filing his patent in 1933 Hollingshead developed a business, Park In Theaters, to take commercial advantage of his patents. In return for the use of his invention,

drive-ins would pay a flat fee of $1,000 and a 5 per cent royalty, based on gross receipts (Austin, 1985, p. 63). Non-paying exhibitors were brought to court. After protracted legal action, Loew's drive-in successfully contested Hollingshead's patent.

6. The two chains that display rules on their websites are Regal Entertainment Group and Kerasotes Theatres. The remaining chains are AMC Entertainment, Cinemark USA, Carmike Cinemas, Cineplex Entertainment, National Amusements, Marcus Theatres, Hollywood Theaters, and Rave Motion Pictures.

7. The adoption of television is by no means a North American phenomenon. Spraos (1962) documents television's rapid spread to the working classes in the UK in the 1950s, which negatively affected theatre attendance among larger families and younger audiences. In the early 2000s, 25 nations had over 500 televisions per 1,000 people while another 53 countries had at least 250 TVs per 1,000 people (US Census Bureau, 2003).

8. This census data include only establishments with payroll and may therefore underestimate the number of cinemas, particularly those that are family owned and operated.

9. For a discussion of land use of former drive-ins in Australia, see Goldsmith (1999).

10. The overall number of establishments we found on drive-ins.com seems credible as it matches the numbers reported for 2008 by the UDITOA and by the National Association of Theater Owners.

11. Admittedly, this number is somewhat arbitrary. Thirty miles is mentioned as the distance people were willing to drive to attend a drive-in in the 1950s (Segrave, 2006, p. 64).

12. One estimate is that film distributors charge approximately $150–$300 for a showing (Loviglio, 2009). Swank Motion Pictures, Inc., founded in 1937, is the world's largest non-theatrical distributor of motion pictures for public performance. Swank does not disclose specific rental fees on their website but states that 'Prices are for a one-day rental. For each additional day shown, a fee of $100 will be charged. If you charge admission, your movie rental rate is a flat rate versus 50 per cent of your gate receipts, whichever is greater.' See: http://www.swank.com/other/faq.html.

13. Anecdotal evidence suggests that this is already happening. The Sub Rosa Guerilla Drive-in faced scrutiny after a front-page article in a local newspaper highlighted their activities. A local video store businessman contacted Swank Motion Pictures, the leading movie distribution licensing firm, who initiated an inquiry. According to Sub Rosa, 'Suddenly, flying under the radar was no longer an option. . . . Our backs to the wall, we had no choice but to work out a deal with Swank to license our movies. . . . License fees for us are $100 a piece' (Sub Rosa Drive-in, 2009).

REFERENCES

Austin, Bruce A. (1983), 'Portrait of a contemporary drive-in movie theater audience', paper presented at the Annual Meeting of the International Communication Association, Dallas, TX, 26–30 May, available at: http://www.eric.ed.gov (accessed 2 December 2009).

Austin, B.A. (1984), 'Portrait of a contemporary drive-in theater audience', *Boxoffice*, May, pp. 33–8.

Austin, B.A. (1985), 'The development and decline of the drive-in movie theater', *Current Research in Film: Audiences, Economics and Law*, **1**, 59–91.

Becker, G. (1965), 'A theory of the allocation of time', *Economic Journal*, **75** (299), 493–517.

Becker, G. and K.M. Murphy (1988), 'A theory of rational addiction', *Journal of Political Economy*, **96** (4), 675–70.

Bell, S. (2003), 'From ticket booth to screen tower: an architectural study of drive-in theaters in the Baltimore–Washington, DC–Richmond corridor', *Perspectives in Vernacular Architecture*, **9**, 215–27.

Bull, Chris, Jayne Hoose and Mike Weed (2003), *An Introduction to Leisure Studies*, Harlow, UK: Pearson Education.

Cameron, S. (1986), 'The supply and demand for cinema tickets: some UK evidence', *Journal of Cultural Economics*, **10** (1), 38–62.

Cameron, S. (1988), 'The impact of video recorders on cinema attendance', *Journal of Cultural Economics*, **12** (1), 73–80.

Cameron, S. (1990), 'The demand for cinema in the United Kingdom', *Journal of Cultural Economics*, **14** (1), 35–47.

Cameron, S. (1999), 'Rational addiction and the demand for cinema', *Applied Economics Letters*, **6** (9), 617–20.

Cameron, Samuel (2003), 'Cinema', in Ruth Towse (ed.), *Handbook of Cultural Economics*, Cheltenham, UK and Northampton, MA, USA: Edward Elgar, pp. 114–18.

Cohen, M.M. (1994), 'Forgotten audiences in the passion pits: drive-in theatres and changing spectator practices in post-war America', *Film History*, **6** (4), 470–86.

Collins, A. and C. Hand (2005), 'Analyzing moviegoing demand: an individual-level cross-sectional approach', *Managerial and Decision Economics*, **26** (5), 319–30.

Collins, A., V. Fernández-Blanco and J. Prieto-Rodríguez (2009a), 'Characteristics of buyers and renters of cultural goods: the case of movies', *Applied Economics*, **41** (2), 195–210.

Collins, A., A.E. Scorcu and R. Zanola (2009b), 'Distribution conventionality in the movie sector: an econometric analysis of cinema supply', *Managerial and Decision Economics*, **30** (8), 517–27.

De Silva, Indra (1998), 'Consumer selection of motion pictures', in Barry R. Litman (ed.), *The Motion Picture Industry*, Needham Heights, MA: Allyn & Bacon, pp. 144–77.

Dolores Park Movie Night (2009), 'About Us', available at: http://www.doloresparkmovie.org/faq.html#about_us (accessed 2 December 2009).

Downs, A. (1953), 'Drive-ins have arrived', *Journal of Property Management*, **18** (March), 149–62.

Durwood, Stanley (2001), 'The exhibitors (1972)', in Gregory A. Waller (ed.), *Moviegoing in America: A Sourcebook in the History of Film Exhibition* (2001), Malden, MA and Oxford: Blackwell, pp. 279–81.

Ferguson, Lisa (2009), 'Guerilla drive-in: creating community, one empty space at a time', available at: http://www.guerilladrivein.ca/articles/GDI_one_empty_space.pdf (accessed 2 December 2009).

Film Daily Year Book of Motion Pictures, The (various years), New York: Film Daily.

Gandossy, Taylor (2007), 'Technology transforming the leisure world', available at: http://www.cnn.com/2007/US/03/29/leisure.overview/index.html (accessed 2 December 2009).

Giles, D. (1983), 'The outdoor economy: a study of the contemporary drive-in', *Journal of the University Film and Video Association*, **35** (2), 66–76.

Goldsmith, B. (1999), '"The comfort lies in all the things you can do": the Australian drive-in – cinema of distraction', *Journal of Popular Culture*, **33** (1), 153–64.

Gomery, Douglas (1992), *Shared Pleasures: A History of Movie Presentation in the United States*, Madison, WI: University of Wisconsin Press.

Hemingway, J. (1988), 'Leisure and civility: reflections on a Greek ideal', *Leisure Sciences*, **10**, 179–91.

Horton, A. (1976), 'Turning on and tuning out at the drive-in: an American phenomenon survives and thrives', *Journal of Popular Film*, **5** (3&4), 233–44.

Jowett, Garth (1976), *Film: The Democratic Art*, Boston, MA: Little, Brown.

Kozak, Jim (2007), *Encyclopedia of Exhibition*, Washington, DC: National Association of Theater Owners.

Krider, R. and C. Weinberg (1998), 'Clustering at the movies', *Marketing Letters*, **9** (4), 393–405.

Leber, Jessica (2008), 'Drive-in movie theaters turn 75. Catch one while you can', Columbia News Service, available at: http://jscms.jrn.columbia.edu/cns/2008-04-01/leber-driveinanniversary/story_syndication (accessed 2 December 2009).

Litman, Barry R. (1998), 'The conduct and performance of the industry', in Barry R. Litman (ed.), *The Motion Picture Industry*, Needham Heights, MA: Allyn & Bacon, pp. 44–60.

Loeffler, W. (2007), 'Drive-in theaters offer a nostalgic entertainment alternative', *Pittsburgh Tribune Review*, 10 June, p. 10.

Loviglio, J. (2009), '"Guerilla drive-ins" turn nostalgia on its head', 9 June, available at: http://www.newsvine.com/_news/2009/06/09/2911380-guerilla-drive-ins-turn-nostalgia-on (accessed 2 December 2009).

Luther, R. (1950a), 'Marketing aspects of drive-in theaters', *Journal of Marketing*, **15** (1), 41–7.

Luther, R. (1950b), 'Television and the future of motion picture exhibition', *Hollywood Quarterly*, **5** (2), 164–77.

Luther, R. (1951), 'Drive-in theaters: rags to riches in five years', *Hollywood Quarterly*, **5** (4), 401–11.

Maxwell, J.A. and M.N. Balcom (1946a), 'Gasoline rationing in the United States, I', *Quarterly Journal of Economics*, **60** (4), 561–87.

Maxwell, J.A. and M.N. Balcom (1946b), 'Gasoline rationing in the United States, II', *Quarterly Journal of Economics*, **61** (1), 125–55.

Monaco, Paul (2003), *The Sixties, 1960–1969* (History of American Cinema, v. 8), Berkeley and Los Angeles, CA and London: University of California Press.

Morse, S.J. (2008), 'Who has Durkheim's number? Cell phones and social interaction', *PsycCRITIQUES*, **53** (47), available at: http://psqtest.typepad.com/blogPost PDFs/200814669_psq-53-47_WhoHasDurkheimsNumberCellPhonesSocialInteraction. pdf (accessed 5 May 2011).

Murray, L.L. (1977), 'Complacency, competition and cooperation: the film industry responds to the challenge of television', *Journal of Popular Film*, **6** (1), 47–74.

National Association of Theater Owners (2009a), 'Average US ticket prices', available at: http://www.natoonline.org/statisticstickets.htm (accessed 2 December 2009).

National Association of Theater Owners (2009b), 'Number of US movie screens', available at: http://www.natoonline.org/statisticsscreens.htm (accessed 2 December 2009).

National Association of Theater Owners (2009c), 'Theatrical release windows', available at: http://www.natoonline.org/windows.htm (accessed 2 December 2009).

Pautz, M.C. (2002), 'The decline in average weekly cinema attendance, 1930–2000', *Issues in Political Economy*, **11** (July), 54–65.

Project for Public Spaces (2000), *How to Turn a Place Around: A Handbook for Creating Successful Public Spaces*, New York: Project for Public Spaces.

Putnam, R.D. (1996), 'The strange disappearance of civic America', *The American Prospect*, **24**, 34–48.

Putnam, R.D. (2000), *Bowling Alone: The Collapse and Revival of American Community*, New York: Simon & Schuster.

Santa Cruz Guerilla Drive-in (2009), available at: http://www.guerilladrivein.org (accessed 2 December 2009).

Sclove, Richard (1998), 'Examples of structural social effects produced by technologies', available at: http://www.loka.org/idt/SocialEffects.htm#Supscript per cent 202 (accessed 2 December 2009).

Segrave, Kerry (2006), *Drive-in Theaters: A History from their Inception in 1933*, Jefferson, NC: McFarland.

Shaw-Smith, M. (2009), 'Drive-ins: the last great picture show', *Cricket*, **36** (6), 34–7.

Spraos, John (1962), *The Decline of the Cinema: An Economist's Report*, New York: George Allen & Unwin.

Stuart, Frederic (1976), *Effect of Television on the Motion Picture and Radio Industries*, New York: Arno Press.

Stuart, Frederic (1982), 'The effects of television on the motion picture industry: 1948–1960', in Gordon Kindem (ed.), *The American Movie Industry*, Carbondale, IL: Southern Illinois University Press, pp. 257–307.

Sub Rosa Drive-in (2009), 'Sub Rosa is officially licensed!', 2 July, available at: http://www. subrosadrivein.com (accessed 2 December 2009).

Taylor, Frank J. (1956) 'Big boom in outdoor movies', reprinted in Gregory A. Waller (ed.)

(2001), *Moviegoing in America: A Sourcebook in the History of Film Exhibition*, Malden, MA and Oxford: Blackwell, pp. 247–51.

Thompson, T. (1983), 'The twilight of the drive-in', *American Film*, **8** (July–August), 44–9.

TV History (2009), 'Television set ownership', available at: http://www.tvhistory.tv/TV-VCR-Remote-Cable_Ownership.JPG (accessed 2 December 2009).

Underhill, Jr, C.R. (1950), 'The trend in drive-in theaters', *Journal of the Society of Motion Picture and Television Engineers*, February, 161–70.

United Drive-In Theater Owners Association (UDITOA) (2009), 'Frequently asked questions', available at: http://www.driveintheatre-ownersassociation.org/FAQs.html (accessed 2 December 2009).

US Census Bureau (1999), *1997 Economic Census*, Washington, DC.

US Census Bureau (2003), 'No. HS-42. Selected Communications Media: 1920 to 2001', in *Statistical Abstract of the United States*, available at: http://www.census.gov/statab/hist/HS-42.pdf (accessed May 2011).

US Department of Commerce (1957), *US Census of Business: 1954*, Washington, DC.

Valentine, Maggie (1994), *The Show Starts on the Sidewalk: An Architectural History of the Movie Theater*, New Haven, CT: Yale University Press.

Variety (1938), 'Spread of drive-in cinemas may become a worry to regular ops: Dixie belt can stay open all year', 6 July, p. 21.

Waller, G.A. (1983), 'Auto-erotica: some notes on comic softcore films for the drive-in circuit', *Journal of Popular Culture*, **17** (2), 135–41.

Yamamura, E. (2009), 'Rethinking rational addictive behaviour and demand for cinema: a study using Japanese panel data', *Applied Economics Letters*, **16** (7), 693–7.

15 Entertainment and economic contributions of the Indian Hindi movie industry
Rajesh K. Pillania and Subhojit Banerjee

INTRODUCTION

The Indian movie industry or 'Bollywood', as it is known colloqui-
ally worldwide, is an apt representation of the subcontinent's cultural
diaspora. The industry has produced approximately 27,000 feature films
and thousands of short documentary films. Having established itself as an
industry and being duly recognized as one, the Indian popular cinema has
over its course made much progress in almost all areas: retail infrastructure, financing, marketing and distribution (Pillania, 2008a). The industry
has come a long way since India's first feature film – *King Harishchandra*
– was released in 1913, produced and directed by Dada Saheb Phalke who
foresaw the march of the leisure business from the stage to the silver screen.
Now film making in India is a multimillion dollar industry employing over
6 million workers and reaching millions of people worldwide. In 2008, the
industry was valued at 107.1 billion rupees (Rs). PricewaterhouseCoopers
estimates that the industry is projected to grow by 11.5 per cent over the
next five years, from Rs 107 billion in 2008 to Rs 184.3 billion in 2013
(PwC, 2009).

Over time, productions have become more elaborate and thus film
budgets are slowly inching towards those of Hollywood productions. In
the past, the financing of a film was done solely by either the producer
or the production house, on a private basis. However, with increasing
budgets, the burden on a sole producer and its potential risk have become
too high. Since the status of 'industry' was conferred on the Indian film
industry in 2000, banks have also been able to provide funding to film
producers.

With the entry of several corporate players, avenues of finance such
as floating on the stock market, both in India and abroad, forging partnerships with regional players in India and foreign players abroad, and
so on are being explored. These players are steadily moving towards
the Hollywood practices of slate financing, co-financing with independent producers and establishing multi-platform distribution networks

(Kavitha, 2010). This chapter outlines the entertainment and economic contributions of the Indian Hindi movie industry, that is, Bollywood.

AN OVERVIEW OF PROGRESS

The Indian movie industry has taken giant leaps since motion pictures first came to India in 1896, when the Lumière brothers' cinematographer unveiled six silent short films in Bombay. India's first feature film *King Harishchandra*, a landmark movie, was released in 1913 (Pillania, 2008a). The first talkie, *Alam Ara*, was released in 1931. A detailed timeline of events in Indian cinema is given in Box 15.1. It highlights various events related to the international character of the industry, namely the import of technology/know-how in the beginning, overseas screening of movies, import/screening of Hollywood movies, organization of international film festivals, liberalization and entry of foreign channels and so on.

ENTERTAINMENT VALUE OF INDIAN CINEMA

The Indian film industry is highly developed and, contrary to popular belief, it is not a 'third-world' art cinema (Tyrell, 1999). The industry is the world's largest in terms of number of films produced as well as the number of cinema-goers. Bollywood produces almost as many films as the next three largest producers – the US, Japan and China – combined. The Indian film industry, with its major centres in Mumbai, Chennai and Hyderabad, produced 1,132 feature films in 2007. In comparison, the American film industry in 2008 produced 520 feature films, Japan 418 and China 400. The fact that India also has the cheapest movie tickets for any major film-producing nation may help explain the high cinematic churn as well as India's huge moviegoing audience (Thakur, 2009).

Movies as Leisure Entertainment

The Indian film industry is among the oldest and the largest in the world, second only to Hollywood in terms of money. Movie watching is among the top leisure activities of Indians in all age groups, geographic regions, economic classes as well as cities and villages. Even in many far-flung villages, movies are shown throughout the night to large audiences in open public spaces, on TV screens. Movies comprise a large part of leisure entertainment at various social gatherings such as weddings or festivals, besides weekend getaways. Ticket prices are the cheapest in the world, averaging

BOX 15.1 TIMELINE OF EVENTS IN INDIAN CINEMA

1895–1910

Landmarks
1896: First film screening at Watson's Hotel, Bombay on 7 July, by the Lumière brothers' cameraman, Maurice Sestier. The Madras Photographic Stores advertises imported 'animated photographs'
1897: First films shown in Calcutta and Madras. Daily screenings commence in Bombay
1898: First gramophone record is released by Gramophone & Typewriter Company, Belgatchia
1898: Hiralal Sen begins making films in Calcutta
1898: Amritlal Bose screens a package of 'actualities' and 'fakes' at the Star Theatre, Calcutta
1898: The Warwick Trading Co., commissions *Panorama of Calcutta* newsreel, other films made include *Poona Races* and *Train Arriving at Churchgate Station* (by Andersonscopograph)
1899: Calcutta receives electricity supply
1899: H.S. Bhatavadekar films a wrestling match in Bombay's Hanging Gardens
1900: Major Warwick establishes a cinema in Madras
1900: F.B. Thanawala starts Grand Kinetoscope Newsreels
1900: Boer War newsreel footage is shown at the Novelty Cinema in Bombay
1901: Hiralal Sen's Royal Bioscope establishes a film exhibition in Calcutta
1901: Bhatavadekar films the return of M.M. Bhownuggree and R.R. Paranjpye to India
1902: J.F. Madan lauches his film distribution and exhibition empire with a tent cinema at the Calcutta Maidan
1903: Bhatavadekar and American Biograph film Lor Curzon's *Delhi Durbar*
1904: Manek Sethna starts the Touring Cinema Co. in Bombay
1906: J.F. Madan's Elphinstone Bioscope Co. dominates indigenous film production

1907: Madan begins the Elphinstone Picture Palace in Calcutta, the first Calcutta cinema house
1907: Pathe establishes an Indian office

1910–1920

Landmarks
1910: Dadasaheb Phalke attends a screening of the *The Life of Christ* at P.B. Mehta's America India Cinema
1911: *The Durbar of George V* in Delhi is the first film extensively filmed in India
1911: Andai Bose and Debi Ghose start the Aurora Film Company, with screenings in tents
1912: *Pundalik*, directed by Tipnis and probably India's first feature film, is shot
1913: Dadasaheb Phalke makes *Raja Harishchandra*, it is shown at Bombay's Coronation Cinematograph
1914: Phalke shows his first three features, *Raja Harishchandra, Mohini Bhasmasur* and *Satyavan Savitri* in London
1914: R. Venkaiah and R.S. Prakash build Madras's first permanent cinema, the Gaiety
1916: R. Nataraja Mudaliar makes the first South Indian feature, *Keechaka Vadham*
1916: Universal Pictures sets up Hollywood's first Indian agency
1917: Baburao Painter starts the Maharashtra Film Co. in Kolhapur
1917: Patankar-Friends & Co. is started. This is the predecessor to Kohinoor Studio
1917: J.F. Madan makes *Satyavadi Raja Harishchandra*, the first feature film made in Calcutta
1917: Dadasaheb Phalke makes *How Films Are Made*, a short on the film-making process
1918: Kohinoor film company founded
1918: Phalke's Hindustan Cinema Films Co. is founded
1918: Indian Cinematograph Act comes into force

1920–1930

Landmarks
1924: First radio programme, broadcast privately with a 40W transmitter, by the Madras Presidency Radio Club Radio. The station ran for three years

1925: *Light of Asia* by Himansu Rai is the first film made as a co-production with a German company

1926: Punjab Film Corporation started in Lahore

1926: Ardashir Irani founds Imperial Films

1927: Indian Kinema Arts, predecessor of New Theatre, is founded in Calcutta

1929: Several important film studios founded – Prabhat Film Co (Kolhapur), Ranjit Movietone (Bombay), British Dominion Films Studio and Aurora Film Corporation (Calcutta) and General Pictures Corporation (Madras)

1930–1940

Landmarks

1931: *Alam Ara*, first talkie released

1932: East India Film Co. starts in Calcutta making films in Bengali, Tamil and Telugu

1932: The Motion Picture Society of India is founded

1933: *Sairandhri* (Prabhat Studios, Pune) is arguably India's first colour film (processed and printed in Germany)

1933: Wadia Movitone is founded

1933: The air-conditioned Regal cinema opens in Bombay

1934: Bombay Talkies is established

1935: South Indian film studios are founded – Madras United Artists and Angel Films (Salem and Coimbatore)

1935: First all-India Motion Picture Convention

1936: Master Vinayak and Cameraman Pandurang Naik co-found Huns Pictures

1939: Vauhini Pictures started by B.B. Reddi (Madras)

1939: S.S. Vasan starts Gemini Studios (Madras)

1940–1950

Landmarks

1940: Film Advisory Board is set up by the Government of India

1942: Filmistan Studios set up by S. Mukherjee and Ashok Kumar

1942: Kardar Studio founded by A.R. Kardar

1942: Rajkamal Kalamandir Studios started by V. Shantaram

1942: Homi Wadia starts Basant Pictures

1942: Mehboob Khan forms Mehboob Studios

1944: Navajyothi Studios started in Mysore
1948: Raj Kapur founds R.K. Studios
1949: Films Division is set up in Bombay

1950–1960

Landmarks
1950: Satyajit Ray, Subrata Mitra, Bansi Chandragupta and Dinen Gupta meet on the sets of Jean Renoir's *The River.* Ramananda Sengupta is operating cameraman for Claude Renoir
1951: The S.K. Patil Film Enquiry Committee reports on all aspects of cinema, noting the emerging shift from the studio system to individual ownership
1952: First International Film Festival of India held in Bombay
1952: Ritwik Ghatak makes his first film, *Padatik*, shot by Ramananda Sengupta
1952: *Aan* and *Jhansi ki Rani* are made in colour
1952: The Indian Cinematograph Act of 1952 replaces the Cinematograph Act of 1918
1952: *Filmfare* is launched as a fortnightly
1953: *Do Bigha Zameen* (Bimal Roy) reveals the influence of Italian neo-realism
1955: Satyajit Ray makes *Pather Panchali*, Subrata Mitra debuts as a cameraman
1956: Experimental television broadcasts begin in Delhi
1958: The Indian Copyright Act comes into force
1958: A festival of documentary films is begun in Bombay
1959: *Kagaz ke Phool*, the first Indian cinemascope film, is made by Guru Dutt and shot by V.K. Murthy

1960–1970

Landmarks
1960: The Film Institute (later the Film & Television Institute of India: FTII) is founded in Pune
1960: The Film Finance Corporation (FFC), later to become NFDC, is founded
1960: K. Asif's *Mughal-e-Azam*, the most expensive feature film until then in Indian film history, is completed

1961: Drastic cuts in the import of raw film stock
1961: Second International Film Festival of India in Delhi
1964: The National Film Archive of India is founded in Pune
1964: The Adyar Film Institute is founded in Madras
1965: Daily hour-long television broadcasts begin in Delhi
1966: Ritwik Ghatak becomes Director of FTII
1967: Hindustan Photo Film makes India self-sufficient in B&W and sound negative film. All colour film is imported and locally perforated
1967: The first 70 mm wide screen film is shown in India
1968: 'Manifesto for a New Cinema' issued by Mrinal Sen and Arun Kaul
1969: FFC finances *Bhuvan Shome* (Mrinal Sen) and *Uski Roti* (Mani Kaul), both photographed by K. K. Mahajan inaugurating 'New Wave Cinema'

1970–1980

Landmarks
1971: Drastic fall in the screenings of Hollywood cinema in India following the expiry between the MPEEA and the Government of India
1971: India becomes the largest producer of films in the world with 433 films
1972: First Art House Cinema is opened by FFC
1972: Chitralekha Co Op, the first cooperative started by film technicians, starts production with Adoor Gopalakrishnan's *Swayamvaram*
1973: FFC becomes the sole channelling agency for the import of raw stock. A 250% import duty on raw stock is imposed
1974: Hindustan Photo Films starts limited production of positive colour stock
1974: The International Film Festival of India becomes an annual event
1974: The Film Institute of India becomes the Film and Television Institute of India
1976: Doordarshan is separated from All India Road and is allowed to take advertising
1979: Malayalam cinema overtakes Hindi Cinema in volume of production

1980–1990

Landmarks
1980: FFC merges with the Indian Motion Picture Export Corporation to form the NFDC (National Film Development Corporation)
1982: Doordarshan begins colour broadcast with Satyajit Ray's *Sadgati* and *Shatranj ke Khiladi*
1985: Doordarshan becomes a fully commercial network, first major TV series, 'Humlog' broadcast
1989: First Bombay International Festival of Short Films and Documentaries

1990–2000

Landmarks
1991: Cable and satellite television comes to India following the Gulf War
1991: Free market restructuring carried out under the tutelage of the International Monetary Fund and the World Bank
1992: The launch of Zee TV and Star TV
1992: The government greatly liberalized the requirements, resulting in a great increase in foreign films being released domestically
1995: VSNL introduced internet services in India

Source: Acharya (2004).

$0.5 (Rs 22). This is a fraction of what moviegoing costs elsewhere: the average price of a ticket in the nine other big film-producing countries ranges from $2.2 in China to $11.7 in Japan (Thakur, 2009). The low price and large pirated market make it affordable even for poor people.

Indian movies are characterized by melodrama and long-drawn-out screenplays, liberally sprinkled with colourful song and dance sequences. It is these ingredients that transform the feature films into 'more than three-hour opuses' (especially when compared to English-language films whose average duration is barely 90 minutes) which command the largest audiences in the world. The leisure value of this industry can be gauged from the fact that even though the Bollywood movies are the ones to be released in the greatest number of cinemas across the country, including in the small cinema halls of small towns, and hamlets of the Hindi belt, the regional language films and their actors also command a very faithful audience and fan following in specific geographic areas of the country. For some actors who choose to capitalize on their popularity, this fan following successfully transcends into the field of politics, especially in South India. It is interesting to note that although the education and awareness levels of southern Indians are overall higher than the national average, they are happy to mix politics with pleasure. In India generally, the popular actors/actresses always win in elections, even against the political heavyweights.

The popularity of movies among the masses is evidenced by the immense fan following that takes the form of ritualistic worship. The Madhuri-Dixit (a famous Indian actress) temple in Jamshedpur, the Amitabh Bachchan (a famous Indian actor) temple in Kolkatta and numerous other such 'shrines' set up all over India to exhibit love, faith and devotion to mortal Bollywood actors, all point towards the fact that Hindi movies project a larger-than-life impact on the psyche of the people. Besides being a stand-alone leisure entertainment industry, it also provides major entertainment inputs to other leisure entertainment sources such as radio, TV, cable, the internet, mobile entertainment, newspapers, magazines and so on.

Consumer Attitude and Demographics

Indian consumers are becoming ever more demanding with regard to their entertainment needs. No longer are entertainment and leisure considered as mere consumption of 'materialistic pleasure'; they are now accepted as part of life. With the increase in household income, Indians are seeking variety in their 'entertainment basket'. With the coming of the digital age, entertainment has taken on a new meaning, with leisure activities extending beyond the playground and movie theatres to computer games and theme parks. But even with a broader product range available to consumers in the entertainment and leisure market, the cinema is still the number one entertainment product for Indians, and is now focusing more on the young urban generation, as evidenced by the new storylines being developed.

The changing consumer trend towards a younger audience can be gauged from the comment made by the President of India, Mrs Devi Singh Patil, in her inaugural speech at the presentation of the national film awards, New Delhi, on 19 March 2010: 'It is true that the audience in India, which is the market for films, is undergoing transformation. There is a new generation of viewers and a growing middle class, more able to and more capable of spending on entertainment' (Patil, 2009).

The report on Leisure and Entertainment Trends 2008 by the Knowledge Company, Technopak, says that those aged between 15 and 19 comprise 15 per cent of all 15–55-year-old urban Indian (those residing in towns with a population above 5 lakh[1]) leisure consumers. A survey conducted on the leisure activities of 15–19-year-olds shows that watching movies is the top entertainment activity among these consumers, followed by reading (second) and socializing (third) as shown in Table 15.1 (BW Marketing Whitebook, 2009–10). Indian audiences are price conscious in general so the low ticket prices are a contributory factor, although in big cities rising incomes make it easier for cinema-goers to afford even relatively higher-priced multiplexes. Audiences look for entertainment and are becoming increasingly demanding.

Indian demographics are dominated by a young population. Whereas the rest of the world is concerned about ageing populations and falling birthrates, India is sitting on a huge demographic dividend (Pillania, 2008b). Around 70 per cent of the total population are below 35 years of age, making it on average the youngest population among major global economies. India is, and will remain for some time, one of the youngest countries in the world. In 2005, a third of India's population was below 15 years of age, and close to 20 per cent were young people in the 15–24 age group. In 2020, the average Indian will be only 29 years old, compared with 37 in China and the US, 45 in Western Europe and 48 in Japan (Chandrasekhar and Ghosh, 2006). With the recognition of the importance of a young population, there are an increasing number of films on the subject of youth and children. Two recent popular and big-hit films focused on child education (*Tare Jameen Par*) and higher education (*3 Idiots*). Indeed, *3 Idiots* has become the biggest hit in the history of the Indian movie industry. Furthermore, there are new young directors coming into the industry and experimenting with newer concepts.

ECONOMIC CONTRIBUTION OF BOLLYWOOD

Contribution of the Film Industry to the National Income

The Indian movie industry is considered part of a larger media and entertainment industry which was worth Rs 587 billion in 2009, a growth of 1.4 per cent despite a global recession (Nandini, 2010). The media and entertainment industry covers eight categories of services, that is, television, films, the printed media, radio, music, animation-gaming and VFX, 'out-of-home' advertising, and online advertising. Of course, there is considerable overlap, and often it is hard to differentiate one from

Table 15.1   Activities stated as entertainment versus percentage of those engaged in activities

Leisure and entertainment activities	15–19 yr olds	
	% stating activities as entertainment	% engaged in activities
Arts and entertainment	100	100
Watching movies	88	83
Other activities – dancing (Indian, Western), visiting art galleries/museums, watching plays, playing a musical instrument	66	48
Fitness/outdoor activities	92	80
Outdoor/indoor sports	52	43
Fitness-related activities (jogging, walking, yoga, cycling, gym, fitness club)	88	69
Adventure sports	16	4
Social activities	98	96
Social activities (eating out, visiting coffee shops)	81	73
Other outdoor recreation	97	94
Religious activities (visiting temples/places of religious interest)	73	69
Other outdoor activities – watching a sport/game, driving out/driving around, picnicking, wildlife viewing	80	70
Indoor recreation	97	95
Reading	85	79
Other indoor recreation (includes cooking, home decoration, painting etc.)	85	78
Travelling out/vacations in the last year	60	46
Leisure on the net	70	50
Surfing the net	45	24
Chatting on the net	43	23
Playing computer games/gaming/video games	58	41

Note: All individuals in the 15–19-year age group from SEC A, B and C households.

Source: The Knowledge Company, Technopak (BW Marketing Whitebook, 2009–10).

another. Film entertainment is the second-biggest earner after television entertainment.

While films, radio and out-of-home advertising witnessed negative growth, sectors that did well include television, the internet, gaming,

Table 15.2   Growth of Indian media and entertainment industry

Rs billion	2004	2005	2006	2007	2008	CAGR 2004–09 (%)
Television	128.7	158.5	191.2	223.9	244.7	17.4
% change		23.2	20.6	17.1	9.3	
Film entertainment	59.9	68.1	84.5	96.0	107.0	15.6
% change		13.7	24.1	13.6	11.5	
Print media	97.8	109.5	128.0	149.0	162.0	13.4
% change		12.0	16.9	16.9	8.7	
Radio	2.4	3.2	5.0	6.9	8.3	36.4
% change		33.3	66.3	38.0	20.3	
Music	6.7	7.2	7.3	7.3	6.3	–1.7
% change		7.3	0.8	0.6	–14.1	
Animation, gaming and VFX			10.5	13.0	15.6	
% change				23.8	20.0	
Out-of-home advertising	8.5	9.0	10.0	12.5	15.0	15.3
% change		6.9	11.1	25.0	20.0	
Online advertising	0.6	1.0	1.6	2.7	5.0	69.9
% change		66.7	60.0	68.8	20.0	
Total E&M industry	304.6	356.5	438.1	511.3	563.9	16.6
% change		17.0	22.9	16.7	10.3	

Source: PwC (2009).

animation and music. The printed media reported a very moderate growth even as the subscription revenues of TV and print grew by 8.5 per cent to reach Rs 241 billion. Advertising spending, whose compound annual growth rate (CAGR) increased by 10 per cent in the previous three years, reported almost flat growth in 2009 (ibid.). However, with the economy firmly on the growth path, consumer sentiment once again buoyant and increasing media penetration, most media and entertainment sectors are expected to record robust growth in the coming years.

Financial Performance

The film industry has been performing very well, having grown by 15.6 per cent in the 2004–08 period as shown in Table 15.2. In 2008, the industry registered a growth of 11.5 per cent over the previous year. Overall, the industry stood at Rs 107 billion in 2008, up from Rs 96 billion in 2007. Domestic box office collections continued to be the largest contributor to the revenues, estimated to be 76 per cent, or Rs 81.2 billion in 2008.

Overseas box office collections, which are steadily becoming an important component, stood at an estimated Rs 10 billion 2008. The home video market has also witnessed dynamic changes, after achieving a growth rate of 14.3 per cent over the 2004–08 period. In 2008, the home video market was estimated to be Rs 5.8 billion, down from Rs 7.4 billion in 2007, translating into a decline of 21 per cent from the previous year. Ancillary revenues are also becoming increasingly important, contributing 9 per cent to the film industry pie in 2008. Satellite rights contribute approximately 75–80 per cent of these revenues. Ancillary revenues are estimated to have grown by 19 per cent over the last four years and 18 per cent in the last year itself on the back of a spurt of satellite rights acquisitions. In 2008, overall, the ancillary revenues were estimated to be Rs 10 billion, up from Rs 8.5 billion in 2007 (PwC, 2009).

Exports of Bollywood Movies

The performance of the film industry has been quite encouraging in the past, with forecasts of a bright future. Entertainment is now, after information and communications technology (ICT), India's fastest-growing sector, and the movie industry is currently growing by 16 per cent annually. After a century of mainly serving the home market, Bollywood is now, with an 87 per cent export growth in 2008, collecting substantial revenues from abroad and is well on its way to becoming integrated in the global economy (Lorenzen and Taeube, 2007).

The film industry has also been recognized as a potent sector for attracting foreign direct investment (FDI). In 2005, in a bid to attract FDI, the government allowed 100 per cent investment in the industry. Prior to this, FDI was allowed only in the area of distribution, which involved Hollywood production houses such as Sony Entertainment, Paramount, Disney and so on investing in the distribution of their own products. More recently, some FDI inflow was also directed towards film exhibitions in multiplexes, with an eye to the wealthy middle-class audiences.

Some of the major FDI inflows in entertainment and the media in 2008 were into Nimbus Communication, Zee Telefilms, Balaji Telefilms Ltd and Times Broadband Services, mainly routed via Mauritius. Film entertainment generated the most interest from foreign investors.

The film industry has been a consistent performer in terms of exports, contributing roughly 0.015 per cent to national exports as shown in Table 15.3, although the same cannot be said about the growth of the film industry's export market, which has seen many ups and downs in the

Table 15.3   Export performance of Indian films

Year	Indian film exports (US$m)	Growth % YOY	% Share of total exports
2001–02	17.53	–29.10	0.0400
2002–03	15.57	–11.18	0.0295
2003–04	13.93	–10.51	0.0218
2004–05	18.22	30.81	0.0218
2005–06	16.30	–10.55	0.0158
2006–07	18.34	12.51	0.0145
2007–08	15.25	–16.82	0.0093
2008–09	28.54	87.13	0.0154

Source: Ministry of Commerce Databank (2010).

last decade. However, this trend is changing rapidly. In 2008, the overall export growth in the industry was more than the overall national export growth, strongly suggesting its important contribution to the national economy. Besides catering to the growing diaspora, Bollywood movies are also becoming popular with overseas audiences in many countries such as Poland, Germany and so on. The Indian diaspora across the globe, particularly in North America, the UK and the Gulf countries, is the second largest diaspora after that of the Chinese (Pillania, 2008b).

The economic slowdown has led to film projects being scaled down, artiste costs have been revised, and film producers are devising new strategies. The Indian film industry is looking to move towards a risk-sharing model, in which costs and benefits are spread across the value chain. With funds for investments drying up, film production companies are becoming more cautious about their selection of movies and their acquisition price and production costs. Examples of cost cutting in film distribution include, among others, limiting the number of languages into which an international film is dubbed; and distribution in select markets, thereby saving on print costs as well as local marketing and promotion costs (PwC, 2009).

CONCLUSION AND DIRECTIONS FOR FUTURE RESEARCH

The Indian film industry is the world's largest in terms of number of films produced as well as the number of cinema-goers. Bollywood produces almost as many films as the next three – the US, Japan and China

– combined. The Indian movie industry, notably Bollywood, has come a long way in the last century. Since it has become recognized as an industry, the Indian popular cinema has made much progress in almost all areas such as retail infrastructure, financing, marketing and distribution.

Bollywood movies are a major source of entertainment and leisure for India and the growing Indian diaspora. Movie watching is the top leisure activity for most Indians. Movies in India are not just a mere 'song and dance' spectacle, but they are an integral part of the Indian culture. Their influence in people's lives can be gauged from the fact that movie stars share 'deity' status, which is not the case in other parts of the world. Besides being a stand-alone leisure entertainment industry, it also provides major entertainment inputs to many other leisure entertainment sources. Bollywood movies are now going beyond national boundaries and are in the process of making their mark on the international movie scene.

The Indian film industry has undoubtedly grown over the years, not only as a major revenue earner for the nation but also as a highly specialized indigenous industry. With the growth of GDP, the spending power of Indians is also changing. Lifestyle changes brought about by changes in economic activity are also spurring the growth of the film industry, which is one of the fastest-growing industries in India and has made a significant contribution to the economy and the export trade.

Future research in this area should be directed at (i) the industry structure and (ii) industry processes. The need for doing research on industry structure lies in the fact that until now the industry has been operating in a rather disorganized manner. But if the industry seeks to be a formidable power globally, it must adopt a structure that will facilitate its international growth. Similarly, research has to be initiated for the different processes involved in the making, distribution and screening of Indian films.

NOTE

1.   One lakh is equivalent to 100,000.

REFERENCES

Acharya, S. (2004), 'Bollywood and globalization', thesis, San Francisco State University, San Francisco, CA, available at: http://www.dishumdishum.com/BollyPresentation/GLOBALIZATION.PDF (accessed 12 January 2008).
BW Marketing Whitebook (2009–10), 'Leisure and entertainment among 15–19 year olds', available at: http://www.bwbooks.in/pdf/Leisure_&_entertainment.pdf (accessed 5 May 2009).

Chandrasekhar, C.P. and J. Ghosh (2006), 'India's potential demographic dividend', Business Line (internet edition), Tuesday, 17 January.

Kavitha, V. (2010), 'Film financing in India', *Media & Entertainment*, **2**, January, Newsletter, Universal Legal.

Lorenzen, M. and F.A. Taeube (2007), 'Breakout from Bollywood? Internationalization of Indian Film Industry', DRUID Working Paper No. 07-06, Danish Research Unit for Industrial Development, available at: www.druid.dk.

Ministry of Commerce Databank (2010), Ministry of Commerce Website, available at: http://commerce.nic.in/eidb/default.asp (accessed 5 March 2010).

Nandini, Raghavendra (2010), 'Media, entertainment to touch $24 bn mark by 2014', *Economic Times*, New Delhi, 17 March.

Patil, P.S. (2009), 'Speech by Her Excellency the President of India, Shrimati Pratibha Devisingh Patil, at the presentation ceremony of the national film awards', available at: http://presidentofindia.nic.in/sp190310.html (accessed 5 December 2009).

Pillania, R.K. (2008a), 'The globalization of Indian Hindi movie industry', *Management*, University of Primorska, Faculty of Management Koper, **3** (2), 115–23.

Pillania, R.K. (2008b), 'Indian diaspora and demographic dividend', *Evolution*, **1** (1), 1–9.

PricewaterhouseCoopers (PwC) (2009), 'Indian Entertainment and Media Outlook', PwC report.

Thakur, A. (2009), 'India dominates world of films', *Times of India*, New Delhi, 28 July.

Tyrell, H. (1999), 'Bollywood versus Hollywood: battle of the dream factories', in T. Skelton and T. Allen (eds), *Culture and Global Change*, New York: Routledge, pp. 260–73.

16 Leisure time, cinema and the structure of household entertainment expenditure, 1890–1940[1]

Gerben Bakker

INTRODUCTION

At the end of the nineteenth century, in the era of the second industrial revolution, falling working hours, rising disposable income, increasing urbanization, rapidly expanding transport networks and strong population growth resulted in a sharp rise in the demand for entertainment. Initially, the expenditure was spread across different categories, such as live entertainment, sports, music, bowling alleys or skating rinks. One of these categories was cinematographic entertainment, a new service, based on a new technology. Initially it seemed not more than a fad, a novelty shown at fairs, but it quickly emerged as the dominant form of popular entertainment. This chapter argues that the take-off of cinema was largely demand driven, and that, in an evolutionary process, consumers allocated more and more expenditure to cinema. It will analyse how consumer habits and practices evolved with the new cinema technology and led to the formation of a new product/service.

These issues provide insight into how new consumer goods and services emerge, how the process works by which certain new goods become successful and are widely adopted while others will disappear and are forgotten forever.

This chapter examines the structure of household expenditure in Britain, France and the United States at the cross-section for benchmark years to get insight into the structure of demand, the differences between countries and expenditure items, and the way in which these affected the industrialization of entertainment.

THE INCREASE IN LEISURE TIME

Time and money both affected entertainment consumption.[2] People had to decide how many hours to spend on labour versus leisure, what to do in the resulting free time, and how much to spend on it. Rising real wages

Table 16.1   Average weekly hours and holidays, US, Britain and France, 1850–1960

Year	Average weekly hours						Holidays per year			
	United States			Britain	France	Western World	US	Britain	France	Western World
	(I)	(II)	(III)							
1850	69.8									
1860	68.0									
1870	65.4		62.0	56.9	66.1	64.3	4	14	19	13
1880	64.0		61.0	56.6	66.0	62.5				
1890	61.9		60.0	56.3	65.9	60.9				
1900	60.2	58.5	59.1	56.0	65.9	59.5	5	20	23	17
1910	55.1	55.6								
1913			58.3	56.0	62.0	57.0				
1920	49.7	50.6								
1929	47.0	48.7	48.0	47.0	48.0	47.8				
1930	45.9	47.1								
1938			37.3	48.6	39	46.1	17	30	33	29
1940	44.0	42.5								
1950	40.0	41.1	42.4	45.7	44.8	45.4	18	24	28	25
1960		41.0	40.2	44.7	45.9	43.2				

Sources: I: Dewhurst (1955), II: Owen (1970); US III both for non-agricultural workers. US III, Britain, France, Western World and holidays: Huberman and Minns (2007), for full-time production workers.

could induce people to work more, because rewards were higher, or less, because consumers could increase leisure time without reducing real income. In addition, changes in preferences – because of, for example, new goods – could affect people's choices of hours. Hans-Joachim Voth (2000) showed how in Britain, during the industrial revolution, the availability of new goods induced people to work longer hours in order to pay for them.

During the second industrial revolution, many of the new goods were time intensive, such as the bicycle, the car, skating rinks, bowling alleys or spectator entertainment. Consumers had to find a balance between working enough hours to buy the goods and having enough time to consume them. The reduction in working hours suggests that the latter became more important. The labour supply had probably turned the kink of a backward-bending curve, as persons exchanged higher wages (and productivity) for fewer hours. So the first choice of consumers appears to have been to increase their amount of leisure time.[3]

In the US, average working hours decreased from 70 a week in 1850 to 60 in 1900 (Table 16.1). In the 1860s and 1880s they declined quickly, in the 1850s, 1870s and 1890s slowly. The American male born in 1900 could expect to be two-thirds of his life in the labour force, out of a total of 48 years.[4] Between 1900 and 1914, the decline accelerated and hours dropped by 6 per cent. Part of the reduction in hours may have been countered by an increase in the travel time between home and work.

Campaigns for the eight-hour workday were organized, and between 1913 and 1919, hours fell by another 8 per cent. The Eight Hours Act (1912) required government contractors to stick to a 48-hour week, or pay a 50 per cent overtime premium. During the 1920s the decline slowed, to only two hours over the decade. Only in 1938, when the Supreme Court approved the Fair Labor Standards Act, did working hours become federally regulated.[5] Holidays also increased substantially, from just four days in 1870, to five in 1900 and 17 in 1938 (Huberman and Minns, 2007: 546).

In Britain, weekly hours decreased from 65 in 1856, to 56 in 1873 and 47 in 1924, 27.7 per cent in all. Annual hours, allowing for holidays, sickness and strikes, fell slightly more, from 3,185 in 1856 to 2,071 in 1937, or 30.3 per cent.[6]

Between 1887 and 1892 workers campaigned for the eight-hour day. The free Saturday afternoon also gave workers more leisure time. In 1894 the Royal Commission on Labour reported that state regulation of hours was not desirable. Some progressive engineering firms adopted eight-hour days, and in 1908 a law secured one for miners. It was not until after the First World War that all workers enjoyed an eight-hour day (Cross, 1989: 71–4, 129–31).

The hours worked a day, the days worked a week, and the weeks worked a year all decreased, although working hours of the middle-class occupations appear to have fallen more rapidly (Benson, 1994: 14). Holidays increased from 14 in 1870 to 20 in 1900, to 30 by 1938. The number of paid holidays increased sharply after 1920. In the mid-1930s 1.5 million workers were entitled to them, and with the Holidays with Pay Act of 1938 nearly eight times as many (Huberman and Minns, 2007: 546).

In France, leisure time increased slightly during the nineteenth century. Before 1850, working hours probably tended to increase. In 1848 legislation limited the working day to 11 hours in Paris and 12 hours in the provinces. However, in practice the average working day remained 12–14 hours until about 1870 and between 11 and 12 hours until 1890. In the 1900s the 10-hour day quickly became the practice. The increase in leisure time was distributed unevenly. For many, the increasing distance and time between home and work countervailed the decrease in working hours. Special craftsmen and domestic workers, for example, benefited disproportionately from falling hours, while it is doubtful whether factory workers benefited overall. In 1906, campaigns for the eight-hour day

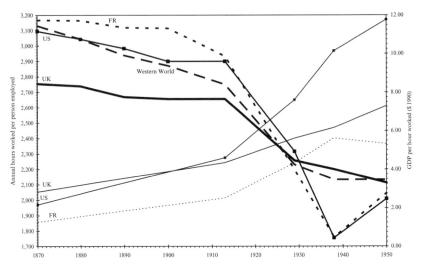

Note: The lines are interpolations from four benchmark years: 1870, 1913, 1929 and 1938. The bold lines represent annual hours worked, the thin lines GDP per hour worked.

Source: Huberman and Minns (2007: 548); GDP/hour derived from Maddison's (1995: 248–9) data on GDP per person employed and Huberman and Minns's annual hours per person.

Figure 16.1   *Annual hours worked per person employed and GDP per hour worked (in 1990 dollars per hour), US, Britain and France, 1870–1950*

started (Dupeux, 1974: 135–8; Berlanstein, 1984; 123–6).[7] Holidays in France increased from 19 in 1870 to 23 in 1900 and 33 in 1938 (Huberman and Minns, 2007: 546).

Although in 1870 total annual hours varied substantially between the three countries, they converged until 1929 (Figure 16.1). Before 1913, hours fell gradually, even if accounts differ on the exact pattern.[8] After the First World War, working hours fell rapidly in all countries. In the 1930s, working hours diverged. In Britain they stabilized, in the US and France they fell more sharply. Labour productivity rose at a similar pace as working hours fell.

Since entertainment takes time, falling working hours were crucial for the rapid rise in entertainment demand.[9] A small elite could not, by buying much more entertainment, be a substitute for the demand of many people with small incomes, since everybody rich or poor had to live with a 24-hour day.[10] Only the elite could enjoy more expensive entertainment. Contemporary observers noted that decreasing working hours would lead to a rapid increase in demand for consumer goods and services, which would offset the cost increase because of higher wages. Authors such as Sidney Webb and Harold Cox (1891) argued that leisure created wants that increased markets for popular services and goods. Henry H. Champion (1890) wrote that the eight-hour day would 'excite a desire for additional means of recreation, amusement and cultivation'. Radical trade unionist Tom Mann (1891) argued that leisure provided workers 'with the desire for the products of manufacture'. French union leader Victor Griffuelhes predicted in 1904 that 'leisure leads the worker to desire to consume more, will increase his needs, and will lead to the proportionate increase in production'.[11]

Some contemporary economists shared this view. George Gunton, in his book *Wealth and Progress* (1887), sets out a demand-side theory which held that capital accumulation depended on wages and working class consumption, rather than investment: 'The development of labor's capacity to consume wealth is as important economically . . . as it is to increase his power to produce'.[12] The European economist Lujo Brentano (1894), later an advocate of the eight-hour day, claimed that employers no longer needed long hours or low pay to ensure profits, a view long held by economists and employers. Rather, advanced consumer needs developed in leisure time would stimulate individual productivity. Growth, rather than redistribution, would be the consequence of shorter hours. By broadening the mass market, they would create jobs.[13]

The question remains how exactly the additional leisure hours translated into more consumption of spectator entertainment. Three long-run changes stand out: the increasing division between labour and leisure, the increase in the planning and timing of work and leisure time, and the rise in opportunity costs. Before industrialization most work was concentrated around the home, and work and private life were inseparable. When people became employed in factories, labour and leisure become more clearly distinguished (Cross, 1988). Additional leisure hours were experienced more as 'real' leisure time, since there was no backlog of work to be done that could interfere with it.

The time that a worker spent in a factory was planned and organized carefully. An organization structure emerged to use the hours as efficiently as possible. Starting with Frederic Winslow Taylor in America, actions of workers were analysed, divided in distinct steps and then performed by separate, specialized workers. Although working hours decreased, the rise in productivity made up for it (Cross, 1989: 103–28). Workers became used to the careful management of time, to the idea of making time productive. They thus also felt a disposition against idleness, in the sense of doing nothing, letting time wither away unplanned, staring out of the window. Leisure time had to be planned, had to be used productively. Increased leisure planning, driven by the conditioning of the worker in the factory, was reinforced by social campaigns for a better spending of free time. An example is the 'rational recreation' movement in Britain, which tried to change workers' leisure time from drowning away in a pub into a carefully planned programme aimed towards self-improvement. Especially the labour movement supported the view that leisure time should be used to improve oneself by following courses, reading literature, going to the theatre or to an exhibition, or making music.

As wages and disposable income grew, leisure time became more valuable in monetary terms. A worker had to make an increasing monetary sacrifice to get one hour of extra leisure time. The cost of leisure was felt more, and so the idea grew that it should be used 'productively'. Increased wages gave workers the choice between longer hours, which became more attractive, and more leisure, which became more affordable. Leisure opportunities thus had to compete with the potential extra working hours. This paved the way for an entertainment industry that could guarantee an enjoyable and carefully timed leisure experience.[14]

HOUSEHOLD EXPENDITURE BEFORE CINEMA

Before the late nineteenth century, only anecdotal quantitative information exists on the household demand for entertainment. Michael Mulhall (1892: 360) quotes a French letter of 1679 of Madame de Maintenon to her sister, in which she advised her sister, who was married and had ten servants, on household expenses: 53 per cent of the budget went on food and rent, and not less than 20 per cent was reserved for the opera. The total budget amounted to 600 pounds sterling, writes Mulhall.

From the mid-century onwards studies of the conditions of the working classes became more common, many inspired by the pioneering work of Frédéric le Play (1855 [1877]). These early studies on family budgets seldom looked at expenditures on entertainment and recreation.[15] In most of Le Play's reports, they are grouped under 'sundries' and thus invisible. Moreover, the early family budgets may be unrepresentative. Often individual cases were studied elaborately, instead of taking sufficiently large and random samples.[16]

Dorothy Brady (1972) constructed representative sample budgets for American families in the 1830s, slightly above the relevant averages for each of three types of residential location: farm, village and city. All types spent much on reading and recreation, about 2 per cent of all expenditures excluding shelter.[17] Expenditures on church and charity were even higher, varying from 9 per cent for farm families to 3 per cent for city families. They may have been overreported, as they were considered socially desirable. Charity expenditure probably functioned not unlike social security contributions, especially in the farm and village communities. For comparison, farm families spent more on tobacco than they spent on reading and recreation, 2.5 per cent, while city dwellers spent only 0.8 per cent, and village families were caught in the middle.[18]

Only in 1889 was the first systematic survey done, with a large number of respondents, and a sample that at least partially started to resemble a random sample. In 1889–90, under the supervision of Carroll D. Wright, the US Commissioner of Labor, the US Department of Labor carried out a survey on family expenditure, as part of a study of costs of production in nine protected industries. The survey was made in preparation for the debate on the highly protective McKinley Tariff of 1890. Data was collected on demographic characteristics, occupations, incomes and expenditure patterns of 8,544 families and their members in these industries in 24 states of the US and five European countries: Britain, France, Germany, Belgium and Switzerland.[19] The nine industries were bar iron, pig iron, steel, bituminous coal, coke, iron ore, cotton textiles, woollens and glass.[20] In America, the researchers interviewed members of 6,809 families in the nine industries, in 25 US states, comprising about 35,500 family members.

The survey is not totally random or representative, for three reasons: it selected only workers in cooperating firms, it selected only cooperating workers who could provide information in sufficient detail, and only industrial workers in families were included. However, research by Michael Haines (1979: 292–5) shows that, at least for the United States, comparison with the US census gives some support to the representativeness of the data.

The survey lists several categories which can be connected to leisure spending: expenditure on amusements and vacation, reading, liquor, religion and charity. The category 'amusements and vacation' includes live entertainment, but it is impossible to say what share of those was used for sports matches, music hall spectacles, theatre, or day trips and vacations.

For the US, the average household income of the respondents, $684, was far higher than national average income of non-farm workers, which was $471 in 1889 and $475 in 1890. The reason for the difference is most likely that more members of the family were working. Expenditure on 'amusements and vacations' was small, only 1.1 per cent of income, on average. Yet this was substantially higher than expenditures on reading, religion and charity (Table 16.2). Only expenditures on liquor and tobacco were substantially higher.

The expenditure on amusements relative to income shows a consistent

Table 16.2   Household expenditure on leisure goods/services, US, UK and France, 1889–1890

	Expenditure (% of income)			Expenditure ($)			Coefficient of variation			Range (max/ min)
	US	UK	FR	US	UK	FR	US	UK	FR	
Amusements/ vacations	1.10	3.47	3.85	7.53	18.46	15.75	2.82	1.38	1.35	2.45
Reading	0.80	0.90	0.46	5.47	4.79	1.88	1.19	0.93	1.36	2.91
Religion	0.97	0.54	0.18	6.64	2.87	0.74	1.42	1 65	3.02	9.01
Charity	0.40	0.26	0.06	2.74	1.38	0.25	2.43	2.36	6.09	11.15
Liquor	1.80	2.36	5.16	12.31	12.56	21.11	2.39	1.41	1.21	1.71
Tobacco	1.30	1.13	0.99	8.89	6.01	4.05	0.92	1.11	1.18	2.20
Total	6.37	8.66	10.70	43.58	46.08	43.77	1.86	1.47	2.37	1.06

Note: Total for coefficient of variation is unweighted average

Source: Data US Commissioner of Labor Survey 1891, provided by Michael Haines.

and almost linear increase with income (Figure 16.2). The fact that amusements expenditure rose substantially faster than income over all intervals, suggests that it was a luxury good for all income groups alike. This is confirmed by the income elasticity, which was above one for households with expenditure on entertainment. Assuming constant elasticity gives an income elasticity of 1.13; assuming that diverging elasticities using ordinary least-squares (OLS) regressions yields an average elasticity of 1.43.[21] The likelihood of households having positive expenditure on amusements shows that this was highly income dependent: as income rises from zero to $500, the probability of any expenditure on amusements doubles from 20 to 40 per cent (Figure 16.3), and as income triples to $1,500, the probability doubles again, to 80 per cent.

If the expenditure, relative to income, is compared with other recreational items, it is clear that amusement expenditure was the item that rose the fastest with income, in a consistent manner (Figure 16.4). Only liquor expenditure rose in a similar way, but only for increases across the lower incomes. The income elasticity of amusement expenditure was also far higher than that of other expenditures, and was higher than all other elasticities across all income intervals except the lowest one, from $200 to $450, where tobacco and religion were higher and that of reading was equal.[22]

In Britain, the average household income was $532 (about £109), which was substantially above the average earnings of general labourers

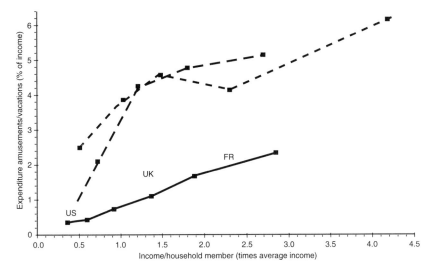

Figure 16.2   Expenditure on amusements and vacations across different income classes, for the US, Britain and France, 1889–1890

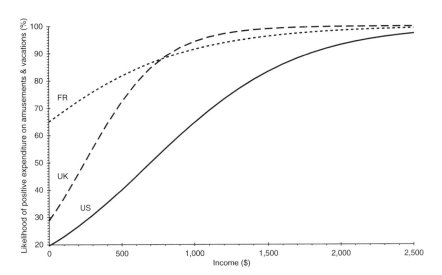

Figure 16.3   Likelihood of positive expenditure of households on amusements and vacations, US, Britain and France, 1889–1890

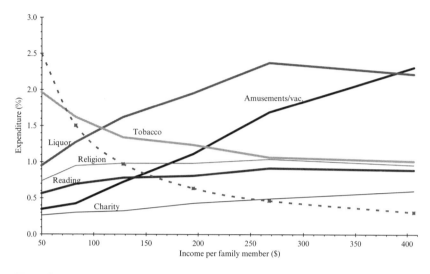

Note: Income groups were made according to income per family member.
The iso-expenditure line shows the slope the expenditure curves should roughly have to reflect a constant expenditure in absolute (dollar) terms. The start value of 2.5 per cent for this line has been taken arbitrarily; what matters is the slope.

Source: Data US Commissioner of Labor Survey 1891, provided by Michael Haines.

Figure 16.4 Leisure and related expenditure of US industrial families, per member, 1889–1890

(£63) and those of skilled labourers (which ranged from £88 to £94).[23] A large part of the difference was probably due to the circumstance that household income often aggregated the income of several family members. The percentage of income spent on amusements was relatively large, about 3.5 per cent, and was far larger than expenditure on the other recreational items. The rise of amusement expenditure with income shows a distinctive pattern; until slightly above the average income, expenditure rises sharply, and after that it rises more gradually and far more slowly (in percentage terms) than income: as income doubles to two times the average, amusement expenditure increases by under a third. The estimated income elasticity was 1.80 assuming constant elasticity and 1.68 assuming changing elasticity.[24] The likelihood of having positive amusement expenditure increased rapidly with income: as income moved to $350, the probability of any expenditure on amusements doubled from 30 to 60 per cent, and as income tripled to $1,000, the probability increased by half to 90 per cent.

None of the other expenditure items showed a similar pattern to

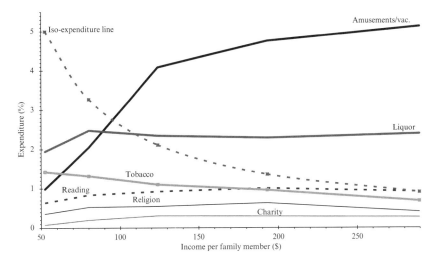

Note: Income groups were made according to income per family member.

Source: Data US Commissioner of Labor Survey 1891, provided by Michael Haines.

Figure 16.5   *Leisure and related expenditure of British industrial families as a percentage of income, 1889–1890*

amusement expenditure. At low incomes, amusement expenditure was comparable with other recreational expenditures, but as incomes rose it became more important than other expenditures (Figure 16.5). This suggests that amusements and vacations were a distinct luxury. Their income elasticity was far higher than that of all other recreational items. Looking at disaggregated income intervals, only across the lowest interval was the elasticity of charity and religion higher; across all other intervals the elasticity of amusements dominated (Bakker, 2001: 102, 391).

An opportunity to compare the British 1889/90 data with other research is provided by a survey of 28 'industrial families' carried out by the Economic Club between 1891 and 1894. The representativeness of the sample cannot be established, and the survey only recorded expenditure, not income. Nevertheless, it can give some rough indications of relative expenditures. Average annual expenditure for the 28 families was £92.16, or $449, considerably below the 1889–90 survey average income of $532 but closer to the national average non-farm wage (Table 16.3). On average, these households spent 1.62 per cent of their income on 'recreation', and 2.41 per cent on 'recreation' and 'travelling', which is more comparable to 'amusements and vacations' in the 1889/90 survey. This suggests that in that survey, the larger part of 'amusements and vacations' may have been

Table 16.3   *Annual leisure and related expenditure of 28 British industrial families, per member, 1891–1894*

	Per expenditure group (£)				All families combined	
	−8.67	8.67–15.17	15.17–21.67	21.67–	2.82–73.02	2.82–73.02
Expenditure/ member (£)	4.97	12.81	18.20	41.17	18.07	
No. of families	7	9	6	6	28	
Average family size	6.29	4.72	4.83	4.61	5.1	

	Expenditure (%)					% reporting
Recreation	3.63	0.33	0.66	2.37	1.62	54
Travelling		0.08	0.16	1.51	0.79	21
Alcoholic drinks	0.02	1.00	4.85	1.33	1.92	43
Tobacco	0.84	0.50	0.20	0.24	0.33	29
Religious observances		0.23	1.38	1.71	1.19	25
Charity and gifts		0.17	0.36	0.88	0.55	43

Note: Expenditure/member refers to average expenditure per family member; % reporting is the share of families that reported any expenditure on the item.

Source: Economic Club (1896).

spent on amusements. The expenditure in 1891–94 is about a third lower than the 3.5 per cent reported in the previous survey.

Like in the previous survey, recreation and travelling are higher than any other leisure item, and recreation itself is lower only than expenditure on alcohol. Expenditure on liquor and tobacco is substantially lower for the 28 families, probably due to more underreporting. Religion and charity expenditure is considerably higher than in the 1890 group. Besides representativeness and comparability, an explanation for the difference may be that the Economic Club, which was an organization of progressive persons, may have selected the more 'progressive' working-class families, which played a role in the temperance movement and would give away more than the average family.[25]

The expenditure on recreation and travelling rises strongly with income, in line with the findings of the earlier survey and confirming that recreation and travelling were strong luxuries. Its income elasticity (1.6) was substantially above one, and lower than the OLS elasticity estimate for the 1889–90 survey (2.2), though not far from the OLS elasticity for cases with positive expenditure (1.7) and the log-log constant elasticity estimate (1.8). Disaggregated elasticity for the two items was also greater than one (1.3

for recreation and 2.3 for travelling), and suggests that, for the 1889–90 survey, the elasticity for 'amusements' expenditure without 'vacations' may be substantially lower than the aggregate. The percentage of families with positive expenditure on 'recreation' and 'travelling' was possibly somewhat lower, 54 and 21 per cent, versus 71 per cent for the 1889–90 survey. The logit model predicts a value of 68 per cent for UK income of $449, suggesting that not all of the difference could be explained by the lower average income in the 1891–94 sample. Overall, the findings of the Economic Club survey are broadly in line with the 1889/90 survey, in terms of directions, and at the very least suggests that the 1889/90 findings are not implausible.[26]

In France, the average household income was $409, about 2,045 francs, which was substantially above the national average for non-farm workers. The average expenditure on amusements and recreation was nearly 4 per cent of income. The rise of expenditure with income shows a discontinuity just below one and a half times average income. Before, amusement expenditure is rising rapidly, but after it is declining somewhat (as a percentage of income, not in absolute terms), and then increasing more gradually.[27] The income elasticity was equal to or greater than one, with a constant elasticity estimate yielding 1.07 and a changing elasticity estimate yielding 1.26.[28]

French expenditure on amusements was substantially larger than all other recreational expenditure, except for liquor, on which over 5 per cent of income was spent, on average (Figure 16.6). Interestingly, the overall income elasticities of religion and charity were substantially higher than amusements. Looking at the disaggregated income intervals, only over the highest income interval did the elasticity of amusements dominate all other elasticities.[29] This suggests that amusements in France were a luxury, but became far more luxurious for the highest income groups.

Comparing the three countries, it is clear that the real income of the US sample was about 30 per cent higher than that of the British one, and that of the latter again 30 per cent higher than the French one. Average expenditure on amusements and vacations as a percentage of income was more than three times higher in Britain and France. The higher expenditure in France compared to Britain appears to be mainly due to a far higher likelihood of positive expenditure for French lower-income groups (see Figure 16.3), with the likelihoods converging quite rapidly as incomes rise. In all three countries, expenditure on amusements and recreation was far higher than that on reading, religion and charity individually, and for Britain and France it was far higher than the combined expenditure on the last three items. The expenditure patterns on liquor and tobacco differ substantially from country to country.

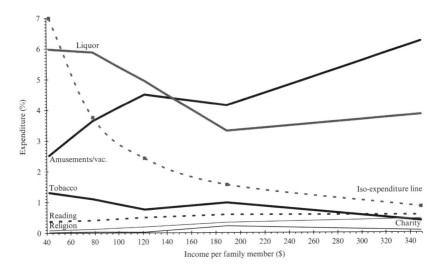

Note: Income groups were made according to income per family member. For a detailed overview of the groups and the sample, see Bakker (2001: 393).

Source: Data US Commissioner of Labor Survey 1891, provided by Michael Haines.

Figure 16.6   *Leisure and related expenditure of French industrial families, 1889–1890*

The expenditure on amusements and vacation relative to income shows sharp differences. In the US, expenditure rises relatively smoothly with income, while both Britain and France have important discontinuities. In Britain, it rises sharply until about 1.2 times average income, and then rises ever more slowly. In France, the expenditure rises until about one and a half times average income, and then shows a mixed pattern. The question remains: what caused this discontinuity in Europe, besides possibly the smaller sample sizes? It is possible that, at the high European expenditure levels, the US would have seen a similar pattern, in which at some point, when a large amount on amusements and vacations has been spent, the marginal utility of further expenditure decreases sharply as income increases. It will be shown below that while US expenditure patterns on amusements only show the same smooth increase in 1917–19 (when expenditure was higher), they start showing discontinuities in 1936–38 (when expenditure was higher again).

Income elasticity was the highest in Britain and the lowest in France, both for assuming constant and varying elasticity. US elasticity was substantially closer to the French one than to the British one. The likelihood of positive expenditure, however, shows sharp differences. At low incomes, British households were about one and a half times as likely to spend on amusements and vacations as their US counterparts, and French households were two to three times as likely to spend on entertainment. In Britain, expenditure was the most income dependent (until about 1.8 times average income), in France the least.

A potential explanation could be differences in the spread of working hours across income groups. Although hours worked in the US do not appear to be higher than in Britain or France at the time,[30] it could be the case that the lowest US income groups worked far longer hours. But even if that were the case, it remains uncertain whether it was an effect of a choice to spend less on amusements and vacation, or the cause of the low expenditure. Another reason may be that the price of spectator entertainment in the US in the late nineteenth century appears to have been significantly higher than in Britain and France (Bakker, 2004a). Part of the price difference could be a result of the relative scarcity of skilled (entertainment) labour in the US.

In all three countries, income expenditure on amusements and vacations rose more sharply than that on other items. In the US and Britain the income elasticity of amusements was far higher than that of all other items, in France religion and charity showed a higher elasticity, but were far lower a percentage of income than in the US and Britain. The expenditure pattern on liquor varied substantially between countries. In Britain, it rose sharply until a certain point, after which it levelled off, in the US it remained more or less stable, and in France, it declined with income (but from a very high income share). It seems that in Britain it was a luxury, while in the US and France it was more of a normal good.

THE STRUCTURE OF DEMAND DURING THE EMERGENCE OF CINEMA

The previous section looked at income elasticity at the cross-section level. The unavailability of reliable data makes it impossible to compare this with the price elasticity of entertainment demand. Particularly good price and capacity data for Boston in 1909, however, enables the making of a rough and ready estimate of the price elasticity of demand for various forms of spectator entertainment and their market shares.[31] A committee in Boston estimated the 'selling capacity' of each category of spectator entertainment, which appears to have been the maximum number of tickets the combined venues in a particular category could sell keeping normal showing hours.[32] As cinemas could have far more showings during one day than, for example, opera, the larger capacity of cinema does not necessarily reflect a proportionately larger number of seats or venues.

Two issues affect the conclusions we can draw from these data. First, in 1909, cinemas had taken off for two to three years and their number was still growing rapidly. The data thus enable no more than a snapshot of a situation that probably was changing rapidly. Second, Boston was a large metropolitan US city, and the findings for Boston may only have a degree of representativeness for other metropolitan areas in the US. In smaller cities, towns and villages, the amount and variety of entertainment supplied was possibly more limited.

From the price and selling-capacity data, the potential weekly revenue can be calculated. This is maximum revenue, assuming that all seats are filled at all show times. The total weekly sales capacity of Boston spectator entertainment venues was $268,070. The real weekly revenues in 1909 were probably substantially lower. These figures cannot easily be transformed into annual figures, because all venues were not open all weeks of the year. Cinema was probably the only venue that was open 52 weeks. If we optimistically assume that opera was operating 30 weeks a year, and the other live entertainment venues 40 weeks a year, we arrive at an annual potential revenue of about $10.5 million. If we then assume that two-thirds of tickets would be sold, on average, we would arrive at annual sales of $7 million, about 4 per cent of total US expenditure of spectator entertainment in 1909.[33] In broad terms, although on the high side, this figure does not seem improbable, given that live entertainment expenditure was heavily concentrated in big cities.

Given the assumptions made to arrive at annual figures, below we shall focus on the weekly data as reported in the source. This is also more relevant if we want to gain insight into consumer expenditure. During about 40 weeks of the year consumers faced all these choices, prices and qualities at the same time, and those are the weeks that matter if we want to compare various forms of entertainment. Using the capacities cumulatively, one can approximate a 'demand' curve, assuming that weekly capacities reflected tickets sold in roughly the same way for each product category (Figure 16.7). Likewise the elasticity of demand can be estimated and the potential consumer surplus generated by each form of entertainment (Table 16.4).

If we look at live entertainment only, first-class theatres sold the most tickets, followed by burlesque and then vaudeville. This suggests that, although burlesque has been less examined in the academic literature than theatre and vaudeville, it was an important form of entertainment for American consumers, probably more significant than vaudeville. In revenue terms, first-class theatres had by far the largest market share, followed at a distance by opera and then vaudeville and burlesque.

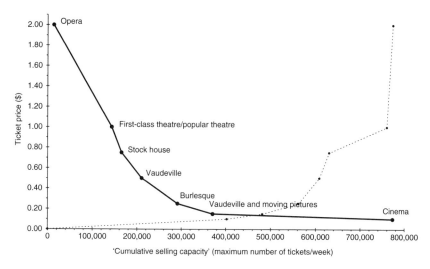

Sources: Table 16.4; compiled from Boston Committee 1909, as reported in Jowett (1974).

Figure 16.7   *Ticket price versus cumulative ticket-selling capacity for entertainment venues in Boston in 1909 ($ and number of tickets)*

From the demand curve (Figure 16.7), one can obtain a rough indication of the consumer surplus of each form of entertainment. Assuming that the demand curve between two points is uncompensated and straight, the surplus is simply the triangle formed by the price line, the 'demand curve' and a vertical line from the first price above the category of which the consumer surplus is calculated. If we look at the consumer surplus generated, opera and first-class theatre together account for as much as 72 per cent of total live consumer surplus, which suggests a far greater economic importance in these terms.[34] If consumer surplus and revenue are added, which may be the least imperfect proxy of economic impact, the share of opera and theatre is still 66 per cent. If all theatre is included, the figures increase to 83 and 80 per cent, respectively.

For spectator entertainment as a whole, it is clear that motion pictures had by far the largest market share in terms of quantity. They accounted for 57 per cent of all capacity, followed by first-class theatre with only 14 per cent and burlesque with 10 per cent. In terms of revenue, however, their market share was far smaller, only 15 per cent. Motion pictures also accounted for only 10 per cent of total consumer surplus, far less than opera and its 'economic impact' (revenue and consumer surplus) was about 15 per cent.[35] First-class theatre held the largest revenue share,

Table 16.4   Prices, capacity, sales potential, price elasticity and consumer surplus for various types of spectator entertainment venues, Boston, 1909

	Price $	Capacity seats	Sales $	Percentage of		sales/ cap	% of all live ent.		'Price elasticity of demand'			Consumer surplus (CS)			CS/ Rev. %	CS+Rev. $	% of total
				Ca-pacity	Sales		Ca-pacity	Sales	Arc	In-formal	Log-log	$	%	average			
Opera	2.00	13,590	27,180	2	10	5.8	4	12	-2.41	-3.86	-0.30	19,230	17	1.42	71	46,410	12
First-class theatres	1.00	111,568	111,568	14	42	2.9	34	50	-2.41	-1.45	-0.30	55,784	48	0.50	50	167,352	44
Popular theatre	1.00	17,811	17,811	2	7	2.9	5	8	-0.96			8,906	8	0.50	50	26,717	7
Stock houses	0.75	21,756	16,317	3	6	2.2	7	7		-1.08	-1.42	2,720	2	0.13	17	19,037	5
Vaudeville houses	0.50	45,744	22,872	6	9	1.4	14	10	-0.61	-0.82	-1.42	5,718	5	0.13	25	28,590	7
Burlesque houses	0.25	80,700	20,175	10	8	0.7	24	9	-0.48	-0.96	-1.42	10,088	9	0.13	50	30,263	8
Vaudeville and moving pictures	0.15	79,362	11,904	10	4	0.4	12	3	-0.48	-0.99	-1.42	3,968	3	0.05	33	15,872	4

Moving-picture theatres	0.10	402,428	40,243	52	15	0.3			-1.76	-1.23	-1.42	10,061	9	0.03	0.15	25	50,304	13
Total	0.35	772,959	268,070	100	100	2.072	100	-1.07	-0.53	-0.78	116,473	100			0.15	43	384,543	100
All live entertainment	0.67	330,850	221,875	43	83	1.9		-1.17			104,428	90				326,304	85
Motion picture entertainment	0.10	442,109	46,195	57	17	0.3		-1.76			12,045	10				58,240	15

Notes: Capacity = the weekly seating capacity as estimated by the Boston committee (venue capacity times number of performances).
Sales = sales potential, when all seats are sold at the listed prices.
Arc elasticity = between respective price and the next price down.
Informal elasticity = based on best tangents to demand curve at datapoint, using mixed log-lin, polynomial and power curves at various stretches of the demand curve
Log-log elasticity = based on constant elasticity log-log model split for two parts of demand curve to get best fit (R2 = 0.998 and 0.945).
CS = consumer surplus = area above price line and under hypothetical demand curve for the respective stretch of the curve. For opera, the intercept at q = 0 is set at $4.83, the price that equalizes arc elasticity for opera
Rev = revenue.

Source: Calculated from data from Boston Committee 1909, as reported in Jowett (1974: 202).

333

with 41 per cent, and opera, which accounted for just 2 per cent of ticket-selling capacity, reached revenues that were two-thirds the size of cinema revenues. Unfortunately, data on profitability are lacking, and these may have shown a different picture.

The forms of entertainment are ranked in order of prices (Table 16.4), and this order more or less coincides with the time when the product category was introduced. This suggests a certain law of diminishing returns. Once high-priced entertainment had been introduced, entrepreneurs tried to capture unserved parts of the market with lower-priced, slightly differentiated entertainment. *Ex post*, once a new product category had been introduced, existing categories might have differentiated their quality further and might have tried to keep up or even increase the price difference with the new product category in a process of dynamic product differentiation, thus operating a system that partially could be characterized as price discrimination.[36] A central question is why dynamic product differentiation did not all happen at the same time, how it could be that only over time, one after the other lower-priced forms of entertainment emerged. Probably, it was increasing disposable income that increased the demand for lower-priced entertainment and made profitable entry feasible. Population growth, rising real wages and falling working hours all increased demand, while urbanization and growing transport networks concentrated the demand spatially. On the supply side a series of technological and organizational innovations reduced costs, increased quality and made capital more readily available. Together these factors probably constituted the process that enabled and limited the speed with which dynamic product differentiation could take place.

The average price for live entertainment was only 67 cents, but the range was wide, from 15 cents for low-class vaudeville (and films) to more than 13 times as much for an opera ticket.[37] Reasons for different prices could have been the intensity of competition – which would also partially depend on the geographic dispersion of venues in a category; differentiated products serving different markets; differences in quality; price discrimination; and relative scarcity of the product. Possibly the differences were caused by a combination of these factors.

The hypothetical demand curve, based on selling capacity and prices, shows a steep curve at high prices and a very flat curve at low prices. First-class theatres faced substantially more demand than opera, but the lower-priced forms of entertainment attracted smaller additional audiences. Only with cinema, at the lowest end of the price range, did demand suddenly more than double. If the curves in Figure 16.7 were actual supply and demand curves, the competitive price (without price discrimination) would have been about 17 cents, which is about half the average price under actual (non-perfect) price discrimination.

A rough and ready indication of the changes in the price elasticity of demand can be obtained by plotting the price and capacity data in logs.[38] This reveals a high elasticity from \$2.00 to \$1.00 (from opera to first-class theatres) and from \$0.15 to \$0.10 (from low-class vaudeville to cinema). The interval between \$1.00 and \$0.15 had a far lower price elasticity.

This pattern is confirmed by a rough estimation of the price elasticities. This has been done in three ways: by calculating arc elasticities; by informally fitting a curve for each pair of adjacent points; and by estimating log-log constant elasticity functions (Table 16.4). The arc elasticity shows the extremely high price elasticity of opera, highly inelastic demand for all intermediate forms, and strongly elastic demand for cinema, below a price of 15 cents.

Using the second approach yields a familiar decrease in elasticity as we go down the demand curve: each further price decrease will result in a lower increase in quantity sold. But when the price falls below \$0.50, the price for vaudeville shows, elasticity increases again and demand becomes elastic when the ticket price of cinema is reached. This suggests that there was a great potential for technologies/product categories that could deliver entertainment at low prices, as demand responded heavily to it. Possibly large groups of consumers, who otherwise could not afford spectator entertainment, would enter the market at these prices. Increasing urbanization probably concentrated these consumers enough spatially to make such lower-priced venues possible over time. This also could explain how every new product category is lower priced. A rough indication of supply (Figure 16.7) shows that the price increase from \$1.00 to \$2.00 yielded limited additional demand, and that therefore providing entertainment at prices and qualities far above opera may not be feasible.

The log-log estimations broadly confirm this pattern, with a few differences. Using the log-log estimation, the data points break into two distinct groups that each fit a log-log function quite well.[39] This suggests increasing price elasticity for lower prices, but also suggests inelastic demand for the higher prices and elastic demand for the lower prices. Cinema entrepreneurs eventually discovered and exploited the sharp increase in entertainment demand at very low ticket prices.

The shape of the demand curve, with high price elasticity at high prices and very low prices, and rather moderate elasticity in between may to some extent explain the time lags in dynamic product differentiation. In a discovery process, entrepreneurs have to find out the demand for new innovative forms of entertainment. The low elasticity in the middle part of the demand curve may have slowed down attempts to provide far lower-priced forms of entertainment, as many entrepreneurs may have guessed that demand would not increase enough to make it worthwhile. Thus it may have taken a long time, and many historical accidents and innovations such as cinema, before entrepreneurs 'discovered' the responsiveness of demand at low prices. This process would not be dissimilar to the 'path dependence' argument that more efficient paths may not be taken because the first few steps seem unattractive and hide the large payoffs later on. At some point in time, the supply-side process would then meet the demand-side process that was driven by the factors mentioned above and was probably increasing elasticity at low prices. Time series of price elasticity, which are unfortunately lacking, would enable the detailed investigation of the interplay between this entrepreneurial discovery process, cost-decreasing technological innovations, and changes in the size and geographic density of demand.[40]

One could argue that the various forms of entertainment were of a different quality, both horizontally (different products) and vertically (better or worse products). These quality differences are not easy to measure. If we assume that all forms of entertainment are part of the same market, one could argue that price differences reflect quality differences and assume that one dollar equals one util,[41] so that the revenue-generating capacity is an indicator of quality-adjusted quantity. This method, though questionable, results in a demand curve that is less steep and flat at its respective ends (Figure 16.8).

The estimates above are based on weekly calculations. If we multiply the weekly quantities by the estimated number of weeks each category was in operation during the year mentioned above, the findings do not change significantly. The share of cinema in quantity increases from 57 to 63.5 per cent, in revenue from 17 to 23 per cent, in consumer surplus from 10.5 to 14.5 per cent and in 'economic impact' from 15 to 20.5 per cent. The arc price elasticity of cinema decreases from 2.1 to 1.8, with all other elasticities not changing significantly.

The findings of the Boston Committee suggest that live entertainment since the second half of the nineteenth century developed in new forms appearing at the margins, in addition to the existing opera and theatre. Through dynamic product differentiation, these forms would partially capture some of the market for pre-existing forms and partially open up a new, underserved market. These data also suggest that cinema initially appeared as such an innovation at the margins. In its early years, it was large in terms of tickets sold, but relatively small in terms of revenue, and at first did not seem a serious competitor to high-value-added entertainment. In subsequent years, however, the price of cinema tickets as well as its quality gradually increased and captured an ever-larger share of the

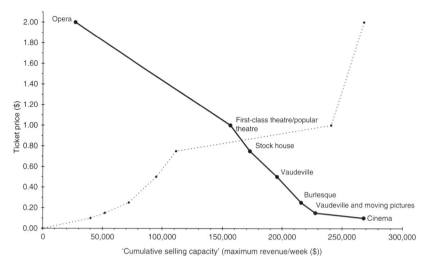

Note: It has been speculatively assumed one dollar equals one util (see text).

Sources: Table 16.4; compiled from Boston Committee 1909, as reported in Jowett (1974).

Figure 16.8 *Ticket price versus cumulative selling capacity for entertainment venues in Boston in 1909 ($ and $ or utils)*

market of pre-existing forms of entertainment, eventually driving some of them to near-extinction.[42]

HOUSEHOLD EXPENDITURE AFTER CINEMA

Fixed cinemas appeared from about 1905 onwards and grew sharply in number during the 1910s. They changed entertainment consumption by offering lower prices and a far wider availability, both in space and in time. Cinemas emerged in neighbourhoods and small towns, and many offered shows even at the marginal hours of the day, the marginal days of the week and the marginal weeks of the year.

Falling ticket prices, wider availability, increased leisure time and easier access to entertainment venues through living in cities and transport networks all had a positive effect on the demand for entertainment. Rising real wages left consumers with more discretionary income, but also increased the opportunity cost of spectator entertainment. Entertainment and other recreations may actually have increased the value of leisure time, making it attractive for workers to strive for more of it. Paradoxically, while during the first industrial revolution workers preferred to work longer hours to pay for new goods (Voth, 2000), during the second one it appears that they chose to reduce hours to be able to enjoy new services.

Falling ticket prices meant that, although the quantity of spectator-hours consumed could go up substantially, the expenditure share might remain limited. The longitudinal fall in ticket prices might have changed the shape of expenditure relative to income at the cross-section for our benchmark years.

A US Department of Labor study surveyed 2,096 'white' families in 92 cities or localities in 42 states between 1917 and 1919. It aimed 'to get representative data that would show living conditions in all sections of the country and in all kinds of localities'.[43] The average household income of respondents was $1,514, 32 per cent higher than that of the 1890 survey, in real terms. The national average income per worker was about $1,224, 15 per cent higher than in 1890.[44]

Households spent 1.2 per cent of income on 'Amusements, vacations, and so on', of which 0.49 per cent on movies, 0.06 per cent on live entertainment and 0.45 per cent on vacations (Table 16.5). The average expenditure per household member on spectator entertainment was at most $1.95, substantially below the national average of $2.84.[45] As a whole, amusements and vacations expenditure was barely higher than 20 years earlier (when it was 1.1 per cent) and one can only speculate how the share of spectator entertainment changed, given the changing aggregate share and substitution of films for live entertainment. The expenditure share of reading was also similar to before. Expenditure shares of liquor, tobacco, religion and charity had all dropped significantly compared to 30 years earlier. Since religion and charity had no price, the lower shares may point to low long-run income elasticity for these items. Liquor consumption dropped by over two-thirds, tobacco consumption by just over 10 per cent. The latter's decline was probably brought to a halt by the rising popularity of the cigarette during the 1910s.

The expenditure patterns of spectator entertainment relative to income reveal an income elasticity of 2.5, substantially lower than in 1890. Elasticities for movies and live entertainment were 2.3 and 4.4, respectively (Bakker, 2007a). For both categories, as well as the average, entertainment consumption increased relatively smoothly with income, with no sharp discontinuities as observed for Britain and France (Figures 16.9, 16.10 and 16.11). It could be the case that as real incomes rise longitudinally, entertainment income elasticity at the cross-section falls. If expenditure increased linearly with income, a big if, then in the long run, income elasticity would go down and approach one.[46] Entertainment income elasticity was substantially higher than that for liquor, tobacco and religion, but lower than that for charity.

Table 16.5 Leisure and related expenditure of US families, 1917–1919 and 1889–1890

Item	1917–1919 survey Expenditure (%)	1889–1890 survey Expenditure (%)
Contributions, dues, gifts		
Church	0.66	0.97
Labour organizations	0.30	
Lodges, clubs, societies, etc.	0.22	
Charity	0.08	0.40
Patriotic purposes	0.50	
Gifts	0.48	
Total	2.24	
Street-car fares		
To work	1.17	
To school	0.04	
Other	0.36	
Total	1.57	
Travel		
Total	0.13	
Amusements, vacations, etc.		
Movies	0.49	
Plays, concerts, etc.	0.06	
Other amusements	0.08	
Excursions	0.07	
Vacations	0.45	
Total	1.16	1.10
Education and uplift		
Newspapers	0.53	
Magazines	0.11	
Books	0.06	
Schools, tuition, books, etc.	0.29	
Music	0.16	
Total	1.15	0.80
Legal drugs		
Liquor	0.49	1.80
Tobacco	1.12	1.30
Total	1.61	3.10

Note: 1917–19: average of 12,096 families, based on income per family member. Average income in 1917–19 was $309, the interval over which elasticity is calculated is $189/$436.
1889–90: average of 6,809 families, based on income per family member. Average income in 1889–90 was $145, the interval over which elasticity is calculated is $50/$406.

Source: US Bureau of Labor Statistics (1924: 1–5; 447–53).

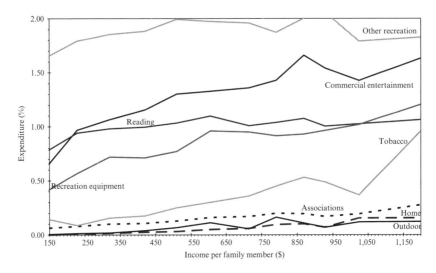

Note: Income groups were made according to income per family member
(Bakker 2001b: 389).
home = entertainment in the home; outdoor = entertainment out of the home; associations
= membership of recreational associations.

Source: Williams and Hansen (1941: 315–16).

Figure 16.9   *Leisure and related expenditure as a percentage of income of
US families, 1934–1936*

A probably unrepresentative survey of single women in Washington
state in 1913 suggests that entertainment expenditure varied substantially
between states, and between married and unmarried consumers. The
women spent between $460 and $570 per annum ($700 to $870 in dollars of
1918, substantially below the national average). Amusement expenditure
was between 1.3 and 2.5 per cent of this, vacation expenditure between
2 and 3 per cent. Paradoxically, those working in hotels and restaurants
spent the least on amusements (1.3 per cent). For laundry workers, mer-
cantile occupations, office personnel, factory workers and telephone and
telegraph personnel average expenditure ranged between 1.6 and 2.6 per
cent. Vacation expenditures were even higher and varied from 2.0 to 3.1
per cent. On average the women spent 2.0 per cent on amusements and 2.4
per cent on vacations (Taylor, 1915).

Between 1934 and 1936 the Department of Labor surveyed 14,469 'white
and negro' families from 42 cities with over 50,000 inhabitants. Families
included had an annual income of at least $500, received no relief and
had at least one person employed for 36 weeks earning at least $300. No

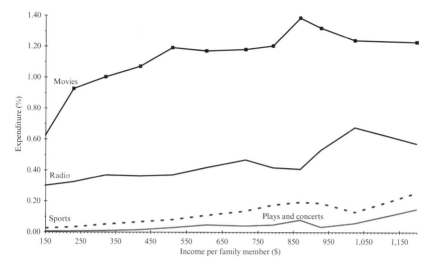

Note: See Figure 16.9.
Sports = spectator sports; radio = radio purchase and radio upkeep.

Source: See Figure 16.9.

*Figure 16.10   Leisure and related expenditure as a percentage of income
of US families 1934–1936*

clerical workers earning over $200 a month or $2,000 a year were included. Within these boundaries, the researchers tried to obtain a random sample (Williams and Hanson, 1941). The average household income was $1,511, 10 per cent higher in real terms than that in 1918. National average income per worker was $1,161, about 5 per cent higher than in 1918.

The average expenditure on spectator entertainment was 1.1 per cent; more than double that in 1918. Over 1 per cent was on movies, more than double the 1918 share. Expenditure per household member was $5.14, compared to national per capita expenditure of $4.72. Live entertainment expenditure was 0.03 per cent, half the 1918 value, or $0.14 per member (compared to a national average of $0.35). The talkies probably increased motion picture expenditure and decreased live expenditure. Tobacco expenditure was up substantially, possibly driven by the prohibition of alcohol, while reading expenditure was also up (Table 16.6).

The income elasticity of motion pictures was 1.5, substantially lower than previously, while that of live entertainment had nearly doubled to 8.2. The increase of expenditure with income was less smooth than before, with substantial fluctuations at above-average incomes (Figures 16.9, 16.10 and 16.11). Compared to Europe, film expenditure increased

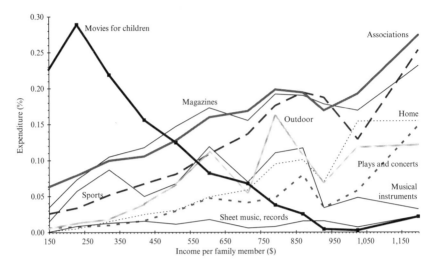

Note: See Figures 16.9 and 16.10.

Source: See Figure 16.9.

Figure 16.11   *Leisure and related expenditure as a percentage of income of US families, 1934–1936*

more sharply with income, suggesting that motion pictures were more of a luxury than in Europe.

In Britain, in 1937 and 1939 two budget studies surveyed 3,580 households.[47] The average household expenditure was £323, substantially higher than the average wage. The difference could probably be explained by the large number of middle-class households in the sample. The average expenditure was 178 per cent higher than in the 1890 survey.

Expenditure on the items that would constitute 'Amusements and Recreations' was substantially lower than in 1890, 2.6 per cent versus 3.5 per cent. Average expenditure on spectator entertainment was 1.3 per cent of all expenditure, slightly higher than in the US (Table 16.7; Figure 16.12). Expenditure per household member was £1.15 (£0.73 for cinema and £0.42 for live), compared to national per capita expenditure of £1.37 (£0.87 and £0.50, respectively).[48]

The pattern of expenditure relative to income showed a rise in the expenditure share until the average income was reached, and then a gradual decline. Both cinema and live entertainment showed a similar pattern, the peak of cinema expenditure at 60 per cent of average income, and that of live at 2.2 times average income. This suggests that live

Table 16.6   Leisure and related expenditure of US families, 1934–1936 and 1889–1890

Item	1934–1936 survey Expenditure (%)	1917–1919 survey Expenditure (%)	1889–1890 survey Expenditure (%)
Commercial entertainment			
Movies (adult admission)	0.96	0.49	
Movies (child admission)	0.14		
Plays and concerts	0.03	0.06	
Spectator sports	0.09		
Total	1.22	0.63	(1.10)
Reading			
Newspapers, street	0.31		
Newspapers, home delivery	0.53		
Magazines	0.14		
Books purchased (except school)	0.02		
Books borrowed from libraries	0.02		
Total	1.01	0.70	0.80
Recreation equipment			
Musical instruments	0.07		
Sheet music, records	0.01	0.16	
Radio purchase	0.32		
Radio upkeep	0.07		
Cameras, films, photogr. equipm.	0.04		
Athletic equipment, supplies	0.05		
Children's play equipment	0.10		
Pets (purchase and care)	0.13		
Total	0.79		
Recreational associations	0.13	0.22	
Entertaining in home	0.04		
Entertaining out of home	0.06		
Other recreation	0.25		
Legal drugs			
Cigars	0.18		
Cigarettes	1.46		
Pipe tobacco	0.18		
Other tobacco	0.08		
Total	1.90	1.12	

Table 16.6 (continued)

Note: 1934–36: average of 14,469 families, based on income per family member.
Average income in 1934–36 was $455, the interval over which elasticity is calculated is
$149/$1198.
'Entertaining in home/out of home': this category excludes food and drink.
For information on 1889–90 and 1917–19 data see Tables 16.11 and 16.14.

Source: US Bureau of Labor Statistics (1941: 315–16).
Williams and Hanson (1941: 315–16).

Table 16.7 *Leisure and related expenditure of British families, 1889–1890
and 1937–1939*

1889–1890 survey		1937–1939 survey	
Item	Expenditure (%)	Item	Expenditure (%)
		Cinema	0.81
		Other spectator entertainment	0.47
		Admissions sports/ games	0.29
		Holiday expenditure	0.60
		Sports and games	0.45
Amusements/vacations	3.47	Total	2.62
Reading	0.90		
Liquor	2.36		
Tobacco	1.13		
Religion	0.54		
Charity	0.26		
Religion and charity	0.80	Religion and charity	0.74
		Gambling	0.11
		Pet food	0.19

Source: US Commissioner of Labor (1890), Prais and Houthakker (1955, appendix).

entertainment was distinctly luxurious and cinema less so. The demand for
cinema was strongly inelastic (0.49), and demand for live entertainment
was moderately elastic (1.22). The role of class in Britain, combined with
the social status of going to the theatre, may have made entertainment
expenditure less income sensitive than in the US.

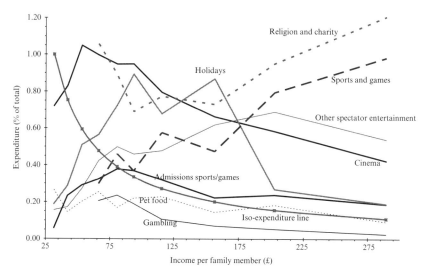

Note: Income groups were made according to income per family member (Bakker 2001: 393).

Source: Prais and Houthakker (1955: appendix).

Figure 16.12   *Annual leisure and related expenditure of British working- and middle-class families, 1937–1939*

All expenditure curves taken together showed the opposite picture of the 1890 survey, which showed a sharply increasing relative expenditure as income rose. The 1930s survey showed an initial rise and then a consistent fall of relative expenditure, sometimes even changing into an absolute decline.

Several explanations are possible. The first survey may have made an error in recording expenditures. The curve's consistent rise suggests that such an error probably would have been a systematic one. That the first survey was specifically aimed at 'industrial families' suggests that it may also have only mapped the first few income brackets of the second survey, if the latter contained more affluent families. Yet a third explanation is that in the 1930s the disposable income at low incomes was substantially higher than in 1890, enabling these households already to spend significantly on entertainment. This would not necessarily have to coincide with increasing income equality, although if the latter took place, the first would probably also. Between 1870 and 1960 Britain experienced a sharp increase in income equality, which may have affected entertainment consumption. The Gini-coefficient decreased from 0.52 in 1867 (or between 0.47 and 0.59 in 1880), to 0.34 in 1962–63 (Kaelble and Thomas, 1991: 26).

Likewise, the share of the top 20 per cent in total income decreased from 62 per cent in 1867 and 58 per cent in 1880, to about 50 per cent in the 1930s, and 43 per cent in 1963.[49]

At the same time, relative prices of several entertainment items probably decreased. Cinema, for example, reduced the average price of spectator entertainment, larger stadiums may have reduced average prices of sports matches and package tours and new seaside resorts the price of holidays. If radio were considered a partial substitute for spectator entertainment, the price per spectator/listener-hour would have decreased even further. Radio in general may be an explanation, as it became an important mass medium in the 1930s, offering the consumer the maximum amount of spectator-hours (24 a day) at a fixed price (equipment costs and licence fee).[50]

Cinema was an inelastic good while other spectator entertainment, sports matches and most other categories were elastic goods. This is a remarkable difference with the 1934–36 US survey, which showed an income elasticity of cinema expenditure of 1.49. However, both in the US and Britain the income elasticity of cinema was lower than that of other entertainment items.

So cinema was a luxury in the US and a normal good in Britain. In the former, nearly all films shown were domestically produced, while in the latter most films were foreign made. This affected consumer expenditure in two ways. First, then as now, across all countries, domestically made talkies attracted on average far more spectators than foreign-made talkies, if production costs are broadly similar.[51] Thus, in the US films may have had a higher quality in the eyes of consumers. Second, in Britain the live entertainment industry would have a competitive advantage over cinema because it offered domestically produced entertainment. British consumers may therefore have felt a far greater urge to supplement their cinema visits with live entertainment than their American counterparts.

Another explanation might be that films were linguistically less demanding than live entertainment. The immigrants in the US therefore may have had a stronger appetite for cinema. Further, British society was probably more stratified by class differences than the US melting pot. Consumers may have used live entertainment to show which class they wanted to belong to.[52] The British sample is probably more unrepresentative than the US sample.

For France, little information on household expenditure is available. A rare study surveyed 92 families in Toulouse between 1936 and 1938 (Delpech, 1938). The sample's representativeness is unclear and the numbers seem too small to yield a robust outcome. The households all consisted of married couples and were divided into working-class '*ouvriers*', and middle-class 'employees' and into four income groups, ranging

*Table 16.8   Annual leisure and related expenditure of 92 French families
in Toulouse, 1936–1938*

Item	Expenditure (%)	Eiasticity		% reporting
		I	II	
Intellectual expenditure	1.76	2.78	2.83	95.65
Cultural expenditure	0.91	1.93	2.07	84.78
Amusements	5.79	1.39	1.32	98.91
Amusements breakdown				
Cinema	2.31	0.63		
Theatre	0.63	2.52		
Cafés	1.35	3.95		
Sports events	0.87	1.18		
Bowling	0.62	0.41		
Total amusements	5.79	1.39		

Note: % reporting is the share of families that reported any expenditure on the item.
Average of 92 families, based on income per family member. Average income was 1,762
francs, interval (I) over which elasticity is calculated is 281 francs/1,208 francs, interval (II)
is 281 francs/533 francs.

Source: Delpech (1938).

from those with an annual family income below 1,200 francs to 'the rich'
(who had an average income of 3,700 francs), with a sample average of
1,705 francs. Because it is unclear how classes were defined and to obtain
a larger sample, only income is examined.

   The average expenditure on amusements was 5.8 per cent (Table
16.8; Figure 16.13). Expenditure on cinema was highest, with 2.3 per
cent, which was substantially above the 0.8 per cent in Britain, and
over three times theatre expenditure. The elasticities of the three broad
expenditure categories – the intellectual, cultural and entertainment
('distractions') expenditure – were above one, suggesting that these were
luxuries. However, disaggregation shows that theatre, cafés and sports
were luxuries, while cinema was a normal good with inelastic demand.

COMPARING THE COUNTRIES

Income elasticity for live entertainment expenditure was far larger in the
US than in Europe, and it doubled between 1918 and 1935. The main

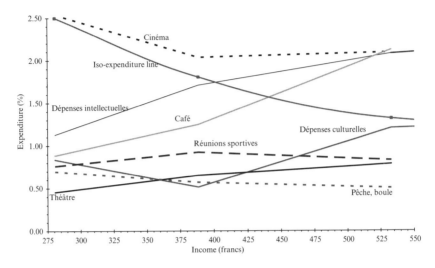

Source: Delpech (1938).

Figure 16.13   *Annual leisure and related expenditure of 92 French families in Toulouse, 1936–1938*

reason seems to be the small and declining share in income; the smaller the expenditure item, the larger the income elasticity if we assume that expenditure increases linearly with income. The decline of live entertainment expenditure was largely caused by cinema, especially by talkies. The large-volume–low-margin–high-profit part of live entertainment was automated away by cinema, while what remained split into a highly commercial metropolitan low-volume–high-margin–high-profit part and a heavily subsidized low-volume–low-margin–low-profit part (Bakker, 2004a). In Britain and France relative live expenditure was far higher, suggesting that cinema was less of a perfect substitute, for example because most films shown were not in the consumers' mother tongue, or that those countries' live entertainment industries had a comparative advantage – lower relative prices – compared to the US.[53]

Although not fully comparable, for all countries the entertainment income elasticities were lower than the amusements and vacations elasticities in 1890. Again, income elasticity could be expected to decline with increasing income over time, although this differs for time series compared to cross-sections. Only for the US, for 1918, was the income elasticity substantially higher than in 1890. When the shape of entertainment expenditure relative to income is examined (Figure 16.14) a similar order to 1890 shows that expenditure was highest in France and lowest in the

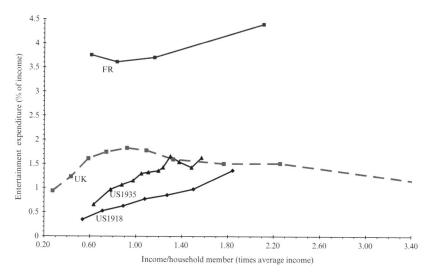

Figure 16.14   Entertainment expenditure across income groups, in share of average income, US, Britain and France, later 1930s

US, roughly across all income classes. US and French income was less dispersed than British income, which contained extremes in both directions. Britain and France had less steep curves than the US. Further, between 1918 and 1935 American relative expenditure increased, consistently for all income groups, although the shape became slightly steeper.

For cinema expenditure (Figure 16.15) the pattern changed and US expenditure overtook British expenditure at about 0.8 of average income. Even 1918 US expenditure overtook British expenditure in the last income class; assuming that the British curve would have been lower in 1918 as well, this suggests a similar US–UK pattern for 1918. France showed a sharp drop in expenditure from the first to the second income class, and then a slightly increasing curve.

For live entertainment (Figure 16.16), the order of magnitude difference between the US and Europe clearly showed, as well as a far slower increase with income in the US. British and French expenditures were close and exhibited broadly similar patterns.

LONG-RUN CHANGES IN EXPENDITURE PATTERNS

The above surveys can be compared at the cross-section level between countries and longitudinally within and between countries. In 1890,

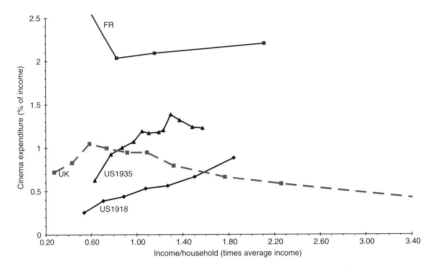

Figure 16.15   Cinema expenditure across income groups, in share of average income, US, Britain and France, later 1930s

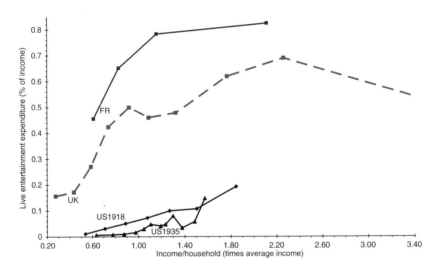

Figure 16.16   Live entertainment expenditure across income groups, in share of average income, US, Britain and France, later 1930s

amusements and vacations had a far lower expenditure share in the US than in Europe. If we compare these findings with the 1900 expenditure share in GDP, estimated from independent sources (Bakker, 2007b), the proportions between the US and Britain remain roughly the same, but French expenditure suddenly becomes far lower than US expenditure. The French survey probably was the most unrepresentative. All three country samples spent far more than the 1900 average per capita expenditure.

In the 1930s, the US again spent less on spectator entertainment than Britain, although the gap narrowed. The entire difference was due to Britain's live entertainment expenditure, which was nearly an order of magnitude larger than that of the US, while cinema expenditure was lower. The US income elasticity was substantially higher. The French household expenditure data again appear unrepresentative, as survey expenditure is about six times the expenditure share of GDP. The share of live entertainment expenditure in the survey was a fifth, compared to over a third nationally. Sample income elasticities were higher than in Britain and lower than in the US. If one exclusively looks at the GDP share, French entertainment expenditure was extremely low, just over half of US expenditure and just over a third of British expenditure (Table 16.9). This does not appear inconsistent with lamentations in the French trade press that the British film market was several times larger. If we look at US expenditure patterns over time, it appears that the expenditure share changed little between 1890 and 1918, both for survey and GDP share indicators, although income elasticity nearly doubled. One reason may have been the rapid adoption of cinema technology, which sharply reduced prices. Between 1918 and 1935 spectator entertainment expenditure doubled, again both for survey and GDP data. The income elasticity for cinema fell substantially, while that for live entertainment nearly doubled.

The British expenditure share in 1934–36 appears to have been lower than that in 1890, according to the survey data, but the 1890 survey may not be fully representative. GDP data suggest that the expenditure share declined somewhat in the 30 years between 1890 and 1920, although part of this may have been due to the war years. In 1920, for example, the expenditure share had increased to 0.95 per cent, and by 1923 it was 1.13 per cent. The 1938 GDP data suggest a modest increase in the expenditure share during the half-century since 1890. Again, the adoption of cinema technology is probably an important reason why this share remained low, when some economists predict that expenditure shares on certain 'low-productivity' services such as entertainment should rise when real income increases, under certain conditions (Baumol, 1967). Income elasticities in 1938 appear to have been somewhat lower than in 1890. The French GDP share of entertainment rose sharply between 1890 and 1940, although it

Table 16.9 Comparison of benchmark year data on entertainment expenditure, US, UK and France, various years, 1890–1938

	US				Britain				France			
	1890	1900	1918	1935	1890	1900	1918	1938	1890	1900	1918	1937
Expenditure share of income (%)												
'Amusements and vacations'	1.11		1.16	1.10	3.50			2.62	3.88			2.31
Cinema			0.49					0.81				0.63
Live entertainment			0.06	0.03				0.47				
Income elasticity												
'Amusements and vacations'	1.13		2.07		1.80				1.07			
Cinema			2.32	1.49				0.49				0.89
Live entertainment			4.40	8.16				1.22				1.54
Average income (current)	684		1,391	1,543	109			323	2,045			1,705
Expenditure as % of GDP:												
All spectator entertainment		0.32–0.43	0.37	0.82		1.00	0.71	1.19		0.07	0.22	0.49
Cinema				0.76				0.76			0.07	0.30
Live				0.06				0.43			0.15	0.19
Long-run GDP elasticity 1900–38												
Annual growth spectator-hours		9.19				3.01				11.10		
Annual real GDP growth		2.26				1.11				1.38		
'Average' elasticity		4.07				2.71				8.06		
Arc elasticity		2.32				2.47				3.79		

Note: US 1900 GDP share shows lower and upper bound estimates (see Bakker, 2007b).
UK data concern expenditure, not income.
The French household expenditure data are probably unrepresentative.

remains comparatively small. One reason appears to be a high live entertainment share, 2.7 percentage points higher than that of Britain, and possibly a lower urbanization level, which may have given cinema technology
less of an advantage.

Comparing the three countries longitudinally reveals some intriguing
patterns. While in the US and Britain the share of spectator entertainment remained stable between 1890 and the late 1910s, in France it
increased sharply. In all three countries it then increased substantially
during the interwar period. In France, the live entertainment expenditure
share dropped dramatically, from over two-thirds of all entertainment
expenditure in 1918 to just over one-third by 1937.

Using estimates on the quantity of spectator-hours sold in 1900 and
1938 (Bakker, 2007b), it is possible to estimate the long-run (arc) GDP
elasticity of entertainment consumption. This was 2.3 for the US, 2.5 for
Britain and as high as 3.8 for France, on average (Table 16.9). For all
three countries, an increase of real GDP by 1 per cent increased spectator
entertainment consumption by at least double the percentage, making the
long-run demand for it highly GDP elastic. That the long-run elasticity
was far higher in France may be due to its relatively low GDP per capita
compared to Britain and the US. All longitudinal GDP elasticities were
higher than the (declining and not comparable) income elasticity at the
cross-section level, which underlines the tremendous impact that cinema
had on spectator entertainment.

Since both GDP and spectator-hours went up quite consistently, and
given that the arrow of time makes it impossible to go in reverse through
this historical period, it appears justified to use the 'average' elasticity
instead of the arc elasticity (Table 16.9). This shows, again, elasticities substantially above one, but a far higher elasticity in the US than in Britain,
and an extremely high elasticity in France.

The lower income elasticities in the 1930s suggest that entertainment
had become less of a luxury, and cinema alone as well. Motion pictures
were less of a novelty, and expenditure was already substantial, even at
lower incomes. Consumers thus found it harder to increase their utility
by consuming relatively more cinema when their income increased.
Moreover, by the 1930s, cinema had outcompeted the low-value-added
live entertainment. The rising price and perceived quality of the remaining
high-value-added live entertainment increased its income elasticity.

The depression may have also played a role in the declining luxury status
of spectator entertainment. This concurs with Owen's (1970) findings that
leisure and recreation expenditure as a percentage of GDP increased substantially between 1900 and 1930, but then that remained stable – at about
5 per cent of GDP – until at least the 1970s.

CONCLUSION

During the first half of the twentieth century, a sharp decrease in working hours and an increase in holidays and leisure time coincided with a sharp rise in expenditure on spectator entertainment. Several differences in the structure of household entertainment expenditure have become apparent between the countries for the benchmark years between 1890 and 1940. Both in the 1890s and in the 1930s, the European expenditure share on amusements was higher than in the US, and in the latter years Europeans spent far more on live entertainment. Second, France had the lowest expenditure share of GDP throughout the period, but by far the highest GDP elasticity, suggesting that it was catching up during this period.[54] The slower urbanization in France may have meant that it could benefit from the scale economies of entertainment venues to a lesser extent.

This chapter also identified several commonalities in expenditure patterns. For all three countries, it found that in 1890, expenditure on 'amusements and vacations' ranged from 1–4 per cent, and that, by the 1930s, spectator entertainment alone varied between 1 and 3 per cent. This suggests a substantial increase in expenditure on 'amusements and vacations' as a whole. Second, for all three countries the data suggest that the income elasticity of demand for these items decreased substantially over this period, although the elasticity generally was higher than that of demand for other recreation items. Third, for all three countries the GDP elasticity of spectator entertainment expenditure was far above one. It was substantially higher than two in all three countries, showing that this is a period in which the GDP share of spectator entertainment increased sharply. This concurs with Owen's findings for the US on the evolution of recreational expenditure as a whole, and suggests that these findings can be extended to European countries as well.

Detailed data on quantity and prices for Boston in 1909 show that cinema had a large share in quantity, but was dwarfed by opera and theatre in terms of revenue share. Cinema thus started as an innovation at the margins that initially captured part of the market previously served by other low-priced entertainment, such as burlesque and vaudeville, and partially it captured an entirely new market of consumers that had not experienced spectator entertainment before. The data also suggest that the price elasticity of demand was U-shaped. It was far above unity both at the highest prices and at the lowest ones, but substantially below one for the price range in between. This indicates that it could have taken a long time before the growth and spatial concentration of consumer expenditure had increased the responsiveness of demand at low prices, before entrepreneurs had discovered it, and before the technology was adopted that could bring down costs concurrently. Most likely, this is what was happening in the late nineteenth century. The U-shaped price elasticity also meant that entrepreneurs that succeeded in matching the changing technology with the changing demand would be disproportionately rewarded by a sharp increase in sales. This makes it understandable why cinema was adopted so rapidly and widely during the 1900s.

NOTES

1. Parts of this chapter have been published in Gerben Bakker, *Entertainment Industrialised. The Emergence of the International Film Industry, 1890–1940* (Cambridge, Cambridge University Press, 2008).
2. Other factors affecting entertainment consumption in the late nineteenth century were urbanization, the population increase and the growth of public transport networks. See Bakker (2008: 79–85).
3. See also Jowett (1974).
4. For comparison, an American male born in 1960 could expect 67 years of life, of which 62.2 per cent (41.7 years) would be spent in the labour force (Owen, 1970: 11).
5. Ibid.: 61–4.
6. Mitchell (1998: 147), based on Matthews et al., 1982: Appendix D). Mitchell mentions Bienefeld (1972), which gives no systematical series like Matthews et al. Also see Huberman and Minns (2007, table 1).
7. Larroque (1988: 44) finds average hours of 13–15 a day for the 1870s. See Huberman and Minns (2007, table 1).
8. Huberman and Minns (2007) find stagnant working hours in Britain and France between 1900 and 1913, while Dewhurst (1955) and Owen (1970) noted substantial falls.
9. Voth (2000: 126, 192–210) found an increase in working hours from 2,795 hours a year in 1760 to 3,070 in 1800 to 3,366 in 1830, according to one of his six measures. This coincided with increased spending on new consumer goods. Voth argued that people worked longer hours to buy those new goods. Towards the end of the nineteenth century they possibly had an increased preference for leisure time to consume more services. Between 1750 and 1830, the three factors discussed below that connected rising free time with rising entertainment consumption – the division between labour and leisure, the increase in planning and timing of work and leisure, and the rise in opportunity costs – were gradually starting to take shape.
10. According to Becker (1965), if an activity become less costly in terms of time or goods, this will result in an increase in its relative amount, while a wage rise will decrease the consumption of those activities that are more time intensive. When incomes rise, for example, people have fewer children or watch movies instead of reading books. Becker (1993: 386) links this theory to economic development in general: 'Economic and medical progress have greatly increased length of life, but not the physical flow of time itself, which always restricts everyone to 24 hours per day. So while goods and services have expanded enormously in rich countries, the total time available to consume has not. Thus wants remain unsatisfied in rich countries as well as in poor ones. For while the growing abundance of goods may reduce the value of additional goods, time becomes more valuable as goods become more abundant. The welfare of people cannot be improved in a utopia in which everyone's needs are fully satisfied, but the constant flow of time makes such a utopia impossible.'
11. Quoted in Cross (1989: 63).
12. Ibid.: 164.
13. Quoted in Cross (1989: 164).
14. When income rises people reduce time-intensive activities (Becker, 1965: note 246).

15. See also, for example, Horrell (1996). The many early nineteenth-century family budget studies Horrell used do not include entertainment expenditure.
16. On early family budget studies, as early as the middle ages, see Nystrom (1931); Zimmerman (1936).
17. On the increasing demand for newspapers and other printed matter, see Bakker (2011).
18. See also Bakker (2007a).
19. The author thanks Michael Haines for generously making available the computerized data.
20. The survey is discussed in detail in Haines (1979).
21. (Biased) OLS income elasticity for the whole sample (including households with zero expenditure on amusements) was 2.14. See Bakker (2007a).
22. See Bakker (2001: 87, 384).
23. This leaves out skilled engineering labour, which earned £107 annually, on average (Williamson, 1982, as quoted in Mitchell 1998: 153).
24. Whole-sample (biased) OLS income elasticity (including households with zero expenditure on amusements) was 2.16 (Bakker, 2007a).
25. This thought is owed to Paul Johnson.
26. According to Feinstein's (1991: 158) rough estimate, based on the Prest (1954) data, in 1900 entertainment and betting accounted for 0.95 per cent of working-class expenditure and 3.07 per cent of middle- and upper-class expenditure, with an average of 1.97 per cent.
27. This could be due to the small French sample size of 263 households, versus 1,024 for Britain and 6,809 for the US. See Bakker (2007a).
28. Whole-sample (biased) OLS income elasticity was 1.41 (Bakker 2007a).
29. See Bakker (2001: 113, 394).
30. See Table 16.1 and Figure 16.1, above.
31. The data are reported in Jowett (1974).
32. Music and concert halls were excluded, apparently.
33. For national expenditure, see Bakker (2008: 99–106).
34. The estimated opera consumer surplus is highly sensitive to the educated guess of the cut-off price (at $q = 0$). The arc elasticity of demand was assumed to be the same between cut-off price and opera price as between opera and first-class theatre prices, yielding a cut-off price of $4.83 for weekly and $4.71 for annualized data. A different value would change opera's consumer surplus significantly.
35. Half of 'Vaudeville and motion pictures' have been included to arrive at these figures.
36. On dynamic product differentiation, see Bakker (2008: 23–6, 69–71).
37. The difference between a ticket for the Metropolitan Opera and the cinema in New York does appear to be within the same order of magnitude today, coincidentally.
38. Figure available from the author.
39. $R^2 = 0.997$ and 0.945, respectively, versus 0.78 for the entire dataset log-log.
40. On entrepreneurial discovery, see Kirzner (1973, 1985).
41. For opera monopoly pricing probably played a role. Other forms sometimes held neighbourhood monopolies, especially if outside the theatre district.
42. That motion pictures were aimed initially at a different market but increased in quality and eventually strongly competed with pre-existing entertainment may not be unlike the experience of 'disruptive innovations' identified by Christensen (1997).
43. 'Cost of living in the United States', in *Bulletin of the United States Bureau of Labor Statistics*, 357 (May 1924).
44. The average income of 1890, $684, amounted to $1,143 in dollars of 1918.
45. National average calculated from 1914 and 1919 expenditure, by geometric interpolation of real expenditure, which is then translated back into nominal expenditure.
46. $\lim_{Y \to \infty} \varepsilon_y = 1/[(a/bY) + 1]$,

    with Y = income, and the line $a + bY$ the estimated expenditure line.

47. For a general discussion, see Massey (1942) and Nicholson (1949). The author thanks Michael Anderson for locating the detailed survey in Prais and Houthakker (1955: appendix). Miskell (2006) also uses these data to compare cinemagoing in Wales and Britain.
48. National data from Prest (1954) and Stone (1966).
49. Williamson (1991: 58). In the US this share fell from 52 per cent in 1935–36 to 48 per cent in 1941, to a low of 44 per cent in 1960, after which it increased.
50. On radio, see Pocock (1988).
51. See Bakker (2004b). Most countries produce only a small share of the films released nationally. Export earnings were relatively limited, so smaller markets were at a disadvantage.
52. Bourdieu (1979) argues that people consume entertainment to distinguish themselves socially, and that attendance of artistic, 'cultural' entertainment is almost exclusively constrained to the upper middle and upper classes. The attendance pattern of the parents predicts the attendance pattern of the children – in post-1945 France at least.
53. Part of the difference may be due to potentially biased samples for Britain and France; national total consumer expenditure estimates, below, show a far smaller difference between Britain and the US, although not between France and the US.
54. This suggests that the French data (which were based on fewer respondents, 244 and 92, respectively) were the most unrepresentative of all three countries, as they do not concur with the national data.

REFERENCES

Bakker, G. (2001), 'Entertainment industrialised: the emergence of the international film industry, 1890–1940', PhD dissertation, European University Institute, Florence.

Bakker, Gerben (2004a), 'At the origins of increased productivity growth in services: productivity, social savings and the consumer surplus of the film industry, 1900–1938', Working Papers in Economic History, No. 81, London School of Economics.

Bakker, Gerben (2004b), 'Selling French films on foreign markets: the international strategy of a medium-sized company', *Enterprise and Society*, **5**, 45–76.

Bakker, Gerben (2007a), 'The evolution of entertainment consumption and the emergence of cinema, 1890–1940', in Marina Bianchi (ed.), *The Evolution of Consumption: Theories and Practices — Advances in Austrian Economics*, Vol. 10, Bingley, UK: Emerald Group Publishing, pp. 93–138.

Bakker, Gerben (2007b), 'Structural change and the growth contribution of services: how motion pictures industrialized U.S. spectator entertainment', Working Papers in Economic History, No. 104, Department of Economic History, London School of Economics, available at: http://www.lse.ac.uk/collections/economicHistory/pdf/WP105Bakker.pdf.

Bakker, Gerben (2008), *Entertainment Industrialised: The Emergence of the International Film Industry, 1890–1940*, Cambridge: Cambridge University Press.

Bakker, Gerben (2011), 'Trading facts: Arrow's fundamental paradox and the origins of global news networks', in Peter Putnis, Chandrika Kaul and Juergen Wilke (eds), *Communication, News and Globalisation: Historical Studies*, New York: Hampton Press/International Association of Media and Communication Research, Chapter 1, forthcoming.

Baumol, William J. (1967), 'The macroeconomics of unbalanced growth: the anatomy of an urban crisis', *American Economic Review*, **57**, 415–26.

Becker, Gary S. (1965), 'A theory of the allocation of time', *Economic Journal*, **75**, 493–517.

Becker, Gary S. (1993), 'The economic way of looking at behavior', *Journal of Political Economy*, **101** (3), 385–409.

Benson, John (1994), *The Rise of Consumer Society in Britain 1880–1980*, London: Longman.

Berlanstein, Lenard R. (1984), *The Working People of Paris, 1871–1914*, Baltimore, MD: Johns Hopkins University Press.

Bienefeld, M.A. (1972), *Working Hours in British Industry. An Economic History*, London: Weidenfeld & Nicholson.

Bourdieu, Pierre (1979), *La Distinction. Critique sociale du jugement*, Paris: Les Éditions de Minuit.

Brady, Dorothy (1972), 'Consumption and the style of life', in Lance E. Davis, Richard A. Easterlin and William N. Parker (eds), *American Economic Growth*, New York: Harper & Row, pp. 61–92.

Brenner, Y.S., Hartmut Kaelble and Mark Thomas (1991), *Income Distribution in Historical Perspective*, Cambridge: Cambridge University Press.

Brentano, Lujo (1894), *Hours and Wages in Relation to Production*, London: Kessinger.

Champion, Henry H. (1890), *The Parliamentary Eight-hour Day*, Pamphlet, London.

Christensen, Clayton M. (1997), *The Innovator's Dilemma. When New Technologies Cause Great Firms to Fail*, Cambridge, MA: Harvard Business School Press.

Cross, Gary (1988), *Worktime and Industrialization. An International History*, Philadelphia, PA: Temple University Press.

Cross, Gary (1989), *A Quest for Time. The Reduction of Work in Britain and France, 1840–1940*, Berkeley, CA: University of California Press.

Delpech, Henri (1938), *Recherches sur le niveau de la vie et les habitudes de consommation (enquête effectué à Toulouse, de 1936 à 1938)*, Paris: Sirey.

Dewhurst, J. Frederic and associates (1955), *America's Needs and Resources. A New Survey*, New York: Twentieth Century Fund.

Dupeux, Georges (1974), *La société française, 1789–1970*, Paris: Armand Collin.

Economic Club (1896), *Family Budgets. Being the Income and Expenditure of 20 British Households 1891–1894*, London: Economic Club.

Feinstein, Charles (1991), 'A new look at the cost of living 1870–1914', in James Foreman-Peck (ed.), *New Perspectives on the Late Victorian Economy*, Cambridge: Cambridge University Press, pp. 151–79.

Gunton, George (1887), *Wealth and Progress: A Critical Examination of the Wages Question and its Economic Relation to Social Reform*, New York: D. Appleton & Company.

Haines, Michael (1979), 'Industrial work and the family life cycle, 1889–1890', *Research in Economic History*, **4**, 289–356.

Horrell, Sara (1996), 'Home demand and British industrialization', *Journal of Economic History*, **3**, 561–604.

Huberman, Michael and Chris Minns (2007), 'The times they are not changin': days and hours of work in old and new worlds, 1870–2000', *Explorations in Economic History*, **44**, 538–67.

Jowett, Garth S. (1974), 'The first motion picture audiences', *Journal of Popular Film*, **3** (Winter), 39–45.

Kaelble, Hartmut and Mark Thomas (1991), 'Introduction', in Brenner et al. (eds), pp. 1–56.

Kirzner, Israel M. (1973), *Competition and Entrepreneurship*, Chicago, IL: University of Chicago Press.

Kirzner, Israel M. (1985), *Discovery and the Capitalist Process*, Chicago, IL: University of Chicago Press.

Larroque, Domique (1988), 'Economic aspects of public transit in the Parisian area, 1855–1939', in Joel A. Tarr and Gabriel Dupuy (eds), *Technology and the Rise of the Networked City in Europe and America*, Philadelphia, PA: Temple University Press, pp. 40–66.

Le Play, Frédéric (1877), *Les ouvriers Européens. Études sur les travaux, la vie domestique et la condition morale des populations ouvrières de l'Europe. D'après les fait observés de 1829 à 1855. Avec des epilogues indiquant les changements survenus depuis 1855*, 2nd edn, Tours: Mame.

Maddison, Angus (1995), *Monitoring the World Economy, 1820–1992*, Paris: Development Centre, OECD.

Mann, Tom (1891), *The Eight Hour Day: How to Get it by Trade and Local Option*, Pamphlet, London.

Massey, Philip (1942), 'The expenditure of 1,360 British middle-class households in 1938–39', *Journal of the Royal Statistical Society*, **105**, 159–96.

Matthews, R.C.O., C.H. Feinstein and J.C. Odling-Smee (1982), *British Economic Growth, 1856–1973*, Oxford: Oxford University Press.

Miskell, Peter (2006), *A Social History of the Cinema in Wales, 1918–1951: Pulpits, Coal Pits and Flea Pits*, Cardiff: University of Wales Press.

Mitchell, B.R. (1998), *International Historical Statistics. Europe 1750–1988*, London: Macmillan.

Mulhall, Michael (1892), *Dictionary of Statistics*, London: George Routledge & Sons.

Nicholson, J.L. (1949), 'Variations in working class family expenditure', *Journal of the Royal Statistical Society. Series A (General)*, **112**, 359–418.

Nystrom, Paul H. (1931), *Economic Principles of Consumption*, New York: Ronald Press.

Owen, John D. (1970), *The Price of Leisure. An Economic Analysis of the Demand for Leisure Time*, Montreal: McGill-Queens University Press.

Pocock, Rowland F. (1988), *The Early British Radio Industry*, Manchester: Manchester University Press.

Prais, Sigbert Jon and Hendrik Samuel Houthakker (1955), *The Analysis of Family Budgets: With an Application to Two British Surveys Conducted in 1937–9 and their Detailed Results*, Cambridge: Cambridge University Press.

Prest, A.R. (1954), *Consumer Expenditure in the United Kingdom, 1900–1919*, Cambridge: Cambridge University Press.

Stone, Richard (ed.) (1966), *The Measurement of Consumer Expenditure and Behaviour in the United Kingdom, 1920–1938*, Volume II, London: National Institute of Economic and Social Research.

Taylor, A.W. (1915), 'The operation of the minimum wage law in the state of Washington', *American Economic Review*, **5**, 398–405.

US Bureau of Labor Statistics (1924), 'Cost of living in the United States', *Bulletin of the United States Bureau of Labor Statistics*, No. 357 (May).

US Commissioner of Labor (1890), *Sixth Annual Report of the Commissioner of Labor*, Part III. 'Cost of Living', US Congress, House of Representatives, House Executive Document 265, 51st Congress, 2nd Session, Washington, DC: G.P.O.

Voth, Hans-Joachim (2000), *Time and Work in England, 1750–1830*, Oxford: Clarendon Press.

Webb, Sidney James and Harold Cox (1891), *The Eight Hours Day*, London: Scott.

Williams, Faith M. and Alice C. Hanson, US Department of Labor, US Bureau of Labor Statistics (1941), 'Money disbursements of wage earners and clerical workers, 1934–36. Summary Volume', *Bulletin of the United States Bureau of Labor Statistics*, No. 638.

Williamson, Jeffrey G. (1982), 'The structure of pay in Britain, 1710–1911', *Research in Economic History*, **7**, 1–54.

Williamson, Jeffrey G. (1991), 'British inequality during the Industrial Revolution. Accounting for the Kuznets curve', in Brenner et al. (eds), pp. 57–75.

Zimmerman, Carl C. (1936), *Consumption and Standards of Living*, New York: D. Van Nostrand Company Inc.

17 Long-run trends and factors in attendance patterns in sport: Australian Football League, 1945–2009
Liam J.A. Lenten

INTRODUCTION AND MOTIVATION

Trends in demand for leisure activities are linked inextricably to many broad factors that are discussed in detail in other chapters in the current volume. A number of well-known dynamics are just as evident in data on professional sport patronage as they are for other leisure activities, such as the arts. Such factors include rising demand in the long run arising from greater leisure time afforded by higher incomes, as well as cyclical effects influencing demand in the shorter-to-medium run, not to mention the standard pricing effects.

However, certain aspects of demand for leisure goods are also highly industry specific, such as the quality of the product, and how that quality is measured. Economists recognize that in the pro-sports industry, the *absolute* level of quality of product is important to fans. A simple example is the tendency for average home attendances of teams in Europe's major football leagues to rise (fall) when they are promoted (relegated) through divisions (see Noll, 2002). Similarly, major league attendances are easily greater than equivalent minor league attendances in North American-style leagues. This is analogous to, for instance, box office revenues rising temporarily during periods in which there are a larger number of movies in release that are rated highly according to movie critic reviews or perceptions of moviegoers. In some cases, there can even be a degree of substitution between forms of leisure, like the anecdotal evidence of Baade and Sanderson (1997, p. 97), who claim that Hollywood had a bumper year in 1994 partly as a result of the Major League Baseball players' strike in that year.

However, the most distinctive feature of demand for sport relates to the importance of *relative* quality of product (that is, competition). Specifically, the underlying economic concept of relevance here is that of competitive balance – this refers to the degree of parity (or otherwise) of the relative quality of teams in sports leagues. League administrators will ideally maintain a given level of competitive balance for the purpose of maximizing demand. This is because fans want to see an even contest – not that they want to see their team lose, but they want to know that there is some chance that their team will lose.[1] Therefore, all other things being equal, a more competitive league should translate into more overall fan interest and therefore demand – this is known as the 'uncertainty of outcome' hypothesis. See Fort (2011, pp. 14–16) for an extended 'textbook' description of the critical distinction between absolute and relative quality of competition.

The relation between match attendances and competitive balance in sport via the 'uncertainty of outcome' hypothesis has been the subject of numerous past empirical studies. Rottenberg (1956) is often credited with pioneering the uncertainty of outcome hypothesis, while Noll (1974) is the first identifiable empirical study, concluding that 'a league benefits from lessening the quality difference among teams' (p. 156). Since then, a significant amount of supporting literature has appeared. Borland and MacDonald (2003) provide a comprehensive survey of these studies, most of which find empirical support for the uncertainty of outcome hypothesis, including Hunt and Lewis (1976), Jennett (1984), Dobson and Goddard (1992), Baimbridge (1997) and García and Rodríguez (2002). The evidence is not entirely unanimous, however, with contrary findings provided by, *inter alia*, Fuller and Stewart (1996) with Australian Football League (AFL) data and McDonald and Rascher (2000), who tie in competitive balance with special promotions, similar to ones now used by the AFL, such as 'Rivalry Round', 'Community Weekend' and 'Heritage Round'.

With respect to AFL data, Lenten (2009) finds strong time-series evidence of higher attendances in more evenly balanced seasons, *ceteris paribus*, though with a low coefficient estimate on the competitive balance term. This demonstrates the habitual and loyal behaviour for which fans of the various AFL teams are well known in Australia. Using this result, Lenten estimates that attendances have risen almost 4 per cent solely from competitive balance gains induced by the introduction of the national player draft and salary cap from the mid-1980s.

However, despite some very strong results from a simple ordinary least squares regression of the series in their disturbances, the question of whether other (lower-frequency) components may have been unfairly ignored remained unanswered. Therefore, the objective of this chapter is to analyse the trend components of the series in an endeavour to link the behaviour of attendance not only to the standard set of candidate economic factors, but also to competitive balance, using known historical information regarding these variables.

The motivation of using AFL data specifically for this exercise relates mainly to a number of intriguing properties of this league as a stand-alone case study. Primarily, the size of the competition is substantial for a relatively small country (also, rugby league is far more popular in Sydney and Brisbane – two of the three largest Australian cities). The most recently announced national broadcasting contract for the years 2012–2016 is worth in excess of AUD 250 million (USD 270 million) per year. Moreover, when other forms of revenues are included (memberships, ticketing, sponsorship and so on), the combined revenue of the 16 AFL teams was AUD 512.7 million in 2007, of which only approximately 20 per cent came from league payments. Even these figures do not include revenues accruing to other parties that benefit from AFL-related trade (stadiums, merchandise retailers, media and so on).

Furthermore, it is one of the very few truly indigenous sports in the world still played professionally only in its primary domicile. Also, it is a very rare contemporary example of a truly professional sports league comprising mainly member-owned (rather than privately owned) teams, whose objectives can be modelled in a win-maximization framework. Finally, there is a lack of long-run time-series studies on demand for sport, due in part to occasional structural and institutional changes to leagues. However, unlike other professional sports leagues where frequent turnover of teams raises the issue of time inconsistency, the composition of teams in the AFL has been remarkably consistent, with the same 12 clubs from 1945 to 1986 (10 of them currently still in their own right). Following league expansion to 16 teams until 1997, there have been no further changes. There is also a distinct shortage of sports economics literature on modelling data from leagues outside the big-four North American leagues or the major European football leagues.

This chapter proceeds with an outline of the series used for the analysis of demand for sport, as well as the modelling procedure used to identify trends in the variables, rather than cycles or shocks. Following that, there is a comprehensive discussion on relating these trends in attendances both to general economic factors, as well as to specific trends in competitive balance. The chapter concludes with a general summary.

AUSTRALIAN RULES FOOTBALL 101

The 'Australian Rules' code is an indigenous winter-season sport originating in 1858 in Melbourne, but with some characteristics vaguely similar to Irish Gaelic football. The elite national competition, the AFL (known as such since 1990) evolved out of the old Victorian Football League, which existed previously as a Melbourne suburban competition. The league still somewhat resembles the competition from its inaugural year of 1897, with all of its eight foundation teams (one has relocated and another merged, however). The popularity of the AFL in Australian society is well understood, with the competition even managing to operate continuously throughout both world wars, although with a shorter season and reduced number of teams. Average match attendances exceeded 20,000 as early as 1924, the year before three new teams were added, and since then has fallen below 14,000 only during the Second World War years (below 10,000 only in 1942). In 2010, the average attendance of 38,423 was the third highest of any professional sports league, with matches in any given city even attracting a rising number of fans of away teams from other cities, although a lower number than in the major domestic football leagues of Europe, owing to higher inter-city travel costs.

As of 2010, there were 16 teams in the AFL – Melbourne having a total of 10 teams (including nearby Geelong), with Adelaide and Perth each having two teams, and both Brisbane and Sydney having a single team (however, expansion in 2011–12 introduces new teams to Gold Coast and Western Sydney. The regular, or 'home-and-away', season runs approximately from late March until the end of August, and consists of 176 games over 22 rounds, followed by a finals series (playoffs) during September. Matches are usually only played on weekends between Friday night and Sunday twilight, although they are now spread relatively evenly across any weekend – a point to be revisited below. The game itself is played on an elliptical playing surface approximately 135–185 metres long by 110–155 metres wide, with each side comprising 18 outfield and four interchange players. Games are played over four 20-minute quarters, with time for stoppages added (typically another 7–10 minutes). A 'goal', scored by kicking the ball between the two goalposts, is worth six points, whereas a 'behind', scored most commonly by kicking the ball between one of the goalposts and the adjacent outer post, is worth one point. The winning team is the team with the most points.

A distinctive feature of the AFL is that, as opposed to the traditional model of each team having its own home stadium, numerous Melbourne-based teams play their home matches at more than one venue. This phenomenon began when incentives to retain suburban grounds in Melbourne declined, and teams were aggregated to a smaller number of larger stadiums. Since 2006, only two grounds, the Melbourne Cricket Ground (MCG) and Docklands, are now used for all matches played in Melbourne. Even Geelong (about 75 kilometres from Melbourne) now plays some home games in Melbourne. Furthermore, due to changing economic incentives, a number of smaller-market Melbourne-based teams now play a few home matches in regional centres. These incentives include higher expected net (less match costs) gate receipts, external financial inducements from municipal or state governments, and the opportunity to build their membership base in these centres. See Booth (2006) for a more detailed discussion on the outcomes arising from changes to AFL revenue-sharing arrangements. Examples of teams doing this in the decade from 2000 to 2009 include Hawthorn (Gold Coast and Launceston), North Melbourne (Canberra and Gold Coast), St. Kilda (Launceston) and Western Bulldogs (Darwin). Teams have even elected to forfeit home advantage, playing home games in opposition territory, specifically Melbourne (Brisbane) and Western Bulldogs and North Melbourne (Sydney).

Finally, the organizational structure of the league combines elements observed commonly in European leagues with others more closely associated with North American leagues. The commonality with Europe can be seen in terms of the win-maximizing behaviour of teams (willing to run minimal profits), stemming from the historically member-owned nature of (the majority of) clubs, as well as the loyal supporter base of various teams. The similarity with the North American model is apparent more in terms of its closed-end (no promotion/relegation) structure, as well as the use of comparable restrictive policies on team behaviour to preserve competitive balance.

DATA AND METHODOLOGY

For the purpose of empirical analysis, we use an annual series (by season) of match attendances and competitive balance, the latter according to some valid measure. While match attendance data go back as far as 1921, the sample used here commences at 1945, in line with many long-term empirical studies in economics, to the time of writing, resulting in 65 annual observations. Also, 1945 corresponds to the beginning of Booth's (2004) 'period four' out of six in his historical analysis of alternative labour market devices and revenue-sharing arrangements over the history of the league. At this time, gate-revenue sharing was introduced for the first time in league history (later rescinded in 2000 as league revenue became more important) as a means of increasing competitive balance.

The series for attendance is simply the average attendance of home-and-away matches, expressed in logarithms. Lenten (2009) argues that AFL attendance data are highly suitable for such a modelling exercise, due to a number of attractive properties, including the long and continuous sample, and the low number of games being sold out fully despite the large average attendance. The latter is the case because of the considerable number of large stadiums in Australia's various cities, allowing attendance to be considered an accurate measure of the underlying demand for top-flight Australian Rules football. In fact, on 2009 figures, the season average attendance in relation to (reported) stadium capacity was 59.8 per cent – much lower than most other major worldwide leagues (for example, the equivalent 2008 figure for the National Football League in the US was 97.3 per cent). Ticket prices are also league regulated and virtually uniform between matches. Finals matches are excluded as they are much more likely to be sold out, misrepresenting demand, especially if held in a smaller stadium – not to mention the independence from the level of competitive balance.

The series for competitive balance is measureable via any number of alternative metrics used in the sports economics literature, based mostly on measures of dispersion applied in other fields of economics, such as the gini coefficient (income distribution) and the Herfindahl index (industrial organization). In a time-series framework, we use a within-season measure that can be calculated annually. The most popular measure within this framework is the common actual-to-idealized (ASD/ISD) ratio, which is simply the quotient of the actual standard deviation of win ratios/percentages to the analogous standard deviation that would be expected for a g round championship if the result of each match were purely random.[2]

The ASD is not affected by changes in the number of teams in the competition, N, over time, since it is calculated as the average squared deviation of the win ratio from the mean (obviously 0.5). This is a crucial numerical property of the measure, as the number of teams has increased over the sample period from 12 to 16 as shown in Table 17.1. Furthermore, the table also reveals that the season length has increased slightly as well, necessitating the inclusion of the ISD, as a league with evenly matched teams should produce a less dispersed league table as the season becomes longer. Formally, this measure can be represented as the following:

$$\text{ASD/ISD}_t = \sqrt{\sum_{i=1}^{N} [(w_i/g)_t - 0.5]^2/N_t} \times 2\sqrt{g_t} \qquad (17.1)$$

where w_i refers to the number of wins for team i. The ASD/ISD ratio can be considered the 'benchmark' measure of competitive balance. Humphreys (2002) describes the ASD/ISD ratio as a 'useful measure', finding that it does a better job explaining competitive balance than the other measures he assesses, although AFL evidence shows the measure to be close to perfectly positively correlated with the gini coefficient and Herfindahl index measures anyway.

The following relates to the chosen econometric methodology for the extraction of trends. The structural time-series model of Harvey (1989) is

Table 17.1   Annual series of teams and rounds in the AFL during the sample period

Year	Teams	Rounds
1945	12	20
1946	12	19
1947	12	19
1948	12	19
1949	12	19
1950	12	18
1951	12	18
1952	12	19
1953	12	18
1954	12	18
1955	12	18
1956	12	18
1957	12	18
1958	12	18
1959	12	18
1960	12	18
1961	12	18
1962	12	18
1963	12	18
1964	12	18
1965	12	18
1966	12	18
1967	12	18
1968	12	20
1969	12	20
1970	12	22
1971	12	22
1972	12	22
1973	12	22
1974	12	22
1975	12	22
1976	12	22
1977	12	22
1978	12	22
1979	12	22
1980	12	22
1981	12	22
1982	12	22
1983	12	22
1984	12	22
1985	12	22

Table 17.1 (continued)

Year	Teams	Rounds
1986	12	22
1987	14	22
1988	14	22
1989	14	22
1990	14	22
1991	15	22
1992	15	22
1993	15	20
1994	15	22
1995	16	22
1996	16	22
1997	16	22
1998	16	22
1999	16	22
2000	16	22
2001	16	22
2002	16	22
2003	16	22
2004	16	22
2005	16	22
2006	16	22
2007	16	22
2008	16	22
2009	16	22

used to estimate an effective decomposition of the series into its various components, allowing a novel approach to modelling such data. The system of series is modelled as a set of components that are not observable directly, though they do have a direct economic interpretation. These components can then be aggregated additively to replicate the realized series. The model is demonstrated by the following relation, represented in vector notation.

$$\mathbf{x}_t = \boldsymbol{\mu}_t + \boldsymbol{\phi}_t + \boldsymbol{\varepsilon}_t \qquad (17.2)$$

such that $\mathbf{x}_t$ is the realized value of the series at t, $\boldsymbol{\mu}_t$ is the trend component (comprising a level and a slope), representing the long-term movement of the series, $\boldsymbol{\phi}_t$ is the cyclical component, and $\boldsymbol{\varepsilon}_t$ is the random component. In addition, the components must not be correlated in any way and the error term must be normally and independently distributed. See Koopman

et al. (2007, Ch. 4), for a full formal representation of each of the components in scalar form.

The estimation of equation (17.2) takes the form of a seemingly unre-
lated time-series equation (SUTSE) model, in which attendance and ASD/
ISD are estimated simultaneously. A general-to-specific methodology is
employed to determine the optimal model for the data. Modelling begins
with the most general version, containing a stochastic level and slope,
as well as the maximum three cycles (each with a different frequency).
The optimal model is determined via goodness-of-fit and diagnostic
results, and proves to be one that in comparison to the general model
contains a fixed slope and is without the lowest-frequency cycle. As a
way of advocating the use of the structural time-series approach with
these particular series, the correlation coefficient between the ASD/
ISD ratio and attendances is –0.1477 over the full sample, which is
insignificant at 5 per cent. Meanwhile, the equivalent correlation coefficient in first differences of the corresponding trend components is
–0.9617, demonstrating strong support for expressing the 'uncertainty of
outcome' hypothesis in this fashion.

DISCUSSION ON THE ESTIMATED TREND COMPONENTS

The estimation of the optimal SUTSE model as described earlier produces
results that, while not reported here, are nonetheless pleasing in terms of
goodness-of-fit and diagnostics, demonstrating the validity of the model.
The following dialogue separates the demand for sport in terms of both: (i)
general economic factors that are thought to affect the demand for leisure
activities generally; and (ii) competitive balance as an industry-specific
factor relating to the relative quality of product offered by competitors (in
this case, teams) in the industry.

General Economic Factors

Figure 17.1 plots four selected variables for Australia over the sample
period. These variables are: (i) total resident population; (ii) male real
weekly earnings; (iii) unemployment rate; and (iv) average hours worked
per week. Both (i) and (ii) are indices, with an arbitrary base value of
1 for 1978, with the latter being used (in favour of an index including
female earnings) merely for data availability back to 1945. Similarly, (iv)
is recorded only from 1967. Meanwhile, Figure 17.2 (labelled with Booth's
periods) displays the average attendance series over the sample (dashed

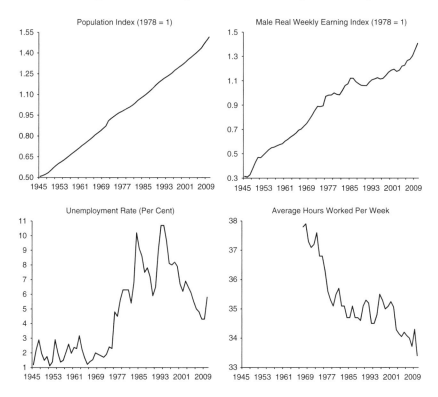

Source: Australian Bureau of Statistics (various databases).

Figure 17.1   *Long-term movement of relevant Australian economic variables*

line), along with its corresponding estimated trend component (solid line). The trend component of attendances is highly time consistent, reducing the standard deviation in first differences of the original series by 40 per cent, allowing a more accurate representation of the true underlying nature of demand for Australian Rules football over time.

The inclusion of population in the analysis accounts simply for 'size of the market' effects. Australia's resident population increased from 7.3 million in 1945 to an estimated 21.8 million in 2009, although as the top left-hand panel shows, the rate of increase (in terms of levels) was highly uniform. Much more important than aggregate population, is the role of national expansion of the league from an inter-suburban competition in Melbourne (2009 greater population estimate of 3.9 million) plus Geelong (municipality population of 210,000), unlocking hitherto unexploited

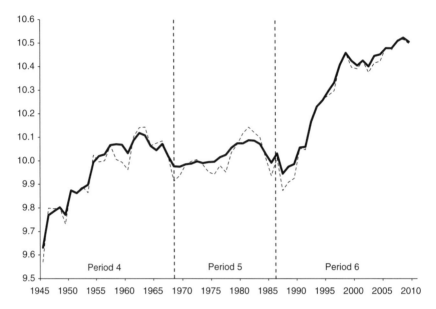

Source: See http://stats.rleague.com/afl/afl_index.html.

Figure 17.2   Original (dashed) and trend (solid) attendance series

market potential. The effect of this is more clearly seen, however, in total (as opposed to average) attendances, with a greater number of matches scheduled as a result of the larger competition, and this is a factor that is revisited in the following subsection.

It may be surprising to note that the move towards a national competition did not commence until the early 1980s. However, it was not until then that travel costs declined to the point such that a national competition became economically viable, long after the same had occurred in European football (much shorter travel distances) and North American pro-sports (larger market size overcoming travel costs). Analogously, the first national leagues in other sports were the National Soccer League (football) in 1977 and the National Basketball League in 1979, while the then New South Wales Rugby League (now National Rugby League) began its own evolution towards a national competition at about the same time as the AFL.

The role of real weekly earnings is to account for income effects on demand. The top right-hand panel, while it may explain much of the variation in trend attendances up until the late 1950s, and again from the late 1980s onwards, does a poor job of doing so in the intervening period. While income effects are a crucial determinant of demand, earnings are also representative of the opportunity cost of time taken to attend sporting events, clouding the analysis (see Løyland and Ringstad, 2009). Indeed, there is some anecdotal evidence that this is a major factor in explaining recent declining attendances, television ratings and participation rates in longer-format sports, such as cricket (especially Test matches) and golf.

The unemployment rate is also a broad indicator of economic activity, but has more built-in informational content on cyclical conditions than earnings. However, a casual look at the bottom left-hand panel of Figure 17.1 in relation to Figure 17.2 reveals little resemblance between cycles in the unemployment rate and attendances. Nevertheless, while cyclical components are not the focus of this analysis, the presence of a cyclical relationship between these variables cannot be discarded, and this remains an empirical issue yet to be resolved (as well as that of cyclicality of competitive balance itself) without further evidence from other leagues.

Finally, the average number of hours worked is exhibited in the bottom right-hand panel as a means of accounting for the general availability of leisure time.[3] Though the series does not extend back to 1945, it is shown clearly that there has been a big reduction in working hours in Australia, as elsewhere. A comparison to Figure 17.2, however, shows that major structural shifts in the hours worked series do not match those in attendances; nor do the peaks and troughs in the series.

Related to this is the current time cost of attending matches itself. In an attempt to construct a series of 'back-of-the envelope' estimates of attending matches throughout a typical season, a game-day estimate of six hours (door to door) is used as a base, for games in the fan's home city. This initial estimate ignores the possibility of combining game day with other social events, and additional time spent following their team and the competition in other forms. If fans attend only their team's 11 home games, the corresponding season estimates range from approximately 65 hours for most teams to 80 hours for smaller-market Melbourne-based teams that opt to play (typically) three home matches elsewhere in smaller regional centres, as outlined earlier. Adding the time to fly between cities (and imposing a range of other assumptions not discussed here for the sake of simplicity), the total season time cost to fans for attending all 22 games rises to between approximately 150 hours (big-market Melbourne teams) to 200 hours (Perth teams). These figures have obviously risen over time with the slightly longer season and nationalization of the league (necessitating interstate travel) affecting especially the 22-game estimates.

The conclusion that can be drawn from this combined (albeit parsimonious) analysis is that over the long term, broad trends in these general economic factors concur with the underlying economic theory. Attendances have risen, both on an aggregate and on an average basis, during a period of history that has seen a growing potential market, rising incomes and a

Table 17.2   Correlation coefficients between attendances and relevant economic variables in levels and first differences

	Levels	First differences
Population index	0.8262	0.3162
Real weekly earnings	0.7649	−0.0540
Unemployment rate	0.4526	−0.1265
Average hours worked	−0.6315	0.0526

reduced working week. The role of unemployment meanwhile could be considered more cyclical. However, none of these series can explain much of the variation in attendances in the short-to-medium run independently.

This conclusion is supported by a brief correlation coefficient analysis, exhibited in Table 17.2, between attendances and each of the respective various economic variables. While each of the correlations is significant in levels, they all become much weaker in first differences (though still marginally above the 5 per cent critical value for population). The correlation coefficient for earnings collapses virtually to zero, possibly suggesting that own-price effects overwhelm income effects. The unemployment rate correlation is arguably even the unanticipated sign in levels, though it changes in first differences.

Clearly, other factors cannot be discounted – not least of which rising competition from other sports, and other forms of leisure generally, many options of which were not available previously, including internet-related activities. Furthermore, it may simply be that factors relating to the competition itself and the quality of product (both absolute and relative) could be more important in explaining this shorter-run variation.

League and Competitive Balance Factors

The original series (dashed) for the competitive balance series, along with its trend component (solid), are displayed in Figure 17.3. As is shown, while there is substantial variation in the ASD/ISD ratio, the trend component eliminates almost 95 per cent of the standard deviation in first differences of the original series. The modelled trend barely ventures outside the range between 1.7 and 1.9, making it measure up favourably against many other comparable professional sports leagues.

The behaviour over time of the trend component also adds considerable weight to Booth's (2004) six-period analysis of AFL competitive balance. In particular, to the assertion that the ASD/ISD ratio increased when it had been a while since previous changes to the combination of revenue-sharing

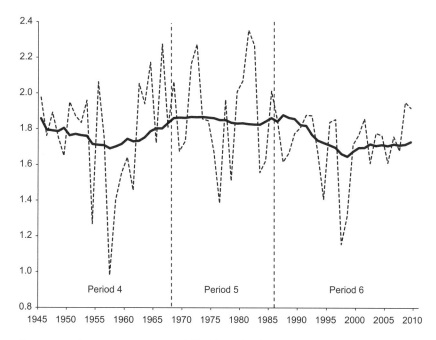

Source: See http://stats.rleague.com/afl/afl_index.html.

Figure 17.3 *Original (dashed) and trend (solid) competitive balance series*

and labour market devices had been made, since clubs would slowly but surely find ways to 'get around' the system. However, whenever competitive balance began to wane (increasing ASD/ISD ratio), the AFL realized that it had to act to restore competitive balance by tinkering with these devices – this corresponds to the end of each period; and that on each occasion, this strategy met with (at least some degree of) success.

Figure 17.3 demonstrates that the introduction of gate-revenue sharing in 1945 met with spectacular success in this regard for over a decade, reducing the ASD/ISD ratio trend component from 1.858 to 1.692 by 1957, until it eventually began creeping up towards its previous level. By 1968, the ASD/ISD trend had reached 1.861, by which time the AFL had reacted by introducing Victorian country zoning to complement Melbourne metropolitan zoning (Hess and Stewart, 1998, pp. 168–88).[4] This was a move in recognition of the fact that by 1967, there were many AFL players from regional and rural Victoria (unlike in 1915 when metropolitan zoning was introduced) which until then were exempt from such zoning regulations. Thus, this move circumvented the ability of the financially stronger teams to procure the best non-metropolitan Victorian talent. Also at this time, the Coulter law (an individual player wage ceiling dating back to 1930) was rescinded.[5]

With these changes, the increase in the ASD/ISD trend was arrested successfully. However, there was no reversal, rather the trend stagnated throughout much of the 1970s, although had decreased slightly to 1.826 by 1982, but then inevitably began increasing again, reaching the 1968 level in 1985. When the geographical zoning and transfer systems were declared illegal labour market restrictions in the early 1980s following the *Hall v Victorian Football League* and *Foschini v Victorian Football League* cases, new devices were required. As a result, the combination of a national player draft and hard salary cap was introduced in 1985 (beginning of period six).[6] Overall, the draft and salary cap have been amazingly successful (more so than any previous regime) in reducing the ASD/ISD trend. However, the effects on the ASD/ISD trend were certainly not immediate. In 1987, the trend had edged higher (1.878) than it was in 1985, but then fell considerably over the nine seasons following 1989, reaching a low of 1.647 in 1998. However, in the decade since, it has risen steadily again, reaching 1.729 in 2009.[7] The recent AFL experience is a marked contrast to the big European football leagues, where competitive balance has clearly declined in the post-Bosman era, that is, since 1996 (see Michie and Oughton, 2004; Brandes and Franck, 2007).

It is clear in particular that, even though the intended effect is the same, the draft is a far superior method to zoning as a means of randomizing talent, not only because of the reverse-order element, but also because zones can themselves contain inherently different levels of talent. Frost (2005, p. 190), for example, provides an anecdotal comparison between the Collingwood and Hawthorn country zones on demographic grounds. The fact that it took a few years for these devices to become effective can possibly be explained by the following factors:

1. Given the player squads that teams had in 1985, it would have taken some years for these squads to become top-heavy with draft-era (that is, talent-equalized) players. Hawthorn (also Carlton to a lesser extent), which dominated much of the early 1980s with an immensely talented side, retained many of their pre-1986 players until the early 1990s, allowing them to continue being very strong until that time. Meanwhile, the salary cap failed to achieve having their better players lured to other clubs for higher salaries, perhaps because they were motivated more by on-field success.
2. Related to point (1), at that time, the competition was still only semi-professional, and in transition towards full professionalism. Thus, the salary cap was not as influential as it would become later on.

3. Anecdotally, levels of club loyalty from players were much stronger than in the current day.
4. There is strong evidence to suggest that in the early years of the draft, high-pick players frequently failed to live up to the reputation bestowed upon them by virtue of being picked early, as their careers progressed. This can be explained by noting that, as a new device, it took clubs with early picks (and the league itself) several years to refine their youth talent identification procedures.[8] Subsequently, the draft did not realize its full talent-equalizing potential until later years, when high-pick draftees more often went on to have successful careers.
5. The gradualism of moving from zoning to the draft, as noted in note 6.

As an aside, it must also be noted that during period six, the AFL has made several (albeit relatively minor) alterations to the combination of various devices, such as changes to the structure of the draft in the annual cycle, and the move to league-revenue sharing from gate-revenue sharing.

Coming back to Figure 17.2, the analogous trend component of the attendance series also picks up the key directional and magnitude changes that conform to known historical information – more so than the original series: the increase during the post-war recovery period, the brief decline beginning around the time of the commencement of television in Australia in 1956, and the stagnation that followed for several years.

However, it is the period from 1980 that is of most interest. With the league (and half of its constituent clubs) in serious financial trouble, the competition's fortunes were declining and so were attendances. The old board of directors (comprising club representatives) agreed to vote themselves out of power and set up an independent commission, designed to run the game on its behalf. As the competition evolved slowly from a Victorian competition to a national competition, trend attendances continued to wane until 1989, from which time the trend rose dramatically over the following nine seasons, plateauing somewhat thereafter, despite increasing competition from other sports. The dramatic rise in attendances during that critical period can be attributed to several league-specific factors, including the following:

1. *The success of various marketing campaigns*, virtually non-existent until that time, many of which were targeted deliberately at previously unpenetrated demographic groups.[9] As a measure of this success, female interest, once negligible, has grown rapidly – according to (undated but recent at time of writing) official AFL figures, women

now account for 43.1 per cent of the total television viewing audience and a similar proportion of total club memberships. Related to marketing is the rise of special promotional rounds, which began during this period and have proliferated since.

2. *The new, or relocated, teams admitted to the league during that period* (Adelaide, 1991; Fremantle, 1995; Port Adelaide, 1997) were much more successful support-wise (on average) than their counterparts of earlier years, especially Sydney (1982) and Brisbane (1987).

3. *Home-ground aggregation*, mainly of the Victorian teams, from their small suburban grounds to the two or three larger, centralized stadiums.[10] This was not a phenomenon strictly confined to this period alone – Richmond had relocated from Punt Road Oval to the MCG as early as 1965 and other teams had also relocated in subsequent years. Meanwhile, the purpose-built Waverley Park had been hosting 'match-of-the-day' from 1970, and the occasional high-drawing game between two non-MCG tenants had been held at the MCG from 1981. However, it was in the period between 1989 and 1998 that this phenomenon gathered pace and proliferated to its near-saturation. Essendon moved from the Essendon Recreation Reserve (a.k.a. 'Windy Hill') to the MCG in 1992, Hawthorn (from Princes Park, 1992) and St. Kilda (from Moorabbin Oval, 1993) both relocated to Waverley Park, and the Western Bulldogs played their last match at the Western Oval in 1997. Furthermore, even though Carlton (Princes Park), Collingwood (Victoria Park) and Geelong (Kardinia Park) were still playing home games at their home grounds, the frequency of these games had slowed to a trickle by 1998, with the remainder being played at the larger venues. Also, Brisbane relocated from Carrara Oval to the larger Wollongabba ground gradually between 1991 and 1993. Finally, Melbourne-based teams playing home games in 'new markets' (see above) began during this time, with Fitzroy's two home games at North Hobart in 1991.

4. *Match scheduling by the league.*   Factor (3) was a sufficient condition for the scheduling of games, exclusively the domain of Saturday afternoons until the early 1980s, to other times – Friday nights, Saturday nights and Sundays – making it possible for Melbourne-based patrons to attend more than one match per week. Originally, it was North Melbourne's full-time move to the MCG in 1985, making it the third co-tenant there, that prompted the Friday night 'experiment', but it was the 1989–98 period that saw the incidence of this phenomenon increase markedly, including the expansion to Saturday night from the early 1990s.[11] In fact, the 2009 fixture contained only 38 (or 22 per cent of the total) matches scheduled on Saturday afternoons, these

being outnumbered by both Saturday nights (45) and Sunday after-noons (52).[12] Also on scheduling, since g has remained at 22, despite N increasing from 12 to 16, each club no longer plays each other twice (eight teams once, seven teams twice). As N increased, the league began rigging the schedule to guarantee that high-drawing fixtures, which they refer to as 'blockbusters' for marketing purposes, were always scheduled twice a season. While this arrangement began with Carlton versus Collingwood (1992), it soon extended to a triumvirate with Essendon (1993), and later to other pairings, such as the two Perth teams and the two Adelaide teams.

5. *The concurrent dramatic surge in (average) club memberships*, stag-nant for years until that time. The figure for 1989 was 7,118 (even lower than the corresponding 1979 figure), but then increased spec-tacularly each year for the following nine seasons, reaching 26,426 by 1998, with only minimal growth since then. This growth (as opposed to attendances generally) was driven by a more specialized set of factors. The main factor was the growing realization among the various clubs that higher memberships (as opposed to attendances) were vital to survival and prosperity, and this resulted in their own orchestrated membership drives and marketing campaigns. However, the explosion in memberships was also attributable to a number of 'one-off' events during this period, such as intermittent revelations that numerous clubs were in desperate financial trouble, such as St. Kilda, Richmond and the Western Bulldogs, rallying their sup-porters. The near-merger of Hawthorn and Melbourne in 1996 was another – the former's membership base increased spectacularly from 12,484 to 27,005 the following year. Admittedly, additional member-ships do not necessarily translate into higher attendances – some people have even been known to register their pets or unborn chil-dren as members. Furthermore, the very nature of membership has changed, with many different 'levels' of membership, some of which provide little or no free entry entitlement, yet they are all counted equally for official AFL record-keeping purposes.[13] However, there would be some level of complementarities present in so far as a fan, who previously might have attended two or three matches a season (paying at the gate), purchases a membership and then attends six to eight matches a season in order to derive value-for-money from his/her membership.

6. *The progression from the* Page *final five system* (in place after 1972) to a final six system in 1991, and then to the (current) final eight in 1994, theoretically keeping fans of a larger number of teams attending until the latter stages of the home-and-away season.

Factors (3) and (4) are the most important in explaining why growth in the trend component of attendances ceased after 1998. Principally, after years of exploiting these (previously unexploited) factors progressively more, most of the potential for *further* gains in attendances had, by then, been mostly exhausted, even though the league still persists with these factors to an even greater degree. Another factor could have been the closure of the larger but less accessible Waverley Park at the end of the 1999 season in favour of the (central) newly constructed Docklands Stadium.

CONCLUSION

This chapter has brought to light further evidence in the relation between competitive balance (as measured by the ASD/ISD ratio) and attendances in the AFL, using the long-term trend components of the series. The sample period of 1945–2009 was a period in which there were profound changes in the demand for sport, driven not only by a range of overwhelming changes in social and economic factors generally, but also by numerous league-specific factors, most notably competitive balance. The trend components were estimated from a SUTSE version of Harvey's structural time-series model, an approach that is highly suited to the series here, given their underlying statistical characteristics, as vindicated by the results of the model.

The trend components reveal a complex and dynamic story regarding the post-Second World War period. This story contains several explanations for the behaviour of the trend components of the variables over the sample period. In terms of general economic factors, long-term changes in the variables conform mostly to what standard economic theory would predict, with respect to market size, income and leisure-time effects. Although these factors do not do as well in explaining shorter-term variations in attendance, the findings are not inconsistent with similar studies on the determinants of demand for alternative forms of leisure.

Nevertheless, the quality of product is also imperative, as espoused here by competitive balance levels from season to season having substantial explanatory power. In the longer term, stagnation of attendances followed by a structural rise in the last generation can be related to the periodic changes to the various labour market and revenue-sharing devices used by the league to bring greater parity to the competition. The period from 1989 to 1998 was identified as being notable for a surge in demand for the AFL, brought about by such events and policies as the expansion of the league from a Victorian-based competition to a national one, venue changes, match scheduling, broadcasting issues, and league and club marketing.

NOTES

1. Quirk and Fort (1992, Ch. 7) provide a case study demonstrating how too much team success can eventually cause even the dominant team's home attendances to fall (not to mention at an aggregate level as well), with primary reference to the All-America Football Conference's Cleveland Browns and Major League Baseball's New York Yankees in the 1940s and 1950s.
2. A higher (lower) value of the ASD/ISD ratio signifies a lower (higher) level of competitive balance.
3. Indeed, the most iconic and revered song about Australian Rules football, Mike Brady's 1979 classic 'Up There Cazaly', begins with the lyrics: 'Well you *work* to earn a living, but on weekends comes the time, you can do what ever turns you on, get out and clear your mind. Me, I like *football*.'
4. Also in 1968, changes were made to membership entitlements, such that members were allowed free entry to home games only, as opposed to all games, which was previously the case.
5. A transfer system, similar to the pre-Bosman system in Europe, was then introduced (to augment those policy changes) from the beginning of the 1972 season.
6. Actually, the first national player draft was held in 1986, and the removal of zoning was phased, not immediate.
7. The 18-season average of the ASD/ISD trend from 1992 to 2009 (post-draft/salary cap transition) of 1.707 compares to 1.850 for the 18-year period from 1968 to 1985: this suggests (arguably) that superior competitive balance *vis-à-vis* all of the previous periods is assured in the medium term as long as the combination of the draft and salary cap are retained, enforced suitably and reformed appropriately.
8. As an obvious example, the annual AFL draft camp did not exist in the formative years of the draft.
9. The AFL was very open in acknowledging that, for example, the 'I'd like to see that' promotion, launched in 1994, was targeted at younger adult women.
10. In a practical sense, this was only made possible, in significant part, by improving ground-keeping technology.
11. The Sydney Swans had previously played a Friday night home match in 1983, although this occurrence had not been by design – this match had been rescheduled due to the state of the playing surface of the Sydney Cricket Ground. However, the 'experiment' rapidly became a success – in 1985, North Melbourne played only two home matches on a Friday night, but in 1986, seven matches involving North Melbourne were Friday night matches (including one away match in Sydney). By 1987, 17 matches were played on Friday night (plenty of them played at venues other than the MCG), of which seven involved North Melbourne. Ironically, given the increasing television ratings of the Friday night slot over time, as television transformed from a substitute for attendances to a complement, North Melbourne found themselves increasingly frozen out of Friday night scheduling, in favour of higher-drawing teams.
12. In addition, round 12 of 2009 (split over two weekends) did not contain a single game on either Saturday afternoon.
13. These different 'levels' of membership essentially represent a form of second-degree price discrimination.

REFERENCES

Baade, R.A. and A.R. Sanderson (1997), 'The employment effect of teams and sports facilities', in R.G. Noll and A.S. Zimbalist (eds), *Sports, Jobs, and Taxes: The Economic Impact of Sports Teams and Stadiums*, Washington, DC: Brookings Institution Press, pp. 92–118.

Baimbridge, M. (1997), 'Match attendance at Euro 96: was the crowd waving or drowning?', *Applied Economics Letters*, **4** (9), 555–8.

Booth, D.R. (2004), 'The economics of achieving competitive balance in the Australian Football League, 1897–2004', *Economic Papers*, **23** (4), 325–44.

Booth, D.R. (2006), 'Some economic effects of changes to gate-sharing arrangements in the Australian Football League', in M. Nicholson, B. Stewart and B. Hess (eds), *Football Fever: Moving the Goalposts*, Hawthorn, Vic: Maribyrnong Press, pp. 111–32.

Borland, J. and R. MacDonald (2003), 'Demand for sport', *Oxford Review of Economic Policy*, **19** (4), 478–502.

Brandes, L. and E. Franck (2007), 'Who made who – an empirical analysis of competitive balance in European soccer leagues', *Eastern Economic Journal*, **33** (3), 379–403.

Dobson, S.M. and J.A. Goddard (1992), 'The demand for standing and seated viewing accommodation in the English Football League', *Applied Economics*, **24** (10), 1155–64.

Fort, R.D. (2011), *Sports Economics*, 3rd edn, Upper Saddle River, NJ: Pearson Education.

Frost, L.E. (2005), *Immortals: Football People and the Evolution of Australian Rules*, Milton, Qld: John Wiley & Sons.

Fuller, P. and M. Stewart (1996), 'Attendance patterns at Victorian and South Australian football games', *Economic Papers*, **15** (1), 83–93.

García, J. and P. Rodríguez (2002), 'The determinants of football match attendance revisited: empirical evidence from the Spanish Football League', *Journal of Sports Economics*, **3** (1), 18–38.

Harvey, A.C. (1989), *Forecasting, Structural Time Series Models and the Kalman Filter*, Cambridge: Cambridge University Press.

Hess, R. and B. Stewart (1998), *More Than a Game: An Unauthorised History of Australian Rules Football*, Carlton South, Vic: Melbourne University Press.

Humphreys, B.R. (2002), 'Alternative measures of competitive balance in sports leagues', *Journal of Sports Economics*, **3** (2), 133–48.

Hunt, J.W. and K.A. Lewis (1976), 'Dominance, recontracting, and the Reserve Clause: Major League Baseball', *American Economic Review*, **66** (5), 936–43.

Jennett, N. (1984), 'Attendances, uncertainty of outcome and policy in Scottish league football', *Scottish Journal of Political Economy*, **31** (2), 176–98.

Koopman, S.J., A.C. Harvey, J.A. Doornik and N.G. Shephard (2007), *Stuctural Time Series Analyser, Modeller and Predictor – STAMP 8*, 4th edn, London: Timberlake Consultants Press.

Lenten, L.J.A. (2009), 'Unobserved components in competitive balance and match attendances in the Australian Football League, 1945–2005: where is all the action happening?', *Economic Record*, **85** (269), 181–96.

Løyland, K. and V. Ringstad (2009), 'On the price and income sensitivity of the demand for sports: has Linder's Disease become more serious?', *Journal of Sports Economics*, **10** (6), 601–18.

McDonald, M. and D. Rascher (2000), 'Does bat day make cents? The effect of promotions on the demand for major league baseball', *Journal of Sport Management*, **14** (1), 8–27.

Michie, J. and C. Oughton (2004), *Competitive Balance: Trends and Effects*, London: Sports Nexus.

Noll, R.G. (1974), 'Attendance and price setting', in Noll (ed.), *Government and the Sports Business*, Washington, DC: Brookings Institution, pp. 115–58.

Noll, R.G. (2002), 'The economics of promotion and relegation in sports leagues: the case of English football', *Journal of Sports Economics*, **3** (2), 169–203.

Quirk, J.P. and R.D. Fort (1992), *Pay Dirt: The Business of Professional Team Sports*, Princeton, NJ: Princeton University Press.

Rottenberg, S. (1956), 'The baseball players' labor market', *Journal of Political Economy*, **64** (3), 242–58.

18 The changing demands of leisure time: the emergence of Twenty20 cricket
David Paton and Andrew Cooke

INTRODUCTION

For the most-gifted individuals, cricket can offer an opportunity to earn a living. The very best can also enjoy the additional opportunity to attract lucrative sponsorship deals to supplement their income from playing professionally. Most people who have an interest in the game have to be content with treating cricket as a leisure outlet, either as an active pursuit within a local team or more passively by attending matches as a spectator or by following the game via the media (for example, television, webcasts, radio, newspapers, dedicated magazines and so on).

One of the key characteristics of cricket is that potential spectators need to invest significant amounts of leisure time in order to watch a game relative to football or rugby. Prior to the advent of one-day cricket in the early 1960s, professional cricket matches were played over several days. Even with the advent of a one-day format (which provides spectators with the opportunity to see the game start and to reach a conclusion within a day), attendance at a cricket game still carries a high opportunity cost. For some individuals this can be seen in terms of forgone earnings, for example overtime wages or the remuneration from a second job. For others, with no intention of working beyond their contracted hours, this opportunity cost can be seen in terms of either forgone non-market work (for example, decorating or mowing the lawn) and/or other leisure activities that might have been undertaken instead (for example, seeing friends and relatives or visiting a tourist attraction).

When real wages increase, so does the opportunity cost of leisure time, generating a 'substitution effect' away from the consumption of higher-priced leisure. Alongside this substitution effect is an 'income effect' reflecting the individual's opportunity to buy more leisure-intensive goods and services. Thus, the impact of an increase in wages depends on the relative strength and direction of these two effects. As Becker (1965, p. 498) notes in a classic paper, householders in richer countries are often willing to forfeit money income in order to obtain additional utility, exchanging money income for 'psychic income'. While this may involve choosing a less unpleasant job, it can also involve taking more leisure time. Becker also observes (pp. 512–16) that wage increases encourage individuals to switch from the consumption of time-intensive commodities to the consumption of goods-intensive commodities. In terms of non-market work, this may result in the greater use of more-expensive pre-prepared food such as microwave meals, whereas in terms of leisure activity, it may involve consumers' preferences shifting away from activities that have a high time input. In many respects, this is the problem that cricket administrators now face. Old newsreel footage of domestic cricket matches picturing spectators spilling over the boundary ropes through sheer weight of numbers is a thing of the past. Now cricket competes against a whole range of other leisure pursuits and as such, has to find a new niche within the leisure market.

The format of cricket in which cricket administrators are placing their faith is Twenty20. This format is the most truncated form of the game to date, emerging in 2003. It is marketed as being fast and furious with a set of incentives that encourage batsmen to adopt a risky and attacking strategy during the game. Particular emphasis is given to providing an exciting family-friendly atmosphere within a self-contained three-hour block of time during a summer's evening. To date, the concept has captured the public's imagination, with many games attracting crowds well in excess of those attending other forms of the game. However, Twenty20 is seen by traditionalists as having a downside as it encourages players to be reckless in the way they approach the game. A negative knock-on effect is predicted in that international Test match cricket, seen as the ultimate examination of a cricketer's mettle, will become diluted in quality. In England and Wales, the receipts from Test matches provide significant incomes to domestic teams as well as to subsidize grassroots development and therefore a potential decline in its attractiveness could have far-reaching consequences.

Twenty20 cricket, as a format, is only seven years old. Nonetheless, enough time has elapsed to enable the undertaking of a preliminary analysis of its impact on the game of cricket. This chapter first examines how cricket has had to reinvent itself in order to keep up with an ever-growing array of competing demands on people's leisure time. Using data provided by the England and Wales Cricket Board (EWCB), we then test empirically whether the advent of Twenty20 cricket has had a negative impact on attendances at four-day domestic matches; specifically is it a complementary or a substitute format for the more traditional four-day version of the game?

THE ORIGINS AND EVOLUTION OF CRICKET IN THE UK

In trying to gain an insight into the demand for any competitive sport, whether it be team based or individual, we need to appreciate Walter Neale's oft-cited view that sport has 'peculiar economics' (1964, p.1), a phrase that underpins a sports economics literature which has been evolving for over 50 years.[1] This peculiarity emerges not only in terms of consumers' relationship with the product (that is, their team and the games played by their preferred team) but also in terms of the conditions under which teams 'compete' against each other. For spectators, there is no assurance as to the quality of the game they are about to see in the same way that consumers might have expectations about a box of cornflakes or the performance of a television they are about to buy. In the case of sport, brand loyalty can be so intense that supporters consume poor-quality performances long after a buyer of a more traditional product would have sought another supplier. With regard to the latter, a central proposition within the sports economics literature is the mutual interdependence that exists between teams – without rivals, clubs cannot supply games to consumers. Teams have to give up some degree of autonomy in order to produce a fixture list that is attractive to potential spectators through the combined impact of 'uncertainty of outcome' (whereby games are, to some degree, evenly matched) and 'competitive balance' (overall competitions are not foregone conclusions too early on in the season; no one team continues to dominate over time).

Cricket's origins in the British Isles can be traced back to the early Middle Ages, (see Birley, 1999, p. 3).[2] In 1744, the rules of cricket were codified for the first time, with amendments added in 1774. By the end of the eighteenth century, informal games of cricket played by 'gentlemen and others' were capable of attracting an audience with teams, such as the Hambledon Club, paying 'non-gentleman' players a match fee. During the nineteenth century, cricket continued to evolve; the game was able to take advantage of not only the rapid growth of the railway system, which brought more opposing teams closer together in distance terms, but also reductions in the working hours of factory workers and the increased number of public holidays.

The formalization of cricket into the game we know today came with its own set of 'peculiarities' when seen alongside other sports such as soccer or rugby league. First, top-tier professional domestic cricket in England and Wales ultimately emerged within a county-based rather than city-based format. Thus, whereas most Yorkshire inhabitants will be united in the cricket team they support, their allegiance in football could focus on one or more of ten professional football teams. Currently 18 fully professional 'first class' counties contest the 'County Championship'; a second tier of 20 'minor' counties also exist, the latter lacking the resources and support to play top-level domestic cricket.[3] The oldest first class county side is Sussex, founded in 1839, followed by Nottinghamshire (1841) and Surrey (1845); the 1860s and 1870s in particular saw a rapid growth in the number of county teams (see Table 18.1). The first official County Championship was contested in 1890.[4]

A second feature that makes professional county cricket particularly distinctive from other professional team sports is that it is played currently within a variety of co-existing formats: four-day,[5] one-day[6] and the aforementioned 'Twenty20'. Thus, spectators are familiar with the idea of their team alternating between the longer and shorter versions of the game and have the opportunity to select the product which best suits their own preferences and leisure-time constraints.

The emergence of the one-day game in England and Wales began in the early 1960s. Although the professional game had been established and evolved within a longer format, it had been recognized that the game was finding it more difficult to attract spectators. A new one-day cup competition, the Gillette Cup, was launched in 1963 following an experimental competition played the year before.[7] This format proved to be attractive to spectators and its success led to the launch of a one-day league in 1969 and an additional cup competition in 1972.[8] Thus, within ten years, domestic teams in England and Wales had found themselves playing in four major competitions over the duration of the regular cricket season instead of one.[9] The success of one-day cricket in the UK led to its adoption throughout the major cricket playing nations. In Australia, the Vehicle and General Knock-Out Cup was introduced alongside the already established 'Sheffield Shield' four-day competition in 1969/70.[10] One-day competitions soon emerged in New Zealand (1971/72), the West Indies (1972/73), India (1973/74) and Pakistan (1974/75).

In this respect, cricket can be seen as a highly innovative sport which has recognized the opportunities that product differentiation can afford with regard to spectator interest and marketing appeal. The general characteristics of one-day cricket make it a more unpredictable form of the game than its first class counterpart. This reflects the fact that the game is limited to a single innings per team and is truncated in terms of the maximum number of balls that each team is asked to face. In the longer version of the game, teams have the opportunity to rectify early mistakes, therefore making it less likely that the weaker team will win.

One-day cricket has also been at the forefront of innovation within the game of cricket, resulting in the emergence of coloured clothing, music and floodlit matches. Despite the significant changes that have surrounded

Table 18.1   The eighteen first class counties

County	Year of formation	Admission into County Championship	County Championship wins[1,2]	List A competition victories[3]	Twenty20 victories[4]
Derbyshire	1870	1895	1 (1936)	3 (1993)	Best QF (2005)
Durham	1882	1992	2 (2009)	1 (2007)	n/q
Essex	1876	1895	6 (1992)	9 (2006)	Best SF (2010)
Glamorgan	1888	1921	3 (1997)	3 (2004)	Best SF (2004)
Gloucestershire	1871	1890	Best 2nd (1986)	9 (2004)	Best F (2007)
Hampshire	1863	1895	2 (1973)	8 (2009)	1 (2010)
Kent	1859	1890	7 (1978)	10 (2001)	1 (2007)
Lancashire	1864	1890	7 (1950)	16 (1999)	Best F (2005)
Leicestershire	1879	1895	3 (1998)	5 (1985)	2 (2006)
Middlesex	1864	1890	12 (1993)	7 (1992)	1 (2008)
Northamptonshire	1878	1905	Best 2nd (1976)	3 (1992)	Best QF (2010)
Nottinghamshire	1841	1890	6 (2010)	3 (1991)	Best F (2006)
Somerset	1875	1891	Best 2nd (2001)	6 (2001)	1 (2005)
Surrey	1845	1890	19 (2002)	6 (2003)	1 (2003)
Sussex	1839	1890	3 (2007)	7 (2008)	1 (2009)
Warwickshire	1862	1895	6 (2004)	11 (2010)	Best F (2003)
Worcestershire	1865	1899	5 (1989)	6 (2007)	Best QF (2004)
Yorkshire	1863	1890	31 (2001)	6 (2002)	Best QF (2007)

Notes:
[1] Year in parentheses denotes the year of the county's most recent victory or highest position.
[2] Win figure includes shared championships.
[3] One-day competitions include all 60, 50, 45 and 40 over competitions.
[4] Where counties have not won the Twenty20 competition, their most recent best performance is noted where F denotes finalist; SF denotes semi-finalist; QF denotes quarter finalist; and n/q means that the county has yet to compete beyond the group stages of the competition.

cricket, both in terms of repackaging its format and organizational structure, there is a limited academic literature that has focused on the factors that influence the demand for the game. Notable exceptions are papers by Schofield (1983) and Paton and Cooke (2005) which focus on domestic cricket, together with Hynds and Smith (1994) and Bhattacharya and Smyth (2003) which have analysed international cricket. In some respects, this is not a big surprise in the sense that the sports economics literature is, to a large extent, driven by North American analysts whose focus is on the 'big four' professional team sports: American football, baseball, basketball and ice hockey. Furthermore, European commentators have tended to gravitate towards soccer, particularly with the large sums of money and media attention given to the game in England, Spain and Italy in particular. Cricket's importance to the population of the Asian sub-continent is not reflected in its academic output, though this may change with the emergence of the Indian Premier League (IPL).

TRENDS IN INTERNATIONAL CRICKET IN ENGLAND

Like domestic cricket, international cricket is now contested in three forms: the 'Test match',[11] the 'one-day international' (ODI)[12] and Twenty20.[13] In England and Wales, five-day Test cricket is highly appealing to spectators with some grounds enjoying sell-out crowds throughout a game's duration.[14] This interest is reflected also in the demand for tickets for international ODIs and Twenty20 games. Since 2000, England (E) has hosted a combination of eight touring teams: Australia (A), Bangladesh (B), India (I), New Zealand (NZ), Pakistan (P), Sri Lanka (SL), West Indies (WI) and Zimbabwe (Z). The letters in parentheses are used to denote each country in Table18.2 which documents the aggregate and average crowds attracted to international cricket in England. Test match average attendance figures pertain to the whole game, rather than to each individual day. Inevitably visiting teams such as Australia are extremely attractive to spectators due to the longstanding cricketing rivalry that exists between the nations and as a result, games sell out long before they are played. Whereas teams such as India and Pakistan can draw upon high levels of 'local' support within England, matches against New Zealand or Bangladesh are less attractive to the viewing public.

Given that most international games played in the UK are played in front of sell-out or near sell-out crowds, the authorities regularly face a pricing conundrum. Assuming that demand is inelastic at current prices (an assumption consistent with the results of numerous empirical sport-based demand studies), revenues could be increased by raising admission prices. This would increase the monies that could be redistributed through the county game to the betterment of the overall domestic product. Inevitably, however, price increases would be extremely unpopular and

Table 18.2   Demand for international cricket in England, 2000–08

	2000	2001	2002	2003	2004	2005	2006	2007	2008
Tests[1]	Z(2)	P(2)	SL(3)	Z(2)	NZ(3)	B(2)	SL(3)	WI(4)	NZ(3)
	WI(5)	A(5)	I(4)	SA(5)	WI(4)	A(5)	P(4)	I(3)	SA(4)
ODIs[1]	10	9[2]	10	10	13[3]	13[4]	10	10	10
2020[1]	–	–	–	–	–	1	2	2	1
Tests									
Agg	388,136	546,450	365,553	437,105	513,014	513,895	562,995	563,124	535,575
Av	55,448	78,064	52,221	62,443	73,287	73,413	80,427	80,446	76,510
ODIs									
Agg	136,972	167,005	190,751	193,108	197,082	165,329	189,113	203,957	189,914
Av	13,697	18,556	19,075	19,310	15,160	12,717	18,911	20,395	18,991
Twenty20s									
Agg						14,097	35,294	42,349	16,817
Av						14,097	17, 647	21,174	16,817
Total	525,108	713,455	556,304	630,213	710,096	693,321	787,402	809,430	737,306

Notes:
[1] Figures denote the number of games played.
[2] One game between Australia and Pakistan was abandoned without a ball being bowled.
[3] Ten games were contested in the triangular tournament between England, New Zealand and the West Indies, together with a further three matches contested between England and India as warm-up matches for a major international competition.
[4] Ten games were contested in the triangular tournament contested by England, Bangladesh and Australia and a further three games were contested between England and Australia.

Source: EWCB (2009).

seen as pricing the 'average' person out of international cricket at a time when it is less accessible since television coverage of international cricket (and indeed, domestic cricket) is only available via a priced sports package available on the standard satellite and cable channels. As a result, cricket may suffer increasingly from underexposure at a time when it is already competing against a growing array of alternative leisure pursuits.

DOMESTIC CRICKET IN THE UK

As noted earlier, 18 first class counties contest the major competitions in the UK. Although the four-day County Championship is hermetically sealed, minor counties, together with Scotland and Ireland, have participated in the Friends Provident Trophy (and its previous incarnations).[15]

In addition, Scotland was given temporary admission into Division Two of the Pro40 competition for three seasons (2003–06).

As Table 18.1 showed, Yorkshire has been the most successful team in the County Championship, with a total of 31 wins since 1890. However, apart from a win in 2001, their 'golden era' was before the Second World War, together with a period of dominance during the 1960s. The second most successful team in the County Championship is Surrey with 19 wins. Surrey dominated the 1950s but has since had three more recent successes either side of the Millennium. More recently, the distribution of championships has been more even. Over the 25-season period from 1986 to 2010, a total of 11 different teams have won the County Championship; between 2000 and 2010, six different counties have been victorious with Durham, which was only admitted into the Championship in 1992, taking the crown in both 2008 and 2009.

The spoils from one-day cricket have been more evenly spread. Since 1963 (when the Gillette Cup was first contested) through to the present, all teams have had at least one victory. Despite its failure to win the County Championship since 1950, Lancashire has been extremely successful in one-day cricket. Up to the end of the 2008 season, it had achieved 16 successes across all one-day competitions. Kent (11 one-day victories, including one Twenty20 win) and Warwickshire (11 victories), have more moderate records in the longer version of the game (with seven and six successes, respectively). The most successful team in domestic cricket's most recent format, Twenty20, has been Leicestershire with two wins since 2003. In total, seven different teams have won Twenty20 in its first eight years. The more even spread of victories in the one-day competitions and Twenty20 in part reflects the greater uncertainty that characterizes more truncated versions of the game. As the County Championship gives two opportunities to bat and bowl, stronger teams have a second chance to redeem a poor performance in the early stages of a game.

IS DOMESTIC CRICKET POORLY ATTENDED IN ENGLAND AND WALES?

A 2009 announcement from domestic cricket's main governing body, the EWCB, revealed that total attendances for all domestic professional cricket (First Class, List A and Twenty20) in 2008 summed to nearly 1.5 million. This figure is well short of the aggregate number of spectators watching football's Premier League (13.73 million), but of a similar order of magnitude to attendances at the main rugby league and union competitions (see Table 18.3).

The vast crowds which attended the inaugural season of the IPL,[16]

Table 18.3   *Attendances at cricket, rugby league, rugby union and soccer,*
                 2008/09

Sport/competition	Season	Total attendance	Average attendance
Cricket[1]			
Championship (4 day)	2008	488,771	3,394
Twenty20	2008	593,717	6,120
Rugby League[2]			
Super League	2008	1,674,809	10,338
Rugby Union[3]			
Guinness Premiership	2008–09	1,590,214	12,047
Soccer[4]			
Premier League	2008–09	13,539,400	35,630
Championship	2008–09	9,867,000	17,875

Sources: [1] EWCB (2009), [2] Sport Industry Group (2008), [3] Premier Rugby (2010),
[4] European Football Statistics (2010).

together with Twenty20's domestic appeal are pushing cricket administrators to expand the supply of Twenty20 games even further (discussed later). However, although the average crowds for the 2007 IPL dwarf anything seen in the UK, it should be noted that: (a) cricket is by far India's most popular sport (equivalent to football in the UK); (b) not all IPL spectators actually paid an entrance fee; (c) the IPL's city-based franchises were located in highly populated centres of a highly populated country; and (d) England's own grounds (see Table 18.5) and size of population centres would provide a constraint to many counties' ability to achieve a dramatic increase in spectators from their current figures.

One of the features of Twenty20 which should also be recognized is that despite its truncated nature (relative to other forms of cricket), the game still lasts for up to three hours (from the bowling of the first ball to the game's conclusion). In reality, many spectators will have entered the ground before the start of the game and therefore the experience may last for nearer four hours. This length of in-ground time is much longer than one would expect for a spectator at a football match or a game of rugby. Thus, the club has more opportunity to attract additional sales beyond the standard ticket charge, not only food and refreshments, but also club merchandise and memorabilia.

In Table 18.4, we compare attendances across the four main types of domestic cricket in England and Wales. It can be seen that there are three versions of one-day cricket: 50 over (regional round robin/knock-out),

Table 18.4   Cricket attendances in English domestic cricket, 2002–08

	Four-day[1]		50-over cup		40-over league		Twenty20		Total attendance
	Agg	Av	Agg[2]	Av[3]	Agg	Av	Agg[2]	Av[3]	
2002	512,494	3,559	60,811	1,090	358,667	2,241	n/a	n/a	1,037,461
2003	530,938	3,687	67,729	1,231	410,536	2,565	257,759	5,603	1,266,962
2004	465,428	3,232	58,809[4]	1,056	352,945[5]	2,205	287,726	5,754	1,164,908
2005	471,488	3,274	68,750[6]	1,938	346,401	2,165	476,174	6,217	1,365,476
2006	488,109	3,390	177,956	1,711	196,927	2,687	500,441	6,281	1,362,633
2007	449,832	3,124	171,829	1,615	186,405	2,553	436,336	7,020	1,244,402
2008	488,711	3,394	159,084	1,482	194,439	2,664	593,717	6,309	1,435,951

Notes:
[1]   Some missing values for four-day attendances are imputed.
[2]   Aggregate attendance covers all games played in the competition.
[3]   Group stage average – this figure increases significantly when the semi-final and final attendances are included, for example in the 2005 C&G competition the figure increases from 1,938 to 4,044.
[4]   This figure excludes 11/31 round two games (involving at least one minor county) for which attendance data are not available.
[5]   This figure excludes two games for which attendance data are not available.
[6]   Figures are available for round 3 of the competition onwards (17 games).

40 over (league) and Twenty20 (regional round robin and knock-out) in addition to the traditional four-day version of the game.

Twenty20's launch in 2003 saw 257,759 spectators come through the turnstiles (EWCB, 2009). In the first round of matches, the 18 teams were arranged geographically into three groups of six, with each team playing a single fixture (home or away) against each of the other teams within the group. The winners, together with the best runners-up, battled out a series of semi-finals and a final over a single day at Trent Bridge, Nottingham. Average figures for the scheduled games (assuming that the three games played on finals day are treated as one), amounted to 5,603. For the 2004 competition, quarter-finals were added to the schedule and with it came a small increase in aggregate and average attendances. The ongoing success of this highly truncated form of the game can be seen in comparison with the average attendances for the longer versions of the game (four day, 50 over and 40 over). As a result the 2005 schedule of Twenty20 games was expanded at the group stages, with each team playing eight matches instead of five. This guaranteed each county four potentially lucrative home games, albeit at the expense of generating an unbalanced format of games.[17] In the wake of the ongoing success of the competition, the number of fixtures played by each team in the group stages of the 2008 competition was further expanded to ten, thereby regenerating a balanced competition. The ongoing success of the competition was maintained despite the fact that poor weather during the three-week Twenty20 'window' meant that a total of 39 games were 'no result' in 2007 (19 games were lost) and 2008 (20 games lost), despite captains' and umpires' attempts to push games to a conclusion in otherwise adverse conditions.

COUNTY-LEVEL ATTENDANCES

Although teams represent counties, rather than towns or cities, they typically play fixtures at one ground. For example, Yorkshire plays the majority of its fixtures at Headingley (Leeds), rather than spread equally across other cities such as Bradford, Sheffield or York. In previous years, counties sought to play a small number of matches at smaller 'outgrounds' but this policy is becoming increasingly undermined by cost considerations and the fear that pitches at smaller grounds may be unsuited for first class cricket.[18] Nonetheless, some county teams still endeavour to maintain some of their traditional games.[19] Table 18.5 lists the grounds and capacities for all 18 first class counties. With the exception of the grounds used for international cricket, county grounds are relatively small, particularly when compared with football grounds. The last two columns set out the largest crowds to attend domestic List A games (Friends Provident or Pro40) and Twenty20 games. Although County Championship matches sometimes attract attendances in excess of these figures, particularly those in the fifth column, it should be recalled that crowds for these games typically embrace the overall four-day period. Thus, when seen in terms of a daily figure, first class matches attract lower daily attendances than their one-day counterparts. A comparison of the fifth and sixth columns emphasizes the popularity of the Twenty20 format and hence the cricket authorities' desire to expand the volume of 20-over matches in the future. The key point to note is that counties' highest attendance rarely comes close to the official ground capacities, even for Twenty20 cricket. Thus, although there seem to be significant disparities between the ground capacities at each of the main venues, demand remains well within the natural constraint that exists.

Since its emergence in 2003, Twenty20 has been highly attractive to the wider cricketing public. Administrators' confidence is reflected in attendances across all counties. For example, figures provided by the EWCB reveal that Surrey's attendances for all forms of cricket in 2008 amounted to 120,552. Of this total, almost two-thirds of those spectators (78,957) were at its five home Twenty20 games. Its games against Kent and Middlesex both attracted in excess of 19,000 spectators. This

Table 18.5   Grounds of first class county cricket teams

County	Main ground	Location	Official capacity	Highest List A crowd 2004–08[2]	Highest Twenty20 crowd 2004–08
Derbyshire	County Ground (F)[1]	Derby	9,500	2,607	4,628
Durham	Riverside*	Chester-le-Street	5,000[3]	5,704	6,139
Essex	County Ground (F)	Chelmsford	6,500	5,250	6,933
Glamorgan	Sofia Gardens*	Cardiff	15,000	7,109	6,519
Gloucestershire	County Ground**	Bristol	7,000[3]	4,808	8,014
Hampshire	The Rose Bowl**	Southampton	6,500[3]	9,100	10,640
Kent	St Lawrence Ground	Canterbury	15,000	5,209	6,372
Lancashire	Old Trafford*	Manchester	19,000	6,626	17,000
Leicestershire	Grace Road	Leicester	12,000	1,914	6,000
Middlesex	Lord's (F)*	London	30,000	8,485	26,812
Northamptonshire	County Ground	Northampton	6,500	2,943	5,327
Nottinghamshire	Trent Bridge (F)*	Nottingham	17,000	8,390	12,325
Somerset	County Ground	Taunton	6,500	4,839	6,501
Surrey	Kennington Oval (F)*	London	23,500	7,706	22,000
Sussex	County Ground	Hove	4,000[3]	5,558	6,844
Warwickshire	Edgbaston*	Birmingham	21,000	7,088	15,067
Worcestershire	New Road	Worcester	4,500	3,763	5,930
Yorkshire	Headingly*	Leeds	17,000	5,530	10,985

Notes:
[1] (F) denotes permanent floodlights. Given the popularity of floodlit cricket in the summer months, some counties bring in temporary floodlights for one or more home games. Grounds identified by a single asterisk (*) are used for test matches and ODIs while grounds identified with two asterisks (**) have been used for ODI matches.
[2] Either Friends Provident Trophy or the Pro40 League.
[3] Capacity is raised for important matches through the use of temporary seating.

Sources: CricInfo (2009: ground locations and capacities), EWCB (2009).

contrasts with Surrey's highest daily crowd of 1,602 for the first day of its four-day game against Somerset. Similarly, Middlesex's highest attendance in the four-day county championship was 1,206 (day two of its game versus Essex) whereas its home Twenty20 games against Essex, Surrey and Sussex were witnessed by 17,463, 16,378 and 18,857, respectively.

Games involving Middlesex and Surrey frequently produce very large attendances. The highest-ever crowd for a domestic Twenty20 game was at Lords in 2005 when Middlesex hosted Surrey. Three other games have generated crowds in excess of 20,000. The highest attendance at a Twenty20 game outside London is a 17,000 crowd that attended the Roses game between Lancashire and Yorkshire at Old Trafford in 2008.

Although less spectacular, figures for the 2008 season seem to justify the use of zonal groups to promote local rivalries: games between Lancashire and Yorkshire, Nottinghamshire and Yorkshire, Warwickshire and Worcestershire as well as the return fixture between Yorkshire and Lancashire all generated attendances well in excess of 10,000 with many other games attracting spectators well in excess of other one-day games or the four-day matches. Similar patterns have emerged for previous seasons.

HAS TWENTY20 CRICKET HAD A NEGATIVE IMPACT ON DOMESTIC FOUR-DAY CRICKET?

As we have seen, traditionalists have been concerned about the potential detrimental effects of limited-overs cricket on the longer version of the game, both domestically and internationally. This concern, which emerged in the 1960s, can be seen in two forms. First, the shorter version of the game encourages batsmen to attempt shots that would be considered fool-hardy within the game's longer format. Similarly, bowlers are encouraged to adopt an overdefensive run-containing strategy, rather than one that emphasizes wicket taking. Thus, too much limited-overs cricket is seen as being potentially detrimental to the ability of the domestic four-day game to nurture players who have Test cricket ambitions. As we have already seen, Test cricket is highly popular in the UK. It is therefore important that the England Test team is competitive to maintain high attendances and hence the revenue stream that goes back into domestic cricket.

Second, the longer version of the game is seen as having more 'gravi-tas'. Limited-overs cricket is perceived as the brash 'new kid on the block' which could kill off an aspect of the game that has a long tradition. If limited-overs cricket becomes too dominant, people may lose interest in the longer form of the game and as a result, lose something that might never be retrieved. The decline of four-day domestic cricket would inevita-bly feed through into the international arena. Of course, it should be noted that there is an opposite viewpoint. The opposite point of view can be put forward not only in terms of the upsurge in attendances at Twenty20 matches but also an increase in the number of new spectators who have been encouraged to sample this form of the game. In other words, instead of being a substitute good, Twenty20 may also serve as a complementary good and may encourage spectators to consume longer versions of the game (50-over or even four-day cricket).

The aim of this empirical section is to focus on the second of these two concerns and to ask the specific question 'has the emergence of Twenty20 cricket had a detrimental impact on attendances at four-day cricket in the UK?' Looking at the descriptive statistics reported in Tables 18.4 and 18.5, it is clear that there is considerable variation in attendances over years and across counties. Twenty20 cricket was introduced in the middle of the 2003 season and there is a mixed pattern of attendance at Championship matches in subsequent years. Average attendance reached a peak of 3,687 in that year but dropped somewhat in subsequent years. These descriptive statistics, however, are not able to take account of factors such as the poor weather conditions experienced in recent years or changes to scheduling such as fewer matches at outgrounds. For example, the average match attendance at outgrounds in 2008 was over 4,600 compared to an average of just under 3,200 at the main grounds. Hence, we now turn to the multivariate analysis of attendance in an attempt to isolate any possible impact of Twenty20 (T20) cricket from other factors.

Our basic approach is to estimate the following econometric model:

$$Attendance_{ij} = \alpha\, trend + \beta\, T20 + \gamma \mathbf{X} + \varsigma_i + v_{ij}$$

where:

Attendance is the total attendance for home county i at County Championship match j.

Trend is a linear time trend included to pick up any long-running trend in County Championship attendances which may have existed prior to the introduction of the Twenty20 competition. We start by specifying a common trend for all counties but we also experiment by estimating a version of the model with county-specific trends.

T20 is a dummy variable covering the period from mid-2003 when the Twenty20 competition was in operation. A significantly negative coefficient on *T20* would be consistent with the Twenty20 cricket acting as a substitute for the County Championship. On the other hand, a significantly positive coefficient on *T20* would be consistent with Twenty20 acting as a complement to the Championship.

It is possible that any effects of Twenty20 would gradually become evident over time. We test this possibility by estimating an alternative specification in which we also include the interaction between *T20* and *Trend*. A negative coefficient on this variable would indicate that the onset of Twenty20 cricket has led to a gradual reduction over time in Championship attendances.

X is a vector of other variables that might affect attendance:

Outground = 1 if match is played at a non-standard venue; = 0 otherwise.

Holiday = number of match days played during school holidays.

Weekend = number of match days played at weekends or bank holidays.

Division 1 = 1 if teams are in division 1; = 0 otherwise.

Local derby = 1 if match is between geographically adjacent counties; = 0 otherwise.

April = 1 if match is played during April.

No play = number of match days on which there were fewer than 20 overs.

Our expectations are that, in line with previous work such as Cooke and Paton (2005), *Outground*, *Holiday*, *Weekend*, *Division 1* and *Local derby* will all attract positive coefficients. *April* and *No play* are included to pick up the effects of poor weather conditions and matches completed in less than the scheduled four days. These are expected to attract negative coefficients.

Finally, ς is a set of fixed effects for each county. We start by including effects for home teams. We also report a version of the model with away-team effects included. v_{it} is an error term.

In common with many other studies of sports attendance, we do not include any price measure. The identification of a consistent method of defining price within sports attendance models has been problematic and has resulted in many studies reporting this variable to be insignificant or, in a small number of cases, assuming a positive sign (which clearly contradicts a priori expectation). A particular issue is that the pricing of sport is associated with extensive price discrimination. Spectators will pay a different price to see the fixture depending on where they sit, their age, when they buy their ticket (on the day or in advance), the nature of the opposition (less attractive fixtures may be discounted whereas more attractive games might carry a premium) or whether there is a special deal available (family tickets, newspaper offers and so on). Furthermore, in the case of cricket, a large proportion of spectators is made up of 'members' who pay an annual fee for the right to attend both Championship and Twenty20 matches. A discussion of these issues can be found in Paton and Cooke (2005) and Forrest and Simmons (2006).

Data and Empirical Results

Attendance data were provided by the EWCB for the period from 2000 to 2008, inclusive. In a few cases, data were missing or unreliable and these observations are deleted. In particular, Glamorgan reported incorrect attendance data for 2008, while match data are missing for Northamptonshire in 2004 and Kent in 2005. That leaves us with a total of 1,263 matches.

Other match-specific data (for example, that related to play lost due to rain or early completion) were obtained from the online Cricket Archive maintained by the Association of Cricket Statisticians and Historians (http://cricketarchive.com/index.html).

Table 18.6 reports the Championship attendance equation estimates. In panel 1 we estimate the impact of Twenty20 cricket using the *T20* dummy variable, while in panel 2 we estimate the impact using the *T20* trend term. The simplest model, reported in column (a) of each panel, includes home-team fixed effects only. In column (b) we also include away-team effects, while in column (c), we allow for county-specific time trends.

The results are very robust to the choice of specification. In common with previous work (for example, Paton and Cooke, 2005) we find that the scheduling of matches is very important for attendance. Each day scheduled during the school holiday period increases match attendance by nearly 300 spectators. Local derbies attract on average about 700 more spectators than other matches, while Division 1 matches are estimated to have between 300 and 400 more spectators than matches in Division 2 (even controlling for home-county fixed effects). Most notably of all, attendances at festival matches played at non-standard venues are estimated to be nearly 1,400 higher than other matches.

Focusing on the impact of Twenty20, when we estimate an average Twenty20 effect (reported in panel 1 of Table 18.6), the point estimates are consistently positive. When we add in the time-trend interaction effect (reported in panel 2), the point estimate on *T20* remains positive, while the coefficient on the trend is negative. This may be suggestive that the introduction of Twenty20 had a positive short-run effect on Championship attendances, while the longer-run impact has been negative. However, none of the Twenty20 effects are even close to being significant at the conventional level. Further, the point estimates of the *T20* variables suggest effects of a very small magnitude both absolutely and in comparison to other effects such as playing at a festival ground.

In Table 18.7, we report estimates in which we allow the average Twenty20 effect to vary for each county. The estimates of the control

Table 18.6   *T20 average effect on County Championship match attendance*

	Panel 1			Panel 2		
	(a) Attend-ance	(b) Attend-ance	(c) Attend-ance	(a) Attend-ance	(b) Attend-ance	(c) Attend-ance
Outground	1,348.9***	1,361.1***	1,384.8**	1,349.5***	1,361.8***	1,385.7***
	(424.70)	(430.905)	(431.24)	(424.74)	(431.03)	(431.09)
Holiday	292.64***	287.41***	290.12***	292.595***	287.34***	290.05***
	(61.40)	(59.86)	(62.55)	(61.38)	(59.83)	(62.51)
Weekend	95.53	88.30	83.06	93.98	86.37	80.87
	(67.55)	(66.93)	(67.47)	(67.53)	(66.76)	(67.03)
Division 1	477.15***	327.44***	368.58***	477.584***	327.67***	369.15***
	(86.62)	(91.55)	(94.65)	(86.19)	(92.01)	(95.46)
Local derby	697.92***	659.77***	701.14***	698.55***	660.64***	702.03***
	(216.36)	(131.99)	(218.48)	(216.60)	(132.38)	(218.74)
April	−98.05***	−102.74***	−96.13**	−99.22***	−104.18***	−97.77**
	(32.31)	(31.25)	(34.40)	(32.62)	(31.08)	(34.84)
No play	−737.52***	−725.24***	−728.05***	−736.67***	−724.17***	−726.76***
	(82.28)	(81.28)	(82.00)	(82.87)	(81.71)	(82.50)
Trend	−25.37	−23.42		−8.07	−2.24	
	(42.35)	(42.82)		(65.08)	(65.59)	
T20	105.60	92.08	127.56	106.27	92.84	128.65
	(173.76)	(176.81)	(184.94)	(173.86)	(176.89)	(185.16)
T20*trend				−21.28	−26.04	−29.93
				(61.30)	(59.29)	(59.32)
Fixed effects						
Home team	Yes	Yes	Yes	Yes	Yes	Yes
Away team	No	Yes	No	No	Yes	No
Home*trend	No	No	Yes	No	No	Yes
N	1,248	1,248	1,248	1,248	1,248	1,248
R-squared	0.58	0.61	0.6	0.58	0.61	0.6

Notes:
Robust standard errors in brackets, clustered according to home team.
* significant at 10%; ** significant at 5%; *** significant at 1%.

variables are not reported in this table but are all very close in magnitude and significance to those reported in Table 18.6. For only four counties is the effect significantly different from zero at the 5 per cent level or better. For two of these (Sussex and Nottinghamshire), Twenty20 appears to have produced a significant boost to Championship attendances while for the others (Surrey and Northamptonshire), the onset of Twenty20 cricket

Table 18.7   County-specific T20 effects

County		County	
Derbyshire	−108.03	Middlesex	370.686*
	(196.743)		(204.376)
Durham	308.18	Northamptonshire	−732.122***
	(189.100)		(202.265)
Essex	239.91	Nottinghamshire	655.159***
	(201.626)		(197.567)
Glamorgan	−341.597*	Somerset	213.13
	(180.772)		(186.867)
Gloucestershire	322.41	Surrey	−741.542***
	(194.813)		(198.436)
Hampshire	165.89	Sussex	1,171.098***
	(189.750)		(202.125)
Kent	242.53	Warwickshire	−191.41
	(195.207)		(201.301)
Lancashire	308.46	Worcestershire	350.11
	(189.684)		(204.762)
Leicestershire	−323.04	Yorkshire	−151.97
	(191.047)		(184.567)

Notes:
Robust standard errors in brackets, clustered according to home team.
*significant at 10%; ** significant at 5%; *** significant at 1%.
The same set of variables is included as in Table 18.6, Panel 1, column (a).
The coefficients indicate the average additional attendance during each match during the T20 period.

appears to have had a significantly negative impact. Consistent with the aggregate effects, other counties have a mix of positive and negative effects but none is significant at better than the 5 per cent level.[20]

Discussion

Overall our results suggest that the onset of Twenty20 cricket has not had the deleterious impact on first class county cricket that some commentators feared. Attendances at County Championship matches have held up well and continue to be particularly strong when matches are scheduled at convenient times, involve local rivals or are played at non-standard (festival) venues.

One potential limitation with the empirical work is the absence of a price measure. It may be that County Championship prices were cut in response to Twenty20 cricket and this explains why attendances have held up. In fact, anecdotal evidence suggests that there has been no significant change in pricing of these matches over the relevant time period.

The fact that County Championship attendances have held up well implies that the overall demand for domestic cricket attendance has increased significantly as a result of the introduction of domestic Twenty20 cricket. At the same time, hopes that Twenty20 cricket might act as a complement to first class cricket and lead to a resurgence in Championship attendance have equally not been realized.

Very few counties appear to have been successful in persuading new spectators at Twenty20 matches to attend first class games. Cricket administrators would do well to conduct qualitative studies of those counties, (such as Sussex and Nottinghamshire) that appear to have managed to make this transition successfully to establish whether these counties have applied particular marketing strategies that could be applied in other areas.

RESTRUCTURING DOMESTIC CRICKET IN 2010: A ROSY FUTURE?

The 2010 season was set to be a landmark season for professional cricket in England and Wales, with Twenty20 being pinpointed as a key driver for protecting the long-term security of domestic cricket. However, deciding upon an appropriate format that would be not only spectator friendly, but also consistent with feeding the England team with high-calibre players has resulted in several major u-turns. One of the early proposals was to create a new Twenty20 competition. This would have involved a major rebranding exercise utilizing a format that incorporated only nine teams (those located at the major international grounds). However, this idea was seen to be undermining the 18-team county system and inevitably lacked support from traditionalists as well as the smaller counties that would have been excluded. In an attempt to placate all parties, a new blueprint was proposed in which the full complement of 18 counties would be joined by two international teams, resulting in a 20-team format instead. However, in the light of the controversy surrounding Allen Stanford[21] (who was to be involved with one of these teams) and the emerging global recession, this proposal was also dropped in favour of a two division twenty-over competition with promotion and relegation. Teams were to have been given the opportunity to sign additional international players in an attempt to capture some of the features of IPL without going down the city-franchise route.

The original blueprint for 2010 involved a format in which the two division four-day competition, the 50-over Friends Provident Cup competition and the existing Twenty20 competition would survive. The expected casualty was to be the Pro40 competition whose format had been popular with spectators since its introduction in 1969. It was to be replaced by a rescheduling of the current Twenty20 competition to Friday and Saturday nights during July, August and early September (previously played predominantly in June) with a new 20-over competition held in June called P20. Its format would take a lead from the success of the inaugural IPL in 2008 and the 2009 IPL (which, for security reasons, had been held in South Africa).

Two 20-over competitions would generate a number of interesting issues: one of the main unknowns was the degree to which P20 will be seen as a substitute good or complementary good for the existing Twenty20 competition and indeed, whether P20's existence will have an impact on the demand for other forms of domestic cricket (50 over and four day). The question of the future impact of a second 20-over competition could have been considered in historical terms; when one-day cricket emerged in the early 1960s, it was a revolutionary format that proved to be highly attractive to spectators. As a result, the authorities were encouraged to establish additional competitions (albeit using different over limits) and ultimately to take the format to the international stage. Thus, if consumers' appetites for an even shorter version of the game have increased, the overall impact may have been positive. However, it would have been wrong to expect the near-full grounds associated with the current Twenty20 competition to be replicated when it was rescheduled. P20 was likely to be marketed heavily and if additional overseas players were available to teams, it would have proved to be a highly attractive product to spectators. Thus, Twenty20 may have appeared to be an inferior product when seen alongside its P20 cousin.

On Wednesday 16 July 2009, the ECB finally declared that the new format for domestic cricket was to involve scrapping the Friends Provident 50-over competition rather than the Pro40 (EWCB, 2009).[22] A repackaged Pro40 competition would regain its former status, with each team playing a completely balanced schedule of 12 games within one of three seven-team divisions.[23] The winners of each group plus the best runner-up will contest a round of semi-finals and finals in September. The four-day game was to remain intact, with its two-division format. Twenty-over cricket was restructured with two groups of nine teams (using a north and south divide to generate as many local derbies as possible) instead of the current format of three regional groups. Games will be played in June and July, targeting days most likely to attract high attendances (Thursday–Sunday, rather than early parts of the week). It is expected that teams will be allowed to field an additional overseas player in P20 games.

This new structure may seem at odds with the fact that ODIs will still be played as 50-over games, a format that is to be erased from England's domestic calendar. However, the repackaging of domestic cricket reflects the fact that 40-over cricket had never become unpopular with spectators – the opportunity to fit a one-day game into a Sunday afternoon was still attractive in consumer survey responses. Furthermore, there remains some degree of doubt as to whether 50-over cricket itself has a long-term future, even at international level. Attempts to introduce innovations, such as 'power-plays',[24] reflect growing dissatisfaction about the time-line of action within games.[25] Thus, the status of the 50-over ODI is itself being debated by the International Cricket Council (ICC), with the possibility that it will adopt a hybrid format played over 40 overs with each team having two innings of 20 overs.

Cricket's ability to repackage itself into a variety of formats is a major product strength. However, it is essential that comprehensive datasets that differentiate between different types of spectator (for example, members, non-members, family tickets, promotional free tickets and so on) are gathered in order to provide researchers and the game's custodians with an opportunity to predict when spectators have reached their saturation with any particular form of cricket before the event rather than after it. Our work shows that the impact of Twenty20 has been mixed. A minority of counties such as Nottinghamshire have enjoyed not only a boost in attendances from the Twenty20 games themselves, but also a rise in attendances in their four-day games. In contrast, Surrey has enjoyed massive Twenty20 attendances, but its four-day attendances seem to have been affected adversely. Despite this caveat, it is hard to avoid the conclusion that the introduction of Twenty20 cricket has been a success story for cricket administrators in England and Wales. Introducing such a fundamentally new product within the crowded marketplace of English domestic cricket was a risky strategy. The administrators have managed to achieve significant new demand for cricket without affecting the demand for the core product. Further, the successful introduction of Twenty20 in the English domestic game paved the way for other national cricket boards to emulate and further develop this strategy, most notably through the Indian Premier League.

NOTES

1. Simon Rottenberg's 1956 evaluation of the baseball players' labour market can be seen as the first example of sport being evaluated within a serious economics journal.
2. According to Birley (1999, pp. 3, 363), Norman French contained the words 'criquet' (itself a diminutive of the old Flemish word 'krick', which means 'stick'), 'wiket' (wiquet), which means 'small gate' and 'beil' or 'cross-piece'.

3. There is no automatic promotion or relegation between first class and minor county leagues. Indeed, minor counties are rarely accorded 'first class' status (equivalent to an expansion franchise in North American sport). The last case was Durham in 1992, prior to which was Glamorgan's admission into the County Championship in 1921.

4. Prior to that date unofficial county champions were crowned (for example, by the sporting press), but the criteria used were not consistent, hampered by the fact that teams played different numbers of games over a season. As a result, cricketing almanacs tend to use 1890 as a starting-point when listing championship winners (see Table 18.1).

5. In four-day cricket, the onus is on both team captains to manoeuvre a game to victory within a four-day period when both teams have two opportunities to bat and bowl. Since there are no formal restrictions on the length of time that a team can bat, other than the desire to force a win, four-day games can frequently end in a draw if one team has been overdefensive (in addition to the possibility that both teams are evenly matched).

6. As its name suggests, one-day cricket is a significantly shortened version of the game with restrictions placed on the number of overs that can be bowled by each team (usually 50 overs per team, though historically games have encompassed 40-over, 45-over, 55-over and 60-over versions). Limits are placed on the number of overs bowled by an individual player and there are restrictions on the fielding positions adopted by a bowling team at different stages of the game. These restrictions favour the batting side with the aim of providing spectators with a more attractive package.

7. The experimental Midlands Knock-Out Competition was contested by Derbyshire, Leicestershire, Northamptonshire and Nottinghamshire in 1962.

8. The Players' County League and the Benson and Hedges Cup, respectively.

9. For statistical purposes, one-day games played between professional counties are referred to as 'List A' whereas longer games are referred to as 'First Class'.

10. It should be noted that the cricket season in the UK typically runs from April to September whereas for other major nations, the season cuts across years, typically November to March.

11. The international Test match is viewed by enthusiasts as the 'purest' form of cricket. Games are contested over five days in which both teams have the opportunity to bat and bowl twice. Currently, nine nations play Test matches against each other within a predetermined tour schedule. The nine Test playing nations are Australia, Bangladesh, England, India, New Zealand, Pakistan, South Africa, Sri Lanka and the West Indies. The first Test match was played between England and Australia on 15–18 March 1877.

12. ODIs are 50 overs per side games. The first ODI was played between Australia and England on 5 January 1971.

13. For logistical reasons, the ODI had been the preferred format for cricket's own World Cup, a competition which has been held every four years since its inaugural competition held in England in 1975 (most recently contested in 2011, a competition hosted jointly by Bangladesh, India and Sri Lanka. Given the rapid rise in popularity of Twenty20, it became inevitable that a separate international competition would emerge for this form of the game. The first was held in South Africa in 2007, followed in 2009 with a competition in England. Within these formats, non-Test-playing nations (such as the Netherlands, Kenya and Ireland) have the opportunity to qualify and play against the major international teams.

14. Particularly popular is the traditional 'Ashes' series with Australia, with all tickets being sold long before the start of the game.

15. Recently Scotland and Ireland have competed against the first class counties in this competition. This may seem something of an anomaly, given that both countries also contest international competitions, such as cricket's World Cup. This reflects their status as minor international cricket nations and as such, provides the opportunity for both countries to develop by engaging in more regular competition.

16. The IPL is a Twenty20 competition first contested in 2008 by eight city-based franchises. It places a strong emphasis on attracting the best of the world's cricketing talent

to play for teams (via an auction system) and packages cricket as a family experience with lots of 'razzmatazz'.

17. Noll (2003) differentiates between 'balanced' and 'unbalanced' competition formats. In the former, teams play all other teams an equal number of times whereas in the latter, some team pairs play against each other more often than other team pairs. Unbalanced competitions can be subdivided further into ones in which all teams play the same number of games and others in which some teams play more games than others. In the case of the evolution of the Twenty20 fixture list, teams have tended to play against their closest geographical rivals twice.

18. Teams that prepare a sub-standard (under-prepared) pitch that over-favours bowlers run the risk of a points deduction. Grounds with less sophisticated maintenance facilities are more likely to encounter this problem.

19. For example, Leicestershire traditionally plays fixtures at Oakham School, Gloucestershire plays at Cheltenham College as part of the Cheltenham Festival and Yorkshire plays fixtures at Scarborough as part of the Scarborough Festival.

20. County-specific estimates using the T20 trend are not reported here but are generally consistent with the average effects.

21. In 2008, Stanford bankrolled a winner-takes-all $20 million Twenty20 match contested by a Stanford West Indies XI and England. The desirability of England committing itself to what traditionalists saw as a vulgar circus split the cricketing community, a perception not helped by England's poor performance in the fixture. This view seemed vindicated when it emerged that Stanford was being investigated for fraudulent business activities in the US. As a result, the EWCB severed its links with Stanford, including an agreement to play further winner-takes-all matches involving England, together with the possibilities of Stanford being involved with the fledgling English Premier League.

22. Counties voted 13-5 in favour of the new proposals.

23. The additional teams are likely to be Ireland, the Netherlands, Scotland and the 'Unicorns', a team made up of former professional cricketers and aspiring players yet to attract a full-time professional contract.

24. Where restrictions are placed on the number of 'defensive' fielders that a captain can employ, thereby encouraging both teams to adopt an attacking strategy.

25. Matches are seen as 'drifting' during the middle part of the innings, with limited excitement for spectators.

REFERENCES

Becker, G. (1965), 'A theory of the allocation of time', *Economic Journal*, **75**, 493–517.

Bhattacharya, M. and R. Smyth (2003), 'The game is not the same: the demand for Test Match Cricket in Australia', *Australian Economic Papers*, **42**, 77–90.

Birley, D. (1999), *A Social History of English Cricket*, London: Aurum Press.

Cricinfo (2009), located at: http://www.cricinfo.com/ (accessed 14 January 2010).

England and Wales Cricket Board (EWCB) (2009) located at: http://www.ecb.co.uk/ecb/about-ecb/media-releases/ecb-unveils-2010-format,307430,EN.html (accessed 14 January 2010).

European Football Statistics (2010), located at: http://www.european-football-statistics.co.uk/attn.htm (accessed 14 January 2010).

Forrest, D. and R. Simmons (2006), 'New issues in attendance demand, the case of the English Football League', *Journal of Sports Economics*, **7** (3), 247–66.

Hynds, M. and I. Smith (1994), 'The demand for Test match cricket', *Applied Economics Letters*, **1**, 103–6.

Neale, W. (1964), 'The peculiar economics of professional sport', *Quarterly Journal of Economics*, **78**, 1–14.

Noll, R. (2003), 'The organisation of sports leagues', *Oxford Review of Economic Policy*, **19** (4), 530–51.

Paton, D. and A. Cooke (2005), 'Attendance at County Cricket: an economic analysis', *Journal of Sports Economics*, **6** (1), 24–45.

Premier Rugby (2010), 'Attendance Table 2008–09', located at: http://www.guinnesspremier ship.com/stats/attendance.php#8913 (accessed 14 January 2010).

Rottenburg, S. (1956), 'The baseball players' labor market', *Journal of Political Economy*, **64**, 242–58.

Schofield, J.A. (1983), 'The demand for cricket: the case of the John Player League', *Applied Economics*, **15** (3), 283–96.

Sport Industry Group (2008), 'Super League Breaks Attendance Record', located at: http://www.sportindustry.biz/news/view/2232/super-league-breaks-attendance-record (accessed 14 January 2010).

PART V

DIVERSIONS AND PERVERSIONS

19 The economics of the video-gaming leisure market
Joe Cox

INTRODUCTION

Video gaming has become a hugely popular activity within the space of the last few decades. The practice of playing video games can take a variety of forms, ranging from feeding coins into traditional amusement arcade machines to the use of dedicated video-gaming hardware or a personal computer and increasingly to mobile devices such as phones and personal organizers. Despite omission as a category in its own right in Aguiar and Hurst's (2007) large-scale study into the use of leisure time over the course of the last five decades in the United States, video gaming is a pursuit that is arguably reaching some semblance of maturity in both market development and depth of cultural content. As a result, video gaming is now being taken seriously within the mainstream as a major commercial force in the entertainment industry and as an art form in its own right. In terms of revenues, video gaming has recently grabbed a number of headlines by recording hugely impressive sales figures, especially in the context of the performance of other, more traditionally heralded constituents of the entertainment industry and of the general economic downturn. For example, the 2008 game 'Grand Theft Auto IV' set a Guinness World Record for the highest ever entertainment earner within the first 24 hours of release, selling 3.6 million units and generating $310 million in revenue (Guinness World Records Gamer Edition, 2008). By comparison, the fastest-selling box-office release ever was *Spiderman 3* (generating $60 million revenue in 24 hours) and the book *Harry Potter and the Deathly Hallows* generated $220 million revenue in the same time period. But how did the video games industry, once regarded as exclusively the domain of the 'geeky' teenage male, come to challenge other, more traditional forms of entertainment? What are the types of game available and how have these different types of game impacted upon usage patterns across demographics and global territories? This chapter will seek to answer some of these questions by detailing relevant aspects of the video-gaming industry from an economic perspective.

A BRIEF HISTORY OF VIDEO GAMING

The introduction of the video game can be traced back as far as the turn of the twentieth century. The alteration of the popular billiards game 'Bagatelle' through the removal of cue sticks and the addition of a plunger created the game known today as 'Pinball'. In the more conventional electronic sense, video gaming as we know it began with the development of 'Pong' by Atari in 1972. The game was so popular that by the middle of 1974, computerized Ping Pong machines were 'in every bar and bowling ally across the United States' (Kent, 2001, p. 58). In terms of video gaming in the home, the real stepping-stone that created the home console industry of today came about in 1975, when Atari released a home version of Pong that connected to a conventional television set. This was followed up by the 1977 release of a home console called the VCS (Video Computer System), which involved consumers being able to vary the game that was played through a system of interchangeable cartridges. This is a feature that has largely endured to this day, albeit with an evolution from software on cartridges to optical disc. Growth in the fledgling industry continued unabated in these early years, cemented by the release of 'Space Invaders' in arcades during 1978. The game was so successful in Japan that it caused a national coin shortage, and additionally met with resounding success in both the US and Europe. Early in 1979, Taito licensed 'Space Invaders' to Atari for release as a cartridge for the VCS, which was the first time that an arcade game was licensed directly for use on a home machine. By 1980, other firms attempted to establish themselves as major players in the market for home video games and, in an effort to win market share from their opponents, each released such a large number of games, gadgets and peripherals that it ultimately led to market saturation and collapse due to widespread consumer confusion over the huge array of products on offer – most being of poor quality.

In the early 1980s, Nintendo (a Japanese firm established 100 years earlier as a playing card manufacturer) attempted to fill the void created by this collapse through the expansion of its activities into toys and electronic games. The company developed and released a home video games machine known as the Nintendo Entertainment System (NES). The NES could produce more colours and better-quality visual effects than any previously available machine, and had more RAM so that it could address more pixels at any one time. However, the most radical departure from any previous console came in the form of its 'joypad' interface system. The pad utilized what has become known as a 'd' pad, shaped like a cross that could be controlled with the gamer's left thumb. Additionally, the conversion of Miyamoto's 'Super Mario Brothers' game onto a NES cartridge ensured its success. This product defined the difference between older systems and games that could be played on Nintendo cartridges. Although the home version of 'Super Mario Brothers' was not identical to the arcade game, it was an extremely close approximation. Competition came in the form of another Japanese firm, Sega, who released a very similar piece of hardware known as the Master System. Finding Nintendo's incumbency a significant barrier to entry, Sega quickly followed up on this initial release with a technically superior successor known as the Genesis (or Megadrive outside the US). Upon its release, Sega adopted an aggressive marketing campaign based on its technical superiority to the NES. When Sega started to siphon a substantial number of consumers away from Nintendo, the incumbent responded by releasing the Super Nintendo Entertainment System (SNES) in 1991. This began a series of iterative technical improvements to available hardware that would become known as the 'console wars', where this initial round continued into the mid-1990s. Sega and Nintendo continued this battle by releasing a further wave of new products – Sega developed the Saturn, which was the first of its consoles to read software from optical discs, while Nintendo released the Nintendo 64 in June 1996. What the two companies failed to account for was the potential for a new entrant to make a decisive impact on what had essentially been a duopoly. Sony, who had originally attempted to work with Nintendo to develop a CD drive add-on to the SNES, developed and released the Playstation console in 1995. This represented one of the most successful products in video-gaming history, marking a move away from children's playrooms and teenagers' bedrooms into the cultural mainstream. The Playstation afforded cheap and easy development of third-party software, which led to a large catalogue of available titles for the machine. As a result of the success of the console, Sega were forced out of the market, and Nintendo's 2001 GameCube console (which was clearly designed to appeal to a younger demographic) also suffered in terms of market share. Microsoft also entered the market at this time with its 'X-Box' console, which was heavily based on PC architecture and contained ports of popular PC games with high-spec requirements to the more affordable console market. It placed a greater emphasis on online play, with its innovative 'X-Box Live' service. Faced with an offering perceived as childlike from Nintendo and a new entrant finding its feet in an unfamiliar market in the form of Microsoft, Sony sought to capitalize on their position with the release of the imaginatively titled 'Playstation 2'. The Playstation brand had quickly developed into a market phenomenon and the sales of the Playstation 2 were massively in advance of any of its competition within that generation. At the peak of the battle in 2002, the X-Box and GameCube had each sold just under 7 million units worldwide, whereas the Playstation 2 had sold over 40 million units as of the same date (Pham, 2002). The Playstation 2 went on to sell over 100 million units by 2005 and became the first console in history to sell over 50 million units in North America by 2008 (SCEA, 2009).

The market, as it currently stands, consists of three market participants competing to establish the dominant technical standard in home video gaming: namely Sony, Nintendo and Microsoft. The present generation of hardware (the Microsoft 'X-Box 360', the Nintendo 'Wii' and the Sony 'Playstation 3') are bringing new innovations to the market in the form of high definition graphics, motion sensitive controllers, wireless connectivity and seamless integration of internet and multimedia features into the field of video gaming (the Playstation 3, for example, contains a Blu-Ray disc drive that also allows for the playback of high definition movies). It would appear that market share will be distributed far more evenly between manufacturers in this generation than in any previous iteration of the console wars. In particular, a principal reason for Nintendo's resurgence from a relatively precarious position revolves around the introduction of a highly innovative control system and a sleek, fashionable design which appeals to a much wider demographic of gamers. By contrast, Sony's latest offering has met with criticism due to a high price point and lack of sufficient volume of high-quality software. In a broader sense, the current struggle also affords the scope for video gaming to have a significant impact on the wider entertainment market, as consumer entertainment products such as PCs, consoles and DVD players inexorably head towards unification. Indeed the triumph of Blu-Ray over HD–DVD as the dominant technical standard for high definition video playback has been suggested to be, in part, linked to the inclusion of a Blu-Ray player within the Playstation 3. This (somewhat costly) tactic saw the adoption of the console in thousands of homes and bedrooms deliver a major blow to the possibility of victory for HD–DVD in the standards war (see Fong et al., 2008 for a detailed discussion of this particular technical contest).

The progression of technology in the video games market has tended to evolve in a series of distinct and iterative stages. Companies that produce hardware will typically release a single product or console to the market at any given time (and possibly one complementary product in the form of a handheld device). Each company will also license the right to produce games for their particular console to third-party games developers. A small volume of software titles account for a large majority of sales: 3 per cent of PlayStation 2, X-Box, and GameCube games released in 2004 accounted for 30 per cent of combined revenues for these three respective firms during that year (Nesbitt, 2004). At roughly the same stage in the product life cycle, all hardware manufacturers will seek to develop and produce a 'next-generation' device that will eventually supersede the current offering and render past models technically redundant. Each of these cycles has historically lasted for around five to six years, with each subsequent generation of console typically being technically superior to the last, while substitutable with other competing products from rival firms. Due to the degree of substitutability and comparability that exists between rival consoles and the limited opportunities available to redress any technical imbalance within a given hardware generation, there has previously existed a clear incentive for firms to meet or exceed the technical characteristics of rivals. However, the strategy adopted in the latest phase of the console wars by Nintendo has turned this paradigm on its head. In their most recent console iteration, the company have forgone the usual focus on graphical capabilities to concentrate on unique methods of motion-sensitive character control and interaction. Thus, the Wii has established a competitive advantage over its rivals via an alternative means rather than simply the ability to render more impressive images. Instead, the Wii has attempted to engage a wider audience in terms of age and gender than is typically associated with home video gaming. This strategy has met with considerable success, with the console taking a clear early lead over equivalent offerings from Microsoft and Sony in this hardware generation.

THE ECONOMICS OF THE VIDEO GAME MARKET

Supply Side: Producers

The video games industry is steadily developing into one of the more prominent global entertainment sectors. Global revenue streams from the video-gaming industry have followed a strong upward trend over the last few years. Table 19.1 contains data from market research group CMSG relating to the size of the video games market globally (that is, the sum of the three main territories: Japan, the US and Europe) between 2007 and 2009, with estimates as to the likely trend that will be observed from 2010 to 2012. As the table clearly shows, the value of the industry is forecast to increase incrementally every year over the six that are presented. Revenue from console gaming has been observed to increase dramatically since 2007, although this is predicted to plateau as hardware models of the current generation reach maturity. A similar trend has been observed and is predicted for both handheld and traditional PC games. The real drive in the growth of industry value is suggested to derive from the take-up of mobile (for example, video games played on mobile phones, PDAs and so on) and online PC gaming. This gives an indication of where the impetus

Table 19.1   The value of the global video games market ($ bn)

	2007	2008	2009	2010	2011	2012
Mobile games	1.6	2.3	3.1	3.8	4.4	4.8
Online PC games	1.9	2.3	2.9	3.6	4.4	5.3
PC games	5.4	5.7	5.7	5.8	5.8	6.0
Portable console games	5.7	6.0	6.1	6.3	6.4	6.4
Console games	15.6	17.8	19.3	20.9	20.9	21.0
Total	30.2	34.2	37.1	39.9	41.9	43.5

Source: IDATE Report (September, 2010).

for market growth is likely to come from, at least until the next generation of console hardware is released, when it is predicted that the current range will remain in place for longer than has been observed in the past. The combination of high development costs, as well as a demonstration on the part of Nintendo that superior graphics are no longer a requisite for differentiating hardware from that of competitors, suggests that manufacturers will be looking to introduce new and innovative methods of interacting with existing platforms as opposed to rushing towards the next iteration of hardware development *per se*. For example, Kazuo Hirai, chief executive of Sony Computer Entertainment, suggested in an interview that the PS3 has been designed with a ten-year lifespan in mind (Reuters Interview, 2008).

Considerable insight into the economics of the video-gaming industry can be derived from industrial organization theory, particularly with regard to the presence of network externalities in small numbers competition. Shankar and Bayus (2003) point out the importance of network externalities in achieving victory in the battle between Sega and Nintendo. Network externalities imply increased utility being derived from the adoption of the same hardware platform by other consumers, specifically in this case in terms of the ability of gamers to discuss, borrow and trade pieces of software between themselves. Additionally, in the age of the internet, similar utility enhancement is also derived from a vibrant and widespread online gaming community with respect to each console. The presence of network externalities in so-called 'standards wars' – a market contest between substitutable yet incompatible technical standards (see Varian and Shapiro, 1999 for a more detailed discussion) – means that there is a significant incentive to quickly achieve a dominant market share, even if the initial push to establish the prevailing technical standard results in short-term loss. Theory suggests that there is likely to be a significant first-mover advantage in the market for home video games consoles, as once an incumbent has established an installed user base, new entrants face considerable entry barriers that become increasingly severe the greater the take-up rate. This is compounded through the analysis of the decision-making process at the margin on the part of the consumer. Once an individual has purchased a particular hardware model at a cost of P_h, the marginal cost of purchasing a piece of software for that machine is P_s, whereas the cost of purchasing software for any other model is $P_h + P_s$ (this brief discussion of marginal expenditure on the part of video games consumers is largely adapted from Mueller, 1997). If there are indeed significant advantages to be derived from the rapid development of a large market share for a particular console, then the question persists as to why PC games tend to sell fewer units at retail than console games (see Table 19.1), considering that such a large number of households have access to this type of hardware – in other words, meaning that the PC has the largest (potential) installation base of any gaming platform. The key contributing factor here is the issue of cost. A PC has to be of a reasonably high technical specification to run the latest games and this is associated with relatively specific configurations of up-to-date (and relatively expensive) components. These components require updating on a regular basis if the gamer is to be able to continue to be able to play newer titles. Contrast this against the video games console, which is designed with a five-year lifespan (or more) in mind, which can be purchased for a fraction of the cost of a high-spec PC (often due to an effective subsidization on the part of the hardware manufacturers through the sale of their hardware at below cost) and requires little or no updating over the course of its lifespan. Although one might assume that PC gamers would be able to enjoy better-quality gaming as a result of the effort and expense required to maintain a gaming set-up, an increasing number of software companies have taken to the practice of releasing identical titles (with the same game play and very similar graphics) across platforms to increase efficiency of development expenditures (Microsoft, for example, release their games both on PC under the title 'games for Windows' and also for the X-Box 360). Thus, the range and quality of games available for console and PC is converging, calling into question the rationality of investing large amounts in maintaining a PC at a suitable spec for gaming, when the economic benefit derived over and above the purchase of a much cheaper home console is negligible.

One means by which the establishment of a dominant technical standard can be achieved other than through strategic entry is by providing a strong early line-up of software – so-called 'killer apps' that define a console and encourage the decision to purchase on the part of the consumer. As a result, early and visible evidence of extensive sunk expenditures on software development by hardware manufacturers can encourage consumers to sign up to a particular model in the period immediately following its release. Additionally, one of the most effective means by which killer apps can be secured is for hardware manufacturers to sign exclusivity deals with software developers whereby they will only release games on a particular platform (this is discussed at length in Katz and Shapiro, 1994). This was a strategy that at one time benefited Nintendo in their rivalry with Sega, and yet also worked against them when key partner Squaresoft switched platforms to support the original Playstation. This tactic continues to be evident in the modern era, with Microsoft notably agreeing a deal worth $25 million in order to secure exclusivity of the latest Grand Theft Auto IV add-on for their console. The ability to attract a good quantity of quality third-party software to a particular brand of hardware is suggested to be of key importance in Rochet and Tirole (2003), who state that an effective means to deliver this is to use the console as a loss-leader to install a wider customer base that will encourage software development. The manufacturers can generate returns based on royalties earned on each unit of software sold (indeed, this is a tactic that Microsoft has employed with the X-Box). Another key element to attracting software developers is the minimization of barriers to games development, such as cost and complexity, which is a much-cited reason as to why the original Sony Playstation met with such success. Finally, in-house game development of sufficient quality can help kick-start demand for the console, which in turn will attract the interest of third-party software developers. This is a strategy that has been employed successfully in the past by Nintendo, who are renowned for their well-known franchises and the rich quality and depth of their game-play experience.

Demand Side: Consumers

Historically perceived as a leisure activity appropriate only for children and teens, it is ironic that the present status of the video games industry has mainly been arrived at due to a shift in demographics. Video games are now largely targeted at the disposable income of adults – according to the US-based Entertainment Software Association (ESA, 2009), the average age of the most frequent game purchaser in the US is 39. With the intention of better understanding the incentives to game, this section outlines a model framework which is similar to that presented in Castronova (2003). It is assumed that video gamers (like any other economic agent) strive to maximize their total amount of utility or happiness. The individual decides how to allocate an amount of their scarce resource, time (T) to playing video games (V), which have a price (p) and earns the gamer some satisfaction (S), where:

$$s = f(C, M). \tag{19.1}$$

Equation (19.1) suggests that satisfaction derived from the game-play experience is a feature of the challenge offered (C) and the level of immersion which satisfies the need for fantasy (M). The exact functional form of equation (19.1) will differ from one consumer to another in accordance with their unique preferences – however, it is suggested below that these 'constraints' could potentially impact upon utility at the margin in a positive *or* a negative fashion, depending on their values in absolute terms.

The other obvious competing use of the individual's scarce time is undertaking paid work (L) which earns an hourly wage of (w). The consumer's income (Y) is a function of time spent working, such that:

$$Y = wL. \tag{19.2}$$

A final choice variable is time spent at leisure in a non-gaming capacity (Z), where Z essentially represents all available time not spent at work or gaming, such that:

$$Z = T - H - L. \tag{19.3}$$

The log-linear utility function becomes:

$$U(H, Y, Z) = s \ln (H) + y \ln (wL + pH) + d \ln (T - H - L). \tag{19.4}$$

The individual seeks to maximize the value of U given the choice of leisure and gaming time. As we would expect, increased wages can potentially have both an income and substitution effect, meaning those on high hourly wages can afford to purchase more normal goods (which we assume is a characteristic of leisure time including video gaming) and those on low wages are incentivized into spending more time gaming, at the margin, due to the lower opportunity cost of allocating their time in such a way. Individuals with hourly wages closer to the average will be those most likely to make sacrifices to their game-playing time in order to spend more time at work as the hourly wage rises, generating a U-shaped Engel curve (a diagrammatic representation of the optimal demand for a good as income increases) for video gaming.

The impact of price and income upon demand for video gaming was studied by Dickerson and Gentry (1983) who showed that the early adoption was associated with very high incomes – suggesting that gaming hardware has traditionally been regarded as a luxury good. However, with real incomes rising and the cost of producing technologically based hardware falling since that time, this contention is unlikely to hold in the present, where video games consoles are more likely to be considered a normal good. In terms of the price elasticity of demand for these goods, Clements and Ohashi (2004) demonstrated that US demand for video-gaming hardware is initially elastic with respect to price, but much less elastic with respect to software variety. The estimates of price elasticity for hardware offered in this paper are derived from US console retail prices along with two instruments designed to control for endogeneity of price: the one-year-lagged monthly exchange rate between the Japanese yen and the US dollar and console retail prices in Japan (introduced to account for cost shocks and quality perceptions in the Japanese market as opposed to the US). The estimations come out on average at –1.07, with the elasticity in the first year being –1.92 and decreasing to –0.52 after the console had been available for a period of seven years. Nair (2007) also attempts to estimate the price elasticity of demand over the life cycle of a game, showing estimated values ranging between –3.29 and –1.27 for the most and least price elastic titles, respectively. This paper also suggests that both prices and quantities of sales for software start high due to strong initial levels of demand, but that these diminish over time as titles are superseded by newer games. This somewhat calls into question the skimming strategy typically exercised by hardware manufacturers, whereby the initial price being charged is relatively high in the period immediately following launch and is then lowered over the course of the product life cyle (sometimes quite dramatically – when it launched in 2006, Sony's Playstation 3 was sold at an RRP of $499 for the 'basic' model and $599 for the 'deluxe' model, whereas the current RRP is $299 and $349, respectively). A strong argument can be made that there are enormous benefits to be derived from establishing a high volume of installed users early in the product life cycle, which combined with the high early price elasticity of demand would create a case for lowering the price. However, it should be noted that the manufacturing costs per unit are very high in the periods surrounding release, which limits the extent to which firms can pursue a strategy of low price and high volume of sales (according to Isuppli, the Playstation 3 was suggested to have cost Sony $840 per unit to manufacture in 2006, which would have led to them making a loss of some $250–$350 per unit: Isuppli, 2006). This may be a principal reason why Nintendo has been more successful this hardware generation, thanks to the relatively low technical standard and low price point of their Wii console. Nintendo have instead elected to focus upon innovative control and software design to derive market share.

Furthermore, cross-price elasticities of demand are found to be very low, illustrating that specific video game titles are generally poor substitutes for one another. Finally on this issue, Crandall and Sidak (2006) explore goods that are complementary to video gaming. For example, the development of more-advanced PC processors are considered to be complementary goods in consumption to video games, as one of the driving forces behind shifts in the technological frontier for personal computers is the extreme demands of cutting-edge games. Other elements, such as enhancements to internet bandwidth and the development of gaming peripherals such as the joystick are also among potential complements.

Consumers of video games around the world are generally divided into three main geographic territories: the USA, Japan and Europe. Historically, many of the current leaders in the market for home video games machines, such as Sony, Nintendo and Sega, have been Japanese firms. As a result, console games have often tended to be more Eastern in their style and approach than their counterparts on, say, the home PC. The USA is also an enormous market in terms of scale and for obvious reasons also ranks highly in the priority of video games companies. The ESA maintains some interesting statistics about the state of the video-gaming industry in the US. For example, it is suggested that 68 per cent of US households play computer or video games and that the average player has been gaming for a period of 12 years. They also suggest that video gaming has become a more popular pursuit among older gamers, with 25 per cent of Americans over the age of 50 playing video games, which represents around a 10 per cent increase from a decade ago. Europe, conversely, seems to attract less attention than its size and potential value as a territory would suggest, with relatively little representation among hardware and software developers. The need for extensive localization of software (that is, games have to be translated into numerous languages before release across Europe, whereas the US and Japan require only a single-language version of any game released) means that there is often significant delay in the release of games in Europe as compared to other territories. This delay can be compounded by the seasonal pattern of video games sales, where top titles are often held back until the winter to avoid the launch being lost in the summer months where demand for video gaming is usually observed to be lower (the exact timing, of course, differing by global region).

Anecdotally, US gamers are supposed to express a general preference for sports and action games, whereas Japanese gamers tend to express a taste for roleplaying games and those with a fantasy content. A study by Ngai (2005) found some evidence to support this, noting that four of the ten top-selling US games in 2004 (accounting for 15 per cent of total game sales that year) were sports titles, while a broadly equivalent level of sales in Japan was observed in relation to RPG or fantasy games. There is an asymmetry in terms of how games with a slant towards either a Western or Eastern philosophy are received outside their home territories

– Japanese-style games tend to be accepted much more readily in the West than the reverse. A good example of this would be the first-person shooter (FPS) 'Halo 3' for Microsoft's X-Box 360, which was among the top selling games of 2007 in the US, but did not make it into the top 100 games in Japan for that year. This may be due to differing perceptions concerning the appropriateness of content and disparities with respect to the morality expressed in Eastern and Western video games. In terms of gaming preferences differing by gender, stereotypically video gaming is perceived very much to be a male pursuit, with an early paper by Braun and Giroux (1989) suggesting that video games culture is strongly masculine, aggressive and violent. Games tend to contain aggressive themes, male voices and male figures on the screen at any given point (Durkin, 1995). The literature up until the mid-1990s is fairly consistent in relation to this point (see articles by Phillips et al., 1995, Funk and Buchman, 1996 and Griffiths, 1997 for examples). Typically, women have been observed in video games as objects or goals for males to work towards, rather than being genuine protagonists within the game in their own right (see Funk, 2001 and Heintz-Knowles et al., 2001 for more on this). Lucas and Sherry (2004) conducted a study to investigate gender differences in gaming. In a survey of young adults, female respondents suggest a reduced frequency of play time, less motivation to play video games in social situations and a preference for software titles that were less competitive in nature and involved a lower incidence of 3D rotation.

There is evidence, however, that this strong gender bias in video gaming is changing. The ESA (2009) state that 40 per cent of American video game players are women and that adult females represent a larger portion of the video game-playing population than males under the age of 18 (34 per cent against 18 per cent, respectively). The rebalancing of the demographic landscape (especially in terms of gender and race) of video-gaming players is at least partially being driven by the ability of gamers to play against one another online (Griffiths et al., 2003). This situation represents a distinct evolution from earlier times when games were primarily played in amusement arcades. While this afforded some opportunity for interaction between players, online video gaming allows for a much more integrated social and cooperative element to game play that would not really be possible in arcades. The online revolution and the shift of gaming to the home have also eliminated barriers to entry for some market participants, especially women (Herz, 1997). Hobler (2007) contends that more women are now playing video games and that so-called 'hardcore' female players were beginning to embrace male-orientated titles, although it is contended that the motivation for such action is not one of rebellion, but instead a desire for the social and interactive aspects of game play. However, problems are still identified in the paper in terms of the willingness of gaming culture to accept female players as being equal in terms of skill or contribution to the game as compared to their male counterparts.

In a broader social context, the practice of video gaming as a leisure pursuit is argued by some to contribute to the so-called decline of civic society in the West (see, for example, Putnam (1995, 1996)). Video gaming in its infancy was perceived to rest in the domain of the solitary gamer and gave birth to the enduring perception of socially inept geeks hunched over a joystick while festering in their bedroom. With technological progress and the advance of the medium towards maturity and mainstream acceptance, this image is increasingly becoming dispelled. The proliferation of social networking sites such as Facebook demonstrate that social interaction can be a central part of leisure activity revolving around technology. Within the medium of video gaming itself, the market has moved in recent years to embrace more socially inclusive concepts that break from the traditional video game. Leaders of this have been Nintendo, who have enjoyed huge success with their DS and Wii consoles as a result of encouraging multiplayer gaming within family and other social groups and pushing as before unheard-of concepts to the gaming fore, such as Brain Training (a series of logic puzzles and mental exercises designed to develop and maintain mental acuity) on the DS and Wii Fit (a motion-sensitive exercise and fitness program) on the Wii console. These games which focus on education and lifestyle improvement have widespread appeal due to their user-friendly control systems, such as the use of touch-screen and motion-sensing technology, which create far lower barriers to entry than the traditional gaming joypad.

Genres of Video Games

In the modern era, there are such a range of game manufacturers and sophistication of technology that a potentially infinite variation is possible in the context of game content. However, over the course of the development of the industry, certain distinct genres of games have become identifiable. The exact names and definitions given to these genres varies by source, but it is possible to extract certain common elements to most sets of definitions that allow us to categorize most video games according to the game play experience that is offered. An attempt is made in Table 19.2 to introduce a fairly concise summary of the different types of video game available.

There are some obvious connections between certain types of video game listed in Table 19.2 and existing media content: strategy and role-playing games as genres represent evolutions of forms of entertainment

Table 19.2   Video game genres

Genre	Example titles	Approximate US sales (2007)
Action	Legend of Zelda, Street Fighter	77 million units
Shoot'em Ups (inc. FPS)	Halo, Half Life, Contra Spirits	85 million units
RPG (inc. MMORPG)	World of Warcraft, Baldur's Gate, Netherwinter Nights	69 million units
Driving	Mario Kart, Gran Turismo	24 million units
Sports	Pro Evolution Soccer, Tiger Woods PGA Tour	215 million units
Platform	Super Mario Bros., Sonic the Hedgehog	38 million units
License	James Cameron's Avatar, Shrek	170 million units
Other	Including: strategy, simulation, puzzle and rhythm action games	72 million units

Source: Curmudgeon Gamer (2007).

(such as pen-and-paper (PnP) roleplaying games, or chess) that existed long before the advent of the video game, while action games can be expressly connected to movies and simulations to non-game computer simulations. However, some of the work appearing in publications relating to genre in video games has suggested that attempts to categorize video games in this way can be misleading, as these genres can be collapsed into very distinct similarities between games that blur these boundaries so as to make them redundant. Apperly (2006), for example, suggested that distinction between games should be made according to the nature of demands made by the game of the player – specifically in terms of either the requirement of constant attention (for example, action games that are 'hyper-performative') or games which require a more distant approach and strategic intervention at key points (for example, strategy titles). A further distinction can be made between games of various types based on the rating given to a game which defines the sort of content displayed in the game. Precise notation for different ratings varies around the world, but these systems typically differentiate between games with particularly violent or mature content, those suitable for teens or children and those with content appropriate for everyone. Thompson and Haninger (2001), however, maintain that the rating system applied to video games can be somewhat misleading. In their paper, 64 per cent of surveyed games that carried an E-rating (that is, 'for everyone') included intentional violence as part of the game and comprised an average of around 30 per cent of time spent on the game. In most of these titles, either violence was found to be a required element of the game for advancement, or the player was rewarded for taking such action in some other way.

Online Gaming and Fantasy

Most genres of game for both PC and the current generation of home consoles include an online element of some sort. This facility varies from offering interaction and competitive play to gamers across the world to the availability of downloadable content for games, such as new music tracks, costumes and map-packs. The practice has become hugely popular, with 62 per cent of all gamers playing games online (NPD Group, 2007). In the previous hardware generation, only the Microsoft X-Box provided a comprehensive, integrated facility for online play via its 'X-Box Live' service. Due to the popularity of this feature, all current hardware offerings (including handheld gaming devices) offer similar levels of online interactivity. However, X-Box Live remains the pre-eminent online service for console gamers, having recently been confirmed as the Guinness World Record holder for most popular online console gaming service, despite the fact that it remains the only online service within the current generation of video games consoles that requires a paid subscription to access most of its available content.

A particularly significant genre of online game in bridging the gender gap is the so-called 'MMORPG' (Massively Multiplayer Online Roleplaying Game), where players meet and interact with one another in rich fantasy worlds, such as that offered in the hugely popular 'World of Warcraft'. This is a game that allows players to take on the role of a fantasy character (such as a warrior, mage and so on) and to interact with millions of other players who simultaneously have a live connection to the game world. This interaction can take the form of cooperation to defeat large monsters or other non-player characters (NPCs), but can also take the form of hostile actions against other players that are associated with opposing in-game factions. This fulfilment of the need for escapism and fantasy is not limited to gaming in particular, being a potential attraction for leisure pursuits in general (in fact, this is not merely limited to computer and video gaming – other types of gaming can also offer similar degrees of fantasy and escapism, such as the table-top RPGs in the fashion of Dungeons and Dragons). However, one factor influencing the rise of this phenomenon is the freedom that games of this nature offer to players to create virtual selves without restrictions. This freedom affords the possibility for players to create avatars that resemble their ideal selves rather than their true selves (a feature that was formally observed by Bessiere et al., 2007). The process of character design may be an important aspect of the derivation of utility from these games on the part of female players in particular – as such, an understanding of the gender motivations behind character selection and customization becomes crucial. DiGiuseppe and Nardi (2007) look at the selection of character class in World of Warcraft, observing that females tended to be less likely to select classes that were specialized in mêlée combat (that is, those that fight monsters face to face), while the ability of a particular type of character to heal or having the inability to wear heavy armour were universally perceived as feminine character traits. Interestingly the choice of character class converged among more experienced players, of both genders, depending upon the usefulness of available traits to a team. Indeed, it is the teamwork and social interaction aspect of these games that seems to be driving their popularity among gamers of both genders.

This element of teamwork essential to the derivation of maximum enjoyment for most games invariably leads to a greater degree of social interaction. Williams et al. (2006) survey a sample of World of Warcraft players, finding that members of guilds (something broadly akin to a society or brotherhood) used the game to extend real-life relationships, as well as to meet new people or form new relationships. The social aspect is compared to that underlying the playing of a team sport, whereby both have rules and restrictions that in fact create a foundation for interaction and the creation of social capital. Additionally, as a testament to the strength of social interaction via this medium, a limited number of respondents to this survey indicated that relationships formed on World of Warcraft were of equal or greater value than their real-world relationships. Another issue that differentiates this genre from any other is the complexity inherent in various aspects of the game. Tychsen et al. (2007) found a positive association made between character complexity and enjoyment value on the part of players representing all genders, ages and levels of experience and that these associations remain constant even where the characters in the game are markedly different from the character of the player themselves. Nardi and Harris (2006) note that the complexity of collaboration in online role-playing games such as World of Warcraft, from the brief and informal to highly formal, organized and structured guild-level interactions, can be enjoyable and provide utility to users even in the case of the former. This is useful when considered in the context of the utility function outlined above, which accounted for the influence of game complexity upon satisfaction derived from marginal increases in hours spent playing games.

Despite the positive strides made by MMORPGs in attracting a wider variety of players to the gaming community, it is perhaps fair to say that the darker side of gaming has been more prevalent for players of this type of game than any other. This calls into question whether or not fantasy relationships formed in game play are substitutes or complements to real-world interaction. Where the two are considered substitutable, the individual afforded unconstrained choice can freely substitute online fantasy relationships for real-world interaction with a view to maximizing utility. Where choice is constrained in some way, the individual may be forced into something approximating a corner solution where a significant number of relationships are of the online/fantasy variety. The most likely scenario whereby an individual would be constrained in this way would be if there were a lack of opportunity for real-world social interaction which would limit the availability of substitutes to those relationships forged in the fantasy environment. It is clear to see how in a rational choice framework, this type of scenario could potentially lead to addiction and something approximating a complete absence of real-world interaction. Frequent game playing could potentially change tastes to such an extent that the individual finds it difficult to interact with others who are not sufficiently interested in gaming. As a result, the utility derived from interaction with non-gamers is diminished, encouraging the deepening of online relationships at the margin and as a result diminishing utility derived from interaction with non-gamers yet further. This issue of spiralling addiction in gaming is not a recent controversy: the use of the term 'addiction' was observed in the context of the proliferation of the (totally non-electronic) Dungeons and Dragons tabletop roleplaying game. In the modern era, these sorts of controversial habits are most likely to be discussed in the context of games set in a persistent online environment, such as that offered in the World of Warcraft, where addiction can have very serious consequences for the gamer's personal life. The following World of Warcraft related tale is recounted (along with several other horror stories) in an online article by Maugans (2007):

> I knew this guy in college that used to be really social. Had a hot girlfriend, lots of friends, was physically fit and looked decent.
> He got WoW and within 6 months his girlfriend was gone. Started fucking his best friend who is also no longer his friend. Guy ended up gaining 30lbs and turned pale as a ghost. I went in his room and he had like 15 bottles of urine stacked up along his desk because he 'couldn't leave the raid'.
> He had 20+ pizza boxes stacked up along the wall of his room. His room smelled like death. His sheets were stained brown from when he did sleep. He lost his job and flunked out of school. He lives at home with his parents now I think. I haven't seen him in a year or so.

This cautionary tale is far from unique. At the most serious end of the spectrum, addiction to games like World of Warcaft has been associated with the most appalling of consequences, such as the story appearing in *The Times* (2005) detailing how a man went into cardiac arrest and died as a result of a 50-hour non-stop online gaming session. In Korea in 2005, a couple were charged with manslaughter after leaving their four-month-old baby alone in their flat while they went to an internet café to play World of Warcraft. The child died after the couple spent longer than anticipated on the game (*Daily Telegraph*, 2008). In 2006, Holland introduced the first clinic for those suffering from gaming addiction, with some of the worst sufferers admitting to playing for 18 hours every day. Initial demand for the services of the clinic has been described as overwhelming, with the issue of video game addiction being 'a greater problem than was imagined' (*Daily Mail*, 2006). Despite these horror stories, studies by the likes of Ng and Wiemer Hastings (2005) have suggested that, while players of MMORPGs devote many more hours to these types of game than to others and find social aspects of the game a strong substitute for real-world interaction, the typical user does not display the characteristics of an addict. This study showed that 13 per cent of players spent between seven and ten hours a week playing this type of game, 25 per cent spent between 11 and 20 hours, 34 per cent spent between 21 and 40 hours and 11 per cent spent over 40 hours playing.

Economic theories of rational addiction would also suggest that high consumption levels *per se* do not mean that a person is addicted in a harmful way. We can introduce fantasy needs, on the part of the individual, into the utility function given above (See Cameron, 2002, pp. 158–61 for a general discussion of addiction and fantasy). Levels of demand are influenced positively by increases in the marginal utility derived from an extra unit of game-play time consumed, which in turn is influenced by level of challenge and fantasy immersion in a way that is not necessarily linear. The crucial factor making it an addictive good in theoretical economic terms is that there is temporal interdependency in marginal utility of consumption. Fantasy can also lead to the tolerance, reinforcement and withdrawal features highlighted in general models of addictiveness. We should finally note, on a broader psychological level, that features of personality may contribute to heavy time use of fantasy games. That is, the individual might be disposed to other activities that serve a similar function if fantasy games were not available.

CONCLUSION

This chapter provides some background information and economic analysis of video gaming, a leisure pursuit that is growing in significance in a large number of territories around the world. A short history of the development of the gaming market has been presented, alongside a consideration of some of the principal issues related to the industry from the perspective of economists. Finally, a comparison of different game-play habits across genres of game, gender and broad geographical location has been offered, with particular attention paid to online gaming and the phenomenon of the 'MMORPG'. Video gaming is undergoing a radical period of change in terms of its significance and perception on the part of the broader entertainment industries. Despite a comparative lack of academic study conducted by economists, it is perhaps only a matter of time before this rich and interesting constituent of popular culture receives the attention that its relative size and potential level of interest would seemingly warrant.

REFERENCES

Aguiar, M. and E. Hurst (2007), 'Measuring trends in leisure: the allocation of time over five decades', *Quarterly Journal of Economics*, **122** (3), 969–1005.

Apperley, T.H. (2006), 'Genre and game studies: towards a critical approach to video game genres', *Simulation and Gaming*, **37** (1), 6–23.

Bessiere, K., A.F. Seay and S. Kiesler (2007), 'The ideal elf: identity exploration in World of Warcraft', *Cyber Psychology and Behavior*, **10** (4), 530–35.

Braun, C.M. and J. Giroux (1989), 'Arcade video games: proxemic, cognitive and content analyses', *Journal of Leisure Research*, **21** (2), 92–105.

Cameron, S. (2002), *Economics of Sin: Rational Choice or No Choice At All?*, Cheltenham, UK and Northampton, MA, USA: Edward Elgar.

Castronova, E. (2003), 'On virtual economies', *Game Studies*, **3** (2), available at: http://www.gamestudies.org/0302/castronova (accessed 1 November 2009).

Clements, M.T. and H. Ohashi (2004), 'Indirect network effects and the product cycle: video games in the US 1994–2002', *Journal of Industrial Economics*, **53**, 515–42.

Crandall, R.W. and J.G. Sidak (2006), 'Video Games: Serious Business for America's Economy', Entertainment Association Report, Washington, DC, March.

Curmudgeon Gamer (2007), 'Another view of sales by genre and publisher', available at: http://curmudgeongamer.com/2007/02/another-view-of-sales-by-genre-and.html (accessed December 2009).

Daily Mail (2006), 'Game addiction clinic overwhelmed by cries for help', available at: http://www.dailymail.co.uk/news/article-397212/Games-addiction-clinic-overwhelmed-cries-help.html (accessed 25 August 2009).

Daily Telegraph (2008), 'World of Warcraft: massive queues expected at launch', available at:http://www.telegraph.co.uk/technology/news/3447598/World-of-Warcraft-massive-queues-expected-at-launch.html (accessed 24 August 2009).

Dickerson, M.D. and J.W. Gentry (1983), 'Characteristics of adopters and non-adopters of home computers', *Journal of Consumer Research*, **10** (2), 225–35.

DiGiuseppe, N. and B. Nardi (2007), 'Real genders choose fantasy characters: class choice in World of Warcraft', *First Monday*, **12** (5) (accessed November 2009).

Durkin, K. (1995), *Computer Games: Their Effects on Young People*, Sydney: Office of Film and Literature Classification.

Entertainment Software Association (ESA) (2009), available at: http://www.theesa.com/facts/index.asp (accessed November 2009).

Fong, M., P. Phan, K. Nghiem and P. Roldan (2008), 'Blu-Ray technology report', available at: http://mr-fong.net/documents/Blu-RayTechnologyReport.pdf (accessed 25 August 2009).

Funk, J.B. (2001), 'Girls just want to have fun', paper presented at the Playing by the Rules: The Cultural Policy Challenges of Video Games conference, University of Chicago, Chicago, IL, 26–27 October.

Funk, J.B. and D.D. Buchman (1996), 'Children's perceptions of gender differences in social approval for playing electronic games', *Sex Roles*, **35** (3–4), 219–31.

Griffiths, M.D. (1997), 'Computer game playing in early adolescence', *Youth Society*, **29** (2), 223–37.

Griffiths, M.D., M. Davies and D. Chappell (2003), 'Breaking the stereotype: the case of online gaming', *CyberPsychology and Behavior*, **6** (1), 81–91.

Guinness World Records Gamer Edition (2008), 'Confirmed: Grand Theft Auto IV Breaks Guinness World Records with Biggest Entertainment Release of All Time', available at: http://gamers.guinnessworldrecords.com/news/130508_GTA_IV_break_record.aspx (accessed 27 August 2009).

Heintz-Knowles, K., J. Henderson, C.R. Glaubke, P. Miller, M.A. Parker and E. Espejo (2001), 'Fair play? Violence, gender and race in video games', *Children Now*, available at: www.childrennow.org (accessed November 2009).

Herz, J.C. (1997), *Joystick Nation: How Video Games Stole Our Quarters, Won Our Hearts and Renewed Our Minds*, Princeton, NJ: Little Brown.

Hobler, M. (2007), 'Games, gender and digital culture: an analysis of three communities', thesis, School of Journalism and Communication, University of Oregon, Eugene, OR.

IDATE Report (2010), 'World Video Game Market', Montpellier, France, September.

Isuppli (2006), 'Playstation 3 offers supercomputer performance at PC pricing: teardown analysis of Sony Playstation 3 gaming console', available at: http://www.isuppli.com/Pages/PlayStation-3-Offers-Supercomputer-Performance-at-PC-Pricing.aspx (accessed 30 November 2009).

Katz, M.L. and C. Shapiro (1994), 'Systems competition and network effects', *Journal of Economic Perspectives*, **8** (2), 93–115.

Kent, S.L. (2001), *The Ultimate History of Video Games*, Roseville, CA: Prima Publishing.

Lucas, K. and J.L. Sherry (2004), 'Sex differences in video game play: a communications based explanation', *Communications Research*, **31**, 499–523.

Maugans, H. (2007), 'World of Warcraft Obsession', available at: http://www.harrymaugans.com/2007/09/03/world-of-warcraft-obsession/ (accessed 25 August 2009).

Mueller, D.C. (1997), 'First mover advantages and path dependence', *International Journal of Industrial Organization*, **15**, 827–50.

Nair, H. (2007), 'Intertemporal price discrimination with forward-looking consumers: application to the US market for console video-games', *Quantitative Marketing and Economics*, **5** (3), 239–92.

Nardi, B. and J. Harris (2006), 'Strangers and friends: collaborative play in World of Warcraft', in *Proceedings of the 2006 20th Anniversary Conference on Computer Supported Cooperative Work*, New York: ACM Press, pp. 149–58.

Nesbitt, H. (2004), 'Interactive entertainment: navigating the transition', cited in R.W. Crandall and J.G. Sidak (2007), 'Video Games: Serious Business for America's Economy', Entertainment Association Report, March, p. 14.

Ng, B.D. and P. Wiemer Hastings (2005), 'Addiction to the internet and online gaming', *Cyberpsychology and Behaviour*, **8** (2), 110–13.

Ngai, A.C.Y. (2005), 'Cultural influences on video games: players' preferences in narrative and gameplay', thesis, University of Waterloo, Ontario, Canada.

NPD Group (2007), 'Online Gaming 2007: The Virtual Landscape', New York, May.

Pham, A. (2002), 'Nintendo's first-half profit drops by 45 per cent', *The Los Angeles Times*, 22 November, 2002, p. C3, cited in M.A. Schilling (2003), 'Technological leapfrogging: lessons from the U.S. video game console industry', *California Management Review*, **45** (3), 6–32.

Phillips, C.A., S. Rolls, A. Rouse and M.D. Griffiths (1995), 'Home video game playing in schoolchildren: a study of incidence and patterns of play', *Journal of Adolescence*, **18** (6), 687–91.

Putnam, R.D. (1995), 'Bowling alone: America's declining social capital', *Journal of Democracy*, **6**, 65–78.

Putnam, R.D. (1996), 'The strange disappearance of civic America', *American Prospect*, **13**, 35–42.

Reuters Interview (2008), 'Sony PS3 sales in line with targets', 16 July, available at: http://uk.reuters.com/article/idUKN1533885420080716?sp=true (accessed 27 August 2009).

Rochet, J.C. and J. Tirole (2003), 'Platform competition in two-sided markets', *Journal of the European Economic Association*, **1** (4), 990–1029.

Shankar, V. and B.L. Bayus (2003), 'Network effects and competition: an empirical analysis of the video game industry', *Strategic Management Journal*, **24** (4), 375–94.

Sony Computer Entertainment America (SCEA) (2009), 'SCEA Milestones', available at: http://www.us.playstation.com/Corporate/About/ThePlayStationStory/Milestones/default.html (accessed 1 November 2009).

Thompson, K.M. and K. Haninger (2001), 'Violence in E rated video games', *Journal of the American Medical Association*, **286** (5), 591–8.

Times, The (2005), 'Korean drops dead after 50-hour gaming marathon', http://www.times online.co.uk/tol/news/world/article553840.ece (accessed 24 August 2009).

Tychsen, A., K. Newman, T. Brolund and M. Hitchens (2007), 'Player-character dynamics in multi-player role playing games', Situated Play, DiGRA Conference Proceedings, Tokyo, September.

Varian, H.R. and C. Shapiro (1999), 'The art of standards wars', *California Management Review*, **41** (2), 8–32.

Williams, D., N. Ducheneaut, L. Xiong, Y. Zhang, N. Yee and E. Nickell (2006), 'From tree house to barracks: the social life of guilds in World of Warcraft', *Games and Culture*, **1**, 338–61.

20 Competitive forces in the US recreational vehicle industry

Mark Fox, David Lane and Grant Black

INTRODUCTION

Michael Porter's Five Forces model is the most frequently used framework for analysing industries. The most recent formulation of his framework appears in a *Harvard Business Review* article (Porter, 2008). Porter's model reconceptualizes the strategy–conduct–performance (SCP) framework that was commonly used by industrial organization economists from the 1950s to the early 1980s (Lee, 2007). In this chapter we show how Porter's framework can be applied to a leisure industry, namely the recreational vehicle (RV) industry in the United States. Before progressing, we should note that the term 'recreational vehicle' can be used to describe various types of motorhomes, travel trailers and caravans. There are five major types of RVs:

- Class A motorhomes are motorized units, built on a bus chassis. Type A and Type C motorhomes feature a kitchen, private master bedroom, bathroom, eating and living areas. Type A motorhomes are the largest and most luxurious, sleeping up to six people. These motorhomes often feature a diesel engine.
- Class B motorhomes are essentially conversions of vans and are not commonplace. Typically featuring high-end craftsmanship, they are no larger than a typical van and are designed to sleep two.
- Class C motorhomes are motorized units built on a van frame, with a bed over the cab.
- Trailers are larger trailers or pop-up camper trailers. Generally, travel trailers are similar to Type C motorhomes, but as they are not self-propelled they often have more interior space. Folding tent trailers have traditionally been designed with a folding tent on a trailer.
- Pickup truck campers are small versions of trailers that rest in the bed of a pickup truck. They feature a large bed, dining and kitchen area, a bathroom and generally sleep up to four people.

These different types of RVs often serve as substitutes for one another. Younger, less-affluent families may aspire to a motorized Class A or C vehicle, but may not be able to afford more than a pop-up trailer. As consumers age and their incomes rise, they may choose to move up to a larger, more expensive trailer and, finally, to a self-propelled (motorized) unit. If this is the case, then we would see a positive income elasticity for RV purchases. Providing support for this proposition, a study for the Recreational Vehicle Industry Association (RVIA) found that motorhome ownership reaches its peak in the 65–74-year-old age group (the group that has typically just entered into retirement), while the age profile for folding camping trailers peaks in the 45–54-year-old group and drops off rapidly thereafter (Curtin, 2005).[1] However, an examination of ownership by income does not produce such clear results for motorhomes. Ownership patterns by income support the hypothesis of owners trading up for travel trailers, folding camping trailers and truck campers. On the other hand, the income profile of motorhome owners shows widespread ownership across all income groups, with the highest rates of ownership among upper-middle-income households. This can likely be explained by the fact that most motorhome sales involve used units, which have undergone substantial depreciation. If they have been well maintained, or (if not used for extended periods) properly stored, such vehicles tend to still be in good working condition.

In the US, the median age of RV owners has remained largely unchanged in recent years, at around 49 (ibid.). From 1997 to 2005, the number of RV owners aged 35–54 rose by 700,000 to 3.9 million by 2005 (ibid.). Ownership rates vary by age, but are highest for those aged between 35 and 74. Indeed, 9.4 per cent of those aged 45–54 own RVs, as well as 10 per cent of those aged 55–64. Even one out of 20 18–34-year-olds own an RV. In 2005, almost 60 per cent of RV owners did *not* have children aged 18 and younger, living at home.

Comprising approximately 78 million people, the baby-boomer market is a key market segment for RVs in the US economy. Boomers are an active, affluent, consumption-oriented consumer group (Schiffman and Kanuk, 2009). By 2030, approximately 20 per cent of the US population will be 65 or older (ibid.). Active lifestyles, substantial disposable income, and increased life expectancy will contribute to their expected strong demand for RVs. Evidence indicates that those 50 and older devote more time and money to vacation travel than younger individuals due to lessening family obligations, sustained income levels and fewer required expenditures (LaMondia et al., 2009). By 2010, consumers aged 50–64 will reach 57 million in the US, 38 per cent higher than in 2000 (RVIA, 2009b).

Regardless of the underlying characteristics of consumers and their motivations, the time allocated for leisure has risen. Time for leisure, narrowly defined as active recreation, entertainment, social activities and relaxation, increased a substantial 4.6 hours per week in the US between 1965 and 2003 (Aguiar and Hurst, 2007). Further evidence indicates that US households devote, on average, approximately half of their total leisure spending to vacation travel (LaMondia et al., 2009).

According to Harris Interactive (2005), a little over half of RV owners used their RVs from one to five times during the year preceding their survey. This represents ten or fewer days of use per year. Surprisingly, about one-quarter of those surveyed took no trips in the preceding year. Those who used their RVs for more than six trips a year constitute only about a quarter of all owners. Lack of free time was cited as the main reason why RV owners did not take more trips. Part of the appeal of RV travel is the convenience that it affords. Examples of this convenience include: the ability to travel without having to pack suitcases; avoiding checking into and out of hotels; and the ability to move at the pace one wants without a rigid schedule. Hitlin (2005) cites the ability to travel on the spur of the moment, escaping to nature and remote locations, an opportunity to rejuvenate, and pursuing hobbies and passions as advantages of RV travel. Hitlin notes that, for parents, teaching respect for nature is also an important benefit of RV camping.

We now turn our attention to a discussion of the five forces that impact competition between RV manufacturers. The forces we examine now involve various demand-side considerations (the power of buyers and substitute products) and supply-side considerations (the power of suppliers, the threat of new entrants, and competitive rivalry).

DEMAND-SIDE CONSIDERATIONS

Here we discuss various factors influencing the demand for RVs, including the market power of buyers, complementary products and the appeal of substitute products.

Buyer Power

The ultimate buyers of RVs are primarily end-use consumers.[2] The power of these buyers is influenced by their ability to negotiate and by their sensitivity to prices (Porter, 2008). The demand for RVs has generally escalated over time. From 1982 to 2007, RV shipments nearly doubled in the US, and annual shipments exceeded the prior year in 17 of the years during that period (RVIA, 2008). More telling is that RV ownership rose from 6.4 million in 1997 to 8.2 million by 2005 (Curtin, 2005). Influencing this growth were increases in the incomes of RV buyers. The average real income of RV buyers increased from $55,000 in 1997 to $60,000 in 2001 and $68,000 in 2005 (ibid.). Average real income grew 9.1 per cent from 1997 to 2001 and 13.3 per cent from 2001 to 2005. In 2005 the average real income of an RV owner was approximately 12 per cent higher than the median income of all households in the US. Those above the median income drove all of the growth in RV ownership in 2005. The highest ownership rate (13.2 per cent in 2005) was for households with incomes of $50,000–$74,999. These upper-middle-income households are likely to be more sensitive to prices and have less disposable income than high-income households. Declines in wealth and disposable income among potential owners, as caused by cyclical economic contractions, increased fuel costs, and tightened access to credit, can increase buyers' sensitivity to RV prices.

With the knowledge that this year's RVs will soon be supplanted by next year's 'new, improved models', the focus of consumers and manufacturers on new models makes RVs somewhat perishable in marketing terms. Hence, while costs matter to RV owners, the features of particular models are typically more important. Only 38 per cent of RV owners indicate that cost was a determining factor in the selection of current RV types (ibid.). Features of the RV itself matter most. In the 2005 survey, the primary factors influencing RV selection by owners were the RV's amenities and features (52 per cent) and vehicle characteristics (44 per cent). Despite manufacturers touting the importance of quality and service, these factors seem to play only minor roles in influencing buyers' selection of an RV.

However, one factor that reduces buyer power relative to manufacturers is that making their own RVs (that is backward integration) is not appealing to most would-be RV buyers. Backward integration would be time-consuming and costly for buyers as it would involve a degree of expertise that the average person lacks.[3] Certainly, individuals may customize their own vehicles (particularly vans), but this too requires a degree of skill that the average consumer lacks.

The consumer behaviour underlying the demand for RVs mirrors Becker's (1965) theory of households' allocation of time. Becker's premise is that individuals within a household jointly act as producers and consumers so as to maximize household utility. Thus, households will allocate time to producing those leisure activities that contribute to utility maximization. Traditional microeconomic theory argues that individuals or households make decisions based on complex, rational calculations. In contrast, Thorstein Veblen suggests that people rely far more on social habits and norms (the prevailing lifestyle) in a given time and community (Starr, 2009). Veblen proposes that people are motivated by two primary considerations, namely a 'distaste' for activities that do not produce utility and a desire to be thought well of by others (Cook, 2006). The ownership and use of RVs provides a means of engaging in exploits that involve a form of conspicuous consumption (namely, ownership of a large vehicle that acts as both a means of pursuing those exploits and a status symbol). The Go RVing campaign states:

> Don't Look Back (Unless It's to Take in the View). Get away at a moment's notice – and take the comforts of home right along with you, including all of your favorite gear. If you like going places and doing things, you'll love RVing. These versatile vehicles are perfect for camping, for exploring our national parks and scenic byways, for tailgating, for weekend excursions – and so much more. (Go RVing, 2009a)

The conspicuous nature of RVs provides a means for families to signify their social status to others. As Cook (2006) observes: 'Leisure and consumption, when made conspicuous, signify social position within the leisure class and between the leisure and non-leisure classes' (p. 306). Starr (2009) argues that the defining components of prevailing lifestyles include: household demographics; modes of transport; and the composition of recreational activities. Veblen's view of consumer choice is helpful in explaining consumer behaviour over the life cycle. In the early-to-mid-prime-age phase of life, households will accumulate new household goods (including vehicles) as social norms establish the foundations of acceptable adult lifestyles (ibid.). As the prime-age years continue, wealth accumulation commonly leads to increased freedom to explore new consumption, including increased spending on leisure; and to prepare for the future, including the retirement years. Then, the retirement phase ushers in a major shift towards increased leisure. Retirement frequently involves major lifestyle changes including downsizing homes, relocating to more appealing areas, and increased travel. This Veblenian view corresponds to observed consumer demand for RVs and to the role of the RV culture. RV ownership expands during the prime-age years and is greatest in the retirement years. The RV culture influences consumer choices about RV ownership, usage, travel routes, campgrounds and other related decisions. Research indicates that households with children, particularly children aged six or older, are more likely to engage in recreational activities outside the home (Bhatt and Gossen, 2004; LaMondia et al., 2009), and that older households are more motivated to travel to socialize and visit others, such as family (ibid.). RV ownership has been increasing among families with children: 94 per cent of parents who own RVs consider them to be the best way to travel with children (Miller, 2005). This finding is consistent with research that sees family leisure as a means of 'facilitating family interaction and bonding, particularly for the married couple' (Harrington, 2006, p. 423). This view is reflected in the advertising campaign promoting RV usage by the Go RVing campaign (2009b), where families are seen engaging in activities such as fishing, swimming, playing sports and exploring nature. Also, Go RVing advertising literature commonly depicts images of children engaging in activities with one another, presumably leaving parents somewhat free to spend time together or with friends. Of course, these ideals may fall short of reality, contributing to 'tensions and conflict arising among family members, and for parents, guilt and disillusionment when the reality falls short of the ideal' (Harrington, 2006, p. 423).

Complements

The demand for RVs is influenced by complementary products – that is, goods and services that are consumed along with RVs. With complementary goods the consumer benefit of the two products combined is greater than the sum of each product's value to the consumer when considered singly (Porter, 2008). One of the more obvious complements to RV ownership is another vehicle (about 80 per cent of all RVs require a motorized vehicle to tow them). In addition to personal vehicles, boats, motorcycles, all-terrain vehicles (ATVs), snowmobiles, hunting and fishing equipment, and camping equipment, are all complementary to RV usage. Gasoline and diesel are other obvious complements to RV ownership. This is true, irrespective of whether the RV is self-contained or towable. However, fuel costs are not a major part of RV ownership costs. Having said this, when the price of gasoline reaches very high levels it can affect the demand for RVs (PKF Consulting, 2010).

In the next subsections we look at two complements to RV ownership, namely camping and owners' clubs.

Camping
RV owners generally exhibit strong family orientations (Harris Interactive, 2005). Approximately one-half of RV owners say that their children had some influence on the plans they made for pleasure trips. Consequently, they were likely to look for places to visit that had plenty of activities for children and teenagers, such as swimming opportunities, theme parks, sporting events, historical places or educational sites. Some of these activities may be also be present when camping. Hitlin (2005) found that camping was given as the major reason for purchasing an RV (87 per cent of respondents), followed by sightseeing (80 per cent), swimming (62 per cent), fishing (62 per cent), shopping (54 per cent), hiking (52 per cent), biking/ATVing (45 per cent), antiquing (45 per cent), and attending

festivals (44 per cent). All of these activities can be complements to RV ownership, with parks and campgrounds being the foremost recreational complements to RV ownership.[4]

The camping culture provides one example of the influence of social context on consumer choice. The broader camping culture (of which the RV community is a part) has been described as a complex social system that involves high levels of social interaction (Clark et al., 2009). As early as the late 1960s, evidence suggests the camping experience was shifting towards larger, more developed and organized camp facilities. Consequently, Clark et al. conclude that a 'new camping style emerged with associated behavioral expectations . . . more compatible with . . . increasingly social conditions' (p. 379). RV owners appear to be moving towards using private campgrounds and parks in place of public ones. Data from the National Park Service (2010) show that RV camping visits declined from over 7.87 million nights in 1979 to around 5.33 million nights in 2009. These data also show that tent camper visits declined from 3.42 million to 3.18 million nights between 1979 and 2009. There are a number of reasons for this decline (YPB&R, 2006). First, almost 70 per cent of RV owners book reservations via phone, as compared to around 30 per cent who book online directly through the campground or RV park/ resort. Many national parks now require online reservations (although they also hold a limited number of spots for 'drive-ups'). Second, among the amenities sought in both RV parks and campgrounds are larger sites, high ratings in national camping directories, attractive landscaping and cooking areas. These features are more prevalent in private campgrounds and parks.

Research by Kyle et al. (2006) illustrates the importance of the social component of the camping experience. Camping provides a mechanism through which to socialize and express one's identity. Even those who seek to escape into solitude through camping do not exclude the presence of close family and friends in that quest. Of further relevance is the work of Howard Becker, which was first conceived to help understand the social world of art lovers, but has been applied to the caravanning culture in the UK (Southerton et al., 2001). The caravanning culture in the UK is somewhat analogous to the RV culture in the US (we say 'somewhat' as there are more class distinctions in the RV culture, where upper-end Class A vehicles can retail at over $1 million). Becker (1984) defines a social world as a 'social organization [that] consists of the special case in which the same people act together to produce a variety of different events in a recurring way' (pp. 368–69). Taking this concept and applying it to caravanning, Southerton et al. observed that caravanners sought to resolve dilemmas regarding three domains: the need for routine versus novelty; security and anxiety; and the need for privacy versus the need to be social. These dilemmas necessitate that decisions be made by campers in order to maximize their utility (and that of their families). Needless to say, conflicts can arise between individual family members when they share differing objectives (for example, when parents desire a quiet vacation, whereas children value lots of socializing with friends, including bringing their friends into the family RV). Part of the appeal of RVing is that it can allow individual family members to pursue different goals, particularly in campground settings where varying activities may cater to the interests of different demographics and ages.

The shift in camping culture would be expected to have influenced both the RV culture and the demand for RVs by broadening the consumer base and enhancing the social nature of the RV experience. More generally, the RV culture parallels the camping culture. RV users form their own communities and cultures. These are expressed in various ways, including: various types of RV parks that appeal to different consumers; the formation of RV clubs; and through interaction outlets such as magazines, websites and festivals. Such social interaction and the sharing of common values bond RV consumers and influence individual consumer behaviour.

The increased socialization and growth in camping and RVing has necessarily led to increased demand for campgrounds as a complementary service to RV use. However, increased competition for parking and campsites could lead to lower utility derived from RV activities and from camping in general. This could influence consumers to allocate less time to these leisure activities. Evidence from a survey of visitors to a US national park indicates that traffic volume and parking affect visitors' level of enjoyment (Hallo and Manning, 2009). However, Clark et al. (2009) find little evidence that campers are put off by behavioural problems in developed campgrounds.

Owners' clubs
Owners of particular RV models or brands frequently participate in owners' clubs that allow for the sharing of experiences. These communities allow owners to network (typically through internet sites and magazines). Clubs also provide benefits to members including discounts at campgrounds. Clubs ostensibly encourage customer loyalty through information sharing and camaraderie. Larger, established RV manufacturers exercise their market power to get better rates and special offers for their members. Despite such efforts to create loyalty, there is relatively low brand commitment on the part of RV owners: 80 per cent of those who have purchased more than one RV do not purchase the same brand as that they owned previously (Harris Interactive, 2005).

Owners' clubs are a means for people with similar characteristics, lifestyles or interests to benefit from socializing with somewhat similar individuals. Historically, RVing has been undertaken disproportionately by Caucasians in traditional male/female partnerships, either with children or empty-nesters. To explain such disproportionate outcomes, it is instructive to consider dominant theories that examine differences in leisure participation across groups. These theories focus on the perspectives of marginality and ethnicity (Bowker and Leeworthy, 1998; Martin, 2004; Philipp, 1999 and 2000). *Marginality* focuses on the role of differences across groups in socioeconomic factors such as income, transport and other resources. *Ethnicity* focuses on the impact of subcultural differences across groups, proposing that groups may have different cultural views on leisure activities. In the context of RVing, marginality theory suggests that the dominant RV users historically emerged, in part, due to the higher disposable incomes of Caucasians compared to minority groups, and due to the presence of asymmetric information about RVing across groups. Ethnicity theories argue that differences in participation have arisen because of distinct differences in how subcultures view the RV lifestyle and activities; evidence suggests, for example, that African-Americans view outdoor recreation differently from Caucasians (Carr and Williams, 1993; Bowker and Leeworthy, 1998).

When a leisure pursuit is dominated by a given group, this can lead to various issues for minority groups. If not addressed, such issues may lead to reduced utility for both minority and majority groups. Writing on the issue of access to leisure for disadvantaged groups, Bull et al. (2003) note:

> The introduction of team and club members from minority groups can lead others to become guarded in informal interactions and social contexts in order to avoid causing offense. This can, however, result in the minority group members being unintentionally marginalized at social events and excluded from more relaxed club interaction and humour. It can also lead to individuals from minority groups becoming subdued and striving to display what may be regarded as conventional behavior in order to conform to expectations and 'fit in'. This, in turn, denies any real chance of an integrated and shared leisure experience. (p. 95)

Thus, in addition to marginality and subculture, the perception or existence of discrimination in leisure activities may contribute to differences in participation between majority and minority groups. For example, evidence indicates that minorities reduce their use of public spaces (such as parks) due to greater perceptions of possible discrimination caused by increased interaction with other (dominant) groups (West, 1989; Blahna and Black, 1993; Floyd et al., 1993). Further, Floyd and Gramann (1995) show that minorities' perceptions of discrimination related to visiting recreational areas are tied to marginality and assimilation in the dominant subculture (in particular, perceptions of discrimination increase with low socioeconomic mobility and assimilation). Importantly, Philipp (1999) finds that middle-class African-Americans and Caucasians in the US perceive similar acceptance for African-Americans to participate in a wide range of leisure activities, suggesting that leisure activities likely have racial information surrounding them that is generally understood across groups. Moreover, African-Americans perceive significantly lower acceptance in many leisure activities than Caucasians believe exists for African-Americans. This would likely influence participation by African-Americans in these forms of leisure. More broadly, given meaningful perceptions of prejudice and discrimination, it could be expected that minorities would limit their participation in majority-dominated activities (or, at least, those activities with less informal or formal social controls against discrimination) and minimize integration with the majority group (Philipp, 2000; Martin, 2004). As a result, minorities have an incentive to participate in leisure in more familiar surroundings with those of the same group, thus perpetuating their limited participation in certain leisure activities (see, Craig, 1972; Philipp, 1994).

Concerns such as those just described (and their resulting impacts on behaviour) may be apparent for various minority groups of RV owners, including those with disabilities, racial and ethnic minorities (such as Hispanics and African-Americans), and gays and lesbians. For example, the Handicapped Travel Club was founded in 1973 and 'encourages people with disabilities and their families to travel, to meet and to share information on making recreational vehicles accessible for the disabled. "Fun and fellowship" is our motto' (Handicapped Travel Club, 2010). One benefit derived from membership of this club is the ability to gain support from others with disabilities, as well as to share ideas on how to gain the most from the RV experience, when living with a disability.

One RV group focusing on a racial minority is the National African-American RVers Association Inc. (NAARVA). Founded in 1993, NAARVA has over 1,400 participants (primarily African-Americans). They promote their membership benefits as follows:

> Experience the tremendous sense of community, see the country and meet new friends. NAARVA brings you the ultimate RV'ing adventure by offering you all these elements and more. NAARVA's members hail from all over the country enjoying the many events and functions scheduled throughout the year by this national organization. You'll meet new people, see new places and become part of a network of friends and professionals that enjoy the freedom that the RV lifestyle provides. (NAARVA, 2009)

Unlike the Handicapped Travel Club (which explicitly focuses on issues of RV use and having a disability), NAARVA does not implicitly focus on the benefits that may accrue from associating with people of the same race *per se*. The Club's reference to becoming 'part of a network of friends and professionals' is, presumably, meant to encourage NAARVA membership on the basis that it may also provide career benefits. However, the concern here is that becoming a NAARVA member may limit one's ability to network with other racial groups who may provide more career support. Having said this, members of NAARVA no doubt assume that they gain greater utility from this membership (and minimize any disutility that may arise from either racism or other factors), compared to belonging to RV clubs that cater predominantly to Caucasians.

Substitutes

The purchase of new recreational vehicles needs to be considered within the context of rival products. The closest substitutes are used or rental vehicles. Vacation and accommodation options that do not require an RV (for example, air travel, cruise ships, rental cars and hotels) also serve as substitutes to RV ownership. When the price/performance ratio of these alternatives improves relative to new RVs, substitutes will draw dollars away from sales of new RVs to end-use consumers. We now discuss two substitutes to new RVs, namely rental and used vehicles.

Rental vehicles

For most consumers the major substitutes for RVs are other forms of travel, accommodation and vacationing: travel in a personal car, by plane or train, hotels, vacation homes or condominiums (purchased or rented), cruise ships, organized tours; or deciding not to travel at all. Which alternatives a given consumer views as a substitute will depend on whether an RV is seen as a means of travel or as a means of vacationing. Hotels may be a substitute for RVs, regardless of whether the goal is travel or vacation, whereas many of the other substitutes listed are more relevant to the vacation-orientated potential RV owner.

Rental RVs serve as a substitute for RV ownership. By renting, potential buyers can explore the possibilities of ownership through an extended 'test drive'/vacation. Renting also allows consumers to try different types of RVs to find out which types and models best meet their needs. Renting is a viable alternative to RV ownership for consumers who want to reduce the long-term costs associated with RV ownership, while still enjoying the benefits of RV use. Rentals work well for vacationers who are seeking to keep costs down and who value flexibility in travel. All types of RVs can be rented, though the most common rentals are self-propelled motorhomes (Types A, B and C). Frequently, rental units are equipped (for a nominal fee) with housekeeping items, such as utensils, pots, pans, sheets and so on (Go Rving, 2009c). Rental rates range from about $100 a night for a pop-up trailer to $400 a night for Type A motorhomes.[5]

Rental demand can be met formally through organizations such as RV dealerships or informally through individual RV owners. Dealers who once only sold RVs now also generate additional revenues by renting out RVs. Much like real estate owners, RV owners can also generate new income by directly renting their RVs when not in personal use. According to Kurowski (2009), 10 per cent of dealers that were members of the national RV Dealers Association offered rentals in 2007. Between 1997 and 2002, the number of RV rental locations expanded 72 per cent while the number of RV dealerships offering rentals increased 14 per cent during the same period (Kurowski, 2005). Sales revenues from rentals at RV rental firms or dealers grew by approximately 63 per cent between 1997 and 2002, reaching $350.3 million in 2002. While systematic data are unavailable on private RV rentals, evidence suggests a sizeable nation-wide market (Owner's Rental, 2010; Private Motor Home RV Rentals, 2009; RVAnytime.com, 2009). RVAnytime.com, an online clearinghouse linking RV owners with individuals desiring to rent, indicates that it supplies over 12,000 site visitors per month who want to rent RVs.

Used RVs
The closest substitute for a new RV is a used vehicle. According to Harris Interactive (2005) slightly more than half of all RV owners have a used RV, and first-time purchasers are more likely to purchase a used RV than repeat owners.

Curtin (2005) provides a detailed breakdown of the used RV market. The majority of used RV transactions involve private parties (dealers sold only about one-third of all used units). According to the 2007 Economic Census Report, dealer sales of used RVs amounted to $4.6 billion in 2007, implying that the used RV market in that year was approximately $13.7 billion (Kurowski, 2009). This compares with retail sales of new units of $14.5 billion for the same year (RVIA, 2008). However, sales of used units are still important to RV dealers. The gross margin as percentage of sales on used units is historically higher than on new units. For the 1998–2008 period, gross margins on used units varied from 18 to 21 per cent, while those on new units varied from around 12 to 15 per cent (Broadus, 2009).

For consumers there are important differences in buying a used RV from a dealer rather than from a private party. Generally, used RVs sold in private party transactions tend to be older than those purchased from dealers. The mean age of used RVs in private party sales was 11.4 years compared to 6.6 years for used RV sales (the respective medians, which are not skewed by the oldest vehicles, are 9.6 and 5.3 years). Although these average ages testify to the construction and durability of RVs, this implies that the majority of used RVs sold have fewer features (or less-modern features) and are likely in poorer condition than those sold by dealers. The older age of RVs sold in the private market also implies higher maintenance and repair costs. These features may lead many consumers to have a lower idea of the overall quality of RVs.

With a mean age of 16.8 years, Class A motorhomes are typically the oldest among used RVs. This is somewhat surprising – given that motorhomes are far more complex than trailers or pickup campers it is to be expected that they would have a shorter lifespan. The average length of ownership is the greatest for motorhomes (7.4 years) as well, compared to an average length of ownership for all RVs (6.6 years). However, the short length of ownership relative to the age of RVs implies that RV owners trade and upgrade their units frequently.

Before discussing supply-side considerations, we shall now discuss the role of intermediate buyers, namely RV dealerships.

INTERMEDIATE BUYERS (RV DEALERSHIPS)

Dealer networks play an important part in the distribution strategies of RV manufacturers. Most RVs are sold through dealerships that sell vehicles directly off the lot, or take orders. For manufacturers with multiple product lines, maintaining separate dealer networks promotes competition among rival brands in similar price ranges, instead of promoting competition between a company's own products. Network agreements are frequently negotiated as renewable fixed-year contracts with little turnover of dealers over time.

Competition is strong among intermediate buyers in the RV market. Over 1,000 dealers are members of the National RV Dealers Association (RVDA).[6] Dealers are more concentrated in the West and South of the US, where RV use is heavier. A disproportionate number of dealers are located in just four states (173 dealers can be found in California, 154 in Texas, 102 in Florida and 60 in Arizona). Dealers play a key role in influencing customer choice as they can encourage customers to select particular brands, models, features and accessories. To take advantage of this influence, formal networks between manufacturers and dealers are common. Thor Industries, for example, had a network of 1,318 dealers in 2009, while Monaco Coach had 364 dealerships for motor homes and 619 for towable RVs and Winnebago had a network of approximately 280 dealers (Monaco Coach Corporation, 2009; Thor Industries, 2010a; Winnebago Industries, 2010b). Dealers entering into relationships with manufacturers can glean geographically exclusive sales rights, sales incentives, training, marketing assistance and other support services. Manufacturers benefit from distributing RVs to different locations and from the strengths of established dealers, including their reputation, financial strength and repair services.

The reliance of RV manufacturers on specific dealers varies greatly. Monaco's top dealer (Lazydays RV Supercenter, in Florida) alone made up over 9 per cent of its sales in 2007.[7] Seven dealers accounted for 25 per cent of Winnebago's unit sales in the 2008 financial year. Fleetwood indicates that no individual dealer contributes significantly to their sales revenues, while Monaco notes that its top-10 largest dealers generate one-third of its sales (Fleetwood Enterprises, 2009; Monaco Coach Corporation, 2008). When manufacturers face concentrated sales from a few dealerships, declines in sales by certain dealers could have substantial adverse effects for RV manufacturers. Such conditions impose greater power on a relatively small number of intermediate buyers who purchase a relatively large portion of a manufacturer's supply of RVs.

Backward integration (that is, making their own RVs) is not appealing to dealers. Intermediate buyers would have an incentive to backward integrate if the manufacturing of RVs were sufficiently profitable to warrant entry into the market.

SUPPLY-SIDE CONSIDERATIONS

Now we consider the market power of suppliers and the extent to which barriers to entry and rivalry impact on the RV industry.

Supplier Power

Suppliers to RV manufacturers can exercise their market power by increasing prices, thereby creating higher production costs for manufacturers. If manufacturers face considerable competition and have little market power they may be unable to shift increased costs on to other market participants (notably dealers and end-use consumers) in the form of higher prices. When all firms within an industry face such constraints, profitability declines throughout the industry.

As we now demonstrate, the power of suppliers is not all that high (the most obvious exception to this is chassis suppliers). While there are numerous competing RV manufacturers, the industry is rather concentrated. The five largest RV manufacturers account for 64 per cent of US sales (Fleetwood Enterprises, 2009). In contrast, suppliers to the RV industry tend to operate in industries that are far less concentrated. For example, Monaco Coach purchases from around 1,000 vendors (Monaco Coach Corporation, 2008). However, not all suppliers are equal in influence. Several major suppliers are very large firms, including Caterpillar, Chrysler, Cummins Onan, Ford, General Motors, Michelin, Workhorse and Yamaha. Many suppliers provide several materials or participate in multiple product markets (for example, General Motors), while others are highly specialized (for example, Workhorse, a chassis manufacturer). Generally speaking, the large number of suppliers and the procurement technologies used by RV firms means that changing suppliers tends to involve relatively little in the way of switching costs, thereby reducing the power of suppliers. Although many suppliers locate close to RV manufacturers (the major locations for RV vehicle manufacturers are Indiana, where 74.5 per cent of RVs are manufactured and Oregon, where 13.3 per cent of RVs are manufactured),[8] the location of multiple vendors close to RV manufacturers makes switching between vendors straightforward.

The primary raw materials needed by RV manufactures are widely available and lack differentiation (for example, aluminium, steel, wood, plastic and fibreglass). Multiple suppliers exist for most materials and for manufactured components. However, several key components (particularly engines, chassis, axles and transmissions) are provided by a limited number of suppliers. Reliance on a single supply source (or on a small group of suppliers) inherently creates greater risks for RV manufacturers. Production disruptions can occur for RV manufacturers if suppliers have problems. Historically, when suppliers (such as large motorhome chassis providers such as Ford and General Motors) faced constraints they allocated parts to RV manufacturers based on the volumes previously purchased. If a key supplier were to cease production or reduce the availability of a given component, RV manufacturers would be adversely affected. Given this, relationships between suppliers and RV manufacturers tend to be somewhat flexible.[9] The cost of purchasing raw materials or manufactured components also depends on fluctuating conditions in various resource markets. The degree to which RV suppliers can pass costs on to manufacturers can impact the profitability of RV manufacturers.[10]

Some RV manufacturers are vertically integrated. In addition to making many of their own component parts, these RV manufacturers act as component suppliers to the other RV manufacturers. For example, Monaco, Fleetwood and Winnebago operate at the supply level so as to exercise greater control over scheduling, parts production and product

Table 20.1   Number of manufacturers, by RV type, January 2010

Vehicle type	Number of manufacturers
Travel trailers	78
Fifth wheel trailers	63
Motorhomes Type C	27
Motorhomes Type A	23
Horse trailer conversions	16
Motorhomes–van campers Type B	14
Sport-utility trailers	14
Truck campers	11
Folding camping trailers	10

Source: http://www.rvia.org/AM/customsource/INCL_manufacturers.cfm?Section=Manufacturers.

quality, and to more ably respond to market fluctuations.   There is little incentive for suppliers to forward integrate and become RV manufacturers. Suppliers are specialized in the areas in which they already operate and generally lack the expertise to forward integrate.

The Threat of Entry

Barriers to entering the RV industry are relatively high. This can be seen to by the relatively low number of RV manufacturers (see Table 20.1). Overall, there are only around 118 manufacturers, with those vehicles that are inherently more complex to manufacture having the fewest manufacturers. The most complex RVs to produce are self-propelled motorhomes (that is RVs that require no additional vehicle for towing). Other forms of RVs involve the manufacture of trailers or campers that are designed to be towed by other vehicles.

Utterback and Suarez (1993) note that when industries mature, barriers to entry increase and an existing distribution network can be a powerful barrier to entry. In our discussion of intermediate buyers we saw that many of the major RV manufacturers have large, established dealer networks. Established relationships between existing manufacturers and dealers make it difficult for new entrants to find dealers.

Capital requirements for entry into the RV industry are relatively small, particularly for towables. This is because towables do not require the same manufacturing expertise or capital to produce as motorhomes as they do not require an engine and cabin. While manufacturing techniques have improved over the years, the RV industry remains labour intensive.

Unlike, say, automobile manufacturing, RV manufacturing does not require costly, high-tech production lines as RVs are typically built up around a chassis provided by a third-party supplier. To some extent, this limits the potential for economies of scale in manufacturing. The scale economies that do exist are largely a function of accumulated employee expertise and specialization. Among North American automotive vehicle manufacturers, the top three manufactures have a 74 per cent market share (Mergent, 2009), compared to 64 per cent for the top five RV manufacturers we mentioned earlier. One likely reason for the higher concentration ratio for auto manufacturers is that they have higher barriers to entry – in terms of sophisticated manufacturing technologies, brand awareness and specialized labour needs (not to mention having to negotiate with unionized labour).

RV manufacturers also need to comply with numerous federal motor vehicle standards. Coachmen Industries notes that the RV industry is 'fairly heavily regulated' and that 'codes, standards, and safety requirements enacted in recent years may act as deterrents to potential competitors' (2008, p. 3). These standards include detailed requirements and performance standards regarding, for example, specific parts, such as inside and outside rearview mirrors. In addition to federal and state requirements, members of the RVIA agree to abide by that organization's standards. This is significant as the RVIA represents manufacturers of over 98 per cent of RVs sold in the USA (RVIA, 2010). Also, compared to RVs made by new entrants, those made by larger, existing RV manufacturers are typically more attractive to consumers. Given that most RV manufacturers also provide after-sales service/repairs, purchasing from a new RV manufacturer rather than an established dealer has an element of risk. Further, large, established RV manufacturers have their vehicles distributed on a national basis, thereby making it easier for customers to find parts and have vehicles repaired wherever they may go. In contrast, smaller manufactures may require that vehicles be shipped back to the factory of origin for repair.

RIVALRY

Major RV manufacturers invariably describe their industry as highly competitive. For example, Fleetwood states that 'The recreational vehicle market is highly competitive, with numerous participants. The five largest manufacturers represented approximately 64 per cent of the retail market' (Fleetwood Enterprises, 2009). These views are consistent with Porter's (2008) observations that competition is more intense when competitors

Table 20.2   Retail market shares

	All %	Class A and C %	Class A %	Travel trailers %	Ownership
Thor	27.8	13.9	13.0	30.5	Public company
Forest River	14.5			16.2	Subsidiary of Berkshire Hathaway, a public company
Jayco	8.8			9.9	Private, family business
Fleetwood	7.6	16.4	20.4	5.9	American Industrial Partners Capital Fund, private company (purchased in July 2009 as part of bankruptcy proceedings)
Monaco Coach	5.4	11.3	16.4	4.2	Owned by Navistar, a public company (purchased in June 2009 as part of bankruptcy proceedings)
Coachmen Industries	3.7	7.8			Subsidiary of Forest River (purchased in December 2008)
Winnebago	3.1	18.6	15.2		Public company
Tiffin			10.0		Private, family business

Source: Statistical Surveys Inc., Year-End 2007 Statistics, available at: http://media.corpo rate-ir.net/media_files/irol/63/63938/reports/Fleetwood08AR_08_14_08.pdf.

are numerous or roughly equal in size. As we mentioned earlier, there are a reasonably small number of RV manufacturers – around 140.

Kydland (1979) noted some stylized facts regarding industry structure, including: many manufacturing industries are characterized by highly unequal market shares; commonly the largest producer is about twice the size of the next largest, who in turn would be substantially larger than the next producer; and rankings of firms according to their market shares are fairly stable over time. Looking at Table 20.2 we see that the first two stylized facts fit the RV industry overall quite well. The market shares for the industry as a whole are clearly unequal, and the proportions follow the pattern predicted by Kydland. This pattern also holds for producers of travel trailers, though not for the Class A and C vehicles. There is no doubt that the major players are constantly vying for market share. Further intensifying competition is that there is no market leader in all market segments. Even though Thor is the overall leader in market share, they do not dominate the Class A motorhome category (where Fleetwood is the market leader), or the combined Class A and C category (where Winnebago is the market leader).

Some might argue that the concentration of RV manufacturers (as evidenced by the number of producers and their geographic locations) implies that the RV industry represents a 'contestable market' rather than a competitive one. Baumol (1982) defined contestable markets as existing where 'entry is absolutely free, and exit is absolutely costless. We use 'freedom of entry' in George Stigler's sense, not to mean that it is costless or easy, but that the entrant suffers no disadvantage in terms of production technique or perceived product quality relative to the incumbent' (p. 3). This is a rather strict definition as it implies that there must be virtually no barriers to entry and exit in a perfectly contestable market. Under such circumstances, existing firms live under the constant threat of 'hit and run' entry if they are charging high prices relative to their costs (that is, if they are making 'abnormal profits'). A more realistic scenario would be one where low barriers to entry and exit exist, thus leaving the market contestable in the sense that there is always the potential for new firms to compete with the existing suppliers. However, as Shepherd (1984) observes, it is highly unlikely that new entrants come in at full scale or that existing suppliers will not respond to the entrance of new competitors, as is implied in the theory of contestable markets. Thus, even if the RV market is contestable, it resembles a competitive market, regardless of the number of producers, because of the intense competition already in place. Market share is not a good guide to market contestability and given that there are barriers to entry and exit, we find the theory of competitive markets to have greater value in understanding this industry.

While none of the major manufacturers dominates all market segments, each competitor is committed to the business and aspires to market leadership. The following quotes demonstrate that market position is used by manufacturers as a selling point to consumers: Winnebago describes itself as 'the leading United States manufacturer of motor homes and related products and services' (Winnebago Industries, 2010b) and Thor states that when they 'joined forces with Keystone RV in 2001, the company achieved an unprecedented dominance within the RV industry' (Thor Industries, 2010b).

While demographic trends (particularly the ageing of baby boomers) are believed to auger well for the growth of the RV industry over time, shorter-term economic fluctuations make for erratic industry growth (see Figures 20.1 and 20.2). Erratic growth trends of the industry mean that

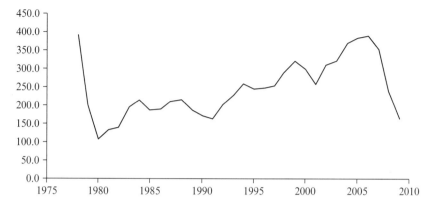

Source: http://www.rvia.org/AM/Template.cfm?Section=Historical_Glance; http://www.
rvia.org/Content/NavigationMenu/MarketDataTrends/Shipments/2008YearinReview/
default.htm.

Figure 20.1   *RV unit shipments, 1978–2009 (000)*

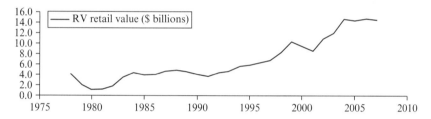

Source: http://www.rvia.org/AM/Template.cfm?Section=Historical_Glance; http://www.
rvia.org/Content/NavigationMenu/MarketDataTrends/Shipments/2008YearinReview/
default.htm.

Figure 20.2   *RV retail value, 1978–2007 ($ bn)*

in lean years, individual firms can only grow at the expense of competitors. Lean years also mean that RV manufacturers often have significant
unused capacity. Of particular concern to the industry have been declines
in shipments and their retail value since around 2006. In 2006, about
353,400 RVs were shipped by manufacturers, yet for 2009 shipments had
declined to 165,700 units. These pressures contributed to some major
changes for the industry. Fleetwood and Monaco Coach went into bank-
ruptcy and had operations purchased by other companies. Coachmen
Industries made losses in 2005 to 2008 and subsequently sold much of their
RV assets to a competitor, Forest River.

CONCLUSION

We applied Porter's Five Forces model to examine the US recreational vehicle industry. Our chapter began with demand-side considerations. The bargaining (market) power of consumers was considered first. Future demand for RVs will likely continue to be widespread across consumers. A 2005 survey of RV owners found that 64 per cent intended to purchase another RV in the future (RVIA, 2008). Of past owners, over one-third planned to buy an RV and one in six of those never owning an RV planned to purchase an RV in the future. As past and current RV owners comprise only one-fifth of all households, potential demand is driven predominantly by those who have never owned an RV. The passage of baby boomers through their peak earning years and into retirement should reinforce this trend towards more widespread ownership for the foreseeable future.

With regard to substitute products, direct substitutes to purchasing new RVs (namely renting or purchasing a used unit) were reviewed as well as comparing the costs of alternative forms of vacationing (flying, using hotels and rental cars, restaurants and so on). Our analysis indicates that the industry appears to be highly competitive with regard to substitute products. Profitability thus depends in part on how the industry deals with these challenges. While the RV industry is intensely competitive, players in the industry also cooperate in an effort to increase the overall size of the RV market. Notable among these efforts is the RVIA's 12-year multimedia Go RVing campaign. This campaign emphasizes the attractiveness and purported cost benefits of RV travel relative to other forms of travel.

We then discussed the supply side of the industry. The third force that we examined, supplier power, indicates that supplier power is in most cases not high and thus less relevant to industry profitability in the RV industry. This follows Porter's observation (2008) that the relative importance of the five forces will differ by industry.

Finally, we considered the threat of new entrants. We found barriers to entry to be relatively high, primarily due to the need to develop an effective dealer network.

Overall, then, we find that the rivalry among existing competitors is influenced more by demand-side than supply-side considerations. As RVs are largely 'luxury' items, the demand side will play the larger role in dictating what vehicles are manufactured and in what quantity. For example, with the relatively recent rises in gas prices and recessionary impact on incomes, there has been an emerging demand for 'greener', more economical RVs (Popescu, 2009).

NOTES

1. Throughout this chapter we rely on a study by Richard Curtin (2005) of the University of Michigan Survey Research Center. However, we should note that the study was conducted for the Recreational Vehicle Industry Association.
2. Foreign buyers also play an increasingly significant role in purchasing US-made RVs. From 1998 to 2002 foreign destinations accounted for only approximately 7 per cent of all US RV shipments (RVIA, 2008, 2009a). By 2004, foreign shipments accounted for more than 10 per cent of all shipments and in 2008 shipments to foreign destinations reached 23 per cent. Canada is the most frequent destination for US RV exports, receiving almost 22 per cent of all RV shipments. This is likely to be because of Canada's proximity to the US, which reduces delivery costs; to its relative prosperity; and to similar leisure/travel preferences to the US.
3. Historically, innovations in RVs arose from users who developed vehicles unavailable in a formal market when few RV manufacturing companies existed. For example, 'housecars', the precursor to the motorhome, were customized vehicles built on standard chassis in the early twentieth century. The necessity for innovations of this nature on the part of users diminished as the formal market for RVs has offered an increasingly wide range of products. Having said this, there are some companies that provide RV kits, although these are mainly for smaller trailers.
4. The amenities offered by campgrounds vary greatly. Traditional campgrounds, such as those in state and national parks, offer hiking, fishing and swimming opportunities, and some may have arcades, shopping and theme-park-like services (such as water parks). Many private RV campgrounds and resorts include flush toilets, hot water and showers, computer hookups, sports facilities, clubhouses, golf courses, lakes, pools, jacuzzis and spas. The locations of private campgrounds are frequently in very desirable areas and some of the luxury campgrounds offer RV timeshare lots.
5. Based on our survey of rates offered on the internet in late 2009. See, for example, http://www.rentrv.com.
6. Based on listings in the RVDA online searchable database (http://members.rvda. org/ScriptContent/Custom/GoRVingDealerSearch_new.cfm). Many dealers also rent RVs: the Recreation Vehicle Rental Association (RVRA) identifies 420 dealers who are members of the RV rental organization. While it is expected that the number of dealerships not affiliated with the RVDA or RVRA would not be inconsequential, the number is unknown.
7. Lazydays advertises as the world's largest RV dealership, with approximately $500 million in sales, 1.25 million visitors annually, over 400 employees, and an inventory of over 1,000 RVs representing 17 brands and 135 models (http://www.lazydays.com/ldadvantage.html).
8. Historically, increased interest in travel trailers occurred partly as a result of a display at the Chicago World's Fair of 1933–34. The motto for the fair was 'Science Finds, Industry Applies, Man Conforms'. Several major distributors located in Elkhart County, Indiana and sold largely to the vaudeville and carnival industries. As demand increased during the 1930s, manufacturers increasingly located in Elkhart (to be closer to distributors). Some employees of these initial companies then gained enough experience to start up their own manufacturing operations. The Second World War proved to be a boom time for the industry. The period saw the rationing of many materials and private trailer manufacturing; however, by securing US government contracts to provide trailers for housing at military bases, for employees in factories devoted to wartime production and so on, the industry was largely exempt from these restrictions on input materials. This also led to dozens of supplier firms moving into the area. By 1949, Elkhart County was known as the 'Trailer Capital of the World' (Hesselbart, 2001, 2010).
9. Monaco Coach, for example, maintains no long-term contracts with suppliers (Monaco Coach Corporation, 2008). The company also tries to minimize risks due to relying on a

single-source supplier by maintaining a 60-day supply of certain key components. Other companies follow similar practices (Fleetwood Enterprises, 2009; Thor Industries, 2010a).

10. The impact of resource prices would diminish if longer-term price contracts between RV manufacturers and suppliers were possible. However, many RV manufacturers maintain relatively short-term inventories, suggesting that fixed resource prices are unlikely.

REFERENCES

Aguiar, M. and E. Hurst (2007), 'Measuring trends in leisure: the allocation of time over five decades', *Quarterly Journal of Economics*, **122** (3), 969–1006.

Baumol, W.J. (1982), 'Contestable markets: an uprising in the theory of industry structure', *American Economic Review*, **72** (1), 1–15.

Becker, G. (1965), 'A theory of the allocation of time', *Economic Journal*, **75** (299), 493–517.

Becker, H. (1984), *Art Worlds*, Berkeley, CA: California University Press.

Bhatt, C. and R. Gossen (2004), 'A mixed multinomial logit model analysis of weekend recreational episode type choice', *Transportation Research, Part B*, **38** (9), 767–87.

Blahna, Dale and Kari Black (1993), 'Racism: a concern for recreation resource managers?', in Paul H. Gobster (ed.), *Managing Urban and High-Use Recreation Settings*, General Technical Report NC-163, St. Paul, MN: USDA, Forest Service, North Central Forest Experiment Station, pp. 111–18, available at: http://nrs.fs.fed.us/pubs/gtr/gtr_nc163.pdf (accessed 30 January 2010).

Bowker, J.M. and V. Leeworthy (1998), 'Accounting for ethnicity in recreation demand: a flexible count data approach', *Journal of Leisure Research*, **30** (1), 74–8.

Broadus, M. (2009), 'Benchmarking for success: analyzing dealership margins and expenses', *RV Executive Today*, June, 10–11.

Bull, Chris, Jayne Hoose and Mike Weed (2003), *An Introduction to Leisure Studies*, Harlow, UK: Prentice-Hall/Financial Times.

Carr, D. and D. Williams (1993), 'Understanding the role of ethnicity in outdoor recreation experiences', *Journal of Leisure Research*, **25** (1), 22–38.

Clark, R., J. Hendee and F. Campbell (2009), 'Values, behavior, and conflict in modern camping culture', *Journal of Leisure Research*, **41** (3), 377–93.

Coachmen Industries (2008), 'Form 10-K, 2007', available at: http://www.secinfo.com/dKmj.tj.htm#ln0h (accessed 11 March 2010).

Cook, Daniel Thomas (2006), 'Leisure and consumption', in Chris Rojek, Susan M. Shaw and Anthony J. Veal (eds), *A Handbook of Leisure Studies*, New York: Palgrave Macmillan, pp. 304–16.

Craig, W. (1972), 'Negro urban community: the role of cultural base', *Economic Geography*, **48** (1), 107–15.

Curtin, R. (2005), 'RV consumer demographic profile: the RV consumer in 2005', University of Michigan Survey Research Center, Ann Arbor, MI.

Fleetwood Enterprises (2009), 'Form 10-K, 2008', available at: http://fleetwood.investor room.com/index.php?s=127 (accessed 30 January 2010).

Floyd, M. and J. Gramann (1995), 'Perceptions of discrimination in a recreation context', *Journal of Leisure Research*, **27** (2), 192–9.

Floyd, M., J. Gramann and R. Saenz (1993), 'Ethnic factors and the use of public outdoor resource-based recreation: the case of Mexican Americans', *Leisure Sciences*, **15** (2), 83–98.

Go RVing (2009a), 'Hit the Road', available at: http://www.gorving.com/pubs/places_to_go_thing.cfm (accessed 19 January 2010).

Go RVing (2009b), 'Phase I–III Print Ad Pages', available at: http://www.gorving.org/pubs/phase_i__iii_print.cfm (accessed 19 January 2010).

Go RVing (2009c), 'Renting an RV', available at: http://www.gorving.org/pubs/renting_an_rv.cfm, (accessed 19 January 2010).

Hallo, J. and R. Manning (2009), 'Transportation and recreation: a case study of visitors driving for pleasure in Acadia National Park', *Journal of Transport Geography*, **17** (6), 491–9.

Handicapped Travel Club (2010), 'About us', available at: http://www.handicappedtravel club.net/htc-about.php (accessed 30 January 2010).

Harrington, Maureen (2006), 'Family leisure', in Chris Rojek, Susan M. Shaw and Anthony J. Veal (eds), *A Handbook of Leisure Studies*, New York: Palgrave Macmillan, pp. 417–32.

Harris Interactive (2005), 'Go RVing Communications Planning Study', New York.

Hesselbart, A. (2001), 'The history of the RV and manufactured housing industry in and around Elkhart Indiana', available at: http://www.amishcountry.org/elkhart.county.rv.history (accessed 20 January 2010).

Hesselbart, A. (2010), 'Personal interview', 27 January 2010.

Hitlin, Robert (2005), 'Campfire canvass survey', Robert Hitlin & Associates, Inc, Washington, DC.

Kurowski, J. (2005), 'RV rental business shows robust growth', *RV Executive Today*, April, 32.

Kurowski, J. (2009), 'New census data shows annual revenue at US RV dealerships approached $20 billion', *RV Executive Today*, August, 17–18.

Kydland, F. (1979), 'A dynamic dominant firm model of industry structure', *Scandinavian Journal of Economics*, **81** (3), 355–66.

Kyle, G., J. Absher, W. Hammitt and J. Cavin (2006), 'An examination of the motivation-involvement relationship', *Leisure Sciences*, **28** (5), 467–85.

LaMondia, J., C. Bhat and D. Hensher (2009), 'An annual time use model for domestic vacation travel', *Journal of Choice Modeling*, **1** (1), 70–97.

Lee, C. (2007), 'SCP, NEIO and beyond', Nottingham University Business School, Working Paper Series, Vol. 2007-05, available at: http://www.icsead.or.jp/7publication/workingpp/wp2007/2007-05.pdf (accessed 17 January 2010).

Martin, D. (2004), 'Racial differences in participation for selected leisure activities: marginality, ethnicity, or fear of discrimination?', paper presented at the annual meeting of the American Sociological Association, San Francisco, CA, August 14, available at: http://www.allacademic.com/meta/p110660_index.html (accessed 30 January 2010).

Mergent (2009), 'North American automotive sectors', available at: http://webreports.mergent.com (accessed 24 January 2010).

Miller, N.B. (2005), 'The joys of RVing' *TravelAmerica*, May/June, 24–7.

Monaco Coach Corporation (2008), Form 10-K, 2007 available at: http://www.secinfo.com/d11MXs.tGuw.htm#1stPage (accessed 9 May 2011).

National African-American RVers Association Inc. (NAARVA) (2009), 'An invitation to our future NAARVAites!', available at: http://www.naarva.com/Join per cent20Us.htm (accessed 23 January 2010).

National Park Service (2010), 'Annual summary report for: 2009', available at: http://nature.nps.gov/stats/viewReport.cfm (accessed 30 January 2010).

Owner's Rental (2010), 'Home page', available at: http://www.ownersrental.com (accessed 30 January 2010).

Philipp, S. (1994), 'Race and tourism choice: a legacy of discrimination?', *Annals of Tourism Research*, **21** (3), 479–88.

Philipp, S. (1999), 'Are we welcome? African American racial acceptance in leisure activities and the importance given to children's leisure', *Journal of Leisure Research*, **31** (4), 385–403.

Philipp, S. (2000), 'Race and the pursuit of happiness', *Journal of Leisure Research*, **32** (1), 121–4.

PKF Consulting (2010), 'RV vacations are least expensive, study finds', available at: http://www.rvia.org/Content/NavigationMenu/MarketDataTrends/VacationCosts/default.htm (accessed 12 January 2010).

Popescu, A. (2009), 'Eco-friendly green RV: the new travel trend', available at: http://www.petergreenberg.com/2009/05/21/new-travel-trend-eco-friendly-green-rvs (accessed 17 January 2010).

Porter, M.E. (2008), 'The five competitive forces that shape strategy', *Harvard Business Review*, **86** (1), 79–93.

Private Motor Home RV Rentals (2009), 'Home page', available at: http://www.privatemo torhomerental.com (accessed 30 January 2010).

Recreational Vehicle Industry Association (RVIA) (2008), 'Industry profile 2007', Reston, VA: Recreational Vehicle Industry Association.

Recreational Vehicle Industry Association (RVIA) (2009a), 'Industry profile 2008', Reston, VA: Recreational Vehicle Industry Association.

Recreational Vehicle Industry Association (RVIA) (2009b), 'Other relevant forecasts', *RV Roadsigns*, **29** (3), 4.

Recreational Vehicle Industry Association (RVIA) (2010), 'About RVIA', available at: http://www.rvia.org/AM/Template.cfm?Section=About_RVIA (accessed 30 January 2010).

RVAnytime.com (2009), 'Home page', available at: http:www.rvanytime.com (accessed 30 January 2010).

Schiffman, Leon and Leslie Kanuk (2009), *Consumer Behavior*, Upper Saddle River, NJ: Prentice-Hall.

Shepherd, W.G. (1984), 'Contestability vs. competition', *American Economic Review*, **74** (4), 572–87.

Southerton, D., E. Shove, A. Warde and R. Deem (2001), 'The social worlds of caravaning: objects, scripts and practices', *Sociological Research Online*, **6** (2), available at: http://www.socresonline.org.uk/6/2/southerton.html (accessed 23 December 2009).

Starr, M. (2009), 'Lifestyle conformity and lifecycle saving: a Veblenian perspective', *Cambridge Journal of Economics*, **33** (1), 25–49.

Thor Industries (2010a), 'Form 10-K, 2009', available at: http://www.thorindustries.com/corporate/10q10k/Thor10K_20090731.pdf (accessed 30 January 2010).

Thor Industries (2010b), 'Home page', available at: http://www.thorindustries.com (accessed 17 January 2010).

Utterback, J.M. and F.F. Suarez (1993), 'Innovation, competition, and industry structure', *Research Policy*, **22** (1), 1–21.

West, P. (1989), 'Urban region parks and black minorities: subculture, marginality, and inter-racial relations in park use in the Detroit metropolitan area', *Leisure Sciences*, **11** (1), 11–28.

Winnebago Industries (2010a), 'Form 10-K, 2009', available at: http://www.ir-site.com/winnebagoind/sec.asp (accessed 30 January 2010).

Winnebago Industries (2010b), 'About us', available at: http://www.winnebagoind.com/company/about-us (accessed 17 January 2010).

Yesawich, Pepperdine, Brown & Russell (YPB&R) (2006), 'The American camper: profiles and perspectives', available at: http://www.funoutdoors.com/files/ARVCStudyOverview.pdf (accessed 30 January 2010).

21 Magazines
Gillian Doyle

INTRODUCTION

Recent research suggests that, on account of factors including changes in the structure of the workforce and technological advances, the amount of leisure time generally available to adults in the US and other developed economies has gradually increased over time. At the same time, the number of pursuits and forms of entertainment and information vying for our attention in any spare moment has multiplied (Davenport and Beck, 2001; Lanham, 2006). A great deal of the extra leisure time available to US adults since the 1960s has been spent consuming media and especially watching television, as opposed to reading (Aguiar and Hurst, 2007: 987). Nevertheless, reading remains a popular leisure pursuit and in many territories including the US, the UK, Western Europe and Scandinavia, the magazine publishing industry enjoyed a sustained period of growth in the 1980s and 1990s.

Focusing mainly on the UK, this chapter introduces some of the key economic characteristics of consumer and leisure magazines and the nature of demand for these products. It examines how publishers structure their activities to spread risk and maximize their returns. This chapter considers the forces that have encouraged trends towards internationalization of high-profile titles such as *Elle*, *Vogue* and *FHM* and towards cross-platform distribution and digital editions. The ability to capitalize on economies of scale and scope through translating popular brands across additional delivery platforms (such as online and mobile), into more product markets and over numerous international territories is increasingly important to economic success in magazine publishing.

THE NATURE OF CONSUMER MAGAZINES

Although magazines are usually categorized alongside other mass media such as television and newspapers, they are different in so far as most consumer magazine titles nowadays are aimed at specific target audience groups rather than at 'the masses' in general. A good starting-point for understanding the economics of special-interest consumer periodical publishing is to be aware that a magazine's main asset lies in its title or, more precisely, the brand associated with its title. A successful brand establishes awareness and sustains appeal among a target group of readers who will purchase each new edition of a magazine, week after week or month after month (Gasson, 1996: 81). So branding and segmentation of market demand are at the heart of the business of magazine publishing.

The magazine industry is generally supported by two sources of income: advertising and direct copy sales to readers (Kaiser and Wright, 2005). The relative weighting between these sources of income varies from one title to another and among different sorts of periodicals. The industry is often subdivided between trade or professional titles (that is, those aimed at groups of people working in specific sectors) and consumer titles (that is, entertainment, lifestyle and hobby), with consumer titles generally earning a relatively lower proportion of their revenue from advertising than professional magazines (Advertising Association/WARC, 2009: 122). So consumer titles, which are the central focus here, are somewhat better insulated against the ravages of advertising recession than professional magazines, albeit that consumer publishing is by no means immune to downturns (Dennys, 2009; Luft, 2009).

Few econometric studies exist which systematically analyse national or international patterns of demand or price income elasticities for magazines. As has been suggested by Malthouse and Calder (2002), consumer experiences of magazines involve complexity and so readership of magazines can be difficult to conceptualize and measure. Nonetheless, in the UK as elsewhere, a wealth of information is publicly available concerning broad readership trends, circulation sales and advertising expenditure on consumer and business magazines. For example, data from the National Readership Survey for January–December 2008 suggests that 57 per cent of UK adults (64 per cent of women and 50 per cent of men) regularly read magazines (NRS data cited in PPA, 2009: 4). The UK Advertising Association compiles statistics on advertising expenditure on magazines while circulation and sales data is collected and analysed by industry bodies such as BRAD (British Rates & Data) and the Audit Bureau of Circulations (ABC), by consumer research organizations such as Key Note and by publishers' trade bodies such as the Periodical Publishers Association (PPA) and the International Federation of the Periodical Press (FIPP). While some of these data are compiled in order to help the sector market itself more effectively to advertisers, it nonetheless offers a useful resource to researchers and scholars interested in questions concerning demand for and expenditure on magazines.

Like all advertising-reliant sectors, magazine publishing is affected by economic cycles (Advertising Association/WARC, 2009: 9). Economic recession was widely regarded as a contributing factor to lower sales and advertising for magazines in 2008 and 2009 (Taylor, 2008: 38; Hughes, 2009: 5). But more generally, long-term trends in demand for magazines are dictated by factors including levels of literacy and, in particular, available leisure time and disposable incomes. Long periods of sustained growth in expenditure on consumer magazines across Europe in the 1980s and 1990s were fuelled by increases in leisure time and in incomes during these periods (Doyle, 2002: 137). Publishers in wealthier European countries (especially Germany, France and the UK) and in the US were well placed to capitalize on growth in demand for high-quality entertainment products in the 1980s and 1990s but, looking to the future, it is in China, India and other developing economies where literacy rates, levels of leisure time and disposable incomes are growing most rapidly. So, in the longer term, these emerging territorities are likely to provide a stimulus for future expansion in demand for magazines.

Like newspapers, magazines are characterized by high first edition and low reproduction costs (Picard, 2002: 54). Many of the costs involved in producing a magazine are editorial (payments for photographs, salaries for journalists, editors and so on) and so they remain fixed, irrespective of circulation sales. There are also important variable elements within publishing costs – paper, printing, distribution and so on. Nonetheless, marginal costs – the cost of supplying a magazine to one extra consumer – tend to be relatively low. So, magazine publishing, in common with other sectors of the media, is strongly characterized by economies of scale. As more copies of a magazine are sold, average production costs are reduced and so economies of scale and higher profits are enjoyed.

The availability of scale economies has naturally encouraged strategies aimed at maximizing circulations. Throughout the 1960s and 1970s, major publishing houses such as IPC in the UK, Condé Naste or Hachette in France, Bauer in Germany or Time Warner in the US tended to produce and print a relatively high proportion of high circulation (often general interest weekly) titles. However, from the early 1980s, a number of changes took place that caused publishers to switch their approach away from offering general interest titles towards specialist or niche publishing (Cox and Mowatt, 2008). Strategies of targeting of particular audience groups with similar tastes or preferences and of segmentation of market demand, whereby audiences are subdivided into ever-narrower specialisms, took over from publication of mass market titles.

A shift from mass market to niche titles took place partly because of increased demand, especially in middle- and upper-market sectors in wealthier countries, for more specialist features and hobbies publications with a focus on, for example, cooking, home improvement, design,

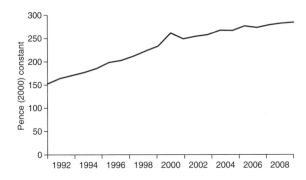

Source: WARC data in Advertising Association/WARC (2009, p. 113).

Figure 21.1   Average cover price of monthly magazines

photography and pets. But supply-side factors also paved the way for more segmentation and targeting. In particular, a move from hot to cold metal technology and the introduction of desk-top publishing around the 1980s radically reduced the costs involved in printing and made it more possible for publishers to introduce new titles with lower print runs. So, many new titles aimed at ever-narrower audience groups – for example, large boat enthusiasts; small boat enthusiasts, and so on – began to appear. In 2009, the number of consumer titles being published in the UK was 3,243 as compared with 1,383 back in 1980 (BRAD/PPA, 2009). As a result, readers are now provided with an unprecedented range and diversity of leisure titles covering a wide range of consumer interests.

Many of the additional titles launched in the 1980s and 1990s were monthly rather than weekly publications. As indicated in Figure 21.1, average cover prices for monthly consumer magazines in the UK rose sharply alongside increased prosperity in 1990s. So the series of new title launches embarked on by magazine publishers to capitalize on changing patterns of demand have been paid for mainly through higher expenditure by consumers on purchasing magazines, as opposed to higher advertising.

But the arrival of desk-top publishing and other technological advances has also been instrumental in bringing down costs and enabling publishers to respond to and indeed lead a process of fragmentation of consumer demand by launching new and innovative low circulation titles (Cox and Mowatt, 2008: 507). The strategy of producing a larger portfolio of niche titles with lower print runs rather just a handful of mass market titles has made it possible for publishers to spread their risks more effectively and

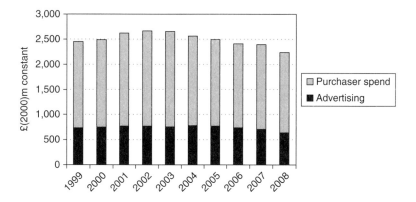

Source: WARC data in Advertising Association/WARC (2009: 122).

Figure 21.2   Total UK expenditure on consumer magazines

to draw on economies of scope rather than relying purely on economies of scale.

Additional cover sales income was a powerful driver for the growth of magazine publishing in the 1990s and, in addition, levels of advertising expenditure on consumer titles held up steadily throughout that decade (Advertising Association, 2000: 134). However, as can be seen from Figure 21.2, the size of the UK market has contracted slightly in real terms over recent years (Advertising Association/WARC 2009: 121). This partly reflects a slowdown for the sector following two decades of very strong growth but also, according to Küng, sales have fallen 'because consumers are increasingly "time poor" and and much of the expert information that [special interest consumer magazines] contain is now easily available online' (Küng, 2008: 44).

A general and ongoing shift in the attention of audiences, especially younger audiences, away from print media towards the internet and other digital media is reflected in all available international data concerning trends in media consumption and, in turn, advertising (Ofcom, 2008: 29, 33). The share of total advertising expenditure accounted for by the internet has risen sharply since the start of the twenty-first century and much of its gain has taken place at the expense of print media, especially newspapers but including consumer magazines – see Table 21.1. Other developments such as the launch of more colour supplements by weekend newspapers have also damaged magazines by siphoning off advertising revenues. As mentioned earlier, recession too has taken its toll with lower levels of magazine purchasing, a contraction in the number of consumer

Table 21.1   Share of advertising expenditure by media (%)

	2003	2004	2005	2006	2007	2008
Newspapers	30.8	30.3	28.5	27.0	25.9	23.8
Consumer magazines	5.0	4.9	4.8	4.7	4.4	4.3
Business magazines	6.6	6.4	6.2	5.9	5.4	4.8
Television	23.6	23.5	23.8	22.5	22.2	22.1
Radio	3.3	3.2	3.0	2.8	2.7	2.6
Direct mail	15.6	14.7	13.8	13.4	12.0	11.8
Other	12.2	12.1	12.0	12.1	11.8	11.3
Internet	2.9	4.9	7.9	11.6	15.6	19.3

Source: WARC data in Advertising Association/WARC (2009: 14).

titles and fewer new launches of new products in the period from 2006 to 2009 (Bilton, 2009: 5; Hughes, 2009: 13).

If understanding and responding to technological shifts and economic cycles is important in consumer magazine publishing, even more crucial is the ability to identify and interpret shifts and changes in culture. With relatively few exceptions, most consumer magazines have a limited life expectancy. So publishers need to identify and value the target market segment for a new title as accurately as possible (Gasson, 1996). This partly involves assessing any underlying cultural developments or fads and fashions that may impact on that segment of the market.

For example, one of the major developments affecting consumer publishing over recent years is the emergence and growth, since the 1990s, of a new 'men's lifestyle' category. Prior to this, the assumption among publishers had been that demand for magazines offering advice on issues such as relationships and appearance was high among women but non-existent in men. However, a gradual redefinition of notions of masculinity and of the concerns which might permissibly be associated with men opened out major new opportunities for publishers. Thanks to lower technological entry barriers to publishing, some of the pioneering titles that emerged initially in response to this opportunity were created by relatively small new players (Cox and Mowatt, 2008). The eventual result was a burgeoning new genre of men's lifestyle or 'lad's mags' (Benwell, 2003). Initially composed of monthly brands such as *GQ* and *FHM*, maturation of the men's lifestyle category and increased competitiveness among rival publishers for a share of this market eventually precipitated the launch of weekly titles too such as *Nuts* and *Zoo* aimed at more-specific demographic segments within the young male category (Andrews, 2006). The proliferation of this sector and its perceived role in fuelling an evolving 'lad culture' is by no means without its critics (Jha, 2006). However, the emergence, rapid growth and eventual cooling off over recent years of 'lad's mags' as a lifestyle category amply demonstrate the value, within leisure magazine publishing, of recognizing, understanding and responding to underlying cultural developments and trends that are going to help shape demand.

In assessing the viability of specific market segments and in calculating the likely profile of returns over the expected life of any given title, many publishers are increasingly turning their sights towards digital distribution platforms and international territories. Full exploitation of the brand image associated with a magazine title may well involve extension of that brand across additional delivery platforms such as mobiles and the internet and also into complementary product and service markets (such as, for example, organization of trade fairs), as well as international growth. Strategies of international and cross-platform expansion, which are central to maximizing the returns from a successful consumer magazine title, are examined more closely below.

INTERNATIONALIZATION

The process of so-called 'globalization' has affected media and communications quite profoundly (Chalaby, 2005). In an economic context, globalization is usually taken to refer to the whittling away, over time, of barriers to international trade – the gradual erosion of any legal or logistical impediments to transnational trade in goods and services because of, for example, more trade agreements, greater mobility of capital, more international inward investment and new technologies. Media are affected by all these factors (Chan-Olmsted and Chang, 2003). But in particular the infrastructure provided by the internet for global distribution of digitized data has had a major impact on media dissemination and on cultures of consumption of content worldwide.

While a globalized approach towards distribution is new to some media players (for example, newspaper publishers), there is a long history of strategies of international expansion in certain areas of media such as films, book publishing, music and, of course, consumer magazine publishing. Within periodical publishing, efforts to internationalize are not new but it is important to recognize that all forms of internationalization of media reflect a basic commercial impetus on the part of suppliers and content owners to try and squeeze as much value as they can out of their assets – their intellectual property – by expanding consumption of their output to as wide an audience as possible.

Because of the 'public good' characteristics of media content (the fact that the stories and messages in which the value of media content mainly resides are generally not destroyed in the act of consumption) and because of the prevalence of economies of scale and scope in the media industry, there is a natural incentive to expand consumption of your output to as wide an audience as possible. This includes expansion across international markets where this is feasible and, thanks to globalization, the opportunities to engage in international expansion have improved over recent years.

Advances in technology including transational satellite broadcasting and growth of the internet have provided opportunities for media companies, when faced with saturation in their own home markets, to instead expand outwards across international territories. Channels such as CNN, MTV, BBC Worldwide and, more recently, Al-Jazeera offer examples of transnationalized television services, and another form of international expansion is globalized exports of television programme formats such as *Big Brother*, *The Office* or *Britain's Got Talent* (Steemers, 2004). As each territory becomes saturated, the life of the product is extended by taking it to new international audiences. Print media publishers have also been engaged in international expansion (Helgesen, 2002). In the US and in Germany, France, the UK and Scandinavia also, major publishing houses when faced with growing competition and increased fragmentation of demand and saturation in their own local markets have turned to international markets to find growth, and many have met with success.

The process of internationalization of media, in which consumer magazine publishing has played a leading role, has been encouraged partly by the needs of the advertising industry (Hafstrand, 1995). Many of the clients of the advertising industry are themselves affected to a significant extent by globalization. More international trade has brought about fierce competition and a desire, where possible, to build brands that have instant international recognition and appeal. In the fashion industry for example, very many retail items (jeans, perfume and so on) are distributed and sold worldwide. Constructing a global brand involves heavy investment in worldwide advertising based on an expectation of higher aggregate returns across numerous international territories (Arvidsson, 2006). Access to global audiences is therefore a commodity which is highly valued by the creators and owners of global retail brands. So, television channels such as MTV or magazines such as *Vogue* that can offer access to a very specific demographic target group worldwide are well placed to cater to the emerging needs of the advertising industry.

In magazine publishing, the tendency to internationalize has a long history and this partly reflects the nature of the product which, relative to other media, has lent itself exceptionally well to overseas expansion (Doyle, 2002). The importance of branding and segmentation techniques in magazine publishing requires that considerable effort be invested in the creation of distinctive brand images that specific readers will identify with and remain loyal to. Often, the strength of a magazine's brand is sufficient to ensure that it will have some appeal for the same lifestyle group or niche across many different geographic and regional markets, albeit that some adaptation at the local level may be required. Because of their emphasis on visual material, many leisure and lifestyle titles are relatively easy to adapt into other languages and will not necessarily lose their core appeal in the process of translation.

Among the options available for expanding the reach of a magazine across multiple international markets, a contract-based approach is a popular model (Cabell and Greehan, 2004). In order to widen the international readership for a magazine, its parent company will adopt a strategy of publishing several different international versions. Doing so under contract-based arrangements means that, instead of setting up numerous wholly owned subsidiaries in other countries, the brand owner enters into licensing or franchising agreements with local publishers who, in partnership with the parent company, will produce a local edition of the magazine. Franchising is potentially very advantageous for both partners, and it minimizes many of the risks and costs associated with international expansion (Deresky, 2006). But sustaining a growing network of international local publishing partners can also involve complexity, particularly in the areas of communication and control over the brand (Doyle, 2006).

The process of extending any cultural product or brand across numerous different international settings is inherently much more difficult than, say, internationalizing sales of shampoos or mobile phones. The main challenge stems from the need to adapt the product appropriately to fit indigenous circumstances, sensitivities, tastes and so on. Franchising is often the chosen route for international expansion because this enables the brand owner to work with a local publishing company. The local partner is provided with a basic format and formula for editorial content, design, physical format and layout. But, in order to 'get it right' for the local audience, the partner publisher also has to be given sufficient freedom and scope to modify and adapt as required to fit local circumstances.

Some would argue that, in the era of the 'global village', local cultural specificities are becoming ameliorated (McLuhan, 1967). Differences in tastes and preferences among international audiences are gradually being eroded by processes of globalization which magazines and other transnational media have facilitated and responded to but, also, which they have accelerated (Cabell and Greehan, 2004: 8). However, the degree to which media globalization is really taking place is disputed by others (Hafez, 2007). In practice, awareness of the particularities of local tastes and values is essential in avoiding offensive or embarrassing editorial misjudgements, as some publishers have discovered only through making costly errors. So striking the right balance between protecting the core brand, which is clearly of paramount importance, and at the same time allowing sufficient editorial and operational latitude or trusting your local partner to understand what adaptations are needed is a major challenge for transational brand-owners (Doyle, 2006). Each company has to find the right sort of local partner to work with, as indicated by international publisher Chris Llewellyn:[1] 'International publishing hangs or falls depending on choice of partners. If you are going to get into a 3-legged race, make sure the other person is going to run as fast as you'.

Notwithstanding the challenges involved, the economic case in favour of extending consumption of a product through means of making minor adaptations to a basic or standard formula so that it appeals in international markets is very compelling. Expansion on this basis, whatever the product, generally involves low investment risks and enables the supplier to capitalize on economies of scale and scope (Deresky, 2006). But expansion of media products on this basis is especially compelling because, in the case of media, the raw material that is being shared between different international versions – the core content or intellectual property – once created then costs little to reproduce. The same story, and/or variations of it, can be 'sold' to multiple different audiences around the globe without its value ever being impaired or diminished.

Advertisers' needs for convenient access to global audiences remains an important driver behind publishers' efforts to extend their footprints across more territories and, notwithstanding the restraining influence of recession, technological advances continue to favour the growth of international magazine publishing. Digitization, and use of electronic communications infrastructures, have made it easier than ever for content (page proofs and so on) to be conveyed and exchanged in international publishing networks. So, the impetus for magazine publishers to embark on strategies of internationalization has increased over recent years and is likely to do so into the future (Cabell and Greehan, 2004).

CROSS-PLATFORM EXPANSION

As well as using international expansion as a means of maximizing the returns from successful brands such as *Newsweek*, *Cosmopolitan* and *Vogue*, magazine publishers have increasingly started to embark on strategies of cross-platform or multi-platform expansion where the strength of a magazine title is used to extend audience relationships and to engage in additional forms of distribution of content to specific groups or constituencies of interest. Many major publishers, as well as producing magazines, are also involved in radio and television broadcasting and in content delivery across online and mobile platforms (Aris and Bughin, 2009). Indeed, some media publishers are now explicitly structured as 'collections of cross-media brands' rather than according to specific divisional activities (such as magazines publishing or radio broadcasting) – an approach which clearly acknowledges that, at root, the business is about devising and building up successful titles or brands and then repackaging them to suit different technologies and audiences (Dowdy, 2005: 5).

The ability to create alternative versions of a core product for different audience groups has long been integral to the business of supplying media and is by no means unique to magazine publishing. Within broadcasting, for example, a strategy commonly found is where groups of broadcasters that operate in different regions form a 'network' and profit by sharing a collective core schedule of programmes, usually with some regional adaptation to fit local needs (Owen and Wildman, 1992: 206). This arrangement is similar to the 'networks' found in magazine publishing in that, in the course of supplying numerous international versions of titles such as *FHM*, all participants reap advantages through shared use of content, shared use of an umbrella brand and (in some cases at least) shared advertising sales.

The recycling of strong content brands across additional delivery platforms is also not unique to magazine publishing but rather is a strategy that is visible across all sectors of the media (Murray, 2005; McDowell, 2006; Ots, 2008). A widespread migration towards cross-platform and multi-platform distribution strategies has been encouraged in recent years by digital convergence and by growth of the internet (Chan-Olmsted and Chang, 2003; Dennis et al., 2006; García Avilés and Carvajal, 2008; Küng, 2008; Küng et al., 2008). Magazine publishers, seeking to capitalize on the strength of their brands, have frequently been at the forefront of this migration. For example the Kerrang! digital television channel part-owned by Bauer Media Group (along with Channel 4 Television) and the Kerrang! radio station broadcasting in the West Midlands region of England are associated in style and ownership with a music magazine called *Kerrang!* published weekly in the UK and also produced by Bauer Consumer Media. The internet has encouraged more cross-platform distribution and most if not all magazine titles now have a significant online presence.

One of the main attractions of sharing content across multiple products or services or delivery formats and across multiple platforms is that such strategies reduce average per-user production costs and so give rise to economies of scale and scope (Küng et al., 2008: 133). Another benefit is that distribution of content across multiple platforms may allow some useful leveraging and additional strengthening of an established magazine brand. So, as with international expansion, the fundamental logic of cross-platform distribution is to utilize a tried-and-tested editorial formula in order to facilitate large increases in output consumption at relatively low marginal cost.

But cross-platform expansion is not just about squeezing additional economies of scale and scope out of content. A significant feature of digital online distribution, albeit one that many conventional mass media suppliers have struggled to capitalize on effectively so far, is that it offers the possibility of engaging with audiences in different ways from before (Doyle, 2010). As earlier research has shown, the two-way mode of communication made possible by the introduction of a digital return path has made it easier for content suppliers to learn about the habits and preferences of their audiences (Shapiro and Varian, 1999). So the use of digital delivery platforms has not only vastly increased the number of avenues and outlets through which content can be mediated to audiences, it has also introduced search tools and systems for signalling of preferences back to suppliers that, in turn, facilitate much more targeted and personalized forms of media provision and consumption.

In the broadcasting industry, the manner in which digitization allows suppliers to forge new sorts of relationships with audiences has been identified and recognized by some players as key to the development of successful strategies for the future. Broadcast television is, as conceded by Channel 4 Chief Executive Andy Duncan, 'no longer the funnel through which entertainment and information are channeled to millions of waiting consumers in a one-way flow' (Duncan, 2006: 21). In the commercial broadcasting sector, an improved ability to gather intelligence about current audience interests and to feed this into production decisions means that suppliers can be much more nimble in addressing audience tastes. In the non-market sector, new ways to relate to audiences are also a source of opportunity. At the BBC, the need for reinvention around closer and more responsive modes of interaction was identified as crucial by the Director-General Mark Thompson when, in 2006, he set out a strategic vision for the corporation's future (Thompson, 2006: 13): 'We need a new relationship with our audiences – they won't simply be audiences but also participants and partners. We need to know them as individuals and communities, let them configure our services in ways that work for them'.

Broadcasters and newspaper publishers, long accustomed to their established positions as 'one-to-many' purveyors of content, have faced considerable challenges over recent years in rethinking their strategies in response to digitization and increased fragmentation of mass audiences (Greenslade, 2009). Magazine publishers, too, have been subject to the harsh winds of change as growth of the internet has brought much more competition for the attention of audiences and advertisers (Küng et al., 2008: 154). But, because of their established strengths in targeting and addressing niche audience segments, it can be argued that magazine publishers are relatively well placed to adapt to the growing predominance of digital forms of delivery.

Magazine publishers, more than other sorts of media suppliers, have long recognized the value of understanding and engaging closely with audiences. Expertise in communicating with specific audience segments has frequently been used by publishers to develop complementary products and services (Doyle, 2002: 139). For example, many magazine publishers are involved in organizing live events or exhibitions and trade fairs related to the themes that their titles focus on (such as cars, interior decoration, weddings, computers and so on). So, despite the threat posed by growing online competition and illegal intermediation of media content, the possibilities offered by the internet for interactivity and closer engagement with particular constituencies of interest play well to established competencies among magazine publishers in building, sustaining and then finding ways to capitalize on relationships with niche audiences.

CONCLUSIONS

Although, spurred on by increases in leisure time and higher disposable incomes in developed economies, consumer magazine publishing enjoyed long periods of growth in the 1980s and 1990s, the industry is now undergoing a period of contraction. A slowdown in expenditures on magazines and a reduction in the number of titles being published partly reflect economic recession and market saturation in wealthier European countries and in the US. In addition, and like other sectors of the print media, magazine publishing is also suffering from the ongoing migration of consumers away from reading as a form of leisure and towards screen-based entertainment activities.

However, a key advantage that magazine publishers can claim is the strength of their brands and the appeal these brands hold for particular audience segments and constituencies of shared interest. Where a magazine's brand appeal is strong enough, the migration of audiences to new delivery platforms need not necessarily be seen as a threat but rather as an opportunity. Virtually all magazines titles now have a well-developed web presence (a small handful are available only in electronic format) and some also offer mobile content services. Digital media platforms, with their capacity for interactivity, are not just venues for electronic versions of the print media version of a magazine but rather they offer an opportunity to deepen and strengthen the relationship between a magazine brand and its target readership and to recruit additional subscribers by providing a more comprehensive and richly layered range of content-based services (Küng, 2008: 49).

Magazines are to some extent like fashion items – titles come and titles go. Although a few well-known titles have survived over numerous decades, most magazines have a much shorter life expectancy. Those that succeed over longer periods require ongoing adaptation to ensure that they maintain a viable constituency (Gasson, 1996: 86). To sustain and replenish the portfolios that help reduce the risks inherent in magazine publishing, new products need to be innovated and launched on a regular basis. So the dynamic nature of markets for magazines is such that publishers must pay close attention to the many cultural and social trends and the transient fads and fashions that help shape demand within and across product genres. Through building expert knowledge of particular lifestyle groups and areas of special interest, publishers do in fact become adept in recognizing shifts and trends and in identifying opportunities for new product launches (Cox and Mowatt, 2008).

So, magazine publishing revolves around identifying viable constituencies of interest and establishing powerful titles that command sufficient brand appeal and will stay in business long enough to cover their initial launch costs and provide a profitable return to their owner. The cost of new magazine launches can be extremely high and so fewer launches will take place in times of recession than normally (Jarvis, 2009: 6). Nonetheless, new launches are essential in sustaining the industry. In calculating the returns available from a title across its expected life, publishers will take into account not only opportunities for domestic and international exploitation of the magazine but also the potential to extend the brand across additional delivery platforms and into complementary product markets (Doyle, 2002). Each of these components will form part of a systematic strategy for maximizing the available returns from any successful magazine brand.

International expansion of successful leisure magazine titles has become increasingly prevalent. Once publishers succeed in developing and perfecting a leading product in the home market, the next step is often to extend the brand internationally through publication of multiple international editions of the magazine adapted suitably in each case for local market circumstances. Although the literature of international management provides numerous warnings about the difficulties of sustaining transnational business alliances, the track record of companies such as Bauer, Hachette Filipacchi and Hearst in developing magazine brands that achieve positions of market leadership right across the globe suggests that, at least in publishing, cross-border partnerships can work highly effectively. This is, perhaps, not surprising given the high financial rewards available to both brand owner and franchisee once a magazine title is successfully translated into new geographic territories.

Cross-platform expansion is another tactic that is increasingly deployed in order to maximize the returns from a popular magazine brand. Again, adaptation is necessary, in this case to suit the strengths and specificities of the delivery platform in question. Although the ability of publishers to adjust fully to internet delivery is doubted by some (Jarvis, 2009: 6), the expertise that most magazine publishers have established in targeting, building relationships with and addressing narrow audience segments is certainly a useful advantage in the context of digital distribution platforms. It is notable that while magazine publishers such as EMAP were early in adopting a 'media neutral' approach towards content delivery, many other media suppliers are now following suit in identifying themselves not purely as broadcasters or publishers but rather as content brand owners and multi-platform distributors.

A reliance on strategies of internationalization and cross-platform distribution is increasingly prevalent. The impetus to capitalize on economies of scale and scope which are naturally present in consumer magazine publishing and other areas of the media has recently been accentuated by the arrival of digital convergence and by the spread of globalization. The implications of these strategies for plurality of content are questionable (Murray, 2005) – whether the predominance of multiple cross-border, cross-platform magazine brands contributes to diversity or rather just to greater standardization of media output is a highly debatable point. What is clear, however, is that such strategies are very likely to continue into the future, not least because maximizing the available market for the firm's output is an obvious economic goal for all media content creators and brand owners.

NOTE

1. Chris Llewellyn, former International Publishing Director at EMAP plc and currently CEO of the International Federation of the Periodical Press (FIPP), interviewed by the author in November 2005.

REFERENCES

Advertising Association (2000), *The Advertising Statistics Yearbook 1999*, Advertising Association, Henley-on-Thames: NTC Publications.

Advertising Association/WARC (2009), *The Advertising Statistics Yearbook 2009*, Advertising Association, London: World Advertising Research Centre (WARC).

Aguiar, M. and E. Hurst (2007), 'Measuring trends in leisure: the allocation of time over five decades', *Quarterly Journal of Economics*, **122** (3): 969–1006.

Andrews, A. (2006), 'Monthly men's magazines battling the weekly grind', *Sunday Times*, Business Section, 29 September, available at: http://business.timesonline.co.uk/tol/business/industry_sectors/media/article653783.ece (accessed 29 July 2009).

Aris, A. and J. Bughin (2009), *Managing Media Companies*, 2nd edn, Chichester: John Wiley & Sons.

Arvidsson, A. (2006), *Brands: Meaning and Value*, London: Routledge.

Benwell, B. (ed.) (2003), *Masculinity and Men's Lifestyle Magazines*, Chichester: Wiley-Blackwell.

Bilton, J. (2009), 'Magazines: cycles, trends and wobbles', *The Guardian*, Media Supplement, Monday, 13 April, p. 5.

BRAD/PPA (2009), *Consumer Magazine Facts and Figures 2009*, available at: www.ppamarketing.net/cgi-bin/go.pl/data-trends/article.html?uid=348 (accessed 29 July 2009).

Cabell, J. and M. Greehan (2004), *International Magazine Publishing Handbook*, prepared by Cue Ball LLC for the International Federation of the Periodical Press, London: FIPP.

Chalaby, J. (2005) 'From internationalization to transnationalization', *Global Media and Communication*, **1**, (1): 28–33.

Chan-Olmsted, S. and B.-H. Chang (2003), 'Diversification strategy of global media conglomerates: examining its patterns and determinants', *Journal of Media Economics*, **16** (4): 213–33.

Cox, H. and S. Mowatt (2008), 'Technological change and forms of innovation in consumer magazine publishing: a UK-based study', *Technology Analysis and Strategic Management*, **20** (4): 503–20.

Davenport, T. and J. Beck (2001), *The Attention Economy: Understanding the New Currency of Business*, Boston, MA: Harvard Business School Press.

Dennis, E., S. Warley and J. Sheridan (2006), 'Doing digital: an assessment of the top 25 US media companies and their digital strategies', *Journal of Media Business Studies*, **3** (1): 33–63.

Dennys, H. (2009), 'Brook keeps wolves from GN&M's new door', *MediaWeek*, 13 January.

Deresky, H. (2006), *International Management: Managing across Borders and Cultures*, 5th edn, Upper Saddle River, NJ: Pearson Prentice-Hall.

Dowdy, C. (2005), 'Why radio offers sound advice on convergence', *Financial Times*, 28 June, p. 5.

Doyle, G. (2002), *Understanding Media Economics*, London: Sage.

Doyle, G. (2006), 'Managing global expansion of media products and brands: a case study of FHM', *International Journal on Media Management*, **8** (3, September): 105–15.

Doyle, G. (2010), 'From television to multi-platform: less from more or more for less?' *Convergence: The International Journal of Research into New Media Technologies*, **16** (4): 431–49.

Duncan, A. (2006), 'Maximising public value in the "now" media world', in C. Sinclair (ed.), *Transforming Television: Strategies for Convergence*, Glasgow: The Research Centre, pp. 18–29.

García Avilés, J. and M. Carvajal (2008), 'Integrated and cross-media newsroom convergence', *Convergence: The International Journal of Research into New Media Technologies*, **14** (2): 221–39.

Gasson, C. (1996), *Media Equities: Evaluation and Trading*, Cambridge: Woodhead Publishing.

Greenslade, R. (2009), 'Online is the future – and the future is now', *Guardian*, Media Supplement, 5 January, p. 4.

Hafez, K. (2007), *The Myth of Media Globalisation*, Cambridge: Polity.

Hafstrand, H. (1995), 'Consumer magazines in transition: a study of approaches to internationalisation', *Journal of Media Economics*, **8** (1): 1–12.

Helgesen, J. (2002), 'The internationalisation of Norwegian newspaper companies', in R. Picard (ed.), *Media Firms: Structures, Operations and Performance*, Mahwah, NJ: LEA, pp. 123–38.

Hughes, K. (ed.) (2009), *Market Report 2009: Consumer Magazines*, Hampton: Key Note Ltd.

Jarvis, J. (2009), 'Digital media: another one bites the dust', *The Guardian*, Media Supplement, Monday, 4 May, p. 6.

Jha, A. (2006), 'Lad culture corrupts men as much as it debases women', *The Guardian*, 30 March, p. 32, available at: http://www.guardian.co.uk/commentisfree/2006/mar/30/comment.prisonsandprobation.

Kaiser, U. and J. Wright (2005), 'Price structure in two-sided markets: evidence from the magazine industry', *Journal of Industrial Organisation*, **24** (1): 1–28.

Küng, L. (2008), *Strategic Management in the Media: Theory to Practice*, London: Sage.

Küng, L., R. Picard and R. Towse (2008), *The Internet and the Mass Media*, London: Sage.

Lanham, Richard (2006), *The Economics of Attention: Style and Substance in the Age of Information*, Chicago, IL: University of Chicago Press.

Luft, O. (2009), 'Magazines: stuck in the middle', *The Guardian*, Media Supplement, Monday 5 January, p. 5.

Malthouse, E. and B. Calder (2002), 'Patterns of readership: a qualitative variable approach', *International Journal Media Management*, **4** (4): 248–60.

McDowell, W. (2006), 'Issues in marketing and branding', in A. Albarran, S. Chan-Olmsted and M. Wirth (eds), *Handbook of Media Management and Economics*, Mahwah, NJ: Lawrence Erlbaum Associates, pp. 229–50.

McLuhan, M. (1967), *Understanding Media*, London: Sphere.

Murray, S. (2005), 'Brand loyalties: rethinking content within global corporate media', *Media Culture and Society*, **27** (3): 415–35.

Ofcom (2008), 'The International Communications Market', London: Ofcom, November.

Ots, M. (ed.) (2008), *Media Brands and Branding*, JIBS Research Report Series No. 2008-1, MMTC, Jönkoping: Jönkoping International Business School.

Owen, B. and S. Wildman (1992), *Video Economics*, Cambridge, MA: Harvard University Press.

Periodical Publishers Association (PPA) (2009), 'Key Facts about the UK Consumer Magazine Industry', PPT presentation available at: http://www.ppamarketing.net/cgi-bin/go.pl/data-trends/.

Picard, R. (2002), *The Economics and Financing of Media Companies*, New York: Fordham University Press.

Shapiro, C. and H. Varian (1999), *Information Rules: A Strategic Guide to the Network Economy*, Boston, MA: Harvard Business School Press.

Steemers, J. (2004), *Selling Television: British Television in the Global Marketplace*, London: BFI.

Taylor, B. (2008), *Market Assessment 2008: Lifestyle Magazines*, Hampton: Key Note Ltd.

Thompson, M. (2006) 'BBC creative future', in C. Sinclair (ed.), *Transforming Television: Strategies for Convergence*, Glasgow: The Research Centre, pp. 10–17.

22 The impact of new technology on leisure networks

Vincent G. Fitzsimons

INTRODUCTION

Previous chapters have looked at leisure choices. In the models associated with this, interaction with others is for mainly instrumental purposes. For example, to play a competitive sport, even in a friendly manner, requires other participants. Obviously, additional utility may arise from social interaction with fellow players. In this chapter, we consider situations where social interaction in itself can become sufficient as an activity. This social interaction has been facilitated by the expansion of information technology which greatly reduces the transaction costs of interacting with another person. It is not without costs, however, mainly in the form of risks to individual safety and well-being, although there may also be 'hidden' pecuniary costs in the way that entry to leisure networks is priced.

While a limited set of opportunities for leisure existed in medieval times, some activities were recognizable forerunners to modern forms of leisure. Religious festivals were particularly important as they provided opportunities for socializing, religious observance, part of which involved public readings of religious tracts, and collective feasting for the community (the basis of the idea of companionship, from *com* and *panis*, or breaking bread with others). In many respects, these were the main forms of social leisure of the period, until the decline in religious feast days following the Reformation. More secular breaks in the routine were the tournaments which feudal nobility participated in at first as competitions of military skills, but later more as symbolic or sporting occasions (Thomas, 1961; Larrabee, 1989). As societies in the seventeenth and eighteenth centuries gradually grew in prosperity, and with the development of trade, towns and proto-industries, many individuals enjoyed greater flexibility in their lives, and used some of this flexibility to enjoy new forms of leisure that became available to them. Thus individuals began to experience more leisure opportunities, and in a more regular pattern. The activities of sports, socializing and artistic display or performance, were all freed from the traditional medieval calendar.

In addition to this 'modernization' of leisure, a distinct transfer towards the purchase of new or rapidly growing categories of leisure goods and services is evident in the period from 1660 to 1760 (Borsay, 1977; McInnes, 1988). This 'commercialization' of leisure or growth of 'marketed' leisure products and activities for those with increasing disposable incomes changed the character of many towns in Britain, with the significant growth of leisure venues such as racecourses, sports grounds, theatres and assembly rooms. This development of new leisure forms was accompanied almost immediately, however, by a parallel tendency for workers' leisure activities to be increasingly dictated by their employers (Thomas, 1961). These trends may have affected different types of labour quite differently, but the 'rationalization' of workers' leisure (Goldman and Wilson, 1977) by employers led to further noticeable changes in the social and leisure lives of the working population. Reid (1976, 1996), for instance, documents the decline of workers' flexibility in taking social leisure, as employers attempted to regularize those social events that might interfere with work. The tendency to hold weddings, baptisms and so on, during the working week met with strong reactions from the new types of employer, and a noticeable trend developed where these moved increasingly to the non-work day of Sunday (Reid, 1996).

Some of the effects of technology on leisure have been a consequence of technological change's broader impact on the behaviour of individuals and societies. Reductions in the time and financial costs of travelling and communicating first affected leisure by affecting the pattern of traditional fairs and markets in which early leisure was often embedded, but have continued their influence by permitting continuous changes in people's behaviour including changing patterns of family life, work and social connections. The studies by Milgram (1967) that produced a (debatable) conclusion that any two individuals unknown and geographically distant to each other in the study were separated by only 'six degrees of separation' can only be possible in a society whose social connections stretch across large distances. The growth of new, capital-intensive industries in particular created a demand for large numbers of workers enabling individuals to migrate away from their traditional family homes to new or growing population centres. As a result of the geographical extension of these social relationships, individuals used communication media more frequently, and in addition as a consequence a greater flow of ideas occurred. The growth of small factory towns led to an increase in population density, at the same time that social connections were stretched over much greater distances. In facilitating these changes, the development of technology for transport and communicating information had profound social effects.

The availability of new forms of leisure changed the way in which societies reacted to events. When Martin Luther nailed 95 theses to the door of a castle church in Wittenberg in October 1517, publicly demonstrating his personal dispute with the church, this might once have had a minor effect in the local area only. The fact that these were copied, set in print, and widely distributed across Germany (and later Europe) was a demonstration of the power of the new technology of the printing press to disseminate information, and so communicate facts, opinions and debates in a way that would have been unthinkable only a short time before. It also demonstrated the inability of authorities to control information once relatively cheap and effective media existed. The spread of ideas reflected that of the pamphleteers of eighteenth- and nineteenth-century Britain, the *samizdat* publications of the twentieth-century Soviet regimes, or the growth of the internet in the face of censorship such as in the recent case of Google's involvement in China.

Social forms of leisure are important not only for individuals, but also for the consequential development of social capital and civil society which acts as an important balance in economic development. These activities depend on an open debate in some 'public space' that exists for the free exchange of ideas, but this in turn depends on the free flow of information, which is enabled by technology. The massive growth in the power of computing and communications technology, alongside its relative decline in cost, has enabled more complex forms of leisure activity and coordination. A particular feature of this change is the development of virtual social network (VSN) sites that provide users with a service combining several characteristics. The fundamental nature of a social networking 'service' involves the provision of relatively cheap or free access space on an internet page that can easily be customized by the user to present various forms of information, and can easily be accessed by others via the internet. This space enables communication of specific messages, but also provides a forum for individuals to express their opinions and portray themselves to a wider audience. The use of the social network page by friends, and strangers (if allowed access), to keep track of life events, arrangements for social engagements, reflections on news, culture, politics and so on, enables the social network to meet several different types of need and does so at very low cost. This may account for the massive growth of social networking sites in recent years. While historically the leisure decision has been increasingly constrained by market and workplace institutions and conventions, these individualized and flexible forms of social interaction may provide a genuinely flexible, and discretionary form of leisure activity for individuals today. This may partly explain their massive and sustained growth in popularity in recent years (Table 22.1).

In addition to the existing trend in VSN membership and use, there continue to be significant advances in the technology that enable more flexible

Table 22.1   Unique visitors (millions) to top US social networking websites

	MySpace	Facebook	Twitter	Classmates. com	iVillage womens net	Total internet users
Jun-09	68.418	77.031	20.111		20.594	193.986
Dec-08	75.909	54.552			20.612	190.650
Jun-08	72.777	37.375				189.873
Dec-07	68.905	34.658			17.234	183.619
Jun-07	70.478	27.965				178.839
Dec-06	60.887	19.105				174.199
Jun-06	52.342			13.963	14.330	172.907
Dec-05	32.209			15.816	13.082	170.285
Jun-05	17.703			18.007	14.175	166.625
Dec-04				13.480	16.931	161.142
Jul-04				15.632	15.941	156.436
Dec-03				13.233	14.556	152.109

Source: comscore.com.

use of social networking including the significant rise in mobile internet services (Horrigan, 2009). It appears that this trend, rather than peaking, is likely to be extended by these further technological developments.

ECONOMICS OF LEISURE NETWORKS

From the broadly macroeconomic analysis above, using historical cases, it is clear that a general relationship exists between the beneficial impact of technology on economic output and wealth, and therefore on the ability of individuals to afford leisure. In this sense, technology is a 'liberating' factor in the determination of leisure. The patterns of consumption of different forms of leisure, however, are partly formed by developments in the types of market that exist for leisure goods (due to the commercialization of leisure – Borsay, 1977), the changes in the market price of leisure goods (Costa, 1996, 1997) and partly to the organization of leisure time by various influential groups (the rationalization of leisure – Goldman and Wilson, 1977). These factors jointly determine the development of particular patterns of leisure. Recently, the impact of specific information and communication technologies on individuals, markets and organizations has caused significant changes in the patterns of leisure, and may have had a particular impact on social leisure. Although leisure networks have existed in many forms, the recent rapid development of VSNs is distinctive, and deserves more specific attention in order to determine the factors that have led to its current form of development.

First, what is a leisure network? Assuming that we can overcome the problems earlier identified in definitions of leisure, it is an extended grouping of individuals who provide each other with utility by interacting even if that interaction has no tangible product in terms of exchange or output. Theoretical economic analysis of this phenomenon is limited to extensions of standard theories of the consumer and the firm. Two distinctive areas of economic theory have attempted to analyse such collective good problems. These both focused initially on the firm in the production of collective consumption goods.

The most notable example is the theory of clubs inspired by Buchanan (1965; see also Sandler and Tschirhart, 1980, 1997), which examined the collective purchase of a public good, including the problems of access, distribution and so on in their provision. Club theory applies to the local public good situation where there are high fixed costs of provision, leading to significant reduction in average costs as consumption increases, along with spillover benefits (positive externalities) of sharing the good combined with sharing the heavy fixed costs of providing a club 'facility'. This has an obvious relevance to the provision of VSNs, although none of the literature on clubs so far has been explicitly applied to VSNs.

In the simplest club model, all members are identical and exclusion is based purely on the cost–benefit calculation, for the group as a whole, rather than personal characteristics. This is typically defined as the 'non-discriminating club' in the literature. Again we have to be careful with words as the term 'discrimination' is used differently from elsewhere such as in Becker's (1965) economic theory of discrimination. Discrimination here simply refers to discrimination of the character of price discrimination in standard economic theory. Confusingly the non-discriminating club would, in essence, discriminate against potential members as it would refuse them entry while letting in otherwise identical people. The usual discussion of club goods then focuses on the role of congestion (responsible for making the good an impure public good) in limiting the size of membership to a level at which net beneficiaries are excluded by the collective group decision.

A more recent literature has examined the impact on individual consumption benefits when purchasing network goods at different levels of collective consumption (Rohlfs, 1974; Katz and Shapiro, 1986). Analysis of the consumption of networked products suggests that the benefits of network membership largely depend on the existence of a number of prior users so that new users enjoy significant externalities from existing users (Rohlfs, 1974). These network externalities typically increase the utility to each consumer as the level of total use increases. This concept of network externality has been widely applied in other areas of economic analysis. Writings in the economics of sport (Boardman and Hargreaves-Heap, 1999; see also Goldman, 1983) have for a long time claimed significant network externalities to fans from simply talking to each other about the game (see also Chapter 12). This benefit that exists separately from that of consumption of a specifically marketed good or service obviously applies to discussion of anything else, whether it is soap operas or the quality of USB sticks. This also appears typical of social networks covering a range of social leisure activities.

Certain common points emerge from the two literatures. Both deal with issues of scale of total consumption of a product and the impacts on relative costs. Club theory's particular focus on problems of congestion, when certain maximum limits to consumption for products are reached, seems in some respects quite different from the analysis of networks which emphasizes the need for consumption to pass certain minimum consumption thresholds, but these problems exist to some extent in both situations. For instance, the performance of communications networks, and many services, suffers significantly from congestion effects during peak-load demand periods. Much of this analysis applies directly to the issues of membership and operation of VSNs.

Several potential models can be suggested to explain the structure of provision of VSNs by producers. Given its network characteristic, they inevitably face relatively complex technical structures. The nature of the content of VSNs was originally relatively simple, however, being used predominantly as a communications platform to 'broadcast' this simple (and therefore relatively cheap) content to a number of users simultaneously using typical web-based systems. The economics of information processing has been analysed as a part of modern technical network analysis, as mentioned above. It is generally accepted that the initial cost of the first unit of any 'information good' is extremely high, but subsequent copies are very cheap (Varian, 1995). These suggest very high set-up costs for establishing VSNs. In addition, with the growth of popularity of digital multimedia products from cameras to phones and music or video players, the nature of content users wish to attach to VSN sites has changed, massively increasing the information processing and storage costs involved in operating VSN services.

Simple subscription services were initially relatively popular in social network provision. The simple subscription model would suggest that the content-related economies of scale would encourage network providers to favour larger individual networks among customers, and attempt to encourage these. Some genealogy sites and social-network-based sites such as Friends Reunited based their business models on this form of payment system, but many have since been forced by competition from other forms of provider to abandon significant charges for their services.

The role of subsidies in the introduction of network products has been examined already (Katz and Shapiro, 1986), and this model is also very relevant to VSNs. The ability to find sponsors for the costly launch of a product and purchase of initial resources, or alternatively the ability to cross-subsidize this from existing products, may enable companies to operate otherwise uneconomic services. The ability of internet firms to operate for significant periods while simultaneously making large losses and easily securing injections of additional funding suggests that the long-term potential of such firms is the main focus of their operations (Parker and Van Alstyne, 2005). If VSN services become sufficiently popular that they become essential goods for a significant number of consumers, then this potential makes them attractive.

Finally, recent analysis of web-based businesses has emphasized the potential benefits to firms managing their resources more efficiently, including the information resources produced as a byproduct of web-based business (Huang et al., 2004). VSN providers can be considered from this perspective. Rather than being a charging service provider, using subsidy or sponsorship to reduce or eliminate service charges, these firms can be seen as producers of information goods, which are of great commercial value. In this view, the VSNs are in essence media for the transfer of information between registered users (and sometimes unregistered observers) via the VSN service provider to information markets. This procedure produces a rich combination of information goods for the service provider, such as targeted advertising (similar to that which finances the expansion of Google), personal characteristics and interests data (which again are heavily used by Google), and information on the level of response of different consumers to different types of information, for either internal use or external sale. Information of this type gives service providers the ability to form valuable information products. The differentiating factor between these is then the quality of the information. If VSN providers can organize and target high-quality information products, a highly profitable market exists for these in the modern information economy. Revenue can also be maximized using product differentiation techniques already discussed in the information goods literature (Varian, 1997). Overall, the commercial value of the information goods appears to significantly exceed the potential value of subscription services, although these will be important in contributing towards the fixed costs of production.

While the discussion above addresses the market for social networks, other aspects of networks also need examination. Significant analysis has gone into the nature of network communication based on Shannon (1948) and related communications models. These emphasize the difficulties of producing accurate 'messages' to communicate, the difficulties of encoding and transmitting these, and the similar problems facing the receiver of the message. The specific extent to which 'noise' distorts the communication at each stage of this process may be questioned, but it emphasizes the fragility of communication of even simple messages.

Despite these difficulties, VSNs have grown massively in popularity, suggesting that the communication they enable provides some significant benefits. While this may be confused by the development of free services by the most popular VSNs, so that communication costs are reduced to internet access costs (which have declined steadily in recent years – see computer and broadband costs in OECD, 2008, 2009; Bureau of Economic Analysis, 2009) and personal time costs, they must appeal to some consumer need. In VSNs, the transmission of users' messages can simply be replaced with a storage and hosting system that breaks the need for simultaneous availability of those who communicate. Just as money, in breaking the acts of buying and selling, facilitates an increase in trade, so the idea of message hosting breaks the act of broadcasting a message from that of receiving it – a simple extension of mailbox and answerphones for telephone services. While the rationalization of leisure, discussed above, has increased the organization of leisure and significantly constrained both opportunities for leisure and scope for self-determination of leisure activities, the flexibility of VSNs and similar technology-based communication enables some form of social leisure communication to take place despite work and other pressures of modern lifestyles.

Social leisure and the accumulation of social capital through social leisure is often highlighted as both beneficial to the individual (Steinfield et al., 2008), and also to the wider society and economy in which they live (Putnam, 1993, 1995a, 1995b). While the impact on the individual is very difficult to prove adequately (particularly as suggesting that declining social leisure injures social well-being is simply true by definition) research has presented support for the idea that social leisure, social group and the support this constitutes are beneficial in many economic and social situations.

IMPACT OF TECHNOLOGY ON INDIVIDUALS

While the relationship between technology and leisure is obvious in its broad implications, analysis of the specific impacts of current technological change and its likely future impact are complicated by a range of issues.

Table 22.2   *Estimated US computer ownership and internet access in the home (%)*

Year	US households with computer at home	US households with internet access at home
2009	–	68.7
2007	–	61.7
2003	61.8	54.7
2001	56.3	50.4
2000	51.0	41.5
1997	36.6	18.0
1993	22.9	–
1989	15.0	–
1984	8.2	–

Source: US Census Bureau.

The economic analysis of technological progress gives us an indication that the potential for leisure increasingly exists in growing economies, but it does not explain the changes in actual labour and leisure hours for individuals, reflecting as they do the choices that firms and individuals make, the environment in which these decisions take place, and the objectives they wish to pursue. It also fails to address specifically the qualitative changes in the forms and patterns of leisure in which individuals participate. The development of computers from calculating and data-handling machines into more general technology used for information and data-processing, communication, and entertainment has led to them becoming embedded in human activity and essential to many types of popular leisure behaviour (Table 22.2). It is therefore necessary to outline some of the key impacts of technology on individuals' social leisure activities.

Analysis of the impact of technology on any human activity is likely to be highly provisional in its nature due to the rapidly changing nature of that technology, but certain basic principles can be established. Spender (1995) emphasized the need to recognize that, when transferring any human activity to a new medium, all of the original characteristics will still be present in some form. Equivalent phenomena will develop paralleling those experienced in other forms of human interaction. What matters is not the technology, but 'the change in society – the shifts in power, wealth, influence, organisation, and the environmental consequences' (p. xiv). Culture, language, attitudes, preferences will all continue to influence behaviour and reproduce problems such as racism, sexism, bullying, inequality in terms of access, manipulation and misrepresentation.

Assumptions of a purely positive and facilitating role of technology must be seen as severely limited in this context. It is also true, however, that existing structures may influence behaviour in different ways following the transfer to technological forms with different characteristics and capacities, such as the emergence of new behaviours due to complex interactions and the effect of systems passing certain 'threshold' levels of activity, or equally the sudden disappearance of certain behaviours. With this in mind, the changes in activity will to some extent be unpredictable, but certain tendencies may hold in the relatively short term, which will be discussed below.

The increasing facilitation of communication by advancing technology has permitted a number of changes, such as the levels of communication, the nature, such as length of communication, and rules or customs relating to these. The use of social networking sites (SNSs) has grown rapidly since their early roots, as can be seen in Table 22.1, above, drawn from US data. As well as looking at the number of users of websites, it is also useful to look at the frequency of use. The statistics show the prominence of SNSs as a proportion of total web use – for the week commencing 26 September 2009, 5.54 per cent of website visits were on Facebook, only beaten by Google who constitute 6.84 per cent of website visits (hitwise.com). While Facebook has only slightly more users than MySpace, the number of visits is considerably higher at 41.8 per cent of all social networking visits. MySpace came a distant second with 21.29 per cent, and YouTube third at 14.12 per cent (again for week commencing 26 September 2009 according to hitwise.com data). It remains to be seen how we can adequately account for this rapid growth in popularity.

In principle, social leisure (in its various forms) is constrained by the cost of leisure-facilitating goods relative to income (Costa, 1996, 1997), the opportunity cost of working time and associated income forgone, as well as the absolute limits of time given and time required for social activities to take place. In this sense, economists see leisure as something that does not suffer a rapidly diminishing utility and as such is viewed as almost an 'absolute good'. This is of course a questionable concept as has been demonstrated in several of the early chapters in this book. Not only does social networking technology reduce financial costs, but it also cuts the time needed for communications. This reduces the opportunity cost of social activities where these are via 'media' – hence mobile and SNS growth. This does not mean that the transfer of social communication to social network sites will leave that communication unaffected, and so the benefits of the SNS-maintained social networks may not be entirely the same as normal social networks.

Certain aspects of leisure appear to be more likely to be affected by the transfer to more technological media. An initial debate revolved around the impact of technology on individual relationships and the resulting impact on social capital, with its economic benefits. The structure of communication as outlined above following Shannon (1948) emphasizes the susceptibility of interpersonal communication to interference causing mistakes and problems. Among other issues, the burden of face-to-face communication which forms the basis of many relationships, falls predominantly on non-verbal elements of communication (Argyle, 1975, 1994). This causes an immediate problem in the transfer of social communication to computer-mediated communication, which removes this nonverbal element entirely. This formed the basis of research by Kiesler et al. (1984) suggesting that there could be negative impacts on business due to the reduction of accuracy in communication when moving to computer-based communication. The negative impact of computers on the quality of communication has been a recurrent concern since this research, but many of the additional media that can be attached to basic electronic communication may in other respects enrich the communication.

Authors such as Kiesler as well as Robert Kraut and others (see Kraut et al., 1998) have continued to examine this sceptical agenda about computer-based communication's effects in investigating the social psychological effects of computers on individuals. The 'internet paradox', suggested by Kraut et al. examined the essentially socially enhancing capacity of computers with convenient email and internet facilities, and found that the introduction of computers to individuals led to an overall decline in psychological welfare in early studies. This led to the suggestion that, following Putnam's (1995b) analysis of declining social involvement and the possible leisure-displacement effect of television, computers displaced other, potentially more beneficial activities, and that this 'social displacement' led to the decline of welfare for many individuals.

Further investigation of this issue first appeared to provide directly contradictory evidence (Kraut et al., 2002). Longitudinal examination of computer use appeared to show that initial impacts of computer use may be negative, but that they will in the long run be more likely to increase individual welfare of individuals. There was a 'social augmentation' effect from the socially enhancing uses of the computer. There were, however, some indications that this followed a 'rich get richer' effect, where those with existing social resources were able to gain more from access to computer-based communication, possibly reflecting their interpersonal ability and general attitudes. Those without such resources tended to be slightly worse off or have little impact from the computer-based communication. Those with these resources tended to be able to strengthen and extend the range of their relationships.

This was also indicated by the findings of Bargh and McKenna (2004) when investigating different forms of self-image and computer-based communication. Bargh and McKenna's work forms the basis of the 'social compensation' hypothesis, that computer-based communication may in fact better suit people with particular characteristics. Typically, the anonymity of the internet and the absence of face-to-face communication may suit those who are unhappy forming relationships in the typical face-to-face way. Applying the concept that individuals may have and present to others multiple selves (Goffman, 1959), Bargh et al. (2002) investigated the ability of individuals to portray their 'true self' in computer-based communications and found that this ability was enhanced by such communications. The ability to express oneself openly when anonymous can be extended to computer-based communications due to the (apparent or actual) anonymity of the communication method. This enhanced ability to communicate can then provide some individuals with access to relationships, and therefore social support structures, that they might otherwise have lacked. The communications can then be seen as enhancing individuals' social and general psychological welfare. Relationships formed this way may be seen as being as strong and beneficial as normal relationships.

These different studies' apparently contradictory findings may cause problems when attempting to draw conclusions on the nature of the impact of social networking on individual welfare. Recent research has attempted to test these hypotheses against each other (Bessière et al., 2008). This work has suggested that different groups are possibly identifiable in the general population, with these hypotheses holding for some users and not others. Evidence from actual studies of internet use has suggested that social augmentation may be one of the most significant effects, as email use for communication with close family and friends has been obvious from early studies up to the present (Center for Digital Future, 2004–2009). In addition, though, there are increasing signs that many people form new relationships on the internet, and that these relationships are counted often as being as important as those relationships formed in face-to-face contact. Data presented in Nie and Hillygus (2002) indicate that heavy internet users typically do suffer from 'displacement' having less total free time, and also use less time for social activities, reading and hobbies than other groups (although they enjoy slightly more TV time and music time than some groups). It therefore appears that the type of individual and type of use jointly determine whether computer-based communication is good or bad for overall individual welfare.

Concerns over the potential problems of anonymity on the internet are also becoming more widespread in such surveys. This negative aspect of the anonymity of the web is damaging in many respects for users of the internet, enabling the unscrupulous to take advantage of their position for malicious or criminal purposes. In addition, it impacts on the validity and therefore quality of the information that service providers possess and use to finance the running of social networking sites. This may ultimately undermine the business model under which many social networks operate at present.

It may in addition, when more widely understood by the public, undermine trust for vulnerable users (social compensation users). Media attention has already focused on the role of social networking sites in coordination of criminal and 'deviant' activity. This may be true, although rare, as any minority views or acts may find relationships with others on the net due to the 'law of large numbers' of the global internet. More frequently cited problems relate to the presence of web 'damagers' such as 'trolls' that attempt to manipulate discussion boards and SNSs, and who have been accused of attempting to destabilize those in need of social support on such sites.

Fundamental concerns surrounding computer-mediated communication revolve around the question of whether virtual networks substitute for real networks, or whether they instead provide better or worse forms of interaction for individuals. Changing the nature of typical communication may also change the communication skills developed by individuals, particularly from 'low-quality' to 'high-quality' communication skills. As this may also in itself be expected to affect the nature of the relationships maintained using these communication techniques, does the strength of attachment decline as numbers increase? The likely impacts on group communication therefore also require further attention.

IMPACT OF TECHNOLOGY ON GROUPS

The impact of technology on groups has been of significant interest to economists and other social scientists for a considerable time, reflecting concerns over the deterioration of social support structures for individuals in modern society and the possible psychological, social and economic consequences of these at the aggregate level. Empirical evidence on social networks, in McPherson et al. (2006), shows that the modal social network has changed considerably in recent years. Social survey data examining social resources and social support (Table 22.3) show that the typical individual's 'confidant' network has changed from one where individuals had three confidants to a society where the modal category had no confidants, this change occurring over the relatively short period from 1985 to 2004 in

Table 22.3   Size of typical discussion networks, 1985 and 2004 US household surveys

Network size	Total discussion network		Kin network		Non-kin network	
	1985	2004	1985	2004	1985	2004
0	10.0%	24.6%	29.5%	39.6%	36.1%	53.4%
1	15.0%	19.0%	29.1%	29.7%	22.4%	21.6%
2	16.2%	19.2%	21.0%	16.0%	18.1%	14.4%
3	20.3%	16.9%	11.7%	9.4%	13.2%	6.0%
4	14.8%	8.8%	5.8%	4.0%	6.8%	3.1%
5	18.2%	6.5%	2.8%	1.3%	3.4%	1.4%
6+	5.4%	4.9%	–	–	–	–
Mean	2.94	2.08	1.44	1.12	1.42	0.88
Mode	3.00	0.00	0.00	0.00	0.00	0.00
SD	1.95	2.05	1.41	1.38	1.57	1.40

Source: McPherson et al. (2006).

the United States. Evidence from household surveys in several countries also suggests that there is in general an international trend for social forms of leisure to go into decline in recent years, with a few exceptions to this trend such as the UK (Gauthier and Smeeding, 2001).

The work of Putnam (1995b), as mentioned above, suggested that one possible reason for the decline in community involvement was the 'displacement' of this form of leisure activity by the rise of television viewing. Furthermore, psychological research has identified this as one of the potential responses to the internet, reinforcing concerns over the social or community involvement and social group-building in modern societies more actively using computer-mediated forms of communication. Nie and Hillygus (2002) provide evidence on this internet displacement effect and examine the effect on a range of leisure activities, including television viewing. Although intuitively it might be expected that internet use may replace television viewing in social displacement, this does not appear to be the case to any significant extent (Table 22.4). In fact computer use appears to rob additional time from other, more traditional leisure pursuits.

Much of the literature on the psychological effects of the internet on users, however, has focused on the formation of relationships or communications between individuals, that is, in 'dyadic ties'. While this level of analysis is important in distinguishing the microeconomic costs and benefits of internet use, economics is also interested in behaviour in the

Table 22.4   Time use (imputed to 24-hour estimate) by levels of home internet use

	Non-user (0 min)	Light user (1–59 min)	Medium user (60 min)	Heavy user (60+ min)	Non-heavy difference
Number of cases (n =)	(4,137)	(474)	(386)	(247)	
Sleep time	467.2	457.8	454.2	446.3	–20.9
TV time	130.2	126.1	120.7	121.3	–8.9
Video/radio/music time	18.1	16.2	16.2	18.8	0.7
Reading time	22.7	21.2	21.0	19.2	–3.5
Social time	58.2	57.3	49.8	48.5	–9.7
Recreation/hobby time	44.5	43.1	42.4	37.7	–6.8
Total free time	292.2	281.6	266.4	262.5	–29.7
Education time	7.4	7.2	7.4	6.7	–0.7
Work time	173.7	156.7	156.7	141.4	–32.3
Housework time	93.0	95.4	93.1	87.1	–5.9
Childcare time	37.3	37.6	35.5	33.1	–4.2
Errands/shop time	42.8	41.4	41.7	38.5	–4.3

Source: Nie and Hillygus (2002).

aggregate and therefore in the impact of communications technology on the presentation of individuals to larger groups. Approaching this problem as one of individual interaction misses the importance of the group that the individual seeks to communicate to and with. The activities and problems of general group behaviour therefore need further, more systematic analysis.

The starting-point for this approach may perhaps be to examine the communication of individuals intended for groups, and the nature of those groups. It is important to point out that individuals may participate in many different groups, each of which may have very different characteristics and for each of which the individual may in fact adopt different behaviours, or portray very different characteristics. One significant issue with the widespread adoption of VSNs that are semi-public or entirely public is the problem of 'leakage' between different groups. As mentioned above, Goffman (1959) and others have discussed the idea of 'self' and different 'selves' – a simple example being between 'true self' which may be some idealized or very internal perception of oneself, and the 'actual self' that may exist or may be the perception of others of the same individual. If we accept that individuals may portray a range of very different selves to different groups in which they participate, then the adoption of a 'global' image in a widely accessible social network can cause obvious problems.

The simple distinction between personal and work life may become blurred, causing either conscious problems for those portraying themselves, or unanticipated problems. These have come to light in recent reports of VSNs where, for instance, individuals are asked by employers to be connected to personal VSNs, removing the ability to communicate views of work privately/anonymously, and so removing one important opportunity to use non-work social resources to deal with workplace pressures (see, for instance, Media Life, 2009; Sky News, 2009).

To illustrate this, it may be useful to look at Mary Douglas's (1973 [1994]) grid–group structure that anthropologists frequently use to classify types of group. Douglas, based on her observation of a range of anthropological cases, developed a system of group classification based on two characteristics of groups, the size of the group (the 'group' aspect) and the extent to which the group was structured or hierarchically controlling (the 'grid' aspect). This can accommodate very 'atomistic' conceptions of economic behaviour as in the microeconomics of the neoclassical synthesis (low grid, low group) as well as more professional/bureaucratic types (high grid, low group), religious groups (low grid, high group) and so on. It is obviously possible for individuals to be relatively involved in several different groups in their day-to-day life, and also to be involved to different extents and in different types of group. The individual's desired presentation of self in each of these contexts may differ significantly, and so individual behaviour and self-portrayal may be adjusted. The idea of SNSs that report on all aspects of an individual's life indiscriminately differs fundamentally from the conceptions of Douglas and of Goffman.

It may well be that, as working hours and working conditions have become more flexible in the modern economy, so groups have become more standardized (perhaps with lower grid and group ties) and the distinction between several distinct selves becomes either blurred or consolidated. The failure to distinguish 'appropriate' communication is much higher in the absence of face-to-face contact and the accompanying non-verbal cues, and this may account for the increasing problems of separation of selves. Some cases have even involved the disclosure of information classified on the basis of national security, such as in the case of the rapid closure of the Facebook page of the spouse of a recent head of the British Security Service's MI6 section (*The Times*, 2009). Ultimately, if VSNs become the dominant form of social portrayal and interaction, then the nature of these will in effect determine the future direction of communication, self-presentation and also of group relationships.

Goffman's (1959) analysis of the role of portrayal of self may, alternatively, provide a partial explanation of the success of multimedia-enabled VSNs. More complex web-based systems in the introduction of 'Web 2.0' are intended to expand the capacity and convenience of the current internet-based media such as SNSs, and also to enrich the content to give a more satisfying form of communication. This explicit recognition of the shortcomings of the older web services underpins much of the current thinking and reflects advice to consider quality as well as speed and quantity in the provision of services to consumers. VSNs provide a platform for presentation of a variety of media, and this may meet a need or desire for a different form of communication, involving a complex, more explicitly designed and constructed portrayal of personal identity as suggested by social theorists such as Goffman. This extent of control, and the absence of the unintentional non-verbal signals that face-to-face communicators depend on to validate the 'self' that individuals present, is an obvious attraction to those who may be socially nervous, or those who wish to maximize the impact of their 'message'. The concomitant reduction in the ability to check the presentation that others construct, however, causes a general and fundamental issue of the validity of information on the internet, and leads to a lower-quality information environment that entails greater burdens of the 'transaction costs' of communication in terms of decoding and checking information. It may in fact lead to a greater risk in the use of the easily and cheaply available information that undoes much of the benefits of the convenient internet.

Groups have been significantly examined in the economics literature, with particular emphasis on concepts such as social capital (Coleman, 1988) being emphasized in particular for the economic benefits of relationships. The definition of social capital by Putnam (1993, 1995a, 1995b) focuses on the instrumental nature of social interaction, very much following the 'instrumental leisure' approach encouraged by the analysis of Becker in the Chicago school tradition. This definition has become widely used, but is obviously quite distinct from the more general concept of social relations in Coleman (1988) and others on the subject. The Putnam approach, while specifically referring to leisure activities such as bowling, is focused very much on political or civil society forms of engagement, not leisure *per se*. This may in fact treat changes in leisure as a symptom of changes in civic engagement, which would appear from the discussion above to be inappropriate. Generally analysis has suggested significant benefits from network memberships, although the mechanisms for this and the types of network relations that are most beneficial are debatable. Granovetter (1973), for instance, emphasizes the extension of networks, suggesting that 'weak ties' are important as close ties tend to be relatively similar and produce little 'new' information to individuals, whereas distant contacts are much more likely to provide additional information. Granovetter suggests that product or job search is much simpler for those embedded in these 'weak ties' networks, demonstrating 'bridging' social ties between distant groups. Putnam (1993, 1995a), however, suggests that close community ties open access to local resources that those without relationships are unable to access. These also strengthen the ability of the community to react to events, creating more resilient and economically successful communities (Putnam, 1993). Olson (1965) suggests a potentially negative side of network membership where the benefits to the group or network can be directed to some within the group more than others. In addition, the potential benefits of 'negative' groups exist, where those groups involved in redistributive conflicts, for instance, may benefit members but not the wider society/economy. In addition, racist groups or others with a negative social theme may benefit members, but are socially divisive. The overall impacts are therefore questionable. Evidence of the benefits to the individual of social capital, and the impacts of modern social technologies generally suggest that there is no clear benefit from the introduction of social technologies to these different types of group (Anderson, 2004), although this is an area in which individual effects are often statistically confounded due to the complex and varied nature of relationships in most samples.

This runs contrary to much of the analysis of social leisure and social activity in earlier social science literature. Riesman (1953), for instance, has influentially stated the de-socializing role of modern economic organization, suggesting a rising interdependence between individuals coinciding with a decline in their social contact and concept of social connection. The 'lonely crowd' that industrialization and population concentration has created may create a significant demand for services such as VSNs. This may well provide an alternative explanation of the 'social compensation' phenomena, where individuals are prevented from socialization due to lifestyle pressures rather than lack of social skills, and so use flexible (not necessarily more anonymous) forms of socialization to compensate for this problem. The implication of Riesman's analysis is that the decline in social activity is economically rather than socially determined, so that the negative economic impact of declining social capital mirrors the weakening effect of the form of economy in operation. The effect of these changes can force people to look outward or inward for their points of reference – those who look outward, despite the social isolation they may experience, would benefit potentially from VSNs and constitute a distinctive element of demand for their services.

Analysis of technology's impact on group activities must also consider whether constraints exist that may restrict the apparent positive impacts of the new technology. One particular area of analysis which is relevant here comes from anthropological and neurological research into socialization. The relevance of anthropological research is sometimes questioned in economic areas, but some of the recent work in the area of cognition and anthropology has significant implications for networks, and consequently for the analysis of modern forms of social and economic virtual networks. The most prominent among these is possibly the work of Robin Dunbar (1993, 1998) whose work on the social groups of animals has produced estimates of the human capacity to maintain relationships, and subsequently to engage in social and other forms of network. Dunbar's work on primate groups demonstrates a relationship between cortex size of different animals and the typical group size of those animals (Dunbar, 1993). Based on an extrapolation of this work, 'Dunbar's number' is widely used in web-network analysis as an approximation for the expected maximum size of virtual networks, at an estimated level of 150 members. The implications of this analysis have led to significant reductions in the estimated value and benefits of virtual networks following overoptimistic predictions made during the dot.com boom and bust in recent years (Fitzsimons, 2006). While the evidence on network activity indicates that 'super-nodes' exist, namely individuals with very high levels of maintained connection, these are rare and typically networks are therefore constrained.

Dunbar's explanation of the relationship revolves around the necessary cognitive costs of 'social grooming' activity in primate groups that is closely equivalent to the activities by which individuals in human networks maintain their connection with other group members. In this analysis, time and cognitive resources devoted to the maintenance of a set of relationships sets an absolute limit on the size of an 'active' network of close ties. The economic implications of this are clear in the case of VSNs where, due to the model of provision that is currently popular, the financial costs of analysis are now minimal and the systems enable widespread communication among a social group simultaneously. The ability to maintain close ties this way, however, may remain largely unaffected by these characteristics, and increasingly network analysis is focusing on the numbers in the 'active' group of social networks, who remain frequently and actively in communication with each other (Ellison et al., 2009). These groups, if they can be identified, are likely to be those whose opinions are of most commercial interest and, if individually persuaded of the benefits of products, are likely to spread these views among the active group quite effectively. This has already become the focus of social networks such as Facebook, and their marketing teams (Mayfield, 2009). There also exists the potential for the flexibility of access to VSNs to reduce the net cognitive costs of social contact, which may raise the effective value of Dunbar's number

Table 22.5 Cybercrime trends in UK

Category	2006	2007	2008
Identity theft and identity fraud	92,000	84,700	86,900
Financial fraud	207,000	203,700	207,700
Online harassment	1,944,000	2,240,000	2,374,000
Computer misuse (excluding viruses)	144,500	132,800	137,600
Sexual offences	850,000	617,500	609,700
Total	3,237,500	3,278,700	3,415,900

Source: Garlik (2009).

for VSNs and other forms of flexible computer-mediated communication relative to that in face-to-face communities.

Every neutral technology may have harmful or negative effects in the ways in which individuals choose to apply them, and the realm of social networking is no different. For a range of reasons, these new social technologies are valuable to those who are intent on harm. These are not caused by the technology, but are enabled by them. The particular increase in the tendency by individuals to put increasing amounts of information about themselves on public show leads to one general area of concern (Wall, 2005; Wall and Williams, 2007). This loss of privacy has resulted in a range of social problems becoming significantly easier for perpetrators, for example, stalking, identity theft, planning burglary and so on, all of which are made increasingly easy by people's use of this technology. More active criminal invention has resulted in the targeting of individuals using computer-based communication, for instance the use by criminals of software to plant items in apparently 'clean' Twitter and Facebook content with malware or spyware, and the use by governments of this openness for other interference (for example, recent accusations of Chinese government involvement in hacking via SNS links). The limited evidence that exists suggests that internet crime affects a significant proportion of the population already, and is likely to rise (Table 22.5). Generally, concerns over internet-based crime are increasing significantly.

A second area of concern arises from the impact on internet-based relationships of the apparent distance and easy anonymity (or false identities) of internet communication. These affect many individuals involved in meeting partners online. While net flirting may be easier than face-to-face flirting, so is net relationship infidelity (Baker, 2000; Whitty, 2009). The confusing range of views over the importance of net relationships also creates a new potential mismatch between the implicit attitudes of those in relationships that may in turn be ultimately damaging. The ability to lie undetectably during the establishment of relationships is an obvious issue (Whitty, 2002). The ability of the internet to provide a tool to use in personal crimes based on 'negative relationships', such as harassment, reflects the capacity to increase access for those in all types of relationships. This results potentially in an extremely intrusive offence but one that is difficult to combat by individuals or even authorities, making it increasingly problematic.

It also causes concern that 'social' networking is apparently being used for serious criminal activity that leads to physical harm to individuals. The criminal grooming of children by paedophile gangs is made much simpler by the creation of false yet convincing identities to entrap children and so on, taking advantage of the difficulties of validation of internet information generally and VSN data in particular. This may be an overstated concern in view of current evidence on such cases (Gallagher, 2007) and may be a consequence of the relative naivety of computer users, but a significant number of cases appear to occur where VSNs have been central to the organization of criminal activities such as paedophilia or murder (Gallagher, 2007; *Telegraph*, 2007, 2008; *Independent*, 2009a, 2009b; *Manchester Evening News*, 2009). This may simply reflect the willingness of criminals like any other people to embrace technology, but the particular characteristics of internet communication particularly suit it to criminal use. VSNs provide a low-cost, rapid and adaptable platform for communicating messages, images and so on; for coordination of activity, for spread of urgent information of different forms, and in a way which leaves attribution unclear and largely untraceable, in some cases, even under official investigation.

CONCLUSION

Leisure networks have been increasingly squeezed by historical changes in the working lives of individuals, the organization of leisure opportunities, and the commercialization of leisure. The capacity for VSNs to increase access to leisure networks in the face of these changes may account for a large proportion of their success in recent years. The ability to 'liberate' leisure, and to make access to it more flexible, goes against a long-running trend that appears to have damaged societies' social leisure considerably in recent years.

The unusual economics of social network providers means that several different models of provision may be considered to finance the massively high costs of purchasing technical infrastructure to store and transfer the material lodged on the individual VSNs. While technically the costs of social networks decline extremely rapidly to near zero due to the minimal costs of reproduction, the increasing demands of users for platforms that accept various forms of content, and the need to store this more resource-intensive content means that costs rapidly advance even as network usage increases. The models of provision vary from, at one extreme, the standard provision of service contracts with standard subscriptions to, at the other, a model that considers VSNs simply as the production process for information goods that are destined for other markets, in various forms.

The position for social networks remains unclear, despite the apparent benefits of 'mechanization' of social interaction using VSNs. There appears to be general agreement that there has been a decline in social involvement of individuals, and that this has consequentially caused problems for individuals lacking social support structures that would help them through social, psychological and economic problems. The negative impact on the resilience of individuals in this position may to some extent be reversible if social networking is developed on VSNs that provide free and flexible social services that enable individuals to develop alternative social resources. Several concerns exist, however, relating to the strength of relationships developed over the internet, and also the validity of information on such sites. The different types of users of the internet may benefit from involvement in additional social networks (social compensation) or may instead neglect other social resources, leaving themselves net losers for their involvement in the VSNs (social displacement). In addition, VSNs constitute a very different form of personal self-presentation that may affect the way individuals perceive others and present themselves in future.

The benefits to the wider economy, rather than to the individual, of social networks derive from their ability to support 'social capital'. The impacts of this may build civic ability to respond to changing conditions, or may enhance an individual's access to important resources. The evidence on actual internet use to date suggests that the dominant patterns of communication have been within existing family groups, suggesting a possible lack of impact on either of the significant forms of social capital, but the increasing use of social networking to meet new people, rather than to service existing relationships more efficiently, may change this. Unfortunately there seems to be significant growth in the illegal uses of VSNs, which appear to be inevitable until honest users become less naive in their attitude to communications on the internet.

Overall, the balance of positive and negative impacts means that it is difficult to predict the future of VSNs. The economic position of VSN providers may also lead to future changes in the system of provision. The value of the information goods produced by VSNs is critical to the provision of the services to consumers for little or no charge. As many consumers of net services feel protected by the anonymity that is possible with VSNs, issues surrounding the identity of users, and the inability to check the validity of information provided via a VSN are likely to remain. It will, in addition, complicate the job of providers who depend on the quality of information they receive through the network to finance their operations. It is possible that, rather than these issues of anonymity being satisfactorily dealt with, VSN providers may need to change to charging subscriptions more widely in order to maintain the standard of service currently expected by users.

REFERENCES

Anderson, B. (2004), 'Information society technologies, social capital, and quality of life', Chimera Working Paper No. 2004-05, January, University of Essex, Colchester.

Argyle, M. (1975), *Bodily Communication*, London: Methuen.

Argyle, M. (1994), *The Psychology of Interpersonal Behaviour*, 5th edn, London: Penguin.

Baker, A. (2000), 'Two by two in cyberspace: getting together and connecting online', *Cyberpsychology and Behavior*, 3 (2), available at: http://oak.cats.ohiou.edu/~bakera/ArticleF.htm.

Bargh, J.A. and K.Y.A. McKenna (2004), 'The internet and social life', *Annual Review of Psychology*, 55, 573–90.

Bargh, J.A., K.Y.A. McKenna and G.M. Fitzsimons (2002), 'Can you see the real me? Activation and expression of the "true self" on the internet', *Journal of Social Issues*, 58 (1), 33–48.

Becker, G.S. (1965), 'A theory of the allocation of time', *Economic Journal*, 75 (299), 493–517.

Bessière, K., S. Kiesler, R. Kraut and B.S. Boneva (2008), 'Effects of internet use and social resources on depression', *Information, Communication and Society*, 11 (1), 47–70.

Boardman, A.E. and S.P. Hargreaves-Heap (1999), 'Network externalities and government restrictions of broadcasting of key events', *Journal of Cultural Economics*, 23, 167–81.

Borsay, P. (1977), 'The English urban renaissance: the development of provincial urban culture, c. 1680–c. 1760', *Social History*, 5, 581–603.

Buchanan, J.M. (1965), 'An economic theory of clubs', *Economica*, 32, 1–15.

Bureau of Economic Analysis (2009), *National Income and Product Accounts (NIPA): Price Indices for Private Fixed Investment by Type*, Washington, DC: US Bureau of Economic Analysis.

Center for the Digital Future (2004), *Surveying the Digital Future: Digital Future Report Year 4*, University of Southern Carolina Annenberg School Center for the Digital Future, Columbia, SC, available at: http://www.digitalcenter.org (accessed 18 September 2009).

Center for the Digital Future (2005), *Surveying the Digital Future: Digital Future Report Year 5*, University of Southern Carolina Annenberg School Center for the Digital Future, Columbia, SC, available at: http://www.digitalcenter.org (accessed 18 September 2009).

Center for the Digital Future (2006), *Digital Future Report Year 6*, University of Southern Carolina Annenberg School Center for the Digital Future, Columbia, SC, available at: http://www.digitalcenter.org (accessed 18 September 2009).

Center for the Digital Future (2007), *Digital Future Report Year 7*, University of Southern Carolina Annenberg School Center for the Digital Future, Columbia, SC, available at: http://www.digitalcenter.org (accessed 18 September 2009).

Center for the Digital Future (2008), *Digital Future Report Year 8*, University of Southern

Carolina Annenberg School Center for the Digital Future, Columbia, SC, available at: http://www.digitalcenter.org (accessed 18 September 2009).

Center for the Digital Future (2009), *Digital Future Report Year 9*, University of Southern Carolina Annenberg School Center for the Digital Future, Columbia, SC, available at: http://www.digitalcenter.org (accessed 18 September 2009).

Coleman, James S. (1988), 'Social capital in the creation of human capital', *American Journal of Sociology*, **94** (Supplement), S95–S120.

Costa, D.L. (1996), 'The wage and the length of the work day from the 1890s to 1991', NBER Working Paper WP6504, Cambridge, MA.

Costa, D.L. (1997), 'Less of a luxury: the rise of recreation since 1888', NBER Working Paper WP6054, Cambridge, MA.

Douglas, M. (1973 [1994]), 'Grid and group', in R. Collins (ed.), *Four Sociological Traditions: Elected Readings*, Oxford: Oxford University Press, pp. 271–80.

Dunbar, R.I.M. (1993), 'Co-evolution of neocortex size, group size and language in humans', *Behavioral and Brain Sciences*, **16** (4), 681–735.

Dunbar, R.I.M. (1998), 'The social brain hypothesis', *Evolutionary Anthropology*, **6** (5), 178–90.

Ellison, N., C. Steinfield and C. Lampe (2009), 'Facebook connection strategies and relationship development: patterns of social network use and communication on campus', paper presented at University of Chicago Booth School of Business, 2 June, available at: http://faculty.chicagobooth.edu/workshops/orgs-markets/archive/pdf/Ellison_et_al_Revised_CONNECTION_STRATEGIES_td.doc (accessed 3 November 2009).

Fitzsimons, V.G. (2006), 'Information society: networks, collective action and the role of institutions', *International Journal of Humanities*, **3** (6), 19–32.

Gallagher, B. (2007), 'Internet-initiated incitement and conspiracy to commit child sexual abuse (CSA): the typology, extent and nature of known cases', *Journal of Sexual Aggression*, **13** (2), 101–19.

Garlik (2009), *UK Cybercrime Report 2009*, London: Garlik, available at: http://www.garlik.com/cybercrime_report.php (accessed 7 October 2009).

Gauthier, A.H. and T. Smeeding (2001), 'Historical trends in the patterns of time use of older adults', mimeo, OECD, available at: http://www.oecd.org/dataoecd/21/5/2430978.pdf (accessed 25 January 2010).

Goffman, E. (1959), *The Presentation of Self in Everyday Life*, New York: Doubleday.

Goldman, R. (1983), '"We make weekends": leisure and the commodity form', *Social Text*, **8**, 84–103.

Goldman, R. and J. Wilson (1977), 'The rationalization of leisure', *Politics and Society*, **7** (2), 157–87.

Granovetter, Mark (1973), 'The strength of weak ties', *American Journal of Sociology*, **78** (6), 1360–80.

Horrigan, J. (2009), 'The mobile difference: wireless connectivity has drawn many users more deeply into digital life', Pew Internet and American Life Project, Washington, DC, available at: http://www.pewinternet.org/Reports/2009/5-The-Mobile-Difference--Typology.aspx (accessed 23 September 2009).

Huang, M.-H., J.-C. Wang, S. Yu and C.-C. Chiu (2004), 'Value-added ERP information into information goods: an economic analysis', *Industrial Management and Data Systems*, **104** (8), 689–97.

Independent (2009a), 'The Facebook paedophile ring', *Independent*, 2 October, available at: http://www.independent.co.uk/news/uk/crime/the-facebook-paedophile-ring-1796373.html (accessed 3 October 2009).

Independent (2009b), 'Man held over death of girl he met on Facebook', *Independent*, 28 October, available at: http://license.icopyright.net/user/viewFreeUse.act?fuid=NTU2MTcyMg%3D%3D (accessed 28 October 2009).

Katz, M.L. and C. Shapiro (1986), 'Technology adoption in the presence of network externalities', *Journal of Political Economy*, **94**, 822–41.

Kiesler, S., J. Siegel and T.W. McGuire (1984), 'Social psychological aspects of computer mediated communication', *American Psychologist*, **29** (10), 1123–34.

Kraut, R., M. Patterson, V. Lundmark, S. Kiesler, T. Mukopadhyay and W. Scherlis (1998), 'Internet paradox: a social technology that reduces social involvement and psychological well-being?', *American Psychologist*, **53** (9), 1017–31.

Kraut, R., S. Kiesler, B. Boneva, J. Cummings, V. Helgeson and A. Crawford (2002), 'Internet paradox revisited', *Journal of Social Issues*, **58** (1), 49–74.

Larrabee, E. (1989), 'The invention of leisure in early modern Europe', *Past and Present*, **146** (1), 136–51.

Manchester Evening News (2009), 'Police warn over murder suspect', *Manchester Evening News*, 9 February, available at: http://www.manchestereveningnews.co.uk/news/s/1095490_police_warn_over_murder_suspect (accessed 28 October 2009).

Mayfield, R. (2009), 'Active networks on Facebook', Ross Mayfield's Weblog: Markets, Technology and Musings, 8 April, available at: http://ross.typepad.com/blog/2009/04/active-networks-on-facebook.html (accessed 21 August 2009).

McInnes, A. (1988), 'The emergence of a leisure town: Shrewsbury 1660–1760', *Past and Present*, **120**, 53–87.

McPherson, M., L. Smith-Lovin and M.E. Brashears (2006), 'Social isolation in America: changes in core discussion networks over two decades', *American Sociological Review*, **71**, 353–75.

Media Life (2009), 'Rachel, my boss wants to friend me', *Media Life*, 18 September, available at: http://www.medialifemagazine.com/artman2/publish/Rachel_speaks_30/Rachel_my_boss_wants_to_friend_me.asp (accessed 18 September 2009).

Milgram, Stanley (1967), 'The small world problem', *Psychology Today*, May, 60–67.

Nie, N.H. and D.S. Hillygus (2002), 'Where does internet time come from?', *IT and Society*, **1** (2), 1–20.

OECD (2008), *Information Technology Outlook 2008*, Paris: OECD.

OECD (2009), *Communications Outlook 2009*, Paris: OECD.

Olson, M. (1965), *The Logic of Collective Action*, Cambridge, MA: Harvard University Press.

Parker, G.C. and M.W. Van Alstyne (2005), 'Two sided network effects: a theory of information product design', *Management Science*, **51** (10), 1494–504.

Putnam, R.D. (1993), *Making Democracy Work: Civic Traditions in Modern Italy*, Princeton, NJ: Princeton University Press.

Putnam, R.D. (1995a), 'Bowling alone: America's declining social capital', *Journal of Democracy*, **6** (1), 65–78.

Putnam, R.D. (1995b), 'Tuning in, tuning out: the strange disappearance of social capital in America', *PS: Political Science and Politics*, **28** (4), 664–83.

Reid, D.A. (1976), 'The decline of Saint Monday: 1766–1876', *Past and Present*, **71**, 76–101.

Reid, D.A. (1996), 'Weddings, weekdays, work and leisure in urban England 1791–1911', *Past and Present*, **153**, 135–63.

Riesman, D. (1953), *The Lonely Crowd* (with Nathan Glazer and Reuel Denney), New York: Doubleday.

Rohlfs, J. (1974), 'A theory of interdependent demand for a communications service', *Bell Journal of Economics and Management Science*, **5** (1), 16–37.

Sandler, T. and J.T. Tschirhart (1980), 'The economic theory of clubs: an evaluative survey', *Journal of Economic Literature*, **18** (4), 1481–521.

Sandler, T. and J.T. Tschirhart (1997), 'Club theory: 30 years later', *Public Choice*, **93**, 335–55.

Shannon, C.E. (1948), 'A mathematical theory of communication', *The Bell System Technical Journal*, **27** (July), 379–423.

Sky News (2009), 'Sacked for calling job boring on Facebook', 27 February, accessed at: http://news.sky.com/skynews/Home/UK-News/Facebook-Sacking-Kimberley-Swann-From-Clacton-Essex-Sacked-For-Calling-Job-Boring/Article/200902415230508 (accessed 22 June 2009).

Spender, D. (1995), *Nattering on the Net: Women, Power and Cyberspace*, North Melbourne: Spinifex Press.

Steinfield, C., N.B. Ellison and C. Lampe (2008), 'Social capital, self esteem, and use of online social network sites: a longitudinal analysis', *Journal of Applied Developmental Psychology*, **29**, 434–45.

Telegraph (2007), 'Facebook takes steps to tackle paedophiles', *Telegraph*, 17 October, available at: http://www.telegraph.co.uk/news/uknews/1566406/Facebook-takes-steps-to-tackle-paedophiles.html (accessed 28 October 2009).

Telegraph (2008), 'Facebook killer jailed for life', *Telegraph*, 17 October, available at: http://www.telegraph.co.uk/news/newstopics/politics/lawandorder/3217888/Facebook-killer-jailed-for-life.html (accessed 28 October 2009).

Thomas, K. (1961), 'Work and leisure', *Past and Present*, **29**, 50–66.

Times, The (2009), 'Wife blows MI6 chief's cover on Facebook', TimesOnline, 5 July, available at: http://www.timesonline.co.uk/tol/news/uk/article6639521.ece (accessed 13 July 2009).

Varian, H.R. (1995), 'Pricing information goods', working paper, Department of Economics, University of Michigan, Ann Arbor, MI.

Varian, H.R. (1997), 'Versioning information good', working paper, Department of Economics, University of Michigan, Ann Arbor, MI.

Wall, David S. (2005), 'The internet as a conduit for criminal activity', in A. Pattavina (ed.), *Information Technology and the Criminal Justice System*, London: Sage, pp. 77–98.

Wall, D.S. and M.L. Williams (2007), 'Policing diversity in the digital age maintaining order in virtual communities', *Criminology and Criminal Justice*, **7** (4), 391–415.

Whitty, M.T. (2002), 'Liar, liar: an examination of how open, supportive, and honest people are in chat rooms', *Computers in Human Behavior*, **18**, 343–52.

Whitty, M.T. (2009), 'Introduction', in M.T. Whitty, A.J. Baker and J.A. Inman (eds), *Online M@tchmaking*, London: Palgrave, pp. 1–14.

23 Girls just want to have fun? Internet leisure and women's empowerment in Jordan
Deborah L. Wheeler and Lauren Mintz

INTRODUCTION

Only a small handful of scholars and policy analysts have examined the meaning of information technology for women in the Middle East.[1] An even smaller community has studied the impact of new media practices on women in Jordan (Wheeler, 2006b; Kaya, 2009; Shunnaq, 2009). There is a particularly significant gap in the literature which looks at women's leisure practices and the internet in the Middle East, a gap which this chapter begins to fill. Jordan is a suitable place to probe the relationship between information technology (IT), leisure and women's empowerment in the Middle East – first, because the desire to empower women by providing IT tools and training is part of a national strategy for economic growth and human development as defined by King Abdullah and Queen Rania of Jordan; and second, because Jordanian women suffer many forms of gender discrimination from unequal access to citizenship rights, to honour killings, to uneven access to jobs. One Jordanian political scientist explains the legal foundations of gender discrimination in her country by observing, 'The only justification for the discriminatory laws, either in text or in practice, is the desire to maintain the status quo of the patriarchal structures within the family and, by extension, within the state' (Amawi, 2000, p. 181). Since potential for grievance is high, one might wonder whether IT access would give women tools with which to better organize and articulate their interests. Manuel Castells has observed that the rise of the network society has 'enabled a mass insurrection of women against their oppression throughout the world, albeit with different intensity depending on culture and country (Castells, 2000, quoted in Senft, 2008, p. 6). Scholars studying such processes in the Arab world have wondered whether the internet and other new media tools will provide women the means to resist deeply entrenched patterns of patriarchy (Wheeler, 2006a, Ch. 4; 2008).

This chapter helps to close the gap in our knowledge of Arab women's internet use by providing a glimpse at the lives of Jordanian women's internet practices. Using their own words, this study provides concrete examples of how women are using the technology to, in the words of Queen Rania, 'reshape their lives'.[2] One of the most important findings of this research is that among the 100 Jordanian female internet café users interviewed for this study, the average number of hours spent online per week in an internet café is nine. This suggests that using the internet is a routine part of everyday life for these women. This finding is of particular importance because one of the arguments for discounting the social and political importance of internet use in the Arab world is an unsubstantiated belief that the technology is not central to the average citizen's life (Alterman, 2000; Rugh, 2004, p. xiii). Also calling into question the belief that the internet is not central to Arab lives is the fact that access to the technology is growing faster in the Middle East than in any other world region, with a diffusion rate between 2000 and 2009 of more than 1,600 per cent.[3]

This study begins to construct a different picture of Arab internet practices. The data below suggest that the internet is slowly becoming an important part of everyday life in Jordan. The women studied in this chapter are not the cosmopolitan elite. Rather, they are the more typical middle- and lower-class women who do not usually have access to the internet at home or work; do not own a car; have limited education; and lack fluency in English. The women tend to come from large families, and also tend to be first-generation internet users. Most of these women have not had any formal IT training. If non-elite women in Jordan are spending on average nine hours a week in an internet café, this suggests that the internet is becoming a mass technology. While penetration rates are just under 25 per cent for Jordanian society as a whole, this number more than likely fails to capture the usership of the high percentage of Jordanians whose only access to the internet is in a public access point.

Imam Yusuf al-Qaradawi, one of twenty-first-century Islam's most prominent conservative voices observes in his book *Love and the Internet* (2006) that 'Since the World Wide Web invaded our lives, we have been going through non-stop transformations' (quoted in Mernissi, 2006, p. 121). The following pages examine in detail what some of the internet-enabled 'non-stop transformations' are for women in Jordan. In a nutshell, the women interviewed observe that the internet enables them to meet new people, to connect with family and friends, to look for jobs, to search for a spouse, to talk about politics, and to learn to develop and express opinions in public (cyber) forums. Supporting al-Qaradawi's observations, the data show that Jordanian women are learning to interact in uncustomary ways with members of the opposite sex. All of these cyber practices are, in the words of the participants, making them more confident, broadening their minds, making life easier, providing entertainment, and sometimes shaping their career/life goals. Being online gives them access to new forms of information, helps them to practise their English, gives them knowledge of foreign cultures and social practices, and invites them to organize for change.

After situating this study within the secondary literature on this subject, and providing an introduction to the case study, research methodology and dataset, the study provides an ethnographic and statistical analysis of the most significant impacts of internet use on everyday life for 100 Jordanian women, as articulated by the participants. While internet café managers and others interviewed often viewed internet practices as 'wasting time chatting', we show that there are potentially significant links between leisure and social transformations in Jordanian women's lives which deserve further study.

SITUATING THIS STUDY: THEORIES OF NEW COMMUNICATIONS TECHNOLOGIES, WOMEN'S LEISURE AND WOMEN'S EMPOWERMENT

This study of women's internet practices in Amman draws upon three areas of social scientific theory: leisure studies, communications studies, and the women's empowerment literature. Based upon six months of ethnographic research in internet cafés throughout a wide sample of neighbourhoods in Amman, from West Amman to Zarqa, the study considers the results of 100 interviews with female internet café users between the ages of 16 and 44. When asked whether time spent online was having any impact on their lives, the two most important responses, as explored more completely below, were first, that the internet expands social networks, including in some cases both cyber and face-to-face meetings with members of the opposite sex; and second, the technology is said to expand the breadth and speed of access to information, including information on subjects sometimes considered sensitive or taboo. A number of women interviewed said that internet cafés provide a socially acceptable public space in which to spend their free time with friends and to escape boredom, thus revealing a 'synergy' between 'gender relations, spatial relations and leisure relations' (Aitchison, 1999, p. 19).

New Media and Civic Engagement

An emerging community of interdisciplinary researchers is examining the ways in which new communications technologies are reshaping leisure and the practice of everyday life – economically, socially and politically. Notable among these researchers is Robert D. Putnam, whose *Bowling*

Alone raised red flags about the potential dangers of TV and the internet use to civic engagement in the US (Putnam, 2000, pp. 216–46). Putnam's basic theory is that 'social networks have value' (p. 19); 'civic virtue is most powerful when embedded in a dense network of reciprocal social relations' (p. 19); and 'civic connections help make us healthy, wealthy and wise' (p. 287). Most importantly for this analysis, Putnam argues that new media technologies are a threat to civic engagement because the more time people spend online, the fewer hours they spend engaging with their communities and peer networks. If these trends continue, which Putnam suggests will be the case, then social capital, which is key for a healthy society, will be on the wane.

This study traces the ways in which internet use, contrary to what Putnam observes in the US, is promoting new forms of civic engagement and empowerment for Jordanian women. For example, Putnam, following Alexis de Tocqueville, sees newspaper reading as a foundation for good citizenship, but argues that with the advent of the TV and internet age, more and more people in the US are seeking entertainment rather than the news, and that the pursuit of that entertainment is increasingly individualized and accessed in more and more socially isolating locations (p. 218). Putnam, quoting Joshua Meyrowitz, notes that 'electronic media allow social ties to be divorced from physical encounters' thus creating processes of 'civic disengagement' (p. 242).

For female internet café users in Amman, however, 85 per cent of those interviewed read a daily newspaper in spite of spending on average nine hours a week online. Most of these women, 74 per cent in fact, prefer to visit internet cafés with someone, suggesting that internet use for them is not a physically isolated experience. Moreover, when asked about their internet practices, 97 per cent stated that they use it for email, 83 per cent said they use it for chatting and 65 per cent use it to get information. The top three uses of the technology all suggest that the tool promotes conversation and social interaction in addition to information awareness, and all of these are potentially important aspects of civic engagement. The most important finding of this study is that women are using online encounters to meet people in real life, thus demonstrating ways in which the technology expands social networks and face-to-face engagements (some of which are leading to marriage . . . sometimes thwarting traditional practices which seek to main strict cultural, tribal and class lines).

Women's Leisure Practices in the Middle East

The study of women's leisure is an increasingly common topic of scholarly debate. However, it seems to be heavily neglected by economists.

Little of the emerging general literature is dedicated to such study. Narges Arab-Moghaddam and Karla A. Henderson in their study of women's leisure in Iran provide the only systematic study to date. They note that the leisure studies literature demonstrates 'a lack of examination of the cultural dimensions of leisure and especially research about women from emerging nations' (2007, p. 110). In their study, they note that Iranian women share in a global problem 'of inequality regarding opportunities for leisure' and that most of women's leisure activities are 'focused on social relationships' (p. 110). Women interviewed for this study of internet leisure practices in Jordan often stated that 'there wasn't much to do in Jordan' and that 'internet cafés were a welcome alternative to boredom'. The fact that 79 per cent of those interviewed found that the most important impact of internet use was that it expanded their social networking capabilities reinforces the view that women's leisure is often focused on social relationships.

In an effort to expand an understanding of 'the leisure of Muslim women from Middle Eastern cultures', Arab-Moghaddam and Henderson conducted a survey of leisure practices among 570 Iranian women between the ages of 24 and 40 living in Shiraz (pp. 110, 115). The findings of their study were that 'the most common leisure activities undertaken were watching TV and listening to the radio, family gatherings, reading books and magazines, outdoor activities, and religious activities' (p. 119). The most important constraint on women's leisure activity was 'lack of structure as it related to opportunities for leisure within the community' with responses ranging from a lack of gender sensitive public facilities for women's leisure, to a critique of government policies (pp. 118–19). In other words, if the Iranian government is going to create policy which segregates the sexes in public, then it will need to provide leisure activities and locations for women only, or women will face public constraints on their leisure access. While Arab-Moghaddam and Henderson do not examine Iranian women's internet use and leisure practices, a growing literature does, as explored below.

The present study illustrates how culturally appropriate public space for leisure can expand women's leisure activities. If women are given easy and culturally sensitive access to leisure activities, they will use them. Some cafés in Jordan, in order to be sensitive to culturally appropriate women's access, provided separate rooms for women to use. Moreover, the female clientele tend to use cafés from morning to late afternoon. Evenings tended to be dominated by men, who often gathered together to surf porn, according to some café managers, making the same café inhospitable to women in the evenings.

IT Access and Women's Empowerment in the Middle East

A handful of scholars have examined the impact of internet use on women's lives in the Middle East. Understanding the social and cultural constraints on women's participation in public life, researchers have wondered whether the internet would open up new opportunities for women's leisure, women's activism, women's empowerment, and ultimately, whether or not access to new media would reshape the role of women in traditionally patriarchal space – from the household to society to the state. For example, a recent study of female bloggers in Iran states that, 'for Iranian women, cyberspace is a liberating territory of one's own'. The author goes on to observe, 'The structure of the interconnections in cyberspace . . . draws participants into ongoing discourses on issues of feminism, patriarchy, and gender politics', which 'offers new possibilities for women's agency and empowerment' (Nouraie-Simone, 2005, p. 61). She explains, 'For women, the internet provides an unfettered, direct connection to the outside world, opening a new horizon for dialogue, self-expression, and dissenting voices. The internet is a medium of empowerment that bypasses traditionally imposed gender identity and roles' (p. 62).

In my own research on women's internet use in Kuwait, I reached a similar conclusion. My study found that the internet enables women in the Gulf to 'carve out spaces for freedom in the face of deeply entrenched hegemonies of patriarchy' (Wheeler, 2006a, p. 108). Similarly, in a comparative study of women's internet use in the Arab world, I found that women in the region saw the internet as 'having a long-term positive impact', in that it 'gives women more of a voice in society, more autonomy in the selection of a spouse, and more authority at work and abroad' (Wheeler, 2004, p. 161).

Several high-profile Arab women have advocated increased access to the internet for women. Her Majesty Queen Rania of Jordan, addressing the Second Arab Women's Summit in 2002 observed: 'it is important for Arab women to make use of the latest technologies, particularly the internet'.[4] Queen Rania, in an effort to teach by example, is an active user of Facebook, Twitter and other new media social networking tools. At Le Web 2009 conference in Paris, she explained the direct link between using social media and creating social change.[5] Similarly, Najat Rochidi, director of the ICTDAR programme at the United Nations Development Programme (UNDP) states that the internet can be leveraged to expand women's leadership skills, provided that 'the culture of machismo in Muslim countries is also changed so that women are valued as clever and accomplished people in their own right outside the tutelage of a father or husband and not only as mothers and caretakers'.[6] The UNDP reinforced these views when in 2002, its *Arab Human Development Report* observed that failing to provide women with easy and equitable access to IT slows the development and progress of society as a whole. This same report ranked expanding women's access to information technology as the third most pressing concern women in the Arab world face, preceded only by domestic violence and poverty (UNDP, 2002, p. 10).

While elite women in positions of political power in the region encourage their sisters to use the internet to expand their social and political capital, for the average woman, the internet seems to be more of a leisure tool at this stage. Only 18 per cent of those interviewed found the internet to be transforming their lives politically. The most important impact as demonstrated below is the ways in which the technology promotes new social networking opportunities (79 per cent) and greater access to information (66 per cent). Some of the narratives examined, however, show that chatting and emailing are not benign leisure activities. On the contrary, many of those interviewed stated that online debates, for example, were making them braver, more socially aware, less shy, and more interested in world affairs. As the technology continues to diffuse throughout society, and women become more skilled in their use of the new tool, we could see increasingly active women pressing for political change. The Kuwaiti suffrage movement and the 2009 Iranian election day protests demonstrate that mobile communications, including the internet, enable women to organize and protest. In both of these cases, new media tools were used to coordinate protests and demonstrations, and to share photos and tweets with the global media.

THE INTERNET IN THE JORDANIAN CONTEXT AND BEYOND

Before we turn to an analysis of female internet café users in Jordan, some background information about IT in Jordan will help to contextualize this study. The internet appeared in the country in 1994. Urban legend states that the internet came so that King Hussein, who was battling cancer at the time, could use the technology to quickly send medical information between his doctors in Amman and those at the Mayo Clinic in Minnesota. During the early years of internet diffusion in Jordan, as in the rest of the region, public access was curtailed because of state concerns about losing an information monopoly. Moreover, low public awareness/ demand for the technology, high cost of access, limited computing skills among the population, and sparseness of Arabic language web content also kept internet communities relatively small and specialized (Wheeler,

Table 23.1   *Regional internet diffusion rates and gross national product*
(PPP)

Country	Population 2009 est.	Internet usage/2000	Internet usage/2009	% population (penetration)	% growth 2000–09	GNP (PPP) in US$
Bahrain	728,290	40,000	155,000	21.0	287.5	38,400*
Iraq	28,945,569	12,500	300,000	1.0	2,300.0	3,300*
Jordan	6,269,285	127,300	1,500,500	23.9	1,078.7	5,530
Kuwait	2,692,526	150,000	1,000,000	37.1	566.7	52,610
Iran	66,429,284	250,000	32,200,000	48.5	12,780.0	10,840
Lebanon	4,017,095	300,000	945,000	23.5	215.0	10,880
Oman	3,418,085	90,000	465,000	13.6	416.7	20,650
Qatar	833,285	30,000	436,000	53.3	1,353.3	121,490*
Saudi Arabia	28,686,633	200,000	7,700,000	26.8	3,750.0	22,950
Syria	21,762,978	30,000	3,565,000	16.4	11,783.3	4,350
UAE	4,798,491	735,000	2,922,000	60.9	297.6	41,800*
Yemen	22,858,238	15,000	370,000	1.6	2,366.7	2,210
Algeria	34,178,188	50,000	4,100,000	12.0	3,740.0	7,940
Egypt	78,866,635	450,000	12,568,900	15.9	2,693.1	5,460
Libya	6,324,357	10,000	323,000	5.1	3,130.0	15,630
Morocco	31,285,174	100,000	10,300,000	32.9	10,200.0	4,330
Tunisia	10,486,339	100,000	2,800,000	26.7	2,700.0	7,070

Sources: Internet World Stats, www.internetworldstats.com, World Bank (www.
worldbank.org) and * *CIA World Factbook* (2009) (www.cia.gov).

2005). Under the present circumstances, state concerns about misuse of
the technology has meant that broadband remains expensive. PC penetration rates are also low, below 10 per cent. These factors keep wi-fi access
beyond the reach of the general population, and internet cafés are popular
among those looking for affordable access to the technology. In spite of
the slow diffusion of wi-fi, there are a growing number of wi-fi hotspots in
Jordan, including a number of high-end cafés, restaurants and shopping
malls, but in most of these locations, there is still a relatively high fee for
access. (See Table 23.1.)

Internet penetration in the Arab world is growing at one of the fastest
rates on the planet. As shown in the table, Jordan had an internet growth
rate of more than 1,000 per cent between 2000 and 2009. Jordan ranks
eighth out of 17 countries in the MENA (Middle East and North Africa)
region in terms of per capita internet penetration. The top two countries
are both oil monarchies with per capita GNP well above the regional
average. The data show that being an oil monarchy is not enough to

guarantee a high level (for the region) of internet penetration. For example, Saudi Arabia and Tunisia both have about the same internet penetration rate, even though Saudi Arabia's GNP per capita is more than three times higher than Tunisia's. Similarly, Jordan's GNP per capita is only a quarter that of Oman, yet Jordan's internet penetration rates are nearly double those in Oman.

Jordan has one of the highest levels of female literacy in the region, with 86.3 per cent of women over the age of 15 being able to read and write. In addition, Jordan ranks third in terms of the share of households with access to a television (97 per cent, almost universal penetration). Surprisingly, given its GNP per capita, Jordan ranks fifth for PC penetration in the region (still, less than 10 per cent of Jordanian society own a PC), with 55 machines per 1,000 people. Jordan is in the *Guinness Book of World Records* for having the highest concentration of internet cafés on a single city block (Irbid, University Avenue). Moreover, Jordan's Ministry of Education has launched a major e.Learning initiative whereby students are taught computer literacy from kindergarten on. The King of Jordan has invested significant government, international and his own private capital in the Jordan Knowledge Station initiative which established 120 public computing/internet access points throughout the country. All of these factors and many others have helped to make Jordan a place where computer and internet literacy are a part of public consciousness and everyday life, even in remote locations.

RESEARCH DESIGN

The analysis below is part of a study begun in 2004 to discover what role internet cafés play in the everyday life of people in the Middle East. The main goal was to see whether internet access was making any significant differences in users' social, political and/or economic life including their leisure practices. This study takes a constructivist approach to understanding the meaning of internet technology in context. It thus relies heavily on user testimonials, by allowing participants to articulate answers to open-ended questions such as 'Has the internet changed your life, and if so, how?' The responses, which were universally 'yes' for women in Jordan, are examined in more detail below.

Figure 23.1 shows the density of the variable 'current age' – representing the age of the women at the time of the interview. It shows that the majority of respondents are young – the mean age is 24.5 years with a standard deviation of 5.6 years.

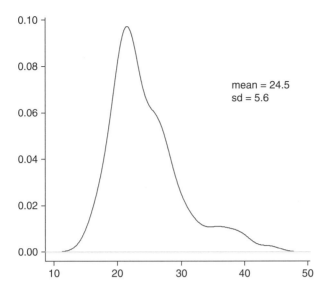

Figure 23.1   Density plot of age

The interviews were conducted face to face, in Arabic, by a Jordanian research assistant in internet cafés throughout Amman, where 68 per cent of the population live. The interviews took place between February and May 2004. The results were verified and supplemented by the findings of another study which conducted fieldwork on women's IT training and practices more widely throughout Jordan (Wheeler, 2006b). The research design was careful to select locations for the interviews covering a cross-section of neighbourhoods and socioeconomic environments in Amman, from wealthy Abdoun to relatively working-class Zarqa. Interviews were conducted at various times throughout the day and evening so as to get a broad spectrum of user patterns. The interviews lasted between 30 and 45 minutes depending upon how much elaboration the participant made to the open-ended questions. (For a complete list of the questions, see Appendix 23A.) In general, the findings suggest that the internet is more of a normal part of everyday life than generally acknowledged. Moreover, the internet is clearly having an impact on users' lives, including giving them important professional development opportunities, expanding their social networks, changing their political/social consciousness, and ending boredom. What this means in terms of individual users' lives is examined below.

Figure 23.2 illustrates how the women interviewed spend their time online.

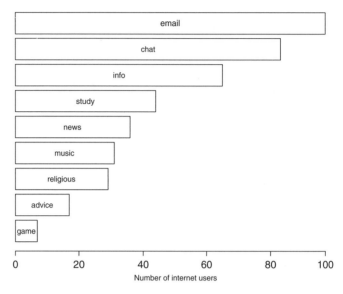

Figure 23.2   Internet uses

IMPACT 1: WIDENING INFORMATION ACCESS

Arab countries are known as some of the most repressive and restrictive in the world. In terms of information access and flow, Arab countries, including Jordan have heavily restrictive press laws which aim to limit oppositional discourse and critique of the government and its allies. In a context of scarcity of access to up-to-date and reliable information regarding politics, news, popular culture and potentially taboo subjects, through state-controlled media channels, citizens have found the internet to provide pathways to new information resources, and means of self-expression. A growing expectation for instant information, on demand, and tailored to one's interests, is changing information environments in the region. Some countries are even abolishing their ministries of information in response to the new information climates in the era of mobile communications (such as Qatar), satellite TV and blogs, all of which lessen state monopolies on information access and distribution channels. Jordanian women have taken advantage of these emerging environments of information abundance. Among the 100 internet users interviewed for this study, 66 per cent said that access to information online was transforming their lives. The following narrative samples are illustrative of the wider process of increased access to information and its impact for women.

A 32-year-old woman who uses the internet for about ten hours a week explains:

> [The internet] has given me information instantly and the variety of information available is vast. It increases my knowledge and through email, it helps me to keep in touch with friends and family. (Interview, Abdoun, Amman, 17 April 2004, evening)

We see in this testimonial that the internet is linked with multiple everyday uses. For this woman, the technology is attractive and useful for getting 'instant' access to 'vast' information (which would be transformative in a conservative Arab context like Jordan, as explained above). At the same time, it 'increases my knowledge' while strengthening her pre-existing social networks by enabling her to 'keep in touch with family and friends'.

This same 'layers of meaning' approach to the technology is characterized by the following narrative. A Jordanian high school student who spends about eight hours a week online at an internet café observes when asked whether the internet has changed her life in any way:

> Yeah, it helped me to keep in touch with my friends abroad, helped me to learn more about certain subjects I like to research. It made it easier to get access to music. When I am bored, it gives me something to do and to have fun. (Interview, Abdoun, Amman, 17 April 2004, evening)

So the primary explanation given is that the technology helps her to maintain her social networks, especially with friends who are abroad. At the same time, the technology gives her access to 'certain subjects I like to research'. When pressed, she explains 'like science projects'. Most importantly for this study, the internet gives her something to do when she is 'bored'. Within these virtual spaces for obtaining information and sharing opinions, 'Arabs have and continue to use the Internet, for reshaping the public sphere through expanding the margins of freedom of expression' and freedom of information (Rinnawi, 2002, p. 1).

IMPACT 2: ESCAPING BOREDOM, FILLING LEISURE TIME

Housewives and the unemployed are two communities significantly drawn to the power of the internet to transport users into meaningful new realities. One in ten of the women interviewed is a housewife. On average, these housewives spend about six hours a week online at an internet café. None of them has access to the internet except through an internet café. When asked whether the internet had changed their life, all of them responded affirmatively. The most common explanations were that they used the internet to fill their free time and to stay in touch with friends and relatives abroad. For example, one 26-year-old housewife observes, 'The internet made a big difference in my life because now I chat with my husband in Saudi Arabia and it is better than letters and phone calls are too expensive'. Similarly, a 30-year-old housewife states, 'The internet made a big difference in my life because with it I talk freely with my husband in the Gulf. We meet online and it is a useful way to communicate'. Another housewife states that she uses the internet 'to contact my sons abroad because with the internet it is cheaper and easier'.

Two other housewives highlight aspects of the other general reasons why Jordanian women are drawn to the internet: (i) to stave off boredom, and (ii) to expand their social networks and global awareness. For example, a 38-year-old housewife with a BA and a working knowledge of English notes:

> The internet is a beautiful thing. I can see and know about the world outside. It is fun for people who have more free time [like housewives] to use it. It gives me access to more news, it's useful and fun at the same time. Now after using it, it made it a lot easier for me to contact friends. (Interview, Internet Café, Amman, Jordan, 19 April 2004)

A 27-year-old housewife with a community college degree who spends on average two hours a week online in an internet café observes:

> The internet makes me very happy and allows me to have fun, relax and to enjoy my free time when I am not with my children. I see and learn new things, very nice things and some are very funny and make me laugh. It added to my general knowledge. Mainly it's fun time. It made it easier for me to get in touch with my friends abroad. The internet is a great thing for housewives and mums like me who don't work. For example, with it, I get information about children and health issues related to them, their food, their upbringing and nutrition. I have two children and I like to learn about all that concerns them. (Interview, Amman, Jordan, 15 April 2004)

Housewives are not the only special niche community to find the internet useful. Unemployed women are also drawn to the technology. Whether this is to use the internet to look for a job, or just to stave off boredom while they explore more traditional means for locating employment, the six women who are unemployed internet café users all testify to their strong attraction to the technology. Incidentally, or perhaps not, four of the six are from Zarqa, an area of Jordan known for being poor, relative to Amman. Zarqa is also a community known to have a high concentration of unemployment. One 24-year-old café user with a high school diploma and no working knowledge of English who spends about seven hours a week in an internet café observes,

> The internet is the best thing that ever happened to me. It's entertaining and especially helps me to fill my free time now that I am unemployed since I left my job two months ago and am still looking for a new one. (Interview, Zarqa, Jordan, 16 May 2004)

Similarly, a 23-year-old female with a BA who spends approximately 12 hours a week at an internet café states:

> The internet is a great thing. I enjoy every minute on the net. I read about many things and I made many new friends in other Arab countries and two in the United States. We chat and exchange jokes, cards and pictures. The internet is also very useful when I need to apply for jobs. (Interview, Zarqa, Jordan, 18 May 2004)

Highlighting once again the link between the technology and occupying one's free time (all too plentiful for the young, educated and unemployed), a 25-year-old woman from Amman who spends on average 15 hours a week in an internet café states:

> Of course the internet has changed my life. If I don't go to the internet café, I'll die of boredom, especially now that I am not working and have nothing to do. I enjoy my time at the café and make new friends and talk and exchange ideas. It also helped me to stay in touch with my brother who is abroad through emails, which I prefer to letters. (Interview, Amman, Jordan, 18 April 2004)

Another interesting juxtaposition of female circumstances in Jordan is revealed by an interview with a 25-year-old, single Christian woman from Zarqa who is unemployed 'because my parents refuse to let me work'. This conservatism reveals Jordan's tribal values (as she is not Muslim, but Christian, and yet her parents want to keep her out of the public sphere). In spite of her family's conservative values, this young woman spends on average ten hours a week in an internet café and notes:

> The net has made my life more interesting and exciting. I get to know men and I met two of them in person in Amman. There is not much to do for outings here in Zarqa. (Interview, Zarqa, 21 May 2004)

IMPACT 3: NETWORKING

One of the recurring themes of these interviews with 100 female internet café users is that the technology enables these women, especially young and single ones, to expand their social networks. Many of those interviewed acknowledged the ways in which the technology enabled them to meet members of the opposite sex. Many of these same online encounters led to meetings in real life, a practice that contravenes Jordan's conservative social practices which discourage interactions across gender lines outside of family members.

Figure 23.3 shows that 66 per cent of the women interviewed made a friend online, 54 per cent of the women made a friend online with someone who was the opposite gender (includes those who went on to meet them in person and those who only communicated with them online), and 29 per cent met the person in real life (both genders).

The internet is known for its ability to connect disparate people; to enable people to reach beyond their own social, political, geographical and economic circumstances. The internet is also said to do the opposite; to link like-minded individuals, wherever they reside, as is the case with terror networks, or hate groups or, in a less sinister way, people who only use the internet to connect with friends and family and people they already know. This latter case, connecting only with people already in one's friend or family networks, characterizes the surfing habits of 34 out of 100

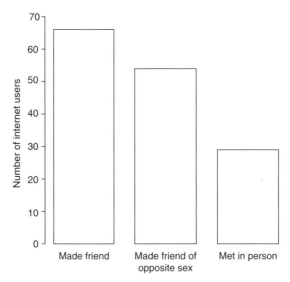

Figure 23.3   Making friends online

women interviewed. These 34 women have never made a friend online. If they chat, they do so with family members abroad. Interestingly, however, a clear majority of those interviewed had made a friend online, 66 in all responded affirmatively to this question. Perhaps more striking is the fact that 54 per cent of those who have made a friend online, have also met that person in real life. Even more surprising, 76 per cent of those women who met their cyber-pals in real life stated that the people with whom they met were men. This number is striking given the conservative nature of Jordanian society, especially when it comes to gender issues. For example, Jordan has one of the highest numbers of honour killings per annum in the Middle East, and yet, many women are not only meeting men online but also meeting them in real life too.[7] The majority of those engaging in this counter-cultural practice are Muslim, not Christian as one might expect. Moreover, all of the women who met male cyber-pals in real life are between the ages of 20 and 27 and are single.

Among the women who have met men on- and offline, clear spillover effects of these encounters are present in their narratives. For example, a 24-year-old, single, Muslim woman from Zarqa who spends on average eight hours a week in an internet café, observes:

> The internet has clearly changed my life. It made my life full. I enjoy my free time and I got to know many girls and made good female friends in Amman and Madaba. I also made a relationship with a man who was my friend in a chat. I have become more open-minded and less conservative since I started talking with people in a chat. (Interview, Zarqa, 20 May 2004)

Similarly, a 21-year-old, single Muslim BSc student majoring in pharmacology who spends on average seven hours a week online in an internet café observes,

> The internet has changed my life in a positive way. It changed my character and I became more social, and less reserved in my relationships with the opposite sex [males]. I became more relaxed; before I used to feel shy. Chat teaches a person to be more relaxed and open with people. It's great! (Interview, Amman, 10 May 2004)

Once again stressing the spillover effects of online encounters with the opposite sex, a 25-year-old, single Christian with a community college degree who is employed as a telemarketer and spends about ten hours a week surfing the internet in an internet café, surfing only in Arabic states:

> The internet has changed my life. It made me more social, less closed minded. I also met a friend that I chatted with. He came to Jordan from Saudi Arabia to meet me, but the relationship didn't work out between us. I made many other

friendships. It's a good way to communicate with people. (Interview, Zarqa, 17 May 2004)

The draw of networking across geographical boundaries, and interacting with different points of view is also a common theme in women's internet transformation narratives. Sometimes these other forms of networking are embedded in interactions across gender lines as well. For example, a 20-year-old, single college student majoring in accounting who spends approximately 20 hours a week surfing the internet at an internet café claims,

> The internet is very good for study, and information. I also made many friends with people in other countries I know I can never travel to because of lack of money. Travel is expensive. It's very interesting to know them and how they [people in other countries] think. Some are strange and weird, but many are nice and friendly with open minds. I'm having a relationship with a man in Syria on the net. He's coming in the summer to get engaged with me. (Interview Zarqa, 20 May 2004)

We see many layers of expanding social networks and minds in the above testimony. Many forms of empowerment are displayed in this single narrative: (i) professional development (she studies and gets information via the web); (ii) expanding social networks (she engages in virtual travel and has met a future spouse online); and (iii) transformations of social and political awareness (she notes that it is interesting to get to know foreigners and how they think; she enjoys those with open minds; in another part of her interview, she explains that she uses the internet to get more detailed information from various sources on the news headlines, demonstrating a link between knowledge, the internet and empowerment).

CONCLUSION

While this study provides a brief snapshot of the importance of internet cafés for Jordanian women, the power of the data suggests that much more careful attention to emerging information societies in the Arab world is warranted. This is especially true if we are to understand the foundations for future change fuelled by internet networks and the new human relationships and leisure practices they enable.

The narratives explored in this chapter demonstrate a clear pattern of the spillover effects linked with surfing the internet for Jordanian women. Even among women who are not wealthy enough to ever travel abroad, who are not well enough educated to have a working knowledge of English, and who are employed in lower-middle-class to lower-class forms of labour, accessing the internet is a regular part of their everyday life. The encounters they have online shape their personalities and character, enable them to travel to places they would never be able to go in real life, and often aid them in choosing a spouse. These forms of empowerment will help to shape and reshape both the public and private spheres in Jordan, as women become more comfortable taking risks and flexing their autonomy. The King of Jordan often reiterates that he wants to build an information society where no Jordanian is left out. The narratives above suggest that many Jordanian women are taking full advantage of the technologies made available to them through such national strategies. In general, to summarize the main findings of this chapter, the Jordanian women interviewed for this study find that the internet provides them with increased speed and breadth in their access to information, expands their social networks, including cross-gender relationships, and provides them with entertainment and a pathway out of boredom. The changes in women's lives occurring in internet cafés in Jordan suggest that women are gaining new expectations for information on demand, developing an awareness of their own voice and its potential power, and losing their inhibitions as they are encouraged to break from customary communication patterns by the anonymity and freedom provided by the internet. Where these micro-changes in women's lives will take Jordanian society and politics in the future is a story yet to unfold.

NOTES

1. For examples of the small community of consultants and scholars attempting to bridge this gap, see: Huyer et al. (2005), esp. p. 11, which has some good data on women's internet access in the UAE, Iran, Yemen and Tunisia; Sakr (2004), esp. Ch. 9; Nouraie-Simone (2005), esp. Ch. 4: 'Wings of freedom: Iranian women, identity, and cyberspace', by Fereshteh Nouraie-Simone; and Mernissi (2006).
2. 'Queen launches Arab Women's Summit' (2002).
3. For detailed statistics on diffusion rates for the Middle East and the global community, see Internet World Stats (www.internetworldstats.com).
4. 'Queen launches Arab Women's Summit' (2002).
5. 'Queen Rania of Jordan at Le Web 09 in Paris' (2009).
6. See www.womenswire.org.
7. A BBC news story states that in Jordan, 'approximately every two weeks, a woman is killed by a male relative because of the shame she has brought upon her family by an alleged sexual transgression' (Murphy, 2003).

REFERENCES

Aitchison, Cara (1999), 'New cultural geographies: the spatiality of leisure, gender and sexuality', *Leisure Studies*, **18**, 19–39.

Alterman, Jon (2000), 'Middle East's information revolution', *Current History*, January, 21–3.

Amawi, Abla (2000), 'Gender and citizenship in Jordan', in Suad Joseph (ed.), *Gender and Citizenship in the Middle East*, Syracuse: Syracuse University Press, pp. 158–84.

Arab-Moghaddam, Narges and Karla A. Henderson (2007), 'Women's leisure and constraints to participation: Iranian perspectives', *Journal of Leisure Research*, **39** (1), 109–26.

Castells, Manuel (2000), *Rise of the Network Society*, 2nd edn, Oxford: Blackwell.

Huyer, Sophia, Nancy Halfkin, Heidi Ertl and Heather Dryburgh (2005), *The Digital Divide to Digital Opportunities: Women in the Information Society*, Quebec: Orbicom/Claude-Yves Charron.

Kaya, Laura Pearl (2009), 'Dating in a sexually segregated sociey: embodied practices of online romance in Irbid, Jordan', *Anthropological Quarterly*, **82** (Winter), pp. 251–78.

Mernissi, Fatima (2006), 'Digital Scheherazades in the Arab world', *Current History*, March, 121–6.

Murphy, Clare (2003), 'Jordan's dilemma over "honour killings"', BBC News Online, 10 September, available at: http://news.bbc.co.uk/go/pr/fr/-/2/hi/middle_east/3094736.stm (accessed 9 December 2006).

Nouraie-Simone, Fereshteh (ed.) (2005), *On Shifting Ground: Muslim Women in the Global Era*, New York: Feminist Press, City University of New York.

Putnam, Robert (2000), *Bowling Alone: The Collapse and Revival of American Community*, New York: Simon & Schuster.

'Queen launches Arab Women's Summit' (2002), *Jordan Times*, 5 November.

'Queen Rania of Jordan at Le Web 09 in Paris' (2009), available at: http://www.demotix.com/news/queen-rania-jordan-leweb-09-paris (accessed 15 May 2011).

Rinnawi, Khalil (2002), 'The internet and the Arab world as a virtual public sphere', available at: http://www.scribd.com/doc/48413268/Khalil-Rinnawi-The-Internet-and-the-Arab-World-as-a-Virtual-Public-Sphere (accessed 15 May 2011).

Rugh, William (2004), *Arab Mass Media: Newspapers, Radio, and Television in Arab Politics*, Westport, CT: Praeger.

Sakr, Naomi (ed.) (2004), *Women and the Media in the Middle East: Power through Self-Expression*, London: I.B. Tauris.

Senft, Theresa M. (2008), *Cam Girls: Celebrity and Community in the Age of Social Networks*, New York: Peter Lang.

Shunnaq, Mohammad (2009), 'Cross cultural cyber-marriages: a global socio-economic strategy for young Jordanians', *Social Identities*, **15** (2: March), 169–86.

United Nations Development Programme (UNDP) (2002), *Arab Human Development Report 2002*, New York: Oxford University Press.

Wheeler, Deborah L. (2004), 'Blessings and curses: women and the internet in the Arab world', in Sakr (ed.), pp. 161–80.

Wheeler, Deborah (2005), 'Digital governance and democratization in the Arab world', in Ari-Veikko Anttiroiko and Matti Malkia (eds), *Encyclopedia of Digital Government*, Hershey, PA: IGI Global, pp. 1–12.

Wheeler, Deborah L. (2006a), *Internet in the Middle East: Global Expectations and Local Imaginations in Kuwait*, Albany: SUNY Press.

Wheeler, Deborah L. (2006b), 'Gender sensitivity and the drive for IT: lessons from the NetCorps Jordan Project', *Ethics and Information Technology*, **8**, 131–42.

Wheeler, Deborah L. (2008), 'What women want from IT: lessons from Western Asia', in Anita Gurumurthy (ed.), *An Empowerment Approach to Gender Equality in the Information Society: Regional Analyses from Asia*, Bangalore: IT for Change; available at: http://www.itforchange.net/images/Empowerment_Approach_to%20_GenderEquality_Full2.pdf.

APPENDIX 23A   JORDAN INTERNET CAFÉ INTERVIEW QUESTIONS

1. Gender?
2. Age?
3. Religion?
4. Married or single?
5. Highest level of education obtained?
6. Age when started using the internet?
7. Who taught you to use the internet?
8. Have you ever taught anyone to use the internet?
9. Do you have internet access at:
   Home?
   Work?
   School/university?
10. Neighbourhood where you live?
11. Are you employed?
12. Number of hours of internet use per week?
13. Do you usually come to cafés alone or with someone?
14. What do you use the internet for:
    Email?
    Chatting?
    Gaming?
    Health-related concerns?
    To get advice?
    For religious purposes?
    Music downloads?
    News sites?
    For study/research?
    For work/business?
    For shopping?
    Sports?
15. Has the internet changed your life? If so, how?
16. Did you receive computer training at school, university, or on the job?
17. Do you read a daily newspaper?
18. Are you comfortable using English?
19. Do you prefer to visit websites in Arabic or English?
20. Do your mum and/or dad use the internet?
21. What are your favourite websites?
22. How many brothers and sisters do you have?
23. Do you have a favourite chat room?
24. Have you ever made a friend online?

25. Were they the same gender as you?
26. Did you ever meet them in person?
27. Do you own a mobile phone?
28. About how many text messages do you send per day?

24 Sexual leisure markets
Alan Collins

INTRODUCTION

Over the entire course of civilized humanity, arguably the single most important leisure pursuit in terms of (i) time and money resources deployed and (ii) a crucial additional role in the continuation of human society, is participation in sexual activity. By this is meant activities that are intended to induce sexual excitement and gratification. This may or may not result in orgasm. For some brands of fundamentalist religious observers, participation in such activities should not or cannot be primarily recreational or a matter of leisure but rather, strictly procreational. The threads of argument set out in this chapter implicitly dismiss such a viewpoint as antiquated and irrelevant in modern society. The 'traditional' view of sexual activity typically seems to cast it as one of the integral binding or reinforcing elements of a relationship, potentially helping afford emotional support, deeper levels of companionship and children. Any departure from this view has been variously deemed as sinful, biologically injurious and degenerative.

It is argued in this chapter that such a traditional view has never really captured the intrinsic psychological and physiological significance of meeting sexual needs. Further, alongside other commentators it is contended that social and technological change now means that companionship, child production and sexual needs can increasingly be met separately or in various combinations. In essence, the notion that people can participate in sexual activity alone, or with one or more other people, just for fun, is generally deemed acceptable if it involves no physical harm and avoids the involvement of minors. Additionally, the range of sexual activities which have featured social stigma or taboo status in the past has diminished including what must be the most extensively participative sexual activity – masturbation (Stengers and Van Neck, 2001). Consequently, this means that the potential repertoires of sexual consumption opportunities have become increasingly extensive. This has translated into the emergence and evolution of a large range of distinct and overlapping sexual leisure markets, many of which are considered in this chapter.

In analysing sexual leisure markets I draw primarily on a pragmatic neoclassical economic perspective but also call upon some concepts in social theory and sociobiological reasoning. As a prelude to the analysis of a selection of sexual leisure markets I set out some simple theoretical and taxonomic considerations to inform the subsequent commentary.

THEORIZING SEXUAL LEISURE

Participating in safe sexual activity can clearly be conducive to both mental and physical well-being and hence people would typically prefer more and frequent sexual activity rather than less and infrequent episodes. Sexual desire can be conceived of as a means to drive domination of the gene pool (Wilson, 1975, 1978; Barash, 1979) and humans, like other creatures, are instinctively driven to reproduce, else the species dies out. Furthermore, humans are not the only species which seek sex far more often than is needed to reproduce (the recreational surplus). Much of it seems to be simply serving recreational objectives. Baker (1999) suggests that it is not just the increasing technological scope for the separation of recreational sexual activity, child production and companionship that is sustaining this recreational surplus. He contends that advances in reproductive medicine, contraception and technology are merely contributing to an increasing existing trend towards single parenting becoming the norm through a process of natural selection. Further, he contends that such individuals will want to share overhead costs and engage in companionship and sexual activity with other single parents in various household and gender configurations.

Sociobiological reasoning might also be advanced as the basis for broad differences in gender contributions to the recreational surplus via the propagation of 'sperm wars' (Baker 1997). The essential nub of this particular thesis is that evolutionary imperatives drive men to conquests and attempts at 'monopolizing' women. This notion is rationalized by reference to the significant percentage of children fathered by men who are not married or partnered to the child's mother. Further, it is contended that given only a small percentage of a given man's sperm would be highly fertile in connection with most women, then the rest of the sperm, it is rationalized, must have another function – specifically to combat other males' sperm. Simultaneously it is contended that women subconsciously search for the best genetic inputs available from the pool of available sexual partners. Further supporting evidence is suggested relating to a higher likelihood to conceive by a woman through a one night stand[1] or other casual sex than through intercourse with her regular partner. It is also asserted that vaginal mucus seems to encourage some sperm but deter others.

An alternative though not necessarily mutually exclusive line of reasoning follows Cameron and Collins (2000) and Collins (2004). Essentially while it is the case that personal relationships do provide marriage-type companionship (M) and recreational sexual services (S) there is no reason to assert or suppose that individuals would require or desire similar levels or proportions of these two relationship elements.

Some individuals could just derive sufficient companionship from their friends and/or family. Alternatively, other individuals could be at a stage in their lives where they do not require high levels of companionship and remain content with a minimal level of companionship from an existing and restricted social circle. In terms of sexual services, libidos do vary widely and may change considerably over life spans. Accordingly, some individuals may feel the need to investigate a wider sexual repertoire than may be provided by a single given partner (Fair, 1978). Bestiality practices aside, acquiring sexual contact takes the form of real, imagined or cyber liaisons between one individual and one or more other individuals. Cameron (2004) classifies such liaisons in terms of those occasioned by direct paid transactions (such as prostitution) or unpaid relationships. The latter of course may involve ancillary transactions for sexual accessories and/or goods with little or no sexual dimension to induce sexual performance (for example, a weekend break in a Paris hotel).

In trying to satisfy needs for S and M, individuals (whether single or partnered) face resource constraints determined by different endowments of wealth, physical attractiveness and various personality traits. Individuals may also have differing levels of efficiency in deploying their personality traits and physical attractiveness to acquire S and M. Clearly for already partnered individuals further resources (both time and money) may also be required to hide participation in extra-relationship sexual activity. The call upon time resources may of course be mediated by limiting the extent of extra-relationship sexual activity to virtual liaisons. Alternatively if real contact is needed then expending time resources can be minimized by physical proximity to a large urban centre. These are, of course, more likely to contain a larger number of similarly minded individuals and also more commercially provided or facilitated recreational sexual opportunities.

Time-dependent search costs will also vary in towns and cities of different ranks and orders. Recourse to commercial markets for sexual contact is thus a possible time-saving strategy for some individuals, and indeed many escort agencies (suppliers of sexual contact) reflect in their promotional material the immediacy and convenience of rapid contact though with some premium for this characteristic featuring in their tariff structure. Using prostitution services may also be perceived as a means of

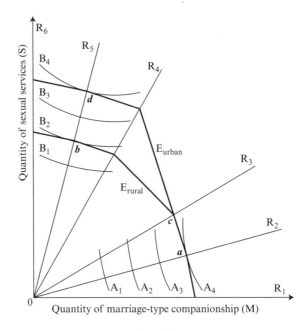

Figure 24.1   Sex and companionship characteristics

better isolating and compartmentalizing extra-relationship sexual encounters to minimize risk of discovery to current partners who may not favour open relationships. Adultery or other extra-relationship partners may be deemed to be of higher risk to existing relationships, though of course paid sex market encounters can present other health or crime proximity related risks.

Recourse to the commercial market for some may also be triggered by dissatisfaction with the quality and quantity of sexual contact they receive in unpaid sex markets. Yet for others it may merely be a convenient means to explore their variety demand (Scitovsky, 1976) for a wider repertoire of sexual consumption activities. For example, in a conventional two-person ostensibly heterosexual relationship it may be the case that one or both partners have a degree of bisexual interest which by definition could not possibly be accommodated by their partner. Hence, these sexual urges may be either suppressed or eventually realized with recourse to other individuals. If the relationship is otherwise providing ample satisfactory companionship and/or child-rearing benefits, then the requirements for some same sex contact may be adequately provided in a paid sex market setting.

These stylized facts are depicted in Figure 24.1 which employs Lancaster's (1966a, 1966b) characteristics approach to analyse the demand for S and

M in an urban and rural setting. In the figure, the resource constraints[2] (efficiency frontiers) for two individuals A and B are set out in an urban or rural setting E_{urban} and E_{rural}. The two individuals differ only with respect to the level of their preferences for S and M. The resource constraints may of course point to a potential level of achievable sexual leisure consumption which some people may feel to be a normal or acceptable level, but for some others a view may be formed that such a level would cross over into problem, compulsive, sexual addictive behaviour. This may be characterized by excessive use of prostitution services but also frequent sex with anonymous partners, considerable time devoted to cruising for sex in real/virtual/phone contexts, extra-relationship affairs including with family friends, members and work colleagues, excessive and repeated use of pornography, considerable sexual partner flux (serial monogamy) and obsessive sexual fetishes.

Thus, like other leisure pursuits, some individuals participating in sexual leisure markets may be described as addicts (or sexual compulsives) which may take the form of 'problem' or 'extreme volume' (in terms of time, money, number of partners) usage. This can be associated with, *inter alia*, unusually high libido, sustaining recurrent mental/sexual fantasies and, in many cases, considerable time and money budgets. For example, men craving high-risk (from HIV and other sexually transmitted infections) sexual intercourse without condoms may be able to realize this desire by simply paying a premium to prostitutes. In the context of Mexico, Gertler et al. (2005) found this premium to be of the order of 23 per cent (46 per cent if the sex worker was particularly attractive) and in other more mature economies this premium could be even higher.

Arguably, however, this focus on compulsivity moves us away from sexual leisure consumption and towards discussion of the suffering of a widespread sexual disorder. That said, there must be some spectrum over which this 'leisure participation to compulsion' transformation takes place, such that a simple dichotomous classification is not readily achievable. Sexual Compulsives Anonymous (SCA) group therapy and meeting groups are now commonplace across US cities and around Western Europe. They have, however, reached public consciousness through several high-profile instances of Hollywood actors publicly declaring their sexual compulsivity. In these groups, members are encouraged to develop their own sexual recovery plans including forming and meeting their own definitions of 'sexual sobriety'. Ultimately this must help provide an upper bound as to what may be deemed an acceptable level of sexual leisure consumption which for some individuals may be to the left of their efficiency frontier and for others some way to the right.

Indifference curves depict all the feasible consumption bundles of S and

M that yield the same level of utility to an individual. Individual A is more M orientated and individual B is more S orientated. The rays R_1 through to R_6 depict readily available combinations of S and M in a sexual leisure market. R_6 depicts a pure sexual relationship type with an absence of an M element (as could be expected from the consumption of standard prostitution services). R_1 depicts a non-sexual (platonic) relationship. Individual A is strongly M orientated but requires some positive level of S. This is achievable in both an urban and a rural setting for this individual at point *a* on R_2. For Individual B who is far more S orientated there is a clear distinction between the maximum achievable utilities available in rural and urban settings (denoted by *b* and *d*, respectively). Given this difference one might expect residency within an urban setting (or at least within a convenient social commuting distance from such a setting). The advent of the internet with websites to commercially mediate sexual contact opportunities even in rural settings may to some extent blur the sharpness of these urban/rural differences.

Yet, even with the opportunities afforded by the internet it should be noted that if extra-relationship sexual contacts are being contemplated without the consent of the other partner then problems remain. Concealment or camouflage costs (associated with use of a prostitute or participating in a one night stand) may reasonably be deemed to be much higher in a more rural context due to typically greater levels of social interaction and visibility within smaller rural populations. Clearly the pool of available partners will also be much richer in an urban context, as would the enhanced scope for participation in various niche sexual leisure markets.

So with recourse to this general framework the chapter proceeds to explore the variety of sexual leisure markets that may be found around the world, concentrating on more contemporary settings, but drawing reference to key markers in their historical evolution and the range of regulatory environments (permissive through to restrictive) that may be found.

PARTICIPATION IN SEXUAL ACTIVITY: SOME GENERAL BACKGROUND

To provide some context on the scale of participation in sexual leisure market activity and what constitutes typical sexual behaviour it is possible to dive into a vast sea of sexual statistics and extract insights from various readily available sources. Yet it is essential to be extremely wary of such data for numerous reasons of varying statistical complexity (Cameron et al., 2009). In many cases one can legitimately question the validity and reliability of the survey data, particularly since many of them are not scientifically rigorous in the way they are conducted. Rather it seems, many are just exercises to generate, in large part, marketing exposure for sponsors designed to supply easily accessed journalistic titillation and thus helping to sell various newspapers and popular magazines. Considerable biases, however, feature in most sexual survey research. These biases relate to the format of the questions posed, the absence of particular questions, the way questions are asked and the characteristics of the people who are being surveyed. Hence, while such surveys may well yield superficially interesting insights such as whether in the last year Mexicans had more sexual intercourse per week than Canadians, the survey deficiencies often mean that the results ought not to be generalized to the scale of an entire population. One popular source of sexual survey data widely employed by journalists since the 1990s is the series of Durex Global Sex Surveys (see, for example, Durex 2005–09) which among other things presents international comparisons of frequency of sexual intercourse and levels of sexual satisfaction.

There is of course also much research produced in an academic vein indicating the average frequency of sexual activity in particular countries, by age group. In summary they generally report (unsurprisingly) a reduction in the frequency of sexual activity (including intercourse) with increasing age and a decreasing frequency of sexual contact as the duration of the relationship or marriage increases (for example, Pfeiffer et al., 1972; Hawton et al., 1994; Call et al., 1995; Thirlaway et al., 1996). These and other studies also generally point to more sexual activity for those in relationships or marriage compared to single/unmarried persons. They also generally indicate a large number of couples reporting no sexual activity between them for long periods. Zero or low frequency of sexual activity in older age groups (which almost by definition is overwhelmingly non-procreational) is often a consequence of some kind of erectile dysfunction rather than a reduced demand for recreational sexual activity among older age groups (for example, Koskimäki et al., 2000). Indeed, the pent-up latent market demand for recreational sex among older age cohorts was dramatically revealed in 1998 with the launch of the blockbuster patented pharmaceutical product Viagra produced by the Pfizer Corporation.

In younger age cohorts, zero frequency of sexual activity may be associated with a preference for abstinence. Sexual abstinence before marriage has become a social movement in some countries such as the USA and a contemporary public policy strategy typically favoured by countries or regional/city jurisdictions characterized by high levels of religiosity and/ or right-leaning political governance. Abstinence or 'pledge' rings have become the hallmark fashion accessory to signal participation in this social movement. That said, Trenholm et al. (2007) present evidence that abstinence-only sexual education programmes actually have no impact on rates of abstinence by youth, though those on such programmes were slightly more informed and less likely to see condoms as protective against sexually transmitted diseases.

SEXUAL ACCESSORIES

There is a vast range of sexual accessories available to add variety in sexual activity or to help sustain participation. Many individuals derive fetishistic sexual satisfaction from a wide variety of objects and materials that may not seem to all people to overtly feature obvious sexual characteristics or connotations including, *inter alia*, nappies or diapers, fur, and chains. Further, many people also derive masturbatory sexual gratification via the aid of commonplace household items such as vacuum cleaners. As the cases of various celebrity fatal accidents show, there has also emerged a key role for commonplace household products such as plastic bags and cord or rope for executing the dangerous sexual practice of auto-erotic asphyxiation. However, this section focuses on those particular product markets which have developed to retail explicitly sexual or erotic accessories.

These markets include those of various pharmaceutical products available in a retail or prescription drug context. The most famous such contemporary product is arguably Viagra. To address erectile dysfunction the lozenge-shaped blue pill is typically advised to be taken from 30 minutes to four hours (depending on the age and health status of the individual) prior to sexual activity. The effects, once active, last approximately four hours. The patent ends this decade, so generic variants seem destined to ultimately dominate in the near future.

Currently, in the UK, Viagra is mainly a strictly rationed prescription-only drug. As a consequence, numerous premium-price web-based 'providers' and email spam operations have also emerged to serve and prey upon those keen and desperate men whose demand was not being met. In 2009 Boots, the largest retail pharmaceutical chain in the country, was permitted to retail the drug without prescription but requiring answers from men aged 30–65 to a short set of questions in a brief 'in-store consultation'. This led to unprecedented queues of men in the store of the trial city of Manchester. Total global sales for Viagra at its market peak exceeded $1 billion, but current annual sales have diminished in 2009 (Q3) to $466 million worldwide (Edwards, 2009). Inevitably emulation and innovation by competitors have over time eaten into market share and there has been some consumer backlash among consumers, especially in the USA, over excessive drug prices across a range of products. Given that the price of Viagra has been increased in some years at least twice, then it is easy to see how these concerns are sustained.

While Viagra currently still dominates global market share, even now there are some regions where market share has diminished markedly to below 50 per cent. In large part this is due to successful market penetration by two key competitor products which (see Lancaster 1966a, 1966b) emphasize and feature some different characteristics appealing to various segments of the market not previously targeted in the product range. Cialis, for example, produced by Eli Lilli and ICOS, is known as the 'weekend pill' in some countries since once taken, the erectile functioning is claimed to be enhanced for a period up to 36 hours, once active (between 30 minutes and 12 hours). The key feature of Levitra, produced by GlaxoSmithKline and Bayer, however, is that it is claimed by some experts to potentially take effect in only 15 minutes, with the duration of the effect lasting up to five hours. Time taken to enhancing erection and duration of effect are clearly the key characteristics taken into account by individuals when contemplating particular time patterns of sexual activity.

Currently, pharmaceutical companies are also engaged in research looking to provide a treatment similar to Viagra for the other half of the population as well – women. The main scientific focus hitherto has been to try to increase the blood flow to the genitals in order to increase lubrication and relax vaginal muscles. In 2007 the drug patch Intrinsa, produced by Proctor & Gamble, was launched in the UK on a prescription-only basis and initially to post-menopausal women reporting low libido. Its active constituent is testosterone (the male sex hormone) which occurs naturally in women, but after menopause, levels may decline dramatically. It seems likely that this drug and others in its wake will eventually develop into a lifestyle drug like Viagra, taken by women who do not actually need it, but who simply seek to boost libido. Many men who regularly take Viagra do not clinically need the product, and as such the drug is unlikely to have any real therapeutic effect on them even though they may perceive such a positive effect.

Of course, other legally and illegally available drugs are consumed because of their real or alleged efficacy in prolonging sexual activity or heightening the quality of sexual activity. Claims of sexual performance enhancement are, for example, accorded to the consumption of cocaine and ecstasy. One of the most common legally available sexual enhancement compounds is Amyl Nitrate, which along with other chemical variants are collectively known more commonly as 'poppers'. The term comes from the early packaging of the substance in small glass ampoules which were crushed (or popped) open to release the vapours. The original drug was developed to aid people with angina. In the liquid form, it is sold under various brand names, such as Liquid Gold and RUSH, ostensibly sold as a room odorants or other cleaning products to conform to some restrictive legal statutes, in the USA and elsewhere, aimed at prohibiting personal consumption of drugs intending to generate feelings of euphoria. In widespread common usage since the 1970s, poppers are inhaled for these euphoric feelings as a means to enhance sexual experience and to relax muscles. This muscle relaxant property can ease initial discomfort in penetrative anal sex in particular. This goes some way to explaining its relative early popularity among men who have sex with men, but over time its popularity has also spread among the heterosexual population for the same reasons. Prices are commonly in the range of £2 to £7 per 15 or 25ml bottle.

While there are a wide range of products designed to enhance and sustain sexual activity, whether as an aid to solo or mutual masturbation and foreplay, arguably the most significant products contributing to the leisure or recreational status of sexual activity are those products designed to ensure that sexual activity does not become procreational – such as the contraceptive pill and the condom. Though not an explicit sexual leisure good *per se*, the contraceptive pill has been accorded a significant role in modern economic history and female emancipation (Shorter, 1973; Jütte, 2008) in allowing and empowering women to choose the timing of life and career choices that govern work/leisure balance as well as the feasibility of more independent sexual lives.

Although it has a long and hotly debated product history (Parisot, 1987; Youssef, 1993; Collier, 2007; Allen, 2008; Jütte, 2008) the worldwide condom market has undergone a phenomenal transformation since the early 1980s given its central and iconic status as one of the best methods for avoiding HIV transmission as well as transmission of various other sexually transmitted infections. The global market for condoms was estimated to be worth $3.1 billion in 2006 (Futura Medical, 2010). The brand leader in the USA is Church & Dwight's main brand, Trojan, with over 70 per cent of the market and the nearest competitor Durex, produced by SSL which is the global brand leader with approximately 25 per cent of the world market. The condom has also now become an erotic sexual accessory given the differentiation of the product by a range of manufacturers. For those seeking to make safe oral sex more appealing, condoms are available in a wide range of taste flavours ranging from various fruit flavours as well as, for example, chocolate, mint, vanilla and cola. There are also semi-therapeutic condoms with anaesthetic gels in the tip to delay ejaculation and scheduled product launches for condoms that are designed to produce a firmer erection. Condoms are also available in various 'ribbed' formats to heighten friction sensation and there are also condoms marketed specifically for anal sex, gay men and non-latex rubber condoms developed for those with latex allergy.

As a consequence of the huge recent growth in the latex condom market, there has also been comparable growth in complementary products. Given the observation that some possible sexual lubricants can cause latex degradation and the growth in continued sexual activity (via Viagra and so on), among older age cohorts who are more prone to vaginal dryness, there has emerged a huge growth in the market for water-based lubricants and massage gels (approximately one-third the size of the over-the-counter condom market). These are also now differentiated by flavour or aroma, tingle sensation and ejaculation-delaying properties.

Dildos and sex toys to add variety to solo or mutual masturbation or to help sustain participation in these sexual activities also have a long and varied history (Taylor, 1997). In the nineteenth century, dildos were typically promoted as a good to support female health 'concerns' such as anxiety and stress. Over the years their overtly sexual nature came to the fore and with it greater sexual stigma. Yet with a global market estimated in 2006 to be around $15 billion (Rosen, 2006), the sex toy industry over the last 20 years has emerged from the shadows to claim high street store frontages in business such as Anne Summers stores in the UK, and has also induced more conservative manufacturers of electrical products to engage with the market. In an interview (Dohmen and Kerbusk, 2010) in *Der Speigel*, the Chief Executive Officer of the Dutch multinational, Philips, Gerard Kleisterlee was nonetheless still acutely conscious of the possible stigma from their recent participation in this market, even though earlier incarnations of ostensibly 'non-sexual' body massagers have been used for similar purposes for decades already:

> We analyzed very carefully, for example, whether such products would damage our brand, especially with our medical technology customers. The reaction was consistently positive. Our sensual massagers are completely different from ordinary sex toys. They're objects that you can leave lying around without feeling ashamed.

A further relatively recent form of product differentiation over the last 30 years which has made some contribution to a complementary good and collection-building motive for dildo purchases, are the ranges purportedly cast and modelled to the exact dimensions of penises of leading performers in adult porn films. Yet one of the next-generation sex toys that have had the most significant market impact over recent years is Vibratex's Rabbit, which came to be an iconic 1990s product. The success of the Rabbit paved the way for more public acceptance of vibrators, particularly after its central plot role in a televised episode of HBO's *Sex and the City* in 1998. Male masturbatory aids have also moved on from standard inflatable sex dolls towards more sophisticated products such as the Fleshlight (www.fleshlight.co.uk) and the Tenga (www.tenga.co.uk) which can be filled with lubricant before use. Some Fleshlight products have the added benefit of discretion by being disguisable as a torch. It is debatable whether for all men the huge range of penis enlargement devices now available on the market constitute a sexual leisure accessory, but there is revealed evidence from sexual partner search literature and reported profiles on sex websites that the use of vacuum pumping devices has also evolved into a solo and with-partner(s) sexual activity and fetish among both gay and straight men.

PORNOGRAPHY

As an aid to masturbation or a prelude to sexual contact with others, pornographic images have a long history at least from the Classical Greek and Roman era (Hyde, 1964; Gillette, 1965). Since then this history has been interspersed in numerous countries with episodic clampdowns arising from moral panic, paving the way for various inhibitory regulations and statutes of some kind (Sigel, 2002, 2005; Peakman, 2003; Toulalan, 2007). There is also a background debate trying to delineate the distinction between pornography and 'erotic art', since the cultural label of the latter term has afforded a line of reasoning by which some individuals and organizations could mount resistance to heavy censorship and stronger regulation.

Consumption of pornographic magazines, films, web images and 'interactive' pages has been charged by some feminist commentators as contributing to demeaning and degradation of women and acting as a stimulus to sexual harassment, sexual assault and rape (for example, Dworkin and MacKinnon, 1988; Dworkin, 1993). Interpretation of evidence from international comparisons of sex-related crime levels is problematic, using official crime statistics, since construction rules vary widely (von Hofer, 2004). It has also been observed that countries which seem to feature very liberal and permissive legal frameworks governing pornography are perceived to have relatively low rates of sexual assault and rape. Kutchinsky (1970, 1973, 1985) and Kutchinsky and Snare (1999), in the context of Denmark, produced some evidence of correlations between availability of hard pornography and a decrease in reported cases of voyeurism and sex offences against children.

Work by Wongsurawat (2006) suggests that the growth of post office boxes was associated with increased pornographic magazine subscriptions. He found that a 1 per cent increase in coverage of US post office boxes (serving as a proxy for pornography magazine subscriptions) was associated with a reduction of 40–50 forcible rapes per 100,000 of the population. Essentially this provides some degree of possible evidence for the inference that pornography and rape are substitutes.

Clearly the advent of the internet has reduced the costs of accessing pornography (and hence led to some switching away from magazine-based pornography) and thus if we follow some lines of feminist reasoning then the increasing market penetration of this technology should have presaged a marked increase in the volume of sexual assaults and rape. To investigate this, Kendall (2006) undertook an analysis of US state-level rape crime data over the 1998–2003 period. He found that the arrival of the internet was associated with a reduction in instances of rape but not of other crimes. Disaggregating the rape data by offender age he found that the rape-reducing effect of the internet was greater in states with higher male to female ratios and for the population segment that enjoyed the greatest non-pecuniary cost reduction (from the internet) in accessing pornography – namely, men aged 15–19, who lived in the family home. Essentially, he found some evidence suggesting that pornography and rape are substitutes in the USA. Specifically a 10 per cent increase in internet access is associated with a decline in reported rape victimization of 7.3 per cent. The policy implications for such sex crime mitigation are that a liberal and permissive policy regarding pornography availability is socially desirable. While this key result of Kendall seems to contradict earlier studies (for example, Jaffee and Straus, 1987), these did not explicitly control for location effects or the age distribution of rape offenders.

EROTIC DANCING VENUES

A relatively widespread and common sexual leisure market presence in the urban landscape is the presence of erotic dance entertainment venues – variously labelled 'lap dancing', 'pole dancing' or 'gentlemen's clubs'. These take the form of licensed drinking establishments with erotic dance entertainment that may be enjoyed on a main stage and additionally in most cases in private sections, recesses or rooms of the venue for an additional charge. Individual firms and several large chain or franchise operations operate in nationwide and international market contexts. The Spearmint Rhino group has perhaps the greatest customer brand recognition among such chain operations, having originated in the USA and then expanded by foreign direct investment into other markets, including the development of new establishments in the UK. In London, the Stringfellows club – owned by the celebrity nightclub owner Peter Stringfellow – is perhaps the best known. Following the liberalization of alcohol licensing in the UK via legislation in 2003, there has been considerable growth in the number of such venues in the UK to well in excess of 300 city establishments nationwide.

Social customs vary markedly across the globe in relation to the degree of permissible customer interaction in such venues, which raises some interesting economic questions. For example, in the USA and Canada it is common to tip dancers, and to do so by placing dollar bills into the skimpy clothing worn (at least in the early phase of the performance) by the dancers. In the UK, by-laws typically restrict any touching of the erotic dancers in this way within the licensed premises. This represents a conspicuous cultural contrast, but such regulation has been challenged in terms of the law and via the deployment of restriction-skirting 'countervailing innovations'. For example, Kenneth McGrath, the owner of the Pussy Cat club in Hove, East Sussex, in the UK petitioned the Brighton and Hove Council (the municipal authority) for a more liberal local licence regime to allow touching by 'blind' men (Sawer, 2000). He contended that their disability did not allow them to fully enjoy the services and contours of the dancers. The request was disallowed on the grounds that the club might not be able to guarantee distinguishing sighted persons pretending to be blind and genuinely visually impaired customers (an information asymmetry). Essentially in economic terms, the Council was concerned that adverse selection might arise since it could reasonably be expected that the club might be inundated by white stick wielding 'bad' (sighted) customers attempting to deceive the club in order to be able to touch the dancers. The Council may also have been concerned that the club would not have been sufficiently concerned about this, particularly if it raised patronage and thus revenue for the club. It may be, however, that such decisions are further challenged in the future in the light of disability discrimination laws.

More recently in the UK the regulatory regime has changed such that erotic dance venues such as the Pussy Cat club have attempted to evade additional restrictions on fully nude dancing. Some clubs have done this by recasting their entertainment as 'life drawing classes' for the enjoyment of stag or hen parties (see, for example, www.pussycatclub.co.uk). In large part, such actions have been a market response in the UK to the required reclassification and licensing of such erotic dance venues (Home Office, 2009) as 'sexual entertainment venues' within a 12-month period commencing from April 2010. These regulatory changes impose additional constraints and restrictions on existing venues and allow local councils to exert stronger controls on the location of potential new venues – essentially providing scope for a moral *cordon sanitaire* around schools and residential areas. The regulations, however, do not apply to one-off or infrequent (say monthly) erotic dance events. This has raised the likelihood of many other regular pubs and clubs holding such events. This seems likely to ultimately raise by a considerable extent the actual number of erotic dancing events and consumption opportunities available in the UK.

Lap dancing clubs have also come under the economic lens in terms of their potential role as a vehicle for engaging in post-entry employee gender discrimination. Essentially, visits to lap dancing clubs have routinely been used for purposes of entertaining business clients or post-work socialization. It has been reported that in London up to 75 per cent of customers were there as part of a business meeting, with this rising to almost 100 per cent during the week (Bennett, 2009). In the UK, firms may claim back 15 per cent value added tax (sales tax) if they take their own staff out to such a venue for business purposes. These alleged purposes may relate to helping to motivate staff and the purported development of team spirit. Additionally, the expenses of entertaining clients may be offset against their corporate tax liability.

Hence, in a work organization context, some female employees have felt either to be excluded by virtue of this practice, or to be humiliated by being required to attend such venues alongside male colleagues. Not surprisingly, such occasions have formed part of constructive dismissal cases and legal appeals against dismissal. Were the tax benefits for firms who engage in the routine use of such venues for work activity to be rescinded, this could be a significant threat to the financial viability of these clubs. This possibility was under active policy consideration in the UK by the Labour Party when it was last in government.

PROSTITUTION, SAUNA AND MASSAGE SERVICES

Bypassing religious, moral and feminist debate there has been a burgeoning of economic and public policy literature in recent years related to the economics of the prostitution (escort) services sector, which in its off-street guises in some cities is virtually indistinguishable from those services operating as sauna and massage services (see, for example, the work surveyed in Cameron, 2002; Collins and Judge, 2008; Munro and Della Giusta, 2008). The key themes analysed comprise: labour market issues trying to explain the supply and relatively high wage levels of some service providers; explanations and measurement of the risk premiums associated with participation in unsafe sexual practices; and the design of regulatory policy. The various dimensions of consumption risk and the nature of the prevailing regulatory policy clearly have the most direct bearing on the level and pattern of participation in this sexual leisure market. These themes are of course intertwined, and public health concerns about the transmission of sexually transmitted infections have led to both increasing and decreasing liberalization of paid sex markets in different countries and jurisdictions.

It seems generally reasonable to economists that such public health risk concerns can form part of an individual's composite risk measure also including risks of arrest, rip-off risks, possible physical violence and so on, and that these can condition the perceived costs of consumption so that they can be set against the benefits of the consumption of this service good.

Although there are few studies focusing on the likely behaviour and responses of consumers, Collins and Judge (2008, 2010) present a formal theoretical analysis of this reasoning in the context of client perceptions of risk under a range of regulatory environments. Under no type of regulatory policy envisaged is zero consumption deemed to ever be a likely long-run equilibrium outcome, but more pragmatic outcomes that can minimize harm on both the demand and supply sides of the market are advanced. Essentially, these are aligned to much greater market liberalization, particularly for licensed off-street providers based in locations where residential neighbourhood disturbance externalities are negligible.

DOGGING, SWINGING AND SEX CLUBS

Dogging, swinging and sex clubs are activities which afford sexual contact with other individuals, either previously known or unknown. Dogging or 'stranger sex' is a 'free good', aside from the travel and risk-related costs, and takes place in alfresco locations which are discreetly situated away from view and/or takes place under cover of darkness. The locations may become known by 'word of mouth' and postings on various dogging or public cruising websites. Swinging, either at home, or in sex club premises relates to similar sexual activity that takes place typically in indoor locations. There are many commercial enterprises across the globe that serve an agency function to provide contact opportunities for swinging individuals or partners either at home or in clubs (see, for example, www.swingeurope.com).

In the monthly magazine published by swingeurope.com – *Swing Europe* – the contact advertisements placed by individuals and couples suggest some conspicuous contrasts with those advertisements placed in newspaper/magazine periodicals and dating websites. Cameron and Collins (1997) was an early study showing that in advertisements for relationship partners, preferred partner age is seen as adjustable according to a trade-off with other attributes – physical appearance and financial

Table 24.1 *French swingers: highlighted characteristics from* Swing Europe *Magazine (January 2009, Issue 200)*

	Single male advertisements	Couples (male/female) advertisements	Others (single female or single sex couples
Percentage of *total* sample	52	45	3
Percentage of *each* *category* declaring interest in fully[1] bisexual activity	77	93	Too small sample
Percentage of *each* *category* expressing *NO* preferred partner age	71	70	Too small sample

Note: [1] For example, for single males this includes: male–male *and* male–female; for male–female couples this includes simultaneously expressed preferences for *both* male–male *and* female–female activity.

security. They estimated age sought as a function of these attributes in a 'hedonic ageing equation' using samples derived from the 'texts' of personal advertisements. There were clear gender differences in these trade-offs and that more financially constrained men seemed more willing to trade down in market desirability (that is, up in potential partner age) and with women offering to buy younger partners with financial signalling.

The advertisements in swinger publications, however, with their focus on soliciting more explicitly recreational sex partners, rather than personal relationship partners, seem to differ markedly. Preferred partner ages, if mentioned at all (most advertisements do not), seem to be expressed in terms of a wider age range or requesting a minimum age for when the individual is keen to meet older partners. One possible explanation for this phenomenon is that given individuals are less likely to be primarily looking for a personal relationship, they can give full vent to sexual experimentalism and a wider repertoire of sexual experiences with partners of a greater range of gender, age, ethnicity as well as sexual practices. This must be the case given that a large number of such advertisements are from couples in established personal relationships looking for group sexual encounters of various kinds. A snapshot of such patterns is presented in Table 24.1. This provides data extracted from an analysis of a representative (20 per cent) sample of swingers advertisements derived from the January 2009 (No. 200) issue of *Swing Europe* magazine containing over 730 advertisements.

As Table 24.1 indicates, single males (or those who advertise themselves as such) and male–female couples dominate this outlet. It seems clear that this avenue of recruiting sexual partners is of particular value to those seeking to practise their bisexuality and seeking to meet their demand for sexual variety. Advertisers (many of whom did signal their own age – ranging from twenties to retirement age categories) seemed more willing to explore the potential of sexual contacts with a broad range of age groups. Further, though not set out in this table, there were also a significant number of advertisements that expressly sought partners from different ethnic groups, again it seems with a view to expressing sexual variety-seeking. Similar such swinger outlets feature across countries throughout the world and have remained a distinctly underresearched topic in behavioural economics and the economics of the household.

CONCLUDING REMARKS

This chapter has sought to give some insight to the contemporary landscape of sexual leisure markets using the perspectives afforded by an established body of relevant economic theory. In such theory, participation in both paid and non-paid sex markets takes time which may be the biting constraint for some wealthier individuals. As such, recourse to commercial intermediation to provide sexual partners seems a rational choice.

While this chapter has not provided a fully comprehensive survey, it has tried to illuminate some aspects of sexual leisure markets that exist beyond prostitution. Paid sex has typically taken centre stage in economic research in the field. For the time being this is likely to continue, given it is still the case that in many economies and societies, there has still been no settlement on the desired long-term regulatory regime choices to permit a stable, less liminal and less stigmatized sexual service sector to operate.

The scale and scope of the sexual accessories and pornography sector has also been explored from a consumer leisure perspective and taken some account of the ancillary discussions as to their societal and economic effects. No attention, however, has been paid to these markets in relation to their pioneer roles in the technological innovation and diffusion of means to protect intellectual property rights across new viewing media. Inevitably the market will continue to advance in surges as new products emerge to tickle consumer interest. There does seem considerable scope (particularly as key patents expire) for the development of safe, flexible and faster sexual recreational pharmaceutical products to emerge. It also seems likely that the new generation of sexual accessories will move beyond a pioneer market to enhance cybersexual activities.

NOTES

1. Cameron (2001) provides an economic analysis of the phenomenon of one night stands.
2. These constraints may comprise both time and budget costs. Fair (1978) develops a formal time allocation model to explore the scope for conducting additional sexual relationships which he shows (in a footnote) can easily be modified to take into account consumption of prostitution services.

REFERENCES

Allen, P. (2008), *Condom: One Small Item, One Giant Impact*, London: New Internationalist.
Baker, R. (1997), *Sperm Wars: The Science of Sex*, New York: Basic Books.
Baker, R. (1999), *Sex in the Future: Ancient Urges Meet Future Technology*, Basingstoke: Macmillan.
Barash, D. (1979), *The Whisperings Within*, New York: Harper & Row.
Bennett, R. (2009), 'Harriet Harman tries to end corporate lap-dancing tax break', *The Times*, 18 September, available at: http://www.timesonline.co.uk/tol/news/politics/article6839221.ece (accessed 18 February 2010).
Call, V., S. Sprecher and P. Schwartz (1995), 'The incidence and frequency of marital sex in a national sample', *Journal of Marriage and the Family*, **57**(3): 639–52.
Cameron, S. (2001), 'The economic analysis of social customs: the case of pre-marital sex', *Journal of Evolutionary Economics*, **11**: 457–73.
Cameron, S. (2002), *The Economics of Sin: Rational Choice or No Choice At All*, Cheltenham, UK and Northampton MA, USA: Edward Elgar.
Cameron, S. (2004), 'Space, risk and opportunity: the evolution of paid sex markets', *Urban Studies*, **41**(9): 1643–57.
Cameron, S. and A. Collins (1997), 'Estimates of a hedonic ageing equation for partner search', *Kyklos*, **50**(3): 409–18.
Cameron, S. and A. Collins (2000), 'Random utility maximiser seeks similar: an economic analysis of commitment level in personal relationships', *Journal of Economic Psychology*, **21**(1): 73–90.
Cameron, S., A. Collins, S. Drinkwater, F. Hickson, D. Reid, J. Roberts, M. Stephens and P. Weatherburn (2009), 'Surveys and data sources on gay men's lifestyles and socio-sexual behavior', *Sexuality & Culture*, **13**(3), 135–51.
Collier, A. (2007), *The Humble Little Condom: A History*, Amherst, NY: Prometheus Books.
Collins, A. (2004), 'Sexuality and sexual services in the urban economy and socialscape: an overview', *Urban Studies*, **41**(9): 1631–41.
Collins, A. and G. Judge (2008), 'Client participation in paid sex markets under alternative regulatory regimes', *International Review of Law and Economics*, **28**(4): 294–301.
Collins, A. and G. Judge (2010), 'Differential enforcement across police jurisdictions and client participation in paid sex markets', *European Journal of Law and Economics*, **29**(1): 43–55.
Dohmen, F. and K.-P. Kerbusk (2010), 'Interview with Philips CEO Gerard Kleisterlee', *Der Spiegel*, available at: http://www.spiegel.de/international/business/0,1518,670164-2,00.html (accessed 18 February 2010).
Durex (2005–09), 'Global Sex Survey', available at: www.durex.com (accessed 18 February 2010).
Dworkin, A. (1993), *Pornography: Men Possessing Women*, London: Women's Press:
Dworkin, A. and C.A. MacKinnon (1988), *Pornography and Civil Rights: A New Day for Women's Equality*, Minneapolis, MN: Organizing Against Pornography.
Edwards, J. (2009), 'Pfizer's Viagra shows signs of flagging: sales down 6 per cent', 22

October, available at: http://industry.bnet.com/pharma/10004956/pfizers-viagra-shows-signs-of-flagging-sales-down-6/ (accessed 18 February 2010).

Fair, R.C. (1978), 'A theory of extramarital affairs', *Journal of Political Economy*, **86**(1): 45–61.

Futura Medical (2010), 'Condoms – the market', available at: http://futura-ir.co.uk/content/products/condoms.asp (accessed 12 February 2010).

Gertler, P., M. Shah and S.M. Bertozzi (2005), 'Risky business: the market for unprotected commercial sex', *Journal of Political Economy*, **113**(3): 518–50.

Gillette, P.J. (1965), *An Uncensored History of Pornography*, Los Angeles, CA: Holloway House.

Hawton, K., D. Gath and A. Day (1994), 'Sexual function in a community sample of middle-aged women with partners: effects of age, marital, socioeconomic, psychiatric, gynecological, and menopausal factors', *Archives of Sexual Behavior*, **23**(4): 375–95.

Home Office (2009), *The Regulation of Lap Dancing Clubs: Consultation on Transitional Arrangements – Government Response*, London: Home Office.

Hyde, H.M. (1964), *A History of Pornography*, New York: Farrar, Straus & Giroux.

Jaffee, D. and M.A. Straus (1987), 'Sexual climate and reported rape: a state-level analysis', *Archives of Sexual Behavior*, **16**(2): 107–23.

Jütte, R. (2008), *Contraception: A History*, Cambridge: Polity.

Kendall, T. (2006), 'Pornography, rape and the internet', Law and Economics Seminar Paper, Stanford University, available at: http://www.law.stanford.edu/display/images/dynamic/events_media/Kendall%20cover%20+%20paper.pdf (accessed 13 February 2010).

Koskimäki, J., M. Hakama, H. Huhtala and T. Tammela (2000), 'Effect of erectile dysfunction on frequency of intercourse: a population based prevalence study in Finland', *Journal of Urology*, **164**(2): 367–70.

Kutchinsky, B. (1970), 'Studies on Pornography and Sex Crimes in Denmark: A Report to the U.S. Presidential Commission on Obscenity and Pornography', New Social Science Monographs, Copenhagen.

Kutchinsky, B. (1973), 'The effect of easy availability of pornography on the incidence of sex crimes: the Danish experience', *Journal of Social Issues*, **14**: 47–64.

Kutchinsky, B. (1985), 'Pornography and its effects in Denmark and the United States: a rejoinder and beyond', *Comparative Social Research*, **8**: 301–30.

Kutchinsky, B. and A. Snare (eds) (1999), *Law, Pornography and Crime – The Danish Experience*, Scandinavian Studies in Criminology, Vol. 16, Oslo: Pax Forlag, available at: www. krim.ku.dk\Jesperkrim.ku.dk\Jesper.

Lancaster, K. (1966a), 'Change and innovation in the technology of consumption', *American Economic Review*, **56**(2): 14–23.

Lancaster, K. (1966b), 'A new approach to consumer theory', *Journal of Political Economy*, **74**(2): 132–57.

Munro, V. and M. Della Giusta (eds) (2008), *Demanding Sex: Critical Reflections on the Regulation of Prostitution*, Aldershot: Ashgate.

Parisot, J. (1987), *Johnny Come Lately: Short History of the Condom*, Newburyport, MA: Journeyman Press.

Peakman, J. (2003), *Mighty Lewd Books: The Development of Pornography in Eighteenth-Century England*, Basingstoke: Palgrave Macmillan.

Pfeiffer, E., A. Verwoerdt and G.C. Davis (1972), 'Sexual behaviour in middle life', *American Journal of Psychiatry*, **128**: 1262–7.

Rosen, D. (2006), 'The global trade in sex toys – made in China', available at: http://www.counterpunch.org/rosen12022006.html (accessed 12 February 2010).

Sawer, P. (2000), 'A touch too much? Lap dancers for the blind', *London Evening Standard*, 26 September, available at: http://www.highbeam.com/doc/1P2-5280602.html (accessed 12 February 2010).

Scitovsky, T. (1976), *The Joyless Economy: The Psychology of Human Satisfaction*, Oxford: Oxford University Press.

Shorter, E. (1973), 'Female emancipation, birth control, and fertility in European history', *American Historical Review*, **78**(3): 605–40.

Sigel, L.Z. (2002), *Governing Pleasures: Pornography and Social Change in England 1815–1914*, New York: Rutgers University Press.

Sigel, L.Z. (2005), *International Exposures: Perspectives on Modern European Pornography, 1800–2000*, New York: Rutgers University Press.

Stengers, J. and A. Van Neck (2001), *Masturbation: The History of a Great Terror*, trans. K. Hoffman, New York: Palgrave.

Taylor, T. (1997), *The Prehistory of Sex: Four Million Years of Human Sexual Culture*, London: Bantam.

Thirlaway, K., L. Fallowfield and J. Cuzick (1996), 'The sexual activity questionnaire: a measure of women's sexual functioning', *Quality of Life Research*, **5**(1): 81–90.

Toulalan, S. (2007), *Imagining Sex Pornography and Bodies in Seventeenth-Century England*, Oxford: Oxford University Press.

Trenholm, C., B. Devaney, B. Fortson, L. Quay, J. Wheeler and M. Clark (2007), *Impacts of Four Title V, Section 510 Abstinence Education Programs – Final Report*, Princeton, NJ: Mathematica Policy Research Inc., available at: http://www.mathematica.org/Publications/PDFs/evalabstinence.pdf (available at 18 February 2010).

von Hofer, H. (2004), 'Crime statistics as constructs: the case of Swedish rape statistics', *European Journal on Criminal Policy and Research*, **8**(1): 77–89.

Wilson, E.O. (1975), *Sociobiology: The New Synthesis*, Cambridge, MA: Harvard University Press.

Wilson, E.O. (1978), *On Human Nature*, Cambridge, MA: Harvard University Press.

Wongsurawat, W. (2006), 'Pornography and social ills: evidence from the early 1990s', *Journal of Applied Economics*, **9**(1): 185–213.

Youssef, H. (1993), 'The history of the condom', *Journal of the Royal Society of Medicine*, **86**(4): 226–8.

Index